THE FIVE

TO SEVEN

YEAR SHIFT

The John D. and Catherine T. MacArthur Foundation
Series on Mental Health and Development

THE FIVE TO SEVEN YEAR SHIFT

The Age of Reason and Responsibility

EDITED BY

Arnold J. Sameroff and Marshall M. Haith

THE UNIVERSITY OF CHICAGO PRESS / CHICAGO AND LONDON

Arnold J. Sameroff is professor of psychology and research scientist in the Center for Human Growth and Development, University of Michigan. Marshall M. Haith is the John Evans Professor of Psychology, University of Denver.

The University of Chicago Press, Chicago 60637
The University of Chicago Press, Ltd., London
© 1996 by The University of Chicago
All rights reserved. Published 1996
Printed in the United States of America
05 04 03 02 01 00 99 98 97 96   1 2 3 4 5
ISBN: 0-226-73447-1 (cloth)

The University of Chicago Press gratefully acknowledges a subvention from the John D. and Catherine T. MacArthur Foundation in partial support of the costs of production of this volume.

Library of Congress Cataloging-in-Publication Data

   The Five to seven year shift : the age of reason and responsibility /
   edited by Arnold J. Sameroff and Marshall M. Haith.
       p.   cm. — (The John D. and Catherine T. MacArthur Founda-
tion series on mental health and development)
   Includes bibliographical references (p.   ) and index.
   1. Cognition in children.   2. Human information processing in children.   I. Sameroff, Arnold J.   II. Haith, Marshall M.,
1937–.   III. Series.
BF723.C5F58   1996
155.42'4 — dc20   96-3304
                                                       CIP

♾The paper used in this publication meets the minimum requirements of the American National Standard for Information Sciences—Permanance of Paper for Printed Library Materials, ANSI Z39.48-1984.

CONTENTS

ACKNOWLEDGMENTS

In 1983 the John D. and Catherine T. MacArthur Foundation began its historic entry into the developmental study of mental health issues through the establishment of its Research Network on Early Childhood Transitions under the leadership of Robert Emde. The focus on transitions was especially significant because it was thought that during such periods the child would be open to many biological, psychological, and social influences that could change trajectories of competence. For some the transition would lead to improved mental health, where for others the result would be a downward course. It was hoped that the study of such processes would enhance scientific understanding not only of the forces that produced such changes but also of opportunities for intervention to increase the probabilities for successful transitions.

The initial concern of the network was to investigate the numerous changes in behavior that occurred during the first years of life as the child moved from the primarily sensory-motor functioning of infancy into the cognitive, linguistic, and social initiatives that characterized the preschooler. The MacArthur Foundation went on to establish a series of developmentally oriented research networks focusing on other periods during the lifespan. These were the Program on Successful Adolescence, the Program on Successful Midlife Development, and the Program on Successful Aging. By definition developmental studies require longitudinal approaches to research, and there was an implicit expectation that as these programs matured, the individuals investigated during one period of time would transition into life periods investigated by others.

But before reaching adolescence, the subjects of the Early Childhood Transitions Network had to cross a major intervening passage, what has come to be known as the 5 to 7 year shift. To begin this effort the editors of this book were given the mandate to review the contemporary state of knowledge on developmental transitions spanning this age range. We were able to recruit a group of experts in the neurobiological, cognitive, emotional, social, and cultural aspects of behavior during this period who shared their wisdom first through a network-sponsored conference and now with the field at large through this book.

We wish to thank Robert Emde for his important support in initiating and maintaining our effort in his role as Network Director and the MacArthur Foundation for providing the wherewithal. The other members of the Network on Early Childhood Transitions—Mark Applebaum, Kathryn Barnard, Elizabeth Bates, Jerome Kagan, and Marian Radke-Yarrow—provided additional enthusiasm and advice as we planned and produced the initial conference and this subsequent volume. We must also mention the support of the network administrator, Joan Deming, who facilitated all our activities and created a positive climte in which we could complete our editorial work, Judy Bandieri, who coordinated the conference, and Suzanna Mroz, who assembled the many chapters into a complete manuscript. In addition, financial support from Research Scientist Awards to both editors from the National Institute of Mental Health enhanced our ability to work on the project.

This effort has been a fascinating and informative one for the editors, and we hope our readers will be able to share in the same excitement we felt as we learned of the multiple processes that are involved in children's lives as they move into the age of reason and responsibility.

PART ONE

Introduction

CHAPTER ONE

Interpreting Developmental Transitions

ARNOLD J. SAMEROFF AND MARSHALL M. HAITH

A 7-year-old came home tearfully one day from school to question her parents about something they had protected her from since birth; her classmates had told her that there was no Santa Claus. When her mother and father admitted that what she heard was true, she stared at them dolefully while reaching an even more disheartening conclusion—"This probably means that there is no Easter Bunny or Tooth Fairy either!"

Many of us have experienced the sad discovery by a child that a favorite belief was not true. But what is especially interesting in the just-mentioned vignette is that a normative but often unnoticed intellectual extension has taken place. The child revealed a belief in the existence of a conceptual category of imagined but unseen figures who brought gifts. When the child discovered that one of these figures did not really exist, she made the logical extension that other members of this cognitive category did not exist. This kind of observation reflects what developmental psychologists have called the 5 to 7 year shift. Children's thinking after age 7 seems to be different from their thinking before age 5. What we present in this book is another shift—a shift in the way developmentalists understand the transition between the behavior of the preschool child to that of the school-age child (Sameroff & McDonough, 1994).

A wide range of scholars representing domains of behavior from the most molecular to the most global were asked to reflect on current thinking about the 5 to 7 year shift in their area. Their specialties range from biological functioning, through cognition, memory, and language, to emotions and conceptions of the self. In the course of their presentation they were asked to reflect on four questions about the transition:

1. Do *7-year-olds* behave differently from *5-year-olds?*

2. If the behaviors do differ, are the differences *quantitative* or *qualitative?* Do they reflect a change in the level of preexisting functions or the appearance of new functions?

3. If the behavioral differences are quantitative, is the change *continuous* or *discontinuous?* Do these behavioral differences occur slowly over a relatively long duration or rapidly in a short period of time?

4. If the behavioral differences are qualitative, are they the result of a *reorganization* of existing processes or the *emergence* of new behaviors?

The understanding of change in mental processes has frequently been related to the degree that they reflect change in biological processes. Are anatomical and physiological changes in the brain associated with changes in behavior, and specifically in this case, do these changes occur between the ages of 5 and 7? Are these changes only in the organization or reorganization of existing structures, or do they reflect the emergence of new processes and structures? In such analyses, bottom-up interpretations often are matched against top-down views. Do changes in behavior reflect underlying biological changes, or do changes in neurophysiological organization reflect changes in behavior?

We hoped that the authors' attempts to answer these questions would provide an overview of current understanding of behavior during this age period. Individual behavior is framed by environmental factors, however, and a full understanding of the 5 to 7 shift would require an examination of changes in overarching cultural processes and social relationships in addition to biological processes. To this end we enlisted a subgroup of contributors who focused on contextual processes in the family, with peers, in the school, and in the culture. Of them we asked each of the four questions in another form:

1. Is the environment of 7-year-olds different from that of 5-year-olds?

2. If the environments differ, are the differences quantitative or qualitative?

3. If the environmental differences are quantitative, are they continuous or discontinuous?

4. If the environmental differences are qualitative, are they the result of a reorganization of existing influences or the emergence of new ones?

The period between 5 and 7 has become of major social concern as the number of children suffering emotional, educational, and social failure has increased. It is usually in the elementary school classroom that children are for the first time rated comparatively and often competitively with their age-mates. Standardized assessments of and expectations for the behavior and achievement of each child reveal that many children are unable to meet these expectations and are not achieving these standards. It is important to understand the sources of these failures. Are they in the school system or in the child? If they are in the child, are they the result of failures in socialization during early childhood, or are they inherent temperamental or intellectual limitations? If they are in the school system, are there problems in the general curriculum or in teacher training, or is it in the uniformity of expectations for a heterogeneous group of 5- and 6-year-old children admitted to kindergarten and first grade? The answer to each of these questions depends on the contributions of the research community to our understanding of child development. This book is an effort to bring these contributions together in the hope not only of achieving understanding but also of making suggestions for change.

The 5 to 7 Year Shift

Although the 5 to 7 year shift was not officially labeled (by Sheldon H. White) until 1965, most formal educational systems are based on a historical recognition of this developmental change. From ancient times there has been cultural awareness of differences in children's behavior after around 6 years of age that permitted children to take on adultlike tasks. These included responsible care of other children, hunting and gathering, and, later, child labor in agricultural and then in industrial societies. Anthropological studies have found that most cultures begin formal training around age 6. Barbara Rogoff and her colleagues (1975) examined ethnographies from 50 communities around the world to determine for what age there was a major change in expectations for children's roles and responsibilities. They found a model pattern of such changes between 5 and 7 years, after which children were given increased responsibility for taking care of younger children, tending animals, and performing household chores, and—most important from the educational perspective—were expected to be teachable. Children after 7 were thought to have common sense or rationality.

White provided a wealth of evidence for this transition, having analyzed 21 developmental studies in a variety of cognitive, linguistic, and perceptual domains where children younger than 5 behaved in one way and those older than 7 behaved in another. Among the architects of those studies he noted Piaget, who in 1965 was just beginning to make an impression on mainstream

American psychological studies and educational practice. It was Piaget (1950), of course, who placed the 5 to 7 year shift at the center of his theory of cognitive development, a period during which children seem to move from dependence on appearance to an understanding of reality, from centering on single aspects of a situation to being able to coordinate multiple perspectives, and from an egocentric focus on their own points of view to an appreciation that other minds have alternative outlooks on the world. It is during this period, Piaget found, that children reach the stage of concrete operations, where an abstracted conservation of the whole replaces perceived changes in the parts.

The water-glass problem is the best known of Piaget's examples of how children's logic changes during this age period. The younger child reports that if water is poured from a short, wide glass into a tall, thin one there is more because the level is higher. The older child recognizes a relation between multiple dimensions in which the increase in height is compensated by a decrease in width, and will frequently state a logical principle, "Because nothing was added or taken away there must be the same amount of water." In classification tasks, the older child is able to consider more than one level in a conceptual hierarchy at a time and knows the difference between *all* and *some*. When younger children are shown a bouquet of roses and daffodils and asked if there are more roses or flowers, they frequently reply that there are more roses. The 7-year-old, understanding the concept of class inclusion, will say that all of them are flowers but only some of them are roses, so there cannot be more roses than flowers.

Piaget believed that the advanced intellectual performance of the older child was not the result of learning but rather the result of developmental processes. Children younger than 5 used a different system of logic than did children older than 7 and needed development to move ahead. Learning taught the names of flowers, more learning more names, but it was *development* that led the child to believe that there were more flowers than roses. Moreover, these changes in the logic of thinking were not restricted to school topics. Developmental advances in the understanding of the physical world were matched by advances in logic children applied to social situations, especially in the area of rules and moral judgments. Where younger children seemed to believe what was right and wrong depended on the consequences, whether or not they got punished, older children recognized that there was a system of morality based on social agreement.

Piaget resolved the classic nature-nurture debate by arguing that every educational achievement was a developmental achievement. The phenomenon of learning wasn't the result of some intellectual trait of the child, as believed in the United States and some other European cultures, or the excellence of the educational system, as believed in most Asian countries (Stevenson, Chen, & Lee, 1993). It was a coconstruction of the child and the teacher in which new knowledge was the result of a creative activity in which the child built upon prior mental constructions and the teacher provided the appropriate building material. Successful learning required a match between the state of the child's understanding and the curricular material. Development is the result of a dialectical partnership in which children transform the world through assimilation as they are transformed by the world through accommodation.

Revising Piaget

Modifications of Piagetian theories are changing the way we understand his contributions as well as leading to new versions of nativism and environmentalism. Neo-Piagetian reformulations are altering our interpretations of what capacities the child brings to the school on the nature side and what makes a successful socialization and educational system on the nurture side. These advances may have major implications for future theory, practice, and training in child development.

The importance of Piaget's work was not lost on educators who began to create Piagetian curricula and assessments where the details of children's knowledge were regarded as secondary to the logical processes by which children arrived at these details. Through the 1960s and 1970s until his death in 1980, Piaget's theories dominated the environment of those interested in the cognitive development of children. However, at about the same time as his physical demise, his work was undergoing a major theoretical demise in scientific circles. The post-Piagetian critique came from two directions, a nativist position arguing that Piaget was wrong in believing that younger children could not engage in logical thinking and an environmental position arguing that Piaget had ignored major environmental influences that produced developmental changes in thought.

New Understandings of the Child's Nature

The heart of the Piagetian position is that children's intelligence develops over time, moving through successive stages, each one building on the achievements of the previous one. Further, Piaget believed that when the child moved from one stage of development to another, for example, from preoperational to operational intelligence, behavior in every cognitive domain changed as children consolidated their new intellectual capacities. The first set of neo-Piagetians argued that there was no general change in children's logic from one stage to the next. There may be stagelike transitions in individual domains of behavior, like the solving of classification problems or the understanding of number concepts or even in moral judgment, but these changes were content-specific and not evidence for a universal shift based on a single central process of cognitive reorganization (Brainerd, 1978; Fischer & Silvern, 1985). Children did not change their thinking across the board. In some areas they might be quite advanced while in others somewhat delayed.

Then other neo-Piagetians argued in an even more serious set of criticisms that what Piaget believed to be changes in the cognitive competence of the child, even within individual domains, were only changes in performance. What Piaget had seen as new intellectual breakthroughs by the 5- to 7-year-old child were already within the capacity of much younger children and perhaps even innate (Gelman & Baillargeon, 1983). Complex understanding of number concepts, spatial transformations, and causality could be found in preschoolers and even infants (Baillargeon, 1994). These critics argued that Piaget confused performance with competence. From this perspective the argument is that children have more cognitive abilities than Piaget could detect in his research because his experiments restricted their ability to show their competence. When experiments are designed especially to reveal logical capacities of young children, surprising precocity is frequently found, even in moral judgment.

New Understandings of the Child's Nurture

The environmental revision of Piagetian theory is based on the contention that he did not pay enough attention to the effects of experience on the course of children's cognitive development. These experiences might arise in the family, in the community, or in the classroom. For example, the shift in behavior between 5 and 7 may be a consequence of schooling rather than the basis for schooling.

The 5 to 7 year shift for children in this country involves a transition from the experiences of the home or preschool to that of the elementary school. Most children do not enter the kindergarten with a clean slate. They have many expectations about the experiences they will encounter based on their previous time spent in school-like settings. Aspects of behavior that are especially salient are the child's prior encounters with social interactions, social comparisons, and self-esteem experiences in the home, day care, and the preschool. There are general differences in these settings that produce problems for children who expect the elementary-school experience to be a continuation of the preschool experience.

Home and preschool social interactions have been collaborative, whereas in the elementary school there is pressure for increasingly individual behavior and self-control. Talking and sharing activities with other children that are often judged by teachers to be evidence of disobedience may be the consequence of previous classroom experience. In the preschool the focus was on individual achievement rather than on comparisons with other children in the class. In the elementary school new enrollees may be confused about the new conditions. Children may perceive their teacher as believing that doing things faster and getting higher scores than other children in the class are more important than doing a good job. All of these changes have an impact on the self-esteem and social behavior of these children with major ramifications for their motivation and achievement in intellectual domains.

Cultural factors constitute another environmental influence on children's cognitive abilities. From a contextualist perspective the abilities of children cannot be understood apart from their participation in the ongoing activities of their family and cultural group. At what age a shift will occur may depend on the social activities of the child. Changes in what children think and do between the ages of 5 and 7 vary widely across different cultures that engage children in different kinds of social activities (Cole, 1984). The period in which a child moves from one stage to another will depend on the meaning and support given that transition by that culture. What is significant in the sociocultural perspective is that developmental transitions are neither in the child nor in the educational system but result from shifts in the roles and responsibilities associated with participation in a social group. From this point of view children will show earlier or later shifts in cognitive skills as a function of earlier or later social participation in activities that require those skills. Nature and nurture are reunited.

Shifts in Social and Emotional Behavior

White's proposal of a 5 to 7 year shift in behavior was originally restricted to cognitive functioning but has been extended by a new generation of developmental scientists into social and emotional domains, especially in regard to children's self-concepts. Although there is considerable debate about contextual contributions to cognitive development, there is more agreement that children's experiences are major determinants of their social and emotional behavior. But here, too, is an embedded question of the relative importance of what the child brings to the situation in terms of temperamental characteristics and what the child takes from the situation in terms of relationship experiences. Are children creators of or are they created by their social experiences?

Although the school is usually regarded as an educational institution, it may be the key determinant of the child's future emotional social adjustment. If development is a function of the child's engagement in cultural activities, then schooling must be reframed as a social activity whose significance goes beyond the training of children in reading, writing, and arithmetic. The nature of activities in the school will impact not only what the child learns, but also how children evaluate themselves as learners and participants in social institutions, in other words, their self-concepts.

Contemporary Views of the 5 to 7 Year Shift

In the plan for what follows we have taken the traditional path from microlevels to macrolevels of organization. This organization derives not from any reductionist faith that more complex levels of functioning are determined by simpler ones but from the practical belief that simpler levels may be easier to understand. After a framing statement by Sheldon White, the book moves from a consideration of neurobiological subsystems, to individual-level domains of cognition, emotion, and self-concept, to relationship-level concerns with siblings, peers, and families, to the institutional influences of social and cultural practices.

White offers an overview that places his own contributions in a historical context leading from ancient times to contemporary concerns with the social organization of cognition. He explores the evidence for a cognitive shift resulting from an inhibition of juvenile levels of thought and the establishment of more adultlike forms. He finds the basis of this change in the relation of the child to society in which the achievement is the ability to reason with and appear reasonable to others.

Neurobiology

Neurological processes are reviewed by Jeri S. Janowsky and Ruth Carper in an immediate contradiction of our premise that subordinate levels of human functioning are any less complex than superordinate ones. In answer to the question of whether there are brain modifications during the 5 to 7 year shift they point out that there are neurobiological changes during any time period. The question to which they address themselves is whether there is a critical brain change that may shape behavioral development during the shift period. They report that there is such a change in prefrontal areas that may be related to complex problem solving and the integration of information across modalities.

Cognition

Differing aspects of cognitive development are considered in the next set of chapters. Robert S. Siegler sets the stage by reviewing the evidence for a shift from unidimensional to multidimensional representations, which is the core of Piagetian-like theories of cognitive development. He concludes that the 5 to 7 year shift is not the result of such an either-or change in abilities but rather a shift in the characteristic tendencies of children's cognitive performances during this age period. He supports White in arguing for a better theory of situations where we can identify those in which children are more likely to demonstrate more complex thought processes.

A neo-Piagetian perspective is presented by Pierre Monoud, who contends that the transition expresses itself in a shift from partial representations of the 4- and 5-year-old to whole representations beginning around age 6. In an innovative analysis of motor behavior he is able to identify what he considers to be a qualitative shift from considering a mechanism as constructed of part processes to a unified conception of an apparatus as a totality. By discussing the unique changes of the 5 to 6 year period he sets the stage for equally important later transitions in the child's understanding of the relations between objects and their constituent dimensions during the period between ages 6 and 10.

Michael Chandler and Chris Lalonde focus their discussion of developing theories of mind toward differentiating 5- to 7-year-old children from younger ones. Confronting the contention that what had previously been thought to be characteristic of older children was already evident in the behavior of preschoolers, they argue against the view that the 3-year-old's ability to understand false beliefs of others is the same thing as the ability to hold an interpretive theory of mind. Moreover, they suggest that after the 5 to 7 shift further cognitive milestones need to be reached during later childhood and adolescence before an adult conception of mental life is fully achieved.

The integration of changes in memory, language, and cognitive functioning are explored by Katherine Nelson. She suggests that changes in memory during the 5 to 7 year shift are a further elaboration of the use of language as a tool for thinking. During this period language becomes a instrument for reflecting on thought and action, enabling the child to bring to mind and reexperience events from the past. The universal effect of being in a linguistic community is that a tool is provided for further advances in cognition and memory. Moreover, variations in the interactions of children with their caregivers produce large individual differences in memory performance. Changes in the ability to remember may be related to the extent to which memories are shared with others.

Another perspective on the relation between experience in social settings and cognitive development is provided by Frederick J. Morrison, Elizabeth McMahon Griffith, and Julie A. Frazier. They examine whether the shift in thinking between 5 and 7 may be a consequence of schooling rather than the basis for schooling. Their research reveals that there is no simple formula for categorizing those intellectual skills that the child brings to the school separately from those that are produced by the school. Children who had been in classrooms for 2 years, kindergarten and first grade, had a number of better memory, language, and quantitative skills than did children with the same chronological ages who had been kept out of school for the first year and had only completed kindergarten. But another set of memory, language, and number skills was no worse in the group of children who were older when they entered school, providing evidence for a developmental effect independent of classroom experience.

A discussion of reading achievement and dyslexia by Richard Olson, Barbara Wise, and Helen Forsberg rounds out the presentations on cognitive issues. There is a clear qualitative shift in performance in which children younger than 5 typically do not read and those over 7 do. Whatever the cognitive prerequisites for this shift in behavior, formal instruction is almost universally required. A negative consequence of the shift is that children with no previous evidence of cognitive dysfunction are revealed to have dyslexia after going through the experience of reading training and ending up failures.

Social and Emotional Behavior

Part of the new look in research during the 5 to 7 year transition has been the increased interest in emotional and social functioning. One aspect of the transition from cognitive to social domains is captured by Susan Harter in her chapter on developmental changes in self-understanding. The self that is considered to emerge through social interactions has more and more come to be viewed as a cognitive construction. As children's cognitive abilities change between 5 and 7, so does their self-system. Embedded within these cognitive changes is a change in affective organization as the child moves from self-descriptions restricted to basic emotions like happiness and sadness to descriptions of more complex self-affects like pride and shame.

The topic of fear is the center of Joan Stevenson-Hinde and Anne Shouldice's presentation on emotional development. When the focus is on transitions in the expression of emotion across the 5 to 7 year shift, individual consistency seems to be the dominant finding. When the focus is on the elicitors of emotions, the effects of cognitive transitions become apparent as children shift from imaginary fears, like ghosts, to realistic ones, like getting hurt or embarrassed.

Another perspective on assessing the stability of individual differences is provided by Judy Dunn in her chapter on sibling relationships and self-competence. She argues that a shift, such as between 5 and 7, would be evident if correlations of behavior across that age period were lower than for durations either before or after the hypothesized shift. She describes a complex picture where some correlations change during the transition and others increase with age with little indication of a shift.

Sociocultural Influences

The sociocultural perspective moves the study of change and transition from a focus solely on individual characteristics or environmental characteristics to one on the nature of the child's involvements in community activities. Barbara Rogoff makes the case that developmental transitions should be analyzed in terms of changes in people's roles and responsibilities in the activities in which they participate. In our culture the major shift in roles and responsibilities is the transition to school that occurs between 5 and 7. In other cultures transitions can be found as early as 3 or as late as 10 if there are major changes in roles for children at those ages. Rogoff presents a holistic view of development in which the change in roles is not entirely a consequence of children's emerging capacities but a cause of new child competencies as well.

Thomas Weisner continues this theme with an emphasis on an evolutionary perspective in which developmental transitions are interpreted in terms of the adaptive problems they resolve. In reviewing the characteristics of the shift in a number of cultures he finds that the major adaptive problem between 5 and 7 years is the transition to help with caregiving and subsistence activities as part of the more fundamental family task of maintaining a daily routine of life. The shift in adaptive tasks for Western children is predominantly the transition into school, which can create much more difficult adjustment problems than those found in more traditional cultures.

School Adjustment

The sociocultural perspective marks a major shift in our understanding of the 5 to 7 transition from a view focused on changes in child capacities as causes of the shift to one focused on changes in society's demands as a causal element. The demand that children go to school is such a change. The school transition produces a new world of peers, greater separation from the intimacy of home, parents, and siblings, and new standards of performance. Increasingly, attention has been devoted to changes in children's adjustment as markers of this transition. The definition of adjustment has expanded at the same time from a singular concern with academic achievement to more attention to the child's ability to understand and function in complex social systems like the classroom and school as well as the child's ability to negotiate new social relationships with teachers and peers.

Joan M. Barth and Ross D. Parke analyze the transition as a shift between two multifaceted social systems, the home and the school. The home is interpreted as a multilevel social system in which parents fulfill a variety of functions including interactors, models, coaches, and managers of children's behavior during the transition into school. Similarly, the complexity of children's behavior in the school is subdivided into a variety of nonacademic domains in which children must regulate those of their behaviors that have major impacts on their school performance. These include interaction with peers, emotional regulation, and attentional regulation.

Gary Ladd continues this theme in his chapter on shifting ecologies of social relationships during the transition. An interesting and important aspect of his contribution is his demonstration of how continuities of children's behavior from the family, the peer group, and the neighborhood into the school setting can produce both continuities and discontinuities of adjustment. For children with a history of cooperative peer interaction patterns there is a continuity of adjustment into the new setting. However, aggressive children are quickly disliked and soon gain a negative reputation that conditions the behavior of their classmates and teachers even when they are not engaged in aggressive behavior. Ladd concludes with a section on possible interventions to promote more successful adaptation of children to the transition into school.

The addition of a historical analysis further complexifies the sociocultural analysis of transition behavior. In their contribution Sharon L. Kagan and Peter R. Neville point out the changing nature of the shift into school. What was formerly a dramatic event beginning with the first day of school when the child was 5, today connotes an extended period of time, for different durations, for different children. Day-care, preschool, transition, and readiness classes are out-of-home experiences shared by more and more children before the classic elementary-school beginnings of formal education. In addition to prior experience with adults and age-mates in the home and the neighborhood, another major contributor to school adjustment is the child's prior experience in these school-like settings. Kagan and Neville contend that many of the problems result from discontinuities from preschool to formal schooling and that the resolution of these problems requires major interventions in our educational system. Here the developmental status of the child returns as a major factor because many of the adjustment problems in preschools are attributed to the unthinking downward extension of educational models designed for more advanced children.

In the second to last chapter of this book Samuel Meisels continues the theme of the necessity for educational reform to facilitate children's transition into school and promotes major changes in child assessment. Where abstract discussions of child development may inform academic research, they have achieved concrete embodiment in the nature of the way children's school performance is evaluated. Meisels indicts current scholastic assessment as based on a narrow perspective on child development that gives us little information on what children actually know and can do. In contrast to standard methods designed to assess decontextualized and isolated skills, he argues for evaluation of children's school performance in the kinds of meaningful contexts propounded by the sociocultural perspective.

Overview

We have raised a number of academic and social questions about the interpretation, causes, and consequences of the 5 to 7 year shift. In what follows the contributors to this book offer their perspectives on these queries. The answers will take a different form from those offered 25 years ago. In these differences will be found changes not only in how we understand child development but in how we understand our efforts to study and treat children in the home and in the school. The bottom line is that understanding children cannot be divorced from the study of the contexts in which they develop. Moreover, there is an implicit link between developmental theory and child adjustment in that the creators of the child's world in the family, the educational system, and society operate on the basis of their own theories of development. The ultimate goals of our effort are to bring the reality and the scientific and popular views of the 5 to 7 year shift into closer accord.

References

Baillargeon, R. (1994). How do infants learn about the physical world. *Current Directions in Psychological Science, 3,* 133–140.

Brainerd, C. (1978). The stage question in cognitive developmental theory. *Behavioral and Brain Sciences, 1,* 173–182.

Cole, M. (1984). Society, mind, and development. In F. Kessel & A. W. Siegel (Eds.), *The child and other cultural inventions* (pp. 89–114). New York: Praeger.

Fischer, K. W., & Silvern, L. (1985). Stages and individual differences in cognitive development. In M. R. Rosenzweig & L. W. Porter (Eds.), *Annual review of psychology* (Vol. 36, pp. 613–648). Palo Alto, CA: Annual Reviews.

Gelman, R., & Baillargeon, R. (1983). A review of some Piagetian concepts. In P. H. Mussen (Ed.), *Handbook of child psychology* (Vol. 3, pp. 167–230). New York: Wiley.

Piaget, J. (1950). *The psychology of intelligence.* London: Routledge and Kegan Paul.

Sameroff, A. J., & McDonough, S. C. (1994). Educational implications of developmental transitions: Revisiting the 5- to 7-year shift. *Phi Delta Kappan, 76,* 188–193.

Stevenson, H., Chen, C. & Lee, S. Y. (1993). Mathematics achievement of Chinese, Japanese, and American children: Ten years later. *Science, 259,* 53–58.

White, S. H. (1965). Evidence for a hierarchical arrangement of learning processes. In L. P. Lipsitt & C. C. Spiker (Eds.), *Advances in child development and behavior.* New York: Academic Press.

CHAPTER TWO

The Child's Entry into the "Age of Reason"

SHELDON H. WHITE

The hypothesis that children show a significant new organization of higher mental processes, enter an "age of reason" at age 7, can be traced back hundreds of years in Europe. Aries's (1962) social history of medieval childhood takes note of this assumption again and again:

> A fourteenth-century poem, reprinted several times in the fifteenth and sixteenth centuries expounds this calendar of the ages.
>> The first six years of life on earth
>> We to January would compare
>> For in that month strength is as rare
>> As in a child six years from birth. . . . (P. 22)
>
> It seems indeed that this age of seven marked a stage of some importance: it was the age usually given in the moralistic and pedagogic literature of the seventeenth century as the age for starting school or starting work. . . . (P. 66)
>
> Once he had passed the age of five or seven, the child was immediately absorbed into the world of adults. . . . (P. 329)
>
> In the Middle Ages, at the beginning of modern times, and for a long time after that in the lower classes, children were mixed with adults as soon as they were considered capable of doing without their mothers or nannies, not long after a tardy weaning (in other words, at about the age of seven). They immediately went straight into the great community of men, sharing in the work and play of their companions, old and young alike. (P. 411)

The Civilizing Vision of Human Development

The hypothesis that there is an "age of reason" was associated with the notion that a growing child should ideally develop civility. In 1530, Desiderius Erasmus of Rotterdam wrote a treatise on the bringing of civility to the young, *De civilitate morum puerilium* (On good manners for boys), which was to have an extraordinary influence. Erasmus's (1530/1985) treatise has been reprinted in 130 editions in many languages, 13 of those editions in the 18th century. The book was used as a textbook in schools. Erasmus declared a standard of perfection, *civility,* by which Europeans came to define what a higher type of human being ought to look and act like (Elias, 1939/1978). Nothing less than a definition of human development was being put forth in that declaration, a telos.

From the perspective of our quite different way of thinking in the 20th century, in an era that might well be called an "age of cognitive development," it is interesting to look back on Erasmus's statement of what happens in the socialization of the young:

> The task of fashioning the young is made up of many parts, the rest and consequently the most important of which consists of implanting the seeds of piety in the tender heart; the second in instilling a love for, and thorough knowledge of, the liberal arts; the third in giving instruction in the duties of life; the fourth in training in good manners right from the very earliest years. This last I have now taken up as my special task. (Erasmus, 1530/1985, p. 273)

Erasmus's treatise on manners discussed, in section after section, proper composure of the face and body, dress, appropriate behavior in church, behavior at banquets, meeting people, play, and behavior in the bedroom. In 16th- and 17th-century Europe, children were widely assumed to have achieved the "age of reason" at age 7, and from that point on were given instruction in civility until the age of 12 (Revel, 1989, p. 174). *Reason* was a less computational word than it is now; then it included the capacity for seemly, courteous behavior that took into account the needs, wishes, and rights of others.

This was a time when philosophical writers and social reformers were just beginning to imagine universal systems of schooling. Inevitably, they based their social designs on what people assumed children's development to look like. Johann Comenius, a 17th-century Moravian bishop, had a vision of peace on earth to be created by universal education, *pansophia,* and so he proposed phases of schooling corresponding to four hypothetical stages of children's development: from birth to age 6, the School of Infancy, or the Mother School; from ages 6 to 12, the Vernacular School; from 12 to 18, the Latin School, or Gymnasium; from 18 to 24, the Collegium Didacticum, or the College of Light (Burnham, 1926).

Jean-Jacques Rousseau in the 18th century also divided the life of the child into periods and designed educational strategies for each period. From birth to age 5, the "age of nature," babies should be given freedom. They should be "hardened" to hunger, cold, and fatigue but should not feel corporal punishment. The child should feel the resistance of things, not the resistance of people. From ages 5 to 12, a tutor, taking over from the parents, should guide without seeming to do so. The tutor should *not* reason with the child but should expose the child to objects and phenomena and invite the child to think about them. Rousseau's tutor should practice "negative education," keeping the child from other children, servants (who corrupt), most books, conventional school studies, learning by rote, and religion. The overarching principle was never to teach what the child cannot understand; otherwise the child will fill its mind with empty words. During later periods of development—12 to 15, 15 to 18, and 18 onward—Rousseau's child would go beyond observations of facts to comparing and reasoning about them. The child would learn a trade, become aware of its moral nature, and begin to study itself in relation to other men and women, something the child would do for the rest of his or her life (Cranston, 1991).

A tradition of writing about child development and educability began with substantial emphasis on development as the *civilization* of the child: the child's movement from lower, simple, brutish thoughts and behaviors governed by animalistic motives toward higher, more spiritual, more human forms of behavior and mental life governed by more refined and altruistic motives. This civilizing vision of child development is, of course, very close to the vision of child development given by G. Stanley Hall in his writings at the beginning of the 20th century. Hall's (1904/1969) definition of stages in children's development and his conceptions of the proper approach to be used in educating each stage were quite consistent with Rousseau's ideas. But in Hall's writings the properties of each stage, and of sequences, were fleshed out by data from studies of children. And Hall's social-biological stages of development (White, 1990, 1992) were conceived within the framework of an evolutionary vision.

From the Civilizing Vision to the Evolutionary Vision

We deal with a historical process of theoretical translation. It was comparatively easy, in the middle of the 19th century, for an older civilizing vision of child development to be aligned with biology and reexpressed as an evolutionary vision of child development. Hall's theory of child development was one realization of such a translation. Freud's evolutionary conception of psychopathology, with its emphasis on "civilization and its discontents," was another. A science-based philosophy arose to become a new basis for educational recommendations.

In his *Adolescence,* Hall (1904/1969) offered a post-Darwinian interpretation of the traditional age of reason. According to Hall this time in human growth reflects an evolutionarily older time of human maturity. Hall's pedagogical recommendations, in the end, are not dissimilar to those of Rousseau:

> After the critical transition age of six or seven, when the brain has achieved its adult size and weight and teething has reduced the chewing surface to its least extent, begins an unique stage of life marked

by reduced growth and increased activity and power to resist both disease and fatigue which . . . suggests what was, in some just post-simian age of our race, its period of maturity. Here belong discipline in writing, reading, spelling, verbal memory, manual training, practice of instrumental technique, proper names, drawing, drill in arithmetic, foreign languages by oral methods, the correct pronunciation of which is far harder if acquired later, etc. The hand is never so near the brain. Most of the content of the mind has entered it through the senses, and the eye- and ear-gates should be open at their widest. Authority should now take precedence of reason. Children comprehend much and very rapidly if we can only refrain from explaining, but this slows down intuition, tends to make casuists and prigs and to enfeeble the ultimate vigor of reason. It is the age of little method and much matter. (Pp. 451–452)

In the 19th century, as laws requiring compulsory and universal education were passed and enforced in one European society after another, and as there was a great growth of services, institutions, and professions for children, philosophical ideas such as Hall's were again and again built into institutional designs. The traditional hypothesis of an age of reason at age 7 has effectively become part of the social architecture that surrounds us all, the *intelligence*—I think that is a fair word—of our contemporary culture. Children begin formal schooling at ages 5, 6, or 7 in all the Western countries. Catholic canon law and English common law, and the several religious and legal practices built upon them, have expressed the assumption that children first know right from wrong, are first capable of guilt, have minds, reason, and are reasonable, at age 7.

The Intelligence of Our Social Architecture

One can study what our society tacitly "knows" about children through a study of the social architecture that surrounds us. The examination of the growing child's development through a consideration of the social discourses, institutions, and practices in which the child lives is, in a formal sense, part of a scientific enterprise that Wilhelm Wundt called *Völkerpsychologie*. Wundt was one of several 19th-century authors who argued that for a full understanding of human mental life the analytical, bottom-up psychology made possible by naturalistic methods must be supplemented by a second, top-down psychology exploring the higher, human mental structures through an examination of the language, myths, and cultural practices that are, in fact, determinants of those higher structures (Cahan & White, 1992).

Can one make some estimation of the phases and stages of children's development through the study of the progression of institutional arrangements for children in different places? Hall made some effort to do this in his *Adoles-*

cence. He surveyed the age of consent in different American states (1904/1969, 374). He looked at the ages at which children assume legal and criminal responsibility in a number of countries (p. 395 ff.). Some years ago, Barbara Rogoff and associates looked at the ages in which children begin to be assigned serious social roles and responsibilities in a number of traditional cultures (Rogoff, Sellers, Pirotta, Fox, & White, 1975; Rogoff, Newcombe, Fox, & Ellis, 1980). There are problems estimating the ages of children in nonliterate societies, but it appears that in a number of such societies children take a first step toward adult roles and responsibilities at age 7. Their movement toward adult standing is partial and probationary with more severe restrictions and judgments being imposed upon them later on, at ages 10 or 11. The sequence is intriguingly like that found in American schools—compulsory entrance into schooling at age 6, with some suspension of judgment about the child's academic ability for a few years. Beginning at the fourth-grade level, the child meets ability and achievement testing and a hardening of the school's estimation. Disadvantaged children, often enough, meet the tests of this period by falling into what has been called "the fourth-grade slump."

What all of this historical and cultural material seems to offer is the Vygotskian argument that theories about children's ages and stages are part of the intelligence of design of human societies. Buried in the architecture of the human world we live in and the day-by-day life that children lead are assumptions about cognitive changes with age. When we study the growth of children's intelligence, to some extent we are also studying the intelligence of the social practices that bring children into society. Common sense, I suspect, "reads" the social practices that surround us—the Book of Culture, no less valuable in everyday life than the Book of Nature. There are reasonable indications that American psychologists, before the onset of significant systematic inquiry into child development, recognized some significant change in children at the age of onset of schooling. In his *Talks to Teachers on Psychology,* for example, William James (1899/1983) remarked as follows:

> In all this process of acquiring conceptions, a certain instinctive order is followed. There is a native tendency to assimilate certain kinds of conception at one age, and other kinds of conception at a later age. During the first seven or eight years of childhood the mind is most interested in the sensible properties of material things. *Constructiveness* is the instinct most active; and by the incessant hammering and sawing, and dressing and undressing dolls, putting of things together and taking them apart, the child not only trains the muscles to coordinate action, but accumulates a store of physical conceptions which are the basis of his knowledge of the material world throughout life. Object-teaching and manual training wisely extend the sphere of this order of acquisition. . . .

It is not till adolescence is reached that the mind grows able to take in the more abstract aspects of experience, the hidden similarities and distinction between things, and especially their causal sequences. Rational knowledge of such things as mathematics, mechanics, chemistry, and biology, is now possible; and the acquisition of conceptions of this order form the next phase of education. Later still, not till adolescence is well advanced, does the mind awaken to a systematic interest in abstract human relations—moral relations, properly so called—to sociological ideas and to metaphysical abstractions. (Pp. 89–90)

James was writing at the very dawning of systematic investigations of child development. Hall began his Clark University questionnaire program in 1894. Yet James gives a relatively substantial picture of children's development, and one ought to reasonably regard this kind of picture as an indication of the substrate upon which systematic investigations of child development were built.

Twenty-four years after the quoted remark by James, the young Jean Piaget published *The Language and Thought of the Child,* the first step in his massive series of studies of children's intellectual development. We tend to look upon psychological theories as models—intellectual constructions that are, or should be, closely built upon research data. But there are indications that Piaget *began* his inquiry into children's thinking with the belief that there is a transition in children's thinking near the onset of schooling; a transition that he sought to explore and clarify with his early studies using the clinical method. Claparede's elegant introduction (1926) describes Piaget's scheme; it is, for that time, a reasonable statement of the 5 to 7 shift:

Our author shows us in fact that the child's mind is woven on two different looms, which are as it were placed one above the other. By far the most important during the first years is the work accomplished on the lower plane. This is the work done by the child himself, which attracts to him pell-mell and crystallizes round his wants all that is likely to satisfy those wants. It is the plane of subjectivity, of desires, games, and whims, of the *Lustprinzip* as Freud would say. The upper plane, on the contrary, is built up little by little by social environment, which presses more and more upon the child as time goes on. It is the plane of objectivity, speech, and logical ideas, in a word the plane of reality. (p. xii)

Systematic Studies of Child Development: The 5 to 7 Shift

There has been a research-based exploration of the "age of reason," and in the bulk of the paper to follow, I discuss the laboratory-based argument that there is a 5 to 7 shift in child development, a move from a more juvenile form of cognition toward a higher-order form of human cognition. The belief that there is such a transition in child development arose in several research literatures in the past half century, and until recently the research-based hypotheses have not been linked with the older tradition of belief. Diverse research traditions— Piagetian studies, Soviet psychology, psychoanalysis, and behavior-theoretical studies of children's learning—have converged on the argument that this is a time of significant change. It seems hard to believe that cultural traditions of belief in an "age of reason" have not played some role in 20th-century readings of the research findings.

The purpose of my paper is threefold:

1. First, I briefly recall the origins of the research-based hypothesis. The very designation of the phenomenon we are discussing, "the 5 to 7 shift," betokens an older, simpler understanding of what such a major change might be and how it should be studied.

2. In the second part of my paper, I discuss the scientific meaning of the study of the transition and what can and cannot be expected from it.

3. In the third part of paper, I contend that there is still a respectable argument that a significant transition does take place as children reach the 5 to 7 age range. The transition is not purely and simply cognitive. It is not—most of what we see is not, at any rate—programmed in the child's biology of growth. It will take new conceptual frameworks and new scientific tactics to fully come to terms with the phenomena of change and their practical meaning.

Origins of the Hypothesis of a 5 to 7 Shift

During the 1940s and 1950s, the study of child development took on a more theoretical cast. The work of the traditional child development institutes and centers began to come together with the work of mainstream psychology. A positive consequence of this was that the study of child development became more theoretical. A negative consequence was that the research program lost some of its multidisciplinary orientation. For a time, at least, researchers sought to account for observed phenomena of children's behavior using purely psychological theories of mind and behavior.

Robert R. Sears's antecedent-consequent analysis of the growth of dependency and aggression in childhood led the way in bringing the theories of mainstream psychology to bear on child development. Sears blended behavior theory and psychoanalytic thinking in his approach to child development. A number of the Sears group advocated a two-factor theory of dependency: a younger form organized around the child's needs for touching, caressing, comforting, and being physically near, and an older form organized around needs for more symbolic tokens of connection with others. Some of the Sears group believed there was an age transition from the younger form of dependency to the older (Sears, 1963), whereas others (Walters & Parke, 1965) felt that elements of both forms of dependency existed at all ages. Discussing the two-factor theory of dependency with members of the Sears group, I had the distinct impression that what they were proposing was a change from one form of dependency to another near the onset of schooling. I believed the transition was real—one could *see* changes in children's motivation when one worked with them in studies—and I have always felt a little regretful that this motivational understanding of the transition was never fully developed by the Sears group.

Most of the experimental child psychologists of the 1950s and 1960s studied children's learning. They gave preschool children tasks like those used with laboratory animals, and they predicted what the children would do from behavior theory. By and large, for preschool children at least, it all worked. The preschoolers were not put off by being given the simple tasks. They enjoyed them. They performed as the theories said they should. When I was a graduate student in Iowa City, it was a standing joke that the children in the university preschool did better by Hull-Spence theory than the laboratory rats of East Hall. But this happy harmony between the children and the animals broke sharply between 5 to 7 years of age.

Margaret Kuenne (1946) in her PhD dissertation had done the classic study of the way in which younger and older children transposed—their tendency, after having been rewarded for choosing the larger of two stimuli, to "transpose" by going on to choose the larger of two stimuli they had never seen before. Kuenne's younger children transposed narrowly, as do laboratory animals. Her older children transposed broadly, as do older children and adults. This difference between the younger and older children seemed rich with meaning. It identified an exact age at which children's learning departed from laboratory animal patterns, and it associated that departure with the use of language. It threw up an unexpected and interesting bridge between the Gestalters and the behaviorists, who were fighting a war about transposition at that time. Kuenne's older children followed Gestalt theory, whereas her younger children followed stimulus-response theory. Perhaps there was a place in the real world for both theoretical approaches.

Some years later, Howard and Tracy Kendler (Kendler & Kendler, 1962) used a somewhat more complex kind of transfer paradigm in which, again, preschool children behaved as laboratory animals do and older children of school age moved to an adultlike pattern of response. The period between 5 and 7 years of age seemed to be a twice-confirmed age in which the use of

mediation carried children away from the associative kinds of learning envis-
aged in behavior theory toward more complex and sophisticated approaches.

Mediation, it might be said, was a largely hypothetical language mechanism.
Presumably, children past a certain age do not respond to stimuli alone. They
look at stimuli and talk to themselves, and what they then do is determined
wholly or in part by what they say. Children's use of language was not very
carefully explored in these learning experiments, nor did any of the mediation
theorists attempt to explain exactly how older children came up with the verbalizations that would help them solve their problems as opposed to the thou-
sands of verbalizations that would be irrelevant or confusing. A large research
literature explored Kuenne's age shift in transposition and the Kendlers'
reversal-nonreversal shifts paradigm, but relatively little was learned. One of
the weaknesses of experimental child psychology—I think it is fair to say this
in 1994—is that experimental procedures are powerful enough to reveal interesting and replicable phenomena, but they offer such a narrow, awkward point
of view that it is often very difficult to pursue the causes of the phenomena by
follow-up experiments alone.

Putting the Transition into a Broader Context of Research and Theory

When I was a graduate student, the Kuenne transposition experiment was well
known and much discussed. A few years later, the work of the Kendlers convinced many experimental psychologists that some significant transition from
animal mechanisms toward uniquely human mechanisms of learning was taking place in the 5 to 7 age range. Mediation, it was said, carried the children
beyond the animals, but mediation, in the offhand way in which it was usually
put forward, seemed to explain very little. It summoned a homunculus that
spoke to the child in exactly the right way to instruct the child about the task at
hand. Some said that mediation meant something more than just language,
without specifying what that something was. The mechanism of mediation had
a short theoretical half-life in the 1960s, just when psychology passed through
what some now call the cognitive revolution. One can suspect that during this
awkward decade *mediation* was simply a polite way for some behaviorists to
say *thinking.*

I became seriously interested in the phenomena of change in the 5 to 7
age range when I accidentally found some age changes in the way in which
children dealt with stimulus-variation problems, changes that could not be
reasonably explained by mediation (White, 1966). Looking beyond the learning literature, I found a great diversity of reported changes in the 5 to 7
age range, and I argued that the learning phenomena had to be understood
in the context of a broad array of reported phenomena of change at this
time. At the bottom of all these changes was a cognitive shift, the inhibition

of a more juvenile level of thought and the establishment of a more adult-like form of thought (White, 1965).

The Child's Entrance into Society

Scientifically speaking, the study of transitions in children near the onset of schooling amounts to an analysis of coincidence and sequence—as, for that matter, does much of the age-related research of developmental psychology. We discover that at age 5 the child approaches a balance-beam problem in one way; at 7 years another way; and at 11 still another. What do these observations tell us about children? Experimental psychologists have from time to time questioned the meaning of research connecting age changes to behavior changes. According to them, age is time and time doesn't cause anything, so let go of age as a variable and look for truly meaningful independent variables. Such criticism reflects the physicalistic bias of traditional experimental psychology and the belief that if an inquiry doesn't work like physics it isn't scientific.

The study of age-related phenomena resembles a stratigraphic analysis. An archaeologist digs down beneath the surface of the earth and discovers 4 feet down, close together, a cup, an arrowhead, a breastplate, and a broken piece of pottery. The four objects are human-made, and a reasonable working assumption is that they are the product of one human group and all reflect some aspect of the group's way of life and system of manufacture. Analysis of what the artifacts imply is highly interpretative and calls upon a great variety of knowledge bearing upon the manufacture and use of objects such as these. We ask where in the world materials such as those in the objects are to be found, what kind of manufacture produced them, and where such manufacture is known to have been undertaken, and what kind of human society might be expected to use this kind of conjunction of objects. This sort of speculative, reconstructive activity aims to put the observed objects within the framework of a functioning human culture.

The stratigraphic analysis is fundamentally an analysis of coincidence, resting on factual observations that all can agree on, yet highly interpretative and argumentative when fully carried out. It does not give the kind of exact, prophetic certainty that once upon a time fond fantasy said that developmental psychologists ought to try for. Yet it is this kind of reconstructive analysis that, I believe, has to be at the heart of our analysis of the transitions found in children near the onset of schooling.

We are faced with some significant interpretative problems with regard to the artifacts of this age range. Consider, on the other hand, what the interpreters of recent research data on children have been telling us and, on the other, what a group of somewhat disparate psychological theorists have been saying.

Recent studies have, at least, complicated the assertion that there is a major change in children's thinking at the "age of reason." We have assumed that this is a time when higher mental processes become a new, strong force in children's thinking. Some new principle—reasoning, symbolic thought, abstract thought, planning, inference, complex conceptualization; all of these have been claimed—comes out in children.

The growing research literature has by no means absolutely denied this possibility, but it has cast doubt on just those features of the earlier research literature that seemed to affirm it. Repeated demonstrations of competence/performance trade-offs have cast doubt on the premise that there is any one age for the emergence of a distinctive intellectual skill. With suitable environmental rearrangements, children's performance on many classes of problems may be advanced or retarded by a half-dozen years. In the 1960s it seemed as though there was an unusually high incidence of qualitative changes in children's thinking near the entrance to schooling. Later research has qualified that judgment. The researchers of the 1960s mostly worked in preschools and elementary schools. As more and more research was done in infancy and the older years, more and more widespread qualitative changes have been found. Most significant have been findings of studies in the earliest years of life that have again and again suggested that the presumptive intellectual novelties of the later years—again, reasoning, symbolic thought, abstract thought, planning, inference, complex conceptualization—may be found in some detectable form in the first year or two of life.

All of this would seem to leave our cadre of developmental theorists—major leaguers such as Freud and Piaget, plus several dozen smaller claimants— somewhat high and dry. Why have so many claimed that a new principle of thought is emergent when reasonably careful research is unable to confirm it? Conceivably, they may have been reading one another. But there are indications that the beliefs and practices of some tribal theorists are in harmony with those of the Western theorists.

My assumption for some time has been that the imputation of an "age of reason" to the child at age 7 is not an absolute fact about child development but is a statement of the relationship of the growing child to the society in which he or she leaves. What happens to children between 5 and 7 is not the acquisition of an absolute ability to reason; it is an ability to reason with others and to look reasonable in the context of society's demands on the growing child to be cooperative and responsible.

The Age of Becoming Reasonable

In order to understand this kind of reasonableness I believe it essential to try to redirect our research on children's development in two important respects: first, to appreciate the full range of real-life situations in which children must act, and second, to understand the psychological requirements that children must reach to act in these situations.

It is essential to look at children in situations other than the tabletop universe of tests, problems, and games that are regularly used by psychologists to explore their cognitive development. The problem is not simply to try to achieve "ecological validity" in our research. There is no one valid environmental place for a growing child. A child lives in a complex ecology of homes, schools, farms, stores, roads, and factories. Part of the growing child's task is to learn how to act in these behavior settings; part of the child's task is to learn how to move among them, selecting some and rejecting others; part of the child's task is to learn how to build them and redesign them. We need a theory of situations that will give us a reasonable sense of the tasks a growing child faces in this environment of adaptation—so different from the legendary "Nature, red in tooth and claw" to which so many of our psychological theories are directed. So far, only Barker and Wright (1955) and Bronfenbrenner (1986) have given us sketches of what such a theory of situations would look like. I have written, with Alexander Siegel, a sketch of what cognitive development might look like in such an environment, cognitive development in time and space (White & Siegel, 1984). What does the "age of reason" look like among the places and spaces and standing behavior patterns and behavior settings of this kind of environment? It looks like a movement out into the school. It looks like a greater and greater investment of the child's time in community behavior settings and away from family behavior settings. It looks like the beginning of the child's participation in not one but three socialities: the society of the family bound by relationships of love and mutual regard; the society of peers organized by relationships of affiliation, friendship, and dominance; and the society of school and community, organized by rules and bureaucratic procedures (White, 1991).

Researchers need to understand what kinds of modifications should be made to the behaviors, motives, concepts, and knowledge of children in order to enable those children to participate in a "community of knowers." Much of what traditional studies of child development have looked at needs to be reconsidered in this regard. Piaget's studies using his revised clinical method—his studies of the child's conceptions of space, time, movement, geometry, chance, causality, and so forth—are usually construed in the terms of his genetic epistemology project. In such studies, Piaget sought to explore the genetic emergence of Kant's categories of thought. But, of course, there are more mundane reasons why a child would acquire socially conventional dimensions of number, time, space, and movement. They are essential devices if children are to locate themselves with respect to others and to cooperate in action and thought. Cooperation in thought with others means, among others things, the ability to share memories. My own interest in the phenomena of infantile amnesia and the development of narrative memories has centered on the child's development of this socially accessible memory system (White & Pillemer, 1979).

The question of what it means for a group of people to think together and to use one another's knowledge synergistically is, of course, profound, and yet I think it is essential to think about what is entailed in the social organization of cognition if we are to understand fully what is happening to children in the "age of reason."

References

Aries, P. (1962). *Centuries of childhood: A social history of family life.* New York: Knopf.

Barker, R. G., & Wright, H. F. (1955). *Midwest and its children: The psychological ecology of an American town.* New York: Row, Peterson.

Brofenbrenner, U. (1986). Ecology of the family as a context for human development: Research perspectives. *Developmental Psychology, 22,* 723–742.

Burnham, W. H. (1926). *Great teachers and mental health: A study of seven educational hygienists.* New York: D. Appleton.

Cahan, E. D., & White, S. H. (1992). Proposals for a second psychology. *American Psychologist, 47,* 224–235.

Claparede, E. (1926). Preface. In J. Piaget, *The language and thought of the child.* (M. Warden, Trans.). New York: Harcourt, Brace.

Cranston, M. (1991). *The noble savage: Jean-Jacques Rousseau, 1754–1762.* Chicago: University of Chicago Press.

Elias, N. (1978). *The civilizing process: The history of manners.* (E. Jephcott, Trans.). New York: Urizen Books. (Original work published 1939.)

Erasmus, D. (1985). On good manners for boys. (B. McGregor, Trans., 3). In J. K. Sowards (Ed.), *Collected works of Erasmus* (Vol. 25). Toronto: University of Toronto Press. (Original work published 1530.)

James, W. (1983). *Talks to teachers on psychology and to students on some of life's ideals.* Cambridge, MA: Harvard University Press. (Original work published 1899.)

Hall, G. S. (1969). *Adolescence: Its psychology and its relations to physiology, anthropology, sociology, sex, crime, religion and education.* New York: Arno. (Original work published 1904.)

Kendler, H. H., & Kendler, T. S. (1962). Vertical and horizontal processes in problem solving. *Psychological Review, 69,* 1–16.

Kuenne, M. (1946). Experimental investigation of the relation of language to transposition behavior in young children. *Journal of Experimental Psychology, 36,* 471–490.

Revel, J. (1989). The uses of civility. (A. Goldhammer, Trans.). In R. Chartier (Ed.), *A history of private life:* Vol. 3. *Passions of the Renaissance* (pp. 167–205). Cambridge, MA: Belknap.

Rogoff, B., Newcombe, N., Fox, N., & Ellis, S. (1980). Transitions in children's roles and capabilities. *International Journal of Psychology, 15,* 181–200.

Rogoff, B., Sellers, M. J., Pirotta, S., Fox, N., & White, S. H. (1975). Age of assignment of roles and responsibilities to children: A cross-cultural survey. *Human Development, 18,* 353–369.

Super, C. M. (1991). Developmental transitions of cognitive functioning in rural Kenya and metropolitan America. In K. R. Gibson & A. C. Petersen (Eds.), *Brain maturation and cognitive development: Comparative and cross-cultural perspectives* (pp. 225–251) New York: Aldine de Gruyter.

Walters, R. H., & Parke, R. D. (1965). The role of the distance receptors in the development of social responsiveness. *Advances in Child Behavior and Development, 2,* 59–96.

White, S. H., (1965). Evidence for a hierarchical arrangement of learning processes. *Advances in Child Behavior and Development, 2,* 187–220.

White, S. H. (1966). Age differences in reaction to stimulus variation. In O. J. Harvey (Ed.), *Flexibility, adaptability and creativity* (pp. 114–132). New York: Springer.

White, S. H. (1990). Child Study at Clark University: 1894–1904. *Journal of the History of the Behavioral Sciences, 26,* 131–150.

White, S. H. (1991). The child as agent: Issues of cognitive style and personal design in human development. In S. Wapner & J. Demick (Eds.), *Field dependence-independence: Cognitive style across the life span* (pp. 7–22). Hillsdale, NJ: Erlbaum.

White, S. H. (1992). G. Stanley Hall: From philosophy to developmental psychology. *Developmental Psychology, 28,* 25–34.

White, S. H., and Pillemer, D. B. (1979). Childhood amnesia and the development of a socially accessible memory system. In J. F. Kihlstrom & F. J. Evans (Eds.), *Functional disorders of memory* (pp. 29–73). Hillsdale, NJ: Erlbaum.

White, S. H., and Siegel, A. W. (1984). Cognitive development in time and space. In B. Rogoff & J. Lave (Eds.), *Everyday cognition: Its development in social context* (pp. 238–277). Cambridge, MA: Harvard University Press.

Wolf, D. (1982). Understanding others: A longitudinal case study of the concept of independent agency. In G. E. Forman (Ed.), *Action and thought: From sensorimotor schemes to symbolic operations* (pp. 297–327). New York: Academic Press.

PART TWO

Neurological Transitions

CHAPTER THREE

Is There a Neural Basis for Cognitive Transitions in School-Age Children?

JERI S. JANOWSKY AND RUTH CARPER

The purpose of this chapter is to describe the neurobiological changes in the brain between 5 and 7 years of age. In addition, we address the possibility that neurobiological changes correlate with behavioral changes in children during this period. Regardless of whether my fellow contributors to this volume conclude that there is a true "shift" in cognitive or emotional processing between 5 and 7 years, there *are* a variety of neurobiological changes in the brain during this period. But there are changes in the brain during any time period, be it the first few months of life, the last few months of life, or on a moment-to-moment basis as we learn and remember the events in our lives. The discovery of changes in the biology underlying cognitive processing is dependent on the level of neurobiological detail one chooses to examine. So the problem we try to address in this chapter is what brain changes are the *critical* events that may shape behavioral development during this time period. We outline a variety of brain maturational changes during this period. We emphasize those that can best be related to the behavioral changes in children during this period, and we speculate about one behavioral example that may be a direct result of maturation of a particular brain system.

Evidence that there are unambiguous neural shifts, and that these unequivocally mediate behavioral changes between 5 and 7 years, would make a nice unifying package between developmental behavioral data and neuroscience. It is a story we would like to endorse. However, there are a set of ground rules, caveats, or warnings that must be considered before we offer for sale such a bill of goods.

Cautions About the Neurobiology of Brain Development and Cognitive Correlates

Does Neurobiology Matter?

One might ask at this point, Why concern ourselves with the brain basis of behavioral transitions at all? After all, if a transition in development is obvious and quantifiable, and its cognitive mechanisms, environmental mechanisms, or both and its triggers can be clearly defined, what does the brain have to do with it? First is the reductionist argument. Since signals between neurons mediate all behavior, knowledge of the development of the mediating neural systems will further inform us about the mechanisms that underlie behavioral development. Granted, this is a promissory note. For those who study abnormal patterns of development, the continuing maturation of the brain, particularly in areas that mediate complex cognition and behavior, may help explain why some neurobehavioral disorders are not apparent until children reach the school-age years. Disorders such as dyslexia (Hynd, Marshall, & Semrud-Clikeman, 1991; Jernigan, Hesseling, Sowell, & Tallal, 1991; Simonds & Scheibel, 1989) and hyperactivity (Shue & Douglas, 1992; Smith, Kates, & Vriezen, 1992) may not be expressed until the brain regions that mediate the cognitive disorder become fully functional. Likewise, the continuing maturation of the brain explains why an early and static brain injury such as a frontal lobe stroke can cause an apparently progressive disorder in behavior (Grattan & Eslinger, 1991, 1992; Janowsky & Finlay, 1986; Williams & Mateer, 1992).

More important is that often the factors that are critical for a behavioral transition are not clear. For instance, there may be conflict about exactly when the "magic moment" of a behavioral transition happens, or why it occurs *then* and not at some other time. The identification of neural changes that are temporally associated with a behavioral transition, or occur in the functional system that most likely mediates the behavior, provides converging evidence on the mechanisms that underlie a transition. Finally, an analogy: looking across one's fence into the playground of your neighbor might get you in trouble. It also might provoke an interaction, a discussion, or a learning experience, even a pleasant one. Such interactions, in this case between the playground of the child development researcher and that of the neuroscientist, might promote a greater understanding of behavior, which, after all, is the research goal of *both* camps. Anyway, who can resist peeping through fences?

What Are the Criteria for a Transition?

We define a *transition* as a *qualitative* change in behavior, mediated by a distinct mechanism that was not previously available to the child. This definition excludes as a transition behavioral change that is strictly quantitative in nature.

It also excludes apparently qualitative behavioral changes that are in fact mediated by the same cognitive processes that mediated an earlier form of the behavior. Two forms of nonlinear change in development often serve as examples of developmental transitions. By *nonlinear* we mean those behaviors that undergo a sudden change in their rate of development or in their character. One form of nonlinear change is the emergence of a new behavior, one that was not previously in a child's repertoire. An example is the onset of expressive speech at around 12 months of age (Bates, Thal, & Janowsky, 1992). A significant change in the quality or frequency of an existing behavior, such as the increased elaborateness of recalled memories in school-age children, might also qualify as a transition (Nelson, 1993; Pillemer & White, 1989). The implication of both of these forms of transition is that a new mechanism emerges to mediate the behavioral change. Several cautions must be voiced at this point: First, nonlinear development of a behavior does not necessarily mean that a new mechanism has emerged to cause or mediate the behavioral change (Bates & Carnevale, 1992). Bates and Carnevale use as their example the language burst that occurs between 16 and 22 months of age, in which toddlers go from having an expressive vocabulary of 50 words to hundreds, seemingly overnight. It could be that a new cognitive and possibly a neural system develops and causes this explosion of words. Alternatively, it could be that an exponential function best describes the process of vocabulary development. Thus, the same mechanism or mechanisms that methodically build vocabulary in the first few months are the same that underlie the explosion of words between 16 and 22 months. In this scenario, each addition of words promotes greater acquisition of words in the subsequent learning phase. Therefore, the "vocabulary burst" of 16 to 22 months is simply the next instantiation of vocabulary development built on the, by this time, rich substrate. Assuming this is the case, if we define *transition* as requiring both the onset or elaboration of a behavior and its mediation by a new cognitive and/or neural mechanism, then the language burst does not qualify as a transition point in language development. The discovery of a neural change that is time locked to the onset of a new behavior would lend support that the *onset* of a new behavior was a true transition. Likewise, if one found a neural change that was causally linked to a qualitative, or quantitative, burst in a behavior, that, too, would help differentiate a true transition from the further development of a nonlinear or exponentially developing behavior.

Nature Versus Nurture

Region-specific brain maturation may correlate with transitions in behavior. However, we do not know if they are the cause or the result of cognitive transitions. Moreover, recent work in neurobiology makes the causal question, that is, the child's environment versus neural and cognitive maturation as mechanisms for cognitive transitions, no longer a viable question. Examples from multiple neurobiological levels show that the formation and function of the brain is determined by an interaction between "hard wired" biological processes and the environment in which they act (Hubel, Wiesel, & LeVay, 1977; Levinthal, Macagno, & Levinthal, 1975; Merzenich et al., 1984). This includes the microenvironment of the neuron, which determines the number and location of synaptic connections, as well as the activity-dependent selection of these connections. The completion of each step in the formation of the brain's architecture has the capacity to then influence the environment in which subsequent processes unfold. Changes in brain function mediate changes in the child's behavior, then the child's behavioral repertoire will, in turn, influence the environment in which the brain operates, from the seeking of warmth to sensory stimulation and to the challenges of solving complex problems (Greenough, Black, & Wallace, 1987). Therefore, we sidestep the question of whether biological change causes, mediates, influences, or modulates cognition or is the *result* of a cognitive transition during development. Instead, we point out the *associations* between cognitive and neurobiological events during development.

Variability in the Brain

Both an obstacle and a blessing to our understanding of the brain bases of cognitive development is the remarkable variations from brain to brain. The variability is obvious from the external morphology of the gyri and sulci (Gilles, Leviton, & Dooling, 1983) to the variability in neuron and synapse number, the length of dendrites, and so forth (Conel, 1939/1967; see Figure 3.1 for a schematic of these neural elements). For example, the number of axons in the major fiber pathway between the two hemispheres (the corpus callosum) varied by as much as 25 million axons in the three monkeys studied (LaMantia & Rakic, 1990). It is also true that the time course and quality of cognition, motor function, or emotional development are also fantastically variable across children. Biological variability makes our search for biological correlates of cognition more difficult. However, variability from one brain to another may help explain the variability between children in the manner and time at which they attain particular milestones. Likewise, different children, attain behaviors in very different environments from each other. Variability in the anatomy and physiology of the brain may allow for the brain to respond to a variety of environments. In fact, if our underlying biology were identical, then one would have to conclude that cognitive development has few, if any, brain correlates. We would be hard-pressed to account for the variability across children of such functions as language or motor development. If the biology is not a constraint on when or what form cognitive development takes place, it might be under-

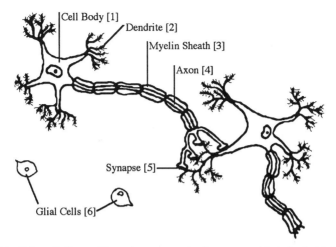

Figure 3.1   Schematic figure of the major components of a neuron and their developmental changes. [1] Neurogenesis is completed prenatally. [2] Dendritic "trees" continue to expand postnatally and change throughout life. [3] Myelination in cortex continues through adolescence. [4] Axon selection and retraction in cortex occur both pre- and postnatally. [5] Synaptogenesis, synapse selection, and reorganization in cortex occur throughout life. [6] Gliogenesis occurs both pre- and postnatally.

stood instead as a source of variance in the behaviors that children express (Segalowitz & Rose-Krasnor, 1992).

Little Human Data

Whereas my colleagues in this volume are often writing with the advantage of exquisitely detailed knowledge concerning behavioral development in children, we are writing from a position of relative ignorance regarding human developmental neurobiology. Not that this should stop one from hypothesizing about brain-to-behavior associations. There are very few studies cataloging growth spurts and changes in the human brain during development. This is because (a) after the perinatal period children are rather robust creatures and the opportunity to investigate their brains through autopsy is rare, and (b) obvious ethical issues prevent us from investigating brain development using the kinds of invasive techniques that would best catalog neurobiological change over the first decade of life. The reluctance to perform invasive investigations, even in the situation of suspected disease, is even more the case when children are the objects of investigation. Although data on brain development from animal models are extremely useful for delineating general principles of biological development, such as the order of neuron birth in different brain regions (e.g., Rodier, 1980), the parallel time course of development in the human can only be estimated. In addition, work from animal models will not help determine the neurobiology of

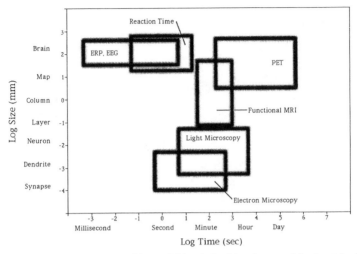

Figure 3.2   Schematic illustration of the spatial (vertical axis) and temporal (horizontal axis) resolution of techniques used to study brain function in humans and human tissue discussed in this chapter. The hazy edges of each box suggest that these are approximations and that these techniques may not be limited to these boundaries in the future. This is particularly true for Functional MRI (magnetic resonance imaging), which is a technique still in development. This figure emphasizes the different spatial and temporal characteristics of methods used to study the neurobiology of behavior, none of which alone is sufficient to understand the neural basis of a behavior or its development. Other abbreviations: EEG, electroencephalogram; PET, positron emission tomography. "Map" refers to functionally specialized brain regions. The figure is substantially modified from that appearing in Sejnowski & Churchland (1989).

human specific behaviors such as language. Therefore, we study human developmental neurobiology through brain imaging and electrophysiological techniques, and occasionally anatomical studies using autopsy material. None of these techniques catalog changes in the brain at the level of analysis that is probably most interesting for making brain-to-behavior associations. However, technological advances over the next few years, such as echo planar functional magnetic resonance imaging, may improve our database considerably (Belliveau et al., 1992; Kim et al., 1993). These techniques will allow us to image and compare region-specific brain activity (e.g., metabolism, or blood flow) in much finer detail than is currently available, while the child performs various tasks and at different stages of brain and cognitive maturation. (See Figure 3.2 for a summary of the temporal and spatial resolution of various imaging techniques).

Levels of Analysis

There are multiple functional levels of complexity in the brain, and it is not clear which of these, or in what combination, will be most informative concerning the brain basis of cognitive development. For instance, will the critical neurobiological key to cognitive shifts be the number of neurons, the number of synapses, changes in connections between cortical columns, or the relationship between inhibitory and excitatory synapses? What level of analysis is the most appropriate one to examine as the associated neurobiological event in behavioral development? To further complicate the picture, this list of candidate anatomical or physiological processes does not capture a change in the conformation or functioning of a neural *network* (e.g., Georgopoulos, Taira, & Lukashin, 1993), that is, interactions between neurons, columns, and structures, which could be yet another means by which qualitative developmental changes are mediated. In this case, shifts in the interaction between different brain areas, both increases and decreases in activity, could mediate a behavioral shift. The infinite levels of the nervous system in which to search causes a "burden of proof" nightmare. That is, does finding no relation between a behavior and a hypothesized neural substrate mean that none exists? If no clear associations are found for a behavior, it may mean that a further search, at a different level of analysis, is in order. It may also mean that the behavior is an emergent result of a wide range of precursor biological processes, none of which alone serves as a trigger or critical element that enables the behavior to unfold. An ideal proof would be one in which a behavioral change is attenuated or absent entirely when a distinct neurobiological process is prevented or slowed, either in the situation of disease or brain damage. However, examples of such cases in the literature are rare.

With these warnings and background, let us examine the neural substrates on which children may or may not build transitions in behavior.

The Brain at 5 to 7 Years of Age—Additive Processes

There are several procedures that are critical for manufacturing a functional brain:

1. The cells of the brain must be made: both neurons and glia.

2. The cells must migrate to the location from which they will operate, as they are often made in "manufacturing plants" distant to the location from which they work.

3. The neurons must make connections to an appropriate target structure—and make just the right number of connections (synapses).

4. Those connections must be functional for behavior to occur. By functional, we mean that the physiological machinery, such as the production and release of neurotransmitter, has to be created and that neurons must be capable of efficient transmission of information.

5. Myelination of axons must occur to increase the efficiency of neural transmission.

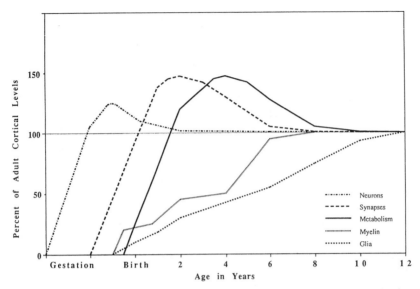

Figure 3.3   Approximation of the time course of additive and regressive events in brain development. The figure is a substantial modification of the original, which appeared in Bates, Thal, & Janowsky (1992).

Each of these steps and its state of completion at the point that children enter school (5 to 7 years) is discussed in turn. (See Figure 3.1 for a diagram of neural elements; see Figure 3.3 for a summary of the time course of maturation of different neural processes.) This discussion focuses on cortical rather than subcortical brain regions because the behavioral questions to be addressed are those that use cortical neural systems for processes such as attention, memory, and problem solving.

Neurogenesis

Current evidence suggests that no new neurons are made in the human brain postnatally (Dobbing & Sands, 1973; Sidman & Angevine, 1962). One exception is the olfactory bulbs where neurons that function as primary olfactory receptors are made throughout life (Graziadei & Monti Graziadei, 1979). Therefore, if new behaviors arise between 5 and 7 years, they are not due to the production of new neurons.

Glia, the other major cell type that constitutes the brain, is made prenatally and postnatally and probably continues to be generated throughout life (Dobbing & Sands, 1973). There are several glial subtypes, each with different functions. Glia transfers nutritive factors to neurons and can act as a shield or barrier that compartmentalizes groups of neurons so that transmitters do not "leak" between them. One specialized glial subtype functions as "insulation" (myelin) around axons to increase the speed of signal transmission. Other specialized glial subtypes serve as guides for neural migration during development or as mechanical barriers that serve to help guide axons to their targets. Glia also serves as the "garbage collectors" of the brain, "digesting" dead neurons or debris in the brain (DeFelipe & Jones, 1988; Kandel & Schwartz, 1981). Although neurons have been considered the information processors of the brain, surprisingly, recent studies suggest that glia may also serve to process and help transfer information (MacVicar, Crichton, Burnard, & Tse, 1987; Matute & Miledi, 1993)! Although it is possible that a change in glial production rate in a localized cortical region could contribute to a significant change in particular behaviors, detailed information on region-by-region rates of glia production in the brain in humans is not available. Other than glia's role in myelination (see "Myelination" section), there simply isn't enough information to consider an active role for glia in behavioral development at this time. If the initial data that glia can process or transfer information are correct, the search for "neural" mediators of behavioral development will get much richer and much more complex in the very near future.

Migration

Neurons and some glia cell types are "born," or generated, in one brain region and migrate to their final destination where they make and receive connections (Rakic, 1972). Neural migration is probably complete by birth in humans. Therefore, migration is not a candidate process to mediate behavioral transitions in school-age children.

Making of Connections

The process of making connections takes place prenatally and through the first several years of life. Rearrangements in connections occur throughout life. Therefore, behavior in the 5 to 7 year period is influenced by the process of making connections in the cortex. After neurons have reached their location of "residence for life," or during the process of migration, they send out axons to target locations and make connections with one or more target structures (Innocenti & Clarke, 1984; Ivy, Akers, & Killackey, 1979). Simultaneously, they expand their dendritic branches, making available "parking places" for connections from other neurons. Examples of the problems that the neuron faces in order to make appropriate connections are (a) how to guide an axon(s) to an appropriate target location, from a few microns away to several feet away; (b) how to decide the number of connections to make or receive from one to several thousand; and (c) in those cases where multiple neurotransmitters are produced by the same neuron, which transmitter should be released to communicate with the postsynaptic cell and under what circumstances.

Some of these problems are solved by careful genetic programming, essentially "predetermination" of the connection and its form. In some invertebrate species neuron number and connections between neurons are completely pre-determined and each animal's nervous system is a replica of every other in its species (e.g., *c. elegans;* Hall & Russell, 1991; but see Levinthal et al., 1975, where genetically identical animals have different dendritic "trees" owing to the influence of local environmental-genetic interactions). This requires rather incredible genetic programming and no behavioral flexibility should a change occur in the animals' environment. It is increasingly clear from recent work that this is not the case for many, if not most, cortical connections in humans. The general blueprint may be programmed, but there are multiple signals and mechanisms that *promote* axon growth, guidance, and synaptogenesis. Signals along the axon's route, as well as local signals at the axon terminal, will promote or inhibit synaptic connections. In addition, there is considerable evidence for relatively unguided exuberant growth and connections (for review, see Purves & Lichtman, 1985). For instance, data from animal models show that motor cortex neurons that must find their way to target structures several inches or even feet away (e.g., the spinal cord) originally send axon branches to a variety of brainstem structures on their way to the spinal cord (Stanfield, O'Leary, & Fricks, 1982). Later during development, the inappropriately spawned branches retract leaving only the appropriate connection between cortex and spinal cord. This "slop" in the system decreases the amount of genetic preprogramming required, increases the possibility for synaptic variability from animal to animal, and increases the role of signals external to the neuron, that is, the environment of the brain in shaping the final neural connections and therefore its function.

Whereas synapses are probably made and remade throughout life, there is a period of synaptic exuberance during the first several months to years of life. Unfortunately, the timing of the exuberant synaptic growth from region to region in humans isn't known, and although there is general agreement that exuberance occurs, there is controversy between findings from human autopsy studies (Huttenlocher, 1979; Huttenlocher & de Courten, 1987; Huttenlocher, de Courten, Garey, & Van Der Loos, 1982) and nonhuman primate studies (Rakic, Bourgeois, Eckenhoff, Zecevic, & Goldman-Rakic, 1986; Zecevic, Bourgeois, & Rakic, 1989). The work of Huttenlocher and colleagues shows that different brain regions have their peak of synaptic density at different times in development. For instance, the primary visual cortex peaks in synaptogenesis rather early (at approximately 3 to 4 months postnatally for Layers I to IV), whereas Layer III in prefrontal cortex reaches a peak in synaptic density at approximately 1 year. These data also show layer-to-layer variability of the time of maximum synaptic density. On the other hand, data from Rakic and colleagues show a peak in synaptic density *across cortex* at approximately the second postnatal month in monkeys, regardless of whether the area was primary sensory, motor, or association cortex. They suggest that there are three "waves" of synaptic change: one at about 2 months of age in monkeys (corresponding to approximately 6 months in humans), one at puberty, and a wave of synaptic decline with aging. Rakic and colleagues interpreted the simultaneous exuberance to suggest that there is a common signal for synaptogenesis across cortex. They have suggested that simultaneous synaptogenesis may promote the competitive interaction between neurons that results in selection and stabilization of some connections and the discarding of others (see "Subtraction and Selection" section).

The morphology of dendrites and dendritic branching often signals the degree or maturation of connections. A classic example is the difference in morphology of dendritic spines in the motor cortex between an 18-week-old fetus and a 7-year-old child. Early in development, the motor cortex dendrites lack spines; later the spines appear long and spindly (33 weeks' gestation); and finally, stubby, mushroom-shaped spines are seen in childhood (Purpura, 1975). Abnormalities in dendrite and dendritic spine development occur in some retarded children and adults in whom there are fewer thickened spines, suggesting "dysmaturation" of dendrites and therefore abnormalities in the location and number of synaptic contacts (Huttenlocher, 1991; Jay, Chan, & Becker, 1990).

Determining Function

Similarly, inequities in dendritic development between brain areas or between the right and left hemispheres can serve as a sign of functional differences between two regions. Pyramidal neuron dendrites in Layer III of frontal cortex are only half their adult length by 2 years of age, whereas Layer III in visual cortex reaches adultlike lengths by 18 months (Huttenlocher, 1990). An autopsy study reported that in the first 2 years of life motor cortex dendritic lengths are greater than those in the speech area and that the right hemisphere appears more advanced than the left hemisphere (Simonds & Scheibel, 1989). By 4 to 5 years of age, distal segments of dendrites predominate in the left hemisphere, and the speech area shows more segments and longer segments than does the motor area. Such data are still preliminary, and the significance of different dendritic morphology from area to area isn't entirely clear. The authors suggest that the longer distal segments of dendrites in the left hemisphere may mean a shift from a fast rate of development of the right hemisphere and predominance of function by the right hemisphere to a shift to dominance by the left hemisphere, which remains for the rest of development. Just when this shift occurs is still unclear (Scheibel, 1991). In addition, there are numerous technical problems with autopsy studies. Still, differences in dendritic development between brain areas may provide clues as to the critical brain regions and time points for transitions in functions, such as language, over the first several years of life.

So what does the time course of connectivity tell us about function? Regardless of whether there is a region-by-region or simultaneous signal for synaptogenesis, and regardless of the exact moment of the synaptogenic peak, or completion of dendritic growth, the early school-age years are a time of connective or synaptic exuberance. This exuberance, at a time of increasing behavioral fine-tuning and behavioral complexity, sets the child up with ample neural material for behavioral development. It may, in fact, be a time of the greatest availability of neural hardware in one's lifetime.

MYELINATION

As the process of synaptogenesis continues, the axons of neurons become myelinated. Specialized glial cells wrap around the axon providing an insulating shield against cross talk from other axons and making the electrical signal travel faster down the axon, thus increasing the rate of signal transduction (Kandel & Schwartz, 1981). For instance, the transmission velocity down an unmyelinated axon is less than 1 m/s but it averages 10 to 100 m/s in myelinated axons (Sejnowski & Churchland, 1989). Periods of myelination correlate with increased metabolic activity seen in positron emission tomography (PET) scans (Dietrich, 1990). This indicates that increasing myelination correlates with increased brain function. Likewise, developmentally delayed infants and children frequently show delayed myelination on magnetic resonance imaging (MRI) scans (Baierl, et al., 1988; Harbord et al., 1990), suggesting that myelination signals the functional maturation of cortical systems. Therefore, the timing of the myelination process in certain brain areas presents itself as a viable candidate mechanism for shifts in cognitive development.

The greatest proportion of the myelination process occurs rapidly during the first 2 years of life in humans, then continues much more slowly until adolescence and possibly even later (Yakovlev & Lecours, 1967). Primary sensory connections myelinate first, followed by myelination of motor pathways (Barkovich, Kjos, Jackson, & Norman, 1988). The behavior of infants and toddlers correlates with the order of myelination in the brain. Sensory systems are fully functional before the fine-tuning of motor performance is finished.

Although there is little conflict about which regions begin to myelinate before other regions (see Dietrich, 1990, for review), there are conflicting data concerning the time course for completion of myelination. This is most likely due to the sensitivity of the measurement technique. The three techniques that have produced data on myelination are autopsy studies, MRI studies, and amount of brain cholesterol as a nonspecific marker of myelin. We focus on four brain structures: association cortex, corpus callosum, internal capsule, and midcerebellar peduncle. This is not to say that myelination in other pathways is unimportant in a 5 to 7 year cognitive transition.

There simply isn't enough information on the time course of myelination in other structures to allow discussion.

ASSOCIATION CORTICES

Association cortices are those brain regions that integrate information from multiple sensory modalities in order to form a plan of action, solve a perceptual problem, or remember an event. These regions are distinguished from primary sensory cortices (e.g., visual, somatosensory, olfactory) and motor cortex, which are less multimodal and are functional earlier in development. Myelination of axons coming from cortical neurons begins in the first year of life but continues into the school-age years and therefore may contribute to behavioral transitions. The increased efficiency of conduction between neurons in the cortex could contribute to a cognitive shift by facilitating complex or abstract thinking and learning by increasing the speed of information processing between regions. Association cortical regions (parietal cortex, prefrontal cortex) appear to myelinate later than do nonassociative regions (e.g., motor cortex and visual cortex; Barkovich et al., 1988), and anterior regions such as frontal cortex myelinates after parietal cortex (Brody, Kinney, Kloman, & Gilles, 1987; Dietrich, 1990; Yakovlev & Lecours, 1967). The increase in myelin in cortex results in a relative decrease in gray matter. However, this "gray matter regression" (Haas, Norman, Holland, Brant-Zawadski, & Newton, 1986; see also Barkovitch et al., 1988) may also be due to an actual loss of neurons (see "Subtraction and Selection"). Different cortical systems have different rates and courses of myelination, and most continue to myelinate from childhood to adolescence. No area of cortex shows a sudden stepwise change in the level of myelination at the 5 to 7 year period (Holland et al., 1986). Therefore, in order for myelination to be a critical feature in 5 to 7 year cognitive shifts one would have to posit that a particular level of maturation of myelin is critical for a particular cognitive process to unfold. Myelin undergoes its own developmental changes. Therefore, while the adult form of myelin may be available in association areas (frontal and parietal lobe) by 2 years of age, these areas do not show the fully adult *pattern* of mature myelin until much later (Brody et al., 1987). According to some MRI studies, myelination of association areas has an adult pattern by 3 years of age (Barkovitch & Truwit, 1990; Martin et al., 1988). Cholesterol measurements that index a major component of myelin support these findings with evidence that myelination is complete by 4 to 5 years of age (Dobbing & Sands, 1973). However, other MRI studies show that myelination continues into the second decade (Holland et al.), and one autopsy study found it continuing through the second decade and possibly into the fourth (Yakovlev & Lecours, 1967). The complete adult myelination pattern as shown by the contrast between white and gray matter may not be reached until

13 to 16 years of age (Salamon Raynaud, Regis, & Rumeau, 1990). In summary, we don't know if myelination of association cortex has a "magic developmental moment," however, it influences the efficiency by which a child processes information and may mediate specific cognitive effects, particularly in conjunction with other physiological changes.

CORPUS CALLOSUM

The corpus callosum is the largest commissure in the brain and includes the majority of the axons that connect the two cerebral hemispheres. This bundle of fibers is important for communication among neurons that send information to the opposite hemisphere. In a study utilizing MRI, myelination in the corpus callosum was comparable with that of an adult by 1 year of age (Holland et al., 1986). Similarly, Baierl et al. (1988) found that myelination was complete by 2 to 3 years. However, Yakovlev & Lecours (1967) found, in an autopsy study, that corpus callosum myelination continued until 7 to 10 years of age and may continue slowly even after the first decade.

INTERNAL CAPSULE

The internal capsule includes axons originating in cortical neurons and connecting to the brain stem and spinal cord. This tract is important for transmission of motor commands and, therefore, might be the final common path for a child's actions upon solving a problem. MRI studies found that myelination in the internal capsule was complete by the third or fourth year of life (Baierl et al., 1988; Holland et al., 1986; Martin et al., 1988). However, the relative size of this structure increased (as compared to other structures) until early adolescence (Holland et al.). This finding supports the report that some portions of the internal capsule do not complete myelination until the seventh year or later (Yakovlev & Lecours, 1967).

MIDCEREBELLAR PEDUNCLE

The cerebellar peduncles connect the cerebellum to the brain stem and the rest of the brain. The cerebellum is responsible for balance and fine-motor coordination. It also plays an important role in classical conditioning and possibly other forms of learning (Yeo, Hardiman, & Glickstein, 1984; for review, see Woodruff-Pak, Logan, & Thompson, 1990). For instance, both delay and trace eye-blink conditioning show developmental changes during the 5 to 7 year period (Ohlrich & Ross, 1968; Werden & Ross, 1972). Both forms of learning require interactions between cerebellum and hippocampus (Berger, 1984; Moore, Goodell, & Solomon, 1976). Therefore, myelination of this pathway could influence new forms of associative learning in the early school years.

However, the time course of myelination of the cerebellar peduncles is not entirely clear. One MRI study showed that myelination is complete in the mid-cerebellar peduncle by 2 to 3 years, (Baierl et al., 1988), whereas another study showed that the midcerebellar peduncle reaches a "fully adult appearance" around 6 years of age (Holland et al., 1986) and an autopsy study showed that myelination continued to increase as late as 4 years (Yakovlev & Lecours, 1967).

None of the studies suggest structures or brain regions that reached adultlike myelin levels just as the 5 to 7 year period. Myelination began before and continued after this period in development. However, it is possible that a point is reached in myelination that enables neurons to carry out new types of processing or changes the efficiency of processing to levels not previously achieved. If this was the case, then myelination, particularly the myelination of association regions such as frontal cortex connections, could make a significant contribution to cognitive development during this critical period. Another scenario to consider is that as myelin increases the efficiency of neural transmission in some brain regions, this efficiency may help stabilize synaptic conditions; that is, the increasing efficiency of some systems over others may influence the activity-dependent selection and stabilization of connections (described in the following "Subtraction and Selection" section). The selection and stabilization of some connections over others could result in the emergence and maintenance of new behaviors (Greenough, 1993; Greenough et al., 1987). In this case, the interaction between the process of myelination and the activity-dependent process of synapse selection would produce significant transitions in behavior. Thus myelination of a neural system could cause a qualitative change in behavior—a transition. The "distinct mechanism," which we said was required as a criterion for a neural mechanism of a transition, would be the increased efficiency of a pathway resulting in the selection and stabilization of some connections over others.

Subtraction and Selection

With the possible exception of myelination, all of the additive or growth processes described thus far are followed by a period of subtraction and selection (see Figure 3.3). Apparently "normal" neurons die off; neurons retract multiple axons to have in the end, only one; and synapse numbers decrease through adolescence and the aging process. Processes of subtraction and selection may be as responsible for developmental behavioral change as are additive processes. The exact time frame of cell death, axon retraction, and synapse subtraction in humans can only be estimated from animal studies because there are few studies of those processes in humans during this period.

If the only mechanism to control the number of neurons, the guidance of axons, and the timing, placement, and number of synapses was through the genetic programming of each cell, one would have an extraordinarily complex programming problem. In addition, preprogramming the entire system negates the possibility of an animal to adapt and respond to a changing environment. Instead, it seems that basic genetic programming provides a rudimentary framework for guiding neurons to make connections and when. After that point, *activity-dependent* selection of neurons and synapses shapes the final networks, microarchitecture, and therefore function of the brain (Changeau & Danchin, 1976). This shaping process is a *competitive one* so that neurons must compete with each other for synaptic space and trophic factors and this competition *requires* neural activity. (Oppenheim, 1981). It is for this reason that Rakic and colleagues (Rakic et al., 1986) reasoned that a single signal for synapse production across the cortex would be the most likely scenario for maximizing competition.

It is highly probable that the period of neuron death precedes other regressive processes and may be nearly complete by the time children enter school. For example, in human frontal cortex, neuron density is well above adult levels (approximately 55%) at 2 years of age, and approximately 10% above adult levels by 7 years of age (Huttenlocher, 1979, 1990; Huttenlocher et al., 1982). It is not clear whether this is due entirely to a loss of neurons, as the density of neurons could decrease owing to increasing size of frontal cortex with the addition of glia, neuropil, and myelin. The *relative* change in neuron number in relation to the expansion of the cortex, or in relation to the number of live neurons, has not been estimated.

Some axons are lost through the process of cell death; however, many neurons send out more than one axon during the process of connecting to a target structure and later retract one branch (Innocenti & Clarke, 1974; Ivy et al., 1979). For instance, axon number is decreased at a rate of about 50 axons per second for the first 3 weeks postnatally in the monkey, and then the callosum loses about 5 per second over the next several months until adult levels are reached (LaMantia & Rakic, 1990). Early in cortical development some neurons may make connections with multiple sensory systems, for instance both the auditory and visual system. Later in development, *and with the appropriate sensory stimulation,* connections to one but not the other sensory system remain. If the "expected" sensory input does not occur, a neuron may retain connections to anomalous regions. The function of such anomalous connections has recently been explored with the event-related potential technique (Neville, 1990, 1991). The data suggest that the sensory deprivation to the auditory system may change connections and function in the visual system, and function in the nonlanguage right hemisphere in the congenitally deaf.

While there is conflict about the time course of the exuberant overproduction of synapses, synapse subtraction appears to be a slower process and most likely continues well into the second decade in humans. This may be prolonged in regions such as frontal cortex (Huttenlocher, 1990). However, region-by-region rates and end points are not known.

This exuberance and the subsequent subtraction of neural elements serve the purpose of selection and stabilization of connections (Changeax & Danchin, 1976). This process of synaptic selection and hypermetabolism may occur in cortex at approximately the time children begin school. It may be a mediator or enable school-age cognitive and behavioral transitions. It is the richest time in terms of neural hardware and activity available to the child. It is also the richest time, possibly with the exception of birth, for new experiences and challenges to the child's mind.

Indices of Functional Neurobiological Maturation: EEG, ERP, and PET

Up to now, we have focused on the acquisition of neural hardware but not on the activity or functioning of that hardware. This section focuses on measures of brain function. For a summary of the temporal and spatial constraints of each technique, see Figure 3.2.

The electroencephalogram (EEG) is a record of brain electrical activity. For purposes of these studies it is usually recorded from the scalp while the child is sitting at rest or performing a repetitive task. The event-related potential (ERP) is a waveform derived from the averaged brain electrical activity while the child performs a task. Therefore it can be used to compare brain activity during the performance of one task with brain activity during another. Both EEG and ERP are records of brain activity *at the moment* a stimulus is presented. This is in contrast to reaction time measures, which can be from 500 msec to seconds after stimulus presentation.

Positron emission tomography (PET) assesses brain metabolism by estimating glucose utilization, changes in blood flow, or changes in oxygenation of the brain. Differences as measured by these indices of function between brain regions can also be assessed as a person performs cognitive or motor tasks (e.g., see Corbetta, Miezin, Shulman, & Petersen, 1993; Squire, et al., 1991).

Electrophysiological Changes

We emphasize that EEG and ERP assess brain function on line because such measurements assess both the maturational state of the brain and behavior, but some cautions are in order. Much has been made of changes in the waveforms or the location of a waveform (e.g., right versus left hemisphere) as signals of biological development. Less emphasized is the fact that a 3- or 4-year-old is quite different from a 7-year-old when it comes to testing, and therefore EEG and ERP also reflect the degree to which a behavioral task performed by a 4-year-old differs from one performed by a 7-year-old. One simple example is the manner in which EEG data are collected. The subject is instructed to lie still and keep his or her eyes closed. To a 4-year-old, in a novel situation, this is an extraordinarily hard task. However, it is a much easier task for an older child. One might then be recording the differences between a child who is trying hard to actively inhibit other behaviors versus a child who is in a resting state. EEG differences, then, between 4- to 7-year-olds may not be due to neurophysiological maturation between these two ages but, rather, to task demands at each age. The maturation of the underlying biology has yet to be disentangled from the behavioral demands of the test session at each age. Basic neurobiological information on neural changes during this period still needs to be correlated with EEG and ERP findings.

With this caveat in mind, let us review what electrophysiological changes have been reported during the 5 to 7 year target age period. There is a gradual but steady change in the waveforms, an increase in the amount of alpha activity, and a decrease in theta activity over the first decade of life (Kiloh & Osselton, 1966). Thatcher and colleagues (Thatcher, 1991, 1992; Thatcher, Walker, & Giudice, 1987) suggest that there is a maturational left to right hemisphere shift during development as well as 2- to 4-year oscillations (increases and decreases) in EEG coherence patterns: in particular, one from birth to 2 years, one in early adulthood (16 to 19 years), and a less dramatic "spurt" from 7 to 9 years. Coherence is the degree to which two brain regions show synchronized or correlated activity. It is not entirely clear what coherence between two brain regions means with regard to behavior or what its biological basis may be. Some have suggested that these oscillations in coherence are due to transient expansion and pruning of synapses in the brain, to an increase and decrease in the number of neurons with each oscillation, or to both. There is as yet little neurobiological data to support spurts or oscillations in neurogenesis postnatally or oscillations in synaptogenesis in 2- to 4-year cycles, and there is ample evidence against the production of substantial numbers of neurons postnatally in humans and other mammals (Rodier, 1980; Sidman & Angevine, 1962). When the generators of the EEG are known, when the neurobiological changes during this time period are cataloged, and when the recording and behavioral conditions for testing children of different ages are equated, we may understand the relationship between EEG findings and neurobiological maturation.

One of the classic transitions in child development is a shift as described by Piaget from the preoperational to the concrete operation stage. An index of this transition is the acquisition of conservation of volume. A recent study examined the neural correlates of conservation performance in 5- to 7-year-old conservers and nonconservers using the ERP technique (Stauder, Molenaar, & Van der Molen, 1993). No difference in ERP of conservers and nonconservers was found on an "oddball" task where the child had to count one stimulus and ignore the other. However, the ERP differed between conservers and nonconservers while they performed the conservation task. This was not due to age differences between the two subject groups. The conservers had a lower amplitude waveform in the frontal and temporal electrode sites as compared with the nonconservers. A dipole analysis to estimate the source of the ERP suggests an anterior (frontal source) for nonconservers but a posterior (parietal) source for conservers 400 ms after the stimulus. The implication of their finding was that conservers and nonconservers used different brain regions during the ERP task, possibly because of differential brain maturation in the two groups. It is important to remember that these electrophysiological techniques measure function. The anterior-posterior differences between conservers and nonconservers may be due to a shift in the brain regions mediating a task once a basic, critical piece of information is acquired. For example, a shift in the motor cortex responses was recently shown when a learner shifted from an implicit to an explicit understanding of a motor sequence (Pascual-Leone, Grafman, & Hallett, 1994). In this case, the shift in neural function was not due to a change in maturation but rather due to the kind of information being processed.

Metabolism

PET studies of children who had seizures in the perinatal period but who later had normal development and no known neurologic problems show an increase in metabolism with adultlike levels reached by 9 to 10 months of age (Chugani & Phelps, 1986, 1991; Chugani, Phelps, & Mazziotta, 1987). Subcortical regions such as brainstem and thalamus become metabolically active before cortex. Primary sensory and motor cortices become metabolically active before association areas such as prefrontal cortex. The lag in metabolic development in the frontal lobes may be a functional signal of later synaptogenesis in this region or later myelination of axons to or from frontal cortex. This pattern of activation correlates with the onset of behaviors in infants. Infants have brainstem "competence" to regulate breathing and heart rate before primary sensory competence, and primary sensation precedes complex voluntary motor behaviors and complex thought. After this point, metabolism increases and *overshoots* adult levels by two to three times, peaking at approximately 4 years of age and slowly decreasing to adult levels by approximately 16 to 18 years of age. This peak in metabolism may signal a "functional exuberance" that is mediated by the exuberance in synaptic hardware. These PET studies were performed "at rest," that is, the child was not performing any particular task. How region-by-region brain metabolism would change if the child were performing simple or challenging age-appropriate tasks is not yet known. The advent of functional MRI imaging may provide such information in the next few years. The point to keep in mind is that as a child enters school, the brain is at its highest metabolic rate for life! It may be this metabolic exuberance that makes this a "special" period of development and signals a period of transition.

The Functional Correlates of Neurobiological Maturation From 5 to 7 Years

There is evidence for neural reorganization and metabolic change during the 5 to 7 year period, occurring predominately in association cortex. We have discussed an electrophysiological study that makes a direct association between the maturation of cognition and brain maturation (Stauder et al., 1993). In this section we speculate about the neural basis for another prominent cognitive shift during development. That is the apparent shift in mnemonic competence and event recall as children enter school. We speculate that the special role of the frontal lobes in memory for the context of events and in metamemory (the ability to reflect upon one's own memory) influences the recall abilities of children during development. We suspect that the frontal lobes go through a significant degree of neurobiological development and reorganization between 5 and 7 years and that this results in qualitative shifts in the manner that children recall memories during this period.

Because of the apparent regulatory role of the frontal lobes, it has been called the "executor" of cognition (Baddeley, 1986). In adults, the frontal lobes play an important role in multiple aspects of memory. The prefrontal cortex is critical for immediate or working memory (Baddeley, 1986; Goldman-Rakic, 1991). In addition, damage to the frontal lobes results in difficulty ordering memories in time (Milner, Petrides, & Smith, 1985; Petrides & Milner, 1982; Shimamura, Janowsky, & Squire, 1990, 1991) and difficulty associating learned information with the context in which it was learned (Craik, Morris, Morris, & Loewen, 1990; Janowsky, Shimamura, & Squire, 1989b). That is, adults may misattribute where or when they learned information to an inappropriate source (source errors; Janowsky et al., 1989b). This is also true in the normal elderly (Spencer & Raz, 1994), particularly when they learn information in an incidental manner (Janowsky et al., 1989b). The quality of memory is such that the adults are not amnesic for the context of the contents of their memory. Rather, in the process of recall, they apparently err in the selection of possible sources from which information comes. Finally, adult patients with frontal lobe damage have difficulty reflecting upon their memory store (metamemory; Janowsky, Shimamura, & Squire, 1989a); that is, despite normal learning and memory for facts and events, these patients are poor at estimating or judging what they know. We found that source errors, metamemory errors, and errors in the temporal ordering of information can occur in patients with frontal lobe damage even when memory for the target information (e.g., facts, or lists of words) is very good. This suggests that these processes are dissociable from the processes involved in the encoding of information.

Nelson, in chapter 7 of this volume, discusses a qualitative shift in memory performance in children during the early school years. Around 5 to 7 years, children show an apparent qualitative shift in the way they speak about their own memories, particularly events in their lives. Previously, this was discussed as a qualitative change in the elaborateness of memory (Pillemer & White, 1989). Without contextual support or ample retrieval cues, younger children report fewer details of events than do older children or adults (Fivush & Hudson, 1990). For example, when asked about the events surrounding a fire drill children will not recall contextual information such as who was with them at the time or what time of day the event occurred. This is despite the fact that when queried about an event and the context surrounding an event, children can recall or recognize facts that they don't spontaneously recall. Over the next several years, the elaborateness of their memory increases until they report the same number and quality of details as adults do. Although recall is commonly improved with retrieval cues and contextual support, it is possible that this information is especially inaccessible or unusable in young children. Nelson's view is that this may be due to a change in the way children *talk* about their memories; that is, between 5 and 7 years children have a qualitative shift in their knowledge and linguistic competence regarding the way one reports events that have occurred.

Our speculative thesis is that the continued development of the frontal lobes during these years enables children to access and flexibly recombine information in memory to include the context of events as well as their metacognition about events in their lives. The frontal lobes may help mediate the elaboration of memory performance, whether the elaboration is due to enhanced memory performance or to enhanced linguistic competence to report multiple facets of remembered events.

But what about the particular form of memory discussed by Nelson, that of *personal* events, or autobiographical memory? Indeed, Tulving (1984) has suggested that in addition to semantic and event memory as categories of declarative memory, a special and separate form of memory exists, that is, autobiographical memory. He reported on a patient who had a selective deficit in autobiographical recall but not in other aspects of declarative memory. This would suggest that there is a specialized neural system for autobiographical memory. One possibility is that autobiographical memory, that is, the recall of events in relation to one's own life, utilizes the temporal lobe memory system for the encoding and storage process, the frontal lobes during the organized recall of the information and its placement in the proper contextual time frame, and finally the frontal lobe mediated self-awareness or metacognition system in order to specify and report reflections about events, as events *about their own lives.* These processes together, having access to the accurate context of events, along with the ability to reflect upon the contents of one's memory, may enhance the recall of events and may particularly enhance the recall of autobiographical events. Several others have suggested that the development of self-reflection and metacognition in children may be due to the development of the frontal lobes (e.g., Segalowitz & Rose-Krasnor, 1992; Smith et al., 1992; Stuss, 1992). Future studies that disentangle a child's memory for an event from a child's memory for the context and metamemory regarding an event will substantiate or eliminate our hypothesis.

Summary

We were asked to address four questions concerning behavioral transitions in the 5 to 7 year period:

1. Do children behave differently at 5 and 7 years? Yes, children "behave" differently at 5 from the way they do at 7 years of age. This is true at the cellular, neural system, and behavioral levels of analysis.

2. Are these changes qualitative? There are certainly qualitative neural changes during this period, and these result in quantitative changes such as improved reaction times, fine motor coordination, and possibly qualitative changes in "higher level" processing.

3. Are the changes continuous or discontinuous? We used a rather strict definition for qualitative change that assumed a discontinuous (non-linear) pattern of change. We conclude that qualitative neural and behavioral changes such as synapse selection occur during this time period in regions (prefrontal cortex) that are critical for complex problem solving and the integration of information across modalities.

4. Is qualitative behavioral change during this period due to the emergence of new behaviors or the reorganization of prior behaviors? At the neural level, both occur (see Figure 3.3). The ERP data of conservation behavior and our proposal that a new and different manner of accessing and reporting memories, owing to frontal lobe development, suggest *new* behaviors emerge at this age.

Although the state of neurobiological knowledge is frustratingly incomplete at this time, the information at hand suggests domains of cognitive and neural investigation whose integration may be particularly fruitful. The neurobiological changes during this time period are not conclusive of behavioral transitions; nevertheless there are sufficient changes in cortical brain systems to enable, mediate, or be a result of cognitive transitions.

Acknowledgments

This work was supported in part by March of Dimes Research Grant 0721. We thank Dr. Janet Davidson for helpful discussions during the development of this chapter, and Dr. Pat Bauer, Dr. Chuck Nelson, and an anonymous reviewer for comments on previous drafts.

References

Baddeley, A. (1986). *Working memory.* Oxford: Oxford University Press.

Baierl, P., Forster, C., Fendel, H., Naegele, M., Fink, U., & Kenn, W. (1988). Magnetic resonance imaging of normal and pathological white matter maturation. *Pediatric Radiology, 18,* 183–189.

Barkovich, A. J., Kjos, B. O., Jackson, D. E., Jr., Norman, D. (1988). Normal maturation of the neonatal and infant brain: MR imaging at 1.5 T. *Radiology, 166,*173–180.

Barkovich, A. J., & Truwit, C. L. (1990). *Practical MRI atlas of neonatal brain development.* New York: Raven Press.

Bates, E., & Carnevale, G. F. (1992). *Developmental psychology in the 1990's: Language development* (Technical Report 9204). San Diego, CA: University of California, Center of Research in Language.

Bates, E., Thal, D., & Janowsky, J. S. (1992). Early language development and its neural correlates. In F. Boller, J. Grafman, S. J. Segalowitz, & I. Rapin (Eds.), *Handbook of neuropsychology* (Vol. *7,* pp. 69–110). Amsterdam, The Netherlands: Elsevier.

Belliveau, J. W., Kwong, K. K., Kennedy, D. N., Baker, J. R., Stern, C. E., Benson, R., Chesler, D. A. Weisskoff, R. M., Cohen, M. S., Tootell, R. B. H., Fox, P. T., Brady, T. J., & Rosen, B. R. (1992). Magnetic resonance imaging mapping of brain function: Human visual cortex. *Investigative Radiology, 27* (Suppl. 2), S59–S65.

Berger, T. W. (1984). Long-term potentiation of hippocampal synaptic transmission affects rate of behavioral learning. *Science, 224,* 627–630.

Brody, B. A., Kinney, H. C., Kloman, A. S., & Gilles, F. H. (1987). Sequence of central nervous system myelination in human infancy: 1. An autopsy study of myelination. *Journal of Neuropathology and Experimental Neurology, 46,* 283–301.

Changeux, J., & Danchin, A. (1976). Selective stabilization of developing synapses as a mechanism for the specification of neuronal networks. *Nature, 264,* 705–712.

Chugani, H. T., & Phelps, M. E., (1986). Maturational changes in cerebral function in infants determined by [18]FDG positron emission tomography. *Science, 225,* 1258–1265.

Chugani, H. T., & Phelps, M. E. (1991). Imaging human brain development with positron emission tomography. *Journal of Nuclear Medicine, 32* (1), 23–26.

Chugani, H. T., Phelps, M. E., & Mazziotta, J. C. (1987). Positron emission tomography study of human brain functional development. *Annals of Neurology, 22,* 487–497.

Conel, J. L. (1939/1967). *The postnatal development of the human cerebral cortex* (Vols. *1–8*). Cambridge, MA: Harvard University Press.

Corbetta, M., Miezin, F. M., Shulman, G. L., & Petersen, S. E. (1993). A PET study of visuospatial attention. *Journal of Neuroscience, 13* (3), 1202–1226.

Craik, F. I. M., Morris, L. W., Morris, R. G., & Loewen E. R. (1990). Relations between source amnesia and frontal lobe functioning in older adults. *Psychology and Aging, 5,* 148–151.

DeFelipe, J., & Jones, E. G. (1988). *Cajal on the cerebral cortex: An annotated translation of the complete writings.* New York: Oxford University Press.

Dietrich, R. B. (1990). Magnetic resonance imaging of normal brain maturation. *Seminars in Perinatology, 14,* 201–211.

Dobbing, J., & Sands, J. (1973). Quantitative growth and development of human brain. *Archives of Disease in Childhood, 48,* 757–767.

Fivush, R., & Hudson, J. A. (1990). *Knowing and remembering in young children.* New York: Cambridge University Press.

Georgopoulos, A. P., Taira, M., & Lukashin, A. (1993). Cognitive neurophysiology of the motor cortex. *Science, 260,* 47–52.

Gilles, F. H., Leviton, A., & Dooling E. C. (1983). *The developing human brain.* Boston: J. Wright PSG.

Goldman-Rakic, P. S. (1991). Relationship of circuitry of primate prefrontal cortex in working functional memory. In H. S. Levin, H. M. Eisenberg, & A. L. Benton (Eds.), *Frontal lobe function and dysfunction.* New York: Oxford University Press.

Grattan, L. M., & Eslinger, P. J. (1991). Frontal lobe damage in children and adults: A comparative review. *Developmental Neuropsychology, 7,* 283–326.

Grattan, L. M., & Eslinger, P. J. (1992). Long-term psychological consequences of childhood frontal lobe lesion in patient DT. *Brain and Cognition, 20,* 185–195.

Graziadei, P. P. C., & Monti Graziadei, G. A. (1979). Neurogenesis and neuron regeneration in the olfactory system of mammals. I. Morphological aspects of differentiation and structural organization of the olfactory sensory neurons. *Journal of Neurocytology, 8,* 1–18.

Greenough, W. T. (1993). Brain adaptation to experience: An update. In M. H. Johnson (Ed.), *Brain development and cognition: A reader.* Oxford, England: Blackwell.

Greenough, W. T., Black, J. E., & Wallace, C. S. (1987). Experience and brain development. *Child Development, 58,* 539–559.

Hall, D. H., & Russell, R. L. (1991). The posterior nervous system of the nematode caenorhabditis elegans: Serial reconstruction of identified neurons and complete pattern of synaptic interactions. *Journal of Neuroscience, 11* (1), 1–22.

Harbord, M. G., Finn, J. P., Hall-Craggs, M. A., Robb, S. A., Kendall, B. E., & Boyd, S. G. (1990). Myelination patterns on magnetic resonance of children with developmental delay. *Developmental Medicine and Child Neurology, 32,* 295–303.

Holland, B. A., Haas, D. K., Norman, D., Brant-Zawadzki, M., & Newton, T. H. (1986). MRI of normal brain maturation. *American Journal of Neuroradiology, 7,* 201–208.

Hubel, D. H., Wiesel, T. N., & LeVay, S. (1977). Plasticity of ocular dominance columns in monkey striate cortex. *Philosophical Transactions Royal Society of London, 278,* 377–409.

Huttenlocher, P. R. (1979). Synaptic density in human frontal cortex: Developmental changes and effects of aging. *Brain Research, 163,* 195–205.

Huttenlocher, P. R. (1990). Morphometric study of human cerebral cortex development. *Neurospychologia, 28,* 517–527.

Huttenlocher, P. R. (1991). Dendritic and synaptic pathology in mental retardation. *Pediatric Neurology, 7,* 79–85.

Huttenlocher, P. R., & de Courten, C. (1987). The development of synapses in striate cortex of man. *Human Neurobiology, 6,* 1–9.

Huttenlocher, P. R., de Courten, C., Garey, L. J., & Van Der Loos, H. (1982). Synaptogenesis in human visual cortex: Evidence for synapse elimination during normal development. *Neuroscience Letters, 33,* 247–252.

Hynd, G. W., Marshall, R. M., & Semrud-Clikeman, M. (1991). Developmental dyslexia, neurolinguistic theory and deviations in brain morphology. *Reading and Writing: An Interdisciplinary Journal, 3,* 345–362.

Innocenti, G., & Clarke, S. (1984). Bilateral transitory projection to visual areas from auditory cortex in kittens. *Developmental Brain Research, 14,* 143–148.

Ivy, G., Akers, R., & Killackey, H. (1979). Differential distribution of callosal projection neurons in the neonatal and adult rat. *Brain Research, 173,* 532–537.

Janowsky, J. S., & Finlay, B. L. (1986). The outcome of perinatal brain damage: The role of normal neuron loss and axon retraction. *Developmental Medicine and Child Neurology, 8,* 375–389.

Janowsky, J. S., Shimamura, A. P., & Squire, L. R. (1989a). Memory and metamemory: Comparisons between patients with frontal lobe lesions and amnesic patients. *Psychobiology, 17,* 3–11.

Janowsky, J. S., Shimamura, A. P., & Squire, L. R. (1989b). Source memory impairment in patients with frontal lobe lesions. *Neuropsychologia, 27,* 1043–1056.

Jay, V., Chan, F. W., & Becker, L. (1990). Dendritic arborization in the human fetus and infant with Trisomy 18 Syndrome. *Developmental Brain Research, 54,* 291–294.

Jernigan, T. L., Hesseling, J. R., Sowell, E., & Tallal, P. A. (1991). Cerebral structure on magnetic resonance imaging in language and learning impaired children. *Archives of Neurology, 48,* 539–545.

Kandel, E. R., & Schwartz, J. H. (1981). *Principles of neural science.* New York: Elsevier North Holland.

Kiloh, L. G., & Osselton, J. W. (1966). *Clinical electroencephalography.* London: Butterworth.

Kim, S., Ashe, J., Hendrich, K., Ellermann, J. M., Merkle, H., Ugubil, K., & Georgopoulos, A. P. (1993). Functional magnetic resonance imaging of motor cortex: Hemispheric asymmetry and handedness. *Science, 261,* 615–617.

LaMantia, A. S., & Rakic, P. (1990). Axon overproduction and elimination in the corpus callosum of the developing rhesus monkey. *Journal of Neuroscience, 10,* 2156–2175.

Levinthal, F., Macagno, E., & Levinthal, C. (1975). Anatomy and development of identified cells in isogenic organisms. *Cold Spring Harbor Symposium on Quantitative Biology, 40,* 321–333.

MacVicar, B. A., Crichton, S. A., Burnard, D. M., & Tse, F. W. (1987). Membrane conductance oscillations in astrocytes induced by phorbol esters. *Nature, 329* (6136), 242–243.

Martin, E., Kikinis, R., Zuerrer, M., Boesch, C., Briner, J., Kewitz, G., & Kaelin, P. (1988). Developmental stages of human brain: An MR study. *Journal of Computer Assisted Tomography, 12,* 917–922.

Matute, C., & Miledi, R. (1993). Neurotransmitter receptors and voltage dependent CA^{+2} channels encoded by mRNA from the adult corpus callosum. *Proceedings of the National Academy of Sciences, 90* (8), 3270–3274.

Merzenich, M., Nelson, R., Stryker, M., Cynader, M., Schoppmann, A., & Zook, J. (1984). Somatosensory cortical map changes following digit amputation in adult monkeys. *Journal of Comparative Neurology, 224,* 591–605.

Milner, B., Petrides, M., & Smith, M. (1985). Frontal lobes and the temporal organization of behavior. *Human Neurobiology, 4,* 137–142.

Moore, J. W., Goodell, N. A., & Solomon, P. R. (1976). Central cholinergic blockage by scopolamine and habituation, classical conditioning and latent inhibition of the rabbit's nictitating membrane response. *Physiological Psychology, 4,* 395–399.

Nelson, K. (1993). The psychological and social origins of autobiographical memory. *Psychological Science, 4,* 7–14.

Neville, H. J. (1990). Intermodal competition and compensation in development: Evidence from studies of the visual system in congenitally deaf adults. *Annals of the New York Academy of Sciences, 608,* 71–91.

Neville, H. J. (1991). Neurobiology of cognitive and language processing: Effects of early experience. In K. R. Gibson and A. C. Petersen (Eds.), *Brain maturation and cognitive development: Comparative and cross cultural perspectives* (pp. 355–380). Hawthorne, NY: Aldine de Gruyter.

Ohlrich, E. S., & Ross, L. E. (1968). Acquisition and differential conditioning of the eyelid response in normal and retarded children. *Journal of Experimental Child Psychology, 6,* 181–193.

Oppenheim, R. W. (1981). Neuronal death and some related regressive phenomena during neurogenesis: A selective historical review and progress report. In W. M. Cowan (Ed.), *Studies of developmental neurobiology.* New York: Oxford University Press.

Pascual-Leone, A., Grafman, J., & Hallett, M. (1994). Modulation of cortical motor output maps during development of implicit and explicit knowledge. *Science, 263,* 1287–1289.

Petrides, M., & Milner, B. (1982). Deficits on subject-ordered tasks after frontal- and temporal-lobe lesions in man. *Neuropsychologia, 20,* 249–262.

Pillemer, D. B., & White, S. H. (1989). Childhood events recalled by children and adults. *Advances in Child Development, 21,* 297–340.

Purpura, D. P. (1975). Dendritic differentiation in human cerebral cortex: Normal and aberrant developmental patterns. *Advances in Neurology, 22,* 487–497.

Purves, D., & Lichtman, J. W. (1985). *Principles of neural development.* Sunderland MA: Sinauer.

Rakic, P. (1972). Mode of cell migration to the superficial layers of fetal monkey neocortex. *Journal of Comparative Neurology, 145,* 61–84.

Rakic, P. (1975). Timing of major ontogenetic events in the visual cortex of the rhesus monkey. In N. Buchwald & M. Brazier (Eds.), *Brain mechanisms in mental retardation.* New York: Academic Press.

Rakic, P., Bourgeois, J. P., Eckenhoff, M. F., Zecevic, N., & Goldman-Rakic, P. S. (1986). Concurrent overproduction of synapses in diverse regions of the primate cerebral cortex. *Science, 232,* 232–235.

Rodier, P. (1980). Chronology of neuron development. *Developmental Medicine and Child Neurology, 22,* 525–545.

Salamon, G., Raynaud, C., Regis, J., & Rumeau, C. (1990). *Magnetic resonance imaging of the pediatric brain.* New York: Raven Press.

Scheibel, A. B. (1991). Some structural and developmental correlates of human speech. In K. R. Gibson and A. C. Petersen (Eds.), *Brain maturation and cognitive development.* Hawthorne, NY: Aldine de Gruyter.

Segalowitz, S. J., & Rose-Krasnor, L. (1992). The construct of brain maturation in theories of child development. *Brain and Cognition, 20,* 1–7.

Sejnowski, T. J., & Churchland, P. S. (1989). Brain and cognition. In M. I. Posner (Ed.), *Foundations of cognitive science.* Cambridge, MA: MIT Press.

Shimamura, A. P., Janowsky, J. S., & Squire, L. R. (1990). Memory for the temporal order of events in patients with frontal lobe lesions and amnesic patients. *Neuropsychologia, 28,* 803–813.

Shimamura, A. P., Janowsky, J. S., & Squire, L. R. (1991). What is the role of frontal lobe damage in amnesic disorders? In H. S. Levin and H. M. Eisenberg (Eds.), *Frontal lobe functioning and effects of injury.* Oxford: Oxford University Press.

Shue, K. L., & Douglas, V. I. (1992). Attention deficit hyperactivity disorder and the frontal lobe syndrome. *Brain and Cognition, 20,* 104–124.

Sidman, R. L., & Angevine, J. B. (1962). Autoradiographic analysis of time of origin of nuclear versus cortical components of mouse telencephalon. *Anatomical Record, 142,* 326.

Simonds, R. J., & Scheibel, A. B. (1989). The postnatal development of the motor speech area: A preliminary study. *Brain and Language, 37,* 42–58.

Smith, M. L., Kates, M. H., & Vriezen, E. R. (1992). The development of frontal-lobe functions. In F. Boller, J. Grafman, S. J. Segalowitz, & I. Rapin (Eds.), *Handbook of neuropsychology* (Vol. 7, pp. 309–330). Amsterdam, The Netherlands: Elsevier.

Spencer, W. D., & Raz, N. (1994). Memory for facts, source and context: Can frontal lobe dysfunction explain age-related differences? *Psychology and Aging, 9,* (1), 149–159.

Squire, L. R., Ojemann, J. G., Miezin, F. M., Petersen, S. E., Videen, T. O., & Raichle, M. E. (1991). Activation of the hippocampus in normal humans: A functional anatomical study of memory. *Proceedings of the National Academy of Science, 89,* 1837–1841.

Stanfield, B. B., O'Leary, D. D. M., & Fricks, C. (1982). Selective collateral elimination in early postnatal development restricts cortical distribution of rat pyramidal tract neurones. *Nature 298,* 371–373.

Stauder, J. E. A., Molenaar, P. C. M., & Van der Molen, M. W. (1993). Scalp topography of event-related brain potentials and cognitive transition during childhood. *Child Development, 64,* 769–788.

Stuss, D. T. (1992). Biological and psychological development of executive functions. *Brain and Cognition, 20,* 8–23.

Thatcher, R. W. (1991). Maturation of the human frontal lobes: Physiological evidence for staging. *Developmental Neuropsychology, 7,* 397–429.

Thatcher, R. W. (1992). Cyclic cortical reorganization during early childhood. *Brain and Cognition, 20,* 24–50.

Thatcher, R. W., Walker, R. A., & Giudice, S. (1987). Human cerebral hemispheres develop at different rates and ages. *Science, 236,* 1110–1113.

Tulving, E. (1984). Precis of elements of episodic memory with open peer commentary. *Behavioral and Brain Sciences, 7,* 223–268.

Werden, D., & Ross, L. E. (1972). A comparison of the trace and delay classical conditioning performance of normal children. *Journal of Experimental Child Psychology, 59,* 19–26.

Williams, D., & Mateer, C. A. (1992). Developmental impact of frontal lobe injury in middle childhood. *Brain and Cognition, 20,* 196–204.

Woodruff-Pak, D. S., Logan, C. G., & Thompson, R. F. (1990). Neurobiological substrates of classical conditioning across the life span. *Annals of the New York Academy of Sciences, 608,* 150–178.

Yakovlev, P. I., & Lecours, A. R. (1967). The myelogenetic cycles of regional maturation of the brain. In A. Minkowski (Ed.), *Regional development of the brain in early life* (pp. 3–70). Philadelphia: F. A. Davis.

Yeo, C. H., Hardiman, M. J., & Glickstein, M. (1984). Discrete lesions of the cerebellar cortex abolish classically conditioned nictitating membrane response of the rabbit. *Behavioral Brain Research, 13,* 261–266.

Zecevic, N., Bourgeois, J. P., & Rakic, P. (1989). Changes in synaptic density in motor cortex of rhesus monkey during fetal and postnatal life. *Developmental Brain Research, 50,* 11–32.

PART THREE

Cognitive Transitions

Unidimensional Thinking, Multidimensional Thinking, and Characteristic Tendencies of Thought

ROBERT S. SIEGLER

I first read Sheldon White's classic description of the 5 to 7 shift in a graduate school seminar in 1972. The paper was exciting, then as now. It marshaled an impressive body of evidence showing that in diverse situations 5- and 7-year-olds' thinking is surprisingly different. It also was critical in motivating the substantial attention that cognitive development in this age range received in the years following the article's publication.

One of the most intriguing hypothesized shifts involved a change from unidimensional to multidimensional thinking. Both before 1965 and since then, a variety of prominent developmental theorists have proposed that 5-year-olds can only represent a single feature of a situation, whereas 7-year-olds and older children can represent multiple aspects of the same situation. Such a difference, if verified, would be of extremely broad significance. Not only would centering on a single dimension affect 5-year-olds' spontaneous efforts to solve many problems, it also would influence their ability to learn more advanced solutions. Thus, it is not surprising that the hypothesized shift from unidimensional to multidimensional reasoning has been the subject of much research since White's (1965) publication.

The present chapter examines what has been learned from this research. The first section examines the roles of the hypothesized shift within a number of prominent theories of cognitive development. The second summarizes some of the large number of studies that have yielded data consistent with it. The third summarizes some of the large number of studies that have yielded findings at odds with at least strong forms of the hypothesis. Finally, the fourth section is a reconsideration of the original idea in the light of current knowledge.

Theories of the 5 to 7 Shift

Both Piaget's theory and prominent neo-Piagetian theories of cognitive development hypothesize profound changes in children's thinking between 5 and 7 years. Changes from unidimensional to multidimensional representations are central to all of the theories. Several of the most influential proposals are briefly described in the following subsections.

Piaget's Theory

Piaget proposed that at roughly age 6 children progress from preoperational to concrete operational reasoning. A critical part of this stage change involves decentration. Children in the preoperational stage are viewed as centering on a single dimension, even when two or more dimensions are relevant, whereas those in the concrete operational stage are viewed as capable of representing multiple dimensions (decentering). This can be illustrated in the context of the class inclusion task, in which children are asked such questions as "If you had 5 dogs and 2 cats, would you have more dogs or more animals?" (Inhelder & Piaget, 1964). Most 5-year-olds say "more dogs." Piaget explained this by hypothesizing that preoperational children cannot simultaneously view an object as both a dog and an animal. Therefore, they focus on the comparison of objects at the same hierarchical level, cats and dogs. In contrast, most 7-year-olds answer the same class-inclusion question by saying "more animals," demonstrating that they can simultaneously view an object as a dog and an animal.

Piaget described a huge number of parallel cases, in which 5-year-olds centered on a single dimension and older children considered multiple dimensions. To cite just one, Piaget (1969) reported that when presented two trains traveling in the same direction along parallel tracks, and asked which train went a greater distance, 5-year-olds focused on the single feature of the trains' stopping points (or, in some cases, stopping time), whereas 8-year-olds considered both starting point and stopping point in their judgments of distance traveled.

This basic perspective has been preserved, with some variation, in a number of leading neo-Piagetian theories that have subsequently been proposed. The commonality can be seen particularly clearly in a book in which a number of leading neo-Piagetian theorists presented their current views (Demetriou, 1988). The following accounts of these theorists' continually evolving positions are taken from their descriptions in that volume.

Case's Theory

Case (1988) posited a major change in which children below age 7 are limited to representing a single dimension, whereas those older than 7 can consider multiple dimensions. In one illustration of this view, he cited a study by Marini (1981) in which children were told of two boys who were having birthday parties. Each boy wanted a certain number of marbles, and each received a certain number of marbles, though the numbers desired and received often were not the same. For example, one boy might want four marbles and get three, and the other might want seven and get four. The question was which boy would be happier. Six-year-olds based their judgments of relative happiness solely on the number of marbles received; whichever boy received more marbles would be happier. In contrast, 8-year-olds considered not only the actual number but also the discrepancy between the hoped-for and the actual number. Case hypothesized that this transition was produced in large part by growth of short-term storage space (STSS), which allowed the older children to represent a greater number of features.

Halford's Theory

Halford (1988) hypothesized a major transition at about the same age, in which 5-year-olds are capable only of forming relational mappings, whereas 7-year-olds are capable of forming systems mappings. According to Halford, a 5-year-old capable only of forming relational mappings will be able to solve a multiple classification task in which only the one dimension varies (e.g., color), but not a task in which matrix entries vary along two dimensions (e.g., shape and color). In contrast, a 7-year-old, capable of systems mappings, can solve both problems. In a hypothesis similar to Case's, Halford posited that the change was due to an increase in the upper limit of information processing capability, in particular the number of dimensions along which the structures used to represent each situation need to be related during formation of a problem-solving strategy.

Fischer's Theory

Fischer and Farrar (1988) also proposed that a critical change in reasoning occurs between 4 or 5 years and 6 or 7 years. The change is from representational mappings to representational systems. As suggested by the similarity in the names, the hypothesized change closely resembles that in Halford's theory. The older children can form representations involving multiple dimensions, whereas the younger ones are more limited in the maximum number of dimensions they can represent. Fischer and Farrar illustrated their distinction in a context in which younger and older children were asked to tell a story about two dolls playing together. Children of age 4 or 5 generally depicted each doll as acting in one way—for example, the doll would be nice or it would be mean. In contrast, children aged 6 or 7 often had each doll simultaneously acting in both a nice and mean way (as when one doll says he would like to be friends but simultaneously hits the other, and the other doll responds by saying that he, too, would like to be friends but not with someone who hits). Once more, the distinction between focusing on a single aspect of a situation and focusing on more than one seems critical to the change hypothesized to occur between age 5 and age 7.

Thus, a number of prominent theories of cognitive development posit a shift between ages 5 and 7, and the change from unidimensional reasoning to multidimensional reasoning plays a central role within each of the hypothesized shifts. The next section examines some of the large body of evidence that such changes occur.

Evidence for the Shift

Spontaneous Performance

Most evidence regarding the shift from unidimensional to multidimensional reasoning comes from assessments of spontaneous performance, that is, performance in the absence of feedback, direct instruction, or other manipulations intended to promote learning. One of the best studied cases involves the balance scale task. Originally studied by Inhelder and Piaget (1958), this task has become something of a benchmark for alternative approaches to cognitive development. It has been studied from a variety of theoretical perspectives: Piagetian (Inhelder & Piaget, 1958; Karmiloff-Smith & Inhelder, 1974); neo-Piagetian (Case, 1985; Halford, 1990; Strauss & Ephron-Wertheim, 1986); psychometric (Wilson, 1989); Vygotskyian (Damon & Phelps, 1988; Tudge, 1992); and information processing (Ferretti & Butterfield, 1986; Siegler, 1976; Wilkening & Anderson, 1982). Its development has been simulated within a variety of modeling frameworks: production systems (Klahr & Siegler, 1978; Langley, 1983); parallel distribution processing models (McClelland & Jenkins, 1991); SOAR (Newell, 1990); and latent trait models (Wilson, 1989). It also has been the subject of many empirical investigations with all age groups from infants to adults, and of particularly intense investigation of the reasoning of 5- to 10-year-olds. Thus, it provides a good place to begin in considering evidence regarding the 5 to 7 shift.

The type of balance scale that most often has been studied is illustrated in Figure 4.1. The scale includes a fulcrum and an arm that can rotate around it. The arm can tip left or right or remain level, depending on how weights (metal disks with holes in them) are arranged on the pegs on each side of the fulcrum. However, the arm is typically held motionless, either by a lever or by blocks underneath each of its ends. The child's task is to examine the arrangement of weights on pegs and to predict which (if either) side would go down if the arm were allowed to move freely.

Two variables determine the balance scale's behavior: the weight on each

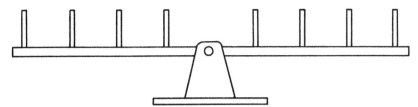

Figure 4.1   The balance scale. From Siegler (1976). Reprinted with permission.

side of the fulcrum and the distance of the weight from the fulcrum. These together determine the torque on each side. Children could represent and base their responses on both variables, on only one, or on some other variable(s).

Inhelder and Piaget (1958) suggested that preoperational stage children rely on the single dimension of weight in solving such problems and that concrete operational children consider both weight and distance. Their conclusions were based largely on the children's verbal explanations. A disadvantage of this way of assessing knowledge was that apparent limitations in reasoning could reflect inarticulateness or lack of awareness of one's cognitive processes, rather than lack of understanding per se. To avoid these methodological problems, Siegler (1976) developed the rule-assessment approach, which allowed assessment of children's rules independent of their ability to express the knowledge verbally. This approach involves hypothesizing rules that people might use and then formulating problem types that yield a distinct pattern of correct answers and errors depending on which rule, if any, is being used. To the degree that an individual's performance adheres closely to that predicted by the rule, and not to that predicted by alternative approaches, the person would be classified as using that rule.

In the case of the balance scale, an analysis of the task, the prior findings of Inhelder and Piaget (1958), and our own pilot studies suggested that children were likely to use one of four rules:

Rule I: If the weight is the same on both sides, predict that the scale will balance. If the weight differs, predict that the side with more weight will go down.

Rule II: If one side has more weight, predict that it will go down. If the weights on the two sides are equal, choose the side with the greater distance (i.e., the side that has the weight farther from the fulcrum).

Rule III: If both weight and distance are equal, predict that the scale will balance. If one side has more weight or distance, and the two sides are equal on the other dimension, predict that the side with the greater value on the unequal dimension will go down. If one side has more weight and the other side more distance, muddle through or guess.

Rule IV: Proceed as in Rule III, unless one side has more weight and the other more distance. In that case, calculate torques by multiplying weight times distance on each side. Then predict that the side with the greater torque will go down.

The 5 to 7 shift hypothesis suggested that 5-year-olds would base their responses on a single dimension, the amount of weight, and thus use Rule I. Children age 7 and older, in contrast, could consider multiple dimensions and thus would more often use Rule II, III, or IV.

To assess which rule, if any, was being used, children were presented examples of each of the six types of problems illustrated in Table 4.1. These problems were defined as follows:

1. *Balance problems:* The same configuration of weights on pegs on each side of the fulcrum.

2. *Weight problems:* Unequal amounts of weights, equidistant from the fulcrum.

3. *Distance problems:* Equal amounts of weights, different distances from the fulcrum.

4. *Conflict-weight problems:* One side with more weight, the other side with its weight farther from the fulcrum and placed so that the side with more weight would go down if the arm could move freely.

5. *Conflict-distance problems:* One side with more weight, the other side with "more distance" and the weight placed so that the side with more distance would go down if the arm could move freely.

6. *Conflict-balance problems:* The usual conflict between weight and distance, and the two sides balance.

A child's pattern of performance on these problems would differ, depending on which rule the child used. For example, a child who used Rule I would consistently be correct on three types of problems and would consistently be wrong on the other three types. Perhaps the most interesting pattern would emerge on conflict-weight problems, where younger children who used Rule I or II would actually be correct more often than older children who used Rule III (see Table 4.1). The reason is that the younger children would consider only weight on such problems and, therefore, would answer them correctly consistently, whereas older children, more aware of the problems' complexity, would consider both weight and distance and, therefore, would sometimes be right and sometimes wrong.

Table 4.1
Predictions for Percentage of Correct Answers and Error Patterns on Posttest for Children Using Different Rules

Problem type	Rules				Predicted developmental trend
	I	II	III	IV	
Balance	100	100	100	100	No change—all children at high level
Weight	100	100	100	100	No change—all children at high level
Distance	0 (Should say "balance")	100	100	100	Dramatic improvement with age
Conflict-weight	100	100	33 (Chance responding)	100	Decline with age Possible upturn in oldest group
Conflict-distance	0 (Should say "right down")	0 (Should say "right down")	33 (Chance responding)	100	Improvement with age
Conflict-balance	0 (Should say "right down")	0 (Should say "right down")	33 (Chance responding)	100	Improvement with age

Table 4.2
Percentage of Children Using Each Rule on Balance Scale Task (Data from Siegler, 1976, Experiment 1)

Age	Rule				
	I	II	III	IV	Unclassifiable
5–6	90	0	0	0	10
9–10	10	40	20	10	20
13–14	10	40	40	0	10
16–17	0	40	50	10	0

In Siegler (1976), 5- to 17-year-olds were presented examples of each of these types of problems and asked to judge whether the left side would go down, the right side would go down, or the scale would balance if the lever were released and the arm could move freely. As shown in Table 4.2, 90% of 5- and 6-year-olds, but only 10% of 9- and 10-year-olds, used Rule I (with use of Rule I defined as generating at least 26 of 30 responses in accord with the predictions of the rule). Thus, a large majority of 5- and 6-year-olds relied on the single dimension of weight, and an equally large majority of older children based their responses on both weight and distance from the fulcrum.

This rule-assessment method has revealed similar differences in problem-solving approaches on a number of other tasks. For example, on a shadows projection task, children were presented a light, a screen, and two T-shaped bars. The bars differed in the lengths of the horizontal part of the bars and in their distance from the light source. The relevant dimensions on this task were the horizontal length of the bar and the ratio of the distance between the light source and the bar to that between the bar and the screen. The task was to judge which bar would cast a longer shadow if the light were turned on. In two experiments, 90% of 5-year-olds but only 17% of 8-year-olds relied on a single dimension (the length of the bars) in judging which bar would cast a longer shadow (Siegler, 1981). Few of the 5-year-olds, but the large majority of 8-year-olds, considered distance from the light source as well as length of the bar in making their judgments.

Similar results emerged in analyses of liquid and solid quantity conservation. As shown in Table 4.3, almost 90% of 5- and 6-year-olds, but only 33% of 7- and 8-year-olds, relied on the single dimension of the length of a clay

Table 4.3a
Percentage of Children Using Each Rule on Conservation of Liquid Quantity Task (Data from Siegler, 1981, Experiment 3)

Age	Rule				
	I	II	III	IV	Unclassifiable
5	75	0	0	8	17
6	92	0	0	8	0
7	42	0	0	33	25
8	42	0	0	50	8
9	8	0	0	67	25

Table 4.3b
Percentage of Children Using Each Rule on Conservation of Solid Quantity Task (Data from Siegler, 1981, Experiment 3)

Age	Rule				
	I	II	III	IV	Unclassifiable
5	83	0	0	8	8
6	92	0	0	8	0
7	33	0	17	42	8
8	33	0	0	42	25
9	25	0	8	67	0

Table 4.4
Studies that Document Unidimensional Reasoning in 5-year-olds

Concept	Source
Class inclusion	Ahr & Youniss (1970)
Conservation	Siegler (1981)
Distance	Acredolo & Schmid (1981)
Emotional reactions	Bruchowsky (1992)
	Case, Hayward, Lewis & Hurst (1987)
Fairness	Marini & Case (1989)
Happiness	Marini & Case (1989)
Monetary value	Griffin, Case & Sandieson (1992)
Morality	Case & Griffin (1990)
Musical sight reading	Capadilupo (1992)
Proportionality	Ferretti, Butterfield, Cahn, & Kerkman (1985)
	Siegler (1976; 1981)
Speed	Strauss & Ephron-Wertheim (1986)
Sweetness	Stavy, Strauss, Orpaz, & Carmi (1982)
Temperature	Strauss (1982)
Temporal duration	Levin, Wilkening & Dembo (1984)
	Siegler & Richards (1979)
Time telling	Case, Sandieson & Dennis (1987)

cylinder in solving solid quantity conservation problems (Siegler, 1981). Simi-larly, 84% of 5- and 6-year-olds but only 43% of 7- and 8-year-olds relied solely on the heights of the liquid columns in judging the amounts of liquid in a conservation of liquid quantity task (Siegler, 1981).

These are far from isolated findings. Table 4.4 lists 15 tasks on which 5-year-olds have been found to base responses on a single dimension and some-what older children (7- to 10-year-olds, depending on the study) on multiple dimensions. The tasks cover a wide variety of concepts, some scientific and mathematical (e.g., time, speed, distance, conservation, sweetness), others so-cial (e.g., understanding of emotional reactions, fairness, morality), yet others involving such concepts as musical sight reading and monetary value. The list is far from exhaustive; a much longer one could easily be assembled. On a great many tasks, then, 5-year-olds rely on a single dimension and older children on multiple dimensions in their spontaneous reasoning.

Learning

Even when both 5-year-olds and older children rely on a single dimension in their spontaneous reasoning, the older children often learn to consider multiple dimensions from experiences that do not help the younger ones. Research on the balance scale again illustrates this phenomenon. In Siegler (1976, Experi-ment 2), 5- and 8-year-olds were tested to identify children of each age who relied on Rule I, that is, who consistently predicted on the basis of relative weight. Then the children were presented feedback experience with one of three types of problems: (a) control problems, which Rule I would solve successfully; (b) distance problems, which Rule I would not solve correctly but which would be solved correctly by the next more advanced approach, Rule II; and (c) conflict problems, which would not be understood even qualitatively until Rule III. (Examples of each type of problem are shown in Table 4.1.)

The 8-year-olds learned to consider both relevant dimensions much more often than did the 5-year-olds. This was particularly marked in the most challenging condition, that involving conflict problems. The 8-year-olds benefited greatly from trying to solve these problems and receiving feedback on their efforts, 70% of them progressing to a more advanced rule, usually Rule III. In contrast, literally none of the 5-year-olds benefited from the same experience; they either continued to rely on Rule I or became confused and stopped relying on any apparent rule.

Intensive observation of a few 5- and 8-year-olds solving balance scale problems suggested a reason. Although the 8-year-olds who were examined did not initially base responses on the distance dimension, they often looked back and forth between the fulcrum and the location of the weights, thus seeming to encode the distance of the weights from the fulcrum. In contrast, the 5-year-olds did not usually look back and forth; they seemed just to look up and down with each pile of weights. This suggested that they encoded the amount of weight on each side but not the distance from the fulcrum. If this impression was accurate, it could explain the differences in learning. A child who was encoding distance could notice that it predicted which side of the balance would go down; in contrast, a child who did not encode distance could not learn this relation.

This hypothesis was tested via a reconstruction task (Siegler, 1976, Experiment 3). On each of 16 problems, children were shown a balance scale with weights on pegs, given 10 seconds to look at it, and then asked to "make the same problem" on an identical balance scale that did not yet have any weights on the pegs. This task allowed independent assessment of the weight and distance dimensions. A child could show encoding of weight by putting the correct number of weights on each side, correct encoding of distance by putting weights on the right peg on each side, both, or neither.

Performance on this task confirmed the impression that the 8-year-olds were encoding both weight and distance dimensions and that the 5-year-olds were encoding only weight. The 8-year-olds correctly reproduced both dimensions on the majority of trials, whereas the 5-year-olds were much more accurate in encoding weight than in encoding distance. A second experiment demonstrated that this was not due to the younger children's having insufficient time to encode both dimensions; given essentially unlimited time to encode, the difference in the younger children's encoding of the two dimensions was just as large.

Most critically, when the 5-year-olds were taught to encode distance information, they, like the 8-year-olds, were able to learn effectively from the experience with the conflict problems that previously had not helped them at all. In particular, having learned to encode distance as well as weight, 70% of 5-year-olds learned Rule II or III from the experience with the conflict problems, versus 0% previously. Thus, it was possible for 5-year-olds to learn to encode and to base responses on two dimensions, but it required instruction in how to encode that was unnecessary with older children.

The tenacity of 5-year-olds' unidimensional reasoning has been observed on many other tasks. They include conservation of number (Kingsley & Hall, 1967), conservation of liquid quantity (Strauss & Langer, 1970), class inclusion (Inhelder, Sinclair, & Bovet, 1974), temporal duration (Siegler, 1983), and many others. Thus, 5-year-olds more often rely on a single dimension in the absence of training and more often continue to reason unidimensionally following training than do older children.

Evidence Against the Shift

Evidence That 5-year-olds Can and Often Do Reason Multidimensionally

Over the past 20 years, many studies have demonstrated previously unsuspected competence in young children. These include demonstrations that 3- to 5-year-olds often consider multiple dimensions even without any special training. Further, they do so on the same concepts on which they reason unidimensionally when understanding is measured in other ways.

The concept of class inclusion provides a number of especially compelling demonstrations of such early competence. One is Markman and Seibert's (1976) study of the effects of alternative phrasings of class-inclusion questions. Like previous investigators, Markman and Seibert found that 5-year-olds rarely answered correctly such questions as, "Here are some blocks; these are blue blocks and these are red blocks; who would have more toys to play with, someone who owned the blue blocks or someone who *owned the blocks?*" (italics added). However, they found that the 5-year-olds do answer correctly when the question is rephrased as "Here are some blocks; these are blue blocks and these are red blocks; who would have more toys to play with, someone who owned the blue blocks or someone who *owned the pile?*" (italics added). With this latter phrasing, the 5-year-olds could view the blue blocks as simultaneously being a subgroup of their own and part of the superordinate group of the pile of blocks.

Studies of temporal duration provide other clear examples of 5-year-olds' ability to consider multiple dimensions on the same concept on which other tasks elicited reliance on a single dimension. For example, Levin (1982) asked 4- and 5-year-olds to judge time under three conditions: (a) a still condition, in which two dolls at the same or different times "fell asleep," "woke up," or did both; (b) a rotational condition, in which two objects rotated on a turntable for varying amounts of time; and (c) a linear condition, in which two trains ran along parallel tracks, starting and/or stopping at the same time but also covering different distances, running at different speeds, and starting, and/or stopping, at different points along the tracks. This last condition was like that studied by Piaget and subsequent investigators. Levin, like them, found that when presented it, most 5-year-olds focused on the single dimension of the stopping points of the trains. In contrast, most of the same children judged correctly on the other two tasks, where there was no visible variation in stopping point to influence judgments. On these tasks, the 4- and 5-year-olds' judgments reflected consideration of both beginning time and ending time.

Table 4.5 lists a number of other concepts on which 5-year-olds have been found to consider multiple dimensions. Note that the list includes many of the same concepts included in the Table 4.4 list of concepts on which 5-year-olds reason unidimensionally. Many task characteristics have been shown to influence whether unidimensional or multidimensional reasoning is obtained: processing demands, phrasing of questions, familiarity of the entities in the problems, ease of mapping the experimental situation onto an everyday situation, presence of salient misleading cues, and many others.

Table 4.5
Studies that Document Multidimensional Reasoning in Children 5 Years and Younger

Concept	Source
Area	Anderson & Cuneo (1978)
	Wilkening (1981)
Class inclusion	Bauer & Mandler (1989)
	Sugarman (1983)
Conservation	Gelman (1972)
	Siegler (1981)
Fairness	Surber & Haines (1989)
	Anderson & Butzin (1978)
Proportionality	Surber & Gzesh (1984)
	Wilkening & Anderson (1982)
Speed	Wilkening (1981)
Temporal duration	Berndt & Wood (1974)
	Levin (1977)

How Should These Findings Be Interpreted?

It seems useful to distinguish among four main classes of interpretations of findings regarding 5-year-olds' unidimensional thinking:

1. *Capacity differences.* Five-year-olds are only capable of focusing on a single dimension.

2. *Order of preference differences.* Five-year-olds can think in terms of multiple dimensions, but while older children and adults prefer to reason multidimensionally, 5-year-olds prefer to focus on a single dimension.

3. *Strength-of-preference differences.* Five-year-olds, like older individuals, can think multidimensionally, and they also have the same relative preferences among modes of thinking, but they have a stronger preference for focusing on a single dimension.

4. *Domain-specific knowledge differences.* Five-year-olds can think multidimensionally and have the same order and strength of preferences as older individuals, but they have less domain-specific knowledge to steer them toward multidimensional thinking on many particular tasks.

These classes of explanations—stressing capacities, relative preferences, degree of preferences, and specific knowledge—can be applied to a wide range of hypotheses regarding developmental differences in thinking. In the following subsections each is evaluated in the context of changes in unidimensional and multidimensional thinking between 5 and 7 years.

Capacity Differences

A great many findings argue against the view that 5-year-olds lack sufficient cognitive capacity to reason multidimensionally. Under many conditions, children 5 years and younger have been shown to consider two or more dimensions. They have been shown to do so on many of the same concepts on which 5-year-olds reason unidimensionally when understanding of the concept is assessed using other tasks. For example, they do not show understanding of the concept of class inclusion using Inhelder and Piaget's (1964) task, but they do show such understanding when the class-inclusion concept is assessed using Markman and Seibert's (1976) task. Even on tasks on which 5-year-olds' spontaneous reasoning is unidimensional, they often can learn to consider multiple dimensions. The evidence seems sufficient to reject the view that 5-year-olds lack the cognitive capacity for multidimensional thinking.

Order-of-Preference Differences

Another possibility is that 5-year-olds prefer to think unidimensionally, whereas older children and adults prefer to consider multiple dimensions. Younger children might adopt a strategy of trying to isolate the single seemingly most important dimension and making predictions based on the values of that dimension. Older children and adults, realizing that the world is complex, might make the opposite assumption and look for multidimensional solutions from the outset.

Evidence from studies of concept formation, however, argues against this view. The reason is that preference for seeking unidimensional solutions is far from unique to 5-year-olds Neisser and Weene's (1962) study of the difficulty of forming different types of concepts illustrates this point. College students needed to classify stimuli as being exemplars or non-exemplars of a concept. Some of the problems that they needed to solve had unidimensional solutions, as when the presence or absence of a single feature determined whether the instance was or was not an exemplar. Other problems had bidimensional solutions, as when both of two features needed to be present for the instance to be an exemplar of the concept. Yet others had tridimensional solutions, as when either both or neither of two features needed to be present. The college students solved the unidimensional problems much more quickly than the bidimensional problems, and the bidimensional problems much more quickly than the tridimensional problems. This pattern suggests that adults, like 5-year-olds, initially form unidimensional hypotheses and move on to considering successively more complex hypotheses only if the simple ones prove inadequate. Lacking evidence to the contrary, both older and younger individuals appear to prefer unidimensional approaches.

Strength-of-Preference Differences

Even if people of a wide range of ages prefer to focus on a single dimension, young children could have a stronger preference than older children and adults for that mode of thinking. This interpretation fits a considerable body of data. It implies that both 5-year-olds and older individuals will sometimes focus on a single dimension and sometimes consider multiple dimensions. It also implies that the younger individuals should focus on a single dimension under a broader range of circumstances. Further, it implies that in situations in which 5-year-olds and older children or adults start with unidimensional hypotheses, the 5-year-olds will be slower and less likely to abandon them in favor of multidimensional approaches. This should be evident both in terms of the number of individuals who consider multiple dimensions following a given type of experience and in terms of the range of experiences that lead to learning. These are precisely the main findings in the developmental literature on unidimensional and multidimensional thinking. Thus, differing strength of preference for unidimensional reasoning seems to be at least part of the explanation for the observed differences in reasoning.

Domain-Specific Knowledge Differences

Many differences among age groups that once were believed to reflect differences in capacity or general strategies now appear to be due to differences in content knowledge about specific domains (see Chi & Ceci, 1987, for a review of this literature). Such differences also seem likely to play a role in the frequency with which children of different ages rely on a single dimension on tasks on which multiple dimensions are relevant. The older children will have more experience, and this experience will have disconfirmed earlier unidimensional hypotheses on particular tasks, leading the older children to consider multiple dimensions on them.

Differing domain-specific knowledge is unlikely to be the whole story, however. The reason is that most tasks on which 5-year-olds have been found to reason unidimensionally and older children multidimensionally are at a specific level unfamiliar to people of any age and are at a general level familiar to people of all ages. For example, at no age are people ordinarily asked whether pouring water from one glass to a differently shaped second glass changes the amount of water (much less told that it does not). At all ages, people frequently see water and other liquids poured into differently shaped containers. Thus, nothing in people's domain-specific experience accounts straightforwardly for 5-year-olds' so often judging the amount of liquid on the basis of the liquids' heights and for 8-year-olds' and older children's judging on the basis of the type of transformation that was performed. This does not mean that changing domain-specific knowledge is unimportant in the shift, but rather that other factors, such as differing strength of preference for unidimensional reasoning, also need to be considered to explain the changes observed in this age period.

Unidimensional Reasoning as a Characteristic Tendency of 5-Year-Olds' Thought

These findings regarding unidimensional and multidimensional reasoning considerably narrow the range of plausible theoretical interpretations. On one extreme, it is clearly not beyond 5-year-olds' capabilities to form multidimensional concepts. At the other extreme, demonstrating that 5-year-olds *can* reason multidimensionally does not explain why they fail to do so in many situations in which older children and adults do. The question is, How should we think of this type of development?

One useful approach may be to conceptualize such developments as *changes in characteristic tendencies of thought.* This conceptualization maintains the recognition that there is something to be explained, while at the same time avoiding untenable claims about multidimensional thinking being impossible for children of certain ages. It goes beyond the typical question of whether children have a given capability at a given age, to the potentially more fruitful issues of the conditions under which they show the capability and the mechanisms that lead them to show it under some circumstances but not others.

Conditions That Promote Unidimensional Thinking in 5-Year-Olds

Analysis of conditions under which 5-year-olds focus on a single dimension and 7- to 10-year-olds consider multiple dimensions indicates four prominent characteristics. The tasks (a) are unfamiliar, (b) require a quantitative comparison, (c) require a discrete choice between two or three alternatives, and (d) include a single perceptually or conceptually dominant dimension that can lead children toward specific incorrect answers.

These phenomena can be illustrated with such prominent exemplars of the 5 to 7 shift as liquid quantity conservation, number conservation, class inclusion, shadows projection, temporal duration, and balance scale problems. Each case illustrates all four qualities. First, the specific tasks typically used to measure these concepts are unfamiliar: Neither children nor adults are ordinarily asked whether pouring water influences the amount of water, whether spreading out a row of objects influences the number of objects, whether there are more objects in the larger subordinate class than in the superordinate class, which object will cast a longer shadow, which side of a balance scale will go down, or which of two toy trains traveled for more time. Second, all of the tasks require a quantitative comparison: Which glass has a *greater amount* of water; which row has a larger *number* of objects; are there *more* blue blocks or more blocks; which side *is more likely* to go down; which object will cast *a longer shadow;* which train went the *longer time;* and so on. Third, the child must choose among two or three discrete alternatives: Does *this glass* have more, does *that glass* have more, or do they *have the same amount;* are there more *blue blocks,* more *yellow blocks,* or is the number *the same;* will *this side* go down, *that side* go down, or will they *balance;* did *this train* travel for more time, did *that train* travel for more time; or did they travel for the *same time;* and so forth. Fourth, the tasks all include a salient but misleading dimension on which young children focus: the height of the water, the length of the row of objects, the number of objects in the greater subordinate class, the weight on each side of the fulcrum, the length of the object whose shadow is being cast, and the stopping points of the trains.

Identification of these four influences suggests predictions regarding the conditions under which 5-year-olds will and will not focus on a single dimension. When all of the properties are present, 5-year-olds are likely to focus on a single dimension; when none are present, they are unlikely to do so; the more that are present, the more likely that the 5-year-olds will reason unidimensionally.

Mechanisms That Promote Unidimensional Reasoning in 5-Year-Olds

The analysis of conditions that promote unidimensional reasoning suggests several mechanisms that may underlie 5-year-olds' tendency to focus on a single dimension: processing capacity, theoretical beliefs, and encoding.

First consider the role of processing capacity. Although 5-year-olds' processing capacity does not preclude them from representing multiple dimensions, it may make them less likely than older children to do so. Unfamiliar tasks tend to stress children's processing limits more than formally isomorphic familiar tasks (Guttentag, 1985). One reaction to tasks that stress processing limits is to narrow one's focus to the seemingly most important part of the task, for example, to the single most salient dimension. This reduces the memory load and makes representing the situation less demanding. If 5-year-olds have less processing capacity than do older children or if new tasks often stress their capacities more because the broad class of tasks is less familiar, they would be likely to engage in such simplification more often than older children.

A second potential source of 5-year-olds' tendency toward unidimensional reasoning is a theoretical belief that quantitative comparisons should have simple one-dimensional solutions. Suggestive of this interpretation, Levin (1977; 1979) found that although young children prefer to focus on conceptually reasonable single dimensions, they will also focus on less reasonable single dimensions when the preferred dimensions are not available in the situation. For example, when cues related to distance or end point are available, 5-year-olds will rely on them to judge relative time (Levin, 1982; Siegler & Richards, 1979). These cues are conceptually quite distinct from time, but at least have an empirical relation to it. A moving object that travels farther and stops farther along a path will, other things equal, have traveled for more time. However, when these cues are not available, young children will rely on cues that seem altogether extraneous. For example, Levin and Gilat (1982) reported that young children judge which of two lamps has been on for the longer time by the brightness of the lights. They also found that young children rely on the single dimension of the size of the bulbs (independent of brightness), which seems even further removed. The 5-year-olds' reliance on such cues may reflect a general belief that it should be possible to make quantitative comparisons on the basis of some simple quantitative dimension and that whichever dimension seems most plausible should be relied upon. Levin (1977) dubbed a related interpretation of young children's reasoning the "more-is-more assumption." As described earlier, adults also first try to identify unidimensional solutions to problems, but 5-year-olds' greater tenacity in maintaining such explanations in the face of negative evidence may reflect a stronger belief in the likelihood of their adequacy.

A third potential explanation for 5-year-olds' frequent unidimensional reasoning is that they encode situations more narrowly than do older children. Such limited encoding may be especially prevalent in situations that include a misleading dimension that is perceptually salient, conceptually salient, or both. Such salient misleading dimensions may capture 5-year-olds' attention and lead them to focus on that dimension to the exclusion of others that they would encode under different circumstances.

The previously described results with the balance scale task directly support this explanation. Five-year-olds' encoding on that task is narrower than 8-year-olds', even when the 8-year-olds initially use the same predictive rule. Promoting encoding of both relevant dimensions allowed the 5-year-olds to learn multidimensional predictive rules, thus showing a causal link between breadth of encoding and ability to learn.

Clearly, these (and other) mechanisms work together to produce 5-year-olds' unidimensional reasoning; it is not a question of either/or. For example, 5-year-olds' narrower encoding under conditions where a salient misleading dimension is present may reflect (a) an adaptation to capacity constraints, (b) a general belief that encoding of a single dimension should be sufficient to make quantitative comparisons, or (c) both. Alternatively, the fact that unidimensional thinking appears so often in situations requiring quantitative comparisons may reflect specific misunderstandings of comparative terms or quantitative dimensions rather than any abstract belief about the types of solutions that should be possible in these situations.

Conclusions

My hope is that viewing this particular change, and age-related changes in general, in terms of changes in characteristic tendencies will shift developmental discussions in useful directions. It will encourage us to identify the situations in which the changes are and are not present and to think about mechanisms that might lead to the changes being evident in some but not all situations. It also will preserve the recognition that there is something important to be explained, without untenable claims about what children cannot do under any condition. In short, identifying and trying to explain changes in characteristic tendencies of thought may help us better understand the large changes that are so omnipresent between ages 5 and 7 and throughout development.

Acknowledgments

Preparation of this article was made possible by grants to the author from the National Institutes of Health (HD-19011), the Spencer Foundation, and the Mellon Foundation.

References

Acredolo, C., & Schmid, J. (1981). The understanding of relative speeds, distances and durations of movement. *Developmental Psychology, 17,* 490–493.
Ahr, P. R., & Youniss, J. (1970). Reasons for failure on the class-inclusion problem. *Child Development, 41,* 131–143.
Anderson, N. H., & Butzin, C. A. (1978). Integration theory applied to children's judgments of equity. *Developmental Psychology, 14,* 593–606.
Anderson, N. H., & Cuneo, D. O. (1978). The height + width rule in children's judgments of quantity. *Journal of Experimental Psychology: General, 107,* 335–378.
Bauer, P. J., & Mandler, J. M. (1989). Taxonomies and triads: Conceptual organization in 1- to 2-year-olds. *Cognitive Psychology, 21,* 156–184.
Berndt, T. J., & Wood, D. J. (1974). The development of time concepts through conflict based on a primitive duration capacity. *Child Development, 45,* 825–828.
Bruchowsky, M. M. (1992). The development of empathic cognition in early and middle childhood. In R. Case (Ed.), *The mind's staircase: Exploring the conceptual underpinnings of human thought and knowledge.* Hillsdale, NJ: Erlbaum.
Capadilupo, A. M. (1992). A neo-structural analysis of children's response to instruction in the sight-reading of musical notation. In R. Case (Ed.), *The mind's staircase: Exploring the conceptual underpinnings of human thought and knowledge.* Hillsdale, NJ: Erlbaum.
Case, R. (1985). *Intellectual development: Birth to adulthood.* New York: Academic Press.
Case, R. (1988). The structure and process of intellectual development. In A. Demetriou (Ed.), *The neo-Piagetian theories of cognitive development: Toward an integration.* Amsterdam: Elsevier Science Publishers.
Case, R., & Griffin, S. (1990). Child cognitive development: The role of central conceptual structures in the development of scientific and social thought. In C. A. Hauert (Ed.), *Developmental psychology: Cognitive, perceptuo-motor, and neuropsychological perspectives.* Amsterdam: Elsevier.
Case, R., Hayward, S., Lewis, M., & Hurst, P. (1987). Toward a neo-Piagetian theory of cognitive and emotional development. *Developmental Review, 8,* 1–51.
Case, R., Sandieson, R., & Dennis, S. (1987). Two cognitive developmental approaches to the design of remedial instruction. *Cognitive Development, 1,* 293–333.
Chi, M. T. H., and Ceci, S. (1987). Content knowledge: Its role representation and restructuring in memory development. In H. W. Reese (Ed.), *Advances in child development and behavior* (Vol. 20, pp. 91–146). New York: Academic Press.
Damon, W., & Phelps, E. (1988). Strategic uses of peer learning in children's education. In T. Berndt & G. Ladd (Eds.), *Children's peer relations.* New York: Wiley.

Demetriou, A. (1988). *The neo-Piagetian theories of cognitive development: Toward an integration.* Amsterdam: Elsevier.

Ferretti, R. P., & Butterfield, E. C. (1986). Are children's rule-assessment classifications invariant across instances of problem types? *Child Development, 57,* 1419–1428.

Ferretti, R. P., Butterfield, E. C., Cahn, A., & Kerkman, D. (1985). The classification of children's knowledge: Development on the balance-scale and inclined plane tasks. *Journal of Experimental Child Psychology, 39,* 131–160.

Fischer, K. W., and Farrar, M. J. (1988). Generalizations about generalization: How a theory of skill development explains both generality and specificity. In A. Demetriou (Ed.), *The neo-Piagetian theories of cognitive development: Toward an integration.* Amsterdam: Elsevier.

Gelman, R. (1972). The nature and development of early number concepts. In H. W. Reese (Ed.), *Advances in child development and behavior* (Vol. 7, pp. 115–167). New York: Academic Press.

Griffin, S., Case, R., & Sandieson, R. (1992). Synchrony and asynchrony in the acquisition of children's everyday mathematical knowledge. In R. Case (Ed.), *The mind's staircase: Exploring the conceptual underpinnings of human thought and knowledge.* Hillsdale, NJ: Erlbaum.

Guttentag, R. E. (1985). Memory and aging: Implications for theories of memory development during childhood. *Developmental Review, 5,* 56–82.

Halford, G. S. (1988). A structure-mapping approach to cognitive development. In A. Demetriou (Ed.), *The neo-Piagetian theories of cognitive development: Toward an integration.* Amsterdam: Elsevier.

Halford, G. S. (1990). *Children's understanding: The development of mental models.* Hillsdale, NJ: Erlbaum.

Inhelder, B., & Piaget, J. (1958). *The growth of logical thinking from childhood to adolescence.* New York: Basic Books.

Inhelder, B., & Piaget, J. (1964). *The early growth of logic in the child: Classification and seriation.* New York: Humanities Press.

Inhelder, B., Sinclair, H., & Bovet, M. (1974). *Learning and the development of cognition.* Cambridge, MA: Harvard University Press.

Karmiloff-Smith, A., & Inhelder, B. (1974). If you want to get ahead get a theory. *Cognition, 3,* 195–212.

Kingsley, R. C., & Hall, V. C. (1967). Training conservation through the use of learning sets. *Child Development, 38,* 1111–1126.

Klahr, D., & Siegler, R. S. (1978). The representation of children's knowledge. In H. W. Reese & L. P. Lipsitt (Eds.), *Advances in child development.* New York: Academic Press.

Langley, P. (1983). Learning search strategies through discrimination. *International Journal of Man-Machine Studies, 18,* 513–541.

Levin, I. (1977). The development of time concepts in children: Reasoning about duration. *Child Development, 48,* 435–444.

Levin, I. (1979). Interference of time-related and unrelated cues with duration comparisons of young children. *Child Development, 50,* 469–477.

Levin, I. (1982). The nature and development of time concepts in children: The effects of interfering cues. In W. J. Friedman (Ed.), *The developmental psychology of time.* New York: Academic Press.

Levin, I., Wilkening, F., & Dembo, Y. (1984). Development of time quantification: Integration and nonintegration of beginnings and endings in comparing durations. *Child Development, 55,* 2160–2172.

Marini, Z. (1981). *The relationship between social and nonsocial cognition in elementary school children.* Unpublished master's thesis, University of Toronto, Toronto, Ontario, Canada.

Marini, Z., & Case, R. (1989). Parallels in the development of preschoolers' knowledge about their physical and social worlds. *Merrill-Palmer Quarterly, 35,* 63–88.

Markman, E. M., and Seibert, J. (1976). Classes and collections: Internal organization and resulting holistic properties. *Cognitive Psychology, 8,* 561–577.

McClelland, J., & Jenkins, E. (1991). Nature, nurture, and connections: Implications of connectionists models for cognitive development. In K. vanLehn (Ed.), *Architectures for intelligence.* Hillsdale, NJ: Erlbaum.

Neisser, U., & Weene, P. (1962). Hierarchies in concept attainment. *Journal of Experimental Psychology, 64,* 640–645.

Newell, A. (1990). *Unified theories of cognition: The William James lectures.* Cambridge, MA: Harvard University Press.

Piaget, J. (1946). *The psychology of intelligence.* London: Routledge & Kegan Paul, 1950. (Trans. by A. J. Pomerans from 2nd French ed.)

Piaget, J. (1969). *The child's conception of time.* London: Routledge & Kegan Paul.

Siegler, R. S. (1976). Three aspects of cognitive development. *Cognitive Psychology, 8,* 481–520.

Siegler, R. S. (1981). Developmental sequences within and between concepts. *Monographs of the Society for Research in Child Development, 46* (Whole No. 189).

Siegler, R. S. (1983). Five generalizations about cognitive development. *American Psychologist, 38,* 263–277.

Siegler, R. S., & Richards, D. D. (1979). Development of time, speed and distance concepts. *Developmental Psychology, 15,* 288–298.

Stavy, R., Strauss, S., Orpaz, N., & Carmi, G. (1982). U-shaped behavioral growth in ratio comparisons. In S. Strauss (Ed.), *U-shaped behavioral growth.* New York: Academic Press.

Strauss, S. (1982). *U-shaped behavioral growth.* New York: Academic Press.

Strauss, S., & Ephron-Wertheim, T. (1986). Structure and process: Developmental psychology as looking in the mirror. In I. Levin (Ed.), *Stage and structure: Reopening the debate.* Norwood, NJ: Ablex.

Strauss, S., & Langer, J. (1970). Operational thought inducement. *Child Development, 41,* 163–175.

Sugarman, S. (1983). *Children's early thought.* Cambridge, England: Cambridge University Press.

Surber, C. F., & Gzesh, S. M. (1984). Reversible operations in the balance scale task. *Journal of Experimental Child Psychology, 38,* 254–274.

Surber, C. F., & Haines, B. A. (1989). The growth of proportional reasoning: Methodological issues. In R. Vasta & G. Whitehurts (Eds.), *Annals of child development* (Vol. 4, pp. 67–103). Greenwich, CT: JAI.

Tudge, J. R. H. (1992). Processes and consequences of peer collaboration: A Vygotskian analysis. *Child Development, 63,* 1364–1379.

White, S. H. (1965). Evidence for a hierarchical arrangement of learning processes. In L. P. Lipsitt and C. C. Spiker (Eds.), *Advances in child behavior and development* (Vol. 2, pp. 187–220). New York: Academic Press.

Wilkening, F. (1981). Integrating velocity, time, and distance information: A developmental study. *Cognitive Psychology, 13,* 231–247.

Wilkening, F., & Anderson, N. H. (1982). Comparison of two rule assessment methodologies for studying cognitive development and knowledge structure. *Psychological Bulletin, 92,* 215–237.

Wilson, M. (1989). Saltus: A psychometric model of discontinuity in cognitive development. *Psychological Bulletin, 105,* 276–289.

CHAPTER FIVE

A Recursive Transformation of Central Cognitive Mechanisms: The Shift from Partial to Whole Representations

PIERRE MOUNOUD

The numerous transitions observed in the behavior of children between 5 and 7 years of age testify, from my point of view, to a general transformation of the central cognitive mechanisms. This transformation expresses itself in particular through the shift from new, fragmentary, and *partial representations* constructed by the child between 4 and 5 years of age to *whole representations,* which appear around the age of 6 years. These whole representations integrate the relevant dimensions previously processed separately. This transition is similar (isomorphic) to the one taking place around 12 months in infancy. That is the reason why I consider it as recursive. I have defended this position for several years and documented it in various ways (Mounoud, 1981, 1986a, 1986b, 1988, 1990a, and 1993a).

Characterizing the transition from 5 to 7 years by the shift from partial representations (fragmentary, piecemeal, elementary) to whole representations (which integrate relevant dimensions previously processed in a split or juxtaposed way) must initially appear as a very traditional position. As a matter of fact, it is the classical shift from uncoordinated (or loosely coordinated) structures (or mental activities) to coordinated structures. Nowadays very few researchers are ready to consider such a transition as general and as related to central cognitive mechanisms. The current credo is in favor of the domain specificity and of the prevailing role of contexts. Furthermore, many examples that seem to contradict the conception I defend immediately come to mind, in particular the whole set of behaviors that can be termed *precocious competencies.* These are defined as 3- to 5-year-old children's successes at tasks that are partly isomorphic to those tasks at which children around 7 years of age are usually successful (for a discussion, see Mounoud, 1986a).

But before considering these contradictory points of view, I examine in more detail how the shift from partial to whole representations affects the way children between 5 and 7 years conceptualize objects (new declarative knowledge) and, consequently, the way they act on them (new procedural knowledge).

This transition corresponds to the shift from conceptions that take into consideration a single *aspect* of a situation, an isolated object *characteristic* (dimension) regarding a given context, or a particular interaction (centration effect) to conceptions involving the *whole set of relevant dimensions* (critical features) of a given object or situation.

Another consequence of this transformation is the shift going from a *successive* to a *simultaneous* organization of behaviors. What the child does, previous to this change, by the juxtaposition or by the succession of distinct, elementary behaviors becomes a single, complex behavior.

Finally, concerning the way actions are connected, the transition has the child going from *local planning of elementary actions* (step-by-step planning) to the *planning of coupled or coordinated action sequences.*

Various descriptions of this transition and analogous or related transitions occurring at different ages can be found in the literature. For instance, authors write about the shift going from piecemeal to whole organization (Keil & Kelly, 1987), from unbounded to bounded engrams (Harnad, 1987), from partial to integrated patterns (Halverson, 1931), or from local to global mappings (Edelman, 1987). It has also been presented as the capacity of integrating and synchronizing subactions in a continuous sequence (Hofsten, 1990). Finally, Diamond (1988) has described this transition in terms of a general capacity to establish relationships between data separated in space, time, or both and the conjoined capacity to inhibit the prevailing responses. Following Diamond I am in favor of considering this major transformation of central cognitive mechanisms as principally determined by internal structural changes (involving mostly frontal and callosal structures) and as secondarily dependent in a nonspecific way on environmental factors (Mounoud, 1993).

Albeit central, this general transformation of cognitive mechanisms does not necessarily manifest itself at the same time in the various cognitive domains by changes in representations. The new cognitive mechanisms intervene only in as much as they are required, that is, depending on the type of experience done by the children relative to the various contexts or domains they confront.

It is possible to show evidence of this transformation of cognitive mechanisms as well as of the visible derived transitions in various domains and at various developmental periods. In infancy, the transformation takes place around 12 months. One of the best examples is the capacity to coordinate differentiated activities of both hands, the capacity to coordinate the various functions involved in complex prehension behavior (reaching, grasping, etc.), or the capacity to coordinate syllables in order to constitute the first words (Mounoud, 1988, 1993a). This transformation is also responsible for the success in the A not B task as well as for the success in detour behavior (reaching for an object located behind a screen or inside a transparent box) ("object retrieval"; cf. Diamond, 1988; Diamond & Gilbert, 1989). In childhood, the transformation takes place around 6 years of age. Behaviors like categorization and seriation activities seem good illustrations, in particular the capacity to consider the relationships between an object and the multiple classes it may belong to, which involves the mastery of concept intension and extension (the all and "some" coordination in Piagetian terms) or the capacity to consider the relationships between a given object and its predecessor and its successor in a series (Bideaud, 1988; Houdé, 1992). The same transformation should still explain the success in conservation tasks: The child must become able to integrate the various aspects taking place in a transformation such as the length and the density concerning number conservation (Fayol, 1990). The shift from partial to whole representations does not explain in itself the emergence of inclusion, of conservation behaviors, or of systematic strategies in seriation. It constitutes a necessary but insufficient condition. Whole representations must be decomposed and analyzed in order to make possible the mastery of the relationships between parts or elements and totality (the partitive or inclusive logical relationships between elements and totalities) as well as the relationships between various totalities regarding one or several of their dimensions.

Although the shift from partial to whole representations sounds familiar to developmental psychologists, it is less common to consider the shift recursive. From this point of view one has to look at the inverse shift, that is, the shift going from whole to partial and fragmentary representations. This transition, recursive as well, occurs at other developmental periods such as, for example, around the age of 4 years (as well as during the first months of life).

The major point of this chapter can be summarized in the following way: The transformation we are trying to capture (the 5 to 7 year shift) could be considered only as one aspect of a more important transformation that constrains the child at different stages, in particular around 3 to 4 years (as well as soon after birth), *to substitute for automatized processes* (performed by constituted knowledge systems) *new processing modes* (coming from new knowledge systems in elaboration). I consider that unfortunately we still are unable to label and characterize these various knowledge systems in a satisfactory way. For the new systems various terms have been used such as *conceptual, conscious, explicit, declarative,* or *discursive knowledge,* to enumerate only some of them. I come back to this topic later in the chapter.

Thus, the transition from 5 to 7 years, as I define it, basically corresponds to one *step* in the genesis of new knowledge systems. Its major characteristic is precisely the shift from partial to whole structures or the shift from centrations on isolated aspects of a situation to their integration.

In contrast, the transition occurring around 3 to 4 years follows a more fundamental transformation, that is, the emergence of new knowledge systems. To understand this transition going from constituted systems to systems in elaboration, it is first necessary to take into consideration the nature and the role played by constituted knowledge systems. These systems, which I call *perceptuomotor,* are characterized by whole representations. They determine behaviors that integrate numerous dimensions of the encountered situations. The emergence of new knowledge systems defines, therefore, an inverse shift to the one observed between 5 to 7 years, going from behaviors determined by whole representations (those of the constituted knowledge systems) to behaviors determined by partial representations (those of the new systems in elaboration). Consequently, in order to understand the transition from 5 to 7 years, it is necessary then to consider the complex relationships between the new systems in elaboration and the previous, constituted ones.

From that perspective it is possible to conciliate the various contradictory claims concerning, in particular, children from 3 to 5. Thus when a 5-year-old child is described as centered on a single aspect of a situation, it is possible to assume that his or her behavior is determined by a new knowledge system in elaboration (or that the child's behavior is controlled by an attentional or conscious supervisory system and not by an automatized one). Nonconservative responses in the classical conservation tasks are good examples of this type of organization. In this connection, it is necessary to consider nonconservative judgments as resulting from a new construction, from an elaboration that initially forces the child to focus on a single dimension. Simultaneously, in a different context the same 5-year-old child could display behaviors that reveal his or her abilities to grasp the whole set of relevant dimensions for a situation more or less similar to the classical conservation tasks, as is the case in Donaldson (1978), for instance. This time the child's behaviors could be determined by an achieved and sedimented knowledge system that operates in an automatized way.

In this chapter I start by illustrating the complex relationships between the two categories of knowledge systems (achieved and in elaboration) by means of an experiment carried out on the construction of simple instruments by children 4 to 9 years old (Mounoud, 1968, 1970). More particularly, I characterize the shift from a conception of instruments as juxtaposed segments or fragments supposed to perform successively various functions (the construction and the corrections consist in adding or subtracting segments at the extremity of the instrument) to a more global conception of instruments, which perform a global transformation (a translation, for example) taking simultaneously into consideration the various functions to be fulfilled (the corrections tend to modify the relationship between the different parts of the instrument in correspondence with the constraints of the task). I explain how this change in the conception of the instrument in children 4 to 9 years old is initially framed or directed by an already constructed knowledge system called perceptuomotor. I then show how this system is later on controlled and integrated by the new conceptual knowledge system in elaboration.

Then I present more extensively a developmental model of the emergence of new skills as resulting from new conceptualizations (owing to new knowledge systems). I will also show how these new conceptualizations are initially directed or framed by the practical forms and automatized behaviors determined by previous systems. The new systems initially reveal themselves as conscious or explicit conceptualizations before transforming themselves into practical or procedural forms of knowledge, more or less automatized, and elaborative processes, which are no longer accessible to consciousness (Mounoud, 1990b).

To conclude, I present the experiments recently conducted by Wilkening and his collaborators (Krist, Fieberg, & Wilkening, 1993) in order to compare competences in intuitive physics in children 5 to 6 years old with those in children 9 to 10 years old as well as those in adults such as expressed through their actions and their judgments.

Construction of Instruments

Before illustrating my point of view, I present these few methodological comments. Some experimental situations are better than others in order to reveal the transformations in children's knowledge during the developmental course and, in particular, to understand the role of experience in this process. The best experimental situations are those that make it possible for children to evaluate their performances in terms of success or failure and to complete or correct them, in other words, to regulate them so as to modify their representations of the task. Practical problem solving is ideal for such an objective. However, most of the situations utilized to evaluate the cognitive abilities of the child do not have such characteristics, as, for example, conservation or classification tasks and all the situations requesting only verbal responses. For these reasons, I became interested a long time ago in tasks requesting the construction of simple instruments in order to solve practical problems. These tasks have been extensively used to study the origins of intelligence and to compare the respective abilities of children and monkeys as well as the transition between so-called practical intelligence and representative intelligence (e.g., Guillaume & Meyerson, 1930, 1931, 1934, 1937; Koehler, 1917/1927). By means of these types of tasks, I consider it possible to understand the modifications in the way children conceive objects, as much from the point of view of their intension (the set of features that define it) as from the point of view of their extension (the set of situations to which the instrument can be applied) and the relations of equivalence between various objects (the set of instruments adapted to solve a given task). This method could be an indirect way to study concept formation or the development of categories. I did not initiate my research for such a purpose. Nevertheless, instruments constitute a special category of objects, intermediary between the subject's actions and the situations to which they apply. This is what I briefly consider.

I had suggested calling an instrument any object the individual associates with his or her actions to execute a task. The instrument constitutes a kind of intermediary world between the person and the object in the sense that it is associated with the individual's actions, which it transmits to other objects, in the sense that it substitutes itself for some of the person's actions for which it then fulfills the functions, and in the sense that it has complementary relationships with the objects to which it applies.

In addition to its static features such as its shape, length, and so forth, the instrument can be characterized by dynamic properties such as the forces that it produces or transmits. In this matter, we have to deal with the problem of the transmission power attributed to the instrument. The instruments also involve causal means-ends relationships that do not exist in the spatial nor logico-mathematical structuration of objects.

I had distinguished two major categories of instruments, those that transmit the individual's actions without transforming them and those that transform them (inversion, demultiplication, etc.). Those instruments I have studied belong to the first category.

Moreover, it is important to make the distinction between the utilization and the construction of instruments. I have been more concerned with their construction.

Finally, among the instruments that transmit actions without transforming them, three different kinds can be described:

1. The simple modification of an object (as, for example, bending a wire to make a hook).

2. The assembly of elements where the meaning of the whole is identical to that of the parts (such as the assembly of small hooks that still constitute a hook).

3. The assembly of elements where the meaning of the whole differs from that of the parts (for example, fitting sticks together in order to construct an instrument that makes it possible to get around obstacles).

Despite the fact that instruments constitute a particular category of objects (which, as we have analyzed, necessitate a causal and physical structuration as well as a physical and logical one), I nevertheless consider the process by which children construct them as revealing some basic aspects related to general developmental mechanisms. More precisely, I hope to discover how children understand, define, and categorize objects at the "concrete" level and to capture directly the transformations of their conceptions by recording their corrections, regulations, and verbal commentaries.

The Experiment

One of the experiments was the following: Children were asked to move a little cube located beside an obstacle by means of an instrument that made a detour. That is a situation belonging to the family of "detour behaviors."

As we know, getting around obstacles can be accomplished in various ways. In infants, for example, it is usual to distinguish the reaching detour (performed with the arm) from the locomotor one (performed with the whole body) (Lockman & Ashmead, 1983). Moreover, the reaching detour can be executed with or without a stick to extend the arm (Guillaume & Meyerson, 1930). Reaching detour studies have been repeated recently by Diamond (1988) and Diamond and Gilbert (1989) under the label of "object retrieval."

The device used was a box without a cover (see Figure 5.1). The rectangular base measured 25 cm × 30 cm and was 4 cm high. An opening of 5 cm was made in the lateral wall of the box, and two partitions labeled v and h were placed inside, making a little entryway. Three squares of different colors (C1, C2, C3) were glued to the bottom of the box. A small wooden cube could be placed in four different locations (P1, P2, P3, P4). The task was to move the cube from one of these starting positions to a new position (C1, C2, C3), by means of an instrument previously constructed by the subject. Four situations were then possible: moving from P1 to C1 (Situation I); from P2 to C2 (Situ-

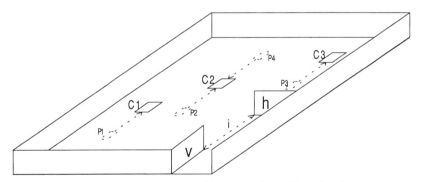

Figure 5.1   Experimental device. Letters *v* and *h* represent the partitions of the box separated by the interval *i*. P_1 to P_4 stand for the starting positions of the cube. C_1 to C_3 correspond to the final positions of the cube.

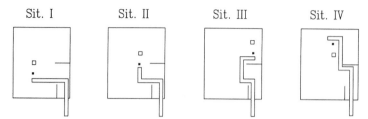

Figure 5.2   Instruments allowing to solve each situation.

ation II); from P3 to C3 (Situation III); and from P4 to C2 (Situation IV). These different displacements could be carried out using instruments such as curved sticks, which could be operated from outside through the lateral opening after the instrument was placed in the box. The amplitude of these displacements was always the same and was slightly smaller than the separating interval between v and h; the variable dimensions were the direction and the kind of detour necessary to reach the cube. It should be noted that the turns made to reach the cube are not necessarily adequate to permit its displacement.

The instruments were constructed with identical rectangular 16 mm × 64 mm plastic pieces called *Legos,* which can interlock with one another, therefore lengthening a part or making a 90° angle. The simplest instruments that were used in order to solve the four situations are shown in Figure 5.2.

After having the child describe the material, the experimenter indicated that the cube had to be pushed onto the square from outside of the box. Then, as an anticipation, the child was asked what would be needed to perform this action; a pencil and a ruler were suggested without letting him or her try. Next, the child was asked to use the Legos to construct "something" that would permit him or her to execute the task.

Once the instrument was placed into the box, the child was asked to move it from outside, without going over the partitions. To make it easier for the younger children to understand, a transparent cover was put on the game once the instrument was introduced. In order to better grasp the degree and type of organization the children were capable of, we asked them the reasons for their errors and the corrections they made.

Children 4 to 9 years old were tested and retested after 4 to 10 months. The children were split into four age groups: 4:6 (4 years 6 months) to 4:11 years ($N = 12$), 5:0 to 5:11 years ($N = 35$), 6:0 to 6:11 years ($N = 20$), and 7:0 to 9:3 years ($N = 16$).

Construction Behavior

Four types of behavior can be characterized on the basis of the children's constructions and corrections. Each of these types is predominant at a given age.

Type I

Type I behavior is predominant among the 4:6- to 4:11-year-old children (90% of the constructions).

It includes two subtypes. The most rudimentary constructions (Type Ia) are simple rectilinear segments ("I need something long") to which children impart rotary motions in order to get around the obstacles. The children often attribute the failures to their own actions. Corrections consist in adding or subtracting elements for lengthening or shortening the instrument at its distal part. (N.B.: To modify the instrument exclusively at its distal part by adding or subtracting elements is related to a very peculiar conception that diverges as we will see later on from the modification of its various segments or of their relationships.) Then bended constructions (Type Ib) can be observed ("I need something to get around it") of which different segments are successively added one to the other after successive trials. Consequently the instrument is constructed step-by-step. Corrections consist again in adding or subtracting segments at the extremity of the instrument.

Type II

Type II behavior is predominant among the 5:0- to 5:11-year-old children (50% of the constructions).

As for Type I, these are bended constructions made step-by-step after successive trials; but all constructions are ended by a vertical segment aimed at pushing the cube in the desired direction ("It can push," say the children). So each segment has a precise role: to lengthen, to get around, to reach, to push, and so forth. The children's conception of the instrument is in a way piecemeal or fragmented; corrections are always made at the extremity of their constructions. Several children entirely destroyed their construction to restart it again. One child restarted his construction four times. At each attempt he produced the same unsatisfactory result!

Type III

Type III behavior is predominant among the 6:0- to 6:11-year-old children (80% of the constructions).

Again, we have two subtypes. The instrument is initially constructed as a whole (without the ultimate segment assigned to push). "I take the instrument, then it turns and then I push," said one child. "It turns around and I can push," said another. Corrections concern initially (Type IIIa) the length of the various segments considered as responsible for the failures, most often paradoxically the length of the first segment (the "handle" is estimated as being too long). Sometimes corrections are produced by adding or subtracting one element to the junction point between the first and the second segment. Children search for a precise location when seeking the cause of the impossibility of moving the instrument. The problem is still conceived in terms of segment length or of distance and not yet in terms of relationships between segments or between parts of the device. Then the corrections do progressively take into consideration the relationships between the parts of the instrument and of the device (Type IIIb) without adding or subtracting elements; children try to modify the relative positions between two parts of the instrument (see Figure 5.3).

Type IV

Type IV behavior is predominant among the 7:0-year-old and older children (60% of the constructions).

As for Type III, the instrument is constructed as a whole without any previous trial. No correction is done on the first segment (or the "handle" of the instrument); its lengthening is recognized as having no effect on the mobility of the instrument. The children anticipate the precise location of the instrument in the experimental device in order to move it. They are also able to justify the equivalence between two instruments having different shapes (see Figure 5.4).

Interpretation of Construction Behavior

Schematically the general developmental trend can be characterized by two major steps.

In the *first step,* typical for children 4 and 5 years old (behavior Types I and II), one can observe the following:

Figure 5.3   Examples of typical Type III corrections.

For sit. II   For sit. IV

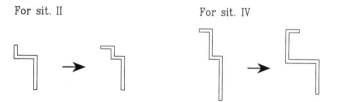

Figure 5.4   Examples of equivalent instruments.

1. How children progressively give up the idea of being able to transmit directly all their actions to the instrument, the instrument being a simple extension of their arm (absolute transmission).

2. How children discover (conceive, become aware of) the functions fulfilled by their actions (lengthening, turning around, pushing), which are then attributed to the instrument that is substituted for the action. In a certain way the instrument is endowed with power. It could be said that it is "lengthening," "passing or turning around," "pushing," and so forth; children discover these various aspects step-by-step while performing the task.

In the *second step,* typical for children 6 to 9 years old, which summarizes the two last behavioral types (Types III and IV), the instrument acquires a global meaning and loses its fragmentary character. It is conceived as a whole. But initially the function of displacing (or moving) transmitted by the instrument is referred to the length of one of its segments before being correctly related to the relationships between the various parts of the instrument and of the experimental device.

In summary, during the first step the instrument progressively loses its initial absolute transmission power in so far as it substitutes itself for the child's actions that it "performs." On the contrary, in the second step, the instrument "recuperates" its relative transmission power, in the sense that the child becomes able to dissociate and to take into account the object's characteristics and those of the action transmitted.

It is now time to express more explicitly my interpretation. At 3 or 4 years of age it is obvious that children are able to solve detour problems in action, the so-called reaching or locomotor detour. They do it by means of a constituted knowledge system that I call perceptuomotor. When the solution is no longer possible in action but requires the use of an intermediary object, 4-year-old children are progressively able, thanks to new capacities, to conceive objects that not only transmit their actions but also substitute themselves for them in order to fulfill various specific functions. Confronted by such situations, children demonstrate the capacity to select, to abstract, and to conceive (to elaborate conceptually) some partial and fragmentary characteristics related to the experimental situation or to their actions. These behaviors illustrate for me the construction of a new knowledge system, the successive construction steps of which I have tried to describe: the progressive discovery of the various *"local" functions* taken up by the action and of the various local aspects of the situation. We are then confronted by a first "realistic" conception of the instrument, conceived by means of representations that can be qualified as partial and fragmentary because they refer only to some local functions or aspects.

The instruments are endowed with power corresponding to these various functions; their particularity is their fragmented nature, as the functions are juxtaposed and not integrated. The major transition, which precisely defines the 5 to 7 year shift, is the transition from a *fragmented conception* of the object as juxtaposed functions, local meanings, or collection of characteristics to a *unified conception* of the instrument as the basic realization of a global function (or transformation) or as the possession of a whole stable meaning. This is in fact a necessary condition (a precondition) for its structuration, for the progressive mastery of the relations between its parts. (Similarly, children must succeed in identifying the objects in a stable way in order to master thereafter the relationships between their dimensions or between various objects concerning one single dimension.)

Finally, I consider the crucial problem of the relationships between knowledge systems. On that topic I do not consider that new cognitive systems are representative redescriptions of previous systems as stated by Karmiloff-Smith (1991), nor abstractions and transpositions from previous systems (Piaget, 1967, 1977; Mounoud, 1979, 1986a), but new original constructions initially framed by previously constituted systems that control the automatized complex exchanges with the encountered situations (Mounoud, 1993b).

By means of new partial (constructed) representations (the new declarative knowledge, the new fragmentary knowledge), subjects can directly assimilate (in a realistic way) some aspects of the situations or of objects encountered.

These partial representations or fragmentary knowledge will be integrated or coordinated into whole representations, owing to or consecutive to the transformation of the central mechanisms on the one hand and to the coherence introduced by the functioning of the previous constituted knowledge systems (which have framed or guided the initial interactions between subjects and environment) on the other hand.

Following this illustration, I now present the general theoretical model I propose to account for the emergence of new skills.

Relationships Between Knowledge Systems: Short Introduction to a Model

In all individuals involved in a learning or developmental process there are simultaneously *two knowledge systems* that differ from each other by their *relative maturity*. A rather achieved and automatized system reveals itself in practical forms of knowledge, and another system in elaboration reveals itself in conceptual forms. These two systems maintain *hierarchical and fairly complex relations* that reverse over time: The "conceptual" forms produced by the new knowledge system are initially directed or framed by the "practical" forms of the previous system but finally end up controlling and integrating them. Such a formulation leads us to a brief comment about the practical-conceptual opposition.

Researchers in human sciences have introduced at least from the beginning of the 20th century an opposition between two types of intelligence or knowledge most often termed *"practical" or "sensorimotor" intelligence* (or situational intelligence) and *"conceptual" or "representative" intelligence* (or discursive or verbal intelligence). This opposition has been used to distinguish *levels of development* (for more details, see Mounoud, 1993a).

This opposition between practical and conceptual knowledge remains present in cognitive psychology under various labels more or less related to the initial ones, for example, between *procedural* and *declarative* knowledge, between *know-how* and *knowledge,* between *symbolic* and *nonsymbolic* processing levels, between knowledge *accessible* to consciousness or *not accessible*, or finally between *implicit* or *explicit* memories.

These oppositions have most often been used in the past to characterize non-contemporaneous *levels* and systems of knowledge; currently, they are used to confront contemporaneous systems of knowledge that are usually considered to be different in *nature* and clearly dissociated.

Ever since 1970 (Mounoud), I have strongly questioned the possibility of using the opposition between "practical" and "conceptual" knowledge in order to differentiate the nature or between the levels of *knowledge systems* (as did Piaget (1936) and Wallon (1945), for instance). By contrast, I suggested that the adjectives *practical* and *conceptual* could be perfectly adequate for characterizing two *forms* (or two distinct states) of any given knowledge system. In the theory I tried to elaborate, the various knowledge systems are called "sensorial," "perceptual," "concrete" (previously labeled "conceptual") and "formal." Each one of these systems (different in nature) can appear under two different forms, that is, conceptual and practical.

It is possible to state the following:

1. The practical forms of a given knowledge system result (ontogenetically or phylogenetically) from the previous conceptual forms of the same system that have become sedimented (or encapsulated) and consequently are no longer accessible to consciousness (no longer explicit).

2. The practical forms of a given knowledge system can only be qualitatively modified or transformed by means of conceptual forms of a new, more abstract knowledge system.

3. The conceptual forms of a given knowledge system do not improve without involving the practical forms of an already elaborated knowledge system.

4. If cognitive development in humans proceeds through stages, differences between two successive stages cannot be reduced to the opposition between practical and conceptual.

Every behavior of an individual involved in a developmental or learning process, and especially that of children from 3 to 4 years of age and on, can be described as determined simultaneously by *two different knowledge systems* (each system being constituted by representations coupled with procedures).

On the one hand, there is a first knowledge system (called "perceptual" system in 3 to 4-year-olds) composed of *constituted and "sedimented" representations* (to which inputs have a direct access) merged with automatized action procedures. This first knowledge system is expressed in practical forms.

On the other hand, there is a second knowledge system (called "concrete" system in 3 to 4-year-olds) composed of *representations in elaboration (status nascendi)* coupled with action procedures in elaboration as well. This second knowledge system initially produces knowledge in conceptual forms, demonstrating a current process of conscious construction, bringing accessible representations into play. The transformation I defined to characterize the 5 to 7 year shift constitutes one of this second system's elaboration steps (the "concrete" system).

In summary, these two contemporaneous representational systems express themselves under two different forms that correspond to the "practical" (or implicit knowledge) and "conceptual" (or explicit knowledge) forms previously described; they simultaneously define two kinds of action planning and control (sometimes called "triggered" and "controlled"), two types of functioning (automatized versus voluntary). It is also possible to compare these two knowledge systems with the two selection systems for thought or action schemes defined by Shallice (1991), that is, the automatized system called "contention scheduling" and the supervisory system, as well as with the two systems of automatic processing and attentional control defined by Posner and Rothbart (1991).

The capacity to produce new behaviors, that is, to elaborate new representations as well as new procedures, is due in children to the fact that new structures or new centers are brought into action (I have previously called these new coding systems). In adults the acquisition of new behavior (or the capacity to solve new problems) could be due to the reactivation of some centers or structures specialized for the conceptual and conscious elaboration of new dimensions or for the reelaboration of some already known dimensions in a new context. These specialized centers may be temporarily brought into action until new routines more or less automatized (practical forms of knowledge) are established (Mounoud, 1988, 1990b).

These new centers or new knowledge systems are supposed to analyze only subsamples of the dimensions or information automatically processed by the previous centers during the execution of complex actions. These analyses give rise to new representations. At the beginning of the process these new representations or conceptions are necessarily elementary. This results precisely from the selection operated by the new centers with regard to the previous ones. These representations are characteristic in 4 to 5-year-olds.

These new elementary representations are used by the knowledge system to elaborate new action procedures (necessarily simple or elementary as well) limited to a single elementary goal, to a simple action, or to a single dimension or idea. These new procedures progressively replace, or inhibit, the previous ones.

Then the various elementary representations and procedures are going to be composed, first by juxtaposition and then by a more organic integration, in order to constitute a new totality, a new set of global representations at the origin of a new complex behavior (as, for instance, the appearance, around 6 years of age, of a conception in which instruments are seen as a whole and in which the diverse functions relevant vis-à-vis a given situation are selected and integrated as a whole; or the ability to integrate diverse dimensions such as height and distance in judgments about ball throwing; cf. "Ball Throwing: Actions and Judgments" section). This is precisely the transition from partial to global representations, that is the main characteristic of the 5 to 7 year shift. Whole representations, when constituted, have to go through a complex process of analysis and decomposition in order to elaborate the relationships between their elements or dimensions.

On the basis of these statements, it is now possible to define what I call the *process of conceptualization* (also previously called "construction of new representations" (Mounoud, 1979) or "thematizing process" (Mounoud, 1988)). This is the process by which, *during activities (mental or material) that are controlled by the constituted knowledge system,* the individual consciously selects or samples information that is relevant regarding the pursued goal, by means of the new knowledge system, which brings this new information into representation. *The simultaneous existence of two knowledge systems in parallel* constitutes the dynamic of the developmental process. The motor of development according to Piaget's formula would not be the action, as he stated it, but rather the dialectical relations between knowledge systems.

By means of these representations the individual will be able to establish new relationships or comparisons between objects or events, between parts of objects, between actions and above all between objects and actions. These comparisons are at the origin of new *inferences,* new links between meanings, temporarily accessible to consciousness or explicit, at least partly.

As a matter of fact, this process would not function in a satisfactory way if the activities of the subject were not initially controlled by *previous knowledge* (resulting themselves of course from a previous developmental process). Without this initial control the explanation of the origin of new behaviors should be sought in randomly produced behaviors. To quote Piaget: "The results (of experience), most of them being fortuitous, acquire nevertheless meanings by means of *hidden but acting schemes* [italics added] that enlighten them" (Piaget, 1937, p. 350). These "hidden schemes" correspond to what one calls sedimented or modularized knowledge.

It is clear that as new conscious inferences, implications, or relations are constituted, new procedures for action planning and control are elaborated. As already mentioned, the previous procedures are going to be replaced by these new ones, which have an inhibitory action before taking the old ones under control and integrating or incorporating them.

Putting so much emphasis on previous knowledge in the process of acquisition of new behaviors leads me to criticize, as I did elsewhere (Mounoud, 1990a), purely inductive theories related to the development of categorization, as for instance those suggested by Harnad (1987) and Nelson (1983) in psychology and by Edelman (1987) in developmental neurobiology. From my point of view, ignoring initial categorization abilities prior to the process they describe gives a wrong picture of the developmental process.

To conclude this presentation, we need to examine what hypotheses can be advanced about the emergence of new behaviors. Four different hypotheses, among others, can be considered:

1. The emergence of new behaviors is preformed; development is only the outcome of progressive maturation of the knowledge systems. Spelke's (1991) position could correspond to this first hypothesis.

2. The emergence of new behaviors comes from a *redescription,* a *transposition,* or an *abstraction* of already organized systems (ahead of the development process under study). This hypothesis corresponds to the reflexive abstraction process suggested by Piaget (1967, 1977), to the representational redescription process suggested by Karmiloff-Smith (1991), and to previous versions of the model I have presented here (e.g., Mounoud, 1979, 1986b).

3. The emergence of new behaviors basically comes from the structure of the situations with which the individual is confronted (with no major role played by the organization of previous systems or of previous knowledge). This hypothesis could correspond to Harnad's model (1987) or Edelman's model (1987).

4. The emergence of new behaviors comes from new processing of experiences done by the individual in his or her different environments but *during activities determined by previously organized knowledge*

systems. It is what I call the indirect link. This hypothesis corresponds to the position I have developed in this chapter and has some similarities with the model published by Morton and Johnson (1991) related to the development of face recognition.

Having described the first illustration borrowed from my previous researches and having briefly presented the theoretical model, I now present more recent studies carried out in order to understand the relationships between children's knowledge such as revealed by their actions and their judgments. These are situations of ball throwing.

Ball Throwing: Actions and Judgments

Wilkening and coworkers (Fieberg, 1992; Krist et al., 1993; Loskill, 1992; Wilkening & Anderson, 1991) conducted several studies aimed at comparing children's and adults' intuitive physics abilities, as revealed in their actions and judgments. To perform their studies, they used a situation of ball throwing in which they varied target distance (on a landing area) and height of throwing (from a horizontal throwing board). Thus, they studied intuitive knowledge about projectile motion. (The authors have written about "throwing speed" ("speed of release"); I consider the term *throwing force* more appropriate.)

Children were tested in two experimental conditions, called action conditions and judgment conditions, respectively. In the action condition, aimed at assessing their perceptuomotor abilities, the children had to throw a ball by varying their movement speed (or force). In the judgment condition, aimed at assessing their cognitive (or judgment) abilities, the children had to turn the knob of an apparatus that was first calibrated for them so they would understand that it estimated throwing speed. The experimenter demonstrated three release speeds (minimum, medium, and maximum) and their corresponding knob position on the apparatus. The goal of the experiment was to understand which aspects of the situation were taken into account by the children in order to adjust their throwing speeds (actual throwing as well as speed rating on the apparatus); in other words, which implicit laws were used to regulate speed (force). Actually, throwing speeds were not recorded; they were computed afterward, on the basis of the landing impacts of the ball.

Five- to 6-year-old kindergartners (mean age 5:11), 10-year-old fourth graders (mean age 10:3), and adults were tested (40 people in each group). In the action condition, all three age groups did behave according to physical laws (to the normative structure) that determine optimal speeds as a function of target distance and height of release. However, mean speed values were far from optimal values; only relative variations were adequate (following physical laws). On the other hand, in the judgment condition, about half the kindergartners did not consistently vary their speed ratings; the other half of the youngest children did vary their speed ratings according to one dimension only: target distance (16 subjects, 40%) or release height (4 subjects, 10%). When evaluating the mean value for the whole group, only target distance was significantly taken into account by the 5- to 6-year-olds. As to the other age groups, twenty-six 9- to 10-year-olds (65%) and eleven adults (28%) took only target distance into account. Now, fourteen 9- to 10-year-olds (35%) and twenty-nine adults (72%) simultaneously took both target distance and release height into consideration.

In the judgment condition, development thus goes from centering on one single dimension to integrating multiple dimensions, whereas in the action condition, all subjects managed a qualitative integration of multiple dimensions (target distance and release height). A control experiment showed that there was no learning effect.

The author's interpretations were inspired by the Piagetian framework; they argued that their subjects' abilities as revealed by their actions and judgments depended upon two kinds of knowledge representation: implicit and explicit knowledge. The authors also seem to have followed Piaget when considering that the cognitive representations are derived from the sensorimotor representations by reflexive abstraction. However, they did not comment on this complex mechanism. On the other hand, actions (i.e., sensorimotor representations) and judgments (i.e., cognitive representations) were said to be independent. Judgments were seen as derived from (or abstracted from) actions, but not as necessarily having an effect back on actions. Their results seem to show an equivalence between the actions produced by children 5 to 6 years old, 9 to 10 years old, and adults. Thus, according to them, there are two parallel knowledge systems, one derived from the other without acting back on it. This interpretation leads to a number of problems.

The first problem has to do with the nature of the so-called sensorimotor abilities revealed by the individuals' actions. Some psychologists call them know-how or procedural knowledge (I call them skills determined by a constituted knowledge system that express themselves in a procedural form). Obviously, these abilities go through a genesis. A study conducted by Fieberg (1992), one of Wilkening's coworkers, showed that it is not before 4 years of age that children manage to take both dimensions (height and distance) into account, in an integrated way, when regulating their actions (ball throwing). These skills are the result of a construction, mainly taking place during the third and fourth years of life. In a similar way, we have demonstrated (Mounoud et al., 1983) how children 3 to 5 years old, when manually tracking a visual target moving periodically, become progressively able to consider first the target's movement amplitude only, and next the target's movement time only, and finally to manage to produce movements that simultaneously take amplitude and movement time into account (without being able, however, to strictly synchronize their own movement with that of the target; these abilities might not only suppose implicit knowledge).

Thus, in direct ball throwing as well as in manual tracking, children go through stages in which they first take only one dimension into account (at about 3 years of age), and later become able to integrate multiple dimensions (around 4 or 5 years of age). This genesis is comparable to the genesis revealed by "judgments," showing a decalage of a few years: The first genesis takes place between 2 and 4 to 5 years, and the second one between 5 and 9 years. What is the reason why one should talk about implicit knowledge in the first case and about explicit knowledge in the second? Is it related to language abilities? This does not seem to be the case, as the judgments do not involve language but only actions. Is it because only the judgments involve symbolic processes? Probably not, as 3- and 4-year-olds are perfectly able to use symbolic processes: Why would they not use symbolizations in regulating their actions? Piaget considered that sensorimotor intelligence or sensorimotor abilities are the result of grasps of consciousness and analytical reasoning that allow babies to *objectivate* the world; in this process, there is already an "explicitation" or a transition from an implicit to an explicit kind of knowledge. In both cases, it seems that the subject does an explication (or objectivation) job that not only involves grasps of consciousness but also declarative and not only procedural forms of knowledge (Mounoud, 1990b).

The second major problem is to understand why explicit knowledge, which, according to Krist et al. (1993), is revealed by the judgments about speed release, does not seem to be involved in the throwing action control. At this point, I wonder whether the individuals' actions are really not influenced by their explicit knowledge, that is, by the kind of knowledge revealed by their judgments. For instance, among 10-year-olds, 65% take only distance into consideration in their judgments. Do they act differently from the 35% who are able to integrate height and distance? Or do those making up the 40% of the 5- to 6-year-olds who consider distance act differently from the 50% of the 5- to 6-year-olds who do not systematically vary their judgments? It does not seem as though the authors tried any of these analyses. Considering other variables might also be necessary to reveal probable differences. As long as such analyses are not done, it seems difficult to claim that the results obtained by the diverse groups in the action condition are equivalent, as the actions themselves were not analyzed. A total independence of judgments vis-à-vis actions would raise important epistemological and pedagogical problems. All the motor abilities I have been studying do transform after 5 years of age: lifting objects that vary in weight (Forssberg, Eliasson, Kinoshita, Johansson, & Westling, 1991; Gachoud, Mounoud, Hauert, & Viviani, 1983), visuo-manual tracking and target pointing (Badan, 1993; Hauert, Zazone, & Mounoud, 1990; Mounoud, Viviani, Hauert, & Guyon, 1985; Zanone, 1990), drawing and writing activities

(Vinter & Mounoud, 1991; Zesiger, 1992; Zesiger, Mounoud, & Hauert, 1993), to mention a few of them. It would be surprising if ball throwing does not transform between 5 to 6 years and 9 to 10 years of age.

In some ways, the experiment presented by Krist et al. (1993) can be considered close to my work on the construction of instruments. In both situations, 4-year-olds did possess an elaborate perceptuomotor knowledge system to solve the task. In both experiments, when individuals were asked to solve the task, not in a direct way, but through an instrument or an apparatus, they had to reelaborate the situation on the conceptual plane (they had to reconceptualize the situation); this led to the appearance of partial and fragmentary solutions, which revealed new knowledge elaboration. In both cases, there was a transition from centering on one single dimension to integration of relevant dimensions. While new conceptual knowledge elaboration does transform the way individuals act in the detour situation drastically, it does not look like ball-throwing behaviors are affected by the explicit knowledge that is revealed by the judgments. But then again, I maintain the hypothesis that a direct analysis of the throwing actions (by contrast to a simple computation of speed based on the landing impact) should reveal changes. Finally, studying age groups in between 6 and 9 years is necessary. In most of our studies, the developmental trends are not monotonic in this age range.

The third problem, certainly the most important of all, is to determine whether the explicit knowledge revealed by the children's judgments is really derived from the knowledge revealed by their actions, as claimed by authors after Piaget. If this is the case, in which way?

Again, I do not consider that the children's new knowledge revealed in their judgments is directly derived from the perceptuomotor knowledge revealed by their actions. There is no representative redescription, nor transposition or complex abstraction of perceptuomotor or procedural knowledge. Conceptual knowledge also does not emerge from the child's simple confrontation with new situations, through simple abstraction of the events or situations, properties, or structure, without an intervention of previous knowledge or structures. Any purely inductive explanation should be rejected. Finally, new knowledge is also not the outcome of the maturation of the child's internal structures. Maturation only makes it possible for new knowledge to be constructed. There is a real reconstruction, an original reconceptualization of the encountered situations, which is elaborated during the child's exchanges with the situations. These exchanges are made possible or determined by the existence of previous constituted knowledge, which is sedimented and is thus not accessible to consciousness anymore (this knowledge became implicit after it had been explicit). In the same way, the action procedures have been automatized to diverse degrees.

In addition, I have to specify that for me new knowledge does not maintain itself in a purely conceptual or declarative form; it also generates new practical or procedural knowledge. This new procedural knowledge is thus also local, partial, and juxtaposed, as is the declarative knowledge that generates it. The new knowledge system in elaboration has progressively an inhibitory action on the previous system.

In summary, there are no practical or procedural knowledge systems, nor conceptual or declarative knowledge systems, but rather knowledge systems that express themselves in a practical or conceptual way. For any given system, the transformation goes from conceptual forms toward practical forms but, again, is initially framed by the practical forms of the previous knowledge system (for more details, see Mounoud, 1993a).

The reflexive abstraction hypothesis is only one of the two main hypotheses formulated by Piaget in order to explain the construction of logical operations based on the sensorimotor coordinations. Reflexive abstraction, as is well known, involves a change in representation level or plane. According to this hypothesis, logico-mathematical operations are defined as the internalization of the general coordinations of actions (see Mounoud, 1992, for a commentary on the other Piagetian hypothesis [Piaget, 1942] to account for the connection between the actions and the operations).

Conclusion

In this chapter I hope I have succeeded in explicating what constitutes for me the major transition of children's behavior between 5 and 7 years and which is supposed to result from the transformation of central cognitive mechanisms. This transition can be viewed as the capacity to integrate or to coordinate in a whole the new partial and fragmentary knowledge about objects constructed by children 4 and 5 years old by means of new knowledge systems. Once they become able to characterize—(re)reconceptualize—objects as stable entities, to conceptually identify them as independent of their actions, children between 6 and 10 years of age still have to elaborate the relations between the dimensions that coexist in the object, as well as the relations between objects related to a given dimension. The critical point is therefore the capacity for grouping or chunking these meaningful juxtaposed units in totalities or the capacity to coordinate or integrate isolated cognitive components, what has sometimes been called the "cognitive chunking" or the "perceptual grouping." The shift going from successive to simultaneous processing could be considered a consequence of this major change. In a recent article (Mounoud, 1993a), I developed the same model but illustrated and concretized at the sensorimotor period. In that article, I took a critical position with regard to Mandler's model (1988), in which she postulated the existence, from birth, of a double representational system (procedural and conceptual systems developing simultaneously and in parallel).

From an experimental point of view, the radical theoretical change I have tried to make consists in looking at the consequences of the new conceptualizations on motoric behaviors instead of studying the conceptualizations for themselves, which has already been extensively done. My project has been to study the restructuration of behaviors, as resulting from new conceptualizations. This is the perspective in which I studied motor development to approach cognitive development from another point of view. It is true that Wilkening's results could constitute a complete denial of my perspective. Nevertheless, changes of behaviors in the construction of instruments as well as in all the other situations I have studied support my perspective. What has to be done in the future is to simultaneously study the respective transformations of the new conceptual and practical knowledge within the same subjects, which is what I have started to do in the studies on the construction of instruments.

To conclude this chapter and as far as it is still necessary I explicate my position on the central question raised by Sameroff and Haith (at least for the nonsedimented parts of my knowledge!). For me it is obvious that the behaviors of 7-year-olds differ from those of 5-year-olds. Originally, the differences are qualitative in nature, but they necessarily generate quantitative differences. Conceiving an instrument in an unified way (as a unity, as a whole) instead of as a constellation of functions constitutes a notorious qualitative change. The corrections brought to the constructions reveal consecutive quantitative changes: Adding a supplementary segment to the construction instead of modifying the relationships between segments is a good illustration. Similarly, taking the various dimensions of a situation into account in a separated or integrated way constitutes qualitative as well as quantitative changes at the same time. This is the case in the genesis of number conservation regarding length and density of collections. These changes result from the emergence of new behaviors, partly dependent on prior behaviors. Eventually, prior behaviors will be controlled by the new ones.

Acknowledgments

I thank Anne Aubert and Pascal Zesiger for their strong support and tireless help all along the gestation of this paper, Claude-Alain Hauert for his critical comments, Denis Page for the figures, and Françoise Schmitt for her valuable secretarial assistance.

References

Badan, M. (1993). *The development of motor control in a sequential pointing task in 6- to 10-year-old children.* Unpublished doctoral dissertation. University of Geneva, Switzerland.

Bideaud, J. (1988). *Logique et bricolage chez l'enfant.* Lille, France: Presses Universitaires de Lille.

Diamond, A. (1988). Differences between adult and infant cognition: Is the crucial variable presence or absence of language? In L. Weiskrantz (Ed.), *Thought without language* (pp. 337–370). Oxford, England: Clarendon Press.

Diamond, A., & Gilbert, J. (1989). Development as progressive inhibitory control of action: Retrieval of a contiguous object. *Cognitive Development, 4,* 223–249.

Donaldson, M. (1978). *Children's mind.* London: Fontana.

Edelman, G. M. (1987). *Neural Darwinism. The theory of neural group selection.* New York: Basic Books.

Fayol, M. (1990). *L'enfant et le nombre: Du comptage à la résolution de problèmes.* Neuchâtel, Switzerland: Delachaux & Niestlé.

Fieberg, E. (1992). *Die Intuitive Physik der Kinematik: Untersuchungen zur Repräsentation des Wissens über Flugbahnen im Handeln, Wahrnehmen und Urteilen* [The intuitive physics of kinematics: Studies on the representation of knowledge about trajectories in action, perception, and judgment]. Unpublished doctoral dissertation, University of Frankfurt, Germany.

Forssberg, H., Eliasson, A. C., Kinoshita, H., Johansson, R. S., & Westling, G. (1991). Development of human precision grip I: Basic coordination of force. *Experimental Brain Research, 85,* 451–457.

Gachoud, J. P., Mounoud, P., Hauert, C. A., & Viviani, P. (1983). Motor strategies in lifting movements: A comparison of adult and children performances. *Journal of Motor Behavior, 15*(3), 202–216.

Guillaume, P., & Meyerson, I. (1930). Recherches sur l'usage de l'instrument chez les singes. I. Le problème du détour. *Journal de Psychologie, 27,* 177–236.

Guillaume, P., & Meyerson, I. (1931). Recherches sur l'usage de l'instrument chez les singes. II. L'intermédiaire lié à l'objet. *Journal de Psychologie, 28,* 481–555.

Guillaume, P., & Meyerson, I. (1934). Recherches sur l'usage de l'instrument chez les singes. III. L'intermédiaire indépendant de l'objet. *Journal de Psychologie, 31,* 497–554.

Guillaume, P., & Meyerson, I. (1937). Recherches sur l'usage de l'instrument chez les singes. IV. Choix, correction, invention. *Journal de Psychologie, 34,* 425–448.

Halverson, H. M. (1931). An experimental study of prehension in infants by means of systematic cinema records. *Genetic Psychology Monographs, 10,* 107–286.

Harnad, S. (1987). Category induction and representation. In S. Harnad (Ed.), *Categorial perception. The groundwork of cognition* (pp. 535–565). Cambridge, England: Cambridge University Press.

Hauert, C. A., Zanone, P. G., & Mounoud, P. (1990). Development of motor control in the child: Theoretical experimental approaches. In O. Neumann & W. Prinz (Eds.), *Relationships between perception and action: Current approaches* (pp. 325–343). Berlin: Springer-Verlag.

Hofsten, C. von. (1990). A perception—Action perspective on the development of manual movements. In M. Jeannerod (Ed.), *Attention and performance* (Vol. 13, *Motor representation and control,* pp. 739–762). Hillsdale, NJ: Erlbaum.

Houdé, O. (1992). *Catégorisation et développement cognitif.* Paris: Presses Universitaires de France.

Karmiloff-Smith, A. (1991). Beyond modularity: Innate constraints and developmental change. In S. Carey & R. Gelman (Eds.), *The epigenesis of mind: Essays on biology and cognition* (pp. 171–197). Hillsdale, NJ: Erlbaum.

Keil, F. C., & Kelly, M. H. (1987). Developmental changes in category structure. In S. Harnad (Ed.), *Categorial perception. The groundwork of cognition* (pp. 491–510). Cambridge, England: Cambridge University Press.

Koehler, W. (1917). *Intelligenzprüfungen an Menschenaffen*. P. Guillaume, (French Trans., 1927), L'intelligence des singes supérieurs. Paris: Alcan.

Krist, H., Fieberg, E., & Wilkening, F. (1993). Intuitive physics in action and judgment: The development of knowledge about projectile motion. *Journal of Experimental Psychology: Learning, Memory, and Cognition, 19*(4), 952–966.

Lockman, J. J., & Ashmead, D. H. (1983). Asynchronies in the development of manual behavior. In L. P. Lipsitt & C. K. Rovee-Collier (Eds.), *Advances in infancy research* (Vol. 2, pp. 113–136). Norwood, NJ: Ablex.

Loskill, J. (1992). *Intuitive Physik im kindlichen Handeln: Ist implizites Wissen ueber Flugbahnen bewegungsspezifisch?* [Intuitive physics in children's actions: Is implicit knowledge about projectile motion effector-dependent?]. Unpublished master's thesis, University of Frankfurt, Germany.

Mandler, J. M. (1988). How to build a baby: On the development of an accessible representational system. *Cognitive Development, 3,* 113–136.

Morton, J., & Johnson, M. H. (1991). Conspec and conlern: A two-process theory of infant face recognition. *Psychological Review, 98,* 164–181.

Mounoud, P. (1968). Construction et utilisation d'instruments chez l'enfant de 4 à 8 ans: Intériorisation des schèmes d'action et types de régulations. *Revue Suisse de Psychologie, 27*(3–4), 200–208.

Mounoud, P. (1970). *Structuration de l'instrument chez l'enfant.* Neuchâtel, Switzerland: Delachaux et Niestlé.

Mounoud, P. (1979). Développement cognitif: Construction de structures nouvelles ou construction d'organisations internes. *Bulletin de Psychologie, 33,* 342, 107–118. [Translation in I. E. Sigel, D. M. Brodzinsky, & R. M. Golinkoff (Eds., 1981), *New directions in Piagetian theory and practice* (pp. 99–114). Hillsdale, NJ: Erlbaum.]

Mounoud, P. (1981). Cognitive development: Construction of new structures of construction of internal organizations. In I. E. Sigel, D. M. Brodzinsky, & R. M. Golinkoff (Eds.), *New directions in Piagetian theory and practice* (pp. 99–114). Hillsdale, NJ: Erlbaum.

Mounoud, P. (1986a). Action and cognition. Cognitive and motor skills in a developmental perspective. In M. G. Wade & H. T. A. Whiting (Eds.), *Motor Development in children* (pp. 373–390). Dordrecht, Netherlands: M. Nijhoff.

Mounoud, P. (1986b). Similarities between developmental sequences at different age periods. In I. Levin (Ed.), *Stage and structure* (pp. 40–58). Norwood, NJ: Ablex.

Mounoud, P. (1988). The ontogenesis of different types of thought. In L. Weiskrantz (Ed.), *Thought without language* (pp. 25–45). Oxford, England: Oxford University Press.

Mounoud, P. (1990a). Cognitive development: Enrichment or impoverishment. In C. A. Hauert (Ed.), *Developmental psychology: Cognitive, perceptuo-motor and neuropsychological perspectives* (pp. 389–414). Amsterdam: North Holland.

Mounoud, P. (1990b). Consciousness as a necessary transitory phenomenon in cognitive development. *Psychological Inquiry, 1*(3), 253–258.

Mounoud, P. (1992). Continuité et discontinuité du développement psychologique. *Revue Suisse de Psychologie, 51*(4), 236–241.

Mounoud, P. (1993a). The emergence of new skills: Dialectic relations between knowledge systems. In G. J. P. Savelsbergh (Ed.), *The development of coordination in infancy* (pp. 13–46). Amsterdam: Elsevier Science Publishers.

Mounoud, P. (1993b). Les rôles non spécifiques et spécifiques des milieux dans le développement cognitif. In J. Wassmann & P. Dasen (Eds.), *Les savoirs quotidiens. Les approches cognitives dans le dialogue interdisciplinaire*. Fribourg, Switzerland: Presses Universitaires.

Mounoud, P., Hauert, C. A., Mayer, E., Gachoud, J. P., Guyon, J., & Gottret, G. (1983). Visuo-manual tracking strategies in the three to five year-old child. *Archives de Psychologie, 51*, 23–33.

Mounoud, P., Viviani, P., Hauert, C. A., & Guyon, J. (1985). Development of visuo-manual tracking in 5- to 9-year-old boys. *Journal of Experimental Child Psychology, 40*, 115–132.

Nelson, K. (1983). The derivation of concepts and categories from event representations. In E. K. Scholnick (Ed.), *New trends in conceptual representation: Challenges to Piaget's theory?* (pp. 129–149). Hillsdale, NJ: Erlbaum.

Piaget, J. (1936). *La naissance de l'intelligence clez l'eufant*. Neuchâtel, Switzerland: Delachaux & Niestlé.

Piaget, J. (1937). *La construction du réel chez l'enfant*. Neuchâtel, Switzerland: Delachaux & Niestlé.

Piaget, J. (1942). Les trois structures fondamentales de la vie psychique: Rythme, régulation et groupement. *Revue Suisse de Psychologie, 1*, 9–21.

Piaget, J. (1967). *Biologie et connaissance*. Paris: Gallimard.

Piaget, J. (1977). *Recherches sur l'abstraction réfléchissante*. Paris: Presses Universitaires de France.

Posner, M. I., & Rothbart, M. K. (1991). Les mécanismes de l'attention et de l'expérience. *Revue de Neuropsychologie, 2*(1), 85–115.

Shallice, T. (1991). Précis of "From neuropsychology to mental structure." *Behavioral and Brain Sciences, 14*, 429–469.

Spelke, E. S. (1991). Physical knowledge in infancy: Reflections on Piaget's theory. In S. Carey & R. Gelman (Eds.), *The epigenesis of mind: Essays on biology and cognition* (pp. 133–169). Hillsdale, NJ: Erlbaum.

Vinter, A., & Mounoud, P. (1991). Isochrony and accuracy of drawing movements in children: Effects of age and context. In J. Wann, A. M. Wing, & N. Sovik (Eds.), *Development of graphic skills: Research perspectives and educational implications* (pp. 113–137). London, England: Academic Press.

Wallon, H. B. (1945). *Les origines de la pensée chez l'enfant*. Paris: Presses Universitaires de France.

Wilkening, F., & Anderson, N. H. (1991). Representation and diagnosis of knowledge structures in developmental psychology. In N. H. Anderson (Ed.), *Contributions to information integration theory: Vol. 3. Developmental* (pp. 45–80). Hillsdale, NJ: Erlbaum.

Zanone, P. G. (1990). Tracking with and without target in 6- to 15-year-old boys. *Journal of Motor Behavior, 22*(2), 225–249.

Zesiger, P. (1992). *Handwriting in 8- to 12-year-old children and adults: Perceptuomotor aspects and linguistic effects.* Unpublished doctoral dissertation, University of Geneva, Switzerland.

Zesiger, P., Mounoud, P., & Hauert, C. A. (1993). Effects of lexicality and trigram frequency on handwriting production in children and adults. *Acta Psychologica, 82,* 353–365.

CHAPTER SIX

Shifting to an Interpretive Theory of Mind: 5- to 7-Year-Olds' Changing Conceptions of Mental Life

MICHAEL CHANDLER AND CHRIS LALONDE

The open question taken up in this chapter is whether, in the wake of more than a decade of research into children's so-called developing theories of mind, it still makes sense to imagine, as we once collectively imagined, that the ages of 5 through 7 years mark a special transition in the ways in which young persons think about their own and others' mental lives. What makes this a matter of special pertinence is that much of the enthusiasm that has fueled the still accelerating literature on children's theories of mind began as an only modestly refined form of otherwise crude Piaget bashing meant to relocate achievements once thought unique to 5- to 7-year-olds to some earlier point well inside the preschool period. Despite this history, the short answer about the continued importance of the classical 5 to 7 year transition that is promoted here is a decided yes; that is, despite mounting evidence demonstrating that even very young preschoolers already possess a great deal of heretofore unsuspected knowledge about their own and others' beliefs and desires, knowledge that previous generations of developmentalists are happy to lay at the door of the 5 to 7 year transition, we still mean to defend in this chapter the view that earlier contributors to the broad social-cognition literature were not altogether mistaken in their assumptions regarding the whereabouts of development's "natural" joints. Instead, as we mean to go on to show, there appears to be new evidence surfacing within the contemporary theories-of-mind literature that adds additional legitimacy to the otherwise classical notion of a major qualitative shift in the way that 5- to 7-year-olds conceptualize their own and others' psychological lives.

In particular, this chapter develops the idea that the lesson best afforded by the new theories-of-mind literature is not, as some would have it, that preschoolers were always secretly capable of just those things once wrongly attributed to 5- through 7-year-olds. Instead, what seems to be closer to the available truth, we argue, is that all that was once imagined to add up to an omnibus

5 to 7 year shift in social-cognitive competence is now better viewed as an admixture of two quite distinct sets of abilities: one of which naturally fits within the province of very young preschoolers; whereas the other continues to more properly define a persistent part of the classical 5 to 7 year transition. That, at least, is the double-barreled thesis that we hope to bring you to prefer over the skimpier "one-miracle" views still being actively touted within certain theory-of-mind circles—a set of middling, compromise views according to which 4-year-olds are held out as categorically distinct from their still younger peers and merely less well practiced than their older and more fully fledged counterparts (Gopnik & Astington, 1988; Perner, 1991; Wimmer & Perner, 1983).

Just so there is no confusion later on, we wish to announce at the outset our own opposition to all such withholding, "one-miracle" approaches and to declare instead allegiance to the wider view that any account of children's emerging beliefs about beliefs needs to make room for what Searle (1983) described as both a "world-to-mind" and a "mind-to-world" direction of fit.[1] As Searle would have it, minds must come to be seen not only as fitting themselves to an independent reality but also as being capable of altering or deforming that reality in such a way as to make it better conform to the particular sorts of intelligence seeking to understand it. By this account, then, anything that might begin to qualify as a fully fledged "interpretive" or "constructive" theory of mind would need to somehow make room for the possibility that mental contents can be actively constructed, as well as copied more or less directly from the environment.

Given this way of thinking we want to go on to promote the idea that young preschool children ordinarily start out their careers as apprentice theorists of the mind by initially subscribing to only the first half of the whole double-edged truth of this matter—that is, they begin by operating as though minds are only obliged to "fit" the world, that only exogenous factors shape mental life, that people can only passively accommodate to the pressures of outside experiences, and that they always copy but never construct the reality with which they interact. In short, mental life, we mean to argue, necessarily proceeds by practicing something like what Piaget termed both "assimilation" and "accommodation"; young preschool children at first fail to appreciate this fact. Instead, they begin their early attempts at psychological theory construction by first employing a view of knowledge and belief that turns upon the limited notion that minds necessarily fit themselves to the world, before going on to make room for the equally critical counterpart idea of a world-to-mind direction of fit that characterizes more mature theories of mind. It is, we suggest, the dropping of this second shoe that serves to define those novel achievements that set 5- to 7-year-olds apart from their still younger preschool counterparts and that marks them as having come to a more fully fledged understanding of mental life.

If, as we propose, early movement toward an increasingly mature conception of belief does ordinarily take place in at least two separate steps or stages, with young preschoolers first coming to a singularly accommodatory view of minds well before their 5- to 7-year-old counterparts eventually arrive at the altogether harder and more assimilatory half of the same puzzle, then the "one-miracle" account of mental life that fails to leave room for such possibilities will end up promoting both of two distinct sorts of errors. One of these ways of falling off the log, and effectively collapsing what is better understood as a two-or-more stage process onto a single point in development, has been to err on the side of caution by overlooking the good abilities of young 3- and even 2-year-olds to understand that ignorance can promote false beliefs. On this withholding view, young preschoolers are accorded no legitimate understanding of the mind unless or until they can successfully acquit themselves on whatever psychometrically inhospitable measures of false belief understanding happen to be currently in vogue.

The even more common way of falling off the other side of this same log has been to mistakenly suppose that whenever preschool children eventually *do* begin subscribing to some clear notion of belief entitlement—that is, whenever they first appreciate that persons who are kept in the dark will consequently get things wrong—they also naturally acquire an *interpretive* or *constructive* view of mental life in the bargain. By these lights the having of a so-called representational theory of mental life, an ability that actually requires for its clear demonstration no more than the recognition of the possibility of false belief, is regularly conflated with the altogether more demanding insight that minds also invariably transform their own inputs—an achievement that necessarily presupposes Searle's "world-to-mind" direction of fit. Of these alternative ways of getting things wrong it is perhaps the second—the mistaken tendency to confuse an understanding of false belief with the accomplishment of having already come to an interpretive theory of mind—that is still least explored and so most deserving of our critical attention.

In order to back our hypothesis concerning the distinction between false belief understanding and a truly interpretive theory of mind at least three things require doing. First, we are under some obligation to back our strong claim that the current theories-of-mind literature has actually undervalued the abilities of young preschoolers by trivializing their real accomplishments by mistakenly viewing them as suffering from a kind of cognitive deficit that, in point of fact, they do not have. Second, we need to offer enough good reasons to convince you that simply acquiring the early arriving metarepresentational competencies necessary to permit an understanding of false belief need not be the same thing as also acquiring those altogether different and later arriving abilities involved in appreciating that knowledge is interpretively constructed. Finally, we close by presenting some new data meant to demonstrate empirically that 4- and 5-year-olds, already shown to have a solid working knowledge of the possibility of false belief, do not, and will not for some years to come, have anything like an interpretive theory of mind.

Taking up this agenda, we begin by briefly summarizing what we take to be the current state of play in the ongoing debate about children's earliest understanding of the possibility of false belief. This summary will be kept brief, primarily as a way of leaving room to discuss adequately those later arriving abilities that we argue are special to the acquisition of genuinely *interpretive* theories of mental life.

Rereading the Evidence on False Belief Understanding

Throughout much of the 1980s an impressive body of research findings accumulated, most of which was read as providing backing for two propositions. The first is that, in so far as clear evidence about children's understanding of mental life is able to show, all former talk about the special accomplishments of 5- to 7-year-olds was simply misguided and arose because poor measurement practices set unnecessary procedural obstacles in the path of still younger preschool children. The second assertion is that children under the age of approximately 4 years all suffer from some general cognitive deficit that is said to disallow them access to any genuine understanding of the real point about beliefs, which is that they can be mistaken. What was offered as proof for these strong if somewhat counterintuitive claims were the facts that, whereas 4- and 5-year-olds regularly succeeded, 3-year-olds consistently failed at various so-called unexpected change and unexpected contents tasks and at false belief versions of the ineffable appearance-reality test (e.g., Gopnik & Astington, 1988; Wimmer & Perner, 1983).

Although we have no special quarrel with the claim that 4- and 5-year-olds regularly pass these various measures of false belief understanding, there is a good deal of room for real disagreement over whether still younger subjects legitimately fail them. Although different in other important respects, it is worth pointing out that essentially all of these measures turn upon comparisons of the beliefs of two persons (either the subject and someone else, or two other, often fictional, characters) one of whom is drawn into a false belief as a result of being carefully kept in ignorance about certain key pieces of information. Josef Perner's story protagonist "Maxi," for example, is made to be out of the room when key facts about the relocation of his chocolate are disclosed, just as other comparable foils are kept partially in the dark by being allowed to see but not to heft or feel John Flavell's celebrated "sponge-rock." The consistent finding arising from the use of these standard measures of false belief and appearance-reality understanding is that children as young as 4 or 5 years old, but *not* still younger children, recognize that the target person, who has been systematically kept in ignorance, will, as a consequence, end up holding to some false belief.

Without wishing to detract from the novelty and relevance of these observations, it needs to be pointed out that an important part of the interest solicited
by these early findings is due, not so much to the actual evidence in hand, as to
the general in-for-a-penny-in-for-a-pound, one-miracle view of belief entitlement within which these findings are customarily couched. That is, if, as proponents of these early views would have it, the process of acquiring a theory
of knowledge and belief does happen in one fell swoop, and if crediting a child
with a truly representational view of the mind also necessarily commits one to
the additional assumption that these same children also automatically grasp the
real interpretive nature of mental experience, then small wonder that 4-year-
olds have already seemed young enough. And so certain battle lines have been
drawn, with a substantial number of investigators strongly committed to and
others in equal numbers staunchly opposed to what we have described here as
the one-miracle view that children as young as 4 years have already bought into
their first and only theory of mind.

While much of the 1980s saw a rush toward an early consensus about the
special abilities of 4-year-olds, the last few years have marked a transition in
this mental models literature. Much of this new energy came to be devoted to
challenging the widely advertised idea that 4-year-olds, but not still younger
children, understand the possibility of false belief and so alone deserve to be
credited with some general theorylike understanding of the mind (see Moses
& Chandler, 1992, for a recent review of this new literature). Most of those
who have contributed to this new literature share a sense of unease with all
claims to the effect that children younger than 4 years wholly lack any genuine
insight into the representational nature of the mind. At present, one might count
some 20 or more recent reports of research that all have this as their common
theme. While this is no place for a detailed accounting of all of these separate
investigations, it may prove helpful at least to list out and illustrate the several
general categories into which these studies tend to fall. Bearing in mind that
the creation of such taxonomic schemes is inherently a suspect trade, we offer
here a set of four arguably distinct groupings.

Asking the Right Question

The first of these categories includes studies (e.g., Siegal & Beattie, 1990;
Lewis & Osborne, 1990) or parts of studies (e.g., Freeman, Lewis, & Doherty, 1991) that undertake to demonstrate that at least one of the reasons that
3-year-olds are so often wrongly judged to have no working knowledge of the
representational character of their own and other's minds is that they frequently
end up badly misunderstanding the test questions that have been put to them
by various theories-of-mind investigators. Contributors of these studies argue,
for example, that when responding to questions about where Maxi "will look
for his chocolate," 3-year-olds, in their impatience, often end up answering

quite different questions about where Maxi "will *eventually* look" or about where Maxi "*should* look" for his chocolate. The obvious repair for this situation is to develop whatever variations upon standard false belief tasks as are required in order to block, or at least discourage, these procedural errors. The common finding reported by those who have attempted such methodological revisions is that when 3-year-olds are further helped to understand what question they are meant to be answering, then some three-quarters of them regularly succeed in making appropriate reference to the existence of false beliefs. The general conclusion to which such findings are said to lead is that 3-year-olds do, in fact, have a real grasp of the possibility of false beliefs, but are often prevented from demonstrating this skill because the measurement procedures in common use work a special hardship upon them.

Making Thoughts More Salient

The second general category of studies includes the work of an additional group of investigators, all of whom have concluded that standard measures of false belief understanding regularly lend a special and disruptive salience to what is objectively the case and so somehow unfairly put in the shade all those more ephemeral thoughts or beliefs that persons actually entertain about such concrete matters of fact. As a consequence, it is maintained, young persons— who are otherwise known to be fools for saliency—end up failing to showcase their real understanding of mental life. Proponents of such views have usually attempted to support their claims by undertaking to show what happens when standard "unexpected change" or "unexpected contents" procedures are followed, except for the taking of some special steps to ensure that "reality" is made somehow less disarmingly salient or that its mental representation is somehow given greater weight.

As one example of these corrective strategies, our colleague Anna Fritz (1991) has undertaken to off-load some of the weight that usually adheres to the concrete realities of standard unexpected change and unexpected contents tasks by substituting, in one case, "pretend" chocolate for the real mind-grabbing chocolate ordinarily employed in Wimmer and Perner's (1983) classic Maxi problem. In a parallel study she has pursued much the same agenda by arranging an altered version of the unexpected contents task in which the surprising fact about the Smarties box employed was not that it unexpectedly contained pencils, but rather that it was unexpectedly empty. The idea obviously at work in these studies was that "pretend chocolate" wouldn't have the same imperious saliency as does the real thing, just as "no contents" would prove to be somehow less salient or attention grabbing than would the reality of actually finding real pencils where candies had been expected. As it turned out, these simple saliency manipulations were enough to allow some 75% of the 3-year-olds that Fritz has tested to pass these otherwise standard false belief measures.

In a comparable line of work, Zaitchik (1991) also attempted to reduce the impact of being a witness to some highly salient and unexpected change by arranging that her subjects only heard rumors about—but did not actually witness—the location of various target objects being changed. As had been the case in Fritz's studies, Zaitchik also found that the lion's share of her 3-year-olds, who had only heard about—but did not actually see—a toy being moved, were remarkably good at recognizing that, while they themselves knew about the crucial transfer, some other less well informed onlooker would not. The general conclusion promoted by these several studies is that if "reality" is not somehow made to seem overweening, and if mental events are allowed to assume anything like the importance ordinarily accorded them in ordinary places where what people are thinking is actually allowed to count for something, then even 3-year-olds will regularly distinguish the truth from what those less well informed than themselves would mistakenly take it to be.

The flip side of this same argument is provided by two further studies by Mitchell and his colleagues (Mitchell & Lacohee, 1991; Robinson, Mitchell, & Nye, 1992; Stevenson & Mitchell, 1992) in which efforts were made not to somehow reduce the salience of reality but to find ways of adding fresh salience to those ordinarily best forgotten beliefs that experience has shown to be mistaken. For example, in the first of these studies, which utilized an otherwise standard version of the usual unexpected contents task, Mitchell and Lacohee (1991) found that the simple act of marking children's original beliefs, by "posting" a version of them in a mailbox, was enough to allow the large majority of their 3-year-old subjects to remember accurately their own now evidently mistaken beliefs regarding the likely contents of a well-marked box.

These studies, in concert with those reported earlier, offer strong support for the view that the poor showings traditionally turned in by 3-year-olds on standardized measures of false belief understanding are unrepresentative and can be explained, in some large measure, by the fact that in most of the assessment procedures in common use the usual importance of mental events is artificially eclipsed by the fact that yesterday's worn-out truths are typically no match for today's hard realities.

Making the Task More Relevant

A third general class of studies aimed at better bringing out the best of 3-year-olds' knowledge about mental life turns upon the odd fact that most of the available investigations of children's false belief understanding seem to presuppose that the assessment contexts of choice are measurement tasks in which young subjects are required to focus attention upon personally irrelevant and usually hypothetical events in the as-if lives of unknown and typically imaginary puppet or story characters. Several teams of investigators (e.g., Chandler, Fritz, & Hala, 1989; Freeman et al., 1991; Hala, 1991; Hala, Chandler, &

Fritz, 1991; Winner & Sullivan, 1993) critical of such impoverished assessment contexts have all taken related methodological steps aimed at better engaging young subjects' serious interests. Freeman et al., for example, have demonstrated that when story protagonists are represented as having a real "need to know," subjects turn out to be quite good at keeping track of what they and others might be thinking. Some of the work going on in our own laboratory, work that demonstrates 3-year-olds' skillful attempts to lead others deceptively into false beliefs, offers a similarly compelling demonstration of just how good young children can be at fathoming the depths of false belief understanding when it is in their own interest to do so.

Some of the clearest demonstrations of this same result are provided by the recent work of Winner and Sullivan (1993) and by the somewhat earlier studies of our colleague Suzanne Hala (1991). In a close replication of the classic Wimmer and Perner (1983) unexpected change procedure, Hala has recently shown that 3-year-olds regularly understand the false beliefs of others when they themselves have taken responsibility for bringing such misunderstandings about. In one of the studies in this sequence, for example, she employed an all but standard version of the unexpected contents task that she had altered only by asking her subjects to themselves empty out the candies with which Smarties boxes ordinarily come equipped, and to go on to choose something to put in the place of these candies from an array of "joke" items such as rubber spiders and snakes. Under these minimally altered but much more interesting circumstances better than 80% of the 3-year-olds tested expressed confidence that another child, who saw only the outside of the box, would be taken in and would wrongly suppose that there were only Smarties in the Smarties box. In a parallel set of studies Hala made similar modifications to the standard unexpected change task by again inviting subjects to relocate the contents of a food container while a second individual was out of the room. Again, more than 80% of a group of 3-year-olds passed this more interactive version of the unexpected change task with flying colors. Interestingly, a sequence of recent control studies (Hala, 1994) has also demonstrated that 3-year-olds who perform exactly the same set of actions, but do so while carrying out someone else's "plan," do not show the same improved performance. Nor does it appear necessary for such young subjects to actually do their own legwork: Much the same good results are obtained when young subjects are made the "brains of an outfit" in which the experimenter actually supplies the "muscle" needed to pull off these substitutions.

Making False Beliefs an Option

Finally, it is possible to identify a fourth category of studies that have as their common feature the fact that, rather than being asked to predict what some target character might potentially do or say, subjects are questioned to determine their readiness to nominate (or accept) the existence of false beliefs as possible explanations for otherwise surprising or anomalous actions that have already taken place. Bartsch and Wellman (1989), for example, found that 3-year-olds attributed false beliefs to a story character who looked for his lost puppy in what the subjects themselves knew to be the wrong place. Similarly, Moses (1993) and Wellman and Banerjee (1991) found that the clear majority of 3-year-olds tested were quick to explain such otherwise anomalous behavioral or emotional reactions by referring to the story character's own evidently mistaken prior beliefs.

These several lines of available evidence go an important distance toward showing that 3-year-olds are not without some resources in navigating the world of true and false beliefs. Our purpose in citing representative studies of each of the four different sorts just enumerated is not, however, simply to reduce by some months the putative age by which children are thought to outgrow whatever cognitive deficit is imagined to be acting as a brake upon the wheel of their thoughts about mental life. What we actually hope to accomplish instead, however, is to more radically alter the nature of the current theories of mind debate itself by persuading you that, while 3-year-olds do genuinely understand the possibility of false belief, and so necessarily subscribe to some truly representational theory of mind, these facts ought not be seen as carrying with them the usual implication that these same young children also hold to anything like an interpretive or constructive theory of mind. Making such a point, however, requires a more head-on attempt to distinguish what might be called merely *representational* accounts from other more genuinely *interpretive* theories of mind.

Representational *Versus* Interpretive Theories of Mind

By way of a reminder about where all of this is supposed to be heading, recall that we began by rehearsing the interesting distinction between "mind-to-world" and "world-to-mind" directions of fit that Searle (1983) introduced as a way of talking about how grown-ups commonly view those epistemic relations that obtain between themselves and their surround. Given this descriptive framework we went on to hypothesize that in the usual ontogenetic course of events young preschool children first come to the view that minds are pure accommodation-side devices that simply "copy" a world that is assumed to be under no reciprocal obligation to do any "fitting" of its own. Not until some years later, it was suggested, do somewhat older school-age children first begin to move toward any real understanding of the mind as a two-way street that also fits or assimilates the world to its own nature. Then, on the assumption that we had gotten things right that far, we went on to consider two of the ways in which contributors to this literature seem to have gotten things the wrong way around by mistakenly supposing that 4-year-olds somehow succeed at completing all of the essentials of epistemic development in one giant all-or-nothing step. One of these mistakes, the one upon which we have just been focusing, is that of wrongly imagining that it is more difficult initially to get into the theories-of-mind game than is actually the case, thus dismissing out of hand young children's earliest insights into the real representational nature of belief. The other way of falling off of this same log, to which we now mean to turn attention, has been to mistakenly assume that having gotten any kind of fledgling grasp upon the accommodatory pole of mental life automatically amounts to the same thing as having come to the fuller realization that minds also assimilate reality by transforming it to match their own nature.

The general contention here is that the contemporary developmental literature is marked by a deep-running confusion about what it could reasonably mean to talk about an "interpretive" as opposed to a "noninterpretive" theory of mind. The root of this confusion, we propose, is to be found in a collective failure to exercise adequate care and concern in our attempts to calculate when it is that two views can properly be said to be *different* views of "one and the same thing." There is, for example, a certain loose but nevertheless familiar way of speaking that gives us license to talk about the fact that Perner's protagonist Maxi and Maxi's mother have different beliefs about the selfsame matter of where Maxi's chocolate happens to be at a given moment (Perner, 1991), just as it seems appropriate to describe "one and the same" item from an appearance-reality test as having been perceived to be a rock by some, while known to be a sponge by others (Flavell, 1988). The "loose" part in all such easy talk about identity is that while the location of the chocolate and the identity of the rock-sponge used in these examples may be in some sense unitary and fixed, the objects of knowledge relevant to the protagonists whose viewpoints are in question are psychologically quite different. Maxi's mother, for example, has access to relevant facts of the matter that are lost upon her son, who has had the bad fortune of being out of the room at just the crucial moment when the question of where the chocolate is really located was settled. Consequently, while the two are fully entitled to their separate opinions, their different beliefs, while focusing on the same topic, don't actually reference "one and the same" phenomenal reality. In exactly the same way, the onlooker who has only seen but not yet touched the sponge-rock in the false belief version of Flavell's task is not playing with the same deck of informational cards that are available to those who are already in on the joke. Of course, for certain purposes, none of this makes any difference. Where it *does* make a lot of difference is when one is trying to establish that point in development at which children come to appreciate that one and the same event can in fact support multiple interpretations.

If all of this is correct, then individuals whose operative theories of mind are still exclusively accommodatory in character should have no special difficulty with standard false belief and appearance-reality problems, for the reason that these measures turn on the fact that all of the persons whose beliefs are in question have access to different information. Nothing about all of this tells us anything one way or another about the ability of children to appreciate (a) that beliefs are underdetermined by matters of fact; (b) that there is a world-to-mind direction of fit operating in our epistemic lives; and (c) that two persons, both of whom have access to *precisely the same* information, can still end up holding to quite different beliefs about their common experience. Consequently, if we are still to somehow decide when it is that young persons actually do come to subscribe to a theory of mind that is legitimately interpretive in the broader and more usual sense, then we will need to pursue that question using procedures other than those that currently make up the roster of standard theories-of-mind tests. Our own attempts, and those of our research colleagues, to develop such alternative procedures have been informed by three sets of studies that need to be mentioned briefly before going on to describe some of the early results of our own research efforts.

In the first of these related studies, undertaken almost 15 years ago by John Flavell and his colleagues (Flavell, 1978; Flavell, Everett, Croft, & Flavell, 1981), children's understanding of what was then called "Level 2 Perspective Taking" was assessed by presenting them with a picture of a turtle that was laid out in front of the subject "feet first," so to speak. The critical question that was posed to these young participants concerned "how" that selfsame turtle would seem to someone who sat opposite them and whose approach to the turtle picture was, consequently, back first. Interestingly, 4-year-old children, but not 3-year-olds responded to the rather cryptic question, "How does X see the turtle?" by reporting that "X" saw it "as if" lying on its back. Clearly, this is a study that, at first blush, seems to be of the sort we are after; one meant to inquire about different accounts of one and the same stimulus object. What is unique and somewhat troublesome about this particular experimental setup, however, is that it too easily supports a confusion over two possible meanings of the key word *how*. What we really want to know about from our subjects when we set out to question them about how "X" sees the turtle is whether they do or do not appreciate something like the fact that different people often find different meanings in the same objective matter of fact. Unfortunately, Flavell's particular way of going about setting this problem would appear to conflate this question with a different and perhaps much simpler one about angles of regard—a question that could literally be gotten to the bottom of by walking around to the other person's side of the table. One could not, we take it, hope to similarly get at *how* you or I might see issues such as capital punishment or abortion by turning the tables in that sort of literal way. Turtles, it would seem, from this side of the table, threaten to lead us down a blind alley.

Second on this list of studies that hold out some promise of informing us about truly interpretive theories of mind is a study by Perner and Davies (1991) that draws upon assessment materials ordinarily used in tests of the appearance-reality distinction. In general, these were brought into play in such a way as to determine whether children would know to discount the mistaken views of persons who themselves were taken in by misleading appearances. What they found was that by approximately 4 years of age children already appreciate that others will set aside what they take to be bad advice or misleading information. Perner and Davies concluded that these data demonstrate that 4-year-olds understand the mind "actively," evaluate incoming information with reference to current beliefs, and already appreciate that individuals with different information at their disposal will evaluate incoming information differently, and so these 4-year-olds must subscribe to an "interpretive" theory of mind. While all of this is quite interesting, it still does not, in our view, tell us anything about the question of when children come to recognize that minds actually interpret in the epistemic sense of differently assimilating, that is, imposing a world-to-mind direction of fit upon experience. It seems unlikely that anyone would seriously doubt that children as young as 4 years see their own or others' minds as "active" in the broad sense of somehow generally operating upon or making good use of the elements of thought. What is at real issue, but unfortunately left unilluminated by the Perner and Davies study, is the question of when children first come to realize that minds not only somehow "crunch" in some procedural way the evidence already at their disposal but also go beyond this to actually reach out to determine what information is taken in and how it is interpreted or construed.

One study sequence that does speak directly to the question of when children do begin acquiring an interpretive view of mind is the work done by Pillow (1991, 1993). Briefly, he has demonstrated that 5-, 6-, and 7-year-olds, but not younger children, seem to appreciate that people's likes and dislikes will dictate how they end up viewing a range of morally and factually ambiguous events. Such findings suggest that, whatever else young children might already know about beliefs and desires, they may have their first inklings of the idiosyncrasies of other people's mental lives during this 5 to 7 year period. While clearly pointing us in the right direction, Pillow's procedures were still not specifically designed to distinguish between children's grasp of simple false belief and their ability to employ a more interpretive theory of mind.

On Recognizing the Possibility of Being Wrong in More Than One Way: Study 1

In view of all of the faults to be found with previous attempts to explore children's first thoughts about the interpretive nature of the knowing process, we felt that we needed to go our own methodologic way. What was required was

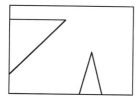

Figure 6.1   Droodle entitled "A ship arriving too late to save a drowning witch."

some procedure that not only would provide a means of assessing children's understanding of what Flavell (1988) has called the "one-many" relation between things in the world and their possible interpretation but also would simultaneously allow for the assessment of children's understanding of the possibility of false belief. Our search was also constrained by our conviction that it is easier to engineer events such that two persons can be differently *wrong* about the same reality than it is to produce circumstances that support multiple *correct* interpretations.

The assessment procedures finally settled upon for use in what is an ongoing series of studies are actually variations upon a "Droodle Task" previously employed in the testing of what were once described as role-taking skills (Chandler & Boyes, 1982; Chandler & Helm, 1984). A *droodle* is a cryptic line drawing or puzzle picture of a type earlier popularized by cartoonist Roger Price (1953) and perhaps better illustrated than explained. Figure 6.1, for example, depicts a variation on a droodle originally published by Price over the caption "A ship arriving too late to save a drowning witch." The humor in this and related drawings by Price is obviously meant to arise from the fact that, given the restricted or keyhole view imposed, it would be ludicrous to imagine that anyone could ever correctly guess about the larger scene of which the droodle itself is only a small, nondescript part. Once oriented by the caption, however, the cryptic fragments of the original drawing fall into place and it becomes possible to imagine—even difficult not to imagine—that the drawing depicts some fractional part of what its caption announces it to be. We set out to take advantage of this property by presenting our young participants with visual information that was analogous to the written caption and then asking them to predict how first one and then another naive observer would interpret the captionless droodle.

Our procedure made use of a set of six such cartoon drawings patterned after those developed by Price and extended in such a way as to include not only the limited details contained within the original droodles themselves but also the more complete scenes suggested by the droodle captions. This series included not only a full picture of a ship coming to save a drowning witch but also an elephant smelling a grapefruit, a shark in a party dress, a giraffe in an engineer's cap, an aerial view of the Eiffel Tower, and Winnie the Pooh clutching a

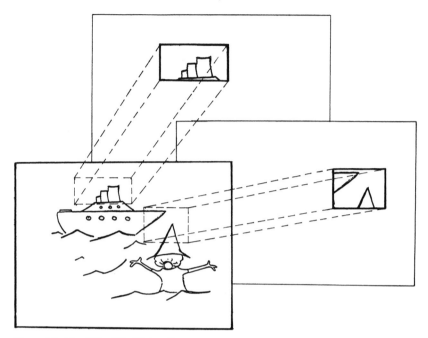

Figure 6.2   The "Ship/Witch" droodle.

honeypot. Each of these drawings was outfitted with a cardboard overlay into which had been cut two different viewing windows. Once in place, these overlays masked most of the extending drawing, permitting only the original droodle portions of the picture to be seen through whichever of the two viewing windows was opened, as illustrated in Figure 6.2.

This procedure has been employed in two separate studies,[2] both aimed at assessing some aspect of the relation between false belief–based and interpretive theories of mind. Although originally conceived as a procedural means of evaluating what was once termed "childhood egocentrism" or the absence of "role-taking competencies," it should be clear that young children who mistakenly suppose that some protagonist such as Raggedy Ann or Andy would somehow mysteriously know, as they themselves know on good evidence, that the sketchy details available in the droodle portion of these pictures would somehow represent "a ship arriving too late to save a drowning witch" can also be fairly said to have committed what the theory-of-mind literature has come to refer to as a *reality error*—In other words, while, of course, these really and truly are pictures of ships and witches, persons who somehow lacked the capacity to understand the possibility of false beliefs would, in their cognitive immaturity, be unable to routinely appreciate that such knowledge would not be available to Raggedy Ann and Andy, who never saw more than a small part of the larger drawing (Perner & Davies, 1991).

Children's false belief understanding was thus assessed by simply asking them what Raggedy Ann would "think" when shown a restricted, or droodle, view. Going on to then ask what Raggedy Andy would "think" of this same droodle offered our subjects the chance to showcase a more sophisticated grasp of mental life under which Ann and Andy were free to entertain different false beliefs or different interpretations of the selfsame reality.

The 5-, 6-, and 7-year-old children who participated in this study were introduced to two dolls—Raggedy Ann and Raggedy Andy—and asked to pretend that the dolls were "real people." Two boxes served as the dolls' "houses," and the children were told that "when Ann and Andy are inside their houses, they can't hear what we're saying, and they can't see what we're doing." They were then shown the full, or unrestricted, view of the first droodle and asked "What do you think this is a picture of?"

The child was then told: "Now we're going to get Andy out of his house and show him the picture. Andy has never seen this picture before, but we're going to show it to him like this" at which point the cover of the droodle was closed and one of the windows covering a restricted view was opened. The child was then instructed to remove Andy from his house and was asked, "What does Andy think that's a picture of?" The child's response was noted and repeated: "So, Andy thinks it's a ———."

The child was then told: "Now we're going to get Ann out of her house and show her the picture. Ann has never seen this picture before, but we're going to show it to her like this," and again a window onto a restricted view was opened (this could be either the same window Andy had been shown or a different window, depending on the experimental condition). The child was then instructed to retrieve Ann from her house and was asked: "What does Ann think that's a picture of?" Again, the child's response was noted and repeated: "So, Ann thinks it's a ———."

A total of six droodles, consisting of three conditions of two droodles each, were presented. In Condition 1, the two droodles shown each contained two windows that opened onto different and nonoverlapping restricted views. Participants were asked to explain what Andy would think of the contents of Window 1 and then what Ann would think of the contents of Window 2. As has been routinely the case in earlier applications of this or similar procedures (e.g., Chandler & Helm, 1984; Perner & Davies, 1991; Taylor, 1988), Condition 2, by contrast, focused attention on children's responses to only one of the available viewing windows. Thus, participants were asked to comment on what first one and then the other of the dolls would say about the contents of one and the same window. Condition 3 was, in most respects, a repeat of Condition 2, in that inquiries were again made about the likely responses of both Ann and Andy to only one of the two available windows. Here, however, the two doll figures were said to actively disagree about the contents of the restricted view. For example, if the subject said of the Ship/Witch droodle that Andy would think "two shark teeth," they were first reminded of that supposed fact and then told, "But Ann doesn't think it's two shark teeth, what does Ann think it is?"

The key hypotheses under examination in this first study were that false belief understanding is (a) an *earlier occurring* condition and (b) a necessary but *not sufficient* condition for the emergence of an interpretive or constructivistic theory of mind. These expectations are taken up here in turn, beginning with children's understanding of the possibility of false belief.

Attributions of False Belief

Regardless of how they otherwise finished up, all participants in all conditions were shown a total of six complete drawings and then immediately asked what either Raggedy Ann or Andy would judge only the restricted or droodle portion of that picture to be. As a way of quantifying each child's apparent capacity for such false belief understanding, their first responses to each droodle, that is, their first attributions as to what either Andy or Ann would judge each of the six droodles to be, was coded as either betraying a reality error (e.g., "Andy would think it was a ship and a witch") or as an expression of legitimate false belief understanding (e.g., "Andy would say it's two knife points"). By these criteria, all but 2 of the 75 children tested (two 5-year-olds) were able to attribute false beliefs to these puppet characters on at least one occasion. The percentage of responses classified as false belief attributions for the 5-, 6-, and 7-year-olds were 50%, 63%, and 98%, respectively.

Summary scores for each child were derived by first assigning them one point for each response coded as a recognition of the possibility of false belief. Scores could thus range from 0 to 6. Using these scores, subjects who failed to evidence any understanding of false belief by responding, at every opportunity, with a reality error (i.e., those with summary scores of 0), were classified *False Belief Understanding Absent*. Subjects whose scores ranged from 1 to 3 were classified *False Belief Understanding Transitional,* and those whose scores ranged from 4 to 6 were classified *False Belief Understanding Present.* Table 6.1 shows the distribution of these classifications by age group.

As can be seen from an examination of this table, only 2 of the youngest children were unremittingly "realistic" never attributing a false belief to Ann or Andy. Slightly more than a quarter of our participants (12) evidenced some partial understanding of false belief, and more than two-thirds of the children (31) appropriately attributed false beliefs to Andy and Ann at nearly every opportunity.

As one might have anticipated, the group of subjects who were most successful in attributing false beliefs to the puppet figures, were, on average, older (6.7 years) than those in both the False Belief Understanding Absent (5.7 years) and Transitional (5.9 years) groups. It should also be noted that, overall, more

Table 6.1
False Belief Understanding: Status by Age Group (Study 1)

Age Group[a]	False Belief Understanding Status		
	Absent	Transitional	Present
5-year-olds	2	5	8
6-year-olds	0	7	8
7-year-olds	0	0	15
	2	12	31

[a]$n = 15$ for each group.

than 95% of the children correctly concluded, on at least one occasion, that these only partially informed puppet figures would end up holding to false beliefs about what they were looking at. Clearly, unless comparable numbers of children also demonstrated an allegiance to an interpretive theory of mind, the one-miracle view that equates such interpretive accounts with simple false belief understanding is automatically mistaken.

Constructive Versus Copy Theories of Mind

A direct measure of when children of various ages first come to an interpretive or constructive theory of mind is provided by a comparison of participants' attributions to Ann and Andy on the various single window conditions of this study. Clearly, children who understand what Flavell (1988) has characterized as the "one-many" relation that obtains between things in the world and their possible representations are in a position to recognize that while Andy might regard the droodle portion of a picture as being one thing (e.g., an arrowhead), Ann might differently judge precisely the same ambiguous stimulus display as being something else entirely (e.g., kitty ears). By contrast, participants who have not yet arrived at such an interpretive view of the knowing process are essentially limited to either throwing up their hands or simply repeating themselves by assuming that since both Ann and Andy are exposed to the same stimulus event, they are obliged to arrive at the same conclusion as to its identity. If, as was the case in experimental Condition 3 where the puppets were said to disagree, such persistently realistic children are directly instructed to assign *different* interpretations to these objectively identical events, they should find it impossible to comply and end up by repeating themselves, by refusing to answer, or by falling back upon the realistic view that either Ann or Andy somehow knows the whole truth and need not make any interpretation at all.

In order to examine these several possibilities each child's responses to the four droodles that made up experimental Conditions 2 and 3 were coded in such a way as to create two different scoring possibilities. The pair of responses attributed to Ann and Andy for any single droodle were considered *Interpretive* if (a) both attributions avoided reality errors and so were scored as expressions of false belief understanding according to the criteria outlined above, and (b) the attributions given to Ann and Andy were legitimately different from one another. In other words, the subject had to attribute a false belief to Andy successfully and then go on to attribute a different false belief to Ann. All other types of response pairs were scored as *Noninterpretive*. These Noninterpretive pairs could be further classified into two subtypes. Pairs of responses were coded as *Repetitive* if the belief attributed to one puppet was automatically attributed to the other (for example, when two reality errors were committed or the same false belief was simply repeated). *Mixed* pairs were noted when a false belief or reality error was followed by a second response that was heavily influenced—yet not quite identical—to the first (for example, "foot" followed by "shoe," or "witch hat" followed by "wizard hat").

Given a total of 60 opportunities, our 5-year-old participants managed to produce Interpretive response pairs on just 20% of these occasions. Repetitive pairs accounted for a full three-quarters of the responses, with Mixed pairs making up 5%. For the 6-year-old children, an even third of the response pairs were classified as Interpretive 57% as Repetitive, and 10% as Mixed. The 7-year-old children were much more consistent, with 88% Interpretive, 12% Repetitive, and no Mixed responses.

The children were then assigned to one of three general scoring categories. Those who reported that the two doll figures would interpret the droodles differently on at least three of these four trials, were categorized as having a *Consolidated Interpretative Theory of Mind*. Those who never made such differential attributions even when pressed to do so were classified as having a *Noninterpretive* Theory of Mind, and the remaining children were classified *Transitional*. By these criteria 40% of our participants were found to be altogether unable to attribute different false beliefs to Ann and Andy, 13% managed to assign different false beliefs to the two doll figures on at least one occasion and so were labeled as Transitional, and 47% qualified as having a Consolidated Interpretive Theory of Mind by attributing different false beliefs to Andy and Ann on nearly every available occasion (see Table 6.2). By these lights, just 60% of our participants gave evidence of possessing at least the beginnings of an interpretive theory of mind capable of generating two different—yet both legitimate—false beliefs to the puppets who had viewed the selfsame image.

Control Conditions

It might have been that some of our participants failed to provide a second interpretation of any droodle simply because they lacked the imagination or

Table 6.2
Interpretive Theory of Mind: Status by Age Group (Study 1)

	Interpretive Theory of Mind Status		
Age Group[a]	Noninterpretive	Transitional	Consolidated
5-year-olds	10	2	3
6-year-olds	8	2	5
7-year-olds	0	2	13
	18	6	21

[a]$n = 15$ for each group.

creativity to actually invent a second reading of the restricted view. To ward off this possible alternative interpretation, we included one final droodle and, after showing our subjects only the restricted view, asked them to "guess what this [the restricted view] might be." Following their initial response, we noted: "That's a good guess, now guess again., What do you think this is?" If any of our participants were to find it difficult to have more than one thing to say about any one picture, they should evidence their lack of imagination here. In nearly all instances, however, they provided interpretations that differed from one another in nontrivial ways—that is, when assessed against the criteria employed in evaluating attributions to Andy and Ann, almost every response was judged Interpretive. In addition, we tested a separate sample of 30 children using our original set of six droodles asking them simply to guess and then guess again at what the contents of a single restricted view might be. These 5-, 6-, and 7-year-olds were all able to give two distinct responses for each droodle, and again nearly all were judged Interpretive. What these control data suggest is that our participants did not suffer any lack of imagination and that, when asked, such children can easily reread the same stimulus picture in a new and different way.

Comparing False Belief and Interpretive Theories of Mind

The final step in this analysis concerned the extent to which our measures of simple false belief understanding, on the one hand, and of the presence or absence of an interpretive theory of mind, on the other, are actually redundant— that is, did all or most of those subjects who evidenced some understanding of false beliefs also go on to show some grasp of the constructed nature of those beliefs as required by so-called one-miracle views of children's developing theories of mind? Or was it rather the case that understanding the possibility of false beliefs was earlier arriving and necessary but not in itself sufficient to guarantee an interpretive theory of mind, as predicted by our own two-miracle view? To answer this question, we first constructed a contingency table that,

Table 6.3
Contingency Table of False Belief Understanding Status by Interpretive Theory of Mind Status (Study 1)

False Belief Understanding Status	Interpretive Theory of Mind Status			
	Noninterpretive	Transitional	Consolidated	
Absent	2	—	—	2
Transitional	12	0	—	12
Present	4	6	21	31
	18	6	21	45

based on their summary scores, boxed each of the children into one cell within the nine-cell matrix shown in Table 6.3.

Our scoring criteria for interpretive responses required that, in order to qualify as Interpretive, the first member of any pair of responses must be a false belief. In other words, by our own working definition, it was impossible for a response pair that did *not* begin with a false belief attribution to be scored as Interpretive. As a matter of definition, then, all of the subjects classified as having a Consolidated Interpretive Theory of Mind are also classified as False Belief Understanding Present. Thus, only one cell in the column labeled Consolidated Interpretive Theory of Mind could contain a number other than zero. Similarly, only the first cell in the row labeled False Belief Understanding Absent could contain a nonzero number. In order to effect a legitimate comparison of false belief and interpretive theories of mind, it was judged prudent to remove the shaded cells from Table 6.3. Lest we risk throwing out the baby with the bathwater, however, note that we are only eliminating subjects whose performances lay either at the ceiling or floor on this procedure—that is, the set of developmentally uninteresting participants who possess either all of none of the required abilities.

The fact that more than 95% of our participants were able to come up with at least one false belief, whereas only 60% of these same children could muster one or more interpretive response pairs, gives us an initial indication that having an understanding of the possibility of false belief is not the same thing as harboring a constructivistic theory of mind. From this distance, then, the measures do not appear to be redundant. Indeed, a chi-square analysis of the non-shaded cells of Table 6.3 offers strong statistical confirmation of this view.

These findings support two general conclusions. First, although subjects were not uniformly successful in attributing false beliefs to the puppet characters, very nearly all of these young persons were able to conclude, on at least one of the occasions afforded them, that Ann or Andy would arrive at a wrong-headed notion about what they were looking at. Second, because just 60% of these same young persons were able, on at least one occasion to attribute *different* false beliefs to the two puppets, it would appear that an understanding of the possibility of false belief does not automatically guarantee one an appreciation of the interpretive nature of beliefs.

These conclusions might be challenged from several perspectives. According to one line of reasoning, the failure of some subjects to attribute different false beliefs to Ann and Andy (i.e., to provide Interpretive response pairs) might arise not from a simple lack of imagination (which our controls rule out) or a pervasive failure to appreciate that beliefs about the picture must be inferred from the ambiguous stimulus (most subjects clearly already appreciate this, as evidenced by their understanding of false belief), but rather because their ability to generate plausible alternative beliefs is at best fragile and easily outstripped in this particular assessment situation. In other words, much like adults made to view a very large window onto a droodle—a window so large that it fails to obscure any meaningful portion of the picture beneath—our young subjects may have been unable to generate or use plausible alternative interpretations because their knowledge of what the picture actually depicts so overwhelms their ability to entertain other possibilities that they are limited either to repeating themselves, to committing a reality error, or to falling silent.

If one could provide participants with some ready alternatives, this reasoning suggests, their performance on the task would improve. One could, for example, add a pretrial condition in which children had access to alternative interpretations of precisely the droodle that was about to become the focus of attention by first showing the children the restricted view and asking, "What do you think that is?" followed by, "That's a good guess, have another guess." On this account, when faced with the task of attributing a plausible belief to Ann and then to Andy, children with even the most tenuous grasp on the interpretive nature of the knowing process could reasonably be expected to take advantage of their own previous "guesses" and to attribute these as legitimate false beliefs to the puppets. Of course, we would need to be convinced that these alternatives were actually available to the subject during the trial itself. Still, a simple posttest recall question ("What did you guess when I first showed you the picture?") could ensure that the alternative representations weren't somehow flushed from the participants' memory when their access to the full picture had proven their guesses "wrong." In a second study, we set out to test another group of 5- to 7-year-olds after making just these modifications to our earlier procedure.

Revisiting the Possibility of Being Wrong in More Than One Way: Study 2

A second sample of thirty 5-, 6-, and 7-year-olds was tested using the same stimulus materials employed in Study 1. Six droodles consisting of three conditions of two droodles each were presented, but here only one-window trials were used—that is, Andy and Ann always viewed the same restricted window onto any droodle. Trials 1 and 2 formed the *Standard Condition* in which participants were asked what first Ann and then Andy would "think" of the restricted view. Trials 3 and 4 formed the *Guess Condition,* which was in all other respects identical to the Standard Condition with the exception that the children were first shown the restricted view and asked to "guess what this is." Following one guess, they were told, "That's a good guess, guess again." Once two guesses had been made, participants were shown the unrestricted view before being asked about Andy and Ann's beliefs as in the Standard Condition. Trials 5 and 6 formed the *Recall Condition.* This trial pair was identical to the Guess Condition except that, at the end of each trial, the children were asked, "Remember when I first showed this to you this [restricted view], what was your first guess? What was your second guess?"

At issue was whether or not having children first guess at the contents of the droodle would serve to provide them with plausible alternative interpretations that could later be attributed to Andy and Ann. Of concern here are (a) whether or not participants' performance on the task in terms of false belief and interpretive understanding would be enhanced by this manipulation; (b) the extent to which their own alternative interpretations (i.e., guesses) would actually be used as attributions to Andy or Ann as false beliefs; and (c) whether, if these guesses were not utilized, we could be sure that they had been available during the trial (i.e., could the children later recall their guesses). Our efforts to address these questions begin with descriptive analyses of participants' understanding of false belief.

Attributions of False Belief

When submitted to the same scoring and coding criteria employed in Study 1, a similar pattern of findings emerges. Among the 5-year-old participants, all were able to attribute at least one false belief, with 48% of all responses classified as expressions of false belief. Among the 6-year-olds, 78% of responses were classified as false beliefs, with all but one subject providing at least one false belief response. All of the 7-year-olds provided at least one false belief with 92% of their responses classified as false belief. Using the same classification criteria employed in Study 1 resulted in the distribution of False Belief Understanding shown in Table 6.4.

As can be seen from an examination of Table 6.4, only one child consistently exhibited errors of intellectual realism and never attributed a false belief, about one-third of the participants (9) correctly made at least one such false belief attribution, and a full two-thirds of the children (20) attributed false beliefs at every opportunity. As was the case in Study 1, the False Belief Understanding

Table 6.4
False Belief Understanding: Status by Age Group (Study 2)

	False Belief Understanding Status		
Age Group[a]	Absent	Transitional	Present
5-year-olds	0	7	3
6-year-olds	1	2	7
7-year-olds	0	0	10
	1	9	20

[a]$n = 10$ for each group.

Table 6.5
Interpretive Theory of Mind: Status by Age Group (Study 2)

	Interpretive Theory of Mind Status		
Age Group[a]	Noninterpretive	Transitional	Consolidated
5-year-olds	6	4	0
6-year-olds	3	3	4
7-year-olds	0	2	8
	9	9	12

[a]$n = 10$ for each group.

Present participants were, on average, older (6.9 years) than those in the False Belief Understanding Transitional group (5.7 years), and the single False Belief Understanding Absent participant (6.5 years). Still, 97% of these children were able to attribute a false belief on at least one occasion.

Constructive Versus Copy Theories of Mind

Using the same criteria for Interpretive, Repetitive, and Mixed response pairs employed in Study 1, the 5-year-old participants in Study 2 managed to produce Interpretive response pairs on just 12% of the possible occasions afforded them. Nearly three-quarters of their response pairs (73%) were coded as Repetitive, and 15% as Mixed. The 6-year-olds produced 45% Interpretive, 43% Repetitive, and 12% Mixed response pairs. The 7-year-olds showed 78% Interpretive, 15% Repetitive, and 7% Mixed responses.

Applying the criteria used in Study 1 to classify individual children, 30% of the participants were classified as Noninterpretive Theory of Mind, 30% as Transitional, and 40% as Consolidated. The results by age group are shown in Table 6.5.

Comparing False Belief and Interpretive Theories of Mind

When, as before, the matrices of False Belief Understanding and Interpretive Theory of Mind are collapsed into a single contingency table, participants in Study 2 align themselves as shown in Table 6.6.

In this second study, all but 1 of the 30 participants could attribute a false belief to Ann, whereas only 21 of these same children attributed a different false belief to Andy. As before, when the cells in table 6.6 should be vacant by definition were eliminated, along with those housing participants whose performance was at ceiling or floor (i.e., the shaded cells of row 1 and column 3), a statistically reliable deviation from the chance placement of participants was found.

Finally, in comparison with the results of Study 1, the guessing manipulation did not enhance false belief performance nor result in reliably higher scores on measures of interpretive understanding.

Use and Recall of Guesses

When asked to provide two guesses in response to viewing the droodles, participants in Study 2 performed in much the same fashion as did children in the control group in Study 1: Children were able to provide two nontrivially different guesses as to the contents of the window on 114 of the 120 (95%) opportunities afforded them. The remaining 6 pairs included four repetitions of the first guess when asked for a second, and two failures—both on the part of a single child—to provide a second guess. During testing, subjects attributed these guesses as beliefs on just 39 of 240 possible occasions (16%) with nearly a third of these coming from just 2 participants (one 5-year-old and one 6-year-old). Finally, the children were able to correctly recall their guesses at the conclusion of 118 of the 120 trials (98%).

What these data suggest is that (1) children find the production and recall of

Table 6.6
Contingency Table of False Belief Understanding Status by Interpretive Theory of Mind Status (Study 2)

False Belief Understanding Status	Interpretive Theory of Mind Status			
	Noninterpretive	Transitional	Consolidated	
Absent	1	—	—	1
Transitional	7	3	—	10
Present	1	6	12	19
	9	9	12	30

such guesses a simple matter, and (2) only rarely do their guesses end up co-inciding with the beliefs they attribute to the puppets.

Justification of Beliefs

In addition to replicating our earlier findings, we also sought a more detailed understanding of how the children themselves viewed the task of attributing beliefs to the puppets. Toward this end, we asked the most competent of our participants (the 7-year-olds) a series of questions meant to prod them into justifying the beliefs they attributed to Andy and Ann. Following both Trial 5 and Trial 6, our 7-year-old participants were asked the following questions:

1. Why would Ann think it was a [belief attributed by child]?
2. Why would Andy think it was a [belief attributed by child]?
3. Why didn't they think the same thing?
4. One child said Andy and Ann would think the *same* thing, is that OK?
5. Would Ann or Andy know it was a [description of full view] from just seeing this [restricted view]?

When asked to justify or explain their attributions, all of the 7-year-old participants were quick to point out features of the droodle that might lead one to hold just the beliefs they had ascribed to the puppets. These off-the-cuff reconstructions of how Ann and Andy had been "led astray" were typically accompanied by gestures and narratives concerning the orientation and composition of the various "parts" of the imagined picture and routinely included allusions to those parts, which could be imagined to extend beyond the borders that framed the restricted view. Indeed, no participant was silenced by this question, and most had to be restrained from continuing their elaborations upon the puppets' supposed beliefs.

Having given what, in their own minds, must have seemed quite adequate explanations, most participants simply scoffed when asked why Ann and Andy had not come to the same interpretation of the droodle. When pressed, however, only two especially disappointed children retreated and claimed not to know. Most were able to revive their narratives and supply some sort of cogent answer. One child noted that, in her experience, Ann and Andy would never agree on anything. Another felt that Andy's mischievous nature had compelled him to listen to Ann's response and then "go her one better" by inventing a more fantastic interpretation. Four of the 10 participants made reference to the context and the ambiguity of the stimulus, claiming that there was no fault to be found in Andy and Ann's disagreement, since "that's just how they saw" the droodle at that particular moment and that their beliefs could easily have been otherwise or even reversed. Two children sought to resolve the differences between Andy's and Ann's interpretations by suggesting that although we might not know what had led them to their differing views, there are *always* reasons for such differences and that more detailed information about Andy and Ann would be required to determine what those reasons were. Finally, one particularly savvy child noted, "They're not a two-headed monster with the same brain! Do you think they both think the *same* thing *all* the time?"

Fully half of the subjects balked when told that "one child said Andy and Ann would think the same thing." A further 3 participants, though incredulous, agreed that while such a thing could conceivably occur, it was extremely unlikely. Though the remaining 2 participants acknowledged that it was indeed "OK" to think such things, it was apparent that they meant "permissible" rather than "plausible."

Finally, all of these 7-year-old participants emphatically denied that it would be possible for Andy or Ann to know what the contents of the larger picture would be given access only to the restricted view.

Discussion

The upshot of evidence just summarized is to go some important distance toward unseating all those more actively rehearsed "one miracle" views of children's tacit epistemologies by whose lights fledgling attempts at false belief understanding are somehow seen to be exactly the same thing as holding to an interpretive theory of mind. Instead, our own evidence serves to show that the emerging ability of young preschoolers to grasp the possibility of false beliefs is at best a necessary, but by no means sufficient condition for their being accorded any sort of constructive or interpretive view of the knowing process. Naturally enough, all such lines of evidence indicating that several steps are required to move children toward some fully adultlike conception of mental life are met with automatic suspicion by those concerned to reduce this developmental course to false belief understanding (carried to some power) plus simple practice. For almost everyone else, however, and especially for those who set out to reexamine classical accounts of the 5 to 7 year transition in children's development in light of recent research, data of the sort reviewed in this chapter can be seen to rescue the study of children's developing theories of mind from the unnecessarily narrow province of the preschool years and can be viewed as making a wider place for such studies not only during the 5 to 7 year transition period but well beyond into middle childhood and adolescence.

What is not settled, of course, by the still controversial findings presented here is whether the tentative insight, characteristic of some of our older participants, that two people can differently interpret one and the same stimulus event, is in fact equivalent to having come to that sort of more fully fledged constructivistic epistemology that dominates the ordinary folk psychology common to most adults. We think probably not. Such middle-school children might well reason, for example, that the fact that they and others do not always see eye to eye only tells us that some people have a perverse way of looking at things or habitually get things wrong—In other words, there is potentially a lot of light between first recognizing that people sometimes disagree about matters open to multiple interpretation and actually understanding that they can some-times *legitimately* disagree. In any case, the seemingly unavoidable conclusion that is forced by the evidence presented here is that the process by means of which children do move toward some reasonably mature conception of their own and other people's mental lives simply could not be, as some would have it, a process essentially completed in the preschool years. Instead, the classical 5 to 7 year shift that has occupied developmentalists for much of this century also appears to mark an important juncture in children's developing theories of mind. So, to the degree that the data presented here can be taken as a guide, it does appear to be the case that roughly within this classical transition period young people first evidence an understanding of the constructive or interpretive nature of the process of belief formation.

Notes

1. As a further way of getting a better grip on what Searle meant by all of this talk of "directions of fit" try imagining that a "world-to-mind" direction of fit comes close to what Piaget meant by assimilation, and a "mind-to-world" direction of fit is the rough equivalent of his notion of accommodation. Better yet, imagine that the mind is a shoe and the world is a foot. Shoe shoppers are naturally in search of mind-to-world directions of fit, by searching out that particular pair of shoes that best conform to their feet. Cinderella's prince, on the other hand, spends his time going about the country trying to find a foot to match up to a specific glass slipper left behind at the ball, and so is in search of a world-to-mind sort of fit.

2. The first of these studies was carried out with the help of Louis Moses.

References

Bartsch, K., & Wellman, H. (1989). Young children's attribution of action to beliefs and desires. *Child Development, 60,* 946–964.

Chandler, M. J., & Boyes, M. (1982). Social cognitive development. In B. Wollman (Ed.), *Handbook of developmental psychology* (pp. 387–402). Englewood Cliffs, NJ: Prentice-Hall.

Chandler, M. J., Fritz, A. S., & Hala, S. (1989). Small scale deceit: Deception as a marker of 2-, 3- and 4-year-olds's theories of mind. *Child Development, 60,* 1263–1277.

Chandler, M. J., & Helm, D. (1984). Developmental changes in the contribution of shared experience to social role-taking competence. *International Journal of Behavioural Development, 7,* 145–156.

Flavell, J. H. (1978). The development of knowledge about visual perception. In C. B. Keasey (Ed.), *Nebraska symposium on motivation* (Vol. 25, pp. 43–76). Lincoln: University of Nebraska Press.

Flavell, J. H. (1988). The development of children's knowledge about the mind: From cognitive connections to mental representations. In J. Astington, P. Harris, & D. Olson (Eds.), *Developing theories of mind* (pp. 244–267). New York: Cambridge University Press.

Flavell, J. H., Everett, B. A., Croft, K., & Flavell, E. R. (1981). Young children's knowledge about visual perception: Further evidence for the Level 1–Level 2 distinction. *Developmental Psychology, 17,* 99–103.

Freeman, N. H., Lewis, C., & Doherty, M. J. (1991). Preschoolers' grasp of a desire for knowledge in false-belief prediction: Practical intelligence and verbal report. *British Journal of Developmental Psychology, 9*(1), 139–157.

Fritz, A. S. (1991, April). *Is there a reality bias in young children's emergent theories of mind?* Paper presented at the biennial meeting of the Society for Research in Child Development, Seattle, WA.

Gopnik, A., & Astington, J. W. (1988). Children's understanding of representational change and its relation to the understanding of false belief and the appearance-reality distinction. *Child Development, 59,* 26–37.

Hala, S. (1991, April). *The role of personal involvement in facilitating false belief understanding.* Paper presented at the biennial meeting of the Society for Research in Child Development, Seattle, WA.

Hala, S. (1994). *The role of personal involvement in accessing false-belief understanding.* Unpublished doctoral dissertation, University of British Columbia, Vancouver.

Hala, S., Chandler, M., & Fritz, A. (1991). Fledgling theories of mind: Deception as a marker of 3-year-old's understanding of false belief. *Child Development, 62,* 83–97.

Lewis, C., & Osborne, A. (1990). Three-year-olds' problems with false belief: Conceptual deficit or linguistic artifact? *Child Development, 61,* 1514–1519.

Mitchell, P., Lacohee, H. (1991). Children's early understanding of false belief. *Cognition, 39,* 107–127.

Moses, L. (1993). Young children's understanding of belief constraints on intention. *Cognitive Development, 8,* 1–25.

Moses, L., & Chandler, M. J. (1992). Traveler's guide to children's theories of mind. *Psychological Inquiry, 1,* 286–301.

Perner, J. (1991). *Understanding the representational mind.* Cambridge, MA: MIT Press.

Perner, J., & Davies, G. (1991). Understanding the mind as an active information processor: Do young children have a "copy theory of mind"? *Cognition, 39,* 51–69.

Pillow, B. (1991). Children's understanding of biased social cognition. *Developmental Psychology, 27,* 539–551.

Pillow, B. (1993, March). *Children's understanding of biased interpretation.* Poster session presented at the biennial meeting of the Society for Research in Child Development, New Orleans, LA.

Price, R. (1953). *Droodles.* New York: Simon & Schuster.

Robinson, E., Mitchell, P., & Nye, R. (1992, September). *Children's understanding of indirect sources of knowledge.* Paper presented at the annual meeting of the British Psychological Society, Edinburgh, Scotland.

Searle, J. R. (1983). *Intentionality: An essay in the philosophy of mind.* New York: Cambridge University Press.

Siegal, M., & Beattie, K. (1990). Where to look first for children's knowledge of false beliefs. *Cognition, 38,* 1–12.

Stevenson, E., & Mitchell, P. (1992, September). *The suggestibility of false belief.* Paper presented at the annual meeting of the British Psychological Society, Edinburgh, Scotland.

Taylor, M. (1988). The development of children's ability to distinguish what they know from what they see. *Child Development, 59,* 703–718.

Wellman, H., & Banerjee, M. (1991). Mind and emotion: Children's understanding of the emotional consequences of beliefs and desires. *British Journal of Developmental Psychology, 9,* 191–214.

Wimmer, H., & Perner, J. (1983). Beliefs about beliefs: Representation and constraining of wrong beliefs in young children's understanding of deception. *Cognition, 13,* 103–128.

Winner, E., & Sullivan, K. (1993, March). *Young 3-year-olds' understand false belief when observing or participating in deception.* Poster session presented at the biennial meeting of the Society for Research in Child Development, New Orleans, LA.

Zaitchik, D. (1991). Is only seeing really believing?: Sources of the true belief in the false belief task. *Cognitive Development, 6,* 91–103.

CHAPTER SEVEN

Memory Development from 4 to 7 Years

KATHERINE NELSON

Sheldon White's 1965 survey of cognitive development focused attention on learning processes and changes therein during the critical years from 5 to 7, and his speculation about the explanation for the shifts in performance resonates in an interesting way today. However, strikingly missing from his documentation was the topic of memory, a topic that subsequently became a major focus of studies in cognitive development.

Memory became important in developmental research primarily because of its emerging general importance in experimental psychology subsequent to what has become known as the "cognitive revolution" of the early 1960s and the development of information-processing models of cognition. Research that had been devoted to verbal learning was transformed in this period into studies of memory.

A general assumption of information-processing models is the existence of a long-term memory store wherein items are organized and made accessible to later recall. Following Tulving's (1972) distinction, long-term memory for general knowledge came usually to be referred to as *semantic memory* and memory for specific items in a specific context as *episodic memory*. Despite many disputes over specific assumptions and terminology, this general model and these terms have been accepted in memory studies of both children and adults for the past two decades and more, and these terms are employed here initially more or less as Tulving defined them (with some later modifications), although the general model from the 1960s does not constrain the discussion.

Peculiarly, neither White's initial survey nor the vast majority of succeeding studies of memory development took notice of the most striking shift in memory in childhood, the release from infantile amnesia—or its inverse, the onset of autobiographical memory—which takes place somewhere between 3 and 8 years for most people. Not much later, however, White and his colleague David

Pillemer (1979) reviewed the evidence for this shift and the theories that had been put forth to explain it. And recently this phenomenon has received more attention from developmental psychologists, although it has yet to enter importantly into the mainstream of cognitive developmental theory. The argument presented here is that understanding this development is critical to our theories and that this shift can shed light not only on memory development but on cognitive development in general in the transition from preschool to the school years.

The chapter proceeds as follows. The first section provides a cursory overview of memory development research in early to middle childhood carried out in the years following White's survey. The emphasis is on the assumptions and conclusions of this research. This summary does not—and could not possibly in the space available—constitute a review of the literature. That task was excellently carried out by Brown, Bransford, Ferrara, and Campione (1983), and additional surveys and theoretical reviews are available (Chi, 1983; Kail & Hagen, 1977; Ornstein, 1978; Weinert & Perlmutter, 1988). The second section is a focused discussion of memory for real-life events and the onset of autobiographical memory in early to middle childhood. This section relates memory to issues of cognitive development, socialization, and language skill. The last two sections set these strands of research and theorizing into the framework of a functional model of development and explore the possibility of a fundamental shift between 4 and 7 years that integrates memory, cognition, and language.

Issues in Memory Development 1965–90

The major paradigm for studying human memory—in adults and children—in the founding years of the cognitive era (post-1960) was that of word list recall. This paradigm was inherited from the earlier period of verbal learning and verbal behavior (as represented in research in *The Journal of Verbal Learning and Verbal Behavior,* later renamed *Memory and Language*). Inherited as well were many well-established findings from that period. For example, words that are high associates are likely to be recalled together, and words from the same semantic category are likely to cluster together in recall. Although information-processing models contained different memory stores (short-term, long-term) in the sequence of processing, memory was basically considered a unitary faculty or resource, an assumption that was reflected in all the research throughout the period. From this perspective children had either good or poor memory; preschoolers in particular were viewed as memory deficient in general. The first studies within this common framework might thus be characterized as Deficiency Studies: Younger children were found to be deficient in memory performance when compared with older children and adults. Thus, if a shift could be observed in the period from 5 to 7 years, it would be—and was—characterized as one from incompetence to competence.

Younger Children Are Incompetent

The free recall paradigm was widely used with schoolchildren and was tried with preschool children as well. A major outcome of the latter studies was that young children had very limited memory capacities in comparison with older children. For example, given a list of 8 to 10 words to recall immediately after presentation, a 3-year-old might recall 2, and a 5-year-old 4 or 5 words. Such results were mirrored as well in the digit span test that is a standard feature of IQ tests. It was easy to conclude that young children have poor memory *because* their short-term-memory (STM) space is very limited. However, the development of STM span appeared to be continuous across the age span from 3 to 12 years without dramatic shifts (Chi, 1977). Thus it could not in itself explain any discontinuous quantitative or qualitative changes in memory if such existed.

One recurrent observation in the early literature was that young children, in comparison with older children and adults, did not show the same clustering effect in recall of lists that contained words from different semantic categories. Nor did they appear to impose any subjective organization on lists repeated over trials, as adults did (Nelson, 1969). Thus it seemed that organizational factors would explain some of the deficiencies in younger children's recall performance. But this left open the questions of whether children lacked categorical knowledge (and so did not recognize the organizational potential in categorized lists) or lacked strategies that would enable them to take advantage of the potential. More recent studies of the effect of the knowledge base on memory (e.g., Bjorklund, 1985) and of memory strategies have suggested a complex interaction of these factors. In the sections that follow, these factors are considered in terms of their sequential emergence as matters of concern, beginning with issues of strategies and metamemory.

A major effort in the early period discussed here was to determine when and under what circumstances children might engage in strategic memory processing. Rehearsal was the primary strategy studied by Flavell and his students, who showed that only in the early school years did children begin to engage in deliberate rehearsal of lists (Flavell, Beach, & Chinsky, 1966; Flavell, Friedrichs, & Hoyt, 1970). This observation seemed to imply that younger children did not engage in voluntary, but only in involuntary, memory processing. In addition to the free recall studies, tests of recognition memory—presumably nondeliberate or involuntary—in both American laboratories and in Piaget's work indicated that recognition of previously seen material was robust in infancy and early childhood, whereas recall was fragile at best (Piaget & Inhelder, 1973).

As discussant in a symposium at the 1971 Society for Research in Child Development (SRCD) meeting, Flavell addressed the question "What is memory development the development of?" He concluded that memory development from the preschool to the school years essentially might consist of the child's deliberate attempts to engage in memory for its own sake, thus beginning to manipulate memory strategies. This idea, first proposed at the 1971 meeting, became known as *metamemory*, the conscious awareness of memory as a process and the deliberate manipulation of strategies for accomplishing memory tasks. The construct of metamemory seemed to cover the results from the studies of organization, strategies, voluntary memory, and recognition memory under one neat umbrella. (See Brown et al., 1983, and Wellman, 1983, for review and discussion of metamemory.)

The idea of metamemory raised the question of its origin, and an obvious suggestion was that children became aware of, and began to engage in, metamemory processing as they entered the school years when memory for school material became a valued product. However, training studies revealed that, although the use of strategies by young children could be improved through training, these beneficial effects did not typically last beyond the test period. If all that was needed was an awareness of metamemory strategies, children should have adapted and used them as their own after training, but they did not (Brown et al., 1983). Thus it appeared that the emergence of metamemory skills might indicate something deep about cognitive development, not simply the shallow effects of learning or the motivation instilled by schooling.

Younger Children Are Competent

A notable advance in understanding the foundation of memory skills from which more sophisticated skills might evolve during the school years took place within a number of research groups in the 1970s, all involving naturalistic studies of memory in preschoolers. The general idea behind these moves was the recognition that the tasks previously used tended to evaluate younger children by the standards applied to older children and adults. By these standards preschoolers were inevitably judged deficient. Researchers began to recognize that such tasks might not be tapping abilities simply because younger children did not understand the task demands in the same way, did not have the same knowledge, or were not motivated to perform as older children were. Different paradigms calling on knowledge accessible to young children and specifically designed to be understandable and motivating to them might reveal abilities that had been missed by the standard laboratory tasks. This was the foundation for a new approach to memory emphasizing the competence rather than the deficiencies of younger children (reflecting as well a general research shift in studies of cognitive development).

INFANT MEMORY

Beginning in the 1960s researchers interested in infant perception and attention began to investigate infant memory as well. Studies soon confirmed that infants retained information about specific stimuli (e.g., faces) over extended periods of time, but by the nature of the evidence the claim was restricted only to recognition memory. Recall in infancy has been difficult to assess because of the lack of viable measures in prelinguistic infants (and, more generally, non-linguistic animals). However, Mandler (1984, 1988) has reviewed the evidence for recall and representation in the first year of life and has theorized that such memorial systems are intact from very early if not from birth. In contrast, Schacter and Moscovitch (1984) argued that there is a shift from an early memory system (common to lower animals and not lost in certain forms of amnesia) to a later memory system, which explicitly accesses new learning. These suggestions are important in building a complete model of the human memory system. However, it should be noted that all theorists now appear to agree that *basic* memory processes—including recall as well as recognition—are present in the human by 1 year of age and are not delayed in development as Piaget originally suggested. Thus the disparate views of competence in infancy are not relevant to the question of changes from early to middle childhood, the transition at issue here.

MEMORY IN THE PRESCHOOL YEARS

As suggested previously, the major new move in studying memory in the preschool years was to view memory in its natural ecological niche. Studies of this kind were first demonstrated in Soviet laboratories, although their results were not widely circulated in the United States until the 1970s (Istomina, 1975). In a classic study (replicated in part by Rogoff, 1990), Istomina demonstrated that when preschoolers were motivated to remember items on a list by appropriate goal-orientation, their performance greatly improved. In particular, her studies contrasted children's requirement to remember items in a school context with their memory for a list of items to buy at the store in order to prepare lunch. This situation presents not only a familiar understandable goal with social consequences but also a familiar, well-structured routine and knowledge of familiar items, all important aspects of memory in natural settings. Significant American studies from this period focusing on these variables include those by Myers and Perlmutter (1978), Wellman and Somerville (1980), and Brown and DeLoache (1978).

During the 1970s and 1980s my colleagues and I investigated the event knowledge base of preschool children and its effects on specific episodic memory (see Nelson, Fivush, Hudson, & Lucariello, 1983, and Nelson, 1986, for summaries of the research). We found that children's knowledge base could be described in terms of scripts for familiar events. The script construct was borrowed from work in artificial intelligence on story understanding by Schank and Abelson (1977). We established that preschool children could give reasonably accurate reports of familiar events, including the people and items that belonged within them, and the appropriate sequence of actions oriented toward goals; such accounts could be viewed as skeletal scripts for familiar events. We also found that script knowledge was reflected in the organization and content of young children's episodic memory, for example, for stories and lists of items to recall. Script organization and content were also apparent in children's memories of their own real-life episodes (Nelson, 1978, 1986; Nelson & Gruendel, 1981).

These studies, together with those from other laboratories, converged on the conclusion that the memory abilities of preschool children had been severely underestimated in earlier work. Under appropriate conditions (e.g., interest in materials, familiarity of context, understandable goals) very young children could remember both specific and general information about scenes, events, stories, and items presented for remembering.

Studies of early memory for personally experienced events soon became increasingly recognized as important with respect to their implications for applied issues and particularly for the case of child witnesses. The question of whether children can be relied on for accurate testimony in cases of child abuse or in other legal cases is an obviously important one. Many studies of the memory of very young children for real events, or for simulation of stressful events, have been developed from this perspective (e.g., Goodman, Rudy, Bottoms, & Aman, 1990). These studies have provided important extensions of the general finding that very young children are generally accurate in what they remember, although they may not remember as much as, or focus on the same things as, do older children. And the effect of factors involved in sexual abuse, for example, are still not well understood and cannot be easily generalized from normative studies.

But Not as Competent as Older Children . . .

Several lines of research emerged over the past 15 years or so that require modification of the conclusions of memory competence in early childhood. One important emphasis has been effects of knowledge on memory. Earlier work on memory, including development of memory strategies, organization, and metamemory, assumed a more or less content-independent faculty. The characteristics of a memory system would be expected to be exhibited regardless of content and, by implication, regardless of other characteristics of the person, such as knowledge about the to-be-remembered material. This assumption was long-standing, deriving initially from Ebbinghaus's experiments and the verbal learning paradigms that used nonsense syllables to control for content (meaning) effects. On this assumption a child could be assumed to be characterized as a memory strategist or as having metamemory ability or as capable of organizing material in a particular way, for example, according to semantic category, regardless of what the material might be.

These assumptions were implicitly challenged in the 1970s. Studies of individual differences in memory within particular domains of expertise (e.g., Chi, 1978; Simon, 1972) indicated that background knowledge, in particular the degree and organization of such knowledge, would determine how items in a specific task would be remembered and how they would be organized for retention. A prime example of the effects of the knowledge base comes from Chi's work, demonstrating how complex relationships in the network of dinosaur knowledge in a young child were reflected in his memory for specific dinosaurs in a recall task (Chi & Koeske, 1983). Chi (1978) also demonstrated the differential effects of knowledge in a comparison of child expert and adult novice on memory for chess positions. The so-called novice-expert shift in knowledge acquisition introduced in these works seems to suggest that many apparently developmental changes in memory capacity or ability are actually effects of increased knowledge. This suggestion must be qualified by consideration of how knowledge is organized and reorganized in development (Bjorklund, 1985; Lucariello, Kyratzis, & Nelson, 1992). A specific case in point is knowledge of one's own life experiences, organized in adults as autobiographical memory.

Autobiographical Memory

The studies that were referred to in the "Younger Children Are Competent" section revealed that young children could remember objects, locations, and events in experimental tasks when they had the knowledge and motivation to do so. Of particular interest are those life experiences that the child might be expected to remember as significant. Children apparently retain specific episodic memories of this kind from a very young age. (Fivush, Gray & Fromhoff, 1987; reviews of this research from a number of different laboratories can be found in Fivush and Hudson, 1990.) Yet we know that autobiographical memory—enduring chronologically sequenced memory for significant events from one's own life—has its onset only during the later preschool years. The puzzle then is why this particular deficiency exists. Is there anything in the memory development literature—or in other developmental studies—that could shed light on this question?

Surprisingly, it is only recently that this onset has been thought of in developmental terms. In the past it has usually been conceived of in terms of childhood (or infantile) amnesia, the phenomenon, first identified by Freud (1938/1905) and familiar to all who reflect on it, that memories for events from the early years of our lives—before about 3 to 4 years—are not available to adult consciousness, although many memories from later childhood usually are easily called up.

The onset of autobiographical memory is simply the inverse of infantile (or childhood) amnesia. Most of the research on childhood amnesia—the later inaccessibility of memories from the period of life before the onset of autobiographical memory—has come from studies of adults' recall of childhood memories, beginning with a questionnaire study by Henri and Henri in 1897 (see review by Dudycha & Dudycha, 1941). As in many studies that followed this one, the Henris asked adults to recall their earliest memories from childhood. Summarizing a large number of such studies, Pillemer and White (1989) found that the earliest memory is reported on average at about 3½ years. Pillemer and White noted that there are actually two phases of childhood amnesia, the first a total blocking of memories, usually prior to about 3 years, and the second a significant lack of many accessible memories relative to later memories between 3 and 6 years. Such a pattern has been verified by the analysis of the forgetting curve for adult recall of childhood memories (Wetzler & Sweeney, 1986). However, it is also important to note that there is considerable individual variability both in age of earliest memory—from 2 years to 8 years or even later—and in number of memories reported from early childhood. In the early empirical literature on the topic, the age of earliest memory has been negatively correlated with IQ, language ability, and social class, and females tend to have earlier memories than males.

Early studies from our laboratory of children's generic and specific memories suggested an explanation for infantile amnesia, namely, that children do not preserve episodic memories, although they may remember bits of information from specific events in their schematic event memory. In early childhood, we believed, all information retained from experience is absorbed by the generic memory system. (Recently, Gopnik & Graf, 1988, and Perner, 1991, have suggested similar "over-write" mechanisms.)

However, this hypothesis—that young children have generic memory only—has not stood up to empirical test. As the previous section indicated, subsequent research found that very young children do remember novel events, within limits, and sometimes quite readily report episodes that they find interesting (Hudson, 1986; Ratner, 1980). When asked about routine events, they simply give routine (scriptlike) answers, but when asked about novel events, children as young as 2 or 2½ years are sometimes able to respond with details. More recent research has verified that children do have specific episodic memories and can remember them for extensive periods—sometimes as long as two years—prior to the age of the earliest autobiographical memories reported by adults (see Fivush & Hudson, 1990, for reviews). Why do these memories not then persist into later childhood and adulthood?

Not only does the research that indicates that children have episodic memories prior to the age of 3 years invalidate the proposal that memory is at first completely generic, but it calls into question some other theoretical proposals as well. For example, there is nothing in this recent evidence to support the idea that young children's memories are especially threatening or either positively or negatively affect laden as Freud's theory would suggest. Nor do they appear to be more banal as his idea of screen memories (i.e., benign memories transformed from the anxiety-producing originals) predicts. A full range of affective states is found reflected in memories from early childhood.

Schachtel (1947) and Neisser (1962) suggested that autobiographical memories are the outcome of a reconstructive process based on schemas or frames of reference, along the lines suggested by Bartlett (1932). Remembering then involves *reconstructing* past events using presently existing schemas, and the claim is that adult schemas are not "suitable receptacles" for early childhood experience; "adults cannot think like children" and thus cannot make use of whatever fragments of memories they may retain. In this view, socialization and the impact of adult linguistic frames of reference force a drastic change in the child's schemas at age 6.

The recent developmental data cast doubt on this proposal as well. Although very young children often need extensive probing to elicit their memories, suggesting that they may retain only random and unschematized fragments, there is also evidence of specific episodic memories that have the same form as we might find in older children. A fragment from a 2½-year-old girl (Emily) talking to herself when alone in her room is illustrative:

> We *bought* a baby, cause, the well because, when she, well, we *thought* it was for Christmas, but *when* we went to the s-s-store we didn't have our jacket on, but I saw some dolly, and I *yelled* at my mother and said I want one of those dolly. So after we were finished with the store, we went over to the dolly and she *bought* me one. So I have one.

In this example, Emily was recounting to herself what apparently was a significant episode in her life; she had not rehearsed this recent episode with her parents or others (see Nelson, 1989a, for details). This recount is well organized with clear and concise temporal and causal sequencing. It—and others like it—do not suggest that the preschool child's schemas are dramatically different from those of the older child and adult.

Indeed, reports of young children's free recall of salient episodic memories gathered by recent investigators (e.g., Engel, 1986; Hudson, 1990; Tessler, 1986) support the conclusion that the basic ways of structuring, representing, and interpreting reality are consistent from early childhood into adulthood. Young children typically tell their experience-based stories in a sequence that accurately reflects the sequence of the experience itself and that has the same boundaries that seem natural to adult listeners (Nelson, 1986, 1989a).

Of course there may be other differences between adult and child memories, including what is noticed and remembered of an event. The extensive cuing and probing often required to elicit details from a young child suggest that adult and child may have different memories of the same event. An analysis of the *content* of crib talk (talk to self alone before sleep) by the child Emily, recorded from 21 to 36 months, supports the suggestion that adult and child may focus on different events and different aspects of events. Emily's memories were mostly concerned with the quotidian, unremarkable, routines of her life. They were not concerned with the truly novel events of her life (from the adult's point of view), such as the birth of her baby brother or her airplane trips to visit relatives (Nelson, 1989a). Children often appear to be interested in—and therefore retain memory for—aspects of experience that seem unremarkable to adults and to be indifferent to what adults find interesting. In addition, their lack of facility with language and relatively undeveloped knowledge base differentiate them from older children and adults. These may all account for why young children may sometimes seem to have organized their knowledge in a form different from, or have remembered only fragments from, an episode that the adult considers memorable.

In summary, recent research on episodic memory in early childhood indicates that children have at least some well-organized specific and general event memories, similar to those of adults; thus the suggestion that a schematic reorganization may account for infantile amnesia is not supported. However, recent research indicating that children *learn to talk* about their past experiences in specific ways does provide some clues as to what may develop and how.

Social Influences on Personal Memory

Over the past decade a number of researchers have studied the ways in which parents engage in talking about the past with their very young children. These studies, some focused on the specific language forms used, others on the content of talk, and still others on narrative forms and differences in communicative styles, have revealed the active role that parents play in framing and guiding their children's formulation of "what happened." Hudson (1990) concluded from a study of her own daughter's memory talk between 21 and 27 months that eventually Rachel began to "interpret the conversations not as a series of questions to be answered but as an *activity of remembering*" (p. 183).

Hudson has endorsed a *social interaction model* of the development of autobiographical memory, a model that Pillemer and White (1989) and Fivush and
Reese (1991) have also invoked. In this view, children gradually learn the
forms of how to talk about memories with others and thereby also how to formulate their own memories as narratives. The social interaction model differs
from the schematic change model put forth by Schachtel (1947) and by Neisser
(1962), noted previously, in that it claims that children learn how to formulate
their memories—assumed to exist in schematic form—as narratives for themselves and others. This format enables their retention for later recovery.

     Several studies have found that parents not only engage in memory talk with
young children, verifying the hypothesized influence of input, but also differ
among themselves in the number of memory-relevant questions they ask, in the
kind of memory they attempt to elicit, and in the ways in which they frame the
talk. Engel (1986) studied mother-child conversations about past episodes with
children from 18 months to 2 years and identified two styles of mother talk,
one described as *elaborative,* the other as *pragmatic.* The elaborative mothers
tended to talk about episodes in narrative terms of what happened when, where,
and with whom. Pragmatic mothers referred to memory primarily in instrumental terms, such as "Where did you put your mittens?" For pragmatic
mothers, memory is useful for retrieving information relevant to ongoing activities. For elaborative mothers, memory provides the basis for storytelling,
constructing narratives about what mother and child did together in the there
and then. Engel found that children of elaborating mothers contributed more
information to the memory talk at 2 years than did children of pragmatic
mothers.

     Tessler (1986, 1991) studied the effect of adult talk *during* an experience on
children's subsequent memory for the experience in two naturalistically framed
experiments. She found differences in mother's style of interaction similar to
those identified by Engel and found that children of narrative (or elaborative)
mothers remembered more from a trip to a natural history museum a week
later, when probed with a standard set of questions, than did the children of
pragmatic-type mothers. Most striking was the finding that none of the children
remembered any of the objects they had viewed in the museum if they had not
talked about them together with their mothers. In a second study Tessler found
that among children experiencing different types of interaction with mothers
during an event there were no differences in *recognizing* elements of the experience, but there were differences in the *amount of information recalled* from
the experience, with the children of narrative mothers recalling significantly
more. Again, things that were not talked about were not recalled. These findings indicated not only that talk about the past is effective in aiding the child to
establish a narrative memory about the past but also that talk *during a present
activity* serves a similar purpose. In both cases, adults who present the activity

in a narrative format, in contrast to a focus on identification and categorization, appear to be more effective in establishing and eliciting memories with their young children. It may be hypothesized, in line with the social-interaction proposal, that specific narrativizing experiences are important in establishing an autobiographical memory system.

Thus there is evidence that the onset of autobiographical memory may be related to the child's experience in talking with others about shared memories. This is one important consequence—among many—of becoming a language user. In this case the consequence results from the opportunity to engage in dialogue with other people about events and to formulate one's memories in the format that is conventional within one's culture. But here a deeper question arises as to why dialogic sharing should have an effect on memory, and particularly on autobiographical memory, which is quintessentially memory for oneself.

Making Sense of It All: A Functional Approach

At this point it may be possible to construct an integrated picture of the development of memory in early childhood and the establishment of an autobiographical memory system (see Nelson 1993a, 1993b for details). The proposal rests on the assumption that the basic episodic memory system is part of a general mammalian learning-memory adaptive function for guiding present action and predicting future outcomes. Memory is considered here as a function of the cognitive system, rather than a modular faculty or a specific skill. Basic memory in humans, as in other animals, is private, a result of individual experience. But as Oakley (1983) has proposed, learning and memory in humans have become augmented and their potential projected explosively through language and external symbolic media, especially writing. By such means memory in humans is no longer private and individual, but social and shared (see also Donald, 1991, for an extensive treatment of human cognitive development in these terms).

From the perspective of a basic individual memory system, the most functional memory is generic memory for routines that fit recurrent situations, that is, a general event schema (or script) memory system. The generic memory system might contain alternative possibilities for what to expect in a particular type of event, based on variation in previous experiences, but these variations would not be embedded in specific memories of the phenomenal kind that seems to present a specific past episode, or even a part of such an episode, for reexperiencing in mental life. Memories for specific episodes presumably become part of the generic system when a new situation is encountered, and thus it becomes apparent that a new schema must be established. A new experience alerts the organism (person, animal) to set up a new schema, which at first may be equivalent to an episodic memory but with further experience with events of the same kind comes to be more and more scriptlike. Indeed, research on novel and repeated events with preschool children found that this was precisely what happened (Hudson & Nelson, 1986). The more frequently an event (such as going to the beach or the zoo) had been experienced, the more scriptlike the child's account became. Children tended to formulate events experienced five or more times in general present-tense terms and to confuse slot-fillers (e.g., animals seen) for different episodes of the event. Linton (1982), based on the analysis of her own memories of life events tracked over many years, described a similar process in adults, a movement from episodic memory to script as similar experiences were encountered. (See Brainerd and Reyna [1990] for an account that has some similarities to the present one but that differs in its conclusions.)

This general scheme leaves us with a problem, however: How is the basic memory system to know whether a novel event is the first of a recurrent series of events that should therefore be remembered (i.e., schematized for future reference) or whether it is an aberration that is of no functional significance? (Of course, if the aberration is life threatening, it is likely to be entered into the general memory/knowledge system as important information for that reason alone.) The point is that the system cannot know on the basis of one encounter what significance the event might have with respect to future encounters.

A reasonable solution for a limited memory system is either to integrate the new information as part of the generic system or to keep the novel memory in a separate, temporary, episodic memory for a given amount of time to determine if it is the first of a series of recurrent events and thus should become part of the generic system. Then if the event reoccurs, the memory may be transferred to the more permanent generic memory system. If a similar event does not recur during that test period, the episode is dropped from memory as of no adaptive significance. In the basic functionally based system being described here, all memory is either generic knowledge—scriptlike—or *temporarily* episodic. The basic episodic system is claimed to be a *holding pattern,* not a permanent memory system. My hypothesis is that this basic system characterizes human infants and young children, and probably also our close primate relatives, and perhaps other mammals.

The persistence of some memories from this early period for as long as 2 years is somewhat puzzling on this account. However, a factor that has been found effective in extending the retention of memory in infants and infrahuman mammals is that of reinstatement, or reactivation through exposure to some aspect of the remembered event before the expiration of the usual retention interval (Rovee-Collier & Hayne, 1987). This effect has been explored with preschool children by Fivush and Hamond (1989) and by Hudson (1991) with similar effects of extension. Such reexposure could be expected to possibly double the period over which a memory for an episode was retained in the temporary episodic store.

Thus far then, the proposed system can account for the good generic event memory found in early childhood, as well as the availability of episodic memories that may persist for 6 months (or longer if there are conditions of reinstatement). But it does not account for the establishment of an autobiographical memory system in which some specific memories may persist for a lifetime. This raises the question as to what *function* the autobiographical system serves beyond that of the long-lasting generic plus temporary episodic system just described, which serves basic functions of preserving individual experience in an efficient form.

The claim here is that the initial functional significance of autobiographical memory is that of sharing memory with others, a function that facility with language makes possible. Memories become valued in their own right—not because they predict the future and guide present action, but because they are shareable with others and thus serve a social solidarity function. Using language to retain memories, stories, and myths within the group is a universal human function, although one with variable culturally specific rules. In this respect it is analogous to human language itself, uniquely and universally human but culturally—and individually—variable. I suggest further that this social function of memory underlies all of our storytelling, history-making narrative activities and thus, ultimately, all of our accumulated knowledge systems. Sharing memories (and stories) in the preschool years is but a first step toward the augmentation of memory in human lives that language—and later permanent written records—make possible.

The research briefly reviewed[1] here supports these speculations. First, children learn to engage in talk about the past, guided at first by parents who construct a narrative around the bits and pieces contributed by the child (Eisenberg, 1985; Engel, 1986; Hudson, 1990). The timing of this learning (beginning at about 2½ years and continuing through the preschool years) is consistent with the age at which autobiographical memory begins to emerge. The fact that the adult data suggest a two-phase process, as noted earlier, covering the absence of memories in the first 2 to 3 years, followed by a sparse but increasing number of memories in the later preschool years, supports the supposition that the establishment of these memories is related to the experience of talking to others about them. Also, the variability in age of onset of autobiographical memory (from 2 to 8 years or later) and its relation to language facility are consistent with the idea that children's experiences in sharing memories of the right kind and to the right degree contribute to the establishment of autobiographical memory (Nelson, 1989b).

The social-interaction hypothesis outlined earlier clearly fits these data well. This proposal is not simply one of cultural transmission or socialization, but rather a dialectical or Vygotskian model in which the child takes over the forms of adult thought through transactions with adults in activity contexts where those forms are employed, in this case in the activities where memories are formed and shared. The problem that the child faces in taking on new forms and functions is to coordinate earlier memory functions with those that the adult displays, incorporating adult values about what is important to remember and the narrative formats for remembering into her or his own existing functional system.

In summary, the theoretical claim here is that language opens up possibilities for sharing and retaining memories in a culturally defined format for both personal and social functions. Following Vygotsky's (1978) model of internalization, after overt recounting becomes established, covert recounting or re-experiencing to oneself may take place and thus provide the conditions for establishing an autobiographical memory system. According to this line of reasoning, the dramatic change from infantile amnesia to a life history in memory results from the child's emerging ability to use language in extended forms of discourse in exchanging "stories" with others and thus acquiring the narrative forms that characterize enduring memories.

What Develops from 4 to 7 years?

If this account is somewhere near correct, it suggests that changes in memory functioning over the years from 4 to 7 result from new functions of language and from cognitive processes that facility with language makes possible. Can this proposal be generalized to other aspects of memory improvement over these years? I consider briefly in this section two aspects that were noted in the earlier part of this chapter: changes in knowledge organization and metamemory.

It is obvious that language makes possible the acquisition of much cultural knowledge ("folk" as well as science) that is otherwise closed off from the individual (Nelson, 1991, 1996). Among the cultural knowledge structures that have been extensively studied are taxonomic hierarchical categories. These, in fact, have entered directly into theories of memory development through the use of lists of categorized words presented to children for recall. A strong case can be made that understanding the structure of such categories requires a level of manipulation of abstract language forms that is achieved only in the early school years. Preschool children's knowledge is organized, and some understanding of category organization is present, but complex taxonomies are structures characteristic of school knowledge and tend to be learned through school instruction. Thus it seems almost trivial to claim that knowledge effects of this kind on memory are the result of increased language understanding and use of language in cognitive tasks.

Metamemory is a kind of reflective process, turning back on one's own schemas, to use Piaget's terms. Reflective processes have been projected by a number of theorists in recent years as emerging at about age 4 (Campbell & Bickhard, 1986; Case, 1992; Karmiloff-Smith, 1986; Perner, 1991). From a Vygotskian perspective this emergence would not be mysterious. Reflection on one's own thinking becomes possible as the child becomes receptive to the comments of others. As adults provide guidance in thinking, planning, talking, and acting, children first use that external guidance provided through the linguistic medium to reflect on their thought and action and, then, through the reciprocal process, use their own language to reflect on their own thought and action. For Vygotsky the role of language in this process was not at all mysterious, but in fact obvious.

Thus the speculations here regarding changes in memory function are in line with the proposal that a new level of thinking emerges toward the end of the preschool years as the child's language matures to the point where language itself can be used as a tool of thinking. Prior to this point language has been used as a mode of communication and to some extent as a means of cognitive organization. By 4 or 5 years, however, language can be used as a system that enables reflection on and manipulation of thought and action that is not in the immediate present. One of the effects of this new capacity is to enable the child to bring to mind and to reexperience events from the past, thus establishing the autobiographical system. Eventually, the child will be able to analyze and re-organize this material for other purposes. The point is that changes in memory function at this age are simply reflections of a general cognitive change that results from the emerging possibility of using language as a cognitive tool. It is important to consider, I think, how many of the changes that take place during the transition period may be traced to the same functional cause.

Note

1. This review was completed in 1992. It has not been possible to update it to take into account subsequent findings, but the general conclusions remain unchanged. See Nelson (1996) for further discussion of the issues raised.

References

Bartlett, F. C. (1932). *Remembering: A study in experimental and social psychology.* Cambridge, England: Cambridge University Press.

Bjorklund, D. F. (1985). The role of conceptual knowledge in the development of organization in children's memory. In C. J. Brainerd & M. Pressley (Eds.), *Basic processes in memory development: Progress in cognitive development research.* New York: Springer-Verlag.

Brainerd, C. J., & Reyna, V. F. (1990). Gist is the grist: Fuzzy trace theory and the new intuitionism. *Developmental Review, 10,* 3–47.

Brown, A. L., Bransford, J. D., Ferrara, R. A., & Campione, J. C. (1983). Learning, remembering, and understanding. In J. Flavell & E. Markman (Eds.), *Cognitive Development* (Vol. 3, P. H. Mussen (Ed.) *Handbook of Child Psychology,* 4th Ed., pp. 77–166). New York: Wiley.

Brown, A. L., & DeLoache, J. S. (1978). Skills, plans and self-regulation. In R. S. Siegler (Ed.), *Children's thinking: What develops?* (Hillsdale, NJ: Lawrence Erlbaum Associates.

Campbell, R., & Bickhard, M. (1986). *Knowing levels and developmental stages.* Basel, Switzerland: S. Karger.

Case, R. (1992). *The mind's staircase.* Hillsdale, NJ: Lawrence Erlbaum Associates.

Chi, M. T. H. (1977). Age differences in memory span. *Journal of Experimental Child Psychology, 23,* 266–281.

Chi, M. T. H. (1978). Knowledge structures and memory development. In R. S. Siegler (Ed.), *Children's thinking: What develops?* Hillsdale, NJ: Lawrence Erlbaum Associates.

Chi, M. T. H. (Ed.). (1983). *Trends in memory development research.* Basel, Switzerland: S. Karger.

Chi, M. T. H., & Koeske, R. D. (1983). Network representation of a child's dinosaur knowledge. *Developmental Psychology, 19,* 29–39.

Donald, M. (1991). *Origins of the modern mind.* Cambridge, MA: Harvard University Press.

Dudycha, G. J., & Dudycha, M. M. (1941). Childhood memories: A review of the literature. *Psychological Bulletin 38,* 668–682.

Eisenberg, A. R. (1985). Learning to describe past experiences in conversation. *Discourse Processes, 8,* 177–204.

Engel, S. (1986). *Learning to reminisce: A developmental study of how young children talk about the past.* Unpublished doctoral dissertation, City University of New York Graduate Center, New York.

Fivush, R., Gray, J. T., & Fromhoff, F. A. (1987). Two-year-olds talk about the past. *Cognitive Development, 2,* 393–410.

Fivush, R., & Hamond, N. R. (1989). Time and again: Effects of repetition and retention interval on two-year-olds' recall. *Journal of Experimental Child Psychology, 47,* 259–273.

Fivush, R., & Hudson, J. A. (1990). *Knowing and remembering in young children.* New York: Cambridge University Press.

Fivush, R., & Reese, E. (1991, July). *Parental styles for talking about the past.* Paper presented at the International Conference on Memory, Lancaster, England.

Flavell, J. H. (1971). First discussant's comments: What is memory development the development of? *Human Development 14,* 272–278.

Flavell, J. H., Beach, D. H., & Chinsky, J. M. (1966). Spontaneous verbal rehearsal in memory tasks as a function of age. *Child Development 37,* 283–299.

Flavell, J. H., Friedrichs, A. G., & Hoyt, J. D. (1970). Development changes in memorization processes. *Cognitive Psychology, 1,* 324–340.

Freud, S. (1938). Three contributions to the theory of sex. In A. A. Brill (Ed.), *The Basic writings of Sigmund Freud.* New York: Random House. (Original work published in 1905.)

Goodman, G. S., Rudy, L., Bottoms, B. L., & Aman, C. (1990). Children's concerns and memory: Issues of ecological validity in the study of children's eyewitness testimony. In R. Fivish, & J. A. Hudson (Eds.), *Knowing and remembering in young children* (pp. 249–284). New York: Cambridge University Press.

Gopnik, A., & Graf, P. (1988). Knowing how you know: Young children's ability to identify and remember the sources of their beliefs. *Child Development, 59,* 1366–1371.

Hudson, J. A. (1991). *Effects of re-enactment on toddlers' memory for a novel event.* Paper presented at the biennial conference of the Society for Research on Child Development, Seattle, WA.

Hudson, J. A. (1986). Memories are made of this: General event knowledge and the development of autobiographic memory. In K. Nelson (Ed.), *Event knowledge: Structure and function in development* (pp. 97–118). Hillsdale, NJ: Lawrence Erlbaum Associates.

Hudson, J. A., & Nelson, K. (1986). Repeated encounters of a similar kind: Effects of familiarity on children's autobiographical memory. *Cognitive Development, 1,* 253–271.

Hudson, J. A. (1990). The emergence of autobiographic memory in mother-child conversation. In R. Fivush, & J. A. Hudson (Eds.), *Knowing and remembering in young children* (pp. 166–196). New York: Cambridge University Press.

Istomina, A. M. (1975). The development of voluntary memory in preschool age children. *Soviet Psychology, 13,* 5–64.

Kail, R. V., Jr., & Hagen, J. W. (Eds.). (1977). *Perspectives on the development of memory and cognition.* Hillsdale, NJ: Lawrence Erlbaum Associates.

Karmiloff-Smith, A. (1986). From meta-processes to conscious access: Evidence from children's metalinguistic and repair data. *Cognition, 34,* 57–83.

Linton, M. (1982). Transformations of memory in everyday life. In U. Neisser (Ed.), *Memory observed: Remembering in natural contexts.* San Francisco: Freeman.

Lucariello, J., Kyratzis, A., & Nelson, K. (1992). Taxonomic knowledge: What kind and when. *Child Development, 63,* 978–998.

Mandler, J. M. (1984). Representation and recall in infancy. In M. Moscovitch (Ed.), *Infant memory: Its relation to normal and pathological memory in humans and other animals* (pp. 75–101). New York: Plenum.

Mandler, J. M. (1988). How to build a baby: On the development of an accessible representational system. *Cognitive Development, 3,* 113–136.

Myers, N., & Perlmutter, M. (1978). Memory in the years from two to five. In P. A. Ornstein (Ed.), *Memory development in children.* Hillsdale, NJ: Lawrence Erlbaum Associates.

Neisser, U. (1962). Cultural and cognitive discontinuity. In T. E. Gladwin & W. Sturtevant (Eds.), *Anthropology and human behavior* (pp. 54–71). Washington, DC: Anthropological Society of Washington.

Nelson, K. (1978). How young children represent knowledge of their world in and out of language. In R. S. Siegler (Ed.), *Children's thinking: What develops?* (pp. 225–273). Hillsdale, NJ: Lawrence Erlbaum Associates.

Nelson, K. (1986). *Event knowledge: Structure and function in development.* Hillsdale, NJ: Lawrence Erlbaum Associates.

Nelson, K. (Ed.). (1989a). *Narratives from the crib.* Cambridge, MA: Harvard University Press.

Nelson, K. (1989b). Remembering: A functional developmental perspective. In P. R. Solomon, G. R. Goethals, C. M. Kelley, & B. R. Stephens (Eds.), *Memory: Interdisciplinary approaches* (pp. 127–150). New York: Springer-Verlag.

Nelson, K. (1991). The matter of time: Interdependencies between language and thought in development. In S. A. Gelman & J. P. Byrnes (Eds.), *Perspective on language and cognition: Interrelations in development.* New York: Cambridge University Press.

Nelson, K. (1993a). Events, narratives, memories: What develops? In C. Nelson (Ed.), *Minnesota symposium: Memory and affect.* Hillsdale, NJ: Lawrence Erlbaum Associates.

Nelson, K. (1993b). Towards a theory of the development of autobiographical memory. In A. Collins, M. Conway, S. Gathercole, & P. Morris (Eds.), *Theoretical advances in the psychology of memory.* Hillsdale, NJ: Lawrence Erlbaum Associates.

Nelson, K. (1996). *Language in cognitive development: The emergence of the mediated mind.* New York: Cambridge University Press.

Nelson, K., Fivush, R., Hudson, J., & Lucariello, J. (1983). Scripts and the development of memory. In M. T. H. Chi (Ed.), *Contributions to Human Development* (Vol. 9, *Trends in memory development research,* pp. 52–70). Basel, Switzerland: S. Karger.

Nelson, K., & Gruendel, J. (1981). Generalized event representations: Basic building blocks of cognitive development. In M. Lamb & A. Brown (Eds.), *Advances in developmental psychology* (Vol. 1, pp. 131–158). Hillsdale, NJ: Lawrence Erlbaum Associates.

Nelson, K. J. (1969). The organization of free recall by young children. *Journal of Experimental Child Psychology, 8,* 284–295.

Oakley, D. A. (1983). The varieties of memory: A phylogenetic approach. In A. Mayes (Ed.), *Memory in animals and humans.* Workingham, England: Van Nostrand Reinhold.

Ornstein, P. A. (Ed.). (1978). *Memory development in children.* Hillsdale, NJ: Lawrence Erlbaum Associates.

Perner, J. (1991). *Understanding the representational mind.* Cambridge, MA: MIT Press.

Piaget, J., & Inhelder, B. (1973). *Memory and intelligence.* New York: Basic Books.

Pillemer, D. B., & White, S. H. (1989). Childhood events recalled by children and adults. In H. W. Reese (Ed.), *Advances in child development and behavior* (Vol. 21, pp. 297–340). New York: Academic Press.

Ratner, H. H. (1980). The role of social context in memory development. In M. Perlmutter (Ed.), *Children's memory: New directions for child development* (Vol. 10, pp. 49–68). San Francisco: Jossey-Bass.

Rogoff, B. (1990). *Apprenticeship in thinking: Cognitive development in social context.* New York: Oxford University Press.

Rovee-Collier, C., & Hayne, H. (1987). Reactivation of infant memory: Implications for cognitive development. In H. W. Reese (Ed.), *Advances in child development and behavior* (Vol. 20, pp. 185–283). New York: Academic Press.

Schachtel, E. (1947). On memory and childhood amnesia. *Psychiatry, 10,* 1–26.

Schacter, D. L., & Moscovitch, M. (1984). Infants, amnesics, and dissociable memory systems. In M. Moscovitch (Ed.), *Infant memory: Its relation to normal and pathological memory in humans and other animals* (pp. 173–216). New York: Plenum.

Schank, R. C., & Abelson, R. P. (1977). *Scripts, plans, goals, and understanding.* Hillsdale, NJ: Lawrence Erlbaum Associates.

Simon, H. A. (1972). On the development of the processor. In S. Farnham-Diggory (Ed.), *Information processing in children.* New York: Academic Press.

Tessler, M. (1986). Mother-child talk in a museum: The socialization of a memory. Unpublished paper. City University of New York Graduate Center, New York.

Tessler, M. (1991). *Making memories together: The influence of mother-child joint encoding on the development of autobiographical memory style.* Unpublished doctoral dissertation, City University of New York Graduate Center, New York.

Tulving, E. (1972). Episodic and semantic memory. In E. Tulving & W. Donaldson (Eds.), *Organization of memory* (pp. 382–403). New York: Academic Press.

Vygotsky, L. S. (1978). Mind in society: The development of higher psychological processes. Cambridge, MA: Harvard University Press.

Weinert, F. E., & Perlmutter, M. (Eds.). (1988). *Memory development: Universal changes and individual differences.* Hillsdale, NJ: Lawrence Erlbaum Associates.

Wellman, H. M. (1983). Metamemory revisited. In M. T. H. Chi (Ed.), *Trends in memory development research.* Basel, Switzerland: S. Karger.

Wellman, H. M., & Somerville, S. (1980). Quasi-naturalistic tasks in the study of cognition: The memory-related skills of toddlers. In M. Perlmutter (Ed.), *Children's memory* (Vol. 10, pp. 33–48). San Francisco: Jossey-Bass.

Wetzler, S. E., & Sweeney, J. A. (1986). Childhood amnesia: An empirical demonstration. In D. C. Rubin (Ed.), *Autobiographical memory* (pp. 191–201). New York: Cambridge University Press.

White, S. H. (1965). Evidence for a hierarchical arrangement of learning processes. In L. P. Lipsitt & C. C. Spiker (Eds.), *Advances in child development and behavior* (Vol. 2, pp. 187–220). New York: Academic Press.

White, S. H., & Pillemer, D. B. (1979). Childhood amnesia and the development of a socially accessible memory system. In J. F. Kihlstrom & F. J. Evans (Eds.), *Functional disorders of memory* (pp. 29–74). Hillsdale, NJ: Lawrence Erlbaum Associates.

CHAPTER EIGHT

Schooling and the 5 to 7 Shift:
A Natural Experiment

FREDERICK J. MORRISON, ELIZABETH MCMAHON GRIFFITH,
AND JULIE A. FRAZIER

The psychological study of cognitive growth has proceeded along four inter-locking fronts. First, developmental and cognitive psychologists have been concerned with how best to describe the *nature, organization,* and *functioning* of the cognitive system. Efforts to more accurately "carve nature at its joints," have evolved from early information-processing models (Atkinson & Shiffrin, 1968; Neisser, 1967) to more sophisticated and elaborate frameworks (Gardner, 1987). Second, incorporating these cognitive frameworks, developmental-ists have attempted to describe how cognitive structures and functions *change with age.* Over the past 20 years, a substantial body of factual information has accumulated on how children of different ages attend to, remember, and reason about their world (Bjorklund, 1988; Flavell, Miller, & Miller, 1992; Siegler, 1992; Small, 1990). Third, more recent research has focused on the *external sources* shaping cognitive change. A growing body of evidence has docu-mented the important roles played by family (Okagaki & Sternberg, 1991), schools (Stevenson & Lee, 1990), communities (Heath, 1983), and culture (Laboratory of Comparative Human Cognition, 1986; Rogoff, this volume, chap. 13) in influencing the nature, magnitude, and timing of changes in cog-nitive skills. Finally, explorations have begun to elucidate the *mechanisms of change* underlying growth of cognitive skills (Siegler, 1989, this volume, chap. 4). At once the most difficult and challenging of tasks facing develop-mental scientists, this relatively new area of inquiry promises to uncover the most fundamental ways in which children's thinking changes.

During the past 30 years, much progress has been made in describing the nature of cognition and developmental changes in thinking skills. Attention has become more focused in the past decade on the sources and mechanisms of cognitive change. This chapter explores the nature and sources of cognitive development using a novel methodology that allows examination of the role of early schooling and related influences during the critical 5 to 7 year age period.

The 5 to 7 Shift

Nature of Cognitive Change

Since children's thinking undergoes significant, perhaps qualitative, shifts from later preschool to early school years, the 5 to 7 age span constitutes a fruitful period within which to examine the nature of cognitive change (White, 1965). Piaget (1960) postulated that one of four major stage transformations in human intellectual development occurred during this time period. Others in the same tradition (Case, 1985; Fischer, 1980) have concurred that important changes in the quality of the child's thought emerge in the 5 to 7 age range. With some exceptions (Fischer, 1980), theorists in the Piagetian structuralist tradition have tended to stress the uniform, more domain-general aspects of cognitive growth while deemphasizing the impact of specific environmental events or specialized experiences. Scientists working in other traditions (e.g., information processing) have also been impressed with the magnitude and range of developmental changes in memory performance (Bjorklund, 1987; Ornstein & Naus, 1978), language skills (Read & Schreiber, 1982; Scribner & Cole, 1973; Treiman & Weatherston, 1992), reasoning (Rogoff, 1981), and metacognitive skills (Butterworth, Harris, Leslie, & Wellman, 1991; Schneider & Pressley, 1989) during this age period. Relative to structural theorists, those in the information-processing tradition have tended to view developments within the cognitive system as somewhat more domain-specific in nature, with changes in one domain of cognitive skill having little direct, immediate influence on changes in another related domain (Ceci & Liker, 1986; Chi, 1978).

Sources of Cognitive Change

While the existence and magnitude of changes between 5 and 7 years of age have been adequately documented, the sources of developmental change have been less well elaborated. For Piaget and others (Case, 1985; Fischer, 1980), changes in thinking across the age period appeared to be regular, universal, and internally driven according to a traditional maturational timetable. In recent years, however, a growing body of empirical research has revealed that relatively specific learning experiences can significantly influence growth of selected cognitive skills during this age period. Cross-cultural research has documented major differences between schooled and unschooled children in growth of perceptual and memory skills, concept development, logical thinking, and concrete operations like conservation (Rogoff, 1981; Wagner, 1981). Research on the development of specialized knowledge or expertise (e.g., on 10-year-old chess masters or 5-year-old dinosaur experts; Chi, 1978; Chi, Hutchinson, & Robin, 1989; Chi & Koeske, 1983) has revealed that intensive learning experiences can improve memory and other thinking skills in the domain of expertise. Finally, the superior mathematics performance exhibited by Asian elementary-school children over American children appears to stem in large part from differing parental expectations and behaviors (Caplan, Choy, & Whitmore, 1992) and specific instructional practices in and outside school (Stevenson & Lee, 1990). As a whole, these findings have reawakened interest in the role that specific learning experiences play in the development of cognitive skills.

Unfortunately, clear interpretation of the cross-cultural and specialized expertise research is hampered by a number of problems, the most serious being subject selection biases. For example, inferring the effects of specific schooling experiences in comparisons between schooled and unschooled children is confounded by the fact that the children who go to school are often those who are thought by parents to be especially bright and likely to benefit from schooling (see Rogoff, 1981, for a more complete discussion of biases in this design). Likewise, the superior cognitive skills demonstrated by 10-year-old chess masters may simply reflect developmental processes in very bright children or in unique learning environments. Therefore, the generality of such effects to the whole population of children remains unknown.

The "School Cutoff" Methodology

For the past few years, we have been experimenting with use of a "natural experiment" (designated "school cutoff") that permits assessment of the influence of a culturally valued learning experience (i.e., schooling) and circumvents some, if not all, of the serious biases found in other research. Each year, North American school boards proclaim that those children whose birth date precedes some specific date will be allowed to go to kindergarten or first grade, whereas other children who just miss the cutoff will be denied entry. Such an arbitrary selection criterion has itself given rise to a voluminous technical and popular literature on the role of school entrance age in school readiness (Shepard & Smith, 1986), a topic that is the focus of separate research investigations (Morrison, Griffith, & Alberts, in press).

In essence, our methodology involves selecting groups of children who just make versus miss the designated cutoff for school entry. By selecting children whose birthdates cluster closely on either side of the cutoff date, we can effectively equate two groups of children chronologically on some target psychological skill or process. Background information gathered from parent questionnaires and direct assessments revealed that the two groups were equated on critical control variables such as intelligence quotient (IQ), socioeconomic status (SES), and preschool experience. With the groups matched on control variables, the children's progress may be compared using a pre-post design with testing in the early fall and late spring of the school year. In other words, comparing the degree of change in the target skill from pre- to post-test (fall to spring) in the children who just make the cutoff versus those who miss it allowed us to assess the impact of a relatively specific schooling experience on the growth of that skill. Though it is tempting to place the learning experience in contrast to general maturation or development, the more neutral comparison is between schooling and related experiences and other experiences at home, with peers or in outside activities.

There are two *potential* subject selection biases in this design. First, some parents of eligible children may elect to either hold their child out a year before beginning kindergarten or retain him or her an extra year in kindergarten because they feel that their child is not optimally "ready" for school. Since children closest to the cutoff date are more likely than older children to be held out or retained, there is some potential for biased sampling to occur (Cahan & Cohen, 1989). In reality, the percentage of children held out or retained in the local school district under study is relatively small—approximately 5% overall, and between 10% and 12% for children born 1 or 2 months prior to the cutoff date. Moreover, in an independent investigation, Morrison, Griffith, and Alberts (in press) compared background characteristics of three groups of relatively young children who had been either held out prior to kindergarten, retained an extra year in kindergarten, or promoted at the appropriate age. On measures of IQ, parental occupation, parental education, and amount of preschool experience, no reliable group differences were revealed. Hence, systematic bias in sampling is unlikely.

Second, some parents of ineligible children (i.e., those who just miss the cutoff) may attempt to enroll them anyway, if legally permissible, since they feel that the children are "ready to learn." Again, current figures from the local school system revealed that only 3 underage children (from a population of 6,700 kindergarten entrants) were permitted to enter school during the year of study.

Methodological Options

In reality, there is more than one way to implement the cutoff method. First, since the method provides flexibility to examine the influences of either kindergarten or first grade, one must decide which grade will be the point of emphasis. In the present series of studies, we have chosen to focus on grade 1 schooling, in part because our preliminary work revealed that the majority of skills under investigation appeared to change more dramatically in first grade. Those children who just make the cutoff for first grade will be young for their grade (young first graders, Y1) and those who just miss the cutoff will be old for their grade (old kindergartners, OK). Yet, focusing on grade 1 raises the obvious concern that Y1 children, having already spent a year in kindergarten, may consequently show superior cognitive performance when compared with OK children. This possibility can be assessed directly by comparing levels of performance on the pretest (Fall) assessment. Finding no group differences would indicate that the skill under investigation was not significantly modified by kindergarten experiences. Conversely, the presence of group differences would reveal a kindergarten schooling effect. In addition, even where initial differences are found, the method permits assessment of the separate contribution of grade 1 schooling over and above that of kindergarten by focusing on the degree of change in Y1 children's performance as compared with that of OK children. Nevertheless, in circumstances where the kindergarten experience appears to produce significant changes in cognitive processing, focusing on kindergarten cutoff remains an option. In this case, the method involves selecting children who just make the cutoff for kindergarten versus those who miss it.

A second decision centers on whether to compare just two groups of subjects—young first-grade (Y1) versus old kindergarten (OK) children—or, alternatively, to include a third group of children: older first-grade children (O1) who just missed the cutoff the previous year and hence are approximately 10 to 12 months older than their grade mates, the Y1 children, and a full year older than the old kindergarten group. In the three-group design, fall comparisons between Y1 and OK children assess the impact of kindergarten on the target cognitive skill, whereas comparisons between O1 and Y1 children evaluate the contribution of age (or the age $\times$ experience interaction) on growth of the target skill. The initial advantage of the three-group design lies in its ability to assess the impact of the age $\times$ experience interaction at the fall testing (the O1 versus Y1 comparison). Additionally, spring comparisons permit assessment of the direct impact of first-grade schooling (Y1 versus OK children), as well as the age $\times$ first-grade experience interaction (O1 versus Y1 children). The drawbacks in the three-group design include greater difficulty of equating all three groups on relevant background variables, as well as increased error variance from the between-subjects manipulation.

The two-group design (Y1 and OK) has the advantage of easier matching of groups on background variables and reduced subject variability in the within-subjects assessment of the age $\times$ experience interaction. In addition, the two-group design permits evaluation of an age $\times$ experience interaction. Specifically, following year one of the study, the OK children will go to first grade. But at that point they will be almost one full year older than were the Y1 children when they attended first grade. If growth of a target cognitive skill is exclusively a product of the schooling experience, the patterns of change shown by the OK children following their grade 1 experience should be identical with those of the Y1 group. If, however, maturational or other age-related influences interact with the schooling experience, the cognitive progress of the OK children should exceed the corresponding pattern shown by the Y1 children. Overall, the advantages of the two-group design overshadow the disadvantage of having to conduct an additional year of testing in order to assess the age × experience interaction.

We have experimented with both procedures in preliminary work and are continuing to evaluate the costs and benefits of the two-group versus three-group option. We have tended to favor the two-group procedure in recent work for reasons just cited. Nevertheless, results from both types of design are presented here.

Focus of Inquiry

Ideally the present method would be wedded to a coherent body of theory and research linking the schooling experience with cognitive changes. Included in such a framework would be theoretically motivated propositions about which cognitive processes were amenable to change via schooling and which were controlled more strongly by a maturational or developmental timetable (Gardner, 1989). Optimally, sources of environmental influence could be isolated and linked in theoretically meaningful ways to identifiable cognitive skills or processes. Unfortunately, no coherent conceptual framework integrating all these elements currently exists. Rather, a series of delimited changes in specific cognitive processes has been linked to different aspects of the schooling experience. For example, memory strategies have been viewed both as a by-product of learning to read (Morrison, Holmes, & Haith, 1974) and as a direct consequence of greater environmental demands for deliberate memory (Rogoff, 1981). Likewise, phonemic awareness has been hypothesized to bear a reciprocal cause-effect relation with reading acquisition (Perfetti, Beck, Bell, & Hughes, 1987).

For the past few years, we have been examining the fruitfulness of the cutoff method in elucidating the independent and interactive influences of schooling (with age) on cognitive growth. Since the field of cognitive development currently lacks a unifying conceptual framework, we have opted initially to identify and investigate a series of individual cognitive domains including memory, language, reasoning and comprehension, and logical operations and problem solving. To date, our findings have been very encouraging. First, we have found that the cutoff method is sensitive to important changes in cognitive processing as a function of schooling. Second, the method is discriminatively sensitive to different patterns of outcomes across different cognitive processes and domains. Third, the method has yielded some valuable insights into the nature and sources of developmental change in cognitive processes during this age period. In the next section, we describe results from three different studies (memory and language skills, quantitative skills, and early literacy skills) conducted on independent samples of children.

The Research

Memory and Language Skills Study

In an initial investigation (Morrison, Smith, & Dow-Ehrenberger, 1995), we chose to examine cognitive growth in two areas that have received significant research attention over the past couple of decades: immediate memory skills and phonological segmentation. These areas have yielded solid empirical bases for developmental phenomena, and in each case, the evidence has suggested that early schooling plays a role in shaping the growth of cognitive skills.

A two-group (OK and Y1) cutoff comparison design was used in this study. Sample sizes for this preliminary investigation were relatively small (10 per group). Nevertheless, OK and Y1 children were equivalent on IQ, maternal education, and preschool experience. On average, the groups were 41 days apart in age.

All children were tested three times. The OK students were tested in the fall and spring of kindergarten (Fall and Spring 1) and again in the spring of first grade (Spring 2). The Y1 students were tested in the fall and spring of first grade (Fall and Spring 1) and again in the spring of second grade (Spring 2).

IMMEDIATE MEMORY SKILLS

From more than 20 years of memory research, we know that performance in free recall tasks improves substantially from 4 through about 12 years of age (Ornstein & Naus, 1978). Moreover, one major source of developmental improvement is increased use of active, cumulative rehearsal strategies, which are indexed indirectly by a heightened primacy effect in serial position analyses (Belmont & Butterfield, 1971; Hagen, Hargrove, & Ross, 1973) and by observed changes in overt rehearsal activity (Ornstein & Naus, 1978). As noted, several authors have hypothesized that changes in memory performance may stem directly or indirectly from experiences in school (Morrison, Holmes, & Haith, 1974; Rogoff, 1981).

In our study of immediate memory skills, four sets of nine pictures of common objects were presented one at a time. Following the presentation of each set, children were asked to report as many of the pictures as they could remember. Before each set of pictures was presented, the children were requested to say aloud anything they were doing to help themselves remember the pictures throughout the presentation. Having the children verbalize their rehearsal

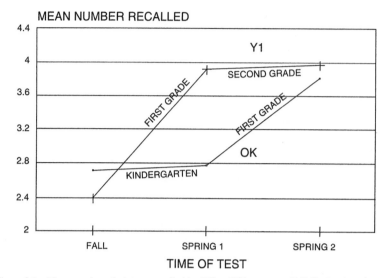

Figure 8.1   Mean number of pictures recalled by OK and Y1 groups at Fall, Spring 1, and Spring 2.

strategies provided some insight into the processes involved in later recall performance.

Changes in memory performance and skill were strongly and uniquely influenced by first-grade schooling experiences. The recall performance of the two groups (OK and Y1) across the three testing periods (Fall, Spring 1, Spring 2) is depicted in Figure 8.1. As shown, there were no reliable group differences in number of pictures recalled in the fall, confirming that kindergarten experiences per se did not directly influence memory performance. This conclusion is buttressed by the fact that OK children showed almost no improvement in memory performance during their year in kindergarten (Fall to Spring 1). In contrast, Y1 children showed a dramatic and statistically significant increase in memory performance following their year in first grade. Hence, experiences in and related to first grade were directly responsible for improvements in immediate memory performance.

What about possible age × experience interactions? Retesting the same children one year later, we found that the original OK group demonstrated a sharp improvement in memory performance following their year in first grade, yet the degree of improvement shown by the OK group did not differ significantly from that shown by the original Y1 a year earlier. Consequently, we could detect no evidence for an age × experience interaction from these findings.

Overall, changes in immediate memory performance were exclusively a product of schooling (and related) experiences during first grade. Corroborating evidence was obtained from analyses of memory across serial positions.

First-grade schooling effects were found for primacy portions of the curve, that is, the first three items on the list, whereas no significant changes were noted on recency portions, that is, the last three items on the list. These results indirectly supported the view that children in first grade had learned a strategy (perhaps verbal rehearsal) for remembering the picture names.

Preliminary analyses of the children's rehearsal activity confirmed this interpretation. Following their year in first grade, Y1 children shifted from predominantly passive rehearsal activity (i.e., saying only the presented item) to more active rehearsal strategies (i.e., saying previous items together with the presented item).

PHONOLOGICAL SEGMENTATION

The growing ability to analyze the speech stream into component segments (e.g., phonemes or syllables) is a hallmark of linguistic development during early childhood. Recently, controversy has arisen regarding the causal nature of the strong association between growth of phonemic segmentation skills or "phonemic awareness" and success in early reading acquisition. Several studies have demonstrated strong correlations between reading scores and phonemic segmentation skills (Fox & Routh, 1976; Share, Jorm, MacLean, & Matthews, 1984; Stanovich, Cunningham, & Freeman, 1984; Tunmer & Nesdale, 1985). More critically, training studies have revealed clear and specific improvements in reading ability following training in phonemic segmentation. For example, Treiman and Baron (1983) trained prereaders in segmentation skills and found that the children later showed success in reading words based on the symbol-sound correspondences used in the training procedure. Hence, evidence has accumulated suggesting that early phonemic segmentation ability may be a prerequisite, or at least a facilitator, for success in early reading.

In contrast, others have argued that significant changes in phonemic awareness come about as a result of exposure to printed materials (Ehri, 1984; Perfetti, 1985; Read, Zhang, Nie, & Ding, 1986). For example, Morais, Carey, Alegria, and Bertelson (1979) found that adult illiterate Portuguese fishermen lacked phonemic awareness skills, whereas their recently educated fishermen counterparts did evidence phonemic segmentation ability. This and other evidence (Ehri & Wilce, 1979) strongly suggest that reading experience exerts a powerful influence on growth of phonemic awareness.

Perfetti (1985) suggested that both views may be correct and that learning to read and growth of phonemic awareness share a reciprocal influence on each other (see also Perfetti et al., 1987). Specifically, some appreciation for the phonemic structure of spoken words probably facilitates initial decoding efforts. In addition, and perhaps more important, exposure to printed materials significantly enhances the child's ability to analyze words and to manipulate their speech segments.

One problem in disentangling the cause-effect relation in this area has been the lack of methodological tools capable of discriminating between the effects of schooling experiences and general age-related influences. The cutoff method afforded a reasonable way to test the nature of the association between phonemic segmentation and early reading acquisition. Although kindergarten children are exposed to letters and are read stories, more formal reading instruction does not really begin until first grade in most North American school systems. If growth of phonemic awareness develops independently of formal instruction, we would expect to see significant changes in children's phonemic segmentation skills over the course of kindergarten. To the extent that phonemic awareness is primarily or more strongly influenced by exposure to formal reading instruction, however, we would expect that Y1 children would show a more marked improvement over the year in phonemic segmentation skills. Evidence of change in both groups of children would confirm precisely Perfetti's notion of reciprocal influence between reading experience and phonemic awareness.

Additional questions addressed in this study include the following: Which segments of speech (phonemic, subsyllabic, and syllabic) do children have knowledge of prior to reading experience? Which segments appear to develop through exposure to written materials? Do changes across the three levels of segmentation skill show a similar (domain-general) pattern or a more domain-specific pattern, perhaps as a function of age, schooling, or both? With regard to the first two questions, existing evidence has documented that prereading children possess some skill in segmenting words into syllables but have great difficulty initially segmenting syllables into phonemes. Evidence obtained by Treiman (1985) points to an intermediate level of segmentation ability (i.e., between syllabic and phonemic) in prereaders, referred to as the intrasyllabic or subsyllabic level. One type of subsyllabic segmentation postulates a split between the onset sound and the rhyme of a word (e.g., in the one-syllable word *grasp*, *gr* would constitute the onset and *asp* the rhyme). Building on Treiman's (1985) work, we examined segmentation ability at the syllabic, subsyllabic, and phonemic levels. We hypothesized that, to the degree children are capable of syllabic and subsyllabic segmentation prior to formal reading instruction, minimal effects specific to first-grade schooling would be observed. In contrast, we anticipated a major increase in phonemic segmentation as a consequence of grade 1 reading instruction because phonemic segmentation is likely a level of analysis that is quite foreign to prereaders. In fact, a completely independent investigation of levels of phonological development using almost the identical procedure was reported recently by Bowey and Francis (1991). They compared performance of OK, Y1, and O1 children on tasks assessing subsyllabic and phonemic segmentation. They found that only the Y1 and O1 groups could successfully perform the phonemic tasks, and they did not differ from each other. Some OK children gave evidence of sensitivity to subsyllabic units. It is noteworthy that in the Bowey and Francis study (1991) the three groups of children did not differ appreciably on background assessments like receptive vocabulary.

The last question addressed by our study focused on the types of changes (domain general vs. domain specific) that may occur across the segmentation levels. Discovery of distinctly different patterns of change across levels of segmentation within the language task or for the memory versus language tasks would reveal the cutoff method to be discriminatively sensitive to uniquely different sources of change in the two domains. If exactly the same pattern of change occurs across tasks or domains, it would raise a question about whether other sources of difference between the groups (e.g., differential motivation or familiarity with testing situations) might be responsible for performance changes. In this regard, it should be noted that Bowey and Francis (1991) found different patterns of schooling effects for subsyllabic versus phonemic levels of segmentation.

Findings for the phonological segmentation tasks yielded different but theoretically meaningful patterns of results, illustrating the discriminative power of the cutoff method. For phonemic segmentation, results (depicted in Figure 8.2) revealed no group differences at fall between OK and Y1 children. Old kindergartners did show a small, but statistically reliable, improvement in phonemic awareness following their kindergarten year. In contrast, Y1 children manifested a much sharper increase in phonemic awareness scores following expo-

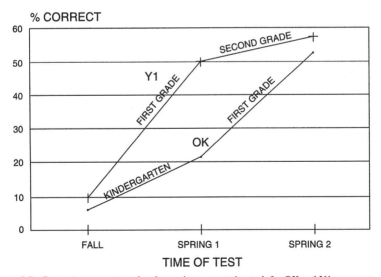

Figure 8.2   Percentage correct on the phonemic segmentation task for OK and Y1 groups at Fall, Spring 1, and Spring 2.

sure to first grade. These findings indicated that the greatest impact on growth of phonemic awareness most likely stemmed from formal reading instruction in first grade. This interpretation was reinforced by the results 1 year later in which the original OK children showed the same degree of improvement in phonemic awareness as had the Y1 group a year earlier. Clearly, first-grade schooling experience constituted a prime source of influence on growth of phonemic awareness.

As depicted in Figure 8.3, a very different pattern emerged for syllabic segmentation; performance on syllabic segmentation was higher than on phonemic segmentation. Surprisingly, little evidence of any improvement, let alone schooling effects, was observed for either group through the end of first grade. Yet, one year later, evidence of a second-grade school effect emerged. Specifically, performance of the OK children in first grade showed almost no change, mirroring the pattern of the Y1 group the previous year. In contrast, the original Y1 children (now in second grade) showed a reliable, rather sharp improvement in syllabic segmentation scores, rising to near ceiling levels by the end of second grade.

Finally, performance on subsyllabic segmentation fell right in between the levels exhibited for syllabic and phonemic segmentation (see Figure 8.4). The pattern of change for subsyllabic segmentation was different from that of the other two levels, showing a modest, reliable increase from kindergarten through second grade, with no evidence of a unique influence of schooling at any grade level.

Altogether, findings from the phonological segmentation task confirmed the

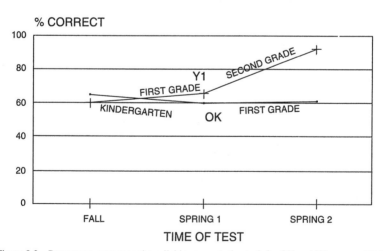

Figure 8.3   Percentage correct on the syllabic segmentation task for OK and Y1 groups at Fall, Spring 1, and Spring 2.

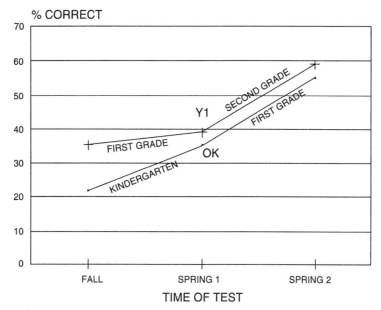

Figure 8.4   Percentage correct on the subsyllabic segmentation task for OK and Y1 groups at Fall, Spring 1, and Spring 2.

sensitivity of the cutoff method to changes in phonological segmentation skills. Moreover, the procedure was sensitive to different patterns of change across levels of word segmentation. On a substantive level, changes over time for the three levels of segmentation showed distinctly different patterns. Hence, growth of phonological segmentation ability did not appear to involve acquisition of a central, domain-general skill that transferred across levels of word segmentation. Each level of segmentation appeared to follow its own unique developmental or experiential trajectory.

Quantitative Skills Study

In a separate investigation involving an independent sample and time period, Bisanz, Morrison, and Dunn (1995) examined the influence of schooling on quantitative skills, a domain of cognitive functioning traditionally conceptualized as different from the domain of language and verbal memory examined in the first study. The two tasks selected, conservation of number and mental arithmetic, differ in the degree to which they are emphasized in formal schooling, provide diverse insights into the nature of children's problem-solving processes, and have been used extensively in previous studies.

Conservation of number and mental arithmetic are both important and pervasive characteristics of cognitive development. Performance on these skills increases dramatically during the very earliest years of elementary school, but the extent to which schooling influences these changes is not entirely clear. Although conservation of number is not taught explicitly in school, there are theoretical and empirical reasons to suspect that formal schooling might facilitate acquisition of this concept. The extent of this facilitation is, however, difficult to predict. In contrast, arithmetic is an important component of instructional curricula, and schooling almost certainly influences improvements in accuracy.

In this study of quantitative skills, we opted to utilize the three-group design comparing groups of old first-grade (O1), young first-grade (Y1), and old kindergarten (OK) children. The groups were essentially matched on background variables, with the exception of a marginally significant difference on IQ, favoring Y1 children over O1 children. Children were tested in the early fall and late spring of the school year.

CONSERVATION OF NUMBER

Conservation of number refers to the concept that the number of objects in a collection remains invariant despite transformations that are irrelevant to quantity (Piaget, 1968). Understanding conservation of number and other features of objects or collections (e.g., length, mass) is a hallmark characteristic of concrete operational thought (Flavell, 1963). Nonconserving children typically are misled by irrelevant cues, such as length or density. For example, when objects in a row are spaced farther apart or closer together than those in the comparison row, these children tend to indicate that one of the two rows of objects has more than the other. Conserving children judge the rows to be equivalent and are capable of giving sophisticated reasons for their judgments. The proportion of children who conserve number increases markedly in Western societies from 5 to 8 years of age.

Predictions about effects of schooling on the acquisition of conservation are not straightforward. To the extent that formal schooling encourages context-independent thinking and a search for general and explicit principles of reasoning (Rogoff, 1981; Scribner & Cole, 1973), schooling might be expected to increase the rate at which conservation is acquired. Schooling also might be expected to help children acquire specific skills that could facilitate the development of conservation. For example, increased accuracy in counting or substitution might provide empirical evidence children can use to induce the concept of conservation (Fuson, 1988; Gelman & Gallistel, 1978; Klahr, 1984). Indeed, training in counting skills has been shown to facilitate performance on conservation tasks (Clements, 1984). If, however, the acquisition of conservation depends primarily on factors not specific to schooling (e.g., extracurricular experiences or biological maturation), then performance may improve as a function of age rather than schooling.

Research on the relation between schooling and the acquisition of conservation is not entirely consistent. Schooled children typically perform at a more advanced level than unschooled children of the same age (Dasen & Heron, 1981; Rogoff, 1981), as would be expected if schooling provides the kinds of instructional experience that improve reasoning. Exceptions to this generalization have been sufficiently frequent, however, to temper strong conclusions. For example, in some studies the effects of schooling were found to be minimal or negligible for performance on conservation tasks, even though performance increased markedly with age (Dash & Das, 1984; Nyiti, 1976). Moreover, the effects of schooling can vary across cultural groups. Posner and Baroody (1979) found that schooled children were more likely to conserve number than unschooled children in an agriculturally oriented African subculture, but schooling had little or no effect among children in a mercantile subculture.

Inconsistency in the results from cross-cultural studies may have arisen, in part, from methodological problems that could bias the results in favor of schooled children and result in underestimation of the competence of unschooled children (Dasen & Heron, 1981; Rogoff, 1981). Often schooled children are more familiar than unschooled children with the stimuli used or with the social, linguistic, and physical characteristics of testing situations. Sometimes schooled children differ from unschooled children in a variety of ways (e.g., parental education and income) that are not evaluated by investigators and that could be related to performance (Rogoff, 1981).

For the conservation of number task in our study, children were first shown two rows of objects containing the same number of items. The objects in each row were arrayed in a one-to-one correspondence, and the rows were equal in length and density. In this phase, the child was asked to say whether the two rows were the same. After responding correctly, the child watched while the experimenter transformed the appearance of one of the arrays by spreading the items apart or scrunching them together. The child was then asked again whether the two rows were equivalent, and justifications for his or her choice were requested.

Results from the conservation of number task (see Figure 8.5) revealed evidence for only age-related changes in conservation skill. At the Fall testing, O1 children outperformed Y1 and OK children, who did not differ from each other. By Spring 1, all children showed marked improvement over the school year, but all groups demonstrated equivalent degrees of change. No evidence of any unique schooling influences on growth in conservation skills was found.

MENTAL ARITHMETIC

The other aspect of the quantitative skills study examined basic arithmetic computations performed without the benefit of calculators or writing tools. Careful analyses of observational, latency, and self-report data have led to the

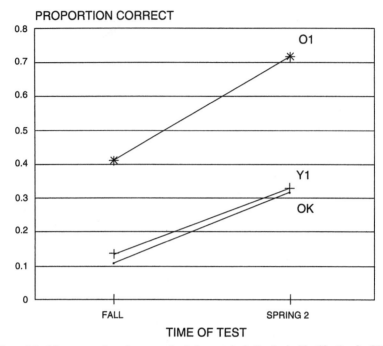

Figure 8.5   Mean proportion of conservation judgments including logical justification for OK, Y1, and O1 groups at Fall and Spring.

conclusion that children of all ages use a variety of solution procedures to solve simple addition and subtraction problems (Geary & Brown, 1991; Siegler, 1987; Siegler & Shrager, 1984). For instance, a child may generate an answer for some problems through either finger counting or mental counting. The same child might retrieve answers rapidly and directly from memory for other problems. As children grow older, counting-based procedures become less frequent, memory retrieval becomes increasingly dominant, and accuracy increases (Ashcraft, 1982, 1990; Bisanz & LeFevre, 1990; Siegler & Shrager, 1984).

According to Siegler's hypotheses about learning (Siegler & Shrager, 1984), the associative strength between a problem and a possible answer increases directly as a function of the number of occasions in which an individual gives that answer in response to the problem. In the normal course of learning, children may make errors but will increasingly give the correct answer to a problem because of self-corrections or feedback from others.

If this theory is correct and if arithmetic facts are practiced in school, then schooling should influence both accuracy and selection of solution procedures. Arithmetic is a central component of the curriculum in nearly all schools, although the focus is on accuracy rather than on the process of solution (Stigler & Perry, 1988). Two types of evidence support the conclusion that schooling influences children's accuracy in arithmetic. First, children's performance in solving arithmetic problems varies considerably according to the instructional practices of the country, even among very young schoolchildren (Song & Ginsburg, 1987; Stevenson, Chen, Lee, & Fuligni, 1991; Stevenson, Lee, & Stigler, 1986). Second, amount of schooling is associated with greater accuracy in timed arithmetic tests for children in upper elementary grades, independent of the effects of age (Cahan & Cohen, 1989; see also Baltes & Reinert, 1969). The effect of schooling may vary, however, depending on the nature of instruction and the level of cultural support for mathematics. For example, Posner (1982) found that schooling was associated with higher levels of accuracy among children of an agricultural tribe in Côte d'Ivoire but had no discernible influence among children of a merchant tribe.

For the number addition task in our study, children were required to add all possible pairwise combinations of the numbers 1 to 5.

In contrast to the results for conservation of number, findings for addition provided evidence of schooling effects. As shown in Figure 8.6, at Fall testing OK children performed much lower than either the Y1 or O1 groups, who did not differ significantly from each other. Likewise, both groups of first graders continued to outperform the OK group at Spring 1. It is evident that growth of addition skills was strongly and additively enhanced by exposure to kindergar-

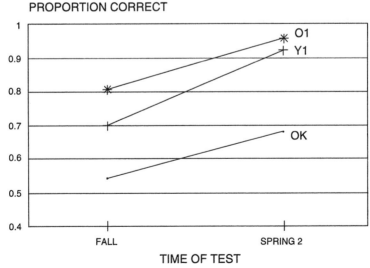

Figure 8.6   Mean proportion of correct answers in the mental arithmetic task for OK, Y1, and O1 groups at Fall and Spring.

ten and first-grade experiences. Notably, we could discern no evidence in these data for an age × experience interaction.

The pattern of findings from this study confirmed the sensitivity of the cutoff method to changes in quantitative cognitive skills. The findings also confirmed those of the earlier experiment in demonstrating a fairly high degree of specificity in patterns of change. Changes in addition skills showed a clear influence of schooling, demonstrating the power of early instruction in addition skills. In contrast, conservation of number, presumably because it is not explicitly taught in the classroom, followed a more age-linked pattern of change. Clearly, the influence of schooling on number manipulation skills like addition did not readily transfer to a reasonably cognate area, namely logical understanding of conservation of number. Nevertheless, conservation skills did show marked improvement. Hence, factors outside of schooling per se helped to shape growth of conservation skills.

Early Literacy Skills Study

The final study to be reported here focused on the role of early schooling in promoting literacy and numeracy skills (Morrison, Griffith, & Frazier, 1993). Patterns of findings from our previous studies had made it abundantly clear that the influences of schooling could be highly specific to those skills heavily emphasized in the local school curricula. Hence, we wondered what skills children were acquiring solely as a function of exposure to formal schooling and related experiences in contrast to other formal or informal experiences in the home, peer groups, or extracurricular settings. The cutoff method appeared to present a reasonable way to examine the impact of schooling across a range of literacy-related skills. The skills selected for study represented those suggested by the literature as important componential skills in growth of early literacy (Adams, 1990). They included alphabet letter naming, phonemic awareness, reading/word recognition (from the Peabody Individual Achievement Test-Revised, PIAT-R), vocabulary (from the Peabody Picture Vocabulary Test-Revised, PPVTR), general knowledge (from the PIAT-R), and narrative skills (Trabasso, Stein, Rodkin, Munger, & Baughn, 1992). The narrative skills included having a story concept and being able to represent, remember, and produce coherent narratives upon request. We also included an assessment of general mathematical skills (from the PIAT-R).

Overall, the pattern of results across tasks confirmed the view that the nature, magnitude, and timing of changes in literacy-related skills during this age period varied considerably. Four of the seven skills showed significant schooling effects, though they differed in timing and magnitude. Growth of alphabet naming was almost exclusively influenced by kindergarten experiences. Young first graders, virtually at ceiling, outperformed OK children at Fall testing; the OK group reached mastery by the end of kindergarten. In contrast, growth in phonemic awareness was most notable during first grade, replicating the first study's results and reinforcing the view that skill at phonemic segmentation derived primarily from exposure to formal reading instruction in first grade. A different pattern emerged for reading/word recognition and mathematical achievement; both kindergarten and first-grade schooling effects were manifested. Although schooling effects were observed for both reading and mathematics, a comparison of the magnitude of the schooling effect for reading versus mathematics revealed that schooling improved elementary reading skills to a greater degree than it improved elementary mathematical skills. This finding confirmed results from other studies (Stevenson & Lee, 1990) documenting the greater emphasis placed upon reading versus math skills in American school systems (see also Morrison, Griffith, & Alberts, in press).

Yet another pattern of change was revealed for vocabulary, general knowledge, and narrative skills. In each of these domains significant, but equal, advances were made by OK and Y1 groups. No evidence was revealed that unique experiences in schooling improved growth of vocabulary, general knowledge, or narrative skills.

Taken together, findings from this study demonstrated that whether, when, and how much a particular literacy skill will improve are highly variable. The most straightforward interpretation of the pattern of results is that changes in important literacy skills will occur if those skills are explicitly targeted for instruction by the school curriculum or teacher. However, it is unlikely that explicit instruction in phonemic awareness forms an integral part of early school teaching in most classes. More likely, growth in phonemic awareness is a by-product of explicit instruction in letter naming, letter-sound correspondence, and word decoding. In fact, we suspect that transfer effects of instruction in one skill on growth of other skills are implicitly assumed by most teachers. Hence, early instruction in word decoding is expected to naturally produce spin-off benefits in vocabulary skills and general knowledge. Findings from this study cast doubt on the validity of this transfer assumption. The pattern of results, like those of the first two studies, revealed a striking degree of specificity in growth of literacy skills that, on the surface, seem cognitively and educationally related to one another.

Working Conclusions

Our results to date utilizing the cutoff method have been encouraging and permit us to derive a preliminary set of conclusions about the method and what it tells us about the nature and sources of cognitive growth:

1. The cutoff method is sensitive to age changes in cognitive skills in the period from approximately 5 to 7 years of age. Given the relatively short time span in which cognitive skills are being assessed

(in some cases only 7 to 9 months), it is noteworthy that reliable changes can be detected by the method.

2. The cutoff method is discriminatively sensitive to different theoretically derived outcomes. The pattern of changes across studies varied greatly but predictably according to theoretical or empirical predictions. Hence, it appears that the method is responsive to real sources of change in cognitive skills and does not simply represent group differences in motivation or familiarity with certain kinds of testing procedures.

3. On a substantive level, the pattern of changes across a broad range of domains and skills appeared to be highly domain-specific and even sub-domain-specific. For example, changes observed in phonological segmentation ability differed greatly depending on the level of segmentation involved (phonemic, subsyllabic, or syllabic). Second, surprisingly little transfer was observed across skills that, on the surface, appear to share cognitive or experiential components (e.g., conservative of number and number addition skills). Finally, schooling influences on growth of literacy skills appeared to be confined to a relatively delimited subset of elementary reading and math skills with little evidence for early schooling effects on or transfer to other important skills such as vocabulary, general knowledge, narrative skills, and conservation. Overall, results from these studies revealed a relatively high degree of specificity in the nature, magnitude, and timing of changes in cognitive skills. An important task for future research will be to link these specific changes to corresponding shifts in sources of variation in the environment and in the child.

4. The cutoff method may permit developmental researchers to move from a relatively coarse to a more fine-grained analysis of the nature and sources of cognitive change during this important developmental epoch. Had we simply plotted age trends from 5 to 7 years of age, we would have observed relatively clear, steady improvements in children's performance across a range of cognitive, linguistic, and literacy skills. Viewed through the "cutoff lens," however, the complexity, timing, and nature of those changes was more clearly discerned. Coupled with the potential to link cognitive changes with sources of influence like schooling, the method holds the promise of yielding a clearer picture of cognitive growth in the 5 to 7 period.

The 5 to 7 Year Age Period

From the evidence gathered to date using the cutoff method, what inferences can we draw about the 5 to 7 shift? Clearly, the cognitive skills of children change in important ways during this age period. Further, as our research documents, one salient environmental change, namely going to school, is responsible for major and, in some instances, unique shifts in those cognitive skills. Children's memory performance (and possibly memory strategies), phonemic segmentation skills, later syllabic segmentation skills, selected quantitative skills including addition, and elementary academic skills such as letter naming, reading, and arithmetic achievement are all enhanced by exposure to early schooling experiences.

Other skills also demonstrated notable change over the same age period, though the influence of schooling appeared to be minimal. Included in this group were subsyllabic segmentation skills, conservation of number skills, vocabulary skills, general knowledge skills, and narrative skills. Across these domains, influences other than those specific to schooling were operating. At present, it is not possible to ascertain the extent to which biological or other maturational processes might play a role in shaping these skills, or whether specific experiences outside of schooling such as family, peer, or extracurricular activities might be influential.

Perhaps the most striking implication emerging from our findings is the need to constrain generalizations about the nature of the 5 to 7 shift. In our view, simple, global conclusions (qualitative vs. quantitative changes or continuous vs. discontinuous changes) about the nature and sources of changes observed during this period will not adequately capture the complexity, intricacy, and specificity of the changes occurring in children at this time. For example, changes observed in memory performance could be interpreted as a relatively straightforward example of a simple quantitative change produced by schooling experiences. Yet the shift from passive to active rehearsal could equally appropriately be viewed as a qualitative shift in type of memory strategy used to aid recall. Likewise, while change in conservation ability could hypothetically be interpreted as involving qualitative shifts in logical operations underlying quantitative reasoning, simultaneous changes in simple addition skills seem most parsimoniously viewed as a quantitative increase in elementary quantitative operations. In both examples it seems most accurate and fruitful to accept the possibility that different kinds of developmental change may occur simultaneously in the same child, depending on the skill in question and on the sources of influence impinging on it. Given the specificity in the nature, magnitude, and timing of developmental changes observed in our data, it seems that the real challenge for future research will require closer scrutiny of the reciprocal interplay between specific domains of cognitive functioning and the specific environmental influences and events. Only then can we hope to reach valid, general conclusions about the nature of the 5 to 7 shift.

References

Adams, M. J. (1990). *Beginning to read: Thinking and learning about print.* Washington, DC: Department of Education.

Ashcraft, M. H. (1982). The development of mental arithmetic: A chronometric approach. *Developmental Review, 2,* 213–236.

Ashcraft, M. H. (1990). Strategic processing in children's mental arithmetic: A review and proposal. In D. F. Bjorklund (Ed.), *Children's strategies: Contemporary views of cognitive development* (pp. 185–211). Hillsdale, NJ: Erlbaum.

Atkinson, R. C., & Shiffrin, R. M. (1968). Human memory: A proposed system and its control processes. In K. W. Spence & J. T. Spence (Eds.), *Advances in the psychology of learning and motivation research and theory* (Vol. 2, pp. 89–195). New York: Academic Press.

Baltes, P. B., & Reinert, G. (1969). Cohort effects in cognitive development of children as revealed by cross-sectional sequences. *Developmental Psychology, 1* (2), 169–177.

Belmont, J. M., & Butterfield, E. C. (1971). Learning strategies as determinants of memory deficiencies. *Cognitive Psychology, 2,* 411–420.

Bisanz, J., & LeFevre, J. (1990). Strategic and nonstrategic processing in the development of mathematical cognition. In D. F. Bjorklund (Ed.), *Children's strategies: Contemporary views of cognitive development* (pp. 213–244). Hillsdale, NJ: Erlbaum.

Bisanz, J., Morrison, F. J., & Dunn, M. (1995). Effects of age and schooling on acquisition of elementary quantitative skills. *Developmental Psychology, 31,* 221–236.

Bjorklund, D. F. (1987). How age changes in knowledge base contribute to the development of children's memory: An interpretive review. *Developmental Review, 7,* 93–130.

Bjorklund, D. F. (1988). *Children's thinking.* Pacific Grove, CA: Brooks/Cole.

Bowey, J. A., & Francis, J. (1991). Phonological analysis as a function of age and exposure to reading instruction. *Applied Psycholinguistics, 12,* 91–121.

Butterworth, G., Harris, P., Leslie, A., & Wellman, H. W. (1991). Perspectives on the child's theory of mind [Special issue] *British Journal of Developmental Psychology, 9* (1, 2).

Cahan, S., & Cohen, N. (1989). Age versus schooling effects on intelligence development. *Child Development, 60,* 1239–1249.

Caplan, N., Choy, M. A., & Whitmore, J. K. (1992, February). Indochinese refugee families and academic achievement. *Scientific American,* 36–42.

Case, R. (1985). *Intellectual development: Birth to adulthood.* Toronto: Academic Press.

Ceci, S. J., & Liker, J. (1986). A day at the races: The study of I.Q., expertise and cognitive complexity. *Journal of Experimental Psychology: General, 115,* 225–266.

Chi, M. T. H. (1978). Knowledge structures and memory development. In R. S. Siegler (Ed.), *Children's thinking: What develops?* Hillsdale, NJ: Erlbaum.

Chi, M. T. H., Hutchinson, J. E., & Robin, A. F. (1989). How inferences about novel domain-related concepts can be constrained by structural knowledge. *Merrill-Palmer Quarterly, 35* (1), 27–62.

Chi, M. T. H., & Koeske, R. P. (1983). Network representation of a child's dinosaur knowledge. *Developmental Psychology, 19,* 29–39.

Clements, D. H. (1984). Training effects on the development and generalization of

Piagetian logical operations and knowledge of number. *Journal of Educational Psychology, 76,* 766–776.

Dasen, P. R., & Heron, A. (1981). Cross-cultural tests of Piaget's theory. In H. C. Triandis & A. Heron (Eds.), *Handbook of cross-cultural psychology: Developmental psychology* (Vol. *4,* pp. 295–341). Boston: Allyn and Bacon.

Dash, U. N., & Das, J. P. (1984). Development of concrete operational thought and information coding in schooled and unschooled children. *British Journal of Developmental Psychology, 2,* 63–72.

Ehri, L. C. (1984). How orthography alters spoken language competencies in children learning to read and spell. In J. Downing & R. Valtin (Eds.), *Language awareness and learning to read* (pp. 119–147). New York: Springer-Verlag.

Ehri, L. C., & Wilce, L. S. (1979). The mnemonic value of orthography among beginning readers. *Journal of Educational Psychology, 71,* 26–40.

Fischer, K. W. (1980). A theory of cognitive development: The control and construction of hierarchies of skills. *Psychological Review, 87,* 477–531.

Flavell, J. H. (1963). *The developmental psychology of Jean Piaget.* New York: Van Nostrand Reinhold.

Flavell, J. H., Miller, P. H., & Miller, S. A. (1992). *Cognitive development.* New York: Prentice-Hall.

Fox, B., & Routh, D. D. (1976). Phonemic analysis and synthesis as word-attack skills. *Journal of Educational Psychology, 68,* 680–688.

Fuson, K. C. (1988). *Children's counting and concepts of number.* Cambridge, MA: Harvard University Press.

Gardner, H. (1987). *The mind's new science.* New York: Basic Books.

Gardner, H. (1989). *The unschooled mind.* New York: Basic Books.

Geary, D. C., & Brown, S. C. (1991). Cognitive addition: Strategy choice and speed-of-processing differences in gifted, normal, and mathematically disabled children. *Developmental Psychology, 27,* 398–406.

Gelman, R., & Gallistel, C. R. (1978). *The child's understanding of number.* Cambridge, MA: Harvard University Press.

Hagen, J. W., Hargrove, S., & Ross, W. (1973). Prompting and rehearsal in short-term memory. *Child Development, 44,* 201–204.

Heath, S. B. (1983). *Ways with words.* Cambridge, MA: Cambridge University Press.

Klahr, D. (1984). Transition processes in quantitative development. In R. J. Sternberg (Ed.), *Mechanisms of cognitive development* (pp. 101–139). New York, W. H. Freeman.

Laboratory of Comparative Human Cognition (1986). Contributions of cross-cultural research to educational practice. *American Psychologist, 41* (10), 1049–1058.

Morais, J., Carey, L., Alegria, J., & Bertelson, P. (1979). Does awareness of speech as a sequence of phonemes arise spontaneously? *Cognition, 7,* 323–331.

Morrison, F. J., Griffith, E. M., & Alberts, D. (in press). Nature-nurture in the classroom: Entrance age, school readiness, and learning in children. *Developmental Psychology.*

Morrison, F. J., Griffith, E. M., & Frazier, J. A. (1993, March). *What literacy skills are children learning in school?* Paper presented at biennial meeting of Society for Research in Child Development. New Orleans, LA.

Morrison, F. J., Holmes, D. L., & Haith, M. M. (1974). A developmental study of the effects of familiarity on short-term visual memory. *Journal of Experimental Child Psychology, 18,* 412–425.

Morrison, F. J., Griffith, E. M., & Frazier, J. A. (1996). Schooling and the 5 to 7 shift: A natural experiment. In A. J. Sameroff & M. M. Haith (Eds.), *The five to seven year shift: The age of reason and responsibility* (chap. 8, this vol.). Chicago: University of Chicago Press.

Morrison, F. J., Smith, L., & Dow-Ehrenberger, M. (1995). Education and cognitive development: A natural experiment. *Developmental Psychology, 31* (5), 789–799.

Neisser, U. (1967). *Cognitive psychology.* New York: Appleton-Century-Crofts.

Nyiti, R. M. (1976). The development of conservation in the Meru children of Tanzania. *Child Development, 47,* 1122–1129.

Okagaki, L., & Sternberg, R. J. (1991). *Directors of development: Influences on the development of children's thinking.* Hillsdale, NJ: Erlbaum.

Ornstein, P. A., & Naus, M. J. (1978). Rehearsal processes in children's memory. In P. A. Ornstein (Ed.), *Memory development in children* (pp. 69–100). Hillsdale, NJ: Erlbaum.

Perfetti, C. A. (1985). *Reading ability.* New York: Oxford University Press.

Perfetti, C. A., Beck, I., Bell, L. C., & Hughes, C. (1987). Phonemic knowledge and learning to read are reciprocal: A longitudinal study of first grade children. *Merrill-Palmer Quarterly, 33,* 283–319.

Piaget, J. (1960). *The psychology of intelligence.* Patterson, NJ: Littlefield & Adams.

Piaget, J. (1968). Quantification, conservation, and nativism. *Science, 162,* 976–979.

Posner, J. K. (1982). The development of mathematical knowledge in two West African societies. *Child Development, 53,* 200–208.

Posner, J. K., & Baroody, A. J. (1979). Number conservation in two West African societies. *Journal of Cross-Cultural Psychology, 10,* 479–496.

Read, C., & Schreiber, P. (1982). Why short subjects are harder to find than long ones. In E. Wanner & L. R. Gleitman (Eds.), *Language acquisition: The state of the art* (pp. 78–101). Cambridge, MA: Cambridge University Press.

Read, C., Zhang, Y., Nie, H., & Ding, B. (1986). The ability to manipulate speech sounds depends on knowing alphabetic spelling. *Cognition, 24,* 31–44.

Rogoff, B. (1981). Schooling and the development of cognitive skills. In H. C. Triandis & A. Heron (Eds.), *Handbook of cross-cultural psychology* (Vol. 4, pp. 233–292). Rockleigh, NJ: Allyn and Bacon.

Rogoff, B. (1996). Developmental transitions in children's participation in sociocultural activities. In A. J. Sameroff & M. M. Haith (Eds.), *The five to seven year shift: The age of reason and responsibility* (chap. 13, this vol.). Chicago: University of Chicago Press.

Schneider, W., & Pressley, M. (1989). *Memory development between 2 and 20.* New York: Springer-Verlag.

Scribner, S., & Cole, M. (1973). Cognitive consequences of formal and informal education. *Science, 182,* 553–559.

Share, D. L., Jorm, A. F., MacLean, R., & Matthews, R. (1984). Sources of individual differences in reading acquisition. *Journal of Experimental Psychology, 76,* 1309–1324.

Shepard, L. A., & Smith, M. L. (1986). Synthesis of research on school readiness and kindergarten retention. *Educational Leadership, 44,* 78–86.

Siegler, R. S. (1987). The perils of averaging data over strategies: An example from children's addition. *Journal of Experimental Psychology: General, 116,* 250–264.

Siegler, R. S. (1989). Mechanisms of cognitive development. In M. R. Rosenzweig & L. W. Porter (Eds.), *Annual review of psychology* (Vol. 40, pp. 3–26). Palo Alto, CA: Annual Review.

Siegler, R. S. (1992). *Children's thinking.* New York: Prentice-Hall.

Siegler, R. S. (1996). Unidimensional thinking, multidimensional thinking, and characteristic tendencies of thought. In A. J. Sameroff & M. M. Haith (Eds.), *The five to seven year shift: The age of reason and responsibility* (chap. 4, this vol.). Chicago: University of Chicago Press.

Siegler, R. S., & Shrager, J. (1984). Strategy choices in addition and subtraction: How do children know what to do? In C. Sophian (Ed.), *Origins of cognitive skills* (pp. 229–293). Hillsdale, NJ: Erlbaum.

Small, M. Y. (1990). *Cognitive development.* New York: Harcourt, Brace, & Janovich.

Song, M. J., & Ginsburg, H. P. (1987). The development of informal and formal mathematical thinking in Korean and U.S. children. *Child Development, 58,* 1286–1296.

Stanovich, K. E., Cunningham, A., & Freeman, D. (1984). Intelligence, cognitive skills, and early reading progress. *Reading Research Quarterly, 19,* 278–303.

Stevenson, H. W., Chen, C., Lee, S. Y., & Fuligni, A. J. (1991). Schooling, culture, and cognitive development. In L. Okagaki & R. J. Sternberg (Eds.), *Director of development: Influences on the development of children's thinking* (pp. 243–268). Hillsdale, NJ: Erlbaum.

Stevenson, H. W., & Lee, S. Y. (1990). Contents of achievement: A study of American, Chinese, and Japanese children. *Monographs of the Society for Research in Child Development, 55,* 3–4).

Stevenson, H. W., Lee, S. Y., & Stigler, J. W. (1986). Mathematics achievement of Chinese, Japanese, and American children. *Science, 231,* 693–699.

Stigler, J. W., & Perry, M. (1988). Cross cultural studies of mathematics teaching and learning: Recent findings and new directions. In D. A. Grouws & T. J. Cooney (Eds.), *Perspectives on research on mathematics teaching* (Vol. 1, pp. 194–223). Hillsdale, NJ: Erlbaum.

Trabasso, T., Stein, N. L., Rodkin, P. C., Munger, M. P., & Baughn, C. R. (1992) Knowledge of goals and plans in the on-line narration of events. *Cognitive Development, 7,* 133–170.

Treiman, R. (1985). Onsets and rhymes as units of spoken syllables: Evidence from children. *Journal of Experimental Child Psychology, 39,* 161–181.

Treiman, R., & Baron, J. (1983). Phonemic-analysis training helps children benefit from spelling-sound rules. *Memory and Cognition, 11,* 382–389.

Treiman, R., & Weatherston, S. (1992). Effects of linguistic structure on children's ability to isolate initial consonants. *Journal of Educational Psychology, 84* (2), 174–181.

Tunmer, W. E., & Nesdale, A. R. (1985). Phonemic segmentation skill and beginning reading. *Journal of Educational Psychology, 77,* 417–427.

Wagner, D. (1981). Culture and memory development. In H. C. Triandis & A. Heron

(Eds.), *Handbook of cross-cultural psychology* (pp. 187–232). Toronto: Allyn and Bacon.

White, S. A. (1965). Evidence for a hierarchical arrangement of learning processes. In L. P. Lipsett & G. C. Spiker (Eds.), *Advances in child development and behavior* (Vol. 2, pp. 1–44). New York: Academic Press.

CHAPTER NINE

The 5 to 7 Shift in Reading and Phoneme Awareness for Children with Dyslexia

RICHARD OLSON, BARBARA WISE, AND HELEN FORSBERG

One of the most significant events in the 5 to 7 age period for most English-speaking children is the development of reading and related language skills. Although some parents successfully teach their children to read during the 4th or 5th year of age, the vast majority of children in the United States and England do not learn to read until the beginning of formal reading instruction in the schools, usually in the first grade beginning around the 6th year of age (Adams, 1990). The critical role of formal instruction has been demonstrated by the comparison of children who were just above or below the age cutoff for beginning school (Morrison, Griffith, & Frazier this volume, chap. 8; Bentin, Hammer, & Cahan, 1991). Nearly all of the development of reading skill and most of an important related language skill, phoneme awareness, are dependent on formal schooling rather than on age. In Germany and the Scandinavian countries, parents are not encouraged to provide informal reading instruction before school begins. Most children in these countries show little development of reading or phoneme awareness until formal schooling begins at age 7 or 8.

There is considerable variation in children's rate of reading development during the early school years. In the United States, much of this variation is associated with large differences in the quality of schools and home literacy environments across different districts. But even in our best schools there is substantial individual variation in reading development, and a significant number of children fail to develop adequate reading skills. The failure of these children is often unexpected in view of their normal instruction, their normal-range performance on standard IQ tests, and the absence of any obvious environmental or neurological cause for their reading difficulty. Children with this type of unexplained reading failure are commonly labeled as *dyslexic*.

In this chapter we provide an overview of recent studies on the etiology of dyslexia and on what can be done to facilitate the age 5 to 7 shift in reading for children with dyslexia. The chapter is organized in three main sections. First we examine correlational and longitudinal studies that point to the role of deficient phoneme awareness in dyslexia. Second, we review behavioral-genetic studies of identical and fraternal twins with dyslexia that reveal both shared environmental and genetic influences on their deficits in reading and phoneme awareness. Third, we examine the results of training phoneme awareness to facilitate the development of reading among children with dyslexia.

Phoneme Awareness in Normal and Abnormal Reading Development

Successful phonological decoding of nonwords and unfamiliar words typically requires the reader efficiently to recognize the mapping between subword speech sounds and letters or letter clusters. Although this mapping is not entirely consistent in English, enough consistency exists to allow skilled readers to decode unfamiliar printed words phonologically with agreement among a few possible pronunciations.

There is now a large body of evidence that a specific type of analytic language skill called phoneme awareness is highly correlated with the broad distribution of skill in phonological decoding and word recognition (Wagner & Torgesen, 1987). Phoneme awareness refers to the ability to isolate and manipulate individual phonemes within spoken words or syllables. A number of different tasks have been used to assess phoneme awareness. These include counting the number of phonemes in a spoken word, blending individually spoken phonemes into a word, and deleting a phoneme from a spoken word and pronouncing the result (e.g., say "cup" without the /k/ sound: "up") (Yopp, 1988). The development of phoneme awareness may be essential for learning to read alphabetic orthographies such as English (Gough, Juel, & Griffith, 1992).

Many theorists have argued from the correlation between phoneme awareness and reading that individual differences in phoneme awareness *cause* individual differences in reading ability. However, there is ample evidence that learning to read is itself a major causal factor in the development of phoneme awareness. Cross-cultural data on illiterate adults have shown very low levels of phoneme awareness before reading instruction and rapid development of phoneme awareness during reading instruction (Morais, 1991). A similar result has been found for young children: Phoneme awareness in preschoolers is quite low but develops rapidly with the onset of reading instruction, regardless of age (Morrison, et. al., this volume, chap. 8; Bentin et al., 1991).

Because of the clear influence of learning to read on the development of phoneme awareness, theorists who wish to argue for its causal role in reading development have used two main research strategies. One has been to train phoneme awareness in preschoolers and to show that this training subsequently facilitates learning to read. Such training effects have been demonstrated in several studies, although the effects have not been very large without concomitant instruction in reading (for a review, see Crowder & Wagner, 1991). (We return to the issue of training in the third section of this chapter.) A second approach has been to assess preschoolers' levels of phoneme awareness and see if these correlate with later reading development. Several of these longitudinal studies have reported significant positive correlations (for a review, see Wagner & Torgesen, 1987). However, some of the preschoolers in these studies may have had some limited reading skills that influenced their phoneme awareness prior to formal reading instruction. Their head start in reading could have led to better reading in school and a positive correlation with preschool phoneme awareness.

A recent longitudinal study by Wagner, Torgesen, and Rashote (in press) carefully measured both phoneme awareness and early reading skills, including knowledge of letter names and sounds, for a large sample ($N = 244$) of beginning kindergarten children. Multiple measures of the different skills allowed the modeling of relations between latent variables. Latent variables were used to estimate the true correlations between phoneme awareness and reading without attenuation from error variance in the individual measures. Only a few of the kindergartners had sufficient home instruction to be classified as readers, but others had some beginning reading skills that included recognition of a few words and knowledge of letter names or sounds. The variability in the kindergartners' early reading skills was significantly correlated with their phoneme awareness ($r = .43$ for phoneme deletion), even though phoneme awareness and reading were generally very low across the whole sample.

Wagner et al. (in press) evaluated the independent relation between kindergarten phoneme awareness and later reading in the first and second grades *after* controlling for the children's initial reading levels and oral vocabulary. The results clearly supported a strong causal link ($r = .67$) between early phoneme awareness and reading at the end of first grade that was independent of reading knowledge and oral vocabulary at the beginning of kindergarten. Thus, although children's phoneme awareness is typically quite low prior to reading instruction, variation in phoneme awareness that is independent of reading level within this limited range appears to play a significant causal role in determining individual differences in later reading skills. Moreover, initial levels of phoneme awareness at the beginning of kindergarten, independent of initial reading and oral vocabulary, were highly correlated with levels of phoneme awareness in the first and second grades. Phoneme awareness increased substantially with formal reading instruction, but children's relative position in the sample was quite stable in the 5 to 7 age range.

This relationship between phoneme awareness and reading in the Wagner et al. (in press) broad longitudinal sample suggests that children with dyslexia will also have low phoneme awareness. This hypothesis has been confirmed in a large number of studies wherein children with dyslexia and children without reading problems have been matched on age (for a review, see Stanovich, 1986). However, the dyslexic children's deficit in phoneme awareness could have been at least partly due to the reciprocal influence of their limited reading development. Several studies have therefore examined the phoneme awareness of older children with dyslexia compared with younger normal groups that were matched on level of word recognition. In these studies, the phoneme awareness of the older children with dyslexia was significantly lower than that of the younger reading-level-matched normal groups. A unique deficit in phoneme awareness compared to reading level has also been found for other populations with dyslexia: for adults (Bruck, 1992; Pennington, Van Orden, Smith, Green, & Haith, 1990), adolescents (Olson, Wise, Conners, Rack, & Fulker, 1989), and 9-year-olds (Bowey, Cain, & Ryan, in press; Manis, Custodio, & Szeszulski, 1993). In contrast, other language skills such as oral vocabulary and oral comprehension were significantly better in the group with dyslexia compared with younger readers without reading problems at the same level of word recognition (Conners & Olson, 1990). These studies suggest that the unique and specific deficits in the analytic language skill of phoneme awareness among people with dyslexia may play an important causal role in the development of their reading problems.

The dissociation in dyslexia between the development of phoneme awareness and other language skills may be linked to a similar dissociation in the development of component reading skills. It is now generally recognized that the primary reading deficit in children with dyslexia involves the decoding of printed words (Stanovich, 1988). These children are also deficient in reading comprehension when compared with same-age normal readers, but their reading comprehension is significantly better when compared with that of younger normal readers matched on level of recognition for individual printed words (Conners & Olson, 1990). This indicates that deficits in reading comprehension among children with dyslexia are at least partly secondary to their deficits in isolated word recognition.

It is also generally recognized that the deficit in word recognition in dyslexia is primarily due to underlying deficits in phonological decoding, which is typically measured by the oral reading of pronounceable nonwords (e.g., *tegwop, framble*). When groups of older children with dyslexia and younger children who read normally have been matched on level of word recognition, the dyslexic groups are usually substantially worse than the normal-reading groups in phonological decoding (Rack, Snowling, & Olson, 1992). This suggests that deficits in word recognition may be secondary to primary deficits in the phonological decoding component of word recognition.

The unique deficits in phonological decoding while reading are mirrored by unique language deficits in phoneme awareness among people with dyslexia. We now turn to behavioral-genetic studies that provide evidence for the common genetic and environmental etiology of deficits in reading and phoneme awareness.

Behavioral-Genetic Evidence

The reading deficits of children with dyslexia place serious constraints on their educational progress. Therefore, the National Institutes of Health has recognized dyslexia as a major public health problem and currently supports several large research programs to explore the etiology and remediation of dyslexia. One of these programs is the Colorado Reading Project, which has conducted twin studies of the genetic and environmental etiology of dyslexia and associated deficits (DeFries, Olson, Pennington, & Smith, 1991).

In the Colorado Reading Project we have compared the similarities of identical and fraternal twin pairs to provide estimates of genetic and shared-environment influence on reading and language deficits. Identical twins develop from the same sperm and egg (monozygotic or MZ) and thus share all their genes. Fraternal twins are derived from two different sperm-egg combinations (dizygotic or DZ), just as ordinary siblings, and they share half their genes on average. The behavioral-genetic interpretation of data from MZ and DZ twins is based on several important assumptions, including additive influence from any relevant genes, no assortative mating, and an equal degree of shared environment for MZ and DZ pairs (Plomin, DeFries, & McClearn, 1990). If these assumptions are not violated to a significant degree, comparing MZ and DZ within-pair differences provides estimates for the proportions of genetic, shared-environment, and non-shared-environment influence on average twin resemblance.

Our dyslexic and normal comparison groups included 3rd- to 12th-grade MZ and same-sex DZ twins ascertained from 27 Colorado school districts. The twins were invited to participate in laboratory testing if either member of a pair's school records (teacher reports, remedial classes, or test scores, or a combination of some or all of these) showed evidence of a reading problem. To provide a normal-range comparison group, a smaller sample of twins with no school record of reading problems was also tested in the laboratory. Some of these twins turned out to have significant deficits and were therefore included in the group with dyslexia for the analyses presented in this chapter. Twins were excluded from the present analyses if they had any of the following: both verbal and performance IQ scores below 90; evidence of neural damage such as seizures; or obvious sensory, social, emotional, or educational conditions such as poor school attendance that might cause reading problems.

The twins were tested with a number of standardized psychometric tests including the full Wechsler IQ test (Wechsler, 1977), the Peabody Individual Achievement Tests (PIAT) for reading comprehension, word recognition, spelling, and math (Dunn & Markwardt, 1970), and several experimental measures of component reading and language skills. In this review we focus on the results for three main skills: word recognition, phonological decoding, and phoneme awareness. Complete descriptions of the measures for these skills are provided in Olson, Forsberg, Wise, and Rack (1994). Word recognition was estimated by combining the results for the PIAT word-recognition test with results for an experimental measure of word recognition. Phonological decoding was assessed by presenting a complete series of 85 one- and two-syllable nonwords on the computer (e.g., *ite, calch, doun, tegwop, framble*). Participants were instructed to pronounce each nonword as quickly and accurately as possible when it appeared on the screen. Phoneme awareness was measured by requiring participants to isolate the initial phoneme of each of 48 spoken target words, place the phoneme at the end of the word, add the sound "ay," and pronounce the result. For example, *pig* would be pronounced "igpay" (this task is much like the children's game and jargon called Pig Latin).

Twin studies of the full range of individual differences across the population usually compare the correlations for MZ and DZ pairs. However, a more appropriate and powerful statistical approach can be used to assess the group heritability for selected characteristics, such as dyslexia, which are deviant from the normal population (DeFries and Fulker, 1985). In this approach, an affected twin (the *proband*) is identified based on a severity criterion for deviation from the mean of the normal population. Genetic and shared-environment influence is then assessed by comparing the MZ and DZ co-twins' regression toward the control group mean.

Suppose that the average proband deficit for both MZ and DZ twins is 2 *SD* below the population mean for a particular measure. If there is no test error and individual differences in performance on that measure are completely heritable, the MZ co-twins should show no regression to the population mean because they share identical genes. DZ co-twins should regress halfway (1 *SD*) to the population mean because they share half their genes, on average. On the other extreme, if there is no heritability for a particular measure, MZ and DZ co-twins would show equal regression to the population mean. Differential co-twin regression between these two extreme examples would indicate an intermediate level of heritability.

Twin data are also informative about the degree to which shared environment, nonshared environment, or both is important for individual differences. If *both* MZ and DZ co-twins showed no regression to the population mean, this would indicate that shared environment accounted entirely for individual differences across the twin pairs. In the more likely case in which MZ co-twins regress somewhat to the mean due to test error and nonshared environment, and DZ co-twins regress more, but somewhat less than halfway to the mean, the combined influence of shared environment and genetic factors is indicated for the probands' group deficit.

The regression procedure used in the present behavioral-genetic analyses was developed by DeFries and Fulker (1985). Their procedure yields estimates and standard errors for the proportion of genetic influence on the probands' group deficit (h^2_g) and the proportion of shared-environment influence (c^2_g). The difference between the sum of these estimates and 1.0 indicates the proportion of twin differences due to nonshared environment, test error, or both.

Estimates and standard errors for heritability (h^2_g) and shared environment (c^2_g) along with the proband and co-twin means for our current sample of MZ and DZ pairs are presented in Table 9.1. For the probands' group deficit in word recognition, it can be seen that the heritability (.47) and shared-environment estimates (.48) are quite similar, leaving a small proportion (.05) of individual differences associated with test error and nonshared environment.

The balance of genetic and environmental influence on the group deficit in phonological decoding was slightly different from that on the group deficit in word recognition (see Table 9.1). The heritability for the group deficit in phonological decoding was higher (.59), and there was a smaller but statistically significant influence of shared environment (.27).

The results for phoneme awareness were similar to those for phonological decoding (see Table 9.1). There was significant heritability (.60) for the group deficit in phoneme awareness, but the effects of shared environment (.20) were not significant. The remaining effect of nonshared environment, test error

Table 9.1
Genetic (h^2_g) and Shared Environment (c^2_g) Influence on Group Deficits in Dyslexic Readers' Word Recognition, Phonological Decoding, and Phoneme Awareness

Task	MZ Proband	MZ Co-Twin	DZ Proband	DZ Co-Twin	h^2_g $(SE)^a$	c^2_g $(SE)^b$
Word Recognition (MZ=183, DZ=129)	−2.65	−2.52	−2.62	−1.87	.47 (.09)*	.48 (.11)*
Phonological Decoding (MZ=151, DZ=105)	−2.63	−2.28	−2.62	−1.50	.59 (.12)*	.27 (.12)*
Phoneme Awareness (MZ=93, DZ=68)	−3.37	−2.67	−2.79	−1.39	.60 (.17)*	.20 (.16)

Note: Probands were selected independently for each measure to be at least 1.5 *SD* below the normal group mean. The numbers of MZ and DZ pairs for each measure are presented in parentheses.
[a]$h^2_g = 2 \cdot$ CMZ/PMZ − CDZ/PDZ. [b]$c^2_g = $ 2CDZ/PDZ − CMZ/PMZ.
* = $p < .01$ for estimates significantly greater than 0.

[1 − (.60 + .20) = .20], or both may be due to the relatively low reliability for this measure.

The significant heritabilities for deficits in word recognition, phonological decoding, and phoneme awareness led us to ask if the same genetic influence might be responsible for deficits in all three measures. Of course, high heritabilities for any pair of measures do not imply that they are influenced by the same genes. This is obvious for measures such as height and word recognition, which are both significantly heritable but not correlated in the population. The age-adjusted measures of word recognition, phonological decoding, and phoneme awareness were significantly correlated within the dyslexic twin sample including probands and co-twins. However, the question we wish to address is the balance of shared-genetic and shared-environment influence on covariation *between* the measures. For example, their correlation could be produced primarily through shared-environment effects rather than genetic effects or vice versa.

The degree of common genetic influence across different variables can be assessed by a bivariate extension of the DeFries and Fulker (1985) univariate multiple-regression procedure. In the bivariate extension, the proband is selected for a deficit on one variable and co-twin regression to the population mean is assessed for the second variable. The resulting bivariate estimate of h^2_g is a function of the group heritabilities for the two variables and the degree to which these group heritabilities are influenced by the same genes. Furthermore, the ratio of the bivariate heritability to the observed standardized covariance between the variables yields an estimate of the proportion of the correlation between the variables that is due to the same genes. For example, the bivariate heritability could be low between two variables because their covariance is low, but most of the variables' shared variance could be due to the same genes.

Table 9.2 presents the results of three bivariate heritability estimates. For each estimate, the proband is selected on the variable that is most highly correlated with the initial group designation of school history for reading problems. This selection is least likely to significantly violate the assumptions of the DeFries and Fulker (1985) multiple-regression procedure. The first column in Table 9.2 presents the estimate of bivariate heritability with its standard error. The second column presents the regression coefficient between the two variables within the proband sample, which provides an unbiased estimate of their linear relationship in selected samples. The third column includes the estimates and their standard errors for the proportion of the correlation between the two variables that is due to common genetic factors.

The first two analyses in Table 9.2 involve proband selection on deficits in word recognition and co-twin regression on a second variable. The bivariate heritability estimates were significantly greater than zero ($p < .05$) for phonological coding and phonological awareness. After dividing these estimates

Table 9.2
Genetic (h_g^2) and Shared Environment (c_g^2) Influence on Covariance for Group Deficits in Word
Recognition, Phonological Decoding, and Phoneme Awareness

Proband Variable	Co-Twin Variable	Bivariate Heritability	Regression Coefficient	Genetic Proportion
Word Recognition	—Phonological Decoding	.43 ± .10	.742	.58 ± .14
Word Recognition	—Phoneme Awareness	.46 ± .16	.613	.75 ± .26
Phonological Decoding	—Phoneme Awareness	.51 ± .18	.656	.78 ± .27

by the regression coefficient, the estimates in the right column represent the proportion of the correlation due to common genetic influences. These estimates are quite high, indicating that the observed covariances are due primarily to heritable influences.

A third bivariate genetic analysis of phoneme awareness was conducted by selecting probands for deficits in phonological decoding. Phonological decoding was highly correlated ($r = .77$) with the primary basis for selection (reading) of our dyslexic sample, so the bivariate estimates with phonological decoding should be valid. The genetic covariance between deficits in phonological decoding and phoneme awareness is substantial (.51) and statistically significant (see Table 9.2).

In summary, we have presented behavioral-genetic evidence that the unique deficits in phonological decoding and phoneme awareness in children with dyslexia are significantly heritable and are largely due to the same genetic influence. It was also shown that much of the genetic influence on deficits in word recognition is shared with phonological decoding. A limitation of our behavioral genetic analyses is that we are only able to assess the heritability of *group* deficits. The degree and specific type of genetic as well as shared-environment influence could vary widely across individuals. Genetic linkage analyses within several different families containing dyslexic probands have suggested heterogeneity in the apparent mode of genetic transmission (Smith, Kimberling, & Pennington, 1991). (The genetic linkage procedure relates reading deficits to specific loci on the chromosomes.) This result raises the possibility of different genetic pathways, perhaps through different profiles of reading and language deficits.

On the environmental side, we noted the strong influence of shared environment on deficits in word recognition. This result was obtained in spite of our exclusion of poor readers with obvious environmental deficits such as poor school attendance or low socioeconomic level. Apparently there was still a wide range of environments for reading development in the twins' homes and schools. It should be noted that the relative balance of genetic and shared-environment influence on probands' group deficits depends on both the strength of genetic factors and the range of relevant environmental differences between twin pairs. If the environmental range were broadened in the sample, estimates of heritability would be lower and shared environment would be higher. Narrowing the environmental range would yield the opposite result.

We have studied environmental influences in dyslexia from two perspectives. One has been to assess subjects' print exposure through tests of magazine and book-title recognition developed by Cunningham and Stanovich (1991). Deficits in print exposure were not significantly heritable, but they did show significant effects of shared environment and significant shared-environment covariance with probands' deficits in word recognition (Olson, 1993, March). Our second approach to understanding environmental influences on dyslexia has been to explore the effects of different types of computer-based training on word recognition, phonological decoding, and phoneme awareness.

Deficits in phonological decoding and phoneme awareness constrain the development of dyslexics' word recognition in two ways. First, their attempts to sound out an unfamiliar word may often be incorrect. If the error is not recognized and corrected, as is often the case for silent reading in the classroom, erroneous print-to-sound associations are reinforced. The incorrect associations may subsequently interfere with memory for those print-to-sound relations in other similarly spelled words. Second, when children with dyslexia look at an unfamiliar word and are told what it says, they typically require many more learning trials with corrective feedback than do children without reading problems to establish an automatized level of recognition for a printed word (Reitsma, 1983). The encoding of a stable relation between the print and sound may be limited by deficits in associating units of orthography and phonology smaller than the word, the essence of phonological decoding. Improved phonological decoding skills should lead to the more rapid development of word recognition. Although we have shown in this section that deficits in phonological decoding may be strongly influenced by genetic factors in many children with dyslexia, this suggests only that some extraordinary environmental intervention may be required, beyond what most of these children currently receive in their homes and schools.

Computer-Based Training for Reading and Phoneme Awareness

The development of high-quality synthetic speech for microcomputers has made possible some promising new approaches to the remediation of dyslexia. Our recent studies using this technology have focused on the long-term training of generalizable phonological-decoding skills and word recognition for second- to sixth-grade children with dyslexia. These children read stories on the computer for half an hour each day over a semester, scheduled during their language-arts and reading instructional time (Olson & Wise, 1992; Wise & Olson, 1992; Wise et al., 1989). The children were trained to target problematic words in order to obtain orthographic and speech feedback presented in words (e.g., *cupcake*) or in word segments of either syllables (e.g., *cup/cake*) or of onsets and rhymes (e.g., *c/up/c/ake*). The subword units were sequentially highlighted and spoken by the computer after the child targeted the word with a mouse. The rationale for the different levels of feedback segmentation was that while whole-word feedback should help children read difficult stories and build their sight-reading vocabularies, segmented feedback might provide additional support for the development of phonological decoding skills.

Pretest to posttest gains over a semester in word recognition and in phonological decoding were compared across the three different feedback conditions. Gains were also compared with an untrained control group matched for having similar reading problems. These control participants received their normal course of instruction in remedial-reading or language-arts classes. Across the three feedback conditions, gains in phonological decoding were 3 to 4 times greater than for the control group, and gains in word-recognition grade levels averaged nearly twice those of the control group. However, the impressive group effects were not found for all participants. When children were divided into high and low groups on an age-adjusted pretest measure of phoneme awareness, the relatively higher phoneme-awareness group showed almost twice the gains of the lower phoneme-awareness group, although children in the high group were still significantly lower in this skill than would be expected for normal readers of the same age.

This relationship between gains and initial phoneme awareness among children with dyslexia suggested that training this skill prior to, concurrent with, or both prior to and concurrent with computer-based reading might be beneficial, particularly for those children whose reading development is constrained by especially low levels of phoneme awareness. Several studies have found that when randomly selected groups of prereaders have been trained in phoneme awareness with various language exercises, their reading development during the first and second grades is slightly faster than for untrained comparison groups (c.f. Lundberg, Frost, & Peterson, 1988). Substantially greater gains in phoneme awareness and later reading come from the combination of phoneme-awareness and letter-sound training (c.f. Byrne & Fielding-Barnsley, 1991). Combinations of phoneme-awareness and reading instruction have also been effectively employed in studies with first graders with reading disabilities (cf Ball & Blachman, 1988; Uhry & Shepherd, 1993).

Most studies have trained phoneme awareness by having participants directly practice some of the language tasks that have traditionally been used in assessment. For example, children might practice blending individual phonemes to form words or delete phonemes from spoken words and pronounce the result. If letters are included in the training, practice is given in associating different phonemes with letters or letter clusters. Clear group benefits have been shown for this type of training, but there are always participants who seem to have extreme difficulty with phoneme-awareness tasks and show relatively small gains in phoneme awareness and reading (Byrne & Fielding-Barnsley, 1991).

Auditory Discrimination in Depth (ADD), a commercially published phonemic-awareness training program (Lindamood & Lindamood, 1975), has special theoretical interest because of its unique emphasis on oral-motor feedback to support conceptualization about phonemes. Children are trained to feel and compare articulatory similarities and differences among phonemes. They manipulate and combine phonemes in isolation and within syllables and words, first using mouth pictures and then abstract blocks and letters to represent the phonemes. Ultimately their training in phoneme awareness is combined with learning about the correspondence between phonemes and print. A similar emphasis on articulatory training has been used by Skjelfjord (1987) and by Lie (1991) in Norway. The use of articulatory awareness as a bridge to phoneme awareness is consistent with A. Liberman's (1982) "motor-theory" that speech is perceived according to articulatory features and with I. Liberman's view that awareness of phonology is necessary for development of the "alphabetic principle" crucial to reading English (Liberman, Shankweiler, Fisher, & Carter, 1974). Montgomery (1981) demonstrated that children with dyslexia cannot access articulatory information as well as children who read normally.

The ADD program (Lindamood & Lindamood, 1975) has been shown to be very effective with children with extreme reading difficulties in two recent studies. One study at a private school used no control group but reported good progress among a group of ten 8- to 14-year-old children with severe dyslexia who had made little progress with previous methods (Alexander, Anderson, Heilman, Voeller, & Torgesen, 1991). Another study at a private school did use a control group, comparing two matched groups of nine 11- to 17-year-old children (Kennedy & Blackman, 1993). The control group received the school's highly regarded phonics-emphasis remedial program. The other group spent 3 hours a day for 6 weeks learning the ADD method before merging it with the school's regular program. All children improved substantially by the end of the school year. The ADD-trained group did not gain significantly more than controls on standardized tests of reading and spelling, although trends favored them, and groups were small. They did make significant improvement relative to the controls in the phonetic quality of their errors in spelling and nonsense-word reading. The greatest differences between the groups occurred in the first semester, when the intensive ADD training occurred. Thus, the program did appear to improve phonological awareness, though with less transfer to reading than one might have hoped.

We recently reanalzyed some previously unpublished data from a clinical training study of two first-grade classes in California (Wise, Olson, & Lindamood, 1993, April). A control class had received the school's normal Ginn basal reading program. The experimental class spent 4 months learning the

ADD program before integrating it with the Ginn reading program. The unpublished report had indicated significant overall gains in four tests: the WRAT (Wide Range Achievement Test) for word recognition, the Lindamood Auditory Conceptualization Test, the Woodcock Word Attack test, and the WRAT spelling test. Our reanalysis examined the progress of the lower 10% of children in each classroom, based on pretest abilities on these same four tests. One would expect these children to be the most at risk for later reading problems. The analysis revealed that in the ADD classroom, the gains of the at-risk children were at least as great as those of the better readers on reading and spelling measures, and gains were significantly greater in nonsense-word reading for the at-risk group. In the control classroom, on the other hand, the at-risk children made the least progress of any of the groups on all measures. Interpretation of this interaction is tenuous owing to the unequal size of the groups, so we conducted another analysis splitting the groups in two based on pretest nonsense-word reading. The significant interaction between ability level and training condition indicated relatively *greater* gains in nonsense-word reading for the low group in the ADD class and relatively lower gains for the low group in the regular class.

These studies suggest that the ADD program is a particularly effective method for boosting poor readers' phoneme awareness and reading skills in beginning and in remedial reading programs. We therefore wondered if pretraining phoneme awareness with the ADD program would significantly improve gains made on our computer-based reading program. Propitiously, the Lindamood-Bell Center is developing a computer-based version of the ADD training program. We are collaborating with Pat Lindamood to test and extend her computerized version of the ADD training program and to interface it with phonological analysis programs and story-reading programs we have designed.

In the fall semester of 1993, we began a study with second- to fifth-grade children with significant reading problems, scheduled three at a time (Wise & Olson, in press). In the fall, the children were pretested on many reading and language measures and were trained to read stories on the computers. In January, strategy training commenced. Half the children had intense phonological analysis (PA) training, beginning with 6 hours of articulatory awareness training based on the Lindamood ADD method. This training was interspersed with practice on the computer, initially utilizing the Lindamood programs using animated mouth pictures for articulatory awareness, and progressing into our own phonological analysis programs using synthetic speech feedback for children's attempts in programs that taught children to analyze and manipulate phoneme and letter patterns; to decode nonwords; and to explore spelling-sound patterns, previously shown to improve phonological coding (Wise & Olson, 1992). As soon as the children could manipulate sound and letter patterns with 80% success at the consonant-vowel-consonant (CVC) level in the phonological analysis programs, they began spending increasing time also reading stories on the computer along with continued practice on the articulatory awareness and phonological analysis programs.

This analytical approach to the training of phoneme awareness and reading was compared to a second condition that began with 6 hours of small-group instruction in comprehension strategies (*CS*) based on the reciprocal teaching method developed by Palinscar and Brown (1984). In this method, the teacher modeled, and children gradually took over, the teaching role while practicing the comprehension strategies of prediction, clarification, question generation, and summarization while reading stories both on and off the computer. Reciprocal teaching has been shown to improve both comprehension and the detection of errors, which should improve children's requests for computer-speech feedback while reading stories.

The CS group had substantially greater practice reading stories on the computer and thus more print exposure compared with the PA group. Total training time and small-group instruction time were the same under the CS and PA conditions. The story-reading computer instruction for both groups used segmented speech feedback for targeted words, which previous research had shown to provide substantial gains in phonological decoding and word recognition for most children (Wise et al., 1989; Olson & Wise, 1992).

Analyses at midsemester indicated interesting and contrasting gains for the two groups, both of which had 10 hours of individualized computer instruction in addition to their 6 hours of small-group instruction (Wise & Olson, in press). However, the PA group had only spent up to 2 hours reading stories on the computer by the midsemester tests, and the rest of their computer time was in the PA programs. The PA group showed significantly greater gains in phoneme awareness and phonological decoding (nonword reading). The PA group was also slightly but not significantly better in an untimed test of word recognition wherein they had adequate time to apply their analytic word decoding skills. However, the CS group showed significantly greater gains in a timed word-recognition test that required rapid responses. We hypothesize that with enough further training time reading stories, the PA children should get faster in applying their skills and should improve in their speed of word recognition as well.

If the advantages of PA training are confirmed in a second sample that was trained during the 1994–95 school year, we will do further studies to learn which components of the PA program are essential for children of varying initial profiles. It may be that children with the lowest phonemic awareness skills require the intense instruction in articulatory awareness as a base, whereas others with moderate problems may do quite well with just the phonological analysis programs leading on into reading. Perhaps those with the least severe deficits may achieve best with the decoding by segmentation and analogy while reading stories with the segmented speech feedback. Another planned extension of our research is to train preschool children who are at risk for reading failure. Our behavioral-genetic research has shown that such children can likely be identified through the presence of dyslexia in their family members. Scarborough (1990) has already used this approach, combined with language analysis, with some success. Catts (1991) has also supported the assessment of prereaders' language skills for early identification of at-risk children. The hope is that intensive early training in the linguistic basis for decoding printed words will be particularly helpful for avoiding the experience of failure during reading instruction in the early grades.

Summary

The 5 to 7 shift in reading and phoneme awareness is usually a qualitative change associated with the explicit instruction in reading that most English-speaking children receive during this period. Compared to the gradual development of language skills such as oral vocabulary during the first 5 to 7 years, most children's basic reading skills and phoneme awareness develop relatively abruptly and rapidly between the ages of 5 and 7. However, the reading skills and phoneme awareness of some children show a substantial deficit during this period that usually continues in later years.

Our research with identical and fraternal twins has shown that the group deficit in dyslexics' reading development and phoneme awareness is substantially heritable, and the covariance between deficits in reading and phoneme awareness is largely due to the same genes. A causal link from deficits in phoneme awareness to deficits in reading has been supported by (1) longitudinal studies of prereaders' phoneme awareness and later reading development, (2) by studies showing that most deficits in phoneme awareness are even worse than the reading deficits among people with dyslexia, and (3) by studies showing that effective early remediation of deficits in phoneme awareness can substantially improve reading development between the ages of 5 and 7, as well as in later years.

Although there appears to be a strong genetic constraint on dyslexics' development of phoneme awareness, the extraordinary environmental intervention of phoneme-awareness training can lead to substantial gains in both phoneme awareness and reading. Early identification and remediation of deficits in preschoolers' and beginning readers' phoneme awareness can facilitate a more normal 5 to 7 shift and avoid the frustration of reading failure in the early school years. Our research on the best way to achieve these goals continues.

Acknowledgments

This work was supported in part by program project and center grants from the National Institutes of Health (HD-11681 and HD-27801) and from the National Institute of Child Health and Development (ROI HD-22223). The contributions of staff members of the many Colorado school districts that participated in our research and the contributions of the twins and their families are gratefully acknowledged.

References

Adams, M. J. (1990). *Beginning to read: Thinking and learning about print.* Cambridge, MA: MIT Press.

Alexander, A. W., Anderson, H. G., Heilman, P. C., Voeller, K. S., & Torgesen, J. K. (1991). Phonological awareness training and remediation of analytic decoding deficits in a group of severe dyslexics. *Annals of Dyslexia, 41,* 193–206.

Ball, E. W., & Blachman, B. A. (1988). Phoneme segmentation training: Effect on reading readiness. *Annals of Dyslexia, 38,* 208–225.

Bentin, S., Hammer, R., & Cahan, S. (1991). The effects of aging and first grade schooling on the development of phonological awareness. *Psychological Science, 2,* 271–274.

Bowey, J. A., Cain, M. T., & Ryan, S. M. (in press). A reading-level design study of phonological skills underlying fourth-grade children's word reading difficulties. *Child Development.*

Bruck, M. (1992). The persistence of dyslexics' phonological awareness deficits. *Developmental Psychology, 28,* 874–886.

Byrne, B., & Fielding-Barnsley, R. (1991). Evaluation of a program to teach phonemic awareness to young children. *Journal of Educational Psychology, 82,* 805–812.

Catts, H. W. (1991). Early identification of dyslexia: Evidence from a follow-up study of speech-language impaired children. *Annals of Dyslexia, 41,* 163–177.

Conners, F., & Olson, R. K. (1990). Reading comprehension in dyslexic and normal readers: A component skills analysis. In D. A. Balota, G. B. Flores d'Arcais, & K. Rayner (Eds.), *Comprehension processes in reading* (pp. 557–579). Hillsdale, NJ: Erlbaum.

Crowder, R. G., & Wagner, R. K. (1991). *The psychology of reading: An Introduction.* New York: Oxford University Press.

Cunningham, A. E., & Stanovich, K. E. (1991). Tracking the unique effects of print exposure in children: Associations with vocabulary, general knowledge, and spelling. *Journal of Educational Psychology, 83,* 264–274.

Defries, J. C., & Fulker, D. W. (1985). Multiple regression analysis of twin data. *Behavior Genetics, 15,* 467–473.

DeFries, J. C., Olson, R. K., Pennington, B. F., & Smith, S. D. (1991). Colorado reading project: An update. In D. Duane and D. Gray (Eds.), *The reading brain: The biological basis of dyslexia* (pp. 53–87). Parkton, MD: York Press.

Dunn, L. M., & Markwardt, F. C. (1970). *Examiner's manual: Peabody Individual Achievement Test.* Circle Pines, MN: American Guidance Service.

Gough, P. B., Juel, C., & Griffith, P. (1992). Reading, spelling, and the orthographic cipher. In P. B. Gough, L. C. Ehri, & R. Treiman (Eds.), *Reading Acquisition.* Hillsdale, NJ: Erlbaum.

Kennedy, K. M., & Blackman, J. (1993). Effectiveness of the Lindamood Auditory Discrimination in Depth program with students with learning disabilities. *Learning Disabilities Research and Practice, 8,* 253–259.

Liberman, A. (1982). On finding that speech is special. *American Psychologist, 37,* 148–167.

Liberman, I. Y., Shankweiler, D. Fisher, F. W., & Carter, B. (1974). Explicit syllable and phoneme segmentation in the young child. *Journal of Experimental Child Psychology, 18,* 201–212.

Lie, A. (1991). Effects of training program for stimulating skills in word analysis in first-grade children. *Reading Research Quarterly, 26,* 234–250.

Lindamood, C. H., & Lindamood, P. C. (1975). *Auditory Discrimination in Depth.* Columbus, OH: SRA Division, Macmillan/McGraw-Hill.

Lundberg, I., Frost, J., & Peterson, O. (1988). Effects of an extensive program for stimulating phonological awareness in preschool children. *Reading Research Quarterly, 23,* 263–284.

Manis, F. R., Custodio, R., & Szeszulski, P. A. (1993). Development of phonological and orthographic skills: A two-year longitudinal study of dyslexic children. *Journal of Experimental Child Psychology, 56,* 64–86.

Montgomery, D. (1981). Do dyslexics have difficulty accessing articulatory information? *Psychological Research, 43,* 235–243.

Morais, J. (1991). Phonological awareness: A bridge between language and literacy. In D. Sawyer & B. Fox (Eds.), *Phonological awareness in reading: The evolution of current perspectives* (pp. 31–71). New York: Springer-Verlag.

Morrison, F. J., Griffith, E. M., & Frazier, J. A. (1996). Schooling and the 5 to 7 shift: A natural experiment. In A. J. Sameroff & M. M. Haith (Eds.), *The five to seven year shift: The age of reason and responsibility* (chap. 8, this vol.). Chicago: University of Chicago Press.

Olson, R. K. (1993, March). *Shared-environment and genetic influences in deficits in phonological and orthographic processes.* Paper presented to the meeting of the Society for Research in Child Development. New Orleans, LA.

Olson, R., Forsberg, H., Wise, B., & Rack, J. (1994). Measurement of word recognition, orthographic, and phonological skills. In G. R. Lyon (Ed.), *Frames of reference for the assessment of learning disabilities: New views on measurement issues* (pp. 243–277). Baltimore, MD: Paul H. Brookes Publishing.

Olson, R. K., & Wise, B. W. (1992). Reading on the computer with orthographic and speech feedback: An overview of the Colorado Remedial Reading Project. *Reading and Writing: An Interdisciplinary Journal, 4,* 107–144.

Olson, R. K., Wise, B., Conners, F., Rack, J., & Fulker, D. (1989). Specific deficits in component reading and language skills: Genetic and environmental influences. *Journal of Learning Disabilities, 22,* 339–348.

Palinscar, A. S., & Brown A. L. (1984). Reciprocal teaching of comprehension-fostering and comprehension-monitoring activities. *Cognition and Instruction, 1,* 117–175.

Pennington, B. F., Van Orden, G. C., Smith, S. D., Green, P. A., & Haith, M. M. (1990). Phonological processing skills and deficits in adult dyslexics. *Child Development, 61,* 1753–1778.

Plomin, R., DeFries, J. C., & McClearn, G. E. (1990). *Behavior genetics: A primer.* San Francisco: W. H. Freeman.

Rack, J. P., Snowling, M. J., & Olson, R. K. (1992). The nonword reading deficit in developmental dyslexia: A review. *Reading Research Quarterly, 27* (1), 28–53.

Reitsma, P. (1983). Word-specific knowledge in beginning reading. *Journal of Research in Reading, 6*, 41–56.

Scarborough, H. S. (1990). Very early language deficits in dyslexic children. *Child Development, 61*, 1728–1743.

Skjelfjord, V. J. (1987). Phonemic segmentation: An important subskill in learning to read: I. *Scandinavian Journal of Educational Research, 31*, 41–57.

Smith, S. D., Kimberling, W. J., & Pennington, B. F. (1991). Screening for multiple genes influencing dyslexia. *Reading and Writing: An Interdisciplinary Journal, 3*, 285–298.

Sanovich, K. E., (1986). Cognitive processes and the reading problems of learning disabled children: Evaluating the assumption of specificity. In J. K. Torgesen & B. Y. L. Wong (Eds.), *Psychological and educational perspectives on learning disabilities.* Orlando, FL: Academic Press.

Stanovich, K. E. (1988). The right and wrong places to look for the cognitive locus of reading disability. *Annals of Dyslexia, 38*, 154–177.

Uhry, J. K., & Shepherd, M. J. (1993). Segmentation/spelling instruction as part of a first grade reading program: Effects on several measures of reading. *Reading Research Quarterly, 28*, 219–233.

Wagner, R. K., & Torgesen, J. K. (1987). The nature of phonological processing and its causal role in the acquisition of reading skills. *Psychological Bulletin, 101*, 192–212.

Wagner, R. K., Torgesen, J. K., & Rashote, C. A. (in press). The development of reading-related phonological processing abilities: New evidence of bi-directional causality from a latent variable longitudinal study. *Developmental Psychology.*

Wechsler, D. (1977). *Examiner's manual: Wechsler Intelligence Scale for Children–Revised.* New York: The Psychological Corporation.

Wise, B. W., & Olson, R. K. (1992). How poor readers and spellers use interactive speech in a computerized spelling program. *Reading and Writing: An Interdisciplinary Journal, 4*, 145–163.

Wise, B. W., & Olson, R. K. (in press). Computer-based phonological awareness and reading instruction. *Annals of Dyslexia.*

Wise, B. W., Olson, R. K., Anstett, M., Andrews, L., Terjak, M., Schneider, V., & Kostuch, J. (1989). Implementing a long-term computerized remedial reading program with synthetic speech feedback: Hardware, software, and real world issues. *Behavior Research Methods, Instruments, and Computers, 21*, 173–180.

Wise, B. W., Olson, R. K., and Lindamood, P. (1993, April). Training phonemic awareness: Why and how it might be done in computerized instruction. Paper presented at the meeting of the American Educational Research Association, Atlanta, GA.

Yopp, H. K. (1988). The validity and reliability of phonemic awareness tests. *Reading Research Quarterly, 23*, 159–177.

FOUR

Social and Emotional Transitions

CHAPTER TEN

Developmental Changes in Self-Understanding Across the 5 to 7 Shift

SUSAN HARTER

Historically, the field of developmental psychology was spawned by the remarkable observations and thoughtful insights of those who documented dramatic age-related changes in the behaviors of children. Thus, the field will forever be indebted to the keen observations of such giants as Gesell, Piaget, Freud, and their colleagues, who documented normative developmental changes that had previously remained undetected. More than 25 years ago, Sheldon White (1965) built upon this legacy and systematized both historical and more contemporary findings revealing the vast number of noteworthy changes that occurred across one particular developmental transition that spanned the ages of 5 to 7 years. At that particular point in the history of our field, broadly defined, there was considerable focus on processes involving cognition, problem solving, and learning. Far less attention had been devoted to issues involving the developing self-system across that same transition.

Since the late 1960s, there has been increasing interest in the self-system, in part influenced by the cognitive zeitgeist that prevailed. Thus, the self came to be viewed as a *cognitive construction,* as a system of descriptive and evaluative representations about the self that, in turn, guided one's behavior. As such, topics involving the self captured the attention of developmentalists who sought to determine whether there were predictable, age-related changes in the self-descriptions and self-evaluations of children and adolescents (Bannister & Agnew, 1977; McGuire & McGuire, 1980; McGuire & Padawer-Singer, 1976; Montemayor & Eisen, 1977; Mullener & Laird, 1971; Rosenberg, 1979).

This groundbreaking work spoke to the issue of developmental shifts across the ages of 5 to 7 years by identifying qualitative differences in the self-descriptions of younger and older children. The typical study involved cross-sectional data in which investigators documented differences on either side of the shift, rather than developmental changes that might occur during the transition. Culling self-descriptions from the findings in the literature, as well from data collected in our own laboratory, one can point to a number of broad, normative, developmental shifts that can be demonstrated to occur across (but not within) what is psychologically a relatively wide age span, at this point in development. Consider the prototypical descriptions of a 4-year-old and an 8-year-old that illustrate the changes to be examined:

> *FOUR-YEAR-OLD.* My name is Jason and I live in a big house with my mother and father and sister, Lisa. I have a kitty that's orange and a television in my own room. I know all of my A, B., C's, listen: A, B, C, D, E, F, G, H, J, L, K, O, M, P, Q, X, Z. I can run faster than anyone! I like pizza and I have a nice teacher. I can count up to 100, want to hear me? I love my dog, Skipper. I can climb to the top of the jungle gym, I'm not scared! Just happy. You can't be happy *and* scared, no way! I have brown hair and I go to preschool. I'm really strong. I can lift this chair, watch me!

> *EIGHT-YEAR-OLD.* I'm in third grade this year, and pretty popular, at least with the girls. That's because I'm nice and helpful and can keep secrets. Most of the boys at school are pretty yukky. I don't feel that way about my little brother Jason, although he does get on my nerves. I love him but at the same time, he also does things that make me mad. But I control my temper, I'd be ashamed of myself if I didn't. At school, I'm feeling pretty smart in certain subjects, Language Arts and Social Studies. I got A's in these subjects on my last report card and was really proud of myself. But I'm feeling pretty dumb in Arithmetic and Science, particularly when I see how well the other kids are doing. Even though I'm not doing well in those subjects, I still like myself as a person, because Arithmetic and Science just aren't that important to me. How I look and how popular I am are more important.

Broad Shifts in the Self-Descriptions of Younger and Older Children

As is characteristic of the discovery of most developmental phenomena, the empirical description of differences precedes the more theoretical explanation of change (see Table 10.1). The cameos of our prototypical 4- and 8-year-olds illustrate several broad developmental shifts in the self-system. I first describe the major themes that characterize these rather dramatic shifts, after which I discuss how the field itself has changed in its approach to such developmental differences.

The Nature of Self-Attributes

Noteworthy in the illustrative cameos are differences in the very nature of the attributes selected to describe the self. First and foremost, in creating a self-portrait, the young child describes concrete, observable behaviors or character-

Table 10.1
Broad shifts in the self-descriptions of younger and older children

Self-Descriptions of Children	
Ages 4–5 Years Old	Ages 7–8 Years Old
Observable, behavioral characteristics	Higher-order generalizations ("traits")
Deny opposite valence attributes, affects	Acknowledge opposite valence attributes, affects
Understand basic emotions but NOT self-affects	Understand and have internalized self-affects
Attributes primarily positive	Ability to criticize the self
Behaviorally manifest self-esteem	Verbalizable concept of global self-esteem

istics (see also Damon & Hart, 1988; Harter, 1983, 1988; Montemayor & Eisen, 1977; Rosenberg, 1979). Thus, Jason can run faster than anyone, can climb to the top of the jungle gym, and knows his ABCs. Particular skills are touted (running, climbing, etc.) rather than generalizations about skills or abilities, such as being athletic or good at sports. Moreover, often these behavioral descriptions spill over into actual demonstrations of one's abilities ("I'm really strong. I can lift this chair, watch me!"), suggesting that these emerging self-attributes are still very directly tied to behavior. They do not represent higher-order conceptual categories through which the self is defined.

In addition to concrete descriptions of behaviors, the young child defines the self in terms of *preferences* (e.g., "I like pizza"; "I love my dog, Skipper") as well as *possessions* ("I have a kitty, . . . a television in my own room, . . . a nice teacher,"). Specific physical features ("I have brown hair") are typically mentioned as are family members ("I live in a big house with my mother and father and sister, Lisa"). As Rosenberg cogently observed, the young child acts as a demographer and radical behaviorist in that his or her self-descriptions are limited to characteristics that are potentially observable by others.

In sharp contrast, the older child, as exemplified by the self-description of Lisa, age 8, is much more likely to describe the self in terms of higher-order generalizations or trait labels such as *popular, smart,* and *dumb.* Such higher-order generalizations typically represent the combination of a number of specific behaviors that provide the basis for such a conclusion. Thus, Lisa's self-evaluation of her smartness is based upon the fact that she received A's in language arts and social studies, that is, she indicated the process through which she had arrived at such a generalization. Similarly, she invoked the trait label of *popular,* documenting it with more specific behavioral attributes, namely that she was nice, helpful, and can keep secrets. Her self-description is also typical of children moving into late childhood in that the trait labels applied to the self become increasingly interpersonal, as one's relationships to others, particularly peers, become an increasingly salient dimension of the self (see also Damon & Hart, 1988; Rosenberg, 1979). Given the changing nature of such self-descriptions, with a greater focus on personality attributes, Rosenberg suggested that the older child functions more like a trait theorist.

The Conceptualization of Opposite Valence Attributes and Affects

Another major developmental shift can be seen in how children conceptualize the possibility of opposite valence attributes and affects experienced by the self. Jason vehemently denied that one could experience both positive and negative affects ("I'm not scared! Just happy. You can't be happy *and* scared, no way!"). In contrast, 8-year-old Lisa volunteered the observation that she was both smart *and* dumb, namely opposite valence attributes within the same domain of scholastic competence. Moreover, she also acknowledged that she could be both proud of herself and ashamed of herself, two opposing self-affects.

A number of investigators have documented the general developmental shift from such all-or-none thinking to a more differentiated portrait of the self. For example, when trait labels such as smart and dumb first enter the self-descriptive repertoire of the child, the self is typically described as all smart (Harter, 1977, 1986a) or, far less commonly, as all dumb. Findings have now systematically documented the fact that young children deny that they can experience both a positive and negative emotion at the same time or toward the same event or person (Harris, 1983a, b; Harter, 1986a). Other investigators in the area of children's person perception converge on the same observation (see Livesley & Bromley, 1973; Rogers, 1978): Young children's descriptions of others appear to be *univalent,* that is, someone is either all good or all bad. Selman (1980) also observed that the young child first believes that both self and others are incapable of having more than one attribute, feeling, or motive at a time, particularly if they appear contradictory. Thus, observations during the 1970s and early 1980s began to document this broad developmental shift descriptively, although little was explored with regard to the underlying processes governing such a change.

Positivity Bias Versus Ability to Criticize the Self

A related developmental shift occurs in the overall valence of the self-descriptions of younger and older children. Most young children describe themselves as paragons of virtue, typically providing a litany of positive attributes and abilities. Jason's account is quite consistent with more systematic findings (Harter & Pike, 1984) revealing that preschoolers give formidable accounts of their running and climbing capabilities, their mastery of words and numbers, as well as their virtuosity in winning friends and influencing others. In contrast, older children typically provide a more balanced self-portrait, offering both positive and negative characteristics. Beginning at about age 8, they are much more likely to be self-critical, an observation first made by Gesell and Ilg (1946) in their description of changes between the ages of 5 and 10. However, as with the preceding developmental shifts, earlier efforts spoke more to the empirical documentation of such differences than to the mechanisms responsible for developmental change.

The Shift From Basic Emotions to Self-Affects

Our prototypic self-descriptions also reveal a developmental difference in the emotion vocabulary available to children at each age. Thus, in describing how he was happy but not scared, Jason made reference to two of the four most basic emotion concepts that have been acquired by young children, happy, sad, mad, and scared (Bretherton & Beeghly, 1982; Dunn & Brown, 1991; Harter & Whitesell, 1988). However, young children do not yet understand or have command of *self*-affects, such as feeling proud or ashamed of the self. In contrast, by age 8, self-affects appear in the child's repertoire of emotion concepts. Thus, Lisa noted that if she didn't control her temper, she would be ashamed of herself. She also described how she felt really proud of herself for getting A's on her report card. As we discuss later in this chapter, there is an intriguing developmental sequence governing the acquisition of such self-affects.

THE MANIFESTATIONS OF SELF-ESTEEM

A final developmental shift involves the manner in which self-esteem is manifest. Our own findings (Harter, 1987, 1990; Harter & Pike, 1984) reveal that it is not until about age 8 that children develop a conscious, verbalizable concept of their overall worth as a person. Thus, Lisa told us "I still like myself as a person," our operational definition of verbalizable self-esteem. The fact that this concept is unavailable to young children does not, however, imply that self-esteem is absent or irrelevant in young children. Rather, what we observe is that young children manifest or exude feelings of self-esteem, through their behaviors, particularly their sense of confidence in their abilities. In Jason's account, we encounter such behavioral demonstrations, for example, his recitation of the alphabet as well as his lifting of a chair to convince us of his strength. In contrast, a young child with low self-esteem would be far less demonstrative, communicating more reluctance, hesitancy, and lack of confidence. Although these behaviors may also be observable among older children, the primary developmental acquisition involves the ability to verbalize one's sense of worth as a person.

How Has the Field Changed in Its Approach to Such Shifts?

Over the past 25 years, we have witnessed a number of highly interrelated changes in how we approach issues involving developmental shifts in the self

Table 10.2
Differences between past and present approaches to developmental shifts in self-understanding

Approaches to Developmental Shifts	
Past	Present
Me self, description	I self, processes
Content of the self-concept	Structure of the self-concept
Major qualitative differences on either side of the shift	Substages during the transition; detailed account of the progression
Discontinuity of development, saltatory leaps from one stage to another	More continuous view of development specifying ministeps and how stages build upon one another

(see Table 10.2). Relevant to a number of these changes is a distinction that William James (1892) introduced in arguing that there are two conceptually distinct, but experientially intertwined, aspects of the self, the I self and the Me self. For James, the I self was the active self as knower, as observer, as the constructor of knowledge, as the architect and subsequent evaluator of the Me self. The Me self, in turn, was the self as known, as observed, as constructed, as evaluated, namely, one's concepts of self. As our prototypical cameos reveal, past efforts focused primarily on developmental differences in the *Me* self, through the presentation of spontaneous descriptions of one's sense of self, of the self as known or constructed. There was little in the way of any explication of the processes responsible for such differences. More recently, as is discussed later in this chapter, far more attention has been paid to changes in the *I* self processes that provide the basis for changes in the Me self. Cognitive-developmental acquisitions, in particular—namely, changes in the capacities of the I self as a constructor of knowledge about the Me self—have increasingly been invoked and examined.

A related recent change is the shift from the singular focus on the *content* of children's self-descriptions to an interest in the *structure* of the self-concept, namely, how features of the self are conceptually organized. Here, investigators have also invoked cognitive-developmental principles to understand changes in the organization of concepts about the self.

Moreover, whereas previous accounts highlighted major qualitative differences on either side of the 5 to 7 shift more recent inquiries have addressed the particular substages during the actual transition. Thus, earlier efforts pointed to the dramatic differences between the accounts of young children, ages 4 to 5, and older children, ages 7 to 8, as the examples illustrated. More recent treatments of self-development fill in these gaps by providing a more detailed account of the progression through the transition.

As a result, we have necessarily had to alter our views about whether the development of the self-concept is best viewed as a discontinuous or continuous process. Employing the framework of the past, self-concept development was viewed as primarily discontinuous, with an emphasis on the saltatory nature of the conceptual leaps from one broadly defined stage to another. Thus, one highlighted the dramatic differences between the self-descriptions and evaluations of young children and those of older children. More recently, we have encountered a framework in which the development of the self is viewed as more continuous, specifying the ministeps or levels that occur during the transition and articulating how the levels build upon, and transform, one another.

Historically, within the field of developmental psychology broadly defined, we can observe these same trends—that is, in the past, we were struck by the most outstanding markers in the psychological landscape, the saltatory leaps across the chasm that defines the 5 to 7 shift, rather than the ministages in between. For example, within the field of cognitive development, we were initially impressed by the dramatic, qualitative differences described by Piaget, differences that defined his four broad stages. Neo-Piagetian accounts (e.g., Case, 1985; Fischer, 1980; Siegler, this volume, chap. 4), in contrast, present a far more continuous portrayal of development in which previous cognitive levels provide the building blocks for subsequent stages.

The development of self-understanding can be viewed quite similarly. Thus, in the remainder of this chapter, I apply such a conceptual lens and address a number of the substantive shifts identified at the outset. However, in so doing, the emphasis, the new look, as it were, focuses on how *I* self processes shape the Me self and are responsible for the changing structure and very organization of the Me self. Moreover, I fill in the gaps, describing the substages during the transition, leading to a perspective in which the development of self-understanding is conceptualized as more gradual or continuous.

A Neo-Piagetian View of the Structure of Concepts About the Self

What do we now know about the more gradual nature of the changes in the structure and organization of concepts about the self, and how can our understanding be enhanced by turning to a neo-Piagetian analysis? For purposes of illustration, I have selected certain constructs from one neo-Piagetian model, Fischer's (1980) skill theory. Although skill theory builds upon Piaget's formulation, it provides a much more differentiated analysis of the stages of cognitive development. Thus, whereas Piaget identified 4 broad stages, Fischer has articulated 10, more differentiated, levels of cognitive development. A complete description of Fischer's theory is beyond the scope of this chapter. However, a basic underlying structural dimension involves the number of representations that a child can cognitively control, which in turn involves processes of

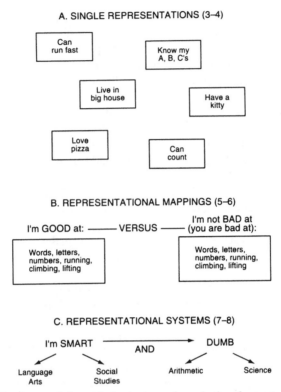

Figure 10.1   Developmental changes in the structure and organization of concepts about the self.

both differentiation and integration or coordination. One can directly apply Fischerian principles to the domain of concepts about the self. Such an analysis not only elucidates the processes underlying the description of younger and older children but also reveals that there are intermediate levels that have been ignored in our previous treatments of the self (see Figure 10.1).

The self-description of our young child (Jason) displays the structural features that define a level that Fischer (1980) has labeled *Single Representations.* At this level, young children can construct very concrete cognitive representations about themselves, (e.g., I can run fast, know my ABCs, live in a big house, have a kitty, love pizza, can count). However, these single representations about the self are highly differentiated or isolated from one another. The young child is incapable of integrating these compartmentalized representations of self, and thus self-descriptive accounts appear quite disjointed. This lack of coherence is a general cognitive characteristic that pervades the young child's thinking across a variety of domains (Fischer, 1980). As Piaget himself observed, the young child's thinking is *transductive,* in that he or she reasons from particular to particular, in no logical order. Moreover, because children at this age also cannot differentiate between their "real" selves and their "ideal" selves, they blur this distinction, resulting in self-descriptions that typically highlight the self that they wish they could be. As a result, self-descriptions often represent overestimations of their abilities. It is important to note, however, that these apparent distortions are normative, in that they reflect the cognitive limitations of this developmental period.

Missing in the earlier illustrations was any discussion of an *intermediate* stage, which corresponds to Fischer's next developmental level, one he has labeled *Representational Mappings.* Self-descriptions at this developmental level, approximately ages 5 to 6, provide us with clues regarding the more gradual nature of change, during the 5 to 7 transition. Consider a portion of a description that I obtained recently from 6-year-old boy when I asked him to tell me about himself:

> **Well, I'm good at schoolwork, I know my words, letters, and my numbers. I can run fast, and I can climb high. I'm also strong. I can throw a ball real far, I'm going to be on a team some day! I can do lots of stuff real good. Let's see, what else can I do? A lot!** (At this point I halted his litany of virtues and said: "You seem to be able to do a lot of things very well. Is there anything you're *not* good at? The 60-second latency seemed like a eternity, as he struggled to come up with an answer to my question.) **Well, if you are good at things, you *can't* be bad at things. I know some *other* kids who are bad at most things, but not me. Wait a minute, maybe I can think of one thing. Yeah, there's something I'm not good at, I'm not a good fighter!** (My subject smiled mischievously when he confessed to his inadequacy. However, I was well aware that he came from a very pacifist family that abhorred violence, and that his parents rewarded him for not being aggressive. Thus, in straining to identify even one limitation, he nevertheless, yet again, cited a virtue.)

How does an understanding of the structural features defined by the stage of representational mappings allow us to better understand this transitional period? The novel acquisition at this level is the child's ability to link or relate representations to each other, to "map" representations onto one another. Thus, a mapping represents some type of connection or relationship between concepts. Of particular interest is one type of mapping that is extremely common in the thinking of young children, namely, a link in the form of opposites. For example, in the domain of physical concepts, the child can relate up to down, over to under, taller to shorter, thinner to wider.

Within the domains of self-description and person perception, the child's ability to relate "good" to "bad" is especially relevant. For example, the child develops a rudimentary concept of the self as "good" at abilities such as knowing one's words, letters, and numbers or at skills such as running, climbing, and lifting. Given that *good* is defined as the opposite of bad, this cognitive construction precludes the young child from being "bad" in any domains. Thus, the mapping takes the necessary form of "I'm good and therefore I can't be bad." At this particular cognitive level the child *over* differentiates good and bad. The very structure of such mappings, therefore, results in the unidimensional or all-or-none thinking that is so pervasive at this level. The application of such structures necessarily leads the child to perceptions of considerable virtuosity. Thus, one continues to see as the norm highly positive self-descriptions at this particular developmental level. For a smaller subset of children, with very negative socialization histories involving maltreatment, neglect, or abuse, perceptions that one is all bad may be maintained. However, what should be noted is that the underlying structure is identical—namely, mappings in the form of opposites that result in all-or-none, unidimensional thinking.

Several developmental acquisitions emerge at the next cognitive-developmental level, which Fischer (1980) has labeled *Representational Systems*. The structures that define this level emerge between the approximate ages of 7 and 8, particularly with regard to self-understanding. There are two very noteworthy acquisitions that are relevant to our analysis. First, the child is now capable of forming higher-order generalizations based upon her or his ability to integrate more specific, behavioral features of the self. In Lisa's account, for example, she was able to form the higher-order concept that she is smart by integrating her observations of success in both language arts and social studies. Similarly, she could construct such a hierarchy for the concept of dumb, coordinating her perceptions that she does not do well scholastically in arithmetic and science.

Representational systems, by definition, involve the integration of concepts that were previously differentiated from one another. Thus, a second major acquisition involves the ability to coordinate dimensions that were previously compartmentalized, for example, smart and dumb. In this way, the older child can acknowledge that he or she can simultaneously be smart and dumb, for example, smart at some school subjects but dumb at others. With this cognitive-structural advance, the child is much less likely to engage in the type of all-or-none thinking observed in the previous stages. The child will much less frequently describe the self as all virtuous. As a result, self-descriptions begin to represent a more balanced presentation of one's abilities in conjunction with one's deficiencies, perceptions that are more veridical with other's views of the self.

To what extent does the transition from the new, intermediate level of representational mappings to the level of representational systems provide us with insights into the processes occurring across the 5 to 7 shift? This particular transition exemplifies certain developmental principles that have their legacy in theorizing of Werner (1957) and Piaget (1963), who argued that differentiation precedes integration. Thus, they illustrate a more gradual developmental process in which newly formed concepts, for example, good and bad, must first be rigidly differentiated and applied accordingly before they can be integrated. That is, the overdifferentiation of good and bad is a necessary precursor, a building block, as it were, to the subsequent integration of attributes that were seemingly contradictory. For the interested reader, a more detailed articulation and application of these principles can be found in the work of Fischer and his colleagues (see Fischer, 1980). The studies on the developmental acquisition of the concepts of nice and mean are particularly relevant to the domain of self-understanding. In this work, Fischer provides a much more complete analysis of the particular transformation rules that govern movement from one level to another, including transitions within as well as across levels.

Developmental Changes in the Understanding of Simultaneous Emotions

The cameos presented at the beginning of this chapter illustrate that the shift from unidimensional to multidimensional representations about the self apply to descriptions of one's emotional attributes as well. Whereas young children will typically describe the self in terms of positive emotions, denying negative affect, older children will provide descriptions of both positive and negative emotional reactions. A growing body of evidence now reveals that young children are incapable of appreciating the fact that they can experience seemingly opposing emotional reactions simultaneously.

Our own sensitivity to this issue began with clinical observations followed by normative-developmental research designed to document and interpret the sequence through which such an understanding emerges. Within a play therapy context, it was initially observed that young clients had particular difficulty in acknowledging the co-occurrence of positive and negative emotions (Harter, 1977). These children would typically deny the simultaneously experience of two emotions, asserting that they could have but one feeling at a time.

This dichotomous thinking was particularly evident in regard to emotional reactions to significant others. For example, a child would be consumed with anger toward a parent, sibling, or friend, staunchly denying any feelings of affection or love. With regard to issues of loss, he or she would be pervasively sad over the departure of a loved one, totally unable to acknowledge the positive emotions that were undoubtedly also felt for the individual. Although one might be tempted to conclude that such difficulties are primarily a function of the presenting problems that brought the child client to therapy, our own work has revealed that such phenomena have a normative, cognitive-developmental basis, although they may well be exacerbated in clinic populations.

Our initial findings were quite consistent with a number of studies in the literature that reveal a general three-stage sequence in children's understanding of simultaneous emotions (Carroll & Steward, 1984; Donaldson & Westerman, 1986; Gnepp, McKee, & Domanic, 1987; Harris, 1983; Harris, Olthof, &

Meerum Terwogt, 1981; Harter, 1982, 1986a; Harter & Buddin, 1987; Meerum Terwogt, 1984; Reissland, 1985; Selman, 1980). These studies documented a sequence in which the youngest children deny the coexistence of two feelings. At the next stage, children acknowledge that two feelings can co-occur in sequence in temporal order, although they cannot occur simultaneously. At the third stage, the oldest children acknowledge that two feelings can occur simultaneously.

Our more recent normative research (see Harter, 1986b; Harter & Buddin, 1987) has focused specifically on the issue of simultaneity. We have now documented a systematic acquisition sequence that describes the emergence of the understanding of simultaneous emotions. Two dimensions govern this sequence. One is the *valence* of the two emotions, whether they are of the same valence (i.e., both positive, such as happy and glad, or both negative, such as mad and sad) or whether they are of opposite valence (one positive and one negative, e.g., happy and mad, or glad and sad). The second dimension involves the *number of targets* toward which the emotions are directed, namely, one target as the focus of the two feelings or two targets, where one of the emotions is directed toward one target and the second emotion is directed toward a different target.

Our strategy was to design a task that would systematically tap children's understanding of the four combinations of valence and target: (1) Same valence, Same target; (b) Same valence, Different targets; (c) Different valence, Different targets; and (d) Different valence, Same target. In this manner, we could determine whether a scalable acquisition might be demonstrated (see Harter & Buddin, 1987, for procedural details).

The findings reveal a highly scalable, age-related sequence that represents five developmental levels of emotional understanding, across the ages of 4 to 12. These levels are defined by which of the combinations of valence and target described in the previous two paragraphs are within the child's repertoire. At the lowest level, young children, like our prototypical subject Jason, staunchly deny that they can have two feelings at the same time. The first acknowledgment of simultaneity involves the first combination, Combination *a*, in which same valence feelings apply to the same target. Subsequently, same valence feelings can be applied to different targets. A major advance occurs with the acknowledgment of different valence feelings first applied to different targets. Our older child, Lisa, represents this stage in that she acknowledged that she would be ashamed about her treatment of others but would be proud about her school accomplishments. At the last stage, one can apply opposite valence feelings to the same target.

With regard to the 5 to 7 shift, the findings provide additional evidence for transitional stages between the earliest steps at which the young child denies the simultaneity of feelings (Level 0 in our analysis) and the stage at which the older child can appreciate opposite valence feelings (Level 3 in our analysis).

Here, as well as in the previous explication of the changing structure of self-understanding, we sought to apply Fischer's theory to provide an interpretation of the lawful progression that our findings demonstrated (see Table 10.3). As in the previous analysis, there is considerable emphasis on developmental changes in the ability to differentiate and integrate concepts about the self.

Level 0

At Level 0 the youngest children (as exemplified by Jason) simply deny that two feelings can simultaneously coexist. While they may acknowledge that two feelings can be experienced sequentially, they are adamant in their belief that it is impossible for two emotions to occur together. That they are firmly entrenched in a theory that precludes the simultaneous experience of two feelings is clear from many of their comments: "There is no way two feelings could ever go together at the same time"; "You can't have two feelings at the same time because you only have one mind!" "I could be happy that I was watching TV and then sad that I had to go to bed, but I couldn't feel both of those at the same time."

Applying Fischer's theoretical principles, the Level 0 child has developed *single representations* for separate emotions (e.g., happy, glad, sad, mad, scared). However, at any time, only one emotional representation can be applied to a given event. The child can deal with emotions that occur in temporal order, since this involves only one emotion at a time. Yet the child denies that he or she can have two feelings at the same time, since he or she cannot simultaneously relate, integrate, or coordinate two representations that refer to different emotions, no matter how similar they appear to be. Thus, the child cannot relate *happy* to *glad* or *sad* to *mad* simultaneously.

Level 1

At the first transitional period, Level 1, children show an initial appreciation for the simultaneous experience of two emotions, but this understanding is restricted to combinations in which emotions of the same valence are directed toward a single target, for example, "If your brother hit you, you would be both mad and sad"; "I was happy and glad that I got a new puppy for Christmas." Children at this level report the two feelings cannot be directed toward two different targets simultaneously, nor can opposite valence feelings co-occur.

According to our theoretical analysis, based upon Fischer, at Level 1 the child is beginning to develop *representational sets* for feelings of the same valence, namely, separate emotion categories, one for positive emotions and one for negative emotions. Thus, feelings within each category are becoming somewhat differentiated from one another (e.g., happy vs. glad within the positive representational set, and mad vs. sad within the negative set). Moreover, the child has some ability to control variations cognitively within each emo-

Table 10.3
A Cognitive-Developmental Analysis of the Five Levels of Emotional Understanding

Level	Diagram of Elements and Relationships	Sample Response	Description of Cognitive Skill	Limitations
Level 0 Temporal Order Denial	$E_1 \rightarrow$ $E_2 \rightarrow$ Target 1 Target 2 Time 1 Time 2	HAPPY that I was watching TV and then SAD that I had to go to bed. You can't have two feelings at the very same time.	Child has single representations for separate emotions. Can attach one feeling to a target at Time 1, and a second feeling to a separate target at Time 2, but cannot handle any combinations simultaneously. Emotions are treated sequentially.	Child cannot integrate two single representations in order to produce two emotions simultaneously.
Level 1 Same Valence Same Target	Positive Emotions Negative Emotions E_1 and E_2 E_3 and E_4 Single Positive Single Negative Target Target Time 1 Time 2	HAPPY and GLAD that I got a new puppy for Christmas. or MAD and UPSET that my brother messed up my stuff	Child develops a representational set for emotions of the same valence (one set for positive emotions and a separate set for negative emotions). Child can relate variations in one set (e.g., different positive emotions to a single target, simultaneously. Child integrates same valence affects, which are brought to bear on the same target.	Child cannot relate variations within a set of emotions to variations in the target(s). Nor can child integrate the sets of positive and negative emotions.

Level	Diagram	Example	What the child can do	What the child cannot do
Level 2 Same Valence Different Targets	Positive Emotions E₁ and E₂ → Positive Target 1, Positive Target 2 (Time 1) Negative Emotions E₃ and E₄ → Negative Target 1, Negative Target 2 (Time 2)	HAPPY I went to Mexico and GLAD to see my grandparents. or MAD that she took my book and SAD that it was raining.	Within one representational set of emotions, the child can simultaneously relate variations in that set to variations in targets, that is, relate one emotion to one target and a second emotion of the same valence to a different target, at the same time.	Child cannot integrate the sets of positive and negative emotions simultaneously. Can only treat different valence emotions sequentially.
Level 3 Different Valence Different Targets	Positive Emotions E₁ and E₂ ⟷ Negative Emotions E₃ and E₄ Positive Target 1 → Negative Target 1 (Time 1)	MAD at my brother for hitting me, but at the same time I was HAPPY that my father gave me permission to hit him back.	Child can simultaneously integrate the sets of positive and negative emotions, but directs the positive emotion to a positive target and the negative emotion to a negative target.	Child cannot bring both a positive and negative emotion to bear on a single, integrated target at one point in time.
Level 4 Different Valence Same Target	Positive Emotions E₁ and E₂ ⟷ Negative Emotions E₃ and E₄ Positive, Negative Aspect Aspect of Same Target	HAPPY that I got a present, but DISAPPOINTED that it wasn't exactly what I wanted.	Child can have a positive emotion and a negative emotion about one target simultaneously, integrating these different valence feelings around aspects of the same target.	Child may not be able to simultaneously direct both a positive and negative emotion to one *person* as the single target.

tional set, that is, to be both happy and glad over one event or mad and sad about one target. However, the emotions within a given set are not yet sufficiently differentiated to allow the child to direct them to different targets simultaneously; The child cannot yet simultaneously control variations within a given representational set of emotions as well as variations in targets in order to relate the two variations to each other. This is the first cognitive limitation of Level 1. The second major limitation is that the child cannot yet integrate the sets of positive and negative emotions, sets that are viewed as conceptually distinct and therefore incompatible. Accordingly, emotions of opposite valence cannot be experienced as simultaneous. This limitation follows directly from Fischer's theory and findings on the difficulty young children have in integrating such conceptual opposites as nice and mean or maleness and femaleness. Such representational sets are viewed as conceptually distinct and therefore incompatible.

Level 2

Another transition is defined by Level 2, during which children can bring two same valence feelings to bear on different targets simultaneously, for example, "I'd be mad if she broke my toy and sad that she went home"; "I was excited I went to Mexico and glad to see my grandparents." However, these children deny the simultaneity of opposite-valence feelings, for example, "I couldn't feel happy and scared at the same time, I would have to be two people at once!" At Level 2, therefore, the child overcomes the first cognitive limitation of Level 1 by developing representational mappings, which, according to Fischer, permit one to control and relate variations within a same-valence emotional set to variations within a set of targets. Thus, the child can map one emotion onto one target, "mad that she broke my toy," and attach the second same valence emotion to a different target, "sad that she went home." However, the child has not yet overcome the second cognitive limitation of the previous level, since she or he cannot yet integrate the sets of positive and negative emotions. This limitation precludes the possibility that one can acknowledge a positive and a negative emotion simultaneously.

Level 3

At Level 3, illustrated by Lisa's cameo, the child demonstrates a major conceptual advance in that he or she can now appreciate simultaneous opposite valence feelings. However, these emotions can only be brought to bear on different targets. Thus, the negative emotion is directed toward a negative event ("I was mad at my brother for hitting me"), and the positive emotion is directed toward a different, positive aspect of the situation ("but at the same time, I was really happy that my father gave me permission to hit him back"). In other cases the two targets are even more discrete, for example, "I was sitting in school feeling worried about all of the responsibilities of a new pet but I was happy that I had gotten straight A's on my report card."

At Level 3, the child advances to what Fischer terms *representational systems* in that he or she can now integrate the representational sets for positive and negative emotions. This allows the child to acknowledge positive and negative emotions simultaneously. However, the child cannot yet bring two opposite valence feelings to bear on a single target. Rather, he or she exemplifies what Fischer terms a *shift of focus,* directing the positive feeling to a positive target or event and then cognitively shifting the focus of the negative feeling to a negative event. The concept that the very same target can simultaneously have both positive and negative aspects is not yet cognitively accessible to the child.

Level 4

There is a final Level 4 during which even older children become able to describe how opposite valence feelings can be provoked by the same target, for example, "I was happy that I got a present but mad that it wasn't exactly what I wanted"; "If a stranger offered you candy you'd be eager for the candy but also doubtful if it was OK"; "I was happy I was joining the new club but also a little worried because I didn't know anyone in it." At this level the child overcomes the limitations of the previous period in that he or she can now acknowledge that the same target can provoke both a positive and negative emotion. The cognitive advance would appear to be the child's newfound capacity to differentiate one target into positive and negative aspects and then coordinate these aspects simultaneously with the corresponding positive and negative emotions.

Thus, each of the levels in this analysis involves developmental change with regard to the number and type of representations that the child can simultaneously control, coordinate, or integrate. The levels examined place increasingly greater cognitive demands on the child, thereby resulting in the systematic, age-related progression that we have documented. As such, they demonstrate the more gradual nature of the transformations that occur within this domain in contrast to the previous focus on dramatic, qualitative shifts in children's understanding of the emotions that define the self.

The Developmental Emergence of Self-Affects: Pride and Shame

Our cameo self-descriptions revealed another developmental feature that differentiates younger from older children. Self-related affects directed at the self (proud of oneself, ashamed of oneself) are absent in the accounts of the younger child, whereas they spontaneously appear in the self-portraits of the older child. In the I self, Me self parlance of James (1892), the I self (as observer and evaluator) comes to be ashamed or proud of the Me self (as observed or evaluated). Within this domain, as well, it behooves us to address the question of the more gradual nature of such an acquisition, as well as to identify the processes that may govern this developmental trajectory.

In the preceding section, we dealt with children's understanding of simultaneous emotions, focusing primarily on the cognitive-developmental factors that help to explain their acquisition. A related topic involves the emergence of certain more complex single emotions that would appear to represent emotion blends. We have been particularly interested in the emergence of an understanding of pride and shame, since not only do they require underlying cognitive advances, but they are heavily dependent upon certain socialization experiences. From a cognitive perspective, pride and shame require more than the single representations that are sufficient for such basic emotions that children label as happy, sad, and scared. An understanding of pride or shame requires the differentiation and integration of several features. For example, pride combines joy over the mastery of a particular skill as well as happiness because the accomplishment was appreciated by others. Shame typically combines the acknowledgment of sadness or regret for hurting or violating another, as well as anger toward the self for committing a transgression.

However, an analysis of the development of an understanding of the concepts of pride and shame must also take into account those socialization experiences necessary for their emergence. This has been the primary focus of our own research. Paradoxically, perhaps, pride and shame have been described as "self-affects," namely, affects in which one aspect of the self, the I self, experiences an emotion about another aspect of the self, the Me self, in the absence of observing others; one can engage in events that provoke the feeling that one is proud of oneself or ashamed of oneself when these events have not been directly witnessed by other people. The ability to experience these self-affects, however, is highly dependent upon one's socialization history.

Cooley (1902), a well-known scholar of the self, was one of the first to devote thoughtful attention to the emotions of pride and shame and their relationship to the social origins of the self. For Cooley, the self was a social construction, the incorporation of the attitudes a person believes significant others hold toward the self. Thus, one adopts the reflected appraisals of these others in the form of what Cooley metaphorically called the looking-glass self. However, the self, so constructed, does not merely represent a cognitive appraisal of one's attributes, imagined in the eyes of significant others, but a self-feeling, namely, an affective reaction to this appraisal. In describing the reactions of the adult self, Cooley singled out in particular the emotions of pride and shame and, in so doing, set the stage for a developmental analysis of how these emotions might emerge.

While pride and shame could clearly be experienced by adults in the absence of others, Cooley (1902) noted that the "thing that moves us to pride and shame is not the merely mechanical reflection of ourselves, but an imputed sentiment, the imagined effect of this reflection upon another's mind" (p. 153). Cooley was clear on the point that this sentiment is social in nature, based upon social custom and opinion, though it becomes somewhat removed from these sources through an implied internalization process. Cooley (1902) wrote that the adult is

> not *immediately* dependent upon what others think; he has worked over his reflected self in his mind until it is a steadfast portion of his thought, an idea and conviction apart, in some measure, from its external origin. Hence this sentiment requires times for its development and flourishes in mature age rather than in the open and growing period of youth. (P. 199)

Cooley (1902) further laid the groundwork for a developmental analysis of shame and pride when he wrote the following:

> The reference to other persons involved in the sense of self may be distinct and particular, as when a boy is ashamed to have his mother catch him at something she has forbidden, or it may be vague and general, as when one is ashamed to do something which only his conscience, expressing his sense of social responsibility, detects and disapproves; but it is always there. There is no sense of "I", as in pride or shame, without its correlative sense of you, he, or they. (P. 153)

These themes have been echoed in more contemporary treatments of shame and pride in which the initial role of external evaluation by socializing agents appears paramount (Erikson, 1963; Harter, 1983, 1985; Lewis & Brooks, 1978; Piers & Singer, 1953; Rogers, 1951; Stipek, 1983). These authors have argued that the ability to experience the emotions of pride and shame requires the internalization of parental values in the form of an ego ideal, a standard, against which one comes to compare one's performance. Thus, pride and shame are socially derived emotions that also have direct implications for one's feelings of worth, given their origins in parental evaluations of the self (see Harter, 1986a, 1987; Stipek, 1983.) As these latter theorists have suggested, this type of analysis leads to the expectation that the young child would require an actual audience that witnesses and reacts to behaviors that are shameful or, alternatively, worthy of pride. However, the need for such a social audience would developmentally decline as one internalized the values or standards of significant others because children could then apply these standards directly in order to feel either proud or ashamed of oneself in the absence of observation.

Until recently this kind of analysis, although very plausible, has been largely speculative. In our work, we have begun to document the emergence of the understanding of the emotions of pride and shame, utilizing a socialization framework. The first findings were rather serendipitous, resulting from an open-ended interview in which we simply asked children, ages 4 to 11, to describe the feelings of pride and shame and to provide a cause for each. We discovered that our youngest subjects, typically the 4- to 5-year-olds, could not provide a compelling description or a very plausible cause, although most were aware of the valence of the two feelings, namely, that pride is a good feeling and shame is a bad feeling.

Interestingly, among our 6- and 7-year-olds, who had some intuitions about these feelings, many of the responses involved descriptions of how parents would be proud or ashamed of them for their actions, that is, significant others were proud or ashamed of the self. Examples of pride included the following: "Dad would be proud of me if I took out the trash"; "Mom would be proud if I cleaned my room"; "My parents would be proud if I won something"; "Dad was proud of me when I made a goal." Examples of shame included these: "Mom would be ashamed of me if I did something bad or got into trouble"; "Dad was really ashamed of me when I broke the window"; "Mom was ashamed of me when I got into her stuff after she had told me not to"; "My parents get ashamed when I do something naughty."

Typically it was not until about the age of 8 that children gave examples of how they could be ashamed or proud of themselves. In these spontaneous accounts, children would report such examples as the following: "I was really ashamed that I broke my friend's bike and didn't tell him"; "I hit my brother for no real reason and felt ashamed of myself"; "I took something of my sister's without asking;" "I hurt my friend's feelings and really felt ashamed." For pride, typical examples were these: "I dived off the high diving board"; "I got all A's on my report card"; "I did a good deed and got a medal"; "When I did something the best."

Although these latter responses did not specify whether an audience was or was not present, we became curious about this dimension. Our open-ended responses did not allow us to determine whether the experience of being proud of oneself or ashamed of oneself required the observation of another or whether one could experience these self-affects in the absence of others. We had some clues, however, from the responses of certain subjects. For example, in pursuing one 9-year-old's description of an experience in which he had felt ashamed of himself, we asked whether he could feel ashamed when he was all alone, or whether someone had to watch what he had done. His thoughtful reply was quite illuminating: "Well I *might* be able to be ashamed of myself if my parents didn't know, but it would sure help me to be ashamed if they were there!"

These preliminary findings suggested the fruitfulness of studying the developmental course of the concepts of pride and shame more systematically, particularly with regard to the role of the audience. In so doing, our focus was on the development of children's understanding of pride and shame, on their ability to conceptualize the causes of these emotions, rather than upon the very first expressions of these emotions in early childhood. In particular, we were interested in the substages that appeared to be precursors of the child's emerging ability to appreciate the fact that one could be proud or ashamed of the self in the absence of any observation by others.

Given our framework, focusing on the socialization component of both pride and shame, we devised a procedure that would be sensitive to the role of the observing parent. We sought to determine whether parents were required to "support" the reported experience of shame and pride. Toward this end we designed two sets of vignettes.

To assess shame, we constructed a set of pictorial vignettes with several frames and a brief story line to accompany the pictures. The story concerns a situation in which the parents have forbidden the child to take any money from a very large jar of coins in the parents' bedroom. However, the child transgresses and takes a few coins. There are two separate story sequences. In one sequence, no one observes the act and no one ever finds out (an outcome we attempted to insure by describing the money jar as very large, whereas the child only took a few coins). In the second sequence, the parent catches the child in the act. The primary dependent measures included the child's description of the emotions that the child would feel in the first story sequence (where the act is not detected) and a description of the emotions that both child and parent would feel in the second story situation (where the parent catches the child in the act).

To assess an understanding of pride, we constructed a set of vignettes that had a gymnastic feat as the demonstration of competence. In the first story sequence, the child goes to the playground on a Saturday when no one else is there and tries out a flip on the bars, one that he or she has been working on at school. The child attempts a flip that he or she has never been able to perform successfully before and does it really well. In the first story sequence, the child leaves the bars, knowing that he or she was the only one at the playground and thus no one else observed the flip. The child is then asked what feeling he or she would have at that time.

In the second story sequence dealing with pride, the parent accompanies the child to the playground and observes the child successfully performing the flip for the first time. The child is asked how he or she would feel as well as how the observing parent would feel having watched the child doing the flip. Here again, pictorial aids in the form of photographs of facial expressions of these emotions—by a child for the first sequence and by a child as well as by a parent for the second sequence—are presented to the child.

The results for both pride and shame revealed a highly age-related, parallel four-stage sequence that is interpretable within our socialization framework (see Table 10.4 and Figure 10.2). The first and the fourth levels represent our previous characterizations of younger and older children. The second and third levels represent transitional levels that were heretofore not identified. At the first level, ages 4 to 5, there is no mention of either pride or shame on the part

Table 10.4

Developmental Sequence of the Acquisition of Concepts about Pride and Shame

| | Emotions Reported by Child Subject for Parent and Child | | | |
| | Transgression | | Successful Feat | |
Age	Parent	Child	Parent	Child
4–5	Mad at child	Scared	Happy for child	Excited
5–6	Ashamed of child	Scared	Proud of child	Excited
6–7	Ashamed of child when observe child	Ashamed of self when observed	Proud of child when observe child	Proud of self when observed
7–8	(Parent doesn't observe act)	Ashamed of self when not observed	(Parent doesn't observe act)	Proud of self when not observed

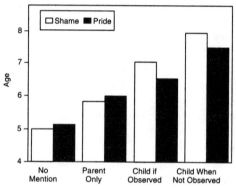

Figure 10.2   Age differences in the four levels defining the developmental sequence for the acquisition of concepts about pride and shame.

of child or parent in either sequence, whether the child is observed or not observed. Subjects give very clear responses about their potential emotional reactions to these situations, reactions that are quite telling. In the transgression situation where they are not observed by the parents, participants report that the child character (with whom they are encouraged to identify) would feel scared or worried about the possibility of detection. In the transgression situation where the child character is caught by the parent, participants report that the child character would also feel extremely scared or worried about the likelihood of punishment. However, there is no acknowledgment of pride or shame.

In the pride sequences of stories, these youngest subjects report that they would feel happy, glad, and excited in the situation where their gymnastic feat is not observed by the parent. In the story sequence where the parent witnesses their performance, they report that both they and the parent would feel happy, glad, and excited; there is no mention of pride, either on the part of the parent or the self.

The second level, ages 5 to 6, represents a very interesting transition period. Children now demonstrate their first use of the terms *ashamed* and *proud*. However, their usage is restricted to reactions of the parents. Thus the parental reaction to the child's transgression is to be ashamed of the child. However, the child does not yet acknowledge that he or she is ashamed of the self. Rather, the child is still scared or worried about the parents' reaction. Similarly, in the case of the gymnastic feat, the child participants describe how the parent is proud of the child. However, the child is not yet proud of the self. Rather, he or she is excited, happy, and glad.

At the third level, children (between the ages of 6 and 7) demonstrate the first acknowledgment of shame and pride being directed toward the self. Thus, in the situation where the act has been observed, not only will parents be ashamed or proud of the child, but children report that they, too, will feel ashamed or proud of themselves, seemingly in response to the parental reaction. However, what also places a child at this level is the fact that she or he does not report any feelings of shame or pride in the story sequence in the absence of parental observation. This seems to be another critical transitional level in our socialization sequence: The act must be observed, in the case of both a transgression (to experience shame) and the demonstration of competence (to experience pride). In the absence of parental observation, no such potential self-affects are acknowledged.

The hallmark of the fourth level (beginning at the ages of 7 to 8) is that in the absence of parental observation children spontaneously acknowledge that they will feel ashamed of themselves or proud of themselves. (It should be noted that the stories in which the child was not observed were always presented first so that any response of shame or pride on the part of the child was not simply a generalization from the sequence in which they were observed.) Therefore, at this level, children appear to have internalized the standards by which shame and pride can be experienced in the absence of direct, parental observation. Interestingly, the large majority of children at this level do not merely report the emotions of shame and pride, but specifically indicate that "I would feel ashamed, or proud, of myself." Thus they appear to be at the stage where these affects do function as self-affects, in the sense that one is truly ashamed or proud of the self.

This sequence not only reveals the more gradual nature of the development of self-affects but also suggests that the critical, underlying processes involve parental socialization. Thus, we have therefore inferred that children must first experience others as models who are proud or ashamed of them in order to internalize these functions themselves. Even when they first develop the ability to acknowledge that they are proud or ashamed of themselves, children still need the scaffolding of parental surveillance or observation. The final stage in the internalization process occurs when these self-affects are experienced in the absence of observations by others: when the I self can be directly ashamed of the Me self, although the person is all by himself or herself.

The Developmental Emergence of the Ability to Observe and Criticize the Self

A theme that characterizes each of the preceding sections is that the child gradually develops the ability to make negative evaluations of the self. One can realize that the self is not totally virtuous and acknowledge one's negative as well as positive attributes or emotions. Self-affects represent the more specific case in which the I self takes the Me self as the target of the emotions. Behaviors or attributes of the Me self provoke the I self to experience pride or shame. As suggested in the description of the pride and shame sequences that have been documented, the very processes involved in self-observation and self-evaluation must undergo a gradual, developmental process deeply embedded within the socialization experiences of the child.

In this section, a more general sequence of the stages of self-observation and self-evaluation is described, drawing upon the historical accounts of Gesell and Ilg (1946), the theoretical formulation of Selman (1980), and our own research in the areas of pride and shame (Harter & Whitesell, 1988), as well as the looking-glass self (Harter, 1986b, 1987, 1990). These stages, depicted in Figure 10.2, directly parallel the four levels presented in the analysis of the emergence of the concepts of pride and shame. This more general analysis is couched in the I self and Me self terminology, where the I self is the observer and the Me self is the observed. As will become apparent, the development of the skills of self-observation and self-evaluation are intimately linked to the interaction of self and other.

At the very first stage (depicted at the top of Figure 10.3), occurring at the approximate ages of 4 to 5, the observing I self is highly capable of observing others. In fact, the young child often seems preoccupied with evaluating the conduct and correctness of friends' and classmates' behavior, often rather critically. However, the young child appears far less aware that others are also observing him or her in this same light, nor can the young child's I self critically evaluate the Me self directly.

At the next stage, approximately 5 to 6, the child comes to appreciate the fact that others are observing and evaluating the self (see B in Figure 10.3). Moreover, as Gesell and Ilg (1946) noted, children at this age begin to be concerned about what others might think of them and are careful not to expose themselves to criticism. They begin to worry about making mistakes and may cringe when they are laughed at or made fun of. Thus, the hallmark can be expressed as "I observe you observing me." Within the context of our pride

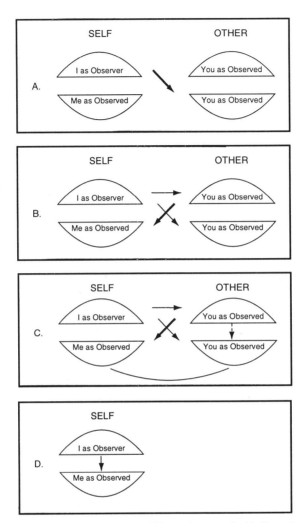

Figure 10.3   Stages in the development of the ability to observe and critically evaluate the self.

and shame sequence, the child observes the parent being proud or ashamed of the self. This second stage, therefore, provides the necessary building blocks for the emergence of the looking-glass self (Cooley, 1902) in which one comes to internalize the attitudes or opinions of significant others toward the self. One must first be sensitive to the fact that one is being observed and evaluated in order to direct one's attention to the specific content of their approval or criticism. The limitation of this period, however, is that the child has not yet internalized these evaluations for the purpose of self-evaluation.

At the third stage, ages 6 to 7, a number of new processes emerge (see C in

Figure 10.3). The child begins to incorporate the observations of others into her or his own self-perceptions, such that the child can directly evaluate the self. Thus, the I self adopts an attitude toward the Me self that parallels the attitude of significant others, although the self-attitude needs to be reinforced by the reactions of others. The pride and shame sequences demonstrate this general principle in that the child must still be observed by parents in order to experience pride or shame toward the self.

Children at this stage become particularly interested in evaluating their own performance based upon the standards that others have set for the self. During this period, they internalize these expectations into self-standards, which pave the way for the capacity to criticize the self if they fail to meet these standards. This third stage also marks the emergence of the ability to compare oneself with others for the purposes of self-evaluation. The child can now simultaneously observe both self and other (as illustrated by the line connecting Me as observed and You as observed in Figure 10.3). This ability to engage in social comparison comes to provide a major index of the self's inadequacy. As was noted earlier, very young children's self-descriptions often represent quite unrealistic inflations of their competencies, in part because they do not yet have the ability to compare their performance with that of others.

In the final and fourth stage (depicted as D at the very bottom of Figure 10.3), these abilities have begun to be consolidated, such that the I self of the older child can now observe the Me self, in the absence of the direct presence or reactions of significant others. Thus, as illustrated by the pride and shame sequence, one can be ashamed of oneself when one is all by oneself.

It should be noted that these developmental trajectories represent acquisition, rather than acquisition/deletion, sequences. Although new stages emerge, the former stages do not drop out of one's repertoire. Therefore, although the child may develop the ability to function at the highest stage in the sequence, he or she will, nevertheless, still manifest lower levels under some circumstances. For example, during environmental transitions, when one is faced with new significant others and new social reference groups, one will necessarily need to operate at the lower levels in order to first observe the characteristics of others, determine their attitudes toward the self, and assess one's own abilities compared with those of others, before such attitudes and standards can be internalized. The general point, therefore, is that the ability to observe, evaluate, and criticize the self must gradually develop through a series of stages that begin with an awareness that others are evaluating the self and with the ability to compare oneself to one's social reference group.

Conclusions

That there are shifts in self-understanding between 5 and 7 years of age is clearly evident. As documented, there are developmental changes in the very nature of self-attributes, in the structure and organization of the self, in the understanding of opposite valence attributes and emotions, in the balance of positive and negative attributes, and in the emergence of self-affects, as well as in the general ability to observe, evaluate, and criticize the self. The goal of this chapter is to move beyond the description of dramatic, qualitative differences that define self-understanding on either side of the 5 to 7 shift. The approach to self-understanding has changed considerably over the past 25 years. Currently there is much more emphasis on the underlying cognitive processes, on structural changes, and on the role of socialization during the transition. As a result, we have a more detailed account of the progression of change, of the more continuous nature of development, and of how previous substages provide the building blocks for the emergence of subsequent stages. We have filled in numerous gaps and, in so doing, have somewhat demystified the saltatory leaps in self-understanding that our previous analyses described if not glorified.

This new look, despite its greater specification of cognitive structures and ministages, does not, however, speak sufficiently to those factors responsible for these more fine-grained changes. What, for example, provokes the underlying cognitive-developmental changes themselves? What endogenous neurological mechanisms are involved? What socialization experiences are implicated? How do experiences and neural development interact or conspire to produce changes that, in turn, directly impact self-understanding? Within the past 25 years, we have definitely altered our level of analysis. However, it now behooves us to direct greater attention to those factors responsible for changes in the I self, which, in turn, have profound implications for changes in the Me self. Therefore, there are still many unanswered questions. Perhaps 25 more years down this yellow brick road we will reach the wizard. However, today, we are intellectually indebted to Sheldon White for charting the course and provoking us to continue down this intriguing developmental path.

Acknowledgments

Support for the research reported in this chapter was provided by NICHD.

References

Bannister, D., Agnew, J. (1977). The child's construing of self. In J. Cole (Ed.), *Nebraska Symposium on Motivation*. Lincoln: University of Nebraska Press.

Bretherton, I., & Beeghly, M. (1982). Talking about internal states: The acquisition of an explicit theory of mind. *Developmental Psychology, 18,* 906–912.

Carroll, J. J., & Steward, M. S. (1984). The role of cognitive development in children's understandings of their own feelings. *Child Development, 55,* 1486–1492.

Case, R. (1985). *Intellectual development: A systematic reinterpretation.* New York: Academic Press.

Cooley, C. H. (1902). *Human nature and the social order.* New York: Scribner's.

Damon, W., & Hart, D. (1988). *Self-understanding in childhood and adolescence.* New York: Cambridge University Press.

Donaldson, S. K., & Westerman, M. A. (1986). Development of children's understanding of ambivalence and causal theories of emotion. *Developmental Psychology, 22,* 655–662.

Dunn, J., & Brown, J. (1991). Relationships, talk about feelings, and the development of affect regulation in early childhood. In J. Garber and K. A. Dodge (Eds.), *The development of emotion regulation and dysregulation* (pp. 69–88). New York: Wiley.

Erikson, E. (1963). *Childhood and society.* New York: Norton.

Fischer, K. (1980). A theory of cognitive development: The control and construction of hierarchies of skills. *Psychological Review, 87,* 477–531.

Gessell, A., & Ilg, F. (1946). *The child from five to ten.* New York: Harper & Row.

Gnepp, J., McKee, E., & Domanic, J. A. (1987). Children's use of situational information to infer emotion: Understanding emotionally equivocal situations. *Developmental Psychology, 23,* 114–123.

Harris, P. L. (1983). Children's understanding of the link between situation and emotion, *Journal of Experimental Child Psychology, 36,* 490–509.

Harris, P. L., Olthof, T., & Meerum Terwogt, M. (1981). Children's knowledge of emotion. *Journal of Child Psychology and Psychiatry, 45,* 247–261.

Harter, S. (1977). A cognitive-developmental approach to children's expression of conflicting feelings and a technique to facilitate such expression in play therapy. *Journal of Consulting and Clinical Psychology, 45,* 417–432.

Harter, S. (1982). Children's understanding of multiple emotions: A cognitive-developmental approach. In W. F. Overton (Ed.), *The relationship between social and cognitive development* (pp. 147–194). Hillsdale, NJ: Erlbaum.

Harter, S. (1983). Developmental perspectives on the self-system. In P. H. Mussen (Series Ed.) and E. M. Hetherington (Vol. Ed.), *Handbook of child psychology: Vol. 4. Socialization, personality, and social development* (4th ed., pp. 275–386). New York: Wiley.

Harter, S. (1985). Competence as a dimension of self-evaluation: Toward a comprehensive model of self-worth. In R. Leahy (Ed.), *The development of the self* (pp. 55–122). New York: Academic Press.

Harter, S. (1986a). Cognitive-developmental processes in the integration of concepts about emotion and the self. *Social Cognition, 4,* 119–151.

Harter, S. (1986b). Processes underlying the construction, maintenance, and enhancement of the self-concept. In J. Suls & A. Greenwald (Eds.), *Psychological perspectives on the self* (Vol. 3, pp. 136–182). Hillsdale, NJ: Erlbaum.

Harter, S. (1987). The determinants and mediational role of global self-worth in children. In N. Eisenberg (Ed.), *Contemporary issues in developmental psychology* (pp. 219–242). New York: Wiley.

Harter, S. (1988). Cognitive development. In S. Shirk (Ed.), *Child psychotherapy* (pp. 119–160). New York: Plenum.

Harter, S. (1990). Causes, correlates and the functional role of global self-worth: A lifespan perspective. In J. Kolligan & R. Sternberg (Eds.), *Perceptions of competence and incompetence across the life span* (pp. 67–98). New Haven, CT: Yale University Press.

Harter, S., & Buddin, B. J. (1987). Children's understanding of the simultaneity of two emotions: A five-stage developmental acquisition sequence. *Developmental Psychology, 23,* 388–399.

Harter, S., & Pike, R. (1984). The pictorial scale of perceived competence and social acceptance in young children. *Child Development, 55,* 1969–1982.

Harter, S., & Whitesell, N. R. (1988). Developmental changes in children's understanding of single, multiple and blended emotion concepts. In C. Saarni & P. L. Harris (Eds.), *Children's understanding of emotion* (pp. 82–107). New York: Cambridge University Press.

James, W. (1892). *Psychology: The briefer course.* New York: Holt, Rinehart, & Winston.

Lewis, M., & Brooks, J. (1978). Self-knowledge and emotional development. In M. Lewis & L. Rosenblum (Eds.), *The development of affect.* New York: Plenum.

Lively, W. J., & Bromley, D. B. (1973). *Person perception in childhood and adolescence.* London: Wiley.

McGuire, W., & McGuire, C. V. (1980). Significant others in self-space: Sex differences and developmental trends in the social self. In J. Suls (Ed.), *Social psychological perspectives on the self.* Hillsdale, NJ: Erlbaum.

McGuire, W., & Padawer-Singer, A. (1976). Trait salience in the spontaneous self-concept. *Journal of Personality and Social Psychology, 33,* 743–754.

Meerum Terwogt, M. (1984). Emotional development in middle childhood: A cognitive view. Unpublished doctoral dissertation, Vrije Universiteit te Amsterdam, Amsterdam.

Montemayor, R., & Eisen, M. (1977). The development of self-conceptions from childhood to adolescence. *Developmental Psychology, 13,* 314–319.

Mullener, N., & Laird, J. D. (1971). Some developmental changes in the organization of self-evaluations. *Developmental Psychology, 5,* 233–236.

Piaget, J. (1963). *The origins of intelligence in children.* New York: Norton.

Piers, E., & Singer, P. (1953). *Shame and guile.* Springfield, IL: Thomas.

Reissland, N. (1985). The development of concepts of simultaneity in children's understanding of emotions. *Journal of Child Psychology and Psychiatry, 26,* 811–824.

Rogers, C. (1951). *Client-centered therapy.* Boston: Houghton Mifflin.

Rosenberg, M. (1979). *Conceiving the self.* New York: Basic Books.

Selman, R. (1980). *The growth of interpersonal understanding.* New York: Academic Press.

Siegler, R. S. (1996). Unidimensional thinking, multidimensional thinking, and characteristic tendencies of thought. In A. J. Sameroff & M. M. Haith (Eds.), *The five to seven year shift: The age of reason and responsibility* (chap. 4, this vol.). Chicago: University of Chicago Press.

Stipek, D. (1983). A developmental analysis of pride and shame. *Human Development, 26,* 42–54.

Werner, H. (1957). The concept of development from a comparative and organismic point of view. In D. B. Harris (Ed.), *The concept of development* (pp. 125–148). Minneapolis: University of Minnesota Press.

White, S. H. (1965). Evidence for a hierarchical arrangement of learning processes. In L. P. Lipsitt & C. C. Spiker (Eds.), *Advances in child development and behavior* (Vol. 2, pp. 187–220). New York: Academic.

Whitesell, N. R., & Harter, S. (1989). Children's reports of conflict between simultaneous opposite-valence emotion. *Child Development, 60,* 673–682.

CHAPTER ELEVEN

Fearfulness: Developmental Consistency

JOAN STEVENSON-HINDE AND ANNE SHOULDICE

In many countries the 5 to 7 year period is one of transition from a familiar home to an unfamiliar school, complete with strange adults and children. Fearful behavior, fears, and worries may become particularly salient during this period in development. If wariness of the unfamiliar is viewed as an adaptive consequence of our evolutionary past (e.g., Bowlby, 1982), then some degree of fearfulness on entering school is to be expected. However, a high degree may form the basis for anxiety disorder (e.g., Bell-Dolan, Last, & Strauss, 1990; Kashani, Dandoy, & Orvaschel, 1991), the most common childhood psychiatric diagnosis (Beidel, 1991).

A Behavior Systems Framework

Using a behavior systems framework, we develop the theme that over the 5 to 7 year period age-appropriate changes occur, in both fear-provoking stimuli and fearful responses. These changes may, nevertheless, reflect an underlying consistency in individuals over time, or what Kagan (1971) refers to as *heterotypic continuity.*

A behavior systems approach is linked with an ethological perspective, embracing the "Four Why's of Behavior" posited by Niko Tinbergen: development, causation, evolution, and function (see, e.g., Hinde, 1987, pp. 15–18). Each aspect of behaviour can illuminate the others. Thus, for a complete understanding of development, questions may be asked concerning the other three areas. Furthermore, according to Fentress (1991), a behavior systems approach stresses organization:

> In the study of behaviour as well as neuroscience the investigator must typically deal with interlocking *networks* of organisational processes, rather than being satisfied with simple linear conceptualisations. . . . [T]he theme of interactive/self-organising systems . . .

exhibits often surprising parallels across problems of neurobehav-
ioural integration and its development. (P. 78)

More specifically, a behavior pattern may reflect a particular motivational
system, which interacts with other systems (e.g., Bischof, 1975). Thus,
"[d]ifferences in responsiveness of one individual at different times can be
understood on the basis of variations in the balance between different motivational systems" (Baerends, 1976, p. 733). For example, Bretherton and Ainsworth (1974) and Greenberg and Marvin (1982) have found coherence in
apparently diverse sequences of behavior by referring to the organization of
four distinct but interacting behavior systems: wary/fear, attachment, exploratory, and sociable. Within this framework, an unfamiliar stimulus would involve activation of fear and attachment behavior systems and deactivation of
exploratory and sociable systems. Thus, fearful behavior is conceptualized as
the product of a motivational system, which interacts with other systems. A
discussion of issues relevant to understanding a behavior system, and in particular a fear behavior system, follows.

Context

With a behavior systems approach, the *context* in which a behavior pattern
occurs is crucial for interpreting the pattern (e.g, Fentress, 1991; Stevenson-
Hinde, 1989). For example, context is implicit in Kagan's (1989) definition of
behavioral inhibition, which is defined not solely in response terms but as "the
initial reaction to unfamiliar or challenging situations" (p. 2). Beyond the immediate challenge, the broader context is relevant as well. Thus, fearful behavior is more likely to occur to challenges within in a strange situation than at
home and more likely to occur with increased distance from mother (e.g.,
Skarin, 1977; Sroufe, Waters, & Matas, 1974).

Furthermore, the level of fearfulness shown by a given child might vary
across different challenging contexts. For example, a child might be particularly wary with an adult stranger but not with a peer or not when faced with a
challenging task. In our own sample of 2.5-year-olds, the correlation between
wariness (latency + behavior ratings) upon entering a strange room and wariness on being addressed by an adult female stranger was only $r = .24$ ($N =
82$; Stevenson-Hinde & Shouldice, 1990).

Behavior

Fearful or inhibited behavior commonly refers to initial withdrawal to unfamiliar or challenging events (e.g., Kagan, 1989). Yet withdrawal may take many
forms: Alternative behaviors may be employed by different children in the
same context or by the same child in different contexts.

To the extent that different children have their own preferred ways of responding, then correlations between different types of fearful behavior within
a particular context may be low. For example, on approaching a stranger, one
child may have a long latency to approach but show few other indications,
whereas another may compliantly approach right away but show wary behavior
while doing so. Thus in our study of 2.5-year-olds invited to approach a female
stranger offering a toy, the correlation between latency to approach and ratings
of wary behavior (including facial expression, gaze, posture, and movement)
was significant, but far from perfect, $r = .44$ ($N = 82$; Stevenson-Hinde &
Shouldice, 1990). Similar levels of intercorrelations among indices of inhibition occur in other studies (e.g., Reznick, 1989).

Outcome

Thus, fearful behavior involves description by consequence rather than by any
particular motor pattern. Its "goal" (used without implying intention, see
Hinde & Stevenson, 1969) is to decrease or avoid proximity to, and/or interaction with, the feared object, either indirectly through alerting a caregiver to
intervene or directly through the child's own behavior. This may increase either
physical or psychological distance from the fear-eliciting stimulus. Psychological avoidance has been likened to cutoff behavior (e.g., Chance, 1962; Tinbergen, 1959), which is assumed to decrease arousal. For example, infant gaze
aversion to a stranger occurred when heart rate acceleration was near its peak,
and the infant again looked at the stranger when the rate neared basal level
(Sroufe & Waters, 1977).

Function

A postulated function of a fear behavior system, as well as an attachment
behavior system, is protection from harm (Ainsworth, Blehar, Waters, & Wall,
1978; Bowlby, 1969/1982, 1991; Sroufe, 1977). Fear of both the unfamiliar
and of being left alone would have been essential for survival in the environment in which humans evolved. Indeed, fears concerning harm that might
have been relevant during the course of evolution were found to have significant heritability estimates, while modern-day fears not involving risk of
life did not. That is, analysis of data from dizygotic and monzygotic twin
pairs (aged 8 to 18 years) revealed significant heritability estimates for fear
of the unknown, fear of animals and minor injury, and fear of danger and
death. Heritability estimates were not significant for fear of failure and criticism or fear of medical procedures (Stevenson, Batten, & Cherner, 1992).
Furthermore, young children's "irrational fears," such as fear of the dark or
fear of snakes, are more ubiquitous than are fears more appropriate to the
present day, such as fears of cars or guns (Marks, 1987). Thus, our propen-

sity to fear particular situations may have been guided by natural selection, with the function being protection from harm.

Developmental Aspects

STIMULUS CHANGES

Stimuli that initially elicit fear may be wide-ranging and then become narrowed through experience. A good example of "tuning" a fear response to a particular stimulus, and of the importance of interactions with others for doing this, is provided by Seyfarth and Cheney's (1986) observations of vervet monkeys. Adult vervets respond with a different alarm call to each of three types of predators: snakes, mammalian predators, and birds of prey. But young vervets initially respond to a wide range of objects. For example, they may give a bird-of-prey alarm call to a falling leaf. However, they come to give appropriate calls to different predators, and not to falling leaves, through observing adults, especially their mothers. Stimuli that do not initially elicit fear may gain fear-eliciting properties through similar observational learning, as when a child acquires a specific fear from his parent.

In addition to the range of appropriate stimuli changing during development, the nature of appropriate stimuli changes as well. Thus, over the first few months, fear-eliciting stimuli are loud noises and loss of support, and around 6 to 9 months, fear of strangers develops (e.g., Skarin, 1977; Waters et al., 1975). Studies at Harvard have shown that while a large mobile may frighten an infant, a more appropriate stimulus for frightening a toddler is an unfamiliar adult, then by 4 years unfamiliar peers, and by 7 years a challenging task (Kagan, Reznick, & Snidman, 1987; Kagan, Snidman, & Arcus, 1993).

Commonly expressed fears of very young children involve imaginary creatures (e.g., MacFarlane, Allen, & Honzik, 1962), certain animals (e.g., Jersild & Holmes, 1935), and the dark (e.g., Bauer, 1976). Starting school may provide an ongoing source of fear, beginning with separation anxiety (e.g., Bauer, 1980). With children's self-ratings of fearful items, the only item to actually increase in level with age (from 8 to 10 years) was "giving a spoken report" (Spence & McCathie, 1993). Thus, "social-evaluative fears" (e.g., Dong, Yang, & Ollendick, 1994) or "fear of negative evaluation" (e.g., Asendorpf, 1986, 1989) may emerge as children acquire the capacity to appreciate that they are being evaluated by others (see Harter, this volume, chap. 10).

RESPONSE CHANGES

Components of fearful behavior, such as crying or startle responses, as well as withdrawal from high-intensity stimuli, are present from birth (e.g., Kagan, 1994). Over the second half of the first year, negative responses to a stranger, such as a frown or gaze aversion, occur (e.g., Schaffer, Greenwood, & Parry, 1972; Waters, Matas, & Sroufe, 1975), and latencies to approach intense and unfamiliar toys increase (Rothbart, 1989). Rothbart observed individual differences in speed of approach before children began to show extended periods of hesitation in approaching novel, high-intensity toys. Thus, fearful behavior, including inhibition of approach responses, may become integrated as a behavior system over the second half of the first year.

The behavior associated with a fear behavior system continues to change, in age-appropriate ways. Whereas motor activity and crying are appropriate expressions of fear for an infant (Kagan et al., 1993), behavioral withdrawal is appropriate for a toddler (Stevenson-Hinde & Shouldice, 1990), and beyond that vocalizations become appropriate, with inhibited children responding minimally (e.g., Evans, 1993; Kagan, Reznick, Snidman, Gibbons, & Johnson, 1988). The association of qualitatively different responses at different ages with a particular behavior system provides grounds for inferring "heterotypic continuity" (Kagan, 1971).

Summing Up

A behavior systems approach permits both a framework and flexibility for conceptualizing fear-related behavior. It encourages thinking about issues beyond the behavior itself—namely, context, outcome, and function—as well as developmental issues. With this background, we shall now go on to consider consistency and change: in general, by postulating a theoretical threshold level of excitation for a fear behavior system; and in practice, by considering some relevant data sets.

Individual Thresholds of Excitation

A behavior systems approach to fearfulness is compatible with theories of childhood temperament, all of which (a) contain a dimension relating to initial approach/withdrawal and (b) emphasize consistency (see, e.g., Goldsmith et al., 1987; Rothbart, 1989). In his commentary on four approaches to childhood temperament, McCall attempted a synthesis with the following definition:

> [T]emperament consists of relatively consistent, basic dispositions inherent in the person that underlie and modulate the expression of activity, reactivity, emotionality, and sociability. Major elements of temperament are present early in life, and those elements are likely to be strongly influenced by biological factors. As development proceeds, the expression of temperament increasingly becomes more influenced by experience and context. (In Goldsmith et al., 1987, p. 524)

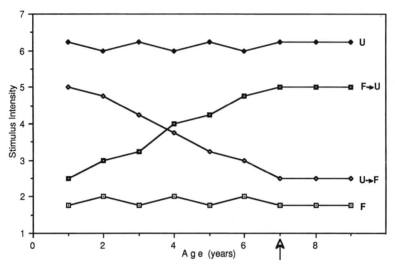

Figure 11.1   Inferred relative thresholds for arousal of a fear behavior system in four different children: Unfearful (U), Fearful (F), changing from Fearful to Unfearful (F → U), and from Unfearful to Fearful (U → F). At each age point, the nature of the eliciting stimuli as well as the responses must be age-appropriate (see text).

One may conceptualize consistent differences or dispositions by postulating individual thresholds of arousal of a fear behavior system, while still acknowledging the complexity of underlying physiological mechanisms (e.g., Kagan, 1989; Kagan et al., 1993). In keeping with a behavior systems approach, the actual eliciting stimuli and fearful responses must be age-appropriate. Each child's threshold is indicated in terms of his or her relative position within the sample. As illustrated in Figure 11.1, the uninhibited individual (U) has a high threshold, requiring relatively strong external stimuli to elicit fearful behavior, whereas the fearful individual (F) with a low threshold requires only a mild stimulus. Additional very short-term fluctuations in state would be expected, due to temporary internal or external factors, such as fatigue or separation from mother (cf. Baerends, 1976).

Similarly, long-term change could be due to internal or external factors. For example, the nature of the child's attachment to her or his mother, which develops over the first year of life (e.g., Isabella, 1993) and then is maintained by ongoing mother/child interactions (e.g., Stevenson-Hinde & Shouldice, 1995a) may influence and be influenced by the child's fearfulness. At 2.5 years, the least fearful children were classed on reunion as "Very securely" attached, whereas the most fearful emphasized dependency to their mothers and were classed as "Secure-ambivalent" or "Insecure-ambivalent" (Stevenson-Hinde & Shouldice, 1990). Additional family variables may raise thresholds, such as levels of parents' education and the variety of social networks provided by the family, including the opportunity to attend nursery school (reviewed in Evans, 1993). This is indicated by the individual (F → U) with an increasing threshold, which might continue to rise into primary school. However, if a child experienced illness or excess stress in primary school and withdrew into the family, the outcome might be a decrease in threshold (U → F).

Finally, a more global level of influence is the culture in which a child is raised. This could push his or her threshold to extremes, depending on the interaction between the child's initial predisposition and cultural pressures. For example, a culture which values individual outgoingness, initiative, and competitiveness too highly could push a threshold one way (i.e., raise the threshold to an extreme) for an initially unfearful child and the other way (i.e., lower the threshold to an extreme) for an initially fearful child. Either extreme might be undesirable, leading to externalizing or internalizing disorders. This example leads to the fundamental issue raised by Rogoff (this volume, chap. 13). She pursues a sociocultural perspective on development, with changes residing neither exclusively in individuals nor exclusively in environments, but rather being a product of individual involvement in sociocultural activity.

In summary, processes of change are not incompatible with a concept of individual thresholds of responsiveness, which may become more resistant to change as a child gets older. We now turn to some relevant empirical results.

Consistency in Fearful Behavior

Behavioral inhibition has been extensively investigated via direct observations rather than questionnaires, from infancy to beyond 7 years (see, e.g., Kagan, 1994; Reznick, 1989; Rubin & Asendorpf, 1993). Within a normative sample, indices of inhibition were significantly correlated, with $r = .51$ from 14 to 20 months; .44 from 14 to 32 months; and .25 from 20 to 32 months (Reznick, Gibbons, Johnson, & McDonough, 1989, Table 3). In a sample of children selected at 21 months as being either extremely inhibited or uninhibited, indices of behavioral inhibition were even more highly correlated over the years, with $r = .67$ from 21 months to 7.5 years (Kagan et al., 1988). About three-quarters within each group kept a similar behavioral profile 6 years later, and original differences in heart rate were preserved as well (Kagan et al., 1988). Over the 5 to 7 year period, both behavior and physiological indices of inhibition were significantly consistent (Table 11.1).

However, in agreement with McCall's overview (discussed in the previous section), Kagan et al. (1988) found that "absolute heart-rate and cortisol level at 7.5 years were not as discriminating of the 2 behavioral groups as they had been 2 years earlier" (p. 1580). "The preservation of behavior, despite weaker contemporary correlations with these biological variables, implies that as

Table 11.1
Consistency in Fearfulness over the 5 to 7 Year Period: Results from Two Samples

Mode of Assessment	4.5 to 7 Years, Madingley Sample[a] (N = 70, unselected)	5.5 to 7.5 Years, Harvard Sample[b] (N = 22 inhibited + 19 uninhibited children, selected at 21 months)
Questionnaires to Mother		
Approach/Withdrawal behavior to unfamiliar people, places, and things	.71***	
Approach/Withdrawal behavior to unfamiliar people only	.46***	
Fears	.48***	
Worries	.30**	
Laboratory Observations		
Behavior during play with unfamiliar peers and cognitive tasks		.57***
Behavior to unfamiliar adult female	.24*	
Heart period during cognitive tasks		.58***
Cortisol level		.40**

[a]From Stevenson-Hinde & Shouldice (1995b).
[b]From Kagan, Reznick, Snidman, Gibbons, & Johnson (1988).
Pearson correlation coefficients: $*p < .05$, $**p < .01$, $***p < .001$, two-tailed.

growing children encounter and cope with new stressors . . . [they may have] developed an automatized response profile that was partially independent of the physiological states that supported their behavior originally (pp. 1588–1589). In addition, according to Kagan (1989), "Children who remained inhibited at 7.5 years were much more consistent across all assessment contexts than they had been two years earlier" (p. 18). All this is in keeping with the view that personality characteristics in general become more organized over that period (Kagan & Moss, 1962).

In our "baseline" longitudinal study, children were selected at 2.5 years without any reference to their behavior patterns, the only criteria involved being the secondborn in two-child, intact families in the Cambridge (England) area (see, e.g., Stevenson-Hinde & Shouldice, 1990; Shouldice & Stevenson-Hinde, 1992). Our concern here is with measures taken at 4.5 and 7.0 years of age, which in Britain covers the transition into primary school at ages 4.5 to 5 years. At 4.5 and 7 years, behavioral observations were carried out in a video-taped laboratory setting and mothers completed both a temperament questionnaire and a questionnaire about their children's worries and fears. In addition, at 7 years each child was interviewed in the laboratory about his or her worries (see Stevenson-Hinde & Shouldice, 1995b).

Initial Approach/Withdrawal refers to one of the nine dimensions of temperament described by Thomas and Chess (1977) and rated by mothers on the McDevitt and Carey (1978) questionnaire. Consistency from 4.5 to 7 years was highly significant (see Table 11.1). Concerning the more specific characteristic of initial reaction to unfamiliar people, consistency was also significant, whether assessed by questionnaires to mothers (three McDevitt and Carey items plus three of our own; see Stevenson-Hinde & Shouldice, 1990, for further details) or by observer ratings made from videotapes of behavior on being spoken to by a female stranger in the laboratory. The ratings included verbal responsiveness as well as inhibited behavior (physical/visual avoidance and tension in the face, body, or voice), and were made on a 9-point scale, from 1 (*relaxed/responsive*) to 4 (a norm for the age) to 9 (*high tension/no verbal response*).

All of the measures were significantly consistent from 4.5 to 7 years (see Table 11.1). However, maternal ratings for the global dimension of Approach/Withdrawal were more consistent than those for the more specific dimension of Approach/Withdrawal to a stranger, which were more consistent than the ratings based on direct observations in the laboratory. The latter were lower than those for the Harvard sample selected for high and low inhibition but similar to those given above for the Harvard sample that was not preselected (Reznick et al., 1989).

Thus, in practice, consistency will be higher with selected samples, with global rather than specific assessments, and with nonindependent observers. One tends to overlook the fact that maternal reports do *not* involve independent observers at each age. Hence, some of the consistency found in typical questionnaire-based studies of temperament could be in the eye of the beholder, in addition to other sources of maternal bias (see, e.g., Sameroff, Seifer, & Elias, 1982; Stevenson-Hinde & Shouldice, 1995a; Vaughn, Taraldson, Crichton, & Egeland, 1981).

Consistency in Worries and Fears

Kagan's finding that with age physiological measures may become dissociated from an adopted response profile implies that people may be feeling anxious and not showing it or vice versa. With older children, it is possible to ask them what they are fearful or worried about. For example, the Fear Survey Schedule for Children (FSSC), first developed by Scherer and Nakamura (1968) and revised by Ollendick (1983), is a list of potentially fearful stimuli (e.g., "being hit by a car or lorry"). Children indicate their level of fear to each item on a 3-point scale: "None"; "Some"; or "A lot." Using the revised FSSC, Spence and McCathie (1993) examined the stability of children's reported fears in an Australian sample over a 2-year period from grades 3 and 4 to grades 5 and 6. For the sample as a whole, the level of fearfulness decreased with age. However, the most frequently feared stimuli remained the same at both ages. These related mainly to fears of danger, death, and physical injury and matched the most prevalent fears found in previous studies (McCathie & Spence, 1991; Ollendick, 1983).

Individual consistency in levels of fear over the 2 years was moderate ($r = .52$). However, children who reported the highest fear levels at the younger age were much more likely to retain extremely high fear scores 2 years later than were children who had moderate or low scores at the earlier age. As with behavioral inhibition (see Kagan et al., 1993; Kagan, 1994), categorizing extreme levels of fear may be more productive than treating all scores as a continuum.

Although girls reported higher levels of fear than did boys on the FSSC, the more frequently reported fearful stimuli were almost identical for boys and girls (e.g., Gullone & King, 1992; Spence & McCathie, 1993). These findings, which are in keeping with previous studies (reviewed in Maccoby & Jacklin, 1975), were significant in Australia, Great Britain, and the United States. Nine of the top 10 fears reported by British children were identical with those reported by Australian and North American children of a comparable age and social class (Ollendick, King, & Frary, 1989).

In our own study, mothers were given two lists, one of common childhood fears and one of common worries. For each item, they were asked to indicate the degree of fear or worry, on a scale from 0 to 3, which was then summed for each list (see Stevenson-Hinde & Shouldice, 1995b). Consistency from 4.5 to 7 years was significant, particularly for fears, which were perhaps more easily observed than worries (see Table 11.1). Indeed, maternal ratings of worries were not significantly consistent for girls. (Because the questionnaires were slightly different at each age, changes in level due to age cannot be assessed.)

The Content of Worries and Fears

Two recent studies involving the 5 to 7 year period used open-ended questions, which did reveal changes in content, not apparent from structured lists. In Bauer's (1976) study, children in kindergarten and in second and sixth grades were asked to describe their fears, as well as to draw them. Using as a guide the system of categories developed by Jersild, Markey, and Jersild (1933), Bauer's study categorized verbatim replies at each age. The frequency of occurrence of imaginary fears (e.g., ghosts and monsters), bedtime fears, and frightening dreams decreased with age, whereas realistic fears involving bodily injury and physical danger increased.

Lentz (1985) used a semistructured doll play technique to investigate fears of 5- and 6-year-olds in three environments: home, school, and baby-sitter's house. Within each environment, specific situations that might evoke fears (e.g., home and bedtime, home and parents arguing) were set up, and the children were asked what the play-child was either afraid of or worried about. Girls were more concerned with bodily injury in the contexts of playing at home and at school than were boys.

When our own sample was aged 7 years, we asked them what they were worried about. During the same laboratory visit as the Approach/Withdrawal to stranger assessment, and after the mother had left the room, each child was given a hand puppet. This was a white rabbit called Bix, to which the experimenter addressed questions primarily about the child's self-concept (based on Cassidy, 1988). The child was asked to answer for the puppet, a technique that is less threatening than direct questions. Of the 20 questions, 2 are relevant here:

> #14. "Bix, does (Name of child) ever worry about things?" (If the child responded "No," the experimenter asked, "Never?")
>
> #15. "What does s/he worry about?"

Each child's response to Question #15 on the Puppet Interview was listed (for the list, see Stevenson-Hinde & Shouldice, 1995b).

Worries were reported by 70% of the sample, with the rest not naming any worries, even when pressed. Both boys and girls (13 boys and 8 girls) mentioned event-related worries. Seven percent of the sample mentioned events that could be related to real life, such as being killed by a car. The other events were nighttime (dark in bed) or imaginary ones (ghostie things)—the "irrational" fears of childhood—mentioned by less than a quarter (23%) of this sample of 7-year-olds. This is consistent with Bauer's (1976) finding that the prevalence of "irrational" fears decreases with age.

Sex differences did occur with the other two categories of worry. Girls were particularly worried about family members and boys about performance ($\chi^2 = 11.62$, $df = 1$, $p < .001$). In particular, family concerns (e.g., her Mum and Dad might have a divorce; when her Mum's feeling tired or sad) were expressed by 14 girls and only 1 boy, who was worried about his brother. Performance-related worries (e.g., when he falls over; football) were reported by 10 boys and only 3 girls. This category included performance at school (when he can't get an "add" right at school) mentioned by 6 children, all boys.

Such differences in the content of worries, with girls being concerned about close relationships and boys about performance, fit with results from asking adolescents what makes them anxious (Magnusson & Oläh, 1981). The direction of the differences also fits with biological theorizing. We may "expect

natural selection in our environment of evolutionary adaptedness to have provided males and females with behavioural propensities that differed between
the sexes" (Hinde, 1987, p. 120). In particular, since a female is restricted in
the number of offspring she can produce, it will "pay" her, in terms of increasing her "inclusive fitness" to invest in raising them to reproductive age. This
may involve promoting close relationships, not only with the offspring themselves but also with other family members who might provide support (and in
so doing maximize their own inclusive fitness as well). On the other hand, a
male is essentially unrestricted in the number of offspring he can produce and
may maximize his inclusive fitness by concerning himself with his performance, expressed in adulthood as gaining as many matings as possible (see,
e.g., Hinde, 1987). A more proximal explanation may lie in the differential
socialization experienced by two sexes. However, this is not incompatible with
an evolutionary explanation, particularly if one considers that socialization
practices themselves may be a product of natural selection.

Conclusions

We have used an ethological perspective, and in particular a behavior systems
framework, to understand the organization of behavior in the midst of contexts
and responses that change with age. With reported fears as well as with fearful
behavior, age-appropriate changes occur while individual consistency remains,
particularly in children with extremely high levels.

Because of age-appropriate changes, it is not possible to consider the development of absolute levels of fearful behavior. However, the relative position of
individuals does appear to be consistent across early childhood. That is not to
deny individual exceptions, as indicated by postulating changes in individual
thresholds of fearful responsiveness (see Figure 11.1). By age 7 years, the Harvard studies indicate a "stabilization of the qualities of inhibition and lack of
inhibition" (Kagan, 1989, p. 18).

When standard lists of fears and worries are used, reported levels decrease
with age. Yet consistency across time is also found, particularly for extreme
cases. With open-ended questions, the content of fears and worries changes
with age. Over the early school years, imaginary fears decrease, whereas realistic fears increase. Furthermore, we identified sex differences in the content of
worries of 7-year-olds. That is, when the children were asked what they worried about, family-related worries were reported mainly by girls and performance worries by boys. These findings are compatible with sociobiological
theorizing. Thus, an ethological perspective—embracing development, causation, evolution, and function—may be used to shed light on consistency and
change in children's fears and worries, as well as fearful behavior.

Acknowledgments

We are grateful to the Medical Research Council, London, for their continued support, and to R. A. Hinde and A. Sameroff for their constructive comments on the manuscript.

References

Ainsworth, M. D. S., Blehar, M. C., Waters, E., & Wall, S. (1978). *Patterns of attachment.* Hillsdale, NJ: Erlbaum.

Asendorpf, J. (1986). Shyness in middle and late childhood. In W. H. Jones, J. M. Cheek, & S. R. Briggs (Eds.), *Shyness: Perspectives on research and treatment* (pp. 91–103). New York: Plenum.

Asendorpf, J. (1989). Shyness as a final common pathway for two different kinds of inhibition. *Journal of Personality & Social Psychology, 57,* 481–492.

Baerends, G. P. (1976). The functional organization of behaviour. *Animal Behaviour, 24,* 726–738.

Bauer, D. H. (1976). An exploratory study of developmental changes in children's fears. *Journal of Child Psychology & Psychiatry, 17,* 69–74.

Bauer, D. H. (1980). Childhood fears in developmental perspective. In L. Hersov & I. Berg (Eds.), *Out of school* (pp. 189–208). New York: Wiley.

Beidel, D. C. (1991). Social phobia and overanxious disorder in school-age children. *Journal of the American Academy of Child and Adolescent Psychiatry, 30,* 545–552.

Bell-Dolan, D. J., Last, C. G., & Strauss, C. C. (1990). Symptoms of anxiety disorders in normal children. *Journal of the American Academy of Child and Adolescent Psychiatry, 29,* 759–765.

Bischof, N. (1975). A systems approach toward the functional connections of fear and attachment. *Child Development, 46,* 801–817.

Bowlby, J. (1982). *Attachment and loss:* Vol. *1. Attachment.* London: Hogarth Press. (Original work published in 1969.)

Bowlby, J. (1991). Ethological light on psychoanalytical problems. In P. Bateson (Ed.), *The development and integration of behaviour* (pp. 301–313). Cambridge: Cambridge University Press.

Bretherton, I., & Ainsworth, M. D. S. (1974). Responses of one-year-olds to a stranger in a strange situation. In M. Lewis & L. A. Rosenblum (Eds.), *The origins of fear* (pp. 131–164). New York: Wiley.

Cassidy, J. (1988). Child-mother attachment and the self in six-year-olds. *Child Development, 59,* 121–134.

Chance, M. R. A. (1962). An interpretation of some agonistic postures: The role of 'cut-off' acts and postures. *Symposium Zoological Society of London, 8,* 71–89.

Dong, Q., Yang, B., & Ollendick, T. H. (1994). Fears in Chinese children and adolescents and their relations to anxiety and depression. *Journal of Child Psychology and Psychiatry, 35,* 351–363.

Evans, M. A. (1993). Communicative competence as a dimension of shyness. In K. H. Rubin & J. B. Asendorpf (Eds.), *Social withdrawal, inhibition, and shyness in childhood* (pp. 189–212). Hillsdale, NJ: Erlbaum.

Fentress, J. C. (1991). Analytical ethology and synthetic neuroscience. In P. Bateson (Ed.), *The development and integration of behaviour* (pp. 77–120). Cambridge: Cambridge University Press.

Goldsmith, H., Buss, A. H., Plomin, R., Rothbart, M. K., Thomas, A., Chess, S., Hinde, R. A., & McCall, R. B. (1987). What is temperament? Four approaches. *Child Development, 58,* 505–529.

Greenberg, M. T., & Marvin, R. S. (1982). Reactions of preschool children to an adult stranger: A behavioral systems approach. *Child Development, 53,* 481–490.

Gullone, E., & King, N. J. (1992). Psychometric evaluation of a Revised Fear Survey Schedule for children and adolescents. *Journal of Child Psychology and Psychiatry, 33,* 987–998.

Harter, S. (1996). Developmental changes in self-understanding across the 5 to 7 shift. In A. J. Sameroff & M. M. Haith (Eds.), *The five to seven year shift: The age of reason and responsibility* (chap. 10, this vol.). Chicago: University of Chicago Press.

Hinde, R. A. (1987). *Individuals, relationships, and culture.* Cambridge: Cambridge University Press.

Hinde, R. A., & Stevenson, J. G. (1970). Goals and response control. In L. R. Aronson, E. Tobach, D. S. Lehrman, & J. S. Rosenblatt (Eds.), *Develpment and evolution of behavior* (Vol. 1, pp. 216–237). San Francisco: W. H. Freeman.

Isabella, R. A. (1993). Origins of attachment: Maternal interactive behavior across the first year. *Child Development, 64,* 605–621.

Jersild, A. T., & Holmes, F. B. (1935). *Child development monographs:* Vol. 20. *Children's fears.* New York: Columbia University Press.

Jersild, A. T., Markey, F. V., & Jersild, C. L. (1993). *Child development monographs:* Vol. 12. *Children's fears, dreams, wishes, daydreams, likes, dislikes, pleasant and unpleasant memories.* New York: Columbia University Press.

Kagan, J. (1971). *Change and continuity in infancy.* New York: Wiley.

Kagan, J. (1989). The concept of behavioral inhibition to the unfamiliar. In J. S. Reznick (Ed.), *Perspectives on behavioral inhibition* (pp. 1–23). Chicago: University of Chicago Press.

Kagan, J. (1994). *Galen's prophecy: Temperament in human nature.* New York: Basic Books.

Kagan, J., & Moss, H. A. (1962). *Birth to maturity.* New York: Wiley.

Kagan, J., Reznick, J. S., & Snidman, N. (1987). The physiology and psychology of behavioral inhibition in children. *Child Development, 58,* 1459–1473.

Kagan, J., Reznick, J. S., Snidman, N., Gibbons, J., & Johnson, M. O. (1988). Childhood derivatives of inhibition and lack of inhibition to the unfamiliar. *Child Development, 59,* 1580–1589.

Kagan, J., Snidman, N., & Arcus, D. (1993). On the temperamental categories of inhibited and uninhibited children. In K. H. Rubin & J. B. Asendorpf (Eds.), *Social withdrawal, inhibition, and shyness in childhood* (pp. 19–28). Hillsdale, NJ: Erlbaum.

Kashani, J. H., Dandoy, A. C., & Orvaschel, H. (1991). Current perspectives on anxiety disorders in children and adolescents: An overview. *Comprehensive Psychiatry, 32,* 481–495.

Lentz, K. (1985). Fears and worries of young children as expressed in a contextual play setting. *Journal of Child Psychology and Psychiatry, 26,* 981–987.

Maccoby, E. E., & Jacklin, C. N. (1975). *The Psychology of sex differences.* Stanford, CA: Stanford University Press.

MacFarlane, J. W., Allen, L., & Honzik, M. P. (1962). *A developmental study of the behavior problems of normal children between 21 months and 14 years.* Berkeley: University of California Press.

Magnusson, D., & Oläh, A. (1981). Situation-outcome contingencies. *Reports from the Department of Psychology.* Stockholm: University of Stockholm.

Marks, I. M. (1987). *Fears, phobias and rituals.* Oxford: Oxford University Press.

McCathie, H., & Spence, S. H. (1991). What is the Revised Survey for Children measuring? *Behaviour Research and Therapy, 29,* 495–503.

McDevitt, S. C., & Carey, W. B. (1978). The measurement of temperament in 3–7 year old children. *Journal of Child Psychology and Psychiatry, 19,* 245–253.

Ollendick, T. H. (1983). Reliability and validity of the Revised Fear Survey Schedule for Children (FSSC-R). *Behaviour Research and Therapy, 21,* 685–692.

Ollendick, T. H., King, N. J., & Frary, R. B. (1989). Fears in children and adolescents: Reliability and generalizability across gender, age, and nationality. *Behaviour Research and Therapy, 27,* 19–26.

Reznick, J. S. (Ed.). (1989). *Perspectives on behavioral inhibition.* Chicago: University of Chicago Press.

Reznick, J. S., Gibbons, J. L., Johnson, M. O., & McDonough, P. M. (1989). Behavioral inhibition in a normative sample. In J. S. Reznick (Ed.), *Perspectives on behavioral inhibition* (pp. 25–49). Chicago: University of Chicago Press.

Rothbart, M. K. (1989). Behavioral approach and inhibition. In J. S. Reznick (Ed.), *Perspectives on behavioral inhibition* (pp. 139–157). Chicago: University of Chicago Press.

Rubin, K. H., & Asendorpf, J. B. (Eds.). (1993). *Social withdrawal, inhibition, and shyness in childhood.* Hillsdale, NJ: Erlbaum.

Sameroff, A. J., Seifer, R., & Elias, P. K. (1982). Sociocultural variability in infant temperament ratings. *Child Development, 53,* 164–173.

Schaffer, H., Greenwood, A., & Parry, M. (1972). The onset of wariness. *Child Development, 43,* 164–175.

Scherer, M. W., & Nakamura, C. Y. (1968). A Fear Survey Schedule for Children (FSS-FC): A factor-analytic comparison with manifest anxiety (CMAS). *Behaviour Research and Therapy, 6,* 173–182.

Seyfarth, R., & Cheney, D. (1986). Vocal development in vervet monkeys. *Animal Behaviour, 34,* 1640–1658.

Shouldice, A. E., & Stevenson-Hinde, J. (1992). Coping with security distress: The Separation Anxiety Test and attachment classification at 4.5 years. *Journal of Child Psychology and Psychiatry, 33,* 331–348.

Skarin, K. (1977). Cognitive and contextual determinants of stranger fear in six- and eleven-month-old infants. *Child Development, 48,* 537–544.

Spence, S. H., & McCathie, H. M. (1993). The stability of fears in children: A two-year prospective study: A research note. *Journal of Child Psychology and Psychiatry, 34,* 579–585.

Sroufe, L. A. (1977). Wariness of strangers and the study of infant development. *Child Development, 48,* 731–746.

Sroufe, L. A., & Waters, E. (1977). Heart rate as a convergent measure in clinical and developmental research. *Merrill-Palmer Quarterly, 23,* 3–25.

Sroufe, L. A., Waters, E., & Matas, L. (1974). Contextual determinants of infant affective response. In M. Lewis & L. Rosenblum (Eds.), *The origins of fear* (pp. 49–72). New York: Wiley.

Stevenson, J., Batten, N., & Cherner, M. (1992). Fears and fearfulness in children and adolescents: A genetic analysis of twin data. *Journal of Child Psychology and Psychiatry, 33,* 977–985.

Stevenson-Hinde, J. (1989). Behavioral inhibition: Issues of context. In J. S. Reznick (Ed.), *Perspectives on behavioral inhibition* (pp. 125–138). Chicago: University of Chicago Press.

Stevenson-Hinde, J., and Shouldice, A. E. (1990). Fear and attachment in 2.5-year-olds. *British Journal of Developmental Psychology, 8,* 319–333.

Stevenson-Hinde, J., & Shouldice, A. (1995a). Maternal interactions and self-reports related to attachment classifications at 4.5 years. *Child Development, 66,* 583–596.

Stevenson-Hinde, J., & Shouldice, A. (1995b). 4.5 to 7 years: Fearful behaviour, fears and worries. *Journal of Child Psychology and Psychiatry, 36,* 1027–1038.

Thomas, A., & Chess, S. (1977). *Temperament and development.* New York: Brunner Mazel.

Tinbergen, N. (1959). The functions of territory. *Bird Study, 4,* 14–27.

Vaughn, B. E., Taraldson, B. J., Crichton, L., & Egeland, B. (1981). The assessment of infant temperament: A critique of the Carey Infant Temperament Questionnaire. *Infant Behavior and Development, 4,* 1–17.

Waters, E., Matas, L., & Sroufe, L. A. (1975). Infants' reactions to an approaching stranger: Description, validation, and functional significance of wariness. *Child Development, 46,* 348–356.

CHAPTER TWELVE

Sibling Relationships and Perceived Self-Competence: Patterns of Stability Between Childhood and Early Adolescence

JUDY DUNN

Children experience major changes in their lives in the years from 5 to 7, with the start of school—a new world of other children and teachers, of novel demands and expectations. Suddenly children are part of a social world in which new social rules apply and new relationships must be formed, and they become aware of a whole set of social comparisons that begin to be applied to them. They also make major advances over these years in their cognitive and communicative development and in their understanding of themselves and of others in their world. How do these experiences and changes affect their social relationships within the family and their feelings about themselves? Should we view this period as a transitional period? Or are the developments that take place in children's socioemotional development and relationships better thought of as continuous rather than discontinuous?

The focus of this chapter is on individual differences over this period rather than on normative changes. Most research on transitions considers only mean age differences, but the perspective of individual differences is also important and for two reasons: First, differences among children at any age are vast, and full description and explanation of transitions must include this range of behavior, not just its average. Second, the societal relevance of developmental changes is chiefly concerned with individual differences—the question of why some children in middle childhood and adolescence lose confidence in themselves, become unhappy, or become delinquent and others weather developmental transitions with grace. Individual differences are particularly important in the transition to middle childhood because it is during this period that individual differences begin to become predictive of later adjustment problems. It is for this reason that middle childhood was targeted for research in the 1993 budget of the U.S. House and Senate appropriations committees. The etiology and explanations of developmental changes in patterns of individual differences, however, are not necessarily related to those of normative developmental change. We may learn little about the influences on individual differences by focusing on average group changes over age and vice versa. Both group changes and individual differences are proper subjects for study, and influences on either one may prove to be good candidates for likely influences on the other. However, there is no necessary connection between them.

The specific question addressed in this chapter is whether there is a significant shift in the patterns of individual differences between children between the years 4 and 8 in two domains of their social development—a shift is of sufficient scale to merit the term *transition*. Such a change could be due either to the major changes in the children's experiences outside the family or to the children's own developmental advances over this period. Changes in patterns of individual differences can be examined in a variety of ways. They are reflected, for instance, in changes in variances of characteristics, in covariances among variables, and in age-to-age correlations (Plomin, Defries, & Fulker, 1988). Of these, most attention has been paid to age-to-age correlations; the idea that we can look at "dips" in age-to-age correlations in considering individual differences models of developmental change has been discussed, for instance, by Wohlwill (1973) and many others since (e.g., Brim & Kagan, 1980). Although the problems in interpreting differences in stability of correlations from age to age are acknowledged (Bateson, 1978), it is argued that in periods of marked developmental change there may be decreases in cross-age correlations. As McCall (1983) put it:

> It is quite possible that individual differences become rearranged at the advent of new skills, a phenomenon that would be reflected in reduced cross-age stabilities at points in development where major discontinuities in the developmental function occur. Consequently, cross-age stabilities should be higher for periods that do not span a discontinuity, and lower for comparable periods that do embrace a discontinuity in developmental function. (p. 120).

During a transitional period in development, it is suggested, there will be a dip in age-to-age correlations. Figure 12.1 demonstrates how differences in developmental timing alone could alter the rank order of individual differences during a period of developmental change. In the example, correlations between years 6 and 7 are low, whereas correlations among years 5, 5.5, 7.5, and 8 are 1.0.

The first domain on which the chapter focuses is the relationship between children and their siblings. The question of interest here is whether differences in this close family relationship, characterized by its uninhibited emotional expression and familiarity with the other, is affected by the major changes in the children's experience outside the family or the developmental changes in their social understanding and communicative skills over this period. The second

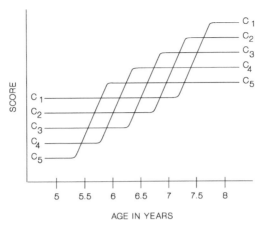

Figure 12.1 Changes in age-to-age correlations with individual differences in the timing of a transition.

domain to be examined is children's perceived self-competence; in contrast to the relationship between siblings, which begins in infancy, children's ability to reflect on themselves—their perception of themselves in relation to others—is a relatively new development over this period (Harter, this volume, chap. 10). Researchers have suggested, however, that individual differences in children's perceptions of themselves are linked to both children's earlier family relationships (Harter, 1986, 1987) and their concurrent experiences with peers (Berndt & Ladd, 1989).

These two domains are not unrelated. The experience of growing up with a sibling who constantly belittles or denigrates a child or with a sibling who apparently effortlessly succeeds in domains in which the child feels less able may well have a long-lasting influence, as the example of Henry James and his older brother, William, amply demonstrates (Edel, 1987; see Dunn & Plomin, 1990, for further consideration of this issue).

The focus of the chapter is primarily upon the first of the four questions posed by the editors of this volume—do 7-year-olds behave differently from 5-year-olds? The question is here considered in terms of stability and change in the rank order of individual differences during this age rather than on average age differences. The distinction made between quantitative and qualitative changes, which underline the subsequent three questions the editors pose, depends surely on the sensitivity of measurements that are made. As a general conceptual point it should be recognized that any behavioral difference over the period between 5 and 7 years of age is likely to be quantitative rather than qualitative if the behavior is measured at a sufficiently fine-grained level. Similarly, whether a measure is described as changing in a discontinuous fashion or a continuous fashion will crucially depend on the nature of measurement that is made. If the behavior is described at a fine-grained and detailed level, it will probably be described as changing continuously. For some of the aspects of behavior that we consider in this chapter, such as the development of intimacy between siblings or sensitivity to others' reactions to oneself—frequently considered "new" aspects of relationships that appear de novo in middle childhood—this may appear to be a controversial position to take; we return to it in the last section of the chapter.

Sibling Relationships

In both early childhood and middle childhood, individual differences in children's relationships with their siblings are marked (Boer, 1990; Boer & Dunn, 1992; Dunn & McGuire, 1992). In middle childhood some children are very hostile and aggressive to their siblings, others are affectionate and supportive, and still others are relatively detached and uninvolved with each other. These differences are of considerable interest to psychologists; links have been described between sibling relationship quality and antisocial behavior (Patterson, 1986; Richman, Stevenson, & Graham, 1982), resilience to marital disharmony (Jenkins, 1992), and sociocognitive development (Dunn, Brown, Slomkowski, Tesla, & Youngblade, 1991). The differences are also of much importance to parents; sibling conflict is commonly cited as a major concern by parents of both 4- to 5-year-olds and 7-year-olds (e.g., Newson & Newson, 1970, 1978).

In spite of the interest in such individual differences, the question of whether they are part of a pattern that has persisted from early childhood has been little studied. In recent years, we have learned something of the mean changes in the structure and quality of sibling relationships during middle childhood and adolescence from cross-sectional studies (Buhrmester, 1992; Buhrmester & Furman, 1990), but the stability of individual differences has remained unexplored. Those longitudinal studies that have been conducted have usually been of short duration and focused on the preschool to early childhood period (e.g., Abramovitch, Corter, Pepler, & Stanhope, 1986).

To the question "Do 7-year-olds behave differently from 5-year-olds?" the answers suggested by the cross-sectional research into mean differences are rather inconsistent. The cross-sectional studies are in agreement that the relationship becomes more egalitarian during middle childhood (Buhrmester & Furman, 1990; Vandell, Minnett, & Santrock, 1987), but there is disagreement about whether this is due to a decrease in dominance by both siblings (Buhrmester, 1992) or an increase in the power exerted by younger siblings (Vandell et al., 1987). Whether there are changes in emotional closeness and conflict is also not clear: Some studies report no age trends (Raffaelii, 1991, April), whereas other studies describe an increase in cooperation, positive emotional tone, and conflict for siblings between 8 and 11 years (Vandell et al., 1987). There are suggestions that the gender composition of a sibling dyad becomes important in middle childhood (Buhrmester, 1992), although in early childhood the evidence for gender effects is much less consistent.

What about changes in the patterns of individual differences between 5 and 7 years? We might well expect to find discontinuities in individual differences in the relationship over this period, given the changes in the structure of the relationship indicated in the cross-sectional research, the major changes in children's lives over this period, and the developments in children's social competence more generally. Starting school can prove for some children a stressful experience (Dunn, 1988a), and it could be that children who find the kindergarten and first-grade experience difficult carry home their problems and are more irritable with other family members, including their siblings. Moreover, in addition to the normative changes such as starting school, many children experience changes in family life such as parental unemployment, parental separation, and house and neighborhood moves, and these may well be linked to changes in family relationships (Dunn, 1988a). Studies of children following divorce indicate increases in hostility in family relationships (for instance, Hetherington, 1988; McKinnon, 1989).

In contrast, it could also be argued that the key influences on individual differences in sibling relationships in the preschool period are likely to continue as important influences through middle childhood and thus to foster stability in the individual differences in the relationship. The temperament of both siblings and the quality of their relationships with their parents, for example, are known to be associated with differences in sibling relationships both in the preschool period (Brody, Stoneman, & Burke, 1987; Munn & Dunn, 1989) and among 4- to 7-year-olds (Stocker, Dunn, & Plomin, 1989).

Two longitudinal studies of families followed from early in the preschool period through middle childhood offer the opportunity to examine these different predictions concerning the stability of the individual differences in sibling relationships over this period. In both studies, unstructured observations of siblings and their mothers were conducted in the home and interviews with mothers conducted concerning the sibling relationship. Table 12.1 gives the outline of the two studies, one of which was conducted in the United States (the Pennsylvania Sibling Study), the other in England (the Cambridge Sibling Study).

In the Pennsylvanian study, 50 sibling pairs were studied when the younger siblings were 33, 40, and 47 months old, then followed up during their kindergarten and first-grade years (Dunn, 1995; Dunn et al., 1991). Their older siblings were on average 43 months older and thus were on average 6 years 4 months at the first visits. In the English study, 40 sibling pairs were studied when the younger sibling was 18, 24, and 36 months old (Dunn & Munn, 1985, 1987), the followed up at the ages of 6, 8, and 10 years old (Dunn, Slomkowski,

Table 12.1
Ages at Which Children Were Studied in the Cambridge and Pennsylvanian Sibling Studies

Pennsylvania Silbings

Years

	2	3	4	5	6	7	8	9	10	11	12	13
YS[a]	X—	X	— X	—	—	X — X_X						
OS[b]						X_X	X	X	— X			

Cambridge Siblings

Years

	2	3	4	5	6	7	8	9	10	11	12	13
YS[a]	X	— X					X —	X		X		
OS[b]				X —				X		X		

[a] YS = Younger Sibling.
[b] OS = Older Sibling.

& Beardsall, 1994). Their older siblings were on average 26 months older and thus were on average 5 years old at the time point when the younger were 36 months, and the older siblings were 8, 10, and 12 years old on average at the subsequent time points. The design of these two projects enabled us not only to examine the stability of individual differences in the children's behavior to their siblings over time but also to study the secondborn children at the ages we had studied their older siblings, thus making it possible to begin to tease apart the significance of birth order and developmental stage. The studies provided a "family cohort sequential" design, by which information was available from the preschool period (for the secondborn children) through to early adolescence (for the firstborn).

Stability or Discontinuity in Individual Differences

To examine the question of whether there was evidence of stability or discontinuity in individual differences in relations with the sibling over the preschool to middle childhood period, we examined age-to-age correlations in maternal interview accounts of the sibling relationship, in observational measures of sibling interaction, and correlations between the early observational measures and later interview accounts by both children and their mothers concerning the relationship (for details, see Dunn, Slomkowski, & Beardsall, 1994). We also examined the coefficient of variance in measures of the sibling relationship at each time point. Four general points stand out from these analyses:

1. There were significant correlations between age points for both the positive and the negative dimensions of the relationships, whatever the source of information on the sibling relationship.

2. These correlations increased in size with the children's age. Thus, in the Cambridge Sibling Study, for example, for the older siblings, the correlations between 8 and 10 years were $r(40) = .72$ and .61 for the positive and negative dimensions, respectively; for the younger siblings, the correlations between 5 and 6 years were .42 and .35.

3. Most important for our present concerns, there was no evidence for a dip in the size of correlations in the 4 to 8 year period. Rather, the data suggested that there were changes in patterns of individual differences between the early preschool period and 5 years and that after 5 years there was considerable stability in the relationship differences. Thus, in the Cambridge study the correlations over the 7 years between 5 and 12 years were .49 and .46 (positive and negative dimensions, respectively), whereas the correlations for the younger siblings between 3 and 10 years were .03 and .01.

4. There was no evidence of a 5 to 7 year change in the coefficients of variance.

These data suggest that it would not be justified to conclude that there is a "transitional" period for individual differences in sibling relationships between 5 and 7 years. However, it still remains possible that the events experienced between 5 and 7 contributed, for some individuals, to changes in their relations with their siblings. As well as studying stability, therefore, we examined the issue of what events were important in accounting for those changes in children's relationships with their siblings that the interview and observational data revealed. We included in the investigations a direct approach to obtaining the family members' own views on the changes in their relationships. For example, in open-ended interviews in the Cambridge study with mothers (at each time point) and with children at the last two time points, we asked the family members whether they felt there had been changes in how the siblings got along and to what such changes were attributable.

A similar pattern of findings emerged from interviews with both mothers and children. First, changes in sibling relationships were described as having occurred at a range of time points between the ages of 4 and 12 years. Figure 12.2 shows the distribution of ages at which negative changes were described as having taken place in those families in which specific ages or stages were mentioned.

It was relatively uncommon for a negative change in the sibling relationship to be described as happening between 5 and 7 years. More frequently, a decrease in closeness between the siblings, an increase in conflict, or both were described as occurring between 7 and 9 years. Indeed, in the children's interviews three times as many children (38) attributed changes in the relationship to one of the siblings starting junior school (a transition from primary school

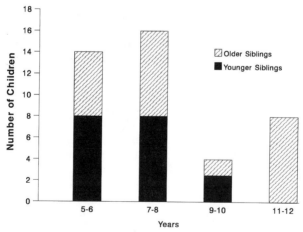

Figure 12.2   Negative changes in sibling relationships: Age of child to whom the change is attributed.

that takes place in England around the age of 8 years) as the number who described changes when one child started primary school at age 5 years (only 12 children). The interviews were coded in detail to examine more specifically the children's view of what had led to changes in their relationship, and three issues emerged that were of general developmental interest.

First, in many of the families negative changes in the sibling relationship were attributed by both siblings and mothers to the new friendships that the children formed outside the family during middle childhood. In 29 families, friendships were described as contributing to negative changes in the sibling relationships, as compared with only 11 families in which such effects were not mentioned. The development of these friendships was associated with jealousy and competitiveness between some siblings; in other siblings the development of friendships was associated with an increase in distance and loss of interest in the sibling.

Second, this pattern of the links between new friendships and deteriorating relations between the siblings was particularly marked in families with firstborn boys. We had found that gender became a more important source of variance in the sibling relationship by the time that the siblings reached middle childhood (Dunn, Slomkowski, & Beardsall, 1994). Gender differences had not been important when the siblings were preschoolers, but by the age of 12 to 13 the firstborn boys were reporting less warmth and intimacy with their younger siblings than were the firstborn girls—a pattern of results that support Buhrmester's (1992) finding that by late middle childhood older sisters were more likely than older brothers to be in confiding relationships with their younger siblings. The interviews showed that in families with older boys and younger sisters changes in the sibling relationship were attributed to the ties that the boys formed with other boys and a male peer group outside the family.

A third source of change that the family members referred to was developmental change in the younger sibling. Thirty-one of the children ascribed changes in their relationship with their sibling to increases in the younger child's assertiveness and powers of argument and reasoning. It was equally common for the siblings to ascribe a cooling or distancing of the relationship to the development of different interests by the two siblings. However, the period between 5 and 7 years was not specifically identified as the stage during which these developmental changes took place.

These results indicate that the transition from primary to junior school—a normative life event for the majority of children around the age of 8—was associated with changes in the sibling relationship for a number of families. The issue of whether other non-normative life events are also associated with changes in the relationship has been a matter of some interest to psychologists, particularly to those concerned with the effects of parental separation and divorce. Some studies report, for example, that sibling conflict and hostility increase following divorce (Hetherington, 1988; McKinnon, 1989); however, others report that some siblings do use each other as sources of comfort and support in the face of parental disharmony (Jenkins, 1992). In the Cambridge study the significance of life events and adversities for the sibling relationship was examined, and the results showed that in the face of adversities the children became more positive and supportive (Dunn, Slomkowski, & Beardsall, 1994). In the detailed interviews, the accounts given by the children amplified these findings: The majority of children volunteered the information that their siblings had provided support for them in the face of difficulties such as problems at school, maternal illness, and illness or accidents they themselves had suffered. This pattern of change differs from that found in the studies of divorce; however, it should be noted that among the adverse events the children in our study faced, marital difficulties were relatively uncommon: Only 8% of the events that were categorized as moderate to severe in negative impact on the children involved marital problems.

To summarize the main points on the individual differences in sibling relationships over the period studied: There were not grounds from the data on age-to-age correlations or from the coefficients of variance for viewing the period from 5 to 7 years old as one of marked change. Rather, the data indicated that changes were more marked during the period between 3 and 5 years. Changes were also described by both children and mothers as occurring around 7 to 8 years. Although developmental changes in the children were mentioned by all three family members interviewed, environmental changes were clearly important from 7 to 8 years onward. For example, socioeconomic status became increasingly important as a correlate of differences in siblings' intimacy and warmth in early adolescence (Dunn, Slomkowski, & Beardsall, in press).

Children's Perceptions of Self-Competence

The second domain to be considered is children's perceptions of their own abilities, attractiveness, social success, and self-worth. Much has been learned about the developmental changes in children's reflections and feelings about themselves over the period of middle childhood and early adolescence, with studies describing the development of a differentiated sense of self-competence, a global sense of self-worth, and the growth of negative self-feelings (e.g., Damon & Hart, 1982; Harter, 1986; Harter, this volume, chap. 10).

Less is known about patterns of change in individual differences in sense of self and perceived self-competence. We have relatively little information, for example, about how the experiences and transitions of the early school years affect children's feelings about themselves or whether the correlates of the different domains of sense-of-self change over these years. In the two longitudinal studies described in the previous sections, we were able to begin to look at these issues, as assessments of the children's perceived self-competence were made at several time points using Harter's (1982) Perceived Self-Competence Scale for Children. In the Cambridge Sibling Study, these assessments were made at each time point after the children were 6 years old. In the Pennsylvania Sibling Study, such assessments were made in the first month after the children began kindergarten and at the end of the kindergarten year. The stability and correlates of individual differences in these assessments were examined. Here the key points that relate to the general issue of whether there was evidence for a lack of age-to-age stability between 5 and 7 years are summarized.

The age-to-age correlations showed there was considerable stability in older siblings' perceived self-competence between 8 and 10 years, 10 and 12 to 13 years, and indeed for the 4-year period from 8 to 12 to 13 years. For each dimension of competence in the assessment (scholastic, social, athletic, physical, conduct, and global), the correlations over 4 years were significant, ranging from $r(40) = .31$ to $.57$. This continuity is striking when we reflect that during this period the children made the transition from primary to secondary school—a change that has been associated with an average dip in self-esteem (Simmons & Blyth, 1987). For the younger siblings, the correlations between 8 years and 10 years were significant and comparable in size to those of the older siblings between 8 and 10; this indicates that there were not birth order differences between the siblings in the stability of their views of themselves. But between 6 and 8 years, the period of particular interest for our present purposes, while the correlations for scholastic, social, and athletic competence were significant—$r(40) = .42, .33,$ and $.45$, respectively—those for physical, conduct, and global competence did not reach significance. And in contrast to the findings for the older siblings for the 4 years between 8 and 12, none of the correlations for the younger siblings for the 4 years between 6 and 10 were significant; they ranged from $r(40) = .07$ to $.26$.

These results do provide some support for the idea that, during the period of the first years at school, children's views of themselves are relatively unstable, at least in the domains of physical attractiveness, conduct, and global self-esteem (Harter, 1986). Prediction from 6 years was poor for all dimensions of perceived self-competence, whereas prediction from 8 years could be made with rather more confidence. In addition to examining stability, we also investigated the sources of change in the children's feelings and perceptions of their own competence; two points are worth noting from the results of these analyses. First, the correlates changed with the age of the children. By early adolescence, for instance, maternal mood and socioeconomic status (SES) were significant correlates of perceived self-competence for the older siblings. Second, the occurrence of life events with negative impact, which were not related to the particular age period 5 to 7 years, was associated with poorer perceived self-competence (Beardsall & Dunn, 1992).

Two final points concerning this study: First, it was notable that the behavior of each sibling was correlated with some aspects of the other's self-esteem at later time points. For example, negative behavior of the older siblings was related to the younger siblings' low sense of their own scholastic competence and conduct at later time points, a contribution to the variance in perceived self-competence that was independent of the variance attributable to other sources. Younger siblings' negative behavior was correlated with older siblings' poorer sense of social competence at a later time point. Second, the quality of the siblings' relationship in the preschool period also contributed independent variance to the children's adjustment in middle childhood, as assessed on the Child Behavior Checklist (Achenbach & Edelbrock, 1983; for details of this study, see Dunn, Slomkowski, Beardsall, & Rende, 1994). Lack of friendliness from the sibling during the preschool period was associated with internalizing behavior later. These connections with sibling relationship quality remind us that continuity in children's self-perceptions and adjustment may reflect continuity of other aspects of children's family world.

The data from the Pennsylvania study, in which assessments of individual differences in children's perceived self-competence were made at the start and at the end of the children's kindergarten year, complement these results from the English study. The children were aged on average 67 months at the time of the first assessment and 76 months at the second assessment. The results showed there was a correlation of .36 in perceived self-competence with peers and .47 in perceived cognitive competence between the start and end of this year. Of particular interest was the change in the pattern of variables that were correlated with the scores on perceived self-competence. At the start of the year, for instance, low scores on perceived self-competence with peers were correlated with high scores on earlier assessments of sociocognitive development. Thus children who as 3-year-olds had scored particularly high on assessments of understanding other's emotions and high on a test of the ability to "read another's mind"—a false belief task (see Dunn, Brown, Slomkowski, Tesla, & Youngblade, 1991)—described themselves as being relatively unpopular with other children (Dunn, 1995). By the end of the kindergarten year, a different set of variables accounted for the variance in perceived self-competence. At this time point, it was the children's contemporary relations with the peers at school rather than their earlier sociocognitive skills that were correlated with their feelings of self-competence.

A Transition Period Between 5 and 7 Years?

The significance of the period between 5 and 7 is rather different for the two domains of development that we have considered here—at least in terms of the patterns of individual differences over time. Children's relationships with their siblings show notable stability over this 5 to 7 year period: It is earlier, between 2 to 3 years and 5 years, that the patterns of individual differences change more strikingly. In spite of the average increases in children's understanding of their siblings and in their ability to negotiate and reason with them when in conflicts that are likely to take place over these years between 5 and 7, the differences between sibling pairs in their friendliness, hostility, support, and companionship do not undergo a marked transition between 5 to 7. Although self-disclosure and intimacy may well increase over these years in this and the children's other relationships, we do not have grounds for seeing this period as one of rapid change in the rank order of individual differences in the sibling relationship. Moreover, a consideration of individual differences in such aspects of children's relationships, which are apparently good candidates for the notion of a "transition" in average differences, raises a general issue concerning the dichotomies of quantitative versus qualitative, or continuous versus discontinuous, change in average group measures.

These distinctions depend on the nature of measurement employed and the level of description used to describe the children's social behavior and understanding. Although 5-year-olds are unlikely to give clear coherent answers to questions about their intimacy with their siblings, whereas 7-year-olds are often articulate on the subject, it would be quite inappropriate to conclude that intimacy and self-disclosure are absent from the relationships of all 5-year-olds. It is evident from observational work that as early as 4 years old some children's sibling relationships are characterized by discussion of feelings and self-disclosure (Brown & Dunn, 1992), by sharing of imaginative worlds (Youngblade & Dunn, 1995), and by understanding the other's feelings and needs (Dunn, 1988b). The parallel with work on close friendships is clear. Some friends even in the preschool period develop intensive, long-term relationships, care about each other, show an awareness of how their actions affect each other's feelings, and indeed may "acquire complex conceptions of friendships at an early age" (Corsaro, 1981, p. 234; for similar evidence on very young friends, see also Blum, 1987; Dunn, 1993; Gottman & Parker, 1986; Howes, 1988).

The pattern of findings on sibling relationships over this period implies that individual differences in the emotional quality of the relationship and differences in the motivation of children to solve sibling conflicts in an amicable way, to help and support one another, and to play together are substantially stable between 5 and 7. The stability suggests that the same influences on individual differences in sibling relationships remain important over this period—a point that the cross-sectional research supports. Changes in the quality of the relationship were in our English study more commonly described as occurring around 7 or 8 years, a time when most of the children changed schools; both children and mothers attributed such changes to the development of close friendships and to the increasing importance of the peer group outside the family.

For the development of perceived self-competence there is a clearer case for seeing 5 to 6 years as a period of instability in individual differences. It appears that children's views of themselves undergo changes at this stage and that difference variables relate to their perceptions of how "well" they are doing in comparison with their peers at the start of kindergarten and at the end of the year. These changes in individual differences fit well with the argument, based on average changes with age, that there are significant changes in how children conceptualize their own self-worth over these years. However, in relation to the questions of whether these changes should be described as quantitative or qualitative, continuous or discontinuous, the same arguments apply here as those given in the context of the developing relationships between siblings. Whether changes appear quantitative or qualitative, continuous or discontinuous, will depend on the nature of measures and methods used.

Take, for example, the proposition that developmental changes in perceived self-competence between 5 and 7 are marked, in part, because there is a major developmental change in average levels of children's understanding of and responses to other people's view of them. It seems quite plausible that such a developmental change contributes to the growth of a new sense of self-worth and new differences in children's perceptions of self. The support for such an argument depends on the way we choose to measure and describe children's responses to others' reactions to them. Experimental studies that examine children's propensity to compare their performance on tasks with those of other children indicate that such comparisons with others are not made by children under 7 or 8 (Ruble, 1983). However, if we choose to study children's responses to others' approval or disapproval, or their propensity to compare themselves with familiar others in situations of emotional significance, signs of such sensitivity to the reactions and performance of others and of self-comparison processes can be seen extremely early.

Consider, for instance, the following incident involving a 2.5-year-old boy, drawn from an earlier study of siblings in England (Dunn, 1988b):

> Andy, aged 30 months, has an ebullient, assertive younger sister Susie, aged 14 months; he himself is a notably cautious, anxious, and sensitive child. . . . He overhears his mother's proud comment on his sister and adds a muted—but accurate—comment on himself in comparison:
>
> M. to sib: Susie, you *are* a determined little devil!
>
> C. to M.:   *I'm* not a determined little devil.
>
> M. (Laughing): No you're not! What are you? A poor old boy!
>   (P. 179)

The general point is this: The concern of 7- to 8-year-olds with the approval and esteem of their peers does not arise de novo. Children are part of a social group from birth and are both interested in and responsive to others' reactions to them from very early in infancy. The behavior of others is extremely salient to them. We can choose to focus on the continuous nature of these phenomena and to trace the early stages of understanding others' reactions that lead to the sophistication of 7-year-olds. Or we can choose to highlight the broad differences between early and middle childhood. It is a matter of theoretical and methodological preference. Either way, we should not lose sight of what a focus on individual differences can tell us.

Acknowledgments

The research in England was supported by the Medical Research Council of the U.K. and by a National Institutes of Health grant (MH-46535); the research in Pennsylvania is supported by a National Institute of Child Health and Development grant (HD-23158).

References

Abramovitch, R., Corter, C., Pepler, D. J., & Stanhope, L. (1986). Sibling and peer interaction: A final follow-up and a comparison. *Child Development, 57,* 217–229.

Achenbach, T. M., & Edelbrock, C. (1983). *Manual for the Child Behavior Checklist and Revised Child Behavior Profile.* Burlington: University of Vermont.

Bateson, P. P. G. (1978). How does behavior develop? In P. P. G. Bateson & P. H. Klopfer (Eds.), *Perspectives in ethology* (pp. 55–73). New York: Plenum.

Beardsall, L., & Dunn, J. (1992). Adversities in childhood: Siblings' experiences and their relations to self-esteem. *Journal of Child Psychology and Psychiatry, 33,* 349–359.

Berndt, T. J., & Ladd, G. W. (1989). *Peer relationships in child development.* New York: Wiley.

Blum, L. (1987). Particularity and responsiveness. In J. Kagan & S. Lamb (Eds.), *The emergence of morality in young children* (pp. 306–337). Chicago: University of Chicago Press.

Boer, F. (1990). *Sibling relationships in middle childhood.* Leiden, Netherlands: DSWO University of Leiden Press.

Boer, F., & Dunn, J. (1992). *Children's sibling relationships.* Hillsdale, NJ: Erlbaum.

Brim, O. G., & Kagan, J. (1980). *Constancy and change in human development.* Cambridge: Cambridge University Press.

Brody, G. H., Stoneman, Z., & Burke, M. (1987). Child temperaments, maternal differential behavior, and sibling relationships. *Developmental Psychology, 23,* 354–362.

Brown, J. R., & Dunn, J. (1992). Talk with your mother or your sibling? Developmental changes in early family conversations about feelings. *Child Development, 63,* 336–349.

Buhrmester, D. (1992). The developmental course of sibling and peer relationships. In

F. Boer & J. Dunn (Eds.), *Children sibling relationships: Developmental and clinical issues* (pp. 19–40). Hillsdale, NJ: Erlbaum.

Buhrmester, D., & Furman, W. (1990). Perceptions of sibling relationships during middle childhood and adolescence. *Child Development, 61,* 1387–1398.

Corsaro, W. A. (1981). Friendship in the nursery school: Social organization in a peer environment. In S. R. Asher & J. M. Gottman (Eds.), *The development of children's friendships* (pp. 207–241). Cambridge: Cambridge University Press.

Damon, W., & Hart, D. (1982). The development of self-understanding from infancy through adolescence. *Child Development, 53,* 841–864.

Dunn, J. (1988a). Normative life events as risk factors in childhood. In M. Rutter (Ed.), *Risk and protective factors in psychosocial development* (pp. 227–244). Cambridge: Cambridge University Press.

Dunn, J. (1988b). *The beginnings of social understanding.* Cambridge, MA: Harvard University Press.

Dunn, J. (1993). *Young children's close relationships: Beyond attachment.* Newbury, CA: Sage Publications.

Dunn, J. (1995). Children as psychologists: The later correlates of individual differences in understanding of emotion and other minds. *Cognition and Emotion, 9,* 187–201.

Dunn, J., Brown, J., Slomkowski, C., Tesla, C., & Youngblade, L. (1991). Young children's understanding of other people's feelings and beliefs: Individual differences and their antecedents. *Child Development, 62,* 1352–1366.

Dunn, J., & McGuire, S. (1992). Sibling and peer relationships in childhood. *Journal of Child Psychology and Psychiatry, 33,* 67–105.

Dunn, J., & Munn, P. (1985). Becoming a family member: Family conflict and the development of social understanding in the second year. *Child Development, 56,* 764–774.

Dunn, J., & Munn, P. (1987). The development of justification in disputes. *Developmental Psychology, 23,* 791–798.

Dunn, J., & Plomin, R. (1990). *Separate lives: Why siblings are so different.* New York: Basic Books.

Dunn, J., Slomkowski, C., & Beardsall, L. (1994). Sibling relationships from the preschool period through middle childhood and early adolescence. *Developmental Psychology, 30,* 315–324.

Dunn, J., Slomkowski, C., Beardsall, L., & Rende, R. (1994). Adjustment in middle childhood and early adolescence: Links with earlier and contemporary sibling relationships. *Journal of Child Psychology and Psychiatry, 35,* 491–504.

Edel, L. (1987). *Henry James: A life.* London: Collins.

Gottman, J. M., & Parker, J. G. (1986). *Conversations of friends.* Cambridge: Cambridge University Press.

Harter, S. (1982). The perceived competence scale for children. *Child Development, 53,* 87–97.

Harter, S. (1986). Processes underlying the construction, maintenance and enhancement of the self-concept in children. In J. Suls & A. G. Greenwald (Eds.), *Psychological perspectives on the self* (Vol. 3, pp. 137–181). Hillsdale, NJ: Erlbaum.

Harter, S. (1987). The determinants and mediation role of global self-worth in children.

In N. Eisenberg (Ed.), *Contemporary issues in developmental psychology* (pp. 219–242). New York: Wiley.

Harter, S. (1996). Developmental changes in self-understanding across the 5 to 7 shift. In A. J. Sameroff & M. M. Haith (Eds.), *The five to seven year shift: The age of reason and responsibility* (chap. 10, this vol.). Chicago: University of Chicago Press.

Hetherington, E. M. (1988). Parents, children, and siblings: Six years after divorce. In R. A. Hinde & J. Stevenson-Hinde (Eds.), *Relationships within families* (pp. 311–331). Oxford: Oxford University Press.

Howes, C. (1988). Peer interaction in young children. *Monographs of the Society for Research in Child Development, Number 217,* Vol. 53, No. 1.

Jenkins, J. (1992). Sibling relationships in disharmonious homes: Potential difficulties and protective effects. In F. Boer & J. Dunn (Eds.), *Children's sibling relationships: Developmental and clinical issues* (pp. 125–138). Hillsdale, NJ: Erlbaum.

McCall, R. B. (1983). A conceptual approach to early mental development. In M. Lewis (Ed.), *Origins of intelligence: Infancy and early childhood* (pp. 107–133). New York: Plenum.

McKinnon, C. E. (1989). An observational investigation of sibling interactions in married and divorced families. *Developmental Psychology, 25,* 36–44.

Munn, P., & Dunn, J. (1989). Temperament and the developing relationship between siblings. *International Journal of Behavioral Development, 12,* 433–451.

Newson, J., & Newson, E. (1970). *Four years old in an urban community.* Harmondsworth, England: Penguin Books.

Newson, J., & Newson, E. (1978). *Seven years old in the home environment.* Harmondsworth, England: Penguin Books.

Patterson, G. R. (1986). The contribution of siblings to training for fighting: A microsocial analysis. In D. Olweus, J. Block, & M. Radke-Yarrow (Eds.), *Development of antisocial and prosocial behavior: Research, theories and issues* (pp. 235–261). New York: Academic Press.

Plomin, R., DeFries, J. C., & Fulker, D. W. (1988). *Nature and nurture during infancy and early childhood.* Cambridge: Cambridge University Press.

Raffaelii, M. (1991, April). *Conflict with siblings and friends in late childhood and adolescence.* Paper presented at the biennial meetings of the Society for Research in Child Development, Seattle, WA.

Richman, N., Stevenson, J. E., & Graham, P. (1982). *Preschool to school: A behavioral study.* London: Academic Press.

Ruble, D. N. (1983). The development of social comparison processes and their role in achievement-related self-socialization. In E. Tory Higgins, D. N. Ruble, & W. W. Hartup (Eds.), *Social cognition and social development* (pp. 134–157). Cambridge: Cambridge University Press.

Simmons, R. G., & Blyth, D. A. (1987). *Moving into adolescence: The impact of pubertal change and school context.* New York: Academic Press.

Stocker, C., Dunn, J., & Plomin, R. (1989). Sibling relationships: Links with child temperament, maternal behavior, and family structure. *Child Development, 60,* 715–727.

Vandell, D. L., Minnett, A. M., & Santrock, J. W. (1987). Age differences in sibling relationships during middle childhood. *Journal of Applied Developmental Psychology, 8*, 247–257.

Wohlwill, J. F. (1973). *The study of behavioral development*. New York: Academic Press.

Youngblade, L., & Dunn, J. (1995). Individual differences in young children's pretend play with mother and sibling: Links to relationship quality and understanding of other peoples' feelings and beliefs. *Child Development, 66*, 1472–1492.

PART FIVE

Cultural Transitions

Developmental Transitions in Children's Participation in Sociocultural Activities

BARBARA ROGOFF

In this chapter, I argue that questions about transitions (such as the 5 to 7 shift) can fruitfully be examined from a sociocultural perspective that asks how children's involvements in the activities of their community change, rather than focusing on change as a property of isolated individuals. It is commonplace in developmental research to attribute change to the properties of individual children without regard to their environments or to include environmental "influences" on children's behavior, with children and environments conceived as separate entities. In contrast, in the sociocultural perspective that I discuss, the changes of individuals are assumed to be inseparable from their involvements in sociocultural activity. So the changes are neither exclusively in the individuals nor exclusively in their environments, but a characteristic of individuals' involvements in ongoing activity.

I argue that the central question is not a matter of determining the onset and course of developmental changes in individuals examined separately from their environments, but of characterizing the nature of the shifts in people's roles and responsibilities in the activities in which they participate. Understanding shifts requires studying how individuals' roles and responsibilities relate to the also-shifting roles and responsibilities of their companions and to changes in community constraints, opportunities, supports, and institutional arrangements. Thus, research cannot focus on the imaginary "generic" 5-year-old, but must focus on particular 5-year-olds involved with their companions in activities of their communities. Transitions cannot be characterized independently of individuals' (or an age group's) activities in their communities.

From a sociocultural perspective, it is thus essential to examine the ongoing processes of children's involvement in particular activities, not simply to assume that their involvement in any particular activity can necessarily be generalized to all. I assume that children's involvements in some activities relate to their involvement in others, but not in an automatic or all-encompassing way. A key empirical question is, How does involvement in some activities relate to involvement in others?

In this chapter, I describe the transitions in my work that have led to this view. I begin by discussing initial work that investigated whether the 5 to 7 shift that White (1965) had abstracted from the research literature involving mostly children in the United States was characteristic of the roles and responsibilities of children around the world. After describing the dilemmas revealed by that work, I turn to a discussion of how the assumptions of a sociocultural approach reorient our questions regarding transitions in development. The question of transitions is an important one for sociocultural research, for it focuses our attention on the changing contributions of people to the activities in which they participate. Developmental research seems to have difficulty in getting beyond exclusive attention to individuals, to attend to social and cultural processes, without *overlooking* individuals in studying social and cultural phenomena. Finally, I describe findings of a study that takes a sociocultural perspective to examine cultural variation in the ages of children's assumption of responsible roles, focusing on young children's coordination with and responsibility to others.

Efforts to Study the Universality of the 5 to 7 Shift

Two decades ago, we extended the evidence of an important transition at age 5 to 7 years in children's learning that White had collected from psychological research and from a few historical accounts by systematically examining ethnographic reports from around the world (Rogoff, Sellers, Pirrotta, Fox, & White, 1975). The study involved examining ethnographies from the Human Relations Area Files (HRAF) of 50 communities around the world to see if at the ages of 5 to 7 years there was a shift in the onset of responsibilities and roles and expectations of the children. (Analysis of the ethnographies collected together in the HRAF is facilitated by the HRAF's indexing system, which locates sections dealing specifically with child development and socialization practices.) We made ratings of age of transitions in 27 categories involving cultural assumptions regarding responsibility or teachability in children or assignment of a more mature social, sexual, or cultural role. Inspection of the 27 histograms obtained from the ratings suggested that for 16 of the 27 categories there appeared to be a modal cultural assignment of social responsibility in the 5 to 7 year age range. We (Rogoff et al., 1975) concluded, cautiously, that it looked like there was something happening about that age range:

> It appears that in the age period centering on 5–7 years, parents relegate (and children assume) responsibility for care of younger children,

for tending animals, for carrying out household chores and gathering materials for the upkeep of the family. The children also become responsible for their own social behavior and the method of punishment for transgression changes. Along with new responsibility, there is the expectation that children between 5 and 7 years begin to be teachable. Adults give practical training expecting children to be able to imitate their example; children are taught social manners and inculcated in cultural traditions. Underlying these changes in teachability is the fact that at 5–7 years children are considered to attain common sense or rationality. At this age also, the child's character is considered to be fixed, and he begins to assume new social and sexual roles. He begins to join with groups of peers, and participate in rule games. The children's groups separate by sex at this time. Concurrently, the children are expected to show modesty and sex differentiation in chores and social relationships is stressed. All of these variables indicate that at 5–7 the child is broadly categorized differently than before this age, as he becomes a more integral part of his social structure. (P. 367)

We accompanied these conclusions with caveats calling for caution in interpretation, pointing out that age estimates in ethnographic literature are unreliable. Most of the communities we included did not categorize children by years or even keep track of time since birth, so ethnographers made age estimates that are likely to be biased by their own expectations. We also pointed out that even in the variables in which an age shift was readily apparent, shifts did not fall into the modal period in a noticeable number of cultures. For most of the 16 variables showing a modal shift in the 5 to 7 range, about 40% of the cultural communities had shifts that fell outside of the modal ages, with ranges of 9 to 15 years. Thus, even for variables with a modal shift at age 5 to 7, in many communities the shifts appeared, for example, at age 2 or 11. We concluded with the hope that these variations could be explained by an understanding of the structure of the cultures.

After that initial study, several of the authors went off to do fieldwork and returned with the impression that the paper on the 5 to 7 shift was an incomplete account—there seemed to be something happening at 8 to 10 years that was very important. We believed that what was happening at 5 to 7 in the ethnographic literature was the beginning of children's being responsible and teachable, but that at 8 to 10, parents could count on children to understand and to help—which was more important to the parents we had talked with.

Sellers (1975) reviewed 19 ethnographies of childhood in rural communities of Mexico and Guatemala and concluded that "although in earlier years children have been exposed to and participated in household work, at ten . . . competence, independence, and responsibility are required in most of the chores delegated to children of this age" (p. 31). Rogoff (1978) observed 100 Mayan children between the ages of 1 and 14 years and found that they began doing chores in the 5 to 7 range, but not until age 10 did they leave behind a period of play combined with supervised apprenticeship in simple chores to assume independent responsibility for some important tasks. These observations are not inconsistent with the earlier study, which focused on *onsets* of responsibilities or changing roles and ignored information regarding the attainment of competence.

We looked at the developmental research literature—in *Developmental Psychology, Child Development,* and *Journal of Experimental Child Psychology*—to see if the literature had information on an 8 to 10 shift and found a fair amount of evidence that something was happening at 8 to 10 as well (Rogoff, Newcombe, Fox, & Ellis, 1980). We noticed that many studies reported the shifts that they observed at ages 8 to 10 as part of the 5 to 7 shift, concluding that the 5 to 7 shift was a little bit late, or that behaviors observed were evidence of the 5 to 7 shift.

That paper also ended cautiously because our conclusion was not that something is happening at 8 to 10 that is more important than changes at 5 to 7, but that if we looked at any age period, we would probably find some important transitions. The research of that era that made age comparisons had focused on ages 4 to 9 or 10, making the 5 to 7 shift quite apparent. Something important may be happening at 5 to 7, 8 to 10, 3 to 5, 11 to 15. Surely 10-year-olds are not the same as 3-year-olds.

However, in order to characterize shifts in development, most approaches seem to have assumed that the shifts are *in* the children and are general across tasks and across communities. Researchers have assumed that the few tasks that have been done are generalizable to something broader and more important than the particular tasks in which the observations have been made. The assumption of generality is being increasingly questioned, owing to observations that infants can be seen doing things that have previously been thought to be only possible for older children, to observations that performance is quite uneven as the same child does different tasks involving logically similar operations, and to observations across cultures that various skills are observed at quite different ages (Feldman, 1980; Fischer, 1980; Flavell, 1977; Gelman & Meck, 1983; Rogoff, 1982).

There are some very compelling examples of variations across communities in the ages at which children are expected to be competent to carry out complicated culturally valued activities. For example, although U.S. middle-class adults often do not trust children below about age 5 with knives, in the Efe community in Zaire, infants routinely use machetes with safety and some skill (D. Wilkie, personal communication, 1989; Figure 13.1)

Another example is the age at which children seem to be responsible enough to take care of themselves or to take care of other children. In middle-class U.S.

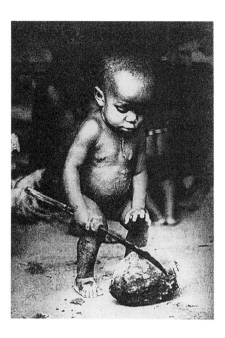

Figure 13.1   This 11-month-old Efe child from the Ituri Forest of Zaire cuts a fruit with a ma-
chete, with a relative supervising in the background. (Photograph courtesy of David Wilkie;
© by David Wilkie.)

families, children seem not to be regarded as capable of beginning to tend
themselves or another child until perhaps age 10 (or later in some regions of
the United States), but in many other communities around the world, children
begin to take on responsibility for tending other children at ages 5 to 7 (Rogoff
et al., 1975), and in some places even younger children begin to assume this
responsibility. Watson-Gegeo (1990) described the roles of young Kwara'ae
children in Oceania:

> Three year olds are skilled workers in the gardens and household, ex-
> cellent caregivers of their younger siblings, and accomplished at so-
> cial interaction. Although young children also have time to play, many
> of the functions of play seem to be met by work. For both adults and
> children, work is accompanied by singing, joking, verbal play and
> entertaining conversation. Instead of playing with dolls, children care
> for real babies. In addition to working in the family gardens, young
> children have their own garden plots. The latter may seem like play,
> but by three or four years of age many children are taking produce
> they have grown themselves to the market to sell, thereby making a
> significant and valued contribution to the family income. Thus for

Kwara'ae children, work and play are often fused, and the leading activity of productive work does not follow chronologically after schooling. (P. 87)

Likewise, Sorenson (1979) noted that Fore (New Guinea) infants handled knives and fire safely by the time they are able to walk. Sorenson stated that he "continued to be surprised that the unsupervised Fore toddlers did not recklessly thrust themselves into unappreciated dangers, the way our own children tend to do" (p. 301). Young children in that community were trusted to be responsible and able to take care of themselves in a way that children in U.S. middle-class communities would not be.

In some cases child development experts in the United States react to accounts like this with the idea that the adults in those communities are irresponsible because we all know that children "can't do such things." But instead, it is reasonable to ask, How do such children become responsible enough to take care of themselves in those ways? It is interesting to note that middle-class U.S. families expect children to be able to do some things that are unexpected or even regarded as dangerous in other places, such as to sleep by themselves from as young as the first months of life (Morelli, Rogoff, Oppenheim, & Goldsmith, 1992) or to engage in school-like discourse or to begin to learn to read in the toddler years (Heath, 1983).

My general point is that some activities that we may regard as having a "natural" point of transition are only natural given the assumptions and the material circumstances and organization of our community. That brings me to a discussion of how a sociocultural perspective changes the ways that we can conceive of transitions in development.

Developmental Transitions in Sociocultural Perspective

The dilemmas that I have mentioned in the previous section have been an impetus for me to reexamine the assumptions on which the field has based research on age transitions in development.[1] The sociocultural approach changes the unit of analysis for observations of development from the individual to the activity (Leont'ev, 1981; Zinchenko, 1985).

The usual unit of analysis has been the isolated individual, with research attempting to extract the individual from the milieu in order to determine what happens within the individual and then to consider which influences on the outside must be added. Differences in development are often considered to be differences in rate along some kind of a natural developmental time course, sped up or retarded by various environmental circumstances.

The sociocultural approach takes as the unit of analysis the activity, which includes the contributions of individuals involved with other individuals, material circumstances, and cultural traditions. The sociocultural approach discards the idea that one can fruitfully study development by searching for the characteristics of the "basic" child and then adding external influences. According to Vygotsky (1987):

> The fundamental aspiration of the whole of modern child psychology . . . [is] the wish to reveal the eternal child. The task of psychology, however, is not the discovery of the eternal child. The task of psychology is the discovery of the historical child, of what Goethe called the transitory child. The stone that the builders have disdained must become the foundation stone. (P. 91)

From a sociocultural perspective, developmental processes are not just within individuals but in group processes and community processes. Hence, individual children are not regarded as developing with everything else static, on the one hand, nor everything else as developing with individuals staying static, on the other. Individual, interpersonal, and community processes are all developmental. Individuals cannot be excised from their involvement in activities to evaluate individual change; rather, individual change is studied as it constitutes and is constituted by interpersonal and community processes in sociocultural activities.

That does not mean that we have to study development in all aspects of activities at once. We can examine the contributions or transitions involving individuals as the focus of the moment, but we must take into account the other aspects of the activity as background information, not separate information (Rogoff, 1995). Individual, interpersonal, and community processes can be analyzed as different "planes" of analysis, but focus on one or another is analytical—that is, the focus is for the purposes of study and communication. The three planes cannot be isolated, and none is primary except with regard to being the current focus of attention when we can focus on one or another, keeping the others in the background for our analysis.[2]

When using activity as the unit of analysis, the emphasis for understanding individual development is on the concept of changing participation in sociocultural activities. Several developmental approaches call attention to the concept of participation for understanding learning and development. I have used the notions of guided participation and participatory appropriation to discuss interpersonal and personal processes (Rogoff, 1990, 1995); Lave and Wenger (1991) have offered the related idea of legitimate peripheral participation; White and Siegel (1984) referred to child development as widening participation in communities of thinkers. In each of these three approaches, the emphasis is on participation in both face-to-face interactions and in indirect interpersonal arrangements of cultural activities (which include times that people are by themselves participating in sociocultural activities).

If we take seriously the idea of participation, we cannot consider the individual to exist in isolation or out of cultural context because participation requires a description or an explanation of how people participate in sociocultural activities that are not formed by individuals alone, but by individuals with other people and in cultural communities.

The way that we have traditionally gone about understanding children's development places a boundary between the children and whatever it is they are learning or the sociocultural world (Figure 13.2), and that boundary is what I am questioning in the idea of participation. If a person is participating in an activity, it is inconsistent to consider the person as separate from it; participation inherently means involvement. Therefore, it is unnecessary to wonder how it is that external information crosses a boundary to be stored internally, a mysterious process that is often referred to as internalization, with either the individual or the environment as the active agent responsible for moving new materials across the boundary (Rogoff, 1995).

Figure 13.3 represents an alternative conceptualization using sociocultural activity as the unit of analysis, with individual, interpersonal, and community

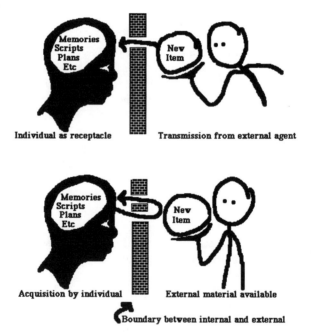

Figure 13.2   Two versions of an internalization model, both with boundaries between individual and external world. One portrays the individual as active, constructing knowledge from a passive environment; the other portrays the environment as active, filling up the individual as a waiting vessel.

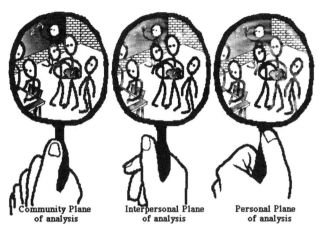

Figure 13.3   Lenses focusing on dynamic processes of participation. A model of participation as individuals contribute, along with others, to using and transforming community practices, in a dynamic sociocultural activity.

planes of analysis portrayed as three lenses in the foreground of the figure. In the whole activity, individuals participate in shared endeavors with some commonality and complementarity of purpose to define the nature of the activity. For example, you and I are engaging in an activity defined by the purpose, at least in part, of communicating understanding within academic traditions. We have complementary purposes as I attempt to write in a fashion that is clear and as you attempt to understand my writing. Of course, we all have other purposes that connect this moment to other activities, such as my attempt to complete this activity in order to meet a deadline so as not to make the editors angry and to do so in a way that fits the canons of academic writing, and your purposes in looking at this chapter to get through a reading assignment or to make use of the ideas to build your own in agreement or disagreement. Hence, the activity in which we are presently collaborating is defined in terms of our shared, complementary, and conflicting purposes.

The role of individual contribution is accessible by focusing on it, with interpersonal and community processes appearing in the background in our lens. The whole activity is still there when one plane of analysis is in focus; in fact, it must be part of the field of vision because without any consideration of the other planes of vision nothing is even visible in the plane that is in focus (the "negative" spaces forming the background around objects are necessary for us to perceive the objects themselves).

In any particular study, one plane of focus can be primary; over the course of a line of research it is necessary for the other planes of focus to take primacy in other studies in order to have a balanced view. Scholarly understanding is itself a sociocultural endeavor, rather than being complete in the accomplishments of an individual study or an individual investigator. A mathematician who solves a problem that has been unsolved for 350 years is participating in an endeavor involving collaborators who devised the problem centuries before and people who in the meantime have ruled out other strategies for finding the solution, as well as participating in an activity constituted by changing cultural and institutional arrangements for the work of scholars.

In the study of human activity, it is not necessary for each participating scholar to address all possible planes of analysis (though the other planes need to play some role for the plane in focus to make sense); however, the overall endeavor of understanding human activity requires the collaboration of scholars using the focus of other planes of analysis. In the social sciences, this collaboration is greatly impacted by sociocultural processes such as those in institutions of learning that solidify boundaries between disciplines, thus making interdisciplinary sharing of information more difficult and forcing narrow specialization of individual scholars who come to regard the disciplines as separate and even in competition for the Truth.

In a sociocultural approach with an emphasis on participation, the emphasis shifts from trying to understand the acquisition of capacities or skills or mental objects to understanding the processes of participation. This contrasts with the internalization perspective in which individuals' development must be explained in terms of purely individual changes (e.g., maturation) or in terms of outside influences (e.g., social "effects"), separately or in interaction. From a participation perspective, individuals are seen as inherently changing through their lifetimes, through their involvement in inherently changing events. Thus, development is inherent in participation, in contrast with being seen as a change of states in the internalization model.

The two models of Figures 13.2 and 13.3 yield different central questions. In the internalization model of Figure 13.2, the central questions are the following:

1. How and where and when is information stored internally?

2. What is the relative importance of the contribution of the individual and the external world?

3. What produces change?

4. How does the external world influence the internal workings of the individual?

In the participation model of Figure 13.3, the central questions are quite different:

1. What activities occur and what is the nature of their transformations?

2. Why and with whom and with what are people engaging in the activity at hand?

3. How do people participate in activities—what are their contributions and how do these change over time?

4. How does the current activity relate to others? Other activities that relate to the activity being studied may be concurrent (such as relating the discourse patterns used in a home activity to those used in school activities), embedded (such as relating discourse patterns in the writing of an article to political issues in the structure of academic institutions), historical (such as relating performance on a test to involvement in prior classroom activities), or future-oriented (such as relating performance on a test to intended involvement in other institutions for which tests serve a preparatory or gatekeeping function).

The internalization model casts development as the acquisition of mental objects such as plans or memories or reading skills and so on (see discussion in Kvale, 1977; Rogoff, Baker-Sennett, & Matusov, 1994). Dropping the internalization model's question of where and how mental objects are stored in the head relates to changes in assumptions regarding how to conceive of developmental transitions.

In a participation model, the focus is on examining transformation in people's actual involvement in activities rather than in attempting to determine which mental objects have or have not yet been acquired. Thus, the effort to infer internal competence (conceived as acquisition of mental objects) from observations of actual performance becomes an uninteresting diversion from attempting to understand the structure of people's developing involvement in inherently changing sociocultural activities. Instead, we would examine how children actually participate in sociocultural activities to characterize how they contribute to those activities cognitively, socially, emotionally, and so on.

Note that in this sociocultural view, boundaries do not exist between cognitive, social, emotional, and motivational processes. Such boundaries may be tied to a model of human functioning that assumes the acquisition of objects in the head that need to be named separately in order to treat them as objects. With a focus on processes of participation in sociocultural activities, one can look at events as involving cognitive, social, emotional, and motivational processes as a function of the focus of the researcher's questions, without assuming that these are "really" separate faculties. This view is profoundly different from much of developmental research, in which cognitive and social processes are regarded as separate (and their influence on each other sometimes examined).

The emphasis changes from trying to infer what children *can* think to interpreting what and how they *do* think. Of course, determining what and how
people think is still inferential and is not simply a matter of recording simple
aspects of behavior or of people's responses to questions or cognitive tasks;
neither the view of observers nor of people themselves is a "true" window on
cognitive processes. Researchers should take advantage of whatever evidence
is available from their own observations as well as from the reports of other
observers and the people involved to create a plausible account that advances
understanding among a community of investigators about the phenomenon under study. (See Kvale, 1977, for a discussion of this point.)

In the sociocultural perspective for which I am arguing, we would observe
the changing participation of children in sociocultural activity rather than aim
to understand what pieces of knowledge or skill they have already "acquired"
and "stored." This is not a suggestion to abandon cognitive research, but rather
an argument that cognitive research can benefit by questioning the assumption
that it is necessary to search for imaginary mental objects stored in the head. I
am arguing that cognitive processes can be well understood through a more
direct examination of processes of thinking, planning, remembering, solving
of problems, and so on, as people engage in them. Meisels (this volume,
chap. 18) makes compatible recommendations for the assessment of children's
intellectual progress by observing children in the context in which they are
trying to puzzle things out and observing that directly.

Dropping the search for assessment of acquisition of mental objects or competence also recasts the question of onset. The question of when a person *begins* to have plans or problem-solving skills or perspective-taking skills or social skills treats transitions as if they were contained in the child, who either
has the skill in question or does not. The onset question in developmental psychology generally searches for the earliest time one can find evidence of the
skill or knowledge in question, yielding continual efforts to demonstrate that
the child has it at an age earlier than that asserted by Piaget or some other
scholar (see Elbers, 1991).

Earlier "attainment" has generally been cleverly demonstrated by changing
the nature of the task situation (in ways that receive insufficient attention) while
continuing to assume that the competence sought is unitary and contained in
the individual, awaiting a pure assessment. From a sociocultural view, no assessment is "pure." All observations involve people participating in one or
more sociocultural activities. The question from a sociocultural participation
view becomes understanding the transformations that occur in children's participation in particular kinds of activities, which are themselves transforming—how do children get from this kind of participation to that kind of participation, and how are the activities in which they participate changing with
the children's involvement along with that of other people?

The question becomes one of understanding children's changing roles as they participate in communities of thinkers. For example, in understanding learning to read, the question would not be focused on identifying the onset of reading skill. Rather, it would examine transformations in how children make sense of letters in certain kinds of texts with specific kinds of social and cultural organization of the reading activity (such as the kind of social support provided for the child's participation in reading and the purpose of the reading effort) and relating similar observations together. There wouldn't be just a child reading (with some inferred level of competence), with those other aspects of the activity treated as potential confounds or features that need to be controlled. The other aspects are inherently part of the process of reading. This involves a larger perspective on what it means to understand text, how texts for children and others are constructed, and how children enter and are brought into communities of readers.

In the participation model, the relation between processes in different activities is a matter for investigation. Processes are not automatically assumed to be general, nor are they assumed to be so particular that we cannot extend from any particular observation to others.[3] Rather, researchers can observe in situations that we want to understand, and they can look to see how those relate to other situations. A key example is the question of how practices in families and in schools relate to each other—some may relate closely, and others may not resemble each other. It becomes essential to try to characterize the relationships among different kinds of activities in which children are involved—the changing participation of children in sociocultural activities such as comprehending texts or studying for a spelling test in school, learning to run a computer program for entertainment with siblings at home, or taking care of younger children.

The question of relating activities to each other is a recasting of the classic question of transfer or generalization. It differs in that the focus is on determining how activities relate to each other and how people move from one activity to another, rather than on determining how mental objects are transferred (as if they existed in isolation in the head) or how physical similarities in the materials elicit transfer (as if the materials carry meaning outside of their use).

In the next section, in order to illustrate how developmental transitions can be studied from a sociocultural perspective, I describe a study focusing on age differences in children's responsible roles. The research does not separate individual processes from interpersonal and community processes but focuses on individual contributions to the whole activity, which includes interpersonal and community processes as background. Explanation focuses on transformations in roles rather than on possession of competence. And variation across communities is taken as an opportunity to see how children's roles everywhere are socioculturally constituted and at the same time constitute the social and cultural processes in which the children participate.

Community Variation in Young Children's Becoming Responsible

One aspect of development that has been identified in the age range 5 to 7 in the research literature is the "capability" to decenter and to take alternative perspectives both with physical objects (like Piaget's three-mountain problem) and with other people (in outgrowing egocentrism). Decentration is a key aspect of the onset of concrete operations in Piagetian theory. As such, it has been challenged over the years, with demonstrations that younger children exhibit perspective taking under some circumstances. For example, U.S. children as young as 2 years turn an object so that it is visible to a viewer (Flavell, Botkin, Fry, Wright, & Jarvis, 1975) and at age 4 they modify their speech in speaking with a toddler (Shatz & Gelman, 1977).

The field has struggled with how, conceptually, to accommodate such variation in age of onset (see Donaldson, 1979; Light, 1986). Piaget's (1971) solution—to refer to the age slippage as *décalage,* owing to varying "friction" in the tasks—is little more than a label for the phenomenon. *Décalage* poses deep problems for the assumptions that development consists of the acquisition of competences in the individual.

The sociocultural participation view that I have outlined in the previous section recasts the perspective-taking findings in terms of understanding developmental transitions that characterize these children's management of these problems as the children participate in sociocultural activities that require investigation to understand the pattern of findings.

Transition to a responsible role requires perspective taking as young children learn to take others' wishes into account. Cultural expectations of when children can take the perspective of a younger child may underlie the assignment of children to be responsible for younger children. Although the modal age in the cultures sampled in the HRAF study (Rogoff et al., 1975) was 5 to 7, in some communities child-care responsibilities were given at age 3 and in others not until age 10. Rather than assuming that Kwara'ae children (for example) are precocious in this skill and U.S. middle-class children (for example) are retarded in it, a sociocultural perspective leads us to examine closely the ways in which responsibility for younger children is structured in each community.

In a Mayan town in the Highlands of Guatemala (San Pedro), 3- to 5-year-olds show responsibility toward 1-year-old siblings, subordinating their own wishes to those of the toddler, in a way that 3- to 5-year-olds from a middle-class U.S. city (Salt Lake City) do not (Mosier & Rogoff, 1995). In order to understand why 3- to 5-year-olds in Salt Lake City do not show such responsibility toward their siblings, and 3- to 5-year-olds in San Pedro do, it is necessary to understand the social organization of family roles and cultural expectations of childhood in each community.

It would be inappropriate to conclude that Salt Lake City 3- to 5-year-olds are less competent, as might occur if we considered skill to be an acquisition of individuals without regard for how the individuals participate in socio-cultural activities composed also of interpersonal and community processes. However, such a conclusion is the usual one in developmental research that compares across cultures or across ages: Those who do not demonstrate the "skill" in question are judged to be less competent, not to have "acquired" the skill, or to be slower along an imaginary timeline of individual development.

The two communities differ in ways that appear related to differences in the children's responsibilities: San Pedro children are learning to become coopera-tive interdependent members of the community; middle-class Salt Lake City children are encouraged to assert individuality and competition. There are also differences in the conception of early childhood that are related to the differ-ences in the two communities. The 3- to 5-year-old siblings in San Pedro re-sponsibly gave over whatever they had or wanted to their younger sibling. If the baby asked for something, the older siblings were expected to respond to the younger sibling by giving something over, and they often did so on their own, seldom needing prompting. In the middle-class Salt Lake City families, the older siblings negotiated and tussled with the baby over whatever they had or wanted, and mothers frequently intervened as judges and more powerful negotiating resources.

Expectations for what can be and should be expected of children in the two communities were very different. The 1-year-olds in Salt Lake City were as-sumed to be ready to learn to follow the rules of sharing and able to understand the consequences of their own actions, and parents treated them by the same rules as their older siblings to enforce sharing and learning to negotiate. The 1-year-olds in San Pedro were assumed not yet to understand how the social world works or how their actions impact others, and they were allowed a spe-cial status, exempt from following rules of fairness. Given the San Pedro toddlers' assumed lack of understanding, their self-interest is assumed to be characteristic of not being ready to be a cooperating member of a group, rather than being a willful antagonist. However, observations of the social interac-tions of toddlers from both communities suggested that if there was a differ-ence between them, it was the San Pedro toddlers who appeared more aware of and in tune with the actions and meanings of the group (see Rogoff, Mistry, Göncü, & Mosier, 1993).

In San Pedro, it is an important social value not to force compliance on any other person, so forcing an infant to cooperate would go against this value. San Pedro caregivers thus treat toddlers with respect for their autonomy, even though toddlers do not yet understand responsibility. Although they encourage toddlers to participate in responsible relations, they do not try to force them to follow other rules of the group. Salt Lake City caregivers, who assume that toddlers understand the consequences of their actions, attempt to make them follow the rules.

The expectations for older siblings in the two communities vary in line with these differences. Children of ages 3 to 5 in both communities are expected to understand the consequences of their actions and to follow the rules of the group. However, in San Pedro, one of those rules is to respect others' autonomy and not force others; children are expected to act interdependently with the group and to understand that toddlers do not yet understand the rules of the group. So San Pedro 3- to 5-year-olds are expected to treat toddlers' wishes with responsibility. They do so without being forced to, giving a desired object to the toddler without prompting, even if they are sorrowful about giving it up.

Treating toddlers' wishes with respect for their autonomy and expecting them later to grow into a voluntarily cooperative role (without being forced) may have something to do with those younger children's moving from a role in a system in which they are treated with respect for their own autonomy into very early responsibility for others. They have not been treated adversarially themselves; they have been treated in a way that gives them a chance to observe what is going on around them and to respect their own and others' autonomy. The 3- to 5-year-olds may act in a socially responsible way with regard to the toddlers in part because that is the way they themselves have been treated. Their transition is that they are no longer the ones who are the object of it; they are no longer the ones who are given the leeway but are already part of the system in which responsibility to other people and respect for each other's autonomy is an inherent part of human relations.

The Salt Lake City middle-class 3- to 5-year-olds follow cultural values in asserting their own rights. Their skillful negotiation and use of adversarial roles is something in which they have participated since infancy, and their treatment of their own toddler siblings is part of a system in which their roles may assist the toddlers in learning to stand up for their own self-interests in an individualistic model of family relations. Perhaps learning to be responsible for others comes later, as it needs to develop with suspension of competition and a stress on individuality. Hence the middle-class Salt Lake City children's apparent "failure" to take a responsible role with regard to nurturing an infant can be reinterpreted in the context of their participation in sociocultural activities with structure different from that of the interdependent, cooperative model of the San Pedro community. Focusing on the 3- to 5-year-olds in isolation would be misleading; they are participants in and contributors to a sociocultural system.

Of course, not only are children making transitions in understanding responsible roles in their communities, but communities themselves are making transitions. Some communities in the United States are seeking ways to encourage children to work well together, using techniques such as reducing age-grading in school and structuring cooperative groups in classrooms. In the Mayan setting, changes involve many more young people leaving the community, especially to go to school, and opportunities for children to serve as caregivers is reduced by increased years of schooling separating children aged 5 and up from others of different ages. The communities and interpersonal relations are continually changing, as are the individuals who participate in sociocultural activities.

Reconceptualizing Transitions

Although some researchers regard focus on "basic" individual processes as a necessary simplification, with addition of interpersonal and cultural processes imposing unwanted complexity, the study of cultural variation in children's responsibility illustrates how interpretation of individual behavior without regard for interpersonal and cultural processes yields a false oversimplification (i.e., that U.S. middle-class 3- to 5-year-olds do not have competence for perspective taking or responsibility to others).

From a sociocultural perspective, parsimony is to be found in recognizing and studying the existing richness of structure of human activity with regularities in terms of how people participate in cultural activities. This contrasts with the separate study of individual, social, and cultural factors and subsequent search for their interactions (the approach followed if the individual is treated as the unit of analysis, Rogoff, 1990). The search for interactions between separately defined individual, social, and cultural factors yields infinite and unanalyzable interactions, leading to "a hall of mirrors that extends to infinity" (Cronbach, 1975, p. 119). Those who become concerned that the study of cultural processes and contextual issues leads toward chaos are likely to be considering those infinite interactions rather than to be aware of the regularities and simplifications of patterns available when sociocultural activity rather than the individual is taken as the unit of analysis.

For example, a researcher attempting to understand the development of children's responsibility for others as an interaction between separate individual and environmental factors would consider the findings in terms of "predictions" of this outcome from characteristics of the individuals (age, gender, birth order, perspective-taking skill, IQ, ethnicity, nationality, social class, etc.) and of the environment (e.g., caregivers' encouragement to share, age of child partner, availability of younger children, presence of attractive novel objects, structure of the society, modernity, climate, presence of formal schooling, technology available). Testing the interactions would be an endless process; reuniting the variables that have been separated out in this way would be a daunting task. Subsequent studies would proceed by varying the identified variables one at a time or (endlessly) including some new ones.

However, when sociocultural activity is taken as the unit of analysis, a coherent account can be discerned in terms of children's transformations of roles having to do with their participation in community practices, which are structured (e.g., in terms of the roles that people play in family responsibilities and public institutions). The account includes reference to something like the "variables" used in the interactional approach, but instead of attempting to define them separately, researchers acknowledge mutual reference to personal, interpersonal, and community planes of analysis. The previous section's account of cultural variation in children's responsibility refers to the relative age and birth order of children and of their partners; to cultural assumptions regarding the development of understanding and responsibility that can be discerned from the inseparable inter-actions of the children and their siblings and caregivers (and researchers); and to cultural values regarding interdependence, autonomy, and fairness that are constituted by the participants together, with changing roles as each person, and his or her relations and community, develop. The resulting account of children's participation suggests principled extensions of the research to examine whether the patterns of regularities observed in these two communities are observed in others and how the children and their caregivers manage the transition in San Pedro from receiver to giver of cooperative respect for autonomy as a responsible member of a community and how they manage the transition in Salt Lake City from defender of individual rights and fairness to nurturant caregiver responsible for others at a later age.

My sociocultural perspective on development as participation thus goes beyond calling attention to the necessity of considering cultural processes in order to understand development; it leads to reconceptualization of some of the central questions of development. A reply to the four organizing questions of this volume (listed here as direct quotations) thus requires recasting of the questions, as they appear to be based on assumptions that individual and environment are separate:

"1. Do 7-year-olds (or environments of 7-year-olds) behave differently than 5-year-olds (or environments of 5-year-olds)?" Yes, but the difference would not be attributed in an either/or fashion to the children or their environments but to differences as a property of the changing involvements of children *in* community activities.

"2. If so, are the differences quantitative or qualitative?" Both. Children begin to do some things more frequently or more skillfully or faster or more deliberately as they and their ongoing activities develop. They also change their roles as activities develop, so they are doing different things and different aspects of things.

"3. If quantitative, are they continuous (i.e., linear) or discontinuous (i.e., nonlinear)?" Sometimes continuous and sometimes discontinuous, depending both on how their involvement is observed (e.g., with what frequency) and how their involvement is structured (e.g., with what periodicity).

"4. If qualitative, are they the result of the emergence of new behaviors or the reorganization of prior behaviors?" Qualitative changes in children's involvements in activities entail (but are not the "result" of) the emergence of new roles and contributions to activities. Emergent roles and contributions themselves involve the reorganization of prior roles and contributions of the children as well as the reorganization of the activities in which children participate.

In sum, this chapter argues that transitions in development can fruitfully be studied as transitions in people's participation in sociocultural activities, building on and further revising community traditions. Expanding our view beyond the individual to the activity as the unit of analysis allows us to understand deeper regularities in children's development and sociocultural processes. Research strategies and questions change with a shift in the unit of analysis (see also Rogoff, Radziszewska, & Masiello, 1995), realigning how we think about developmental transitions. Of course, research done according to other perspectives is still of interest, but its contribution may require an interpretation different from that within which it was carried out. In large measure, attention turns from trying to determine when a competence that is assumed to reside within an individual first appears or how it transforms, to studying how the nature of individuals' participation in sociocultural activities changes as individuals, groups, and communities all develop.

Notes

1. Although age comparisons are commonly used in this endeavor, the more interesting questions remain (as Piaget pointed out) those having to do with sequences of transitions and possible variations in organization of transitions, rather than questions of age per se. A focus on age as an aspect of individual identity is itself a somewhat local concern, as may be apparent from the fact that in many communities people do not keep track of age.

When I began fieldwork in a Mayan community years ago, I was surprised to note that upon meeting a child, adults' next question after "What is your name?" was not "How old are you?" but "What are your mother's and your father's names?" Instead of a focus on identity as defined by individuals' progress on a timeline (as is habitual in the U.S. middle class), the Mayan questions suggest a focus on identity as defined by social relationships or place in the community.

2. Although biological processes are not the focus of my attention here, it would be

consistent with the sociocultural perspective to consider phylogenetic changes as well as brain development as other planes of analysis, without which understanding is incomplete. In a sociocultural approach, biology and culture are not in opposition; rather, phylogenetic and physical developmental processes are regarded as essential but at a different grain of analysis (see Rogoff, 1990; Scribner, 1985).

3. The query of "Baffled in Buffalo" to Ann Landers (1993) and Ann's rejoinder express the dilemma of assumptions of generality: "Dear Ann Landers: A friend of mine who is considered a pretty dim bulb (she ends almost every sentence with 'you know') can sit down and work out a crossword puzzle in nothing flat. How come?" Ann's response: "Dear Baff: Practice makes for proficiency. Crosswords are games, and people who work at them learn the tricks of the trade. It's as simple as that."

Acknowledgments

Recent research reported in this chapter was supported by the Spencer Foundation. I deeply appreciate discussion over the decades with Shep White, as well as the commentary and assistance of Pablo Chavajay, Jacyn Lewis-Smith, Eugene Matusov, and Cindy White. I am also grateful for the persistent interest in this chapter of Marshall Haith and Arnie Sameroff.

References

Cronbach, L. J. (1975). Beyond the two disciplines of scientific psychology. *American Psychologist, 30,* 116–127.

Donaldson, M. (1979). *Children's minds.* Glasgow, Scotland: Fontana.

Elbers, E. (1991). The development of competence and its social context. *Educational Psychology Review, 3,* 73–94.

Feldman, D. H. (1980). *Beyond universals in cognitive development.* Norwood, NJ: Ablex.

Fischer, K. W. (1980). A theory of cognitive development: The control and construction of hierarchies of skills. *Psychological Review, 87,* 477–531.

Flavell, J. H. (1977). *Cognitive development.* Englewood Cliffs, NJ: Prentice-Hall.

Flavell, J. H., Botkin, P. T., Fry, C. L., Wright, J. W., & Jarvis, P. E. (1975). *The development of role-taking and communication skills in young children.* Huntington, NY: Robert E. Krieger.

Gelman, R., & Meck, E. (1983). Preschoolers' counting: Principles before skill. *Cognition, 15,* 343–359.

Heath, S. B. (1983). *Ways with words: Language, life, and work in communities and classrooms.* Cambridge: Cambridge University Press.

Kvale, S. (1977). Dialectics and research on remembering. In N. Datan & H. W. Reese (Eds.), *Life-span developmental psychology: Dialectical perspectives on experimental research* (pp. 165–189). New York: Academic Press.

Landers, A. (1993, June 29). Memories are tough to forget. *Santa Cruz Sentinel,* p. A10.

Lave, J., & Wenger, E. (1991). *Situated learning: Legitimate peripheral participation.* Cambridge: Cambridge University Press.

Leont'ev, A. N. (1981). The problem of activity in psychology. In J. V. Wertsch (Ed.),

The concept of activity in Soviet psychology (pp. 37–71). Armonk, NY: M. E. Sharpe.

Light, P. (1986). Context, conservation and conversation. In M. Richards & P. Light (Eds.), *Children of social worlds: Development in social context* (pp. 170–190). Oxford, England: Polity Press.

Meisels, S. J. (1996). Performance in context: Assessing children's achievement at the outset of school. In A. J. Sameroff & M. M. Haith (Eds.), *The five to seven year shift: The age of reason and responsibility* (chap. 18, this vol.). Chicago: University of Chicago Press.

Morelli, G. A., Rogoff, B., Oppenheim, D., & Goldsmith, D. (1992). Cultural variation in infants' sleeping arrangements: Questions of independence. *Developmental Psychology, 28,* 604–613.

Mosier, C., & Rogoff, B. (1995). Cultural variation in young children's roles in the family: Autonomy and responsibility. Manuscript in preparation.

Piaget, J. (1971). The theory of stages in cognitive development. In D. R. Green, M. P. Ford, & G. P. Flamer (Eds.), *Measurement and Piaget.* New York: McGraw-Hill.

Rogoff, B. (1978, February). *Companions and activities of Highland Mayan children.* Paper presented at the meetings of the Society for Cross-Cultural Research, New Haven, CT.

Rogoff, B. (1982). Integrating context and cognitive development. In M. E. Lamb & A. L. Brown (Eds.), *Advances in developmental psychology* (Vol. 2, pp. 125–170). Hillsdale, NJ: Erlbaum.

Rogoff, B. (1990). *Apprenticeship in thinking: Cognitive development in social context.* New York: Oxford University Press.

Rogoff, B. (1995). Observing sociocultural activity on three planes: Participatory appropriation, guided participation, and apprenticeship. In J. V. Wertsch, P. del Rio, & A. Alvarez (Eds.), *Sociocultural studies of mind* (pp. 139–164). Cambridge: Cambridge University Press.

Rogoff, B., Baker-Sennett, J., & Matusov, E. (1994). Considering the concept of planning. In M. Haith, J. Benson, R. Roberts, & B. Pennington (Eds.), *The development of future-oriented processes* (pp. 353–373). Chicago: University of Chicago Press.

Rogoff, B., Mistry, J., Göncü, A., & Mosier, C. (1993). Guided participation in cultural activity by toddlers and caregivers. *Monographs of the Society for Research in Child Development, 58* (7, Serial No. 236).

Rogoff, B., Newcombe, N., Fox, N., & Ellis, S. (1980). Transitions in children's roles and capabilities. *International Journal of Psychology, 15,* 181–200.

Rogoff, B., Radziszewska, B., & Masiello, T. (1995). Analysis of developmental processes in sociocultural activity. In L. Martin, K. Nelson, & E. Tobach (Eds.), *Cultural psychology and activity theory.* Cambridge: Cambridge University Press.

Rogoff, B., Sellers, M. J., Pirrotta, S., Fox, N., & White, S. H. (1975). Age of assignment of roles and responsibilities to children. *Human Development, 18,* 353–369.

Scribner, S. (1985). Vygotsky's uses of history. In J. V. Wertsch (Ed.), *Culture, communication, and cognition: Vygotskian perspectives* (pp. 119–145). Cambridge: Cambridge University Press.

Sellers, M. J. (1975). The first ten years of childhood in rural communities of Mexico and Guatemala. Unpublished manuscript, Harvard University, Cambridge, MA.

Shatz, M., & Gelman, R. (1977). Beyond syntax: The influence of conversational constraints on speech modifications. In C. E. Snow & C. A. Ferguson (Eds.), *Talking to children.* Cambridge: Cambridge University Press.

Sorenson, E. R. (1979). Early tactile communication and the patterning of human organization: A New Guinea case study. In M. Bullowa (Ed.), *Before speech: The beginning of interpersonal communication* (pp. 289–305). Cambridge: Cambridge University Press.

Vygotsky, L. S. (1987). *Thinking and speech.* (N. Minick, Trans.) In R. W. Rieber & A. S. Carton (Eds.), *The collected works of L. S. Vygotsky* (pp. 37–285). NY: Plenum.

Watson-Gegeo, K. A. (1990). The social transfer of cognitive skills in Kwara'ae. *The Quarterly Newsletter of the Laboratory of Comparative Human Cognition, 12,* 86–90.

White, S. H. (1965). Evidence for a hierarchical arrangement of learning processes. In L. P. Lipsitt & C. C. Spiker (Eds.), *Advances in child development and behavior* (Vol. 2, pp. 187–220). New York: Academic Press.

White, S. H., & Siegel, A. W. (1984). Cognitive development in time and space. In B. Rogoff & J. Lave (Eds.), *Everyday cognition: Its development in social context* (pp. 238–277). Cambridge, MA: Harvard University Press.

Zinchenko, V. P. (1985). Vygotsky's ideas about units for the analysis of mind. In J. V. Wertsch (Ed.), *Culture, communication, and cognition: Vygotskian perspectives* (pp. 94–118). Cambridge: Cambridge University Press.

CHAPTER FOURTEEN

The 5 to 7 Transition as an Ecocultural Project

THOMAS S. WEISNER

The 5 to 7 transition involves changes in internal states and competencies of the maturing child—shifts in cognitive capacities, self-concept, visual-perceptual abilities, and social abilities. The transition marks the emergence of increasing capacities for strategic and controlled self-regulation, skills at inhibition, the ability to maintain attention and to focus on a complex problem, and planfulness and reflection. These changes are well described by other chapters in this volume. But the 5 to 7 transition is a transition period not only within the child, but also in interpersonal relationships, and in the wider cultural contexts that surround the child.

Maturational transitions in development shape cultural contexts and interpersonal relations through their effects on family adaptation. They create new constraints on and opportunities for adaptation for families and communities, just as they do for the individual. This is a two-way transaction: The community defines the meaning of the transition, as well as responding to changes in children's abilities. The child may be prepared to develop new competencies, but it is only in the particular cultural place in which new cultural activities develop that they can be understood.

In many cultures, for example there is a quite striking shift in children's roles and cultural opportunities during and after the 5 to 7 period. From a cross-cultural perspective, children from around 4 to 9 participate in more nurturant, caretaking interactions with other children (Rogoff, Sellers, Pirrotta, Fox, & White, 1975; Rogoff, Newcombe, Fox, & Ellis, 1980; Whiting & Whiting, 1975; Whiting & Edwards, 1988; Weisner & Gallimore, 1977). They also take on new domestic task responsibilities, and are expected by parents and other adults to have the social skills to manage these domestic tasks and to act appropriately in social situations. Children in many cultures around the world appear to be participating more extensively and creatively in a cultural world of "socially distributed" care, nurturance, and task responsibility, as Robert Serpell has recently called these practices regarding social support and obligation (Serpell, in press). The 5 to 7 transition for the family and community in these societies is one in which children increasingly are capable of actively participating in socially distributed support and work.

Children moving through the 5 to 7 shift in many cultures, then, begin to assist in shared caretaking and help with domestic tasks. Finding such assistance and help is of course an adaptive problem facing parents in all societies. Developmental transitions, whatever else they may be, generate adaptive changes in families, and these changes may well help to solve a variety of problems faced by families and communities. Transitions, of course, present adaptive problems as well as opportunities, such as possible competition, jealousy, and disruptiveness of children; the increased complexity and sophistication of the children's ability to understand their own role and position in the family adaptation process; and children's efforts to manipulate others. Regardless of whether some aspect of this transition is viewed positively or negatively in a particular family or cultural community, the 5 to 7 period represents a predictable "perturbation" (Chisholm, 1983) in development that is associated with changes in cultural context and family adaptation. Developmental transitions like the 5 to 7 period create and help resolve important adaptive problems in families and cultures.

Anthropologists have long recognized another feature of cultural transitions: They are potentially dangerous as well as hopeful. They represent changes in the social order, in social relationships, and in personal identity, changes in which many in the community have a stake. They are often, therefore, marked through rituals, initiations, ceremonies, and special, culturally marked events. Children and their families passing through such transitions enter a liminal state with heightened symbolic recognition of the changes that are occurring in them and their social world. In this transitional state, specialized teaching occurs; ritual participants leave their normal routines; and foods, housing, sleep periods, and bodily security are all changed. The end point of these events is a socially recognized return to "normal society," but in a new social role. It is interesting that the 5 to 7 transition is not as often marked by such cultural practices as are other periods such as adolescence, marriage, survival at the early infancy period, and so forth. Although not as culturally marked, it is nonetheless widely recognized in cultures around the world through changes in the child's participation in the tasks important for family assistance and caretaking. The 5 to 7 transition is less dangerous and more hopeful to the family and community than are other periods.

An Ecocultural Model of Development Transitions

What, then, is the adaptive problem for which the 5 to 7 transition is both a solution (i.e., a help and opportunity for families and children) and a concern?

The example of socially distributed support and work is, of course, a specific family adaptive problem—an 8-year-old caretaking young children or doing domestic tasks assists in family adaptation. But what is the more general adaptive problem of which this is but one aspect?

One approach to finding an answer is ecological-cultural (ecocultural) theory (Gallimore, Weisner, Kaufman, & Bernheimer, 1989; Weisner, 1984, 1993). Ecocultural theory proposes that the adaptive problem is constructing and sustaining a daily routine of life that has meaning for culture members and that fits with the competencies of available members of the family and community. The construction and sustenance of a daily routine are adaptive problems that challenge all families. "Constructing" a routine reminds us that this is a proactive process in which families shape and are shaped by the social world around them as they try and create and change their routines. "Sustaining" a daily routine means adapting it to a local ecology and the family resource base— that is, the family adaptive problem involves survival, work, and wealth. A "meaningful" routine is one that has moral and cultural significance and value for family members. Although there is always variation within a cultural community in daily routines and practices, any possible one will not do: There are always moral and social preferences that matter. The "competencies" of family members depend on many maturational and cultural indicators, such as age, gender, temperament, kinship status, and cultural beliefs about competencies and status. A developmental transition like the 5 to 7 shift, filled as it is with gradually emerging, powerful new social and cognitive potentials, surely presents enormous new opportunities for familial and community responses to the adaptive task of constructing and sustaining a meaningful daily routine of life.

A central argument of ecocultural theory is that a child's participation in such routine everyday family activities is the preeminent experience shaping the child's development. The construction of the daily routine by families provides these activities for children. Even a cursory glance at the great variety of cultures around the world reminds us that the single most important influence on the developmental trajectory of a child is the particular, local cultural place into which the child is born. The meaning and adaptive use of the 5 to 7 transition by families and cultural communities depend on the transition's use in each cultural place.

Ecocultural theory draws on anthropological and cross-cultural human developmental research (LeVine, 1977; Munroe, Munroe, & Whiting, 1981; Nerlove & Snipper, 1981; Super & Harkness, 1980, 1986; Weisner & Gallimore, 1985; Weisner, Gallimore, & Jordan, 1988; B. Whiting, 1976, 1980; B. Whiting & Edwards, 1988; Whiting & Whiting, 1975). The focus on cultural context, the daily routine, and behavior settings—and their power to shape interaction and cognition—come from this research transition. The ecocultural model also draws on sociocultural and activity theory and research (e.g., Cole, 1985; Rogoff, 1982, 1990; Tharp & Gallimore, 1988; Vygotsky,

1978; Wertsch, 1985). This different, but related, line of work emphasizes the socially constructed nature of cognition and mind, as well as the role of activities and practices as the constitutive elements of the daily routine producing developmentally sensitive interactions.

The general idea that developmental transitions are interchanges between person and environment—that development is always occurring in a social context—is, of course, a well-known and well-understood approach in the study of development generally (Bronfenbrenner, 1979; Kessen, 1979; Sameroff & Chandler, 1975). Super and Harkness, (1980, 1986) have called this changing, interactive environment around the child the developmental niche, consisting of physical and social settings, customs of child care, and cultural beliefs and goals, and have long called for the study of its development alongside the developing child.

What ecocultural theory adds to this general exhortation to consider social context is its focus on the activities and practices of the daily routine as the locus for this contextual influence, its focus on the task of family adaptation in constructing this routine as a common adaptive task around the world, and its attention to cross-cultural variations in ecocultural context. The model also proposes 12 ecocultural domains that seem to be involved in shaping family adaptation everywhere (Weisner, 1984). These domains represent resources and constraints for families that seem related to the 5 to 7 transition, such as the family domestic workload, subsistence adaptations of parents, supports for mothers, gender role training, peers and child activity groups, and others. The involvement of children in caretaking and domestic tasks directly relates to a number of these domains.

The cross-cultural literature is filled with examples of the assumption of caretaking and domestic tasks by children of about ages 5 to 7 (Rogoff et al., 1980; Rogoff et al., 1975; Weisner & Gallimore, 1977). Children during and after this stage are better able to both learn and recall a general social schema or plan for action, as well as keep track of the details of interaction. For instance, they can mind a child moment-to-moment by responding to his or her cries, but they can also keep tabs on and manage the larger task of organizing the domestic routine so that a shop is open for selling, a fire is maintained, food prepared, and animals tended to. It is, then, a plausible hypothesis that the 5 to 7 maturational shift has the adaptive benefit for families around the world of preparing a child who will be able to assist in caretaking and domestic tasks, and who will be able to do so increasingly in the wider social community, and so is better prepared to assist in the maintenance and survival of the family daily routine of life.

To summarize the argument so far: Developmental transitions like the 5 to 7 period are cultural projects for families and communities—that is, they are a part of the universal adaptive problem of constructing and sustaining a meaningful daily routine of life for family members, a routine that is congruent with the competencies of family members. In the ecocultural model, the 5 to 7 transition may create new adaptive problems for families, but it also provides opportunities for the solution of many existing adaptive problems. An example of this, the primary topic of this chapter, is the role of children in providing caretaking, social support, and task assistance in the family during and after the 5 to 7 transition.

The Western cultural project surrounding the 5 to 7 transition is reflected in the name often given to it: the "school-age" transition. This Western concern with cognition, literacy, numeracy, and verbal skills reflects what the West has made of some—only a small portion—of the emerging abilities of children during this period. It reflects specific sociohistorical concerns over what defines competence in children, much as other cultures show concern over doing family and community tasks to assist in their survival. Although the school setting may have indirectly taken advantage of certain psychological abilities afforded by evolution and past cultural experiences, it hardly capitalizes on most of the competencies I argue evolved in the past.

Why Is There a 5 to 7 Transition in Development?
A Family Adaptation Hypothesis

A focus on the adaptive uses of the 5 to 7 transition today leads to asking about its adaptive origins. If there is a 5 to 7 developmental transition, an assumption that appears broadly correct based on many of the chapters in this volume, it may have originated in human evolution as a solution to adaptive problems, just as it can be situated today in the context of the human adaptive problem of organizing family and community routines of life. What were the adaptive problems in our human evolutionary past, including our nonhuman primate past, that might have led children of about this stage in their maturation to develop the kinds of skills that have been identified: increased complexity in reasoning abilities; strategic decision making; empathy; memory and cognitive abilities; social communication; and self-concept changes?

Perhaps one of these problems was assistance for parents in caretaking of infants and other juveniles. Assistance must have included direct care of full siblings or related individuals in the community, as well as other tasks essential for providing a sustainable daily routine, such as improving communication and signaling skills, protecting the group against predators, seeking and defending food supplies, and fully learning group roles and social positions through a combination of play and apprenticeship. All of these behaviors assist in the survival of a domestic group and in caretaking.

My argument is based on the general notion in studies of the evolution of human growth that both juveniles and their families would have benefited from continued sharing of food and from age-graded caretaking by older children of younger (Bogin, 1988, pp. 92–93). But my argument extends this notion by focusing on the wider adaptive problem—sustaining a meaningful, coherent routine of everyday life—which continues today. Some of the psychological mechanisms assisting in this adaptive task include the tendency to analyze problems in terms of social costs and benefits, to be able to grasp the complex network of social roles and relationships in a community, and to do so by taking into account the reference points of others' minds. These are among the abilities that appear to emerge, or significantly increase in complexity and generalizability, during the 5 to 7 transition.

These are abilities that assist children and adults alike in acquiring, remembering, and using cultural models for action. D'Andrade (1987, p. 112; 1992) defined cultural models as "a cognitive schema that is intersubjectively shared by a social group," and that is hierarchically organized. "Buying something," for example, is a cultural activity that is schematically organized, involves shared knowledge, and includes concepts like money, seller, and price. "Taking care of an infant," "delivering messages to an uncle's house," "herding cattle," and "guarding the house and minding younger siblings" are practices embedded in cultural models. Children's abilities to use such cultural models and schemas appear to increase dramatically during the 5 to 7 period. Older children can manage complex, hierarchically organized sequences of tasks essential to families because they have acquired cultural models of great complexity (Nerlove, Roberts, Klein, Yarbrough, & Habicht, 1974). This is one of the achievements that emerge at the 5 to 7 transition.

An understanding of the psychological mechanisms that might have evolved during the 5 to 7 transition is central to understanding how the 5 to 7 transition may have evolved and what its enduring adaptive value for families and children may have been. This is because selection operates on these mechanisms as well as on behaviors that might be adaptive. Chisholm (1992) has summarized this point:

> [W]e cannot confuse a trait—like the chin, or infanticide—with genes "for" that trait. We must instead understand how the trait works and where it comes from. Selection acts not only on behavior, but also on the developmental biological and psychological mechanisms that produce behavior. (P. 130)

Thus, although the abilities emerging at the 5 to 7 transition may have evolved in part to assist in caretaking and related aid in family and community survival, they need not be tied to a specific past ecological environment. The 5 to 7 transition may have somewhat different functional-adaptive behavioral patterns in varied ecologies (Borgerhoff-Mulder, 1991) as well as a set of interrelated psychological mechanisms gradually favored by natural selection (Cosmides

& Tooby, 1989; Tooby & Cosmides, 1989). Some of the psychological characteristics of the 5 to 7 transition are abilities that would be adaptive for both caretaking other infants and juveniles and for adapting to survival in the social group, in situations in which juveniles are less and less under the mother's immediate gaze.

This seems to be a "sensible paradigm" (Blurton-Jones, 1990, p. 353) for thinking about the evolution of the 5 to 7 transition. It seems useful to view the process as a mix of functional utility (without tying behavior to some necessarily adaptive function in what are, after all, highly changing behavioral environments) and a study of the evolved psychological processes or mechanisms in children that might have enhanced fitness under varying ecological and social conditions. These mechanisms included the child's ability to use cultural models in complex ways to solve problems in changing and uncertain, new environments. These abilities assisted in meeting adaptive problems facing families as they attempted to construct a meaningful, sustainable routine of everyday life, one which would be congruent with the ages and abilities of those in the domestic group.

Of course, the fact that the 5 to 7 transition may have current utility for family adaptation in contemporary cultures does not necessarily mean that this same functional utility is the basis of its evolutionary origins. There are many ways that the juvenile period in human development likely evolved in addition to an adaptation related to caretaking and family-group survival. Indeed, the juvenile or extended childhood period has a series of adaptive advantages in addition to caretaking, as outlined in Bogin (1988, p. 75), including a general opportunity for cultural learning and brain development, small juvenile body size, which reduces parent-offspring conflict and competition over resources, delayed eruption of molars, and others. Some of the characteristics associated with the 5 to 7 transition could have coevolved with other traits that were selected for in some past environment of evolutionary adaptedness. These past environments may have favored practices different from shared caretaking or domestic task maintenance or group protection of children in the family, yet the same cognitive abilities and social communication skills successful in that other environment might be now focused on those new practices.

The 5 to 7 period is when children enter the juvenile period—defined as a stage of life when children could probably survive if their caretakers died or if they were to lose some or all of what their parents provide them, but they are not yet mature sexually (Pereira, 1993, p. 19). In human communities, children could survive alone in large numbers, but only with the social assistance of individuals other than their parents. In fact, this is what occurs in human communities—other kin or non-kin often do take in such children, and adoption, fosterage, and child lending are common practices. In nonhuman primate communities, the arrival of a new infant is often the time when the young juveniles are pushed out of the mother's immediate social group and into the wider group. This is simultaneously the time, then, when social awareness and social communication skills are needed for survival and when, in many primate groups, juveniles start assisting in the care of infants.

In the literature dealing with nonhuman primates, researchers have discussed a number of ways in which juvenile members of a primate group who are not actually breeding new offspring themselves contribute to group and offspring survival (Periera & Fairbanks, 1993). These contributions include reducing the carrying load of the mother or in other ways providing direct child care (alloparenting); acting as "sentinels" detecting and warning against predators; or defending feeding sites from competitors. Juvenile vervets in Amboseli, Kenya, for instance, learn to recognize the calls and signals of dangerous animals in their environment, as well as learn to produce the calls their own primate group will recognize as warnings (Cheney & Seyfarth, 1990). Such social cooperation among maternal kin (full and half siblings) does affect reproductive success in primates. If an infant is orphaned, siblings are most likely to care for it and help it survive. Juvenile care also promotes independence and assists in the weaning transition of the younger offspring. There is evidence that juveniles in many primate groups dramatically increase their caretaking, social communication skills, and reciprocal social roles during this period. The nonhuman primate evidence is at least not inconsistent with the evidence from human groups, who clearly begin to deploy children of these ages for such tasks.

Why do these developing abilities in reasoning, decision making, social competencies, and self-understanding begin around age 4, and why do changes continue through about age 8? The reason for this may have to do with adaptive concerns not exclusively having to do with the 5- or 6-year-old himself or herself, but rather with the parents and any younger infant or toddler who would have by this time been born into the child's domestic group. The new child would require the mother's time and would place the older children more often in a daily routine shared with peers or other adults. It would be valuable to the domestic group and family unit if the juvenile could in various ways assist the parent and other caretakers of the infant. These forms of assistance could include direct infant care or performance of domestic tasks that the mother would otherwise have done or the sharing of food or the insuring of the safety and the physical and social viability of the family unit so that the mother could safely care for the new infant. The new competencies that emerge during the 5 to 7 period are compatible with a child's being able first to assist others and then more independently to assist by undertaking caretaking and domestic tasks.

Although birth spacing varies widely today and probably has in the past, birth-spacing data on human foragers such as the !Kung suggest that there is about a 50-month interval between births of children who survive to a year

(Blurton-Jones, 1986) and that this is a theoretically optimal interval in that particular environment. However, other foragers have different patterns of birth intervals, and it appears unlikely that the wide variations in environments faced by our nonhuman primate ancestors and our human ancestors would have selected for a single such interval such as between age 4 and 5. The expectable, rather high demographic variability, owing to mortality and fertility variations within human communities, also means that spacing will vary across domestic groups within any society (Hewlett, 1991). Although births may occur more or less often than at a median interval of 50 months, the 5 to 7 period as the onset of juvenality could well have emerged due in part to birth spacing.

Age in the study of this transition is a relational or positional index variable. Age is not only elapsed time (on some scale of years or life expectancy or age-specific mortality) but also relative status and position in a group. It is not the juvenile's absolute age of 5 that is important, but rather the juvenile's relative position of age 5 or so compared to the timing of the birth of younger children and the normal juvenile maturational period. The age range of this transition is more gradual than precisely 5 to 7 because there are anticipatory beginnings of some aspects of this transition early on and others do not fully emerge until later. Furthermore, the complex set of intellectual, emotional, social, linguistic, visual, and other competencies are not changing in lockstep, nor do children move through this period at the same rate with respect to each ability. Since diverse cultures place different expectations and pressures on children for different kinds of change, one or another of these competencies might appear at an earlier chronological age among children in one culture than in another. In addition, although the onset and end points of the transition may differ in different individuals, nevertheless, there may be a relatively clear demarcation within a social group around the 5 to 7 period.

The reason for the evolution of any development-maturational transitional period is that those genetic tendencies that encouraged the development of these competencies during roughly the 5 to 7 age period, or equivalent period for nonhuman primates, would have increased the direct or indirect fitness of the individuals who had those tendencies. Fitness in this sense is the survival of an individual's own genetic material (direct fitness) or survival of the genetic material of one's relatives, who on average share some of one's own genetic material (indirect fitness). If one reason for the evolution of the 5 to 7 transitional period was because juveniles could assist in infant caretaking and assist the new mother in other tasks related to family and group survival, then those offspring who had competencies that assisted them in those activities would have been more likely to survive, as would their kin. In this way, these competencies developing during the 5 to 7 period would be more likely to persist in a community. As I will show in the next section, families and cultural communities throughout the world do, in fact, provide opportunities for children to assist in care of younger children and to assist in family adaptive tasks after this transition—and children are prepared to do these tasks.

Cultural Opportunities and the 5 to 7 Transition: Caretaking, Tasks, and Social Support

Families and communities in a wide range of cultures recognize the cognitive and maturational changes in children between about ages 4 to 9 (Rogoff et al., 1980; Rogoff et al., 1975). Among the ways they do so is to assign children more responsibility for doing tasks and chores around the house and in the community. Children are also involved in caring for younger children. Some cultures have codified these changes in children's activities by defining clear roles for children as child caretakers or assistants in managing the domestic domain. Others have not culturally elaborated the roles, but the practice is widely shared. Whether or not these roles are defined explicitly or assigned more to girls or boys or to particular ages, such changes in children's activities very often appear. Children's participation in the family adaptive task of shared support and maintenance of the family routine is a clear example of the patterned expression of the 5 to 7 developmental transition at the cultural and interactional levels.

The provision of nurturance and social support for kin and community is a universal adaptive problem. Although its form and content and cultural meaning varies widely around the world, there are universal features recognizable in cultures everywhere. One can have a deep appreciation of the very important and meaningful local cultural differences and also recognize that it is not necessary to "start over" conceptually or methodologically each time we visit a new cultural community, in the hope of studying activities in the daily routine that involve support and nurturance. These activities include affection, physical comfort, assistance in doing tasks, shared solving of problems, provision of food and other resources, and protection against harm and aggression (Weisner, 1993). Nurturance and support involve anticipating, intuiting, and recognizing the needs and the circumstances of others and then acting to assist the other person or persons. Domestic tasks assigned to children also share many common features and have been systematically compared in cultures around the world (Bradley, 1993).

The examples of cultural practices, children's caretaking, social support, and task involvement presented here come primarily from sub-Saharan African societies, particularly East African (Weisner, in press). The African data are from studies done among the Abaluyia of Kisa location in western Kenya, a group of Bantu, horticultural communities. These groups also have a history of extensive wage-labor migration throughout Kenya and East Africa (Wagner, 1949/1970; Were, 1967). The Abaluyia live in dispersed homesteads connected by paths and surrounded by their fields of maize, potatoes, vegetables, cassava, plantains and bananas, sugarcane, groundnuts, and other crops. Their homes and lands sit on green, gently rolling hills, with rainfall adequate for two crops a year when the region is not affected by drought. Well over half the adult males, and substantial numbers of women and children, are away from the community at wage jobs, or trying to find such jobs, or living with kin in Nairobi or other urban centers (Weisner, 1976b). The Abaluyia have been in extensive contact with national and international economies for generations, and schools have been operating since the 1920s. Hence, the circumstances of children's 5 to 7 transition in these communities, which I describe in this chapter, are not from some long-past "traditional" history; these are the practices of contemporary generations. Because Abaluyia are living in cities and towns as well as in rural communities, data are presented from urban-resident families as well as rural ones.

Some of the characteristics of the 5 to 7 child transition in these places can stand for other cultural places around the world, but some cannot. For example, the gender preference for girls doing caretaking and domestic activities appears widely around the world. The activities children do together, the extent of maternal and paternal involvement, and the styles of caretaking, all vary much more widely. There is a useful contrast worth making between preindustrial, less technologically developed societies, on the one hand, and industrial or postindustrial societies in Europe and North America, on the other. (For convenience, recognizing the enormous diversity within each grouping, I will gloss this contrast as preindustrial and Western, respectively. Preindustrial societies include the horticultural, peasant, and simple agricultural communities, such as the East African or Polynesian communities described in the chapter.) By no stretch of the imagination are these two distinct and homogeneous categories, nor have they been isolated from one another. Indeed, some of the characteristics of the cultural transition for children in African communities can be found in the West, and Western children, of course, do child-care and domestic tasks. There are elites and middle-class families and communities with similar characteristics throughout the preindustrial world. Active child participation in socially distributed nurturance and support is a family adaptive pattern that can be found in more culturally elaborated forms in preindustrial communities but is available and found in some degree everywhere.

Patterns of Child Nurturance, Support, and Family Task Assistance That Develop During the 5 to 7 Transition

In a system for caretaking and support based on age-graded care by juvenile children, children are expected to turn to parents, siblings, cousins, aunts, grandparents, and socially recognized others for help. In turn, they are often expected to assist others in their family. Parents may manage and direct their family caretaking system without directly providing care themselves. Children may spend time living with other kin and participating in the care of others away from their natal home. Interdependence, more so than independence, is culturally expected of children at these ages particularly (Weisner, 1982).

Although the qualities of social interaction and role that characterize child caretaking and domestic task participation for children vary widely around the world, there are some patterns frequently found in field studies of children and parenting. Although no one characteristic of this pattern defines the transition for children and families, some subset of these features is very often found accompanying the 5 to 7 transition (Weisner, 1989).

Other Children Provide Assistance and Support

Children look to other children for assistance and support as much or more than to adults. Figure 14.1 shows data from observational studies done among the Abaluyia (Weisner, 1979, 1987). These naturalistic observations were done in and around children's homes throughout the day and were subsequently coded jointly by Kenyan students and American researchers. Mothers were the exclusive providers of nurturance and social support in only 23% of all supportive acts in the sample. The remainder of the support either included other children or occurred in the absence of the mother. Girls do about as much caretaking as mothers. Abaluyia children in urban Nairobi do not differ substantially in the amount of care they provide compared with children in the rural community.

Nor are the Abaluyia unusual. Cross-cultural samples showed that older children were the caretakers of younger children after infancy about 35% of the time (Barry & Paxson, 1971). Leiderman and Leiderman (1974a, 1974b) found that polymatric care was widely practiced among Kikuyu in the Central Highlands of Kenya. Reed and Leiderman (1981) demonstrated that infants show attachment behaviors with sibling caretakers similar to that shown toward their mothers, although the nature of the caretaking provided by mothers and siblings differs. Grace Shibadu (1978) interviewed women in Kenya, who reported that 90% of girls 5 to 9 did child-care tasks, as did 82% of boys. However, boys drop to 38% during ages 10 to 12, whereas 82% of girls remain involved in child care. Pamela Reynolds (1991) reported similar observational data from Tonga families in Zimbabwe; the Tonga are a community dependent on wage-labor migration and are a mixed horticultural economy in a relatively dry and arid part of the country. Child care clearly was the predominant work activity for girls and was done in the context of a heavy overall domestic workload. Tonga women spent 20% of their work time caring for children, girls 33%, and boys 4%. Girls under 10 spent 56% of their time caring for infants

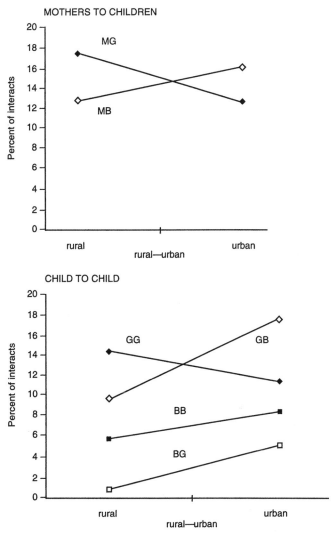

Figure 14.1 Nurturant interactions (direct care and emotional support), by dyad and rural-urban residence. From T. S. Weisner, 1987, "Socialization for Parenthood in Sibling Caretaking Societies," in *Parenting Across the Lifespan: Biosocial Dimensions,* (p. 254), J. B. Lancaster, J. Altman, A. S. Rossi, and L. R. Sherrod (Eds.). New York: Aldine de Gruyter. Copyright 1987 by Aldine de Gruyter.

and young children. These data include being directly involved in attending to a child—not merely being around children while doing other tasks (Reynolds, 1991, p. 80).

Indirect Chains of Support

Children care for other children within indirect chains of support in which one child (under a mother's or other adults' management) assists another, who assists a third, who shares help for others, and so on. For instance, an Abaluyia toddler of 3 years or so will fall down and cry. The child's mother and a teenage sibling will not necessarily run to assist, although they will be aware and perhaps glance over at the situation. A 7-year-old sister will come over and help the child up. Later on, if the 7-year-old needs help in gathering wood or in weeding, the teenage sibling will help the girl out.

The cultural practices of the 5 to 7 transition not only assist children to participate in such intrafamily chains of support but also carry the expectation that children will learn about and understand such networks of support and avoidance across families as well. A 4-year-old may learn and display rules of greeting and avoidance; an 8-year-old learns why these are important rules and how to apply them to novel situations. Whom to avoid or approach in the wider community and how to successfully negotiate visits and exchanges across families is an important concern children learn by age 8 or so. Learning to run errands all around one's community successfully is a sign of maturity (Super, 1983), as is an appropriate understanding of complex kinship connections and community political alliances. There is a cultural value placed on children's interdependence and on hierarchical age structures, more than on autonomy and independence.

Gender Differences

Although boys and girls are capable of doing the full range of caretaking, domestic tasks, vigilance, food gathering, play, and social negotiations that assist their family, they begin to specialize at the 5 to 7 period. Girls in societies with age-graded caretaking, for example, are more likely than boys to be involved in caretaking or other activities that entail doing caretaking, such as tasks done in or near the home.

Girls do over twice as much caretaking and domestic tasks as boys do according to the Abaluyia data, but boys clearly provide support, caretaking, and nurturance to other children as well, although more infrequently as they reach late middle childhood. Figure 14.1 shows this pattern in the Kenya samples, with girls doing two to three times more caretaking and nurturant interaction with other children than do boys. Infant care is particularly common among girls right after the 5 to 7 transition. Edwards (1993) found that cross-cultural studies support the view that "involvement with infants is one of the most consistent sex-differentiated behavioral domains of middle childhood" (p. 336). This same difference appears in virtually all primate studies. Bradley (1993) examined the patterns of domestic task performance in a large cross-cultural sample and found that, though both boys and girls assist in women's domestic tasks, girls seldom do men's tasks. Furthermore, "the most common children's tasks are women's tasks"; both boys and girls are under the supervision of women, who use both boys' and girls' labor to assist in their often heavy workloads. As boys reach later middle childhood, they are more likely to leave the domestic domain controlled by women, and they gradually do fewer tasks done by and allocated by women or older girls managing the household. Family adaptation seems to capitalize on boys' and girls' abilities at the 5 to 7 transition by involving both genders in work and child care. However, girls do more of such tasks than boys do.

Children self-ascribe cultural standards and beliefs about their appropriate role according to age and gender and are also socialized through apprenticeship learning of their family roles and responsibilities. Native Hawaiian girls, living in a working-class neighborhood in Honolulu, for instance, tended to overreport to others that they were responsible for caring for others, whereas boys tended to underreport (Weisner, Gallimore, & Tharp, 1982).

Boys and girls divided themselves, and cultural practices divide them, into sex-segregated peer groups right at the 5 to 7 transition period in many cultures (Edwards, 1993; Ember, 1981). For instance, as Figures 14.2a and 14.2b show (data are from the Giriama in the coastal region of Kenya, described by Wenger, 1983, 1989), boys and girls spend more time with peers (± 2 years) of their own gender as they move through the 5 to 7 period (Figure 14.2b). But girls spend more time with both boys and girls (Figure 14.2a) of all ages, not only peers, because they are more often involved in caretaking and domestic tasks with boys and girls, whereas boys spend more time exclusively with boys (Figure 14.2a). Abaluyia children's interactions show a similar gender shift (Figure 14.3): Up to age 5, Abaluyia boys are about as likely to interact with girls 10 or older, who are often their caretakers or working around them doing domestic tasks, as they are with boys. But older boys spend most of their time with other boys.

Relevant in speculating about gender differences in the transition is the distinction between the psychological abilities emerging during the transition and the specific behavioral patterns. It seems, from the capability of both boys and girls to do a wide range of tasks, that psychological abilities are transferable across tasks like caretaking, family protection, play, domestic tasks, food gathering and sharing, and so forth. But the differences between juvenile girls and boys specifically in caretaking experiences or in threat and defense, although these might have led to specialization in abilities, is much more likely due to

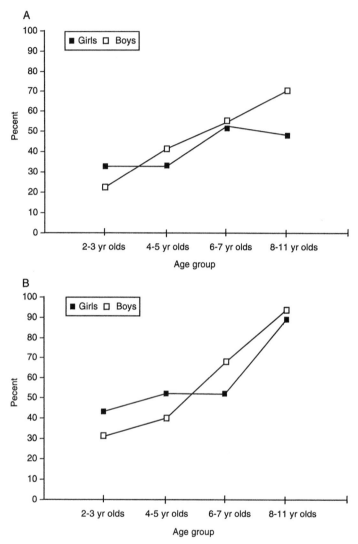

Figure 14.2 Children's interactions with other children and with their peers. (a, top) Percentage of home and courtyard observations of children ages 2 to 11 in which all children within a child's interactional space are of the same sex as the child observed. (b, bottom) Percentage of home and courtyard observations of peers (±2 years of age) in which all children within a child's interactional space are of the same sex as the child observed. All data for Fig. 14.2 are from *Children of Different Worlds: The Formation of Social Behavior* (pp. 229–230), by B. Whiting and C. Edwards. Cambridge, MA: Harvard University Press.

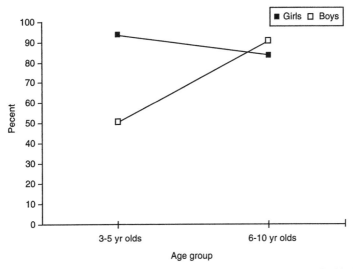

Figure 14.3   Percentage of all social interactions of Abaluyia children ages 3 to 10 with children of the same sex.

the nearly universal sociocultural fact that most "mothering" (e.g., parenting in the prejuvenile years) is done by women and girls (Chodorow, 1974; Maccoby & Jacklin, 1973).

Indirect Care by Parents

Parenting during and after the 5 to 7 period increasingly involves indirect care. Parents provide support and nurturance for children as much by ensuring that others will consistently participate in providing this support after the 5 to 7 transition as in doing so directly themselves (Whiting & Edwards, 1988). Children are expected to provide such care, with a more indirect, managerial parenting role than when children were 4 or under. Of course, this is not to say that children under 4 are not cared for by others, nor that children of age 7 or 8 have no direct interactions and continuing close relationships with their parents. Rather, the pattern of cultural activities shifts to place children more often with peers, and multiage groups of children and other adults, and less often in close proximity to their parents or primary caretakers for most of the day. It structures increasingly independent responsibility for children about these ages. As many mothers in Kenya told me in interviews and conversations, indirect care by others and good parenting go together; insuring good placement of one's children and seeing sibling caretaking functioning in everyday practice in the family daily routine are good parenting (Weisner, 1987).

Complex Responsibility Training

Nurturance and support are learned and practiced in the context of increasingly complex responsibility training for many other tasks. Child care and nurturance as part of a specific, baby-sitting role, are both more and less important during and after the 5 to 7 shift. They are more important in that for 7-year-olds child care and nurturance are often more culturally elaborated, with clear expectations, and with mistakes in their enactment strongly sanctioned. Gender differences further elaborate on the role. But it is less important in that the tasks of child minding are merged in everyday cultural activities with other tasks. Super (1983), for instance, showed that children among the Kipsigis of western Kenya increase their domestic work time from around 30% at age 4 to more than 50% by age 7 and older, while play and idle time decline. The typical Kipsigis girl is likely to be in charge of a younger child while doing such tasks, whereas boys increasingly move away from the home, doing herding. Among the Abaluyia, some 9% of all interactions between mothers and children involve instructions and requests regarding child care, and another 17% (20% for girls, 14% for boys) involves other domestic tasks and chores (Weisner, 1987). Children minding other children are also tending the fire, selling in a shop, weeding in a garden, minding small animals, husking corn, playing games, doing their school homework in a group, and running errands. Child minding is culturally an important kind of domestic task, rather than the highly specialized "baby-sitting" activity, kept somewhat separate from family adaptation and survival in the wider world, that it is in the West.

Varied Emotional and Affective Climate

The emotional and affective climate that surrounds caretaking and social support by children of other children is varied across cultures. Children's caretaking is not necessarily characterized by warmth or empathy, for instance. Among the Abaluyia, where child caretaking and support are common and where children have substantial responsibility for managing their domestic tasks and assisting parents, aggression, teasing, and dominance often accompany support. For instance, a 9-year-old Abaluyia child will be carrying a toddler around, and the younger child wants some food. The older child refuses to give the younger child food, proceeding to eat the food herself. At the same time, food is frequently used to soothe and comfort children and adults and child caretakers alike. Or a younger child gets teased by having a burning stick from the fire poked at him or her; the younger child is scared and cries; the older children laugh. Later that same morning, the older child (age 9) comforts the younger sibling, whom he has often caused to cry, get scared, and run out of the house.

Comfort and support thus co-occur, in children's experience and in activities in the daily routine, with dominance, teasing, and fear (Weisner, 1979). Broch has observed the following among the Bonerate, an isolated small island community in Indonesia (1990):

> One day I observed two children, a boy and a girl, who were looking after their younger siblings. They moved to the edge of the village where the toddlers were teased until they started to cry, to the great amusement of the caretakers. They continued to trouble their charges for a while before they picked them up. Then they returned, hugging the crying youngsters and showing all villagers how kindly they tried to comfort them! (P. 81)

The same kin network that (usually) can be counted on for support can also be counted on to dominate, tease, even exploit.

Similarly, verbal exchanges and elaborated, question-framed discourse do not necessarily accompany support and nurturance for children. For instance, in some 49 hours of observations of support and nurturance among the Abaluyia, there were no instances of support accompanied by the kind of empathic, verbal interactions more common in Western, middle-class relationships (Weisner, 1979). The kinds of verbal and visual contingent responsiveness commonly associated with mother-child interactions in Western studies and learned by siblings (Dunn, 1985; Dunn and Kendrick, 1982; Mendelson, 1990) are not necessarily found in either parents or children in many preindustrial samples. The Western cultural script of treating the young child as a coequal interlocutor, even though the younger child is not yet linguistically capable, is highly elaborated in Western models of maternal responsiveness, but not in other cultural places (Ochs & Schieffelin, 1984). This is both a cross-cultural difference and a difference owing to low or no maternal formal schooling (LeVine et al., 1991; Richman, Miller, & LeVine, 1992). The point for purposes of understanding children's participation in caretaking and support is that appropriate and responsible care and support are culturally encouraged in children during the 5 to 7 transition, but the same kind of emotional climate and the verbal responsiveness associated with such support in Western cultures are present much less often.

But a deep sense that socially distributed support is both available to children and an activity in which children are expected to participate is present. The culturally elaborated ways—the styles and routinely expected activities—in which this support is manifested and culturally organized differ. Western children do not necessarily experience more nurturance and support but rather, a different way of culturally organizing it.

Children's Social and Intellectual Competence

Social and intellectual competence in children is judged by the children's competence in doing child-care and domestic tasks, as well as by their successful social functioning in the wider community. Sending children on errands that require knowledge of kinship terms and rules for interaction marks their developmental maturity, and doing this task well is a sign of "responsible intelligence," as well as skill at verbal quickness, which is often used later in development and when they become adults (Harkness & Super, 1982, 1992). Serpell has pointed to the many variations within the diverse meanings of intelligence in many African societies, including (a) cognitive cleverness, (b) cooperativeness, and (c) social responsibility (Serpell, 1977, 1982, 1993). He quoted this definition of intelligence among the Chewa in Zambia: *"to be able to be sent out; . . . one who is willing to go."* The Abaluyia described as "bright" or intelligent those children who could mind others with little supervision or discussion *and* those who did well in school. Nerlove described two criteria for local community folk judgments of "smartness" among children in the Guatemalan villages she studied: the ability to sustain self-managed sequences of activities (e.g., in doing tasks by oneself) and the ability to engage in and sustain social exchanges throughout the community (Nerlove, Roberts, & Klein, 1975). Children living in Bonerate are given tasks and child-care responsibilities at the same time (Broch, 1990):

> When children are from five to six years old they are delegated their first chores of importance in the daily activities of the household. . . . The assignments are, however, always adjusted to their physical age and mental maturity, as interpreted by their parents. (P. 79)

Abaluyia mothers in western Kenya use evidence that a child had the ability to give and receive social support and assist others as markers of a child's more general intellectual development level, much as an American parent might use literacy skills such as knowing the alphabet or numbers or displaying verbal facility to show how grown-up or precocious his or her child is. African mothers proudly include helpfulness and task competence as evidence that their children are maturing successfully. Intelligence as a mental ability and competence in social context are tied to the abilities of children to provide social support and nurturance. Motor skills in children and responsible compliance to others' requests are used as signs of intelligence (Super, 1991). Being "smart" yet *not* being socially competent is a difficult idea to grasp for communities that depend on socially distributed support.

Literacy, urban residence, and formal schooling are changing this picture, of course (Kilbride & Kilbride, 1990). Children are watched closely for success in school grades and national examinations and are encouraged where possible to continue schooling if they do well. Yet other skills are still valued in both rural and urban contexts, and change may sometimes have altered the form of cognitive skills or the way in which they are displayed, more than they have changed underlying cognitive capacities (Weisner, 1976c). For instance, cognitive assessments of Abaluyia children ages 5 to 11 in both Kisa and Nairobi showed urban-rural differences in how children approached cognitive tasks, but only small differences in the children's overall ability owing to urban or rural residence. For instance, urban-resident children were bolder with the testers and tried out more solutions to the problems presented to them, but the proportion of correct responses did not differ between city-resident and country-resident children. Urban-resident and schooled children did give more partially correct answers to most of the cognitive tasks administered, however, and had better facility in English and Kiswahili because of their greater exposure to both languages in Nairobi.

Furthermore, those children observed to participate more actively in sibling caretaking in either setting, in fact, did somewhat better in primary school (assessed by final exams administered at the school or by the national Kenya Primary Examination, as shown in Figure 14.4. Children involved in caretaking and domestic tasks talked together about schoolwork, used English and Kiswahili more often, and played games children played in school. They integrated their school-acquired abilities into their tasks and caretaking. Education levels of parents (in a range from none to about 2 years of secondary school, with a median of 4 years) were unrelated to parents' beliefs about and commitment to shared caretaking. There is no evidence that the two kinds

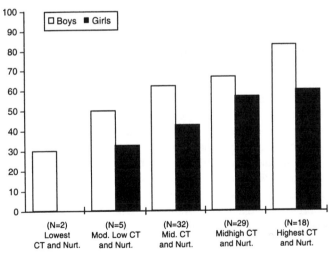

Figure 14.4   Relationship between caretaking experience (CT) and nurturing (Nurt.), and rank in upper primary school, for Abaluyia children ($n = 86$). The x-axis shows the mean percentile rank in upper primary school class (ages $11-17+$). The y-axis charts the times observed in caretaking (CT) role/proportion of nurturant (Nurt.) interactions (ages $4-11$).

of competence—schooled and community-social—are mutually exclusive or cannot both continue as valued indicators of child competence.

Families living in Nairobi often left part of their sibling group behind, and the nature of tasks and shared management changed dramatically because of the breakup of the sibling group. Partly as a result, urban-resident children, compared with rural-resident children, showed more disruptive and aggressive behaviors, less sociability, and less shared task performance, and sought out their mothers for interaction (and disturbed them) more than did rural-resident children (Weisner, 1987). This is primarily due to the absence of older children from the Nairobi households. Older children were more likely to be needed for farmwork, remained in school in the rural areas, had difficulty finding appropriate city housing, and were kept home owing to parental concerns over the dangers and bright lights of the city and the costs of supporting children there. Because these rural and urban families were carefully matched by the father's age, education, and kinship affiliation, it was clear from parents' reports and ethnographic comparisons that the breakup of the child caretaking and sibling group support network led to this change in interaction—not selective migration or changes in parents' beliefs about appropriate caretaking or education for children.

The Cultural Complex Sustaining Shared Management

There is a culture complex that seems to favor the cultural elaboration of socially distributed support in an age-graded, shared-management family caretaking system for children, beginning around age 5 to 7. A culture complex includes characteristics of community beliefs and values, ecology, demography, and social history, which often occur together and which mutually support and reinforce each other. The competencies emerging in children at the 5 to 7 period are then used by families to solve some of the adaptive problems characteristic of their culture complex.

None of the features clustered together in such a culture complex, whether alone or in combination, are necessary or sufficient for child involvement in shared domestic-management and socially distributed support. Many aspects of child caretaking and shared support can and do occur in families and communities around the world in the absence of the features defining any particular culture complex. Similarly, features related to children's involvements in shared support are found at least to some degree most everywhere in the world regardless of a particular culture complex. For instance, low-fertility and low-mortality demographic patterns do not preclude such child activities nor do relatively egalitarian gender roles in childhood, formal schooling, or more egalitarian family relationships. However, culturally elaborated and sanctioned child caretaking and support typically occur along with at least some of the following ecological-cultural complex of features:

- High total fertility and declining child and parent mortality (Caldwell, 1982; Hewlett, 1991; LeVine & White, 1986). A consequence of these conditions often means that there are many children who are available for caretaking and who require care, and much work to be done, and that children are close in age, with an interbirth interval smaller than 5 years.

- Sibling caretaking an accepted and well-understood cultural practice (Weisner & Gallimore, 1977). Not all families necessarily follow the practice, but it is a routine option, among others, for raising children. Parents and children do not have to explain why or what they are doing. It is a shared cultural script for a child's and parents' development together. Preindustrial cross-cultural samples show that about 35% of the time older children are the caretakers of younger children after infancy (Barry & Paxson, 1971).

- High moral importance placed on shared family social support and child caretaking (Edwards, 1993; Nsamenang, 1992). This is a transition for children that is culturally significant, one that matters to parents and to the community. The sibling relationship may stand as high or higher than do other close relationships (mother-child; husband-wife, etc.) as the culturally idealized close relationship (Marshall, 1983).

- Mobile families may be living in more than one household or exploiting more than one resource for subsistence and support (Weisner, 1976a). Families with members gone for wage labor elsewhere will often commute from one place to another and will have children live in different places to assist in child care and work for the family (Ross & Weisner, 1977). Child lending, fosterage, and adoption practices are frequently present as well (E. Goody, 1982; J. Goody, 1969).

- High variability in family composition, size, and fertility within the community (Hewlett, 1991). Families will be at different points in their development cycle; others will not have high total fertility or low mortality. This variability encourages the sharing of children between households of related kin to assist in child care or work and perhaps to permit children to attend school while living with kin.

- Heavy maternal domestic workload (Minturn & Lambert, 1964; Munroe, Munroe, & Shimmen, 1984; Reynolds, 1991; Whiting & Whiting, 1975). Work that takes mothers out of the home for long periods of time and domestic work that requires help from others mean that children and other adults are needed for the maintenance of the domestic routine.

- Gender role differences (Bradley, 1993; Burton, Brudner, & White, 1977; Munroe, Shimmen, & Munroe, 1984). Tasks for boys and girls and for men and women are relatively clear, and gender roles are often segregated.

- Clear status and authority distinction between child and adult. There is unlikely to be a strong cultural presumption of even pseudo-equality between parents and children. Children are expected to invest in the family "estate," both economically with their labor and socially. Hierarchy and deference distinctions within the family are usually clearly marked (Caldwell, 1982).

- Child apprenticeship for caretaking and domestic tasks during and following the 5 to 7 transition. Seldom are there formal instructions or "schooled" learning that begin at this period. Rather, children learn through "enterprise engagement" in the tasks themselves, learning through observation and direct experience. Children are familiar with "pivot roles" (Mead, 1928/1961), in which they are often simultaneously a caretaker or doing a task and being taken care of and supervised in a task by an older, more competent or senior child or adult (Gallimore, Boggs, & Jordan, 1974; Jordan, 1985). Although cultural training is usually apprentice-based, schooling is not incompatible with such training. Indeed, as shown in Figure 14.4, the two kinds of competencies can co-occur.

An Ecocultural Approach to the 5 to 7 Transition: Four Developmental Questions

The ecocultural approach to the 5 to 7 transition focuses on the cultural project of constructing a daily routine and on the shift in interactions and practices that occur very widely around the world during this period. From this point of view, the questions raised in the introduction to our volume—whether there is a 5 to 7 transition, whether changes are quantitative or qualitative, whether there are continuous or discontinuous transitions, and whether there is a reorganization of existing patterns or new ones—can be answered, but in a form somewhat revised from the way they are presented there.

By age 8, children clearly interact differently and participate in cultural practices differently from the ways they did when they were 4. Cultures around the world recognize this in the roles and expectations they have for children at the beginning and end of this period. Families in many societies have utilized the developmental transition as an opportunity for new adaptations that have assisted in child care and domestic tasks specifically and shared social support generally.

At the same time, the adaptive value of both the cultural practices and the children's abilities has evolved because children were maturing in families where younger siblings, following after the 5- to 7-year-old child, were being born. Caretaking and assistance in sustaining the family domestic routine—features of the developmental context around the child—would encourage many of the abilities seen in children of that age. There is an interaction between child abilities afforded by evolution and cultural projects shaping children's development.

These differences at the cultural level are differences in both quantity and quality. Children participate as younger apprentices in caretaking and domestic activities, which as older children they continue in, but now as more active organizers and managers. These pivot roles are characteristic of the 5 to 7 transition. The interactional opportunities and cultural practices are there at both younger and older ages; but the quality of the child's participation shifts.

These shifts are continuous for the same reason. Children are less competent at age 4, but they are, nonetheless, gaining the experience, through redundant participation with older children and parents, that will, in turn, lead them to take on much more competent roles by age 8. The child makes a gradual transition in cultures prepared for such gradual assumption of new tasks.

Hence, the transition is the reorganization of existing patterns of interaction and cultural practices for the child. This follows from the view that the 5 to 7 transition is an opportunity and a challenge for family and community adaptation. From the point of view of the cultural tools for adaptation available to parents, the transition is a reorganization of practices encoded in cultural beliefs and values regarding children of different ages. These beliefs are encoded because, at least to some degree, they have been found useful in prior adaptive efforts.

Conclusion

The 5 to 7 period transition influences and is influenced by different cultural projects for children and for families around the world. It is a period in many cultures when children are asked to assume new functions in the family, such as caretaking, social involvements in the wider community, subsistence tasks, and increased involvement in domestic tasks within the family. These changes are a part of the more fundamental family adaptive task of sustaining a daily routine of life.

The 5 to 7 transition is striking in how well children seem to fit into varying requirements of their cultural settings. This is a period of life when children in most societies seem able to meet relatively well the developmental task of understanding the social rules and cultural meanings around them and seem able to use creatively those rules and meanings in everyday interactions rather than to resist or rebel against cultural expectations. This is not to underemphasize the workload, emotional struggles, and conflicts that children do have, a number of which are mentioned in this chapter, or to present this transition in an overromanticized, idyllic way. Nonetheless, the 5 to 7 period is characteristically not a period of rebellion from social conventions but, to the contrary, a time when children seem to hunger to acquire more and more skill in using and understanding those conventions. It is a period when children appear capable of achieving a significantly more complex and subtle ability to understand and model the roles of their parents and of older children; they want to do this and want approbation at success.

Some Western parents struggling with their children's transition to formal schooling may be surprised at this characterization. The "school-age transition" can be a time of great uncertainty and concern for parents and children. But the nature of the tasks and activities of classrooms may produce the struggle, not something inherent in the 5 to 7 transition. A whole new world of peers; a new everyday routine; greater separation from home, parents, and siblings; and new and perhaps invidious evaluations of competence can all make for a difficult transition. Age-graded classrooms run by a single adult manager-teacher provide little opportunity for the development of the kinds of competencies described in this chapter. The 5 to 7 transition viewed as a shift in the competence of children to participate in tasks of family caretaking and survival is not without struggle. But the transition does not have such sharp and different developmental tasks as literacy and numeracy training in a room with 30 children of the same age in classrooms with a cultural routine very different from the home and family.

There is a relative lack of attention to the emergence of social support and caretaking skills during the 5 to 7 period and after in Western psychology, perhaps because of the focus on school changes and on individual, rather than cultural, transitions. The ecological circumstances of early middle childhood in the middle class of the industrialized world, although they do not eliminate support and caretaking activities, nonetheless do not encourage their cultural elaboration. This may have to do with the decline within some middle-class cultural communities of shared activities providing the opportunity for the expression and cultural elaboration of such skills. This pattern is recent, however, and is not necessarily characteristic of other ethnic and immigrant communities in the United States. Historically, children in North America were routinely involved in their families' farm, trade, or business activities. Various ethnic minority communities throughout North America, such as some African American, Latino, or Asian American groups, have continued to emphasize shared support and child caretaking responsibility, as do many European American families. There are many reasons for this having to do with economic and ecological pressures, historical traditions in these communities, the need for self-reliance owing to threat and discrimination, or moral and religious values. And there are signs that increasing work pressures on dual-income families, on single-parent households, and on others may be increasing the roles that children are playing in caretaking and tasks.

But families in the West attempt socially distributed caretaking and support under very difficult circumstances. Families are separated by divorce and by residential norms and cultural expectations of autonomy driving apart those who might co-participate with children in shared support. The middle-class legal system may define care of young children by older, preadolescent children as exploitative of the children, or illegal in some circumstances. Although such care can become exploitative, it need not. There is considerable evidence that under appropriate adult direction and cultural supports, children are prepared for active participation in such systems of shared child care and domestic management.

During a period of history as rapidly changing and uncertain as the present one, it is important to keep available as much knowledge as we have about the many ways that cultural communities around the world have defined and utilized the abilities of children during the 5 to 7 period. This is a storehouse of cultural knowledge—of tools for family adaptation—worthy of renewed comparative study. These adaptive cultural tools should be studied in cultural context, along with their costs and benefits to children, families, and communities. Cultural practices of shared social support are a widespread example of such tools and clearly have taken advantage of children's abilities that develop at the time of the 5 to 7 transition.

Acknowledgments

This chapter was originally presented as a paper at a conference, "The 5–7 Shift: Biopsychosocial Transitions," sponsored by the MacArthur Foundation Transitions Network, Marco Island, Florida, November 1992. NIMH; Carnegie Corporation of New York; the Child Development Research Unit of Kenyatta University College, Nairobi; the Academic Senate research grant program, University of California, Los Angeles; the Kamehameha School/B. P. Bishop Estate, Hawaii; and the Department of Psychiatry and Biobehavioral Sciences of UCLA had all provided support for the Kenya and Hawaiian research presented. Portions of this chapter are adapted from Weisner, 1989, and Weisner, in press.

References

Barry, H., & Paxson, L. M. (1971). Infancy and early childhood: Cross-cultural codes 2. *Ethnology, 10,* 466–508.

Blurton-Jones, N. (1986). Bushman birth spacing: A test for optimal interbirth intervals. *Ethology and Sociobiology, 7,* 91–105.

Blurton-Jones, N. (1990). Three sensible paradigms for research on evolution and human behavior? *Ethology and Sociobiology, 11,* 353–359.

Bogin, B. (1988). *Patterns of human growth.* Cambridge: Cambridge University Press.

Borgerhoff-Mulder, M. (1991). Human behavioural ecology. In J. R. Krebs & N. B. Davies (Eds.), *Behavioural ecology: An evolutionary approach* (pp. 69–98). New York: Blackwell.

Bradley, C. (1993). Women's power, children's labor. *Cross-cultural research: The Journal of Comparative Social Science, 27* (1 and 2), 70–96.

Broch, H. B. (1990). *Growing up agreeably: Bonerate childhood observed.* Honolulu: University of Hawaii Press.

Bronfenbrenner, U. (1979). *The ecology of human development: Experiments by nature and human design.* Cambridge, MA: Harvard University Press.

Burton, M. L., Brudner, L. A., & White, D. R. (1977). A model of the sexual division of labor. *American Ethnologist, 4,* 227–251.

Caldwell, J. (1982). *Theory of fertility decline.* London: Academic Press.

Cheney, D. L., & Seyfarth, R. L. (1990). *How monkeys see the world.* Chicago: University of Chicago Press.

Chisholm, J. S. (1983). *Navajo infancy: An ethological study of child development.* Hawthorne, NY: Aldine de Gruyter.

Chisholm, J. S. (1992). Putting people in biology: Toward a synthesis of biological and psychological anthropology. In T. Schwartz, G. M. White, & C. A. Lutz (Eds.), *New directions in psychological anthropology* (pp. 125–149). New York: Cambridge University Press.

Chodorow, N. (1974). *The reproduction of mothering: Psychoanalysis and the sociology of gender.* Berkeley: University of California Press.

Cole, M. (1985). The zone of proximal development: Where culture and cognition create each other. In J. Wertsch (Ed.), *Culture, communication, and cognition* (pp. 146–161). New York: Cambridge University Press.

Cosmides, L., & Tooby, J. (1989). Evolutionary psychology and the generation of culture, Part II. *Ethology and Sociobiology, 10,* 51–97.

D'Andrade, R. (1987). A folk model of the mind. In D. Holland & N. Quinn (Eds.), *Cultural models in language and thought* (pp. 112–148). New York: Cambridge University Press.

D'Andrade, R. (1992). Schemas and motivation. In R. D'Andrade & C. Strauss (Eds.), *Human motives and cultural models* (pp. 23–44). New York: Cambridge University Press.

Dunn, J. (1985). *Sisters and brothers.* Cambridge, MA: Harvard University Press.

Dunn, J., & Kendrick, C. (1982). *Siblings: Love, envy and understanding.* Cambridge, MA: Harvard University Press.

Edwards, C. P. (1993). Behavioral sex differences in children of diverse cultures: The case of nurturance to infants. In M. E. Pereira & L. A. Fairbanks (Eds.), *Juvenile primates: Life history, development, and behavior* (pp. 327–338). New York: Oxford University Press.

Ember, C. (1981). A cross-cultural perspective on sex differences. In R. H. Munroe, R. L. Munroe, & B. B. Whiting (Eds.), *Handbook of cross-cultural human development* (pp. 531–580). New York: Garland Press.

Gallimore, R., Boggs, J. W., & Jordan, C. (1974). *Culture, behavior, and education.* Beverly Hills, CA: Sage Books.

Gallimore, R., Weisner, T. S., Kaufman, S. Z., & Bernheimer, L. P. (1989). The social construction of ecocultural niches: Family accommodation of developmentally delayed children. *American Journal of Mental Retardation, 94* (3), 216–230.

Goody, E. (1982). *Parenthood and social reproduction: Fostering and occupational roles in West Africa.* Cambridge: Cambridge University Press.

Goody, J. (1969). Adoption in cross-cultural perspective. *Comparative Studies in Society and History, 11,* 55–78.

Harkness, S., & Super, C. M. (1982). Why African children are so hard to test. In L. L. Adler (Ed.), *Cross-cultural research at issue* (pp. 145–152). New York: Academic Press.

Harkness, S., & Super, C. M. (1992). Shared child care in East Africa: Sociocultural origins and developmental consequences. In M. E. Lamb, K. J. Sternberg, C.-P. Hwang, & A. G. Broberg (Eds.), *Child care in context: Cross-cultural perspectives* (pp. 441–459). Hillsdale, NJ: Erlbaum.

Hewlett, B. (1991). Demography and childcare in preindustrial societies. *Journal of Anthropological Research, 47* (1), 1–37.

Jordan, C. (1985). Translating culture: From ethnographic information to educational program. *Anthropology and Education Quarterly, 16,* 106–123.

Kessen, W. (1979). The American child and other cultural inventions. *American Psychologist, 34* (10), 815–820.

Kilbride, P. L., & Kilbride, J. C. (1990). *Changing family life in East Africa: Women and children at risk.* University Park: Pennsylvania State University Press.

Leiderman, P. H., & Leiderman, G. F. (1974a). Affective and cognitive consequences of polymatric infant care in the East African highlands. *Minnesota Symposium on Child Psychology, 8,* 81–109.

Leiderman, P. H., & Leiderman, G. F. (1974b). Familial influences on infant development in an East African agricultural community. In E. J. Anthony, & C. Koupernek (Eds.), *The child in his family: Children at psychiatric risk* (Vol. 3). New York: Wiley.

LeVine, R. (1977). Child rearing as cultural adaptation. In P. Leiderman, S. Tulkin, & A. Rosenfeld (Eds.), *Culture and infancy* (pp. 15–27). New York: Academic Press.

LeVine, R. A., LeVine, S. E., Richman, A., Uribe, F. M. T., Correwa, S. C., & Miller, P. M. (1991). Women's schooling and child care in the demographic transition: A Mexican case study. *Population and Development Review, 17* (3), 459–496.

LeVine, R., & White, M. I. (1986). *Human conditions: The cultural basis of educational development.* London: Routledge & Kegan Paul.

Maccoby, E., & Jacklin, C. (1973). *The development of sex differences.* Stanford, CA: Stanford University Press.

Marshall, M. (Ed.). (1983). *Siblingship in Oceania: Studies in the meaning of kin relations* (ASAO Monograph No. 8). Lanham, MD: University Press of America.

Mead, M. (1961). *Coming of age in Samoa.* New York: New American Library. (Original work published 1928).

Mendelson, M. J. (1990). *Becoming a brother: A child learns about life, family, and self.* Cambridge, MA: MIT Press.

Minturn, L., & Lambert, W. (1964). *Mothers of six cultures.* New York: Wiley.

Munroe, R. H., Munroe, R. L., & Shimmin, H. S. (1984). Children's work in four cultures: Determinants and consequences. *American Anthropologist, 86,* 369–379.

Munroe, R. H., Munroe, R. L., & Whiting, B. B. (Eds.). (1981). *Handbook of cross-cultural human development.* New York: Garland STPM Press.

Munroe, R. H., Shimmin, H. S., & Munroe, R. L. (1984). Gender understanding and sex role preference in four cultures. *Developmental Psychology, 20,* 673–682.

Nerlove, S. B., Roberts, J. M., & Klein, R. E. (1975, April). Dimensions of listura ("smartness"): Community judgments of rural Guatemalan children. In P. Draper (Chair), *Experimental correlates of cognitive abilities.* Symposium conducted at the biennial meeting of the Society for Research in Child Development, Denver, CO.

Nerlove, S. B., Roberts, J. M., Klein, R. E., Yarbrough, C., & Habicht, J. P. (1974). Natural indicators of cognitive development: An observational study of rural Guatemalan children. *Ethos, 2* (3), 265–295.

Nerlove, S., & Snipper, A. (1981). Cognitive consequences of cultural opportunity. In R. H. Munroe, R. L. Munroe, & B. B. Whiting (Eds.), *Handbook of cross-cultural human development* (pp. 423–474). New York: Garland STPM Press.

Nsamenang, B. A. (1992). Early childhood care and education in Cameroon. In M. E. Lamb, K. J. Sternberg, C.-P. Hwang, & A. G. Broberg (Eds.), *Child care in context: Cross-cultural perspectives* (pp. 419–439). Hillsdale, NJ: Erlbaum.

Ochs, Eleanor, & Schieffelin, B. B. (1984). Language acquisition and socialization. In R. A. Schweder & R. A. LeVine (Eds.), *Culture Theory* (pp. 276–320). New York and London: Cambridge University Press.

Pereira, M. E. (1993). Juvenality in animals. In M. E. Pereira & L. A. Fairbanks (Eds.), *Juvenile primates: Life history, development, and behavior* (pp. 17–27). New York: Oxford University Press.

Pereira, M. E., & Fairbanks, L. A. (Eds.). (1993). *Juvenile primates: Life history, development, and behavior.* New York: Oxford University Press.

Reed, G., & Leiderman, P. H. (1981). Age-related changes in attachment behavior in polymatrically reared infants: The Kenyan Gusii. In T. H. Field, A. M. Sostek, P. Vietze, & P. H. Leiderman (Eds.), *Culture and early interactions* (pp. 215–234). Hillsdale, NJ: LEA Press.

Reynolds, P. (1991). *Dance Civet Cat: Child labour in the Zambezi Valley.* Athens: Ohio University Press.

Richman, A. L., Miller, P. M., & LeVine, R. A. (1992). Cultural and educational variations in maternal responsiveness. *Developmental Psychology, 28* (4), 614–621.

Rogoff, B. (1982). Integrating context and cognitive development. In M. E. Lamb & A. L. Brown (Eds.), *Advances in developmental psychology* (Vol. 2, pp. 125–170). Hillsdale, NJ: Erlbaum.

Rogoff, B. (1990). *Apprenticeship in thinking: Cognitive development in social context.* Oxford: Oxford University Press.

Rogoff, B. Newcombe, N., Fox, N., & Ellis, S. (1980). Transitions in children's roles and capabilities. *International Journal of Psychology, 15,* 181–200.

Rogoff, B., Sellers, M. J., Pirrotta, S., Fox, N., & White, S. H. (1975). Age of assignment of roles and responsibilities to children: A cross-cultural survey. *Human Development, 18,* 353–369.

Ross, M., & Weisner, T. S. (1977). The rural-urban migrant network in Kenya: Some general implications. *American Ethnologist, 4,* 359–375.

Sameroff, A., & Chandler, M. (1975). Reproductive risk and the continuum of caretaking casualty. In F. D. Horowitz, M. Hetherington, S. Scarr-Salapatek, & G. Siefel (Eds.), *Review of child development research* (Vol. 4, pp. 84–104). Hillsdale, NJ: Erlbaum.

Serpell, R. (1977). Estimates of intelligence in a rural community of eastern Zambia. In F. M. Okatcha (Ed.), *Modern psychology and cultural adaptation* (pp. 179–216). Nairobi, Kenya: Swahili Language Consultants and Publishers.

Serpell, R. (1982). Measures of perception, skills and intelligence: The growth of a new perspective on children in a third world country. In W. W. Hartup (Ed.), *Review of child development research* (Vol. 6, pp. 392–440). Chicago: University of Chicago Press.

Serpell, R. (1992). African dimensions of child care and nurturance. In M. E. Lamb, K. J. Sternberg, C. P. Hwang, & A. G. Broberg (Eds.), *Child care in context: Cross-cultural perspectives* (pp. 463–476). Hillsdale, NJ: Erlbaum.

Serpell, R. (1993). *The significance of schooling: Life-journeys in an African society.* Cambridge: Cambridge University Press.

Serpell, R. (in press). Afrocentrism: What contribution to the science of developmental psychology?

Shibadu, G. C. (1978). Children's labour contributions in Hamisi Division (Kakamega). Unpublished B.A. dissertation, Department of Sociology, University of Nairobi, Kenya.

Super, C. (1983). Cultural variations in the meaning and use of children's "intelligence." In J. B. Deregowski, S. Dziurawiec, & R. C. Annis (Eds.), *Expiscations in cross-cultural psychology* (pp. 199–212). Lisse, The Netherlands: Swets & Zeitlinger.

Super, C. (1991). Developmental transitions of cognitive functioning in rural Kenya and metropolitan America. In K. Gibson, M. Konner, & J. Lancaster (Eds.), *The brain and behavioral development: Biosocial dimensions* (pp. 225–257). Hawthorne, NY: Aldine de Gruyter.

Super, C., & Harkness, S. (Eds.). (1980). *Anthropological perspectives on child development: New directions for child development, No. 8.* San Francisco: Jossey-Bass.

Super, C. M., and Harkness, S. (1986). The developmental niche: A conceptualization at the interface of child and culture. *International Journal of Behavior Development, 9,* 1–25.

Tharp, R. G., & Gallimore, R. (1988). *Rousing minds to life: Teaching, learning, and schooling in social context.* Cambridge: Cambridge University Press.

Tooby, J., & Cosmides, L. (1989). Evolutionary psychology and the generation of culture, Part 1. *Ethology and Sociobiology, 10,* 29–49.

Vygotsky, L. (1978). *Mind in society: The development of higher psychological processes,* M. Cole, V. John-Steiner, S. Scribner, & E. Souberman, Eds. Cambridge, MA: Harvard University Press.

Wagner, G. (1970). *The Bantu of western Kenya.* Vol. *1.* London: Oxford University Press. (Original work published in 1949.)

Weisner, T. S. (1976a). The structure of sociability: Urban migration and urban-rural ties in Kenya. *Urban anthropology, 5,* 199–223.

Weisner, T. S. (1976b). Kariobangi: The case history of a squatter resettlement scheme in Kenya. In W. Arens (Ed.), *A century of change in Eastern Africa* (pp. 77–99). The Hague and Paris: Mouton Publishers.

Weisner, T. S. (1976c). Urban-rural differences in African children's performance on cognitive and memory tasks. *Ethos, 4,* 223–250.

Weisner, T. S. (1979). Urban-rural differences in sociable and disruptive behavior of Kenya children. *Ethnology, 18* (2), 153–172.

Weisner, T. S. (1982). Sibling interdependence and child caretaking: A cross-cultural view. In M. Lamb & B. Sutton-Smith (Eds.), *Sibling relationships: Their nature and significance across the lifespan* (pp. 305–327). Hillsdale, NJ: LEA Press.

Weisner, T. S. (1984). Ecocultural niches of middle childhood: A cross-cultural perspective. In W. A. Collins (Ed.), *Development during middle childhood: The years from six to twelve* (pp. 335–369). Washington, DC: National Academy Press.

Weisner, T. S. (1987). Socialization for parenthood in sibling caretaking societies. In J. B. Lancaster, J. Altmann, A. S. Rossi, & L. R. Sherrod (Eds.), *Parenting across the lifespan: Biosocial dimensions* (pp. 237–270). New York: Aldine de Gruyter.

Weisner, T. S. (1989). Social support for children among the Abaluyia of Kenya. In D. Belle (Ed.), *Children's social networks and social supports* (pp. 70–90). New York: Wiley.

Weisner, T. S. (1993). Siblings in cultural place: Ethnographic and ecocultural perspectives on siblings of developmentally delayed children. In Z. Stoneman & P. Berman (Eds.), *Siblings of individuals with mental retardation, physical disabilities, and chronic illness* (pp. 51–83). Baltimore: Brooks.

Weisner, T. S. (in press). The crisis for families and children in Africa: Change in shared social support for children. *Health matrix: The journal of law and medicine.* Cleveland, OH: Case Western Reserve University.

Weisner, T. S., & Gallimore, R. (1977). My brother's keeper: Child and sibling caretaking. *Current Anthropology, 18,* 169–190.

Weisner, T. S., & Gallimore, R. (1985, December). Ecocultural and neo-Vygotskian models of cultural acquisition. Paper presented at the annual meeting of the American Anthropological Association, Washington, DC.

Weisner, T. S., Gallimore, R., & Jordan, C. (1988). Unpackaging cultural effects on classroom learning: Hawaiian peer assistance and child-generated activity. *Anthropology and Education Quarterly, 19,* 327–353.

Weisner, T. S., Gallimore, R., & Tharp, R. (1982). Concordance between ethnographer and folk perspectives: Observed performance and self-ascription of sibling caretaking roles. *Human Organization, 41* (3), 237–244.

Wenger, M. (1983). Gender role socialization in an East African community: Social interaction between 2 to 3 year olds and older children in social ecological perspective. Unpublished doctoral dissertation, Harvard University, Cambridge, MA.

Wenger, M. (1989). Work, play, and social relationships among children in a Giriama community. In D. Belle (Ed.), *Children's social networks and social supports* (pp. 91–115). New York: Wiley.

Were, G. S. (1967). *A history of the Abaluyia of western Kenya, c. 1500–1930.* Nairobi, Kenya: African Publishing House.

Wertsch, J. V. (1985). *Vygotsky and the social formation of mind.* Cambridge, MA: Harvard University Press.

Whiting, B., Edwards, C. (1988). *Children of different worlds: The formation of social behavior.* Cambridge, MA: Harvard University Press.

Whiting, B., & Whiting, J. W. M. (1975). *Children of six cultures: A psycho-cultural analysis.* Cambridge, MA: Harvard University Press.

Whiting, B. (1976). The problem of the packaged variable. In K. Riegel & Meacham (Eds.), *The developing individual in a changing world: Historical and cultural issues,* Vol. *1.* The Hague, The Netherlands: Mouton.

Whiting, B. (1980). Culture and social behavior: A model for the development of social behavior. *Ethos, 8,* 95–116.

PART SIX

The Transition to School

CHAPTER FIFTEEN

The Impact of the Family on Children's Early School Social Adjustment

JOAN M. BARTH AND ROSS. D. PARKE

Development can be viewed from a variety of viewpoints, but it has traditionally been approached from a developmental status perspective. According to this view, children's cognitive, social, emotional, and biological capacities are assumed to be linked to age status, and age will, in turn, determine children's level of understanding, behavior, and adaptation. A less frequently utilized approach to understanding development is the cultural agenda perspective, which assumes that culture organizes and determines the timing of children's entry into various social settings such as elementary or junior high school (Parke, 1988; Rogoff, 1990; Sameroff & Fiese, 1991) and that the management of these transitions will markedly alter children's subsequent development (Alexander & Entwisle, 1988). These two viewpoints are not independent: The concept of *readiness* is a classic example of the interplay between developmental assumptions about maturational progress and societal decisions about the optimal timing of entry into formal school environments.

In the United States age 5 is a culturally mandated turning point that signals a shift in the setting for child development from the family and other small, intimate groups (e.g., nursery school) to a larger, less intimate public context. Although the cultural agenda and developmental status viewpoints have set the timing for the transition to school, neither perspective has attended to the consequences of individual variability in the ability to negotiate this transition. Evidence suggests that children's academic and social trajectories are formed in the early stages of the transition to school (e.g., Alexander & Entwisle, 1988; Entwisle & Alexander, 1992; Kupersmidt, Coie, & Dodge, 1990; Lambert, 1988; Parker & Asher, 1987). Moreover, research suggests that family factors antecedent to the transition to school are associated with later school adjustment (Barth, 1988; Barth & Parke, 1993; Cowan, Cowan, & Heming, 1989; Cowan, Cowan, Heming, & Miller, 1992; Cowan, Cowan, Schulz, & Heming, 1994).

The goal of this chapter is to examine the role of family factors in accounting for variations in early social adaptation to school. Our decision to orient our review to social adjustment flows from the fact that most prior work has focused on the family's role in children's academic achievement and scholastic performance (Eccles & Midgley, 1989; Entwisle & Alexander, 1992). However, school adjustment involves a variety of social tasks, including understanding the complex social systems of the classroom and school, as well as the negotiation of new social relationships with teachers and peers. Hence, we view our focus on social adjustment as corrective to the relatively cognitive orientation of prior work.

As Cowan, Cowan, and Heming (1989) have noted, research examining the relations between family and school systems suffers from "contextual myopia," tending to only consider a narrow range of family or school variables. Consequently, we first provide a description of the structure of the family and school systems. A discussion of three possible mechanisms through which the family promotes school social competence follows. After presenting the model, relevant literature is reviewed, employing the model as a framework. It should be noted that an adequate understanding of family-school linkages requires that these relations be studied using longitudinal methodologies that assess family and child functioning prior to school entrance and continue to do so in the context of the school setting. Such research is rare, however (e.g., Barth, 1988; Barth & Parke, 1993; Cowan et al., 1989; Cowan et al., 1994. Concurrent analyses that rely on a "snapshot" of family-school relations fall short of describing the adjustment process. Nevertheless, key findings in these studies are often consistent with findings in longitudinal studies and point to important issues for future research. Consequently, this review includes both concurrent and longitudinal research. Finally, based on the research reviewed, some suggestions are made for future research.

Family and School as Social Systems

Families and schools are multifaceted social systems, and a description of linkages between the two systems requires the consideration of their structure (Cowan et al., 1989; Cowan et al., 1994; Parke, 1988). Both consist of subsystems that can be hierarchically organized in terms of their complexity. Describing a child's embeddedness in each system aids in understanding not only the relation between the two systems but their impact on the child as well.

Families as a Context for Social Development

Children participate in a multitier family system (e.g., Cowan et al., 1989; Cowan et al., 1994; Parke, 1988), and behavior is influenced by events at each level. Family experiences that impact on children include those that occur within the family system and those that operate outside the family but impact on family members, for example, work (Bronfenbrenner, 1979). Figure 15.1

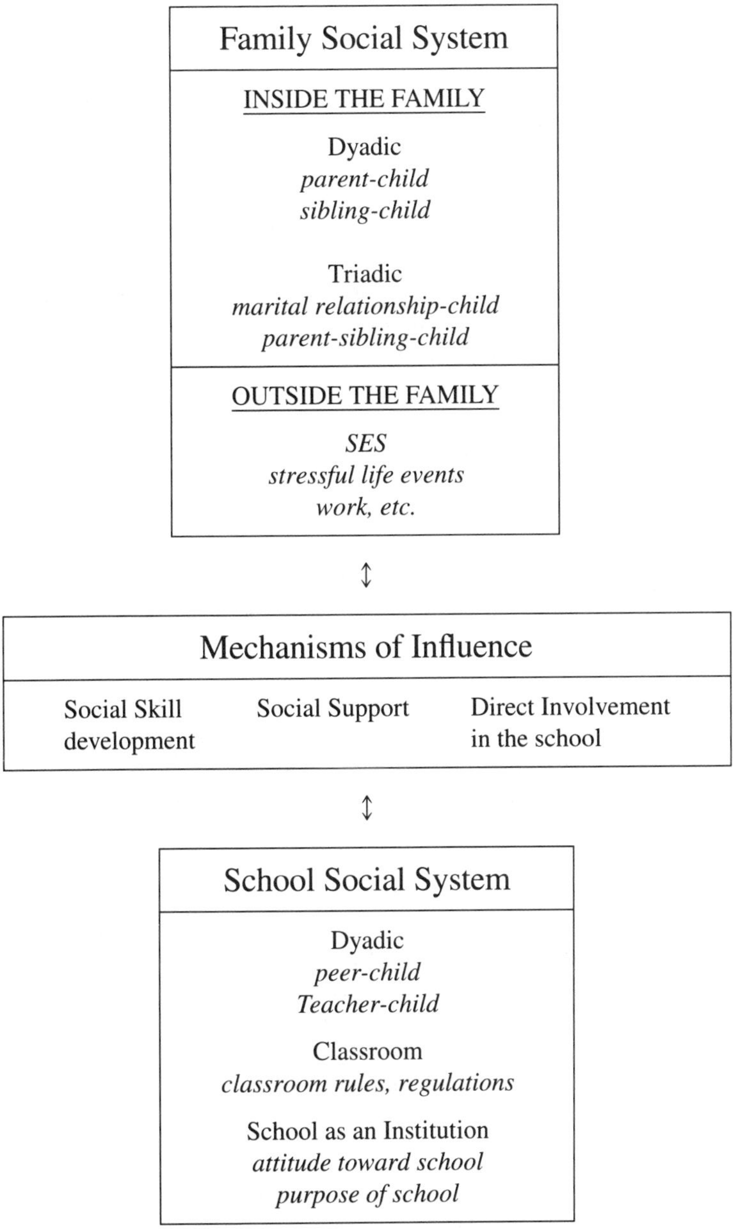

Figure 15.1   Model of family influence on children's adaptation to school.

shows a model of family influence on children's adaptation to school. At the simplest level within the family, children's school adjustment is influenced by dyadic relationships that include the child (i.e., parent-child and sibling-child relationships). The availability, quality, and style of interactions children have with each family member may influence school adjustment. Our focus is on the parent-child relationship rather than the sibling-child relationship because of the clear importance of parents during early childhood and because there is relatively little research on the impact of child-sibling relationships on school social adjustment.

Family relationships that do not directly include the child, such as the marital and parent-sibling relationships also influence children. They may impact on a child's dyadic family relationships or affect the nature of observational learning experiences in the family (Cowan et al., 1989; Emery, 1982; Howes & Markman, 1989). Influences such as these are labeled triadic because they involve at least three family members, including the child. Relatively little research has been conducted on the influence of the parent-sibling relationship on children in school. Consequently, our focus is on the impact of marital relationships on children in school.

Both dyadic and triadic relationships are affected by social systems outside the family. Low socioeconomic status (SES) has traditionally been used as an overall indicant of family hardship; however, more specific factors like parental employment and work conditions have received attention over the past decade and a half (e.g., Berndt, 1981; Bronfenbrenner, 1986; Bronfenbrenner & Crouter, 1982; Crouter, 1994; Hoffman, 1984). These social systems may promote personal stress that may impact on the quality of family relationships and the availability of family members. A child's school functioning may be affected by the resulting alterations in the more proximal family environment.

The three levels described provide a useful heuristic for describing the family's influence on a child. Functioning in one subsystem clearly has implications for the functioning in other subsystems and for the child's behavior in school. To better understand the impact of the family during the early school years, it is necessary to consider the structure of the school system and how this structure is related to social adjustment tasks.

Schools as a Context for Social Development

The family and school social systems have differences, but they also share some similarities. Compared to families, schools provide less personalized attention, more heterogeneous beliefs and values, formal evaluation, and more same-aged playmates (Farnham-Diggory, 1990; Hess & Holloway, 1984; Minuchin & Shapiro, 1983; Shipman, 1972). However, like the family system, the school system consists of interrelated multiple levels, including relations with both individuals and larger subsystems. At the simplest level, a child experiences a number of dyadic relationships with peers and teachers. Peer interactions provide opportunities for both social and cognitive development and are an integral part of school life. Teacher-student relationships are especially important during the early school years because children are more emotionally attached to teachers compared to other periods (Entwisle & Alexander, 1992).

Children experience the classroom system at a level somewhat more complex than the level of dyadic relationships with peers and teachers (Eccles & Midgley, 1989; Hamilton, 1983; Rohrkemper, 1984; Weinstein, 1989). The classroom system includes rules and norms for classroom behavior. Teachers, of course, play a major role in determining the quality of the classroom environment through their management techniques.

At an even more complex level, the child must cope with the larger school institution. Children develop a general attitude toward school as an educational and social institution (Chall, Jacobs, & Baldwin, 1990). This is important because a general dislike of school is a common and persistent problem among children with school difficulties (Moore, 1966). To summarize, the school social system incorporates teacher and peer relationships, the classroom system, and the larger school institution. Children's school adjustment concerns tasks at each level of the school system.

Dimensions of Children's Adjustment to School

At the dyadic level, children must establish favorable peer and teacher relationships. Social adjustment to peers includes peer acceptance, peer social skills, and a child's feeling toward classmates (e.g., loneliness). The importance of peer relationships for school adjustment is evident in research that shows that poor peer relationships are a significant predictor of both short-term school adjustment (Ladd, this volume, chap. 16; Ladd & Price, 1987) as well as long-term school adaptation and retention (Kupersmidt, Coie, & Dodge, 1990; Parker & Asher, 1987). Particular aspects of poor peer relationships early in school are associated with problems later: Male aggressive behavior is a predictor of increased teenage delinquency (Kellam, 1994), and children who are both shy and aggressive (e.g., loners who break rules and fight) have even higher levels of delinquency than those who are only aggressive (Kellam, 1994).

Both the teacher's perception of the student and the student's perception of the teacher are important dimensions of the teacher-student relationship. Teachers' perceptions of children's academic potential are associated with later cognitive and academic performance (Entwisle & Hayduck, 1988; Rist, 1970, 1973; Rosenthal & Jacobson, 1968; Weinstein, 1989; Weinstein, Marshall, Sharp, & Botkin, 1987). Students' expectations for achievement and classroom behavior are associated with patterns of teacher praise and criticism (Parsons, Kaczala, & Meece, 1982; Pintrich & Blumenfield, 1985; Stipek, 1992).

Adjustment at the classroom level overlaps to some degree with adjustment to teachers because of the major role teachers play in establishing the classroom environment. It includes adoption of classroom rules set by teachers and appropriate social behavior in large classroom situations. The nature of classroom regulations established by teachers may influence helpfulness (Rohrkemper, 1984), competitiveness (Marshall & Weinstein, 1984; Weinstein, 1989), and student self-expectations (Stipek, 1992). In addition, a child's perception of order and organization in the classroom is associated with more favorable classroom peer relations (Haertel, Walberg, & Haertel, 1979).

Adjustment at the institutional level is not totally independent of social adjustment at other levels. However, adjustment at the institutional level differs in that it reflects a more pervasive attitude toward school independent of particular social agents. For example, some children may approach school as an opportunity for play and socializing, whereas others may see it as a place of excessive evaluation and unpleasant work. Children with such varying attitudes may behave quite differently in school and develop distinct peer and teacher relationships. In summary, adjustment to school is best viewed as a multidimensional construct that reflects the multitier school system. We now turn to discussing how early functioning in school may be influenced by elements in the family.

Mechanisms Linking the Family and School Social Systems

Descriptions of the family and school social systems help to target aspects of each system that may affect children's behavior. However, this description does not indicate the means by which one system may influence another. Specifically, how might functioning in the family influence children's interaction with peers, teachers, the classroom, and the school system? Social adjustment research on linkages between the family and school makes evident at least three family influence roles: social skill development, social support, and direct involvement in the school setting. Social skill training may occur in a variety of contexts in the family. For example, through their interactions with family members, children may learn how to share, negotiate, and influence peers and teachers. Some skills may deliberately be encouraged by parents, whereas others may develop through the course of everyday interactions and observational learning experiences.

The social support and buffering functions of the family are evident when school experiences are the source of stress (e.g., being teased, being ostracized from group play). The quality of family relationships and the degree to which families themselves are stressed may influence the ability to accommodate their children's needs.

Furthermore, parents may be active in school programs that directly or indirectly affect the school environment and consequently influence their children's social adjustment. For example, they may volunteer to be teacher aides in classrooms, which may ease teacher overload, or they may serve on advisory committees that help determine school curriculum.

The three processes are clearly interrelated. For example, parents who have endured a number of stressful events are not likely to be school aides and may be less effective at providing social skill training and social support. The family's ability to serve in these capacities is determined by the relations among family members and their interactions with the larger social context. The influence of the family system on school adjustment through the social skill, social support, and school involvement mechanisms is the focus of the remainder of this chapter. The family system levels provide the organizing structure for the discussion, beginning with the parent-child relationship. As the review moves to more complex levels of the family, interaction between family subsystems is also discussed. As noted earlier, there are only a limited number of studies that look at adjustment over time. Consequently, the following review includes longitudinal as well as concurrent research which is pertinent to the model.

Parent-Child Relationship Influences on School Social Adjustment

Compared to other points in their children's school careers, parents of young school-aged children have considerable influence over their children's school behavior (Cowan et al., 1994) because their children are more reliant upon them for their emotional, cognitive, and physical needs. Children may develop social skills out of their day-to-day interactions with parents and by being deliberately taught skills by parents. Parents are a primary source for social support, and the parent-child relationship may buffer a child against stressful events. Outside of the family context, parents continue to exert an influence over their children's social behavior by becoming involved in the school system itself. The discussion that follows describes the multiple roles parents play in children's school adjustment.

Parent-Child Relationships and Social Skills
and Social Adaptation to School

In recent years, some consistency has emerged in the types of parent-child relationships and interaction styles associated with favorable school social adjustment. Two bodies of research can be distinguished: an attachment approach, which focuses on the impact of early infant-parent attachment, and a parenting or parent-child interaction-style approach. A sizable body of research supports the link between early mother-child attachment relationships and children's adaptation to peers in both the preschool (Arend, Gove, & Sroufe, 1979; Sroufe, 1983; Sroufe & Fleeson, 1986) and early elementary school (Renken, Egeland, Marvinney, Mangelsdorf, & Sroufe, 1989). More recently, Young-

blade and Belsky (1992) have reported links between father attachment relationships and children's friendships at age 5. This work has been extensively
reviewed elsewhere (see Sroufe, 1983; Sroufe & Fleeson, 1986).

The second tradition is illustrated by studies of the relationship between particular child-rearing styles or styles of parent-child interaction and children's
social adaptation in the early years of elementary school. Longitudinal and
concurrent studies are considered separately.

SHORT-TERM LONGITUDINAL EVIDENCE

One limitation of much previous research is that it does not permit a clear
inference that familial factors are predictive of subsequent social adjustment.
Two exceptions are studies by Barth (1988; Barth & Parke, 1993) and Cowan
and Cowan and colleagues (Cowan et al., 1989; Cowan et al., 1994) focusing
on the transition to school. These studies permit a careful examination of the
relationship between parent-child interactions prior to school entrance and
children's social adaptation in kindergarten.

Barth and Parke (1993; also Barth, 1988) observed mothers and fathers separately with their 5-year-old children in physical play sessions 1 or 2 months
prior to kindergarten entrance. Parent-child physical play interactions were
used in this research because such physical play is an emotionally arousing
activity that requires skillful and coordinated interaction between parents and
children in order for play to succeed. School social adjustment was assessed 2
weeks after school began and at the end of the first semester.

Both mother-child and father-child interactions predicted subsequent school
social adaptation. First, the amount of time that the parent and child were engaged in sustained-play interaction was a significant predictor of school adjustment. For mothers, play engagement was associated with more considerate
and less dependent child classroom behavior and more favorable school attitudes by children across both school assessment periods. Low play engagement
was associated with loneliness immediately after school began and hostile
classroom behavior at the end of the first school semester. For father-child dyads play engagement was associated with more favorable home behaviors both
prior to the onset of school and at the 2-week postschool assessment. These
results deserve special attention because physical play engagement has been
linked to children's emotional skills (MacDonald, 1987; Parke et al., 1989) and
to other peer acceptance measures (MacDonald, 1987; MacDonald & Parke,
1984; Parke et al., 1989).

Second, the style of interaction was an important correlate of children's social adjustment. Children who were highly directive with their mothers and
unwilling to accept her input were more hostile and less considerate in the
classroom at both school assessment periods. In addition, these children experienced higher levels of loneliness after the initial onset of school, but greater

dependency on the teacher at the end of the first school semester. Dyads with a controlling mother and an uncooperative, resistant child were related to dependency after the onset of school and hostility at the end of the semester. Similarly, father-child dyads characterized by this control-resist pattern were associated with school loneliness and home behavior problems immediately after school entrance and low consideration at the end of the semester. Finally, nondirective dyads in which fathers relied on questions rather than directives were related to favorable home behaviors at the onset of school and at the end of the semester and with reports of low hostility at the end of the semester. Although the results of this research are generally consistent with the concurrent research that is described later, they also show that relations between family interactions and school adjustment may change over time.

Cowan and Cowan and colleagues (Cowan et al., 1989; Cowan et al., 1994) evaluated parents during the prebirth period and assessed parents and children again in the preschool period and finally during kindergarten when they also examined children's academic competence and social relationships with peers. Ineffective parenting, characterized by low warmth and structuring, in the preschool period predicted low academic achievement and shy-withdrawn behaviors. In addition, low warmth (but not structuring) in the preschool period was related to aggression 2 years later in kindergarten. "Parenting effectiveness during the preschool period predicts academic and social competence at the end of kindergarten, but the specific qualities of parenting are related to specific indices of social competence" (Cowan et al., 1994, p. 34).

Taken together, these results support past research that shows controlling and directive parenting styles and noncompliant demanding child behaviors are negatively related to social adjustment in school settings and peer sociometric assessments. Most important, these data suggest that earlier observed parent-child interaction patterns have value in predicting later social adjustment in school and peer contexts. Although the Barth and Parke (1993) and Cowan et al. (1989, 1994) studies do not imply a causal relationship between parent-child interaction and later behavior in peer contexts, they suggest the plausibility of this direction of effect, in view of the fact that parent-child interaction was observed prior to the transition to school.

Concurrent Evidence

In general, studies on concurrent family-school linkages follow a similar two-step paradigm. In one phase, parents and children are observed interacting together, usually in a gamelike or play context, while separate and independent measures of peer competence are collected as well. The relationship between variations in the parent-child interaction and social adjustment outcome is then examined. Two classic dimensions that have characterized parent-child interaction for several decades, warmth and control, emerge as common themes.

To briefly summarize, when playing with their parents, children with poor social relationships and less skillful peer interactions tend to exhibit a high degree of noncompliance and negative affect (Campbell, Breaux, Ewing, & Szumoski, 1985; MacDonald, 1987; Putallaz, 1987) and have poor regulation of arousal (MacDonald, 1987). Parents of such children also exhibit a high degree of noncompliant and disagreeing behaviors (Campbell et al., 1985; Gottman & Fainsilber-Katz, 1989; Putallaz, 1987), are more controlling and directing (MacDonald, 1987; MacDonald & Parke, 1984; Pettit, Dodge, & Brown, 1988; Putallaz, 1987), and are characterized as cold, unresponsive, angry, and low in limit setting and structuring (Gottman & Fainsilber-Katz, 1989). In contrast, children with more favorable and skillful peer relationships have more balanced interactions with their parents, (Baldwin, Cole, & Baldwin, 1984) and use less coercive and more indirect (vs. direct and demanding) influence strategies (Parke et al., 1989; Putallaz, 1987). Parents are more agreeable and responsive to their children's requests (Baldwin et al., 1984; MacDonald, 1987; MacDonald & Parke, 1984; Putallaz, 1987).

Longitudinal research findings on parent-child physical play are also corroborated in concurrent analyses employing this observational paradigm. (Burks, Carson, & Parke, 1987; MacDonald, 1987; MacDonald & Parke, 1984; Parke et al., 1989). In findings similar to those of the longitudinal research, parent-child dyads who were able to initiate and maintain physical play were more likely to have children with favorable social behaviors in school. Negative affect, negative responses by the child to parent play initiations, and coercive interactions, characterized by a high usage of directives and physical play initiations (e.g., grabbing a parent or child), were common in dyads with children with greater peer social problems.

The consistency of these findings with those from studies of parental disciplinary styles increases our confidence in the ecological validity of the laboratory-based findings. Other evidence suggests that the same styles of parent-child interaction that characterize social adjustment predict academic performance and school achievement as well (e.g., Baumrind, 1991; Hess & Holloway, 1984; Steinberg, Elmen, & Mounts, 1989).

The association between interaction styles and social skills may be due to the opportunities that parent-child interactions provide for modeling, practicing, or reinforcing prosocial behaviors (Putallaz, 1987; Putallaz & Heflin, 1990). For example, disagreeable-demanding and agreeable-feeling behaviors by parents toward children are associated with comparable behaviors by children toward parents and playmates (Putallaz, 1987; Putallaz & Heflin, 1990). The similarity of behaviors across the two settings suggests that the parent-child relationship may reinforce, model, or provide practice for these skills.

In summary, there is considerable evidence that parent-child relationship quality plays a role in the development of children's social skills and that these social skills are associated with children's peer relationships in preschool and early grade school. However, little is known about the development of school social skills for areas outside of peer relations (e.g., teacher relations), and these areas need further consideration.

Parents as Coaches and Teachers of Social Skills

Another way that parents may influence children's school adjustment is by explicitly teaching children appropriate social behavior, such as how to share or take turns. Although parents' intentional involvement in social skill development seems an obvious predictor of school social adjustment, it has received little attention, and that research has only used concurrent assessments of families and school social skills. Studies focusing on academic performance find that mothers who provide early academic or educational experiences have children who perform better in school and score higher on measures of cognitive ability (Schaefer & Hunter, 1983). Other investigations targeting parents' preparation for dealing with peer social situations (such as being teased or entering a group) find that mothers who offer advice that is specific, affectively positive, sensitive to the peer group, and rule oriented have children who are more accepted by peers (De Aenlle, 1976; Finnie & Russell, 1988). Mothers of children with low peer involvement (peer-neglected) provide minimal assistance when their children are faced with a group entry situation and often focus on play materials rather than on suggesting ways for the child to socially integrate themselves (Russell & Finnie, 1990). Advice that involves relationship enhancement, assertiveness, or disruptive techniques is not strongly associated with peer acceptance or rejection (Putallaz, 1987; Russell & Finnie, 1990). It should be noted that preschool children have been targeted in some of this research (Finnie & Russell, 1988; Russell & Finnie, 1990), and further work is needed to determine if the specific nature of parental advice and its relation to peer acceptance change as children develop over the early grade school years.

Parents may influence children's adjustment to the more general classroom situation and school context by explaining classroom and school procedures (e.g., raising hands to talk). Hess and Shipman (1967) found that the use of rationales by mothers to explain school rules was associated with school adjustment and varied with socioeconomic status. Lower-class mothers, whose children performed relatively poorly in school, provided their children with unqualified directives for school behavior (e.g., "Don't talk!"), in contrast with middle-class mothers, who provided rationales for school rules. This issue needs further investigation, focusing on the social consequences for these different orientations.

Although research on parents as coaches of social skills is promising, a distinction needs to be made between parents' ability to give quality advice and the actual frequency at which advice is given and taken. The affective quality of the parent-child relationship may influence the degree to which parents' instruction attempts are actually successful (Johnson & McGillicuddy-Delisi, 1983). In addition, relationships outside the parent-child dyad (e.g., marital relationship, work) may decrease the opportunities for and quality of instruction. Unfortunately, the hypothetical problem tasks employed in most research cannot address these issues, and other research strategies, including those that look at these variables over time, are clearly needed.

Parents as Social Support Providers

General qualities of the parent-child relationship, such as attachment, (Baldwin et al., 1984; Campbell et al., 1985; Garmezy, 1988; Maccoby, 1980; Sroufe, 1983), as well as parents' specific social support behaviors, for example, involvement in intervention and provision of advice (Cohen, Rubin, & Woody, 1986; Elizur, 1986), are associated with children's functioning under stress. Attachment theorists suggest that through early child-care experiences infants develop expectations for the behaviors of parents during times of stress (Sroufe, 1983). Parents who are unavailable and insensitive do not function as effective social supports later in childhood. Some evidence supports this hypothesis: Early mother-child affective and attachment relationships are related to preschool children's ability to approach and persist at difficult tasks (Arend, Gove, & Sroufe, 1979; Estrada, Arsenio, Hess, & Holloway, 1987). Furthermore, in clinical populations a key mitigating element in the relation between poor school functioning and a parent's mental illness is the responsiveness and emotional availability of parents (Baldwin et al., 1984).

Whereas the studies described in the previous paragraph suggest that general qualities in the parent-child relationship foster stress-resistance, children's adjustment after destabilizing events is in part due to the quality of caretakers' responses to that specific event. For example, evidence suggests that the eventual improvement of children with school difficulties is related to parents' active involvement with their children's problems (Elizur, 1986).

Children's perceptions of the quality of parental social support and involvement in schools vary with peer rejection and acceptance in school (Cohen et al., 1986). Cohen et al. (1986) interviewed fourth- and fifth-grade children and reported that fathers' involvement increases with the aggressiveness of the children's behaviors, perhaps because such children "require more active parental attention" (Cohen et al., 1986). Mothers are perceived by isolated or unpopular girls as uninvolved; whereas mothers of "average" girls are perceived as providing advice and emotional support. Interestingly, "average" boys see their mothers as less involved in their problems. The conflicting findings for average boys and girls may be due to different socialization practices on the part of the mother: "By middle childhood, mothers of boys may be hesitant to demonstrate physical affection and support for their sons" (Cohen et al., 1986). In light of this hypothesis, it is important to extend this line of research to younger children.

In summary, parent-child relationship qualities and parents' active support and intervention for children may be related to school social adjustment. Perceived parental support and involvement in school problems are associated with peer acceptance-rejection and improvement in school. Parental qualities such as warmth, availability, and sensitivity may facilitate parents' social support role during the early school years.

Parental Direct Involvement in the School System

Parents may directly influence their child's adjustment to school through their own involvement in the school system. They may become involved in the classroom and school as teacher assistants, library aides, lunchroom assistants, and a variety of other activities in order to help their children in school. Parental school involvement may have several effects on the child. First, by providing services to the school in general, parents are providing these services to their own children and thus improving their children's school experiences. For example, parental school involvement has been associated with favorable teacher ratings of school performance in a sample of 5- to 17-year-olds (Stevenson & Baker, 1987). In addition, a school-based behavior modification program that involved parents as reward providers increased second- through fifth-grade children's school performance (Blechman, Kotanchick, & Taylor, 1981). Parental involvement is associated with academic gains in older children as well (Dornbusch & Ritter, 1988; Smith, 1968; also see Walberg, 1984, for a general review of research on the effectiveness of parental involvement for educational gains).

Parent volunteers may help shape the classroom environment as classroom assistants by lessening teachers' loads and allowing more time for individualized student attention (Lightfoot, 1978). Parental involvement may give parents direct teacher contact that may be used to inform teachers how to be more responsive to their child's needs (Lightfoot, 1978).

Finally, parents participate in organizations that influence school policy and classroom programs, such as school boards. Through involvement in such organizations, parents may help determine the values and cultural perspective that are transmitted to their children. Lightfoot (1978) pointed out that schools that are successful are those incorporating familial and cultural values acquired at home. She suggested that this results in a more fluid and less conflictive transition from home to school. The notion that "school-home match" is bidirectional suggests that families whose members use strategies and have values similar to those in the school are likely to fare better (Comer, 1988; Lightfoot, 1978). For example, Hansen (1986) found that students who experienced teaching styles in school that were similar to their parents' instructive style achieved higher grades than did mismatched students.

Although it is clear that there are several avenues for parents to influence their child's school adjustment through school involvement, the major focus of research on young children has been on academic gains. Few studies have focused on children's social adjustment. For example, it is not known if teacher-student relationships improve as a result of a parent's classroom involvement. It is possible that some of the academic gains that are associated with more parental input into the school systems are due, in part, to smoother social adjustment. However, this issue needs investigation.

Summary of Parent-Child Relationship Influences on Social Adjustment in School

The evidence presented indicates that parents can potentially have a sizable impact on their children's social adjustment in school through their daily interactions, coaching, teaching, and involvement in the school system. However, with few exceptions, research to date has primarily focused on peer relations at the expense of other aspects of the child's school behavior. An important area for future research to explore is how parents may impact on the child's adjustment to the teacher, the classroom, and the school as an institution. In addition, a majority of the research cited has focused on the mother-child relationship, ignoring the potential contributions of fathers. Furthermore, this research has neglected the issue of how relations develop and change over time. Moreover, parents' interactions with their children and involvement in the school are influenced by other elements in the family including the quality of marital relationships and external family circumstances.

Marital Relationship Influences on School Social Adjustment

Marital relationships have both indirect and direct effects on children's social adaptation in school settings. Most models of parenting assume that marital relationships impact on children's behavior indirectly due to shifts in patterns of parent-child interaction (e.g., Belsky, 1984). In addition, marriages may directly impact on children's development: Marriages in which there are high degrees of discord and conflict may promote maladaptive coping behavior in children and provide inappropriate and ineffective models for conflict resolution (Cummings & Cummings, 1988).

Marital Relationship as a Context for Social Skill Development

Marital conflict may provide a background of anger that may influence social skill development by (a) promoting specific child behaviors for dealing with conflict, (b) providing models of aggression or prosocial behaviors, and (c) altering the quality of parent-child interactions (Cowan et al., 1989; Cowan et al., 1994; Cummings & Cummings, 1988; Easterbrooks & Emde, 1988; Emery, 1982; Grych & Fincham, 1990; Hetherington, Cox, & Cox, 1979).

Children who are exposed to a high degree of conflict at home may develop maladaptive behavior patterns for managing conflict at school (Grych & Fincham, 1990, 1993). Child behaviors that are effective in reducing marital conflict are likely to be repeated in future family conflict situations and may generalize to situations outside the home. For example, during a marital argument a child may act out to distract attention away from the conflict. However, such a strategy applied to the school setting is highly maladaptive. Marital conflict may also oversensitize children to conflict (Grych & Fincham, 1990). Consequently, children may see conflict where there is none, and behave in appropriately. The marital relationship may also provide a model for children for dealing with others in school. Precise imitation of parent behaviors is rare, but observational experiences may influence behavior in other ways (Cummings & Cummings, 1988). These experiences may weaken inhibitions over socially unacceptable behaviors, resulting in a range of negative behaviors outside the family setting.

The specific type of marital conflict is related to the type of subsequent child difficulties in school contexts. In a longitudinal study, Fainsilber-Katz and Gottman (1994) assessed the school adjustment of children at age 5 and again at age 8. Children whose parents were mutually hostile when they were entering school were rated by teachers at age 8 as being higher in externalizing behavior. In families where the husband was angry and withdrawn, the children were rated by teachers as higher in internalizing behavior. Clearly marital conflict is not a unitary concept, and "the results highlight importance of specifying the nature of marital conflicts to understand its effects on children" (Fainsilber-Katz & Gottman, 1994, p. 948).

Finally, marital conflict may influence a child's social skill development by altering the parent-child relationship. A longitudinal study by Cowan et al. (1989) found that fathers' marital adjustment during toddlerhood was positively associated with a parenting style characterized by warmth, responsivity, engagement, and the setting of limits. This parenting style was negatively associated with externalizing and internalizing child behaviors in kindergarten. For mothers, similar links were found between marital satisfaction, parenting style, and internalizing behaviors. In general, parents who are competitive and hostile in their marital interactions and do not work cooperatively in front of their preschooler tend to have children who are shy and withdrawn with their classmates or who show higher levels of aggression in kindergarten (Cowan et al., 1994). Further evidence for the mediating role of the parent-child relationship comes from research that shows that a favorable parent-child relationship can mitigate some of the negative effects of divorce (Easterbrooks & Emde, 1988; Emery, 1982; Hetherington et al., 1979).

In summary, marital quality may affect social skills by promoting behaviors for dealing with conflict, providing observational learning opportunities, and altering the quality of the parent-child relationship.

Marital Relationship Influence on Family Social Support

Marital relationship quality may influence parents' emotional and physical availability to children and thus affect their ability to provide social support or function as a stress buffer (Cowan et al., 1989; Easterbrooks & Emde, 1988; Goldberg & Easterbrooks, 1984). Parents' psychological availability and support may be mitigated by depression, which often accompanies marital problems (Cowan et al., 1989; Shaw & Emery, 1987). The longitudinal study conducted by Cowan et al. (1989) found that parents' depression 18 months after childbirth predicted marital dissatisfaction at 42 months, which subsequently predicted children's behavior problems at entrance to kindergarten. Depending on the particular behavior problem and the parent, the influence of marital satisfaction on school behavior may be direct or mediated through the parent-child relationship. A possible interpretation of these findings is that depression associated with dissatisfaction from the marriage spills over into other aspects of family life, rendering parents unavailable to help children with problems at school.

Children's perceptions of their parents' emotional support and availability are also an important consequence of marital discord (Easterbrooks & Emde, 1988) and need further investigation. Although children in families with a high degree of marital conflict may feel that their parents are accepting, they may also believe that their parents cannot provide adequate help for them (Cohen et al., 1986).

In summary, the degree to which marital discord results in depression or withdrawal from the family may determine the influence it has on parental social support. Furthermore, even if children perceive that parents are accepting, the perception of the quality of that support may vary depending on the degree of marital discord.

Marital Relationship and Family Involvement With the School System

Just as other forms of parental influences are altered by marital relationships, it is likely that direct parental involvement in school activities is altered by the quality and structure of the marital relationship, but this research is scarce. Intact families who are experiencing marital discord may not have the emotional and psychological resources to take on the added responsibility of school activities. It may be possible that some events and activities are relatively un-affected by marital discord (e.g., attending parent conferences); whereas others that require a more extended commitment are affected (e.g., advisory commit-tees). Recently divorced or separated parents are likely to have diminished re-sources as well. Moreover, Dornbusch & Ritter (1988) found that stepparents and single parents participate less in school activities than do families with two natural parents. Single parents' low participation in schooling may be due to the fact that responsibilities that might normally be shared between two parents are carried by one (Leitch & Tangri, 1988). It should be noted that educators seem increasingly aware of the need to adapt school activities to the schedules of divorced and single parents (e.g., Espinoza, 1988; Seefeldt, 1985). In light of the prevalence of marital discord and divorce and changes in school systems, this issue needs further consideration.

Summary of Marital Relationship Influence on School Social Adjustment

A great deal of research has focused on how marital relationship quality im-pacts on children's social behavior by altering the quality and quantity of parent-child interactions and parents' involvement in children's lives. Much of this research, however, has failed to focus on the school environment as a spe-cific setting in which negative behaviors occur. A focus is needed on early school years because this is a time when children may be more susceptible to marital disruptions.

External Family Influences on School Social Adjustment

In this section the influences of factors outside the family on social skill devel-opment, social support, and family involvement in the school system are ex-amined. Lower SES and stressful events (e.g., financial problems, family ill-nesses and deaths) are the focus here. Similar to marital relationship quality, in many cases extrafamilial influences are hypothesized to have their greatest im-pact on children by altering relationships within the family.

External Family Influences on Children's Social Skill Development

Social economic status (SES), is a broad term encompassing a wide range of work, economic, and environmental factors. SES is associated with chil-dren's understanding of rules (Johnson & McGillicuddy-Delisi, 1983) and peer acceptance in school (Dishion, 1990; Patterson, Griesler, Vaden, & Ku-persmidt, 1992; Patterson, Vaden, & Kupersmidt, 1991). However, it is also correlated with parenting styles that may influence the development of social skills in the family. SES is associated with parents' use of rationales (Hess

& Shipman, 1967). Parents' affective feedback to children may mediate the relation between SES and children's understanding of rules (Johnson & McGillicuddy-Delisi, 1983).

Other research focuses more narrowly on the frequency of stressful family events and also finds relations to children's behavior in school. Barth (1988) found that the number of acute stressors that a family experienced before a child enters school was associated with dependency on the teacher and low consideration and extroversion toward peers. Children who are classified as rejected by peers in grade school often have experienced more stressful life events than children who are not rejected (Patterson et al., 1992; Vaden, Patterson, & Kupersmidt, 1988). Consistent with the Sameroff, Seifer, Baldwin, and Baldwin (1993) cumulative risk hypothesis, Patterson et al. found that the impact of multiple chronic adversities appears to be cumulative: The greater the number of adversities, the greater a child's likelihood of being rejected by peers.

Both SES and stress include factors related to parents' work, but another line of research has focused on work specifically. Whereas past research has emphasized fathers' job status (i.e., white- vs. blue-collar workers) and parenting style (Kohn, 1977; Mortimer, 1976), more recent research has emphasized maternal employment and its influence on children. Research on the influence of work on mothers' availability has compared families of mothers who are employed outside the home to those of mothers not employed outside the home. While past research has not shown consistent links between maternal work stats (i.e., employed vs. non-employed) with social adjustment, recent longitudinal research indicates relations between maternal work attitudes and children's social development (Crouter, 1994; Gottfried, Gottfried & Bathurst, 1988; Lerner & Galambos, 1988). Mothers with favorable attitudes toward work and their dual roles as mother and worker have high educational aspirations for their children (Gottfried et al., 1988) and may promote academic skills in their children: Social, behavioral, and cognitive functioning of young school-age children is greater if mothers are satisfied with their dual roles (Gottfried et al., 1988).

In summary, SES, stressful events, and work may influence children's social skill development, and this influence may be mediated by the more proximal family environment. In addition to social skills, external familial circumstances may alter the social support function of the family.

External Family Influences and Family Social Support

Stressful circumstances from outside the family are likely to impact on the parent-child relationship by affecting both the quality and availability of support. For example, demanding work that is either extremely satisfying or dissatisfying may cause parents to return home too exhausted to carefully attend to the concerns of their children (Hoffman, 1984; Piotrkowski, 1979; Repetti, 1989, 1993). In their longitudinal study, Lerner and Galambos (1988) reported that mothers' dissatisfaction with their parent and worker roles is associated with maternal rejection of their preschool children. Using a path analysis technique, they found that the path from role dissatisfaction to child difficulties was mediated by parent rejection of the child.

Work schedules and other social obligations may also affect the amount of contact between parents and children. Parents who work night shifts or who have extensive evening commitments may not be able to provide support because of decreased contact with their child (Biller, 1992).

During the early school years the negative effects of external events on social support may be more marked. Mothers often return to work at this time, and new child-care arrangements must often be made. This points to the need to focus on the early school years as a special time, perhaps more vulnerable to the influence of external family circumstances.

External Family Influences and Family Involvement in the School System

The degree to which families must attend to circumstances outside the home (other than school) is associated with school involvement. A good deal of research suggests that the general quality of the social context in which families function, as measured by SES, is positively associated with parental involvement in schools and children's education in general (e.g., Lareau, 1987; O'Donnel & Steuve, 1983). Explanations for such effects have focused on parental values and attitudes that co-vary with SES. For example, Lareau (1987) suggested that social class differences are, in part, a function of parents' comfort with teacher and school interactions. Lower SES parents may feel less at ease in schools because of their own low educational attainment. However, it is also possible that other factors associated with SES, such as employment circumstances and stressful events, play a role.

A number of researchers have implicated parents' work as a major factor in low levels of volunteerism and participation in school (Epstein, 1988, 1989; Espinoza, 1988; Letich & Tangri, 1988; Seefeldt, 1985). Mothers, who have traditionally been involved in school activities, are now working full-time. Although consistent differences are often not found for maternal employment per se, the number of hours employed (full- vs. part-time) and flexible work hours seem to be important factors (Espinoza, 1988; Hayes & Kamermann, 1983; O'Donnel & Steuve, 1983). For example, in a series of interviews with employed and non-employed mothers, O'Donnel and Steuve (1983) found that full-time employed mothers are more likely to set limits on the amount of time they will volunteer. However, employed mothers are more likely to be involved in school activities if they work under a flexible time schedule compared with a rigid time schedule (Espinoza, 1988).

Summary of External Family Influences on Children's School Adjustment

A recurring theme in this discussion is that external family influences create difficulties for individual family members that are then "carried over" in to family life. Thus, it is commonly hypothesized that the impact of external family factors on children is mediated by their impact on intrafamilial relationships. Recent research has focused on maternal employment as a major source of perturbation in the family system. Although recent secular changes in maternal employment perhaps warrant this concern, it should also be recognized that in the majority of families both parents are employed. The inclusion of both parents' employment characteristics is likely to provide a better understanding of how children's school adjustment is affected.

Summary, Critique, and Future Directions

The model described in this chapter contributes to our understanding of the family's impact on school social adjustment by presenting some of the pathways linking the two systems. Each level of the family provides a set of circumstances that influence its capacity to promote social skills, provide social support, and become involved in the school system. Furthermore, these processes influence multiple aspects of children's school adjustment, including peer and teacher relationships, classroom adjustment, and general attitudes toward school as an institution. Although the model in Figure 15.1 is far from comprehensive, it provides a useful heuristic for describing family-school linkages. Based on the review provided, some suggestions and criticisms can be offered for improving family-school research.

Family and School Social Systems

Throughout the discussion it has become apparent that the parent-child relationship is a major conduit linking family experiences to children's social adjustment in school. Nevertheless, there are some suggestions that marital quality and external family systems influence children directly by providing observational learning experiences and a background of conflict, warmth, or neglect. However, these pathways of influence are less explored than others and are in need of further research.

At the beginning of the chapter a multilevel description of school social adjustment was provided. Research on family-school linkages has ignored the multifaceted nature of social adjustment, tending to focus on peer relationships (Cowan et al., 1994) or broad descriptions of functioning (e.g., conduct, compliance, aggression). The emphasis on peer relationships is perhaps driven by indications that peer rejection is relatively stable over time and is associated with later difficulties in school (see Asher & Coie, 1990, and Parker & Asher, 1987, for reviews). However, evidence is accumulating that suggests teacher relationships, classroom adjustment, and school attitudes are important as well (Kellam, 1993). Family factors that play a role in adjustment at these levels need further examination.

Mediating Adaptation Processes: Emotional and Attentional Processes

A major limitation of prior work is the lack of focus on specific mediating processes that are critical for social adaptation in school and thus underlie children's adaptation to peers, teachers, the classroom, and the institution of school. Thus, the degree to which social skill development, social support, and family involvement influence these adaptational process will determine the degree to which they influence children's adjustment to school. We propose that two sets of important adaptation processes are emotional behaviors—including regulation, recognition, and production skills—and attentional regulation.

A number of theorists have suggested that the ability to regulate both emotional experiences and expression is an important task for young children (Kopp, 1989; Maccoby, 1980). Fainsilber-Katz and Gottman (1994) argued that the inability to regulate emotions may disrupt the child's ability to focus attention and coordinate actions to attain a goal. The disruption of attention and goal-related activity "may be an important step in the development of more severe behavior problems" (pp. 15–16). In support of their claim, they have found that children who experience a great deal of anger during parent-child interactions also show certain physiological signs that are associated with difficulty in focusing attention and coordinating actions. Additional evidence indicates that rejected children are generally more aggressive than their more popular peers (Asher & Coie, 1990; Pelligrini, 1991) and, more specifically, that their rough-and-tumble peer play is more likely to result in aggressive versus nonaggressive rule-bound play (Pelligrini, 1991).

The recognition and production of emotional expression has also been identified as an important task for young children's social development that may underlie many other social skills necessary for social adaptation (Philippot & Feldman, 1990). In support of this hypothesis, Zuckerman and Przewuzman (1979) reported that kindergarten children's adjustment to school is related to their ability to express and recognize facial expression of emotion. Additional studies have indicated that both recognition (Barth & Bastiani, 1993; Beitel & Parke, 1985; Philippot & Feldman, 1990) and production skills (Buck, 1975, 1977; Carson, Burks, & Parke, 1993; Field & Walden, 1982) are strong associates of peer sociometric status and social competence during the preschool and early school years.

How do families contribute to emotional behaviors? It is our view that emotional regulation, decoding, and encoding are practiced and learned in the context of parent-child interactions and that parent-child play is one of the more important interaction contexts for their development. This assumption has led us to focus our studies on parent-child physical play because it requires a subtle and complex ability on the part of the parent and child to keep stimulation within an optimal range and regulate the child's affective displays. During physical play, overstimulation of the child and approach-withdrawal behaviors are common, yet it is these very behaviors that must be regulated in order for play to succeed. In the course of play, "[c]hildren may be learning the social communicative value of their own affective displays as well as how to use these signals to regulate the social behavior of others" (Parke et al., 1989, p. 77).

In support of this argument, MacDonald (1987) has found that parents of rejected children tend to overstimulate their children during physical play. The differences in the regulation of arousal in dyads of parents with rejected children may, in fact, be evident in peer-peer interactions as well (Carson, Burks, & Parke, 1993). If this hypothesis is correct, the low acceptance of rejected children by their peers may in part be due to rejected children's tendency to be overly aroused during peer interactions. While it is certainly possible that this skill may be acquired outside of parent-child interactions, this work suggests that parent-child play is a viable context for its development.

Further evidence suggests that marital quality may affect parent-child interaction patterns that, in turn, are related to poor emotional regulation among children. In their work, Fainsilber-Katz and Gottman (1994) found that in families in which wives were withdrawn during marital interaction, both parents were negative listeners during parent-child interaction (i.e., they made negative facial expressions or withdrew from interactions). In turn, this pattern of parent-child interaction was associated with anger and low vagal tone in 5-year-old children—a pattern that may bode poorly for later peer interaction. Together, these findings underscore the role of emotional regulation as a potential mediator between family and school contexts.

Research examining emotional decoding and encoding skills and parent-child play interactions indicates that there may be a relation between the two. Beitel and Parke (1986) found that father-child physical play, but not mother-child physical play, was associated with the child's ability to correctly decode pictures of unfamiliar children posing emotional expressions. Their findings were stronger for girls than for boys. Interestingly, Muth, Burks, Carson, and Parke (1988) found associations between the amount of physical play in both mother- and father-child play interactions and children's ability to decode. The difference between the two studies is most likely due to the fact that the Muth et al. study selected children who were more extreme in their peer acceptance and that they asked children to decode their parents' faces, which were more likely to vary in their quality.

Muth et al. also examined encoding skills and found that the length of both parents' physical play is associated with children's encoding skills and peer acceptance. Interestingly, these relations were only found when encoding skill was assessed by judges outside the family. Taken together, these findings have led us to propose that there may be a "family-centric" bias (Parke et al., 1989) in emotional decoding and encoding skills: Parents of rejected children become skilled at recognizing their children's emotional expressions, but others, unfamiliar with the child, have difficulty with the same task. The theory implies that some emotional behaviors that children acquire in the context of the family may be maladaptive for interactions outside the family.

The role of attentional processes in accounting for children's adaptation to school also requires more research. Several lines of work, however, suggest that this is a promising direction. Kellam (1993) has found that a teacher-rated index of concentration problems predicted shy and aggressive behavior and poor achievement in both boys and girls and depressive symptoms among females. Kellam (1994) has suggested that

> concentration problems are a common latent condition underlying both social maladaptation and psychological well-being. Rather than a categorical attentional disorder, concentration/attention problems may be evidence of general developmental psychopathology with potential for expression in many forms including maladaptive shy and/or aggressive behavior, depressed affect, and poor learning. (P. 19)

An open question that continues to intrigue researchers is whether to treat attentional problems as individual differences with a significant developmental history (Fagan, 1984) or as a stage-like issue that shows significant shifts in the 5 to 7 year period due to underlying changes in brain maturation. Some evidence (R. Canfield, personal communication, November 1992) suggests that children improve on attentional tasks that require inhibition of a response in the 5 to 7 year period. Some have suggested that shifts in frontal lobe development may underlie these apparent changes (Diamond, 1990). Unfortunately, the studies of shifts in attentional abilities have not been placed in a sociocultural context in which the influence of variations in family, peer, and school environments on the emergence of these processes could be measured.

Longitudinal studies that trace shifts in attentional and emotional regulatory abilities before and after school entry, as well as family and school socialization strategies that might alter these abilities, would be worthwhile. One of the provocative questions that needs to be addressed is whether or not parents socialize attentional or emotional regulatory abilities differently during the 5 to 7 age period or during the transition-to-school period. A simultaneous focus on both developmental shifts in attention and emotional regulation and their related socialization practices would clearly be worthwhile.

Methodological and Design Considerations

The subject populations, methods, and designs employed in past studies have limited the conclusions that can be drawn about family and school linkages. First, past research on familial influences on children in school has generally focused on mothers. As a result, our understanding of the effects of families on children in school is primarily an understanding of maternal influences. Studies that include father-child, sibling, and marital relationships will enhance our understanding of familial influences on social adjustment.

A second concern lies in the description of a child's functioning in school. Reports from teachers, peers, or mothers or direct observations have been the primary choices in past research. Noticeably lacking is the child's perspective on school, for example, school attitude. Because school adjustment must occur at a number of levels, it is important to consider a variety of sources within a single study to truly characterize the quality of a child's school adjustment.

Third, researchers need to consider a wider variety of research designs. The predominant approach to family-school relationship studies has been to examine correlations between concurrent measures of home and school functioning. Longitudinal studies allow a more dynamic examination of family influences on school adjustment. They can uniquely describe how previous functioning within the family affects later school adjustment. Experimental designs that manipulate a family or school experience through a planned intervention can be used in conjunction with longitudinal designs to test hypotheses about the direction of causal relations between home and school variables. For example, instruction on how to provide effective social support could be provided to a randomly selected group of parents. Adjustment difficulties of these children could be compared with those of others who did not receive the intervention. Two recent studies illustrate the value of this kind of approach. Cowan and Cowan (1992) have reported data on a project in which parents receive a supportive intervention prior to their child's entry into school. In comparison to a nonintervention control group, children in the parent support group adjusted better in kindergarten. Similarly, Kellam (1993) has focused on the classroom as an intervention site. Separate interventions aimed at either reducing aggression or improving reading skills have both yielded significant changes. In view of the poor prognosis for children who are low academic achievers, aggressive, or both (Asher & Coie, 1990; Kellam, 1993), these indications of the malleability of these behaviors are encouraging. Together these two pioneering intervention efforts provide guidelines for later work that focuses on the testing of specific theoretical models and processes that may underlie successful early adaptation in school contexts.

A fourth concern is our lack of knowledge of the duration and development of school problems. For some children the early school years may be associated with relatively short-term difficulties, whereas for others it may mark the beginning of long-term problems. Alternatively, for some children, problems that are evident in the school setting may have existed long before school entrance. It is reasonable to expect that the families of children whose problems begin after entrance to school are different from those whose problems were evident before school entrance. This highlights the value of considering family-school linkages as children make the transition to school.

This raises the next concern, namely, the need for more studies of the actual transition to school. Studying children and families as they begin school permits the examination of processes that are evident later in school as well as the examination of developmental factors in the family-child-school relationship. The transition to school may magnify processes that are in place at other time points in a child's school career. For example, social skills such as initiating peer interaction will have a heightened importance as children make new friends at school. The family's social support function may also be intensified at this time. Attachment security, which describes parents as providing a "secure base" from which the child explores, may have increased importance for the strange and new school setting. It should be noted that the paths through which the family may affect school adjustment are not likely to be affected by the time point in a child's school career. Rather, the transition time point permits researchers to examine these pathways at a time of increased activity and importance and at the same time observe the ontogeny and development of school adjustment.

Secular Changes in Families and Schools

Rapid changes occurring in the family and school systems may alter our views of "normal" family-school relationships. Increases in single-parent families and families with two working parents may indicate a decrease in the availability of parents (Dornbusch & Ritter, 1988; Epstein, 1988). Dornbusch and Ritter (1988) found that stepparents and single parents participate less in school activities than do families with two natural parents. Work has been cited as a major reason parents do not become involved in school activities (Leitch & Tangri, 1988). However, flexible work schedule policies are positively associated with parents' involvement in children's education (Espinoza, 1988). If such work policies become more common, then an increase in parental involvement may be possible in the near future.

Accompanying the trend toward two working parents are children's earlier and more frequent contacts with child-care institutions and educational programs. The fact that most children have been exposed to educational television, child care, and preschools expands the range of factors that must be considered when studying early school adjustment. (See Ladd & Price, 1987, for research on the transition from preschool to kindergarten.) Perhaps as a result of pre-school experiences, the early educational experiences of children are under-going changes. There is a recent reemergence of full-day kindergarten pro-grams, longer school days, and suggestions that formal schooling should begin at age 4.

The organization of the family and the organization of the school system have also changed so that the tasks of adjustment during the early school years may have been altered. For example, families have become smaller, with the result that many children do not have the benefit of older siblings' experiences in school and thus may have fewer opportunities for learning and practicing social skills within the family. Alternatively, as a result of more adult attention because of fewer siblings, children may show increases in intellectual devel-opment (e.g., the confluence model of Zajonc & Markus, 1975).

It can be seen that families and schools are continually changing and devel-oping. By attending to these secular changes, researchers will be better able to understand the process of adjusting to school and select more effective means of intervention and remediation for children at risk and their families.

Conclusions

Although many dimensions of the family and school systems have been dis-cussed, the relation between the two systems during the early school years has many unexplored avenues. The model described in this chapter suggests that a better understanding of the pathways between the two social systems can be achieved by considering the child's embeddedness in multiple tiers of the family as well as children's interactions at numerous levels within the school. More attention needs to be given to the interplay between changing environ-ments that the child encounters at age 5 when school entry begins and indi-vidual and family factors that aid or impede the child's adjustment to these changing environments.

Acknowledgments

Preparation of this chapter and the research reported herein were supported in part by National Science Foundation grant SBR 9308941 and National Institute of Child Health and Development grant R01 HD32391. Thanks to Karin Horspool for her assistance in preparation of this manuscript.

References

Alexander, K. L., & Entwisle, D. R. (1988). Achievement in the first two years of school: Patterns and processes. *Monographs of the Society for Research in Child Development, 53* (2, Serial No. 218).

Arend, R., Gove, F., & Sroufe, A. (1979). A continuity of individual adaptation from infancy to kindergarten: A predictive study of ego-resiliency and curiosity in pre-schoolers. *Child Development, 50,* 950–966.

Asher, S. R., & Coie, J. D. (Eds.). (1990). *Peer rejection in childhood,* Cambridge: Cambridge University Press.

Baldwin, A., Cole, R., & Baldwin, C. P. (1984). Parental pathology, family interaction and the competence of the child in school. *Monographs of the Society for Research in Child Development, 47* (5, Serial No. 1197).

Barth, J. M. (1988). Transition to school. Unpublished doctoral dissertation, University of Illinois at Urbana-Champaign.

Barth, J. M., & Bastiani, A. (1993, March). *Emotional skills and preschool children's peer relationships.* Paper presented at the biennial meeting of the Society for Research on Child Development, New Orleans, LA.

Barth, J. M., & Parke, R. D. (1993). Parent-child relationship influences on children's transition to school. *Merrill-Palmer Quarterly, 39,* 173–195.

Baumrind, D. (1991). Effective parenting during the early adolescent transition. In P. A. Cowan & M. E. Hetherington (Eds.), *Advances in family research* (Vol. 2, pp. 111–163). Hillsdale, NJ: Erlbaum.

Beitel, A., & Parke, R. D. (1985). Relationship between preschooler's sociometric status, parent interaction and emotional decoding ability. Unpublished manuscript, University of Illinois at Urbana-Champaign.

Belsky, J. (1984). The determinants of parenting: A process model. *Child Development, 55,* 83–96.

Berndt, T. (1981). Peer relationships in children of working parents. In C. Hayes & S. B. Kamerman (Eds.), *Children of working parents* (pp. 13–43). Washington DC: National Academy Press.

Biller, H. B. (1993). *Fathers and families.* Westport, CT: Auburn House.

Blechman, E. A., Kotanchick, N. L., & Taylor, C. J. (1981). Families and schools together: Early behavioral intervention with high risk children. *Behavioral Therapy, 12,* 308–319.

Bronfenbrenner, U. (1979). *The ecology of human development.* Cambridge, MA: Harvard University Press.

Bronfenbrenner, U. (1986). Ecology as a context for human development: Research perspective. *Developmental Psychology, 22,* 723–742.

Bronfenbrenner, U., & Crouter, A. (1982). Work and family through time and space. In S. B. Kamerman & Hayes, C. D. (Eds.), *Families that work: Children in a changing world* (pp. 39–83). Washington, DC: National Academy Press.

Buck, R. (1975). Nonverbal communication of affect in children. *Journal of Personality and Social Psychology, 31,* 644–653.

Buck, R. (1977). Nonverbal communication of affect in preschool children: Relationships with personality and skin conductance. *Journal of Personality and Social Psychology, 35,* 225–236.

Burks, V., Carson, J., & Parke, R. D. (1987). Parent-child interaction styles of popular and rejected children. Unpublished manuscript, University of Illinois at Urbana-Champaign.

Campbell, S. B., Breaux, A. M., Ewing, L. J., & Szumoski, E. K. (1985, April). *Family characteristics and child behaviors as precursors of external symptomology at school entry.* Paper presented at the biennial meeting of the Society for Research on Child Development, Toronto, Canada.

Carson, J., Burks, V., & Parke, R. D. (1993). Parent-child physical play: Determinants and consequences. In K. MacDonald (Ed.), *Parent-child play: Descriptions and implications* (pp. 197–220). Albany: State University of New York Press.

Chall, J. S., Jacobs, V. A., & Baldwin, L. E. (1990). *The reading crisis: Why poor children fall behind.* Cambridge, MA: Harvard University Press.

Cohen, J. S., Rubin, K. H., & Woody, E. Z. (1986, June). *Parental support and children's peer relationships.* Paper presented at the annual meeting of the Canadian Psychological Association, Toronto, Canada.

Comer, J. (1988, November). The education of low-income black children. *Scientific America, 259,* 42–48.

Cowan, C. P., & Cowan, P. A. (1992). *When partners become parents: The big life change for couples.* New York: Basic Books.

Cowan, C. P., Cowan, P. A., Heming, G., & Miller, N. B. (1992). Becoming a family: Marriage, parenting, and child development. In P. A. Cowan & E. M. Hetherington (Eds.), *Family transitions: Advances in family research* (Vol. 2, pp. 79–109). Hillsdale, NJ: Erlbaum.

Cowan, P. A., Cowan, C. P., & Heming, G. (1989, April). *From parent adaptation in pregnancy to child adaptation in kindergarten.* Paper presented at the biennial meeting of the Society for Research in Child Development, Kansas City, MO.

Cowan, P. A., Cowan, C. P., Schulz, M. C., & Heming, G. (1994). Prebirth to preschool family factors in children's adaptation to kindergarten. In R. D. Parke & S. Kellam (Eds.), *Exploring family relationships with other social contexts.* Hillsdale, NJ: Erlbaum.

Crouter, A. C. (1994). Processes linking families and work: Implications for behavior and development in both settings. In R. D. Parke & S. Kellam (Eds.), *Exploring family relationships with other social contexts* (pp. 9–28). Hillsdale, NJ: Erlbaum.

Cummings, E. M., & Cummings, J. S. (1988). A process-oriented approach to children's coping with adults' angry behavior. *Developmental Review, 8,* 296–321.

De Aenlle, C. R. (1976). Parental involvement in children's peer relations: Their role as problem solvers and teachers of social skills. Unpublished master's thesis, University of Illinois at Urbana-Champaign.

Diamond, A. (1990). Rate of maturation of the hippocampus and the developmental progression of children's performance on the delayed non-matching to sample and visual paired comparison tasks. *Annals of the New York Academy of Sciences, 608,* 394–426.

Dishion, T. J. (1990). The family ecology of boys' peer relations in middle school. *Child Development, 61,* 874–892.

Dornbusch, S. M., & Ritter, T. L. (1988). Parents of high school students: A neglected resource. *Educational Horizons, 66,* 75–77.

Easterbrooks, M. A., & Emde, R. N. (1988). Marital and parent-child relationships: The role of affect in the family system. In R. A. Hinde & J. Stevenson (Eds.), *Relationships within families: Mutual influence* (pp. 83–103). Oxford: Oxford University Press.

Eccles, J. S., & Midgley, C. (1989). Stage/environment fit: Developmentally appropriate classrooms for early adolescents. In R. C. Ames & C. Ames (Eds.), *Research on motivation in education* (Vol. 3, pp. 139–186). New York: Academic Press.

Elizur, J. (1986). The stress of school entry: Parental coping behaviors and children's adjustment to school. *Journal of Child Psychology and Psychiatry, 27,* 625–638.

Emery, R. E. (1982). Interparental conflict and the children of discord and divorce. *Psychological Bulletin, 92,* 310–330.

Entwisle, D. R., & Alexander, K. L. (1992). Early schooling as a "critical period" phenomena. In K. Namboodiri & R. G. Corwin (Eds.), *Sociology of education and socialization* (Vol. 8, pp. 27–55). Greenwich, CT: JAI Press.

Entwisle, D. R., & Hayduck, L. A. (1988). Lasting effects of the elementary school. *Sociology of Education, 61,* 147–159.

Epstein, J. L. (1988). How do we improve programs for parent involvement? *Educational Horizons, 66,* 58–59.

Epstein, J. L. (1989). Family structures and student motivation: A developmental perspective. In C. Ames & R. Ames (Eds.), *Research on motivation in education:* Vol. 3. *Goals and cognitions* (pp. 259–293). New York: Academic Press.

Espinoza, R. (1988). Working parents, employers, and schools. *Educational Horizons, 66,* 62–65.

Estrada, P., Arsenio, W. F., Hess, R. D., & Holloway, S. D. (1987). Affective quality of the mother-child relationship: Longitudinal consequences for children's school-relevant cognitive functioning. *Developmental Psychology, 23,* 210–215.

Fainsilber-Katz, L., & Gottman, J. M. (1994). Patterns of marital interaction and children's emotional development. In R. D. Parke & S. Kellam (Eds.), *Exploring family relationships with other social contexts* (pp. 49–74). Hillsdale, NJ: Erlbaum.

Farnham-Diggory, S. (1990). *Schooling.* Cambridge, MA: Harvard University Press.

Field, T. M., & Walden, T. A. (1982). Production and discrimination of facial expressions by preschool children. *Child Development, 53,* 1299–1311.

Finnie, V., & Russell, A. (1988). Preschool children's social status and their mother's behavior and knowledge in the supervisory role. *Developmental Psychology, 24,* 789–801.

Garmezy, N. (1988). Stressors of childhood. In N. Garmezy & M. Rutter (Eds.), *Stress, coping and development in children* (pp. 1–42). Baltimore, MD: Johns Hopkins University Press.

Goldberg, W. A., & Easterbrooks, M. A. (1984). Role of marital quality in toddler development. *Developmental Psychology, 20,* 504–514.

Gottfried, A. E., Gottfried, A. W., & Bathurst, K. (1988). Maternal employment, family environment, and children's development. In A. E. Gottfried & A. W. Gottfried (Eds.), *Maternal employment and children's development* (pp. 223–283). Chicago: University of Chicago Press.

Gottman, J. M., & Fainsilber-Katz, L. F. (1989). Effects of marital discord on young children's peer interaction and health. *Developmental Psychology, 25,* 373–381.

Grych, J. H., & Fincham, F. D. (1990). Marital conflict and children's adjustment: A cognitive-contextual framework. *Psychological Bulletin, 108,* 267–290.

Grych, J. H., & Fincham, F. D. (1993). Children's appraisals of marital conflict: Initial investigations of the cognitive-contextual framework. *Child Development, 64,* 215–230.

Haertel, G. D., Walberg, H. J., & Haertel, E. H. (1979, April). *Socio-psychological environments and learning: A quantitative synthesis.* Paper presented at the biennial meeting of the American Educational Research Association, San Francisco.

Hamilton, S. F. (1983). The social side of schooling: Ecological studies of classrooms and schools. *Elementary School Journal, 83,* 313–334.

Hansen, D. A. (1986). Family-school articulations: The effects of interaction rule mismatch. *American Educational Research Journal, 23,* 643–659.

Hayes, C. D., & Kamerman, S. B. (1983). Conclusions and recommendations. In C. D. Hayes & S. B. Kamerman (Eds.), *Children of working parents* (pp. 220–247). Washington, DC: National Academy Press.

Hess, R. D., & Holloway, S. D. (1984). Family and school as educational institutions. In R. D. Parke, R. N. Emde, H. P. McAdoo, & E. P. Sackett (Eds.), *Review of child development research* (Vol. 7, pp. 179–221). Chicago: University of Chicago Press.

Hess, R. D., & Shipman, V. C. (1967). Cognitive elements in maternal behavior. In J. P. Hill (Ed.), *Minnesota symposia on child psychology* (Vol. 1, pp. 57–86). Minneapolis: University of Minnesota Press.

Hetherington, E. M., Cox, M., & Cox, R. (1979). Play and social interaction in children following divorce. *Journal of Social Issues, 35,* 26–49.

Hoffman, L. W. (1984). Work, family, and the socialization of the child. In R. D. Parke, R. N. Emde, H. P. McAdoo, & G. P. Sackett (Eds.), *Review of child development: Vol. 7. The family* (pp. 223–283). Chicago: University of Chicago Press.

Howes, C., & Markman, H. (1989). Marital quality and child functioning: A longitudinal investigation. *Child Development, 60,* 1044–1051.

Johnson, J. E., & McGillicuddy-Delisi, A. (1983). Family environment factors and children's knowledge of rules and conventions. *Child Development, 54,* 218–226.

Kellam, S. G. (1994). The social adaptation of children in classrooms: A measure of family child rearing effectiveness. In R. D. Parke & S. G. Kellam (Eds.), *Exploring family relationships with other social contexts.* Hillsdale, NJ: Erlbaum.

Kohn, M. L. (1977). *Class and conformity.* Chicago: University of Chicago Press.

Kopp, C. (1989). Regulation of distress and negative emotions: A developmental view. *Developmental Psychology, 25,* 343–354.

Kupersmidt, J. B., Coie, J. D., & Dodge, K. A. (1990). The role of poor peer relationships in the development of disorder. In S. R. Asher & J. D. Coie (Eds.), *Peer rejection in childhood* (pp. 274–305). Cambridge: Cambridge University Press.

Ladd, G. W. (1996). Shifting ecologies during the 5 to 7 year period: Predicting children's adjustment during the transition to grade school. In A. J. Sameroff & M. M. Haith (Eds.), *The five to seven year shift: The age of reason and responsibility* (chap. 16, this vol.). Chicago: University of Chicago Press.

Ladd, G., & Price, J. M. (1987). Predicting children's social and school adjustment following the transition from preschool to kindergarten. *Child Development, 58,* 1168–1189.

Lambert, N. (1988). Adolescent outcomes for hyperactive children: Perspectives on general and specific patterns of childhood risk for adolescent educational, social, and mental health problems. *American Psychologist, 43,* 786–799.

Lareau, A. (1987). Social class differences in family-school relationships: The importance of cultural capital. *Sociology of Education, 60,* 73–85.

Leitch, M. L., & Tangri, S. S. (1988). Barriers to home-school collaboration. *Educational Horizons, 66,* 70–74.

Lerner, J. V., & Galambos, N. L. (1988). The influence of maternal employment across life: The New York longitudinal study. In A. E. Gottfried & A. W. Gottfried (Eds.), *Maternal employment and children's development* (pp. 59–84). New York: Plenum.

Lightfoot, S. L. (1978). *Worlds apart: Relationships between families and school.* New York: Basic Books.

Maccoby, E. E. (1980). *Social development: Psychological growth and the parent-child relationship.* New York: Harcourt, Brace & Jovanovitch.

MacDonald, K. B. (1987). Parent-child physical play with rejected, neglected, and popular boys. *Developmental Psychology, 23,* 705–711.

MacDonald, K. B., & Parke, R. D. (1984). Bridging the gap: Parent-child play interaction and peer interactive competence. *Child Development, 55,* 1265–1277.

Marshall, H. H., & Weinstein, R. S. (1984). Classroom factors affecting students' self-evaluations: An interactional model. *Review of Educational Research, 54,* 301–325.

Minuchin, P., & Shapiro, E. K. (1983). The school as a context for social development. In P. H. Mussen (Ed.), *Handbook of child psychology:* Vol. 4. *Socialization, personality and development* (pp. 195–274). New York: Wiley.

Moore, T. (1966). Difficulties of the ordinary child in adjusting to primary school. *Journal of Child Psychology, 7,* 17–38.

Mortimer, J. T. (1976). Social class, work and the family: Some implications of the father's occupation for familial relationships and son's career decisions. *Journal of Marriage and the Family, 38,* 241–256.

Muth, S., Burks, V., Carson, J., & Parke, R. D. (1988). Peer competence: Parent-child interaction and emotional communication skills. Unpublished manuscript, University of Illinois at Urbana-Champaign.

O'Donnel, L., & Steuve, A. (1983). Mothers as social agents: Structuring the community activities of school-aged children. *Research in the interweave of social roles: Jobs and Families* (Vol. 3, pp. 113–129). Greenwich, CT: JAI Press.

Parke, R. D. (1988). Families in life-span perspective: A multilevel developmental approach. In E. M. Hetherington, R. M. Lerner, & M. Perlmutter (Eds.), *Child development in life-span perspective* (pp. 159–190). Hillsdale, NJ: Erlbaum.

Parke, R. D., MacDonald, K. B., Burks, V. M., Bhavnagri, N., Barth, J. M., & Beitel, A. (1989). Family and peer systems: In search of the linkages. In K. Kreppner & M. Lerner (Eds.), *Family systems of life-span development* (pp. 65–92). Hillsdale, NJ: Erlbaum.

Parker, J. G., & Asher, S. R. (1987). Peer relations and later personal adjustment: Are low acceptance children at risk? *Psychological Bulletin, 102,* 357–389.

Parsons, J. E., Kaczala, C. M., & Meece, J. L. (1982). Socialization of achievement attitudes and beliefs: Classroom influences. *Child Development, 53,* 322–339.

Patterson, C. J., Griesler, P. C., Vaden, N. A., & Kupersmidt, J. B. (1992). Family economic circumstances, life transitions and children's peer relations. In R. D. Parke & G. W. Ladd (Eds.), *Family-peer relationships: Modes of linkage* (pp. 385–424). Hillsdale, NJ: Erlbaum.

Patterson, C. J., Vaden, N. A., & Kupersmidt, J. B. (1991). Family background, recent life events, and peer rejection during childhood. *Journal of Social and Personal Relationships, 8,* 347–361.

Pelligrini, A. (1991). A longitudinal study of popular and rejected children's rough and tumble play. *Early Education and Development, 2,* 205–213.

Pettit, G., Dodge, K., & Brown, M. (1988). Early family experiences, social problem solving patterns and children's social competence. *Child Development, 59,* 107–120.

Philippot, P., & Feldman, R. S. (1990). Age and social competence in preschoolers' decoding of facial expression. *British Journal of Social Psychology, 29,* 43–54.

Pintrich, P. R., & Blumenfield, P. C. (1985). Classroom experience and children's self-perceptions of ability. *Journal of Educational Psychology, 77,* 646–657.

Piotrkowski, C. S. (1979). *Work and family systems: A naturalistic study of working class and lower middle class families.* New York: Free Press.

Putallaz, M. (1987). Maternal behavior and children's sociometric status. *Child Development, 58,* 332–340.

Putallaz, M., & Heflin, A. H. (1990). Parent-child interaction. In S. R. Asher & J. D. Coie (Eds.), *Peer rejection in childhood.* Cambridge: Cambridge University Press.

Renken, B., Egeland, B., Marvinney, D., Mangelsdorf, S., & Sroufe, L. A. (1989). Early childhood antecedents of aggression and passive-withdrawal in early elementary school. *Journal of Personality, 57,* 257–281.

Repetti, R. L. (1989). Effects of daily workload on subsequent behavior during marital interaction: The roles of social withdrawal and spouse support. *Journal of Personality and Social Psychology, 57,* 651–659.

Repetti, R. L. (1993). Short-term and long-term processes linking job stress to father-child interaction. *Social Development, 3,* 1–15.

Rist, R. C. (1970). Student social class and teacher expectations: The self-fulfilling prophecy in ghetto education. *Harvard Educational Review, 40,* 411–451.

Rist, R. (1973). *The urban school: A factory for failure.* Cambridge, MA: MIT Press.

Rogoff, B. (1990). *Apprenticeship in thinking.* New York: Oxford University Press.

Rohrkemper, M. (1984). The influence of teacher socialization on students' social cognition and reported interpersonal classroom behavior. *Elementary School Journal, 85,* 245–275.

Rosenthal, R., & Jacobson, L. (1968). *Pygmalion in the classroom.* New York: Holt, Rinehart & Winston.

Russell, A., & Finnie, V. (1990). Preschool children's social status and maternal instructions to assist group entry. *Developmental Psychology, 26,* 603–611.

Sameroff, A. J., & Fiese, B. H. (1990). Transactional regulations and early intervention. In S. J. Meisels & J. P. Shonkoff (Eds.), *Handbook of early childhood intervention* (pp. 119–149). New York: Cambridge University Press.

Sameroff, A. J., Seifer, R., Baldwin, A., & Baldwin, C. (1993). Stability of intelligence from preschool to adolescence: The influence of social and family risk factors. *Child Development, 64,* 80–97.

Schaefer, E. S., & Hunter, W. M. (1983, April). *Mother-infant interaction and maternal psychological predictors of kindergarten adaption.* Paper presented at the biennial meeting of the Society for Research in Child Development, Detroit, MI.

Seefeldt, C. (1985). Parent involvement: Support or stress? *Childhood Education, 62,* 98–102.

Shaw, D. S., & Emery, R. E. (1987). Parental conflict and other correlates of the adjustment of school-age children whose parents have separated. *Journal of Abnormal Child Psychology, 15,* 269–281.

Shipman, M. D. (1972). *Childhood: A sociological perspective.* Windsor, England: NFER Publishing Co.

Smith, M. B. (1968). School and home: Focus on achievement. In A. H. Passow (Ed.), *Developing programs for the educationally disadvantaged.* New York: Teachers College Press.

Sroufe, L. A. (1983). Infant-caregiver attachment and patterns of adaptation in preschool: The roots of maladaptation and competence. In M. Perlmutter (Ed.), *Minnesota symposium in child psychology* (Vol. *16,* pp. 41–81). Hillsdale, NJ: Erlbaum.

Sroufe, L. A., & Fleeson, J. (1986). Attachment and the construction of relationships. In W. W. Hartup & Z. Rubin (Eds.), *Relationships and development* (pp. 51–72). Hillsdale, NJ: Erlbaum.

Steinberg, L., Elmen, J. D., & Mounts, N. S. (1989). Authoritative parenting, psychosocial maturity, and academic success among adolescents. *Child Development, 60,* 1424–1436.

Stevenson, D. L., & Baker, D. P. (1987). The family-school relation and the child's school performance. *Child Development, 58,* 1348–1357.

Stipek, D. (1992). The child at school. In M. H. Bornstein & M. E. Lamb (Eds.), *Developmental psychology: An advanced textbook* (pp. 579–625). Hillsdale, NJ: Erlbaum.

Vaden, N. A., Patterson, C. J., & Kupersmidt, J. B. (1988, March). *Family background, life events, and personal characteristics as predictors of peer rejection during childhood.* Paper presented at the Conference on Human Development, Charleston, SC.

Walberg, H. J. (1984). Families as partners in educational productivity. *Phi Delta Kappan, 65,* 397–400.

Weinstein, R. S. (1989). Perceptions of classroom processes and student motivation: Children's views of self-fulfilling prophecies. In R. Ames & C. Ames (Eds.), *Research on motivation in education: Vol. 3. Goals and cognitions* (pp. 359–369). New York: Academic Press.

Weinstein, R. S., Marshall, H. H., Sharp, L., & Botkin, M. (1987). Pygmalion and the student: Age and classroom differences in children's awareness of teacher expectations. *Child Development, 58,* 1079–1093.

Youngblade, L. M., & Belsky, J. (1992). Parent-child antecedents of 5-year-old close friendships: A longitudinal analysis. *Developmental Psychology, 28,* 700–713.

Zajonc, R. B., & Markus, G. B. (1975). Birth order and intellectual development. *Psychological Review, 82,* 74–88.

Zuckerman, M., & Przewuzman, S. J. (1979). Decoding and encoding facial expressions in preschool-aged children. *Environmental Psychology and Nonverbal Behavior, 3,* 147–163.

CHAPTER SIXTEEN

Shifting Ecologies During the 5 to 7 Year Period: Predicting Children's Adjustment During the Transition to Grade School

GARY W. LADD

During early childhood, children participate in a variety of ecological transitions that require adaptation to new or altered environments. For most children who are raised in the United States, the 5- to 7-year age period begins with a significant ecological shift—the transition to kindergarten. In many respects this transition constitutes a rather abrupt change in early nonfamilial rearing conditions and, thus, represents a major qualitative environmental discontinuity. This overall qualitative change can be viewed as the summation of quantifiable changes in a number of dimensions, including temporal, physical, and interpersonal features of the child's school environment.

From a temporal perspective, entrance into kindergarten is not a gradual process, that is, a series of steps that children undertake until they are ready for a full day of school. Nor is kindergarten entrance timed to correspond with the individual child's developmental achievements or timetables. Rather, chronological age alone determines when children will begin school—the timing of children's birthdays, not their developmental states or achievements, determines when they will enter kindergarten.

Entrance into formal schooling typically exposes children to substantial changes in physical environments. To attend kindergarten, most children move from smaller settings with higher adult-child ratios, such as the home, family day care, or preschool, to larger settings with lower adult-child ratios, as found in grade-school complexes with large class sizes. Also, because kindergarten classrooms tend to be housed in elementary schools, young children are often faced with physical challenges such as traveling greater distances from home, riding school buses, and finding their way through larger school buildings.

Children also experience a significant "cultural" shift as they start grade school because, unlike most family, day-care, or preschool environments, kindergartens are specifically designed to prepare children for the rigors of formal schooling. Thus, compared to what happens in preschool, important shifts occur in the types of academic and social demands that are placed on children and in the value systems that are used to evaluate their development and progress. Kindergartens, for example, tend to be more scholastically focused than most preschool or day-care programs and, thus, place greater demands on children's physical and intellectual resources. Compared to their time spent in preschool, children spend less time engaging in semi- or unstructured activities such as "play" and more time working on structured preacademic tasks such as reading-readiness activities. Accordingly, many new rules and regulations are introduced to govern children's behavior and their use of time. Children are also introduced to higher levels of critical feedback about their academic skills and abilities, and increasingly, their achievements are judged against explicit performance standards.

In addition to these changes in socialization settings and "cultures," the transition to grade school creates a significant shift in children's social ecologies. Compared to many family and preschool environments, the adult to peer ratio is often smaller in kindergarten classrooms. As a result, children are required to spend more time interacting with peers than with adults and must engage in higher levels of competition for adult attention. In addition, opportunities for mixed-age companionship are less common in kindergarten than in many preschool environments because grade-school classrooms tend to be segregated by age. Thus, children in kindergarten are under greater pressure to achieve among equals. They must succeed at forming relationships with agemates and, at the same time, compete with them for resources and recognition.

The transition to kindergarten also brings about a significant shift in the composition of children's peer networks. As they begin school, children are likely to lose many of their preschool friends and playmates and meet many new peers in their kindergarten classrooms. In fact, studies show that children are often thrust into new peer groups with unfamiliar classmates as they enter kindergarten (see Ladd & Price, 1987). Thus, the peer groups that children join as they enter kindergarten tend to be not only larger and more homogeneous in age but also novel.

Furthermore, school entrance may also bring about important changes in children's families and in the relationships they have with caretakers. As children enter grade school, they often leave behind ties that were formed with preschool caretakers, sitters, and day-care teachers, and begin a relationship with their kindergarten teacher. Moreover, once children are in school, full-time parents may return to work, and those who are employed may no longer rely on people outside the home for child care.

The Role of Child Characteristics and Relational Supports in Early School Adjustment

It is also likely that major environment shifts, such as the transition to kindergarten, precipitate important transformations in the child. When environments change radically, children are confronted with new tasks and demands. School transitions, as we have seen, are likely to present children with an array of challenges or perturbations that they must adapt to during their first year of grade school. A number of factors may affect children's success in dealing with these challenges. For example, the manner in which children embrace these challenges, and the resources they have at their disposal as they attempt to do so, may ultimately shape their development and adjustment in these settings.

A Person-by-Environment Model of Early School Adjustment

The conceptual framework we have used to explore the precursors of children's early school adjustment has evolved from recent person-by-environment theories of adaptation (cf. Garmezy, Masten, & Tellegen, 1984; Heller & Swindle, 1983; Ladd & Price, 1987). This model, which is summarized in Figure 16.1, depicts school adjustment as an outcome of children's attempts to adapt to the demands of the school environment. The types of adjustment outcomes children experience are hypothesized to be a function of both their personal-social characteristics, including organismic factors, and features of their interpersonal environments. Thus, a central assumption of this model is that the origins of early school adjustment lie both in the child and in his or her interpersonal environment.

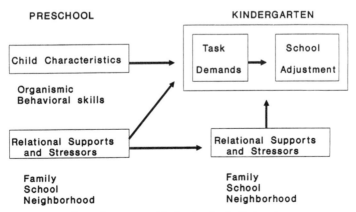

Figure 16.1   A person-by-environment model of early school adjustment.

Characteristics That Children "Bring" to Transitions

One set of variables that can be located within the child are organismic characteristics, such as the child's age or gender. These characteristics represent features of the child's biological makeup or developmental status and may influence both the kinds of responses children can make to new demands and the types of responses that agents such as parents or direct toward the child during environmental shifts.

Children's behaviors, or the types of responses they generate in the face of new challenges, represent another set of variables that can be located within the child. When children are presented with new demands or altered contingencies, they may cope or react to these demands in different ways (see Rutter, 1983). Research with children and adolescents suggests that coping can be an active or passive process and may take a variety of forms, including positive coping, projective coping, denial coping, and noncoping (Compas, Malcarne, & Fondacaro, 1988; Connell & Ilardi, 1987; Tero & Connell, 1984). Active coping occurs when children directly confront or respond to environmental challenges. Children who engage in active forms of coping may address novel demands with "old" behaviors, such as responses that they have developed previously for other purposes, or they may rely on experimentation or improvisation to invent "new" behaviors. Passive forms of coping occur when children fail to confront new demands or take action; passive forms of coping may include not responding to environmental demands, blaming others, or undertaking efforts to escape, avoid, or deny challenging contexts.

Along with more immutable child characteristics, it is assumed that coping behaviors produce differing outcomes in challenging contexts. Coping behaviors can be viewed as adaptive if they tend to maximize positive outcomes such as caretaker approval, cognitive or emotional equilibrium, favorable self-esteem or positive self-perceptions, and achievement, and they tend to minimize negative outcomes such as punishments, negative emotional states, cognitive disequilibrium or dissonance, and academic failures. Thus, some of the coping processes children employ in challenging or stressful circumstances may increase the risk of maladjustment, whereas others may enhance the likelihood of adaptation (Lazarus, Cohen, Folkman, Kanner, & Schaefer, 1980).

Consistent with this premise, there is growing evidence to suggest that children's personal and behavioral attributes are associated with school adjustment and progress. Certain organismic attributes and child competencies appear to be important predictors of school progress. Girls, for example, are more likely to develop lower or inaccurate perceptions of their competence (Block, 1983; Dweck, 1986; Dweck & Elliott, 1983; Ladd & Price, 1986), and boys are at greater risk for conduct problems in the classroom (Garmezy et al., 1984; Ladd & Price, 1987). Children's mental abilities and basic academic skills predict achievement in the early primary grades (Stevenson, Parker, Wilkinson, Hegion, & Fish, 1976), and their behavioral styles (e.g., prosocial vs. aggressive) forecast later peer rejection, classroom disruption, and school avoidance (Ladd & Price, 1987; Parker & Asher, 1987). Less is known, however, about the contributions of specific child characteristics to different forms of school adjustment such as school perceptions and performance.

Relational Supports and Stressors in the Child's Environment

Another set of variables that may influence children's success in dealing with changing environmental demands lies in the child's interpersonal relationships. Included among these are the interpersonal relationships that children have formed with parents, teachers, and peers. Children's relationships may serve a number of functions that may enhance or impede their adaptation to new environments. Moreover, children's relationships may make important contributions to adjustment not only during the process of adaptation but also before they confront new challenges.

Prior to environmental shifts, relationships may serve important preparatory or formative functions. Some parents, for example, may anticipate the demands of future transitions and prepare children for these challenges before they occur. During transitions, children's relationships may function as supports, stressors, or both and thereby exert a positive or negative impact on their coping strategies and adjustment outcomes. A close relationship with the teacher or access to friends, for example, may provide children with resources that mitigate adaptive demands, such as instrumental assistance or instrumental instruction or emotional support (e.g., a "secure base"). In contrast, relationships that negatively impact on the child or the absence of supportive relationships may interfere with children's adaptation to new environments. For example, peer bullying or victimization may exacerbate the demands of new or challenging situations and may have a debilitating effect on children's adjustment.

Evidence that supports these contentions has begun to accumulate in the research literature. A number of studies show that children's experiences and relationships in the family, school, and neighborhood are related to school adjustment outcomes. Families are a primary support system for most children, and their experiences in this context may play an important role in early school adjustment. Exposure to stressful life events in the family may place children at risk for school maladjustment (see Cowen, Lotyczewski, & Weissberg, 1984; Garmezy et al., 1984; Sandler & Ramsay, 1980), and the form of family stress may affect the type of adjustment problems children display in the classroom. Felner, Stolberg, and Cowen (1975), for example, found that children who had recently suffered the death of a parent tended to be withdrawn at school, whereas those who had lost a parent through divorce were more likely to be disruptive and disorderly in the classroom. Prior theory and research (Bronfenbrenner, 1979) has also suggested that cooperative linkages between the home and school environment, such as exchanging information about the child and fostering schoolwork at home, can facilitate children's progress in school. Beyond this, various socialization practices in the family, such as parents' management of children's peer relations, may have a bearing on children's school adjustment. Parents who arrange opportunities for their children to meet and play with age-mates during the preschool years may help their children to develop the interpersonal skills needed to establish relationships with unfamiliar peers as they enter grade school and move from grade to grade (see Ladd & Golter, 1988).

Experience with schooling and features of the school environment may also affect the degree to which children adapt to educational demands. Prior school experience may facilitate school adjustment, especially as children enter grade school. For example, as Ladd and Price (1987) have argued, children with considerable preschool experience may well have mastered tasks such as separating from parents, accepting the teacher's authority, meeting new peers, and negotiating large group settings. The result may be that these children face fewer adjustment demands as they enter school or, perhaps, that the demands they do face are perceived as less discrepant with past experience and, therefore, less stressful to accommodate.

Once children are in grade school, features of the school environment may have an important bearing on adjustment processes and outcomes. Within this context, it is hypothesized that children's interpersonal relationships with teachers and peers play an important role in their school adjustment by serving as sources of support or stress. Recent evidence indicates that young children who develop close relationships with their teachers (i.e., "attachments") appear to develop more sophisticated interpersonal skills (Howes, 1991). Similarly, the importance of supportive peer relationships is underscored by evidence indicating that the quality of children's classroom peer relations forecasts school avoidance, disruption, and failure (Coie & Krehbiel, 1984; Kupersmidt, 1983; Parker & Asher, 1987). Moreover, children's self-esteem and achievement appear to suffer in the absence of supportive school friendships (Bukowski & Hoza, 1989; Krappman, 1985).

School adjustment may also be influenced by children's friendships in the neighborhood or nonschool settings (see Cowen et al., 1984; Ladd & Price, 1987). It is hypothesized that the features of the friendships children form outside the school context may vary in ways that facilitate or impede school adjustment. One potentially important feature is the type of companionship children pursue in the neighborhood. For example, children who choose to relate with younger companions in the neighborhood may find grade-school classrooms, which tend to consist of age-mates, a less familiar or more stressful environment (Ladd & Price, 1987). It is also possible that children may compensate for failures to develop supportive peer relationships at school by doing so in the neighborhood.

Another relevant feature may be the stability of children's friendships in the neighborhood. A number of researchers have argued that the continuity of an individual's social networks or close personal relationships is related to his or her success in coping with life's demands (e.g., Blyth & Traeger, 1988; Howes, 1983, 1988). Recent evidence has suggested that this may also be the case for children who develop stable friendships in the neighborhood, especially during the transition to grade school (Ladd & Price, 1987).

The Interplay Between Child Characteristics and Relational Supports or Stressors

In all likelihood, children's adjustment to ecological transitions is determined in multiple ways—that is, influenced not only by their organismic and behavioral characteristics but also by their access to supportive or stressful relationships. Investigators have in the past decade or so begun to develop hypotheses about how these factors may combine to influence adjustment, and some of the most promising models have evolved from person-by-environment theories of adaptation (e.g., Garmezy et al., 1984; Heller & Swindle, 1983; Ladd, 1989). Two hypotheses, analogous to the compensatory and protective models proposed by Garmezy et al. (1984), are especially germane to this question.

One hypothesis that emerges from this literature is that, in the context of new environmental demands, children's attributes and relational ties make "additive" contributions to their adjustment. An additive model implies that, in addition to the effects of specific child characteristics, environmental supports or stressors may contribute uniquely to adjustment outcomes. For example, in the context of a school transition, personal attributes that reduce children's motivation or success at dealing with changing environmental demands, such as low intellectual ability, may be partially offset by relational supports (e.g., a supportive relationship with the teacher) or exacerbated by interpersonal stressors (e.g., rejection by classmates). Similarly, attributes that increase the likelihood of adjustment may be mitigated or enhanced by stressful or supportive relationships, respectively. Consistent with this model, Ladd and Price (1987) found that children with antisocial behavioral styles in preschool and early kindergarten achieved higher levels of school adjustment in kindergarten if they began school in classrooms with familiar peers—a supportive interpersonal context.

Equally plausible is the hypothesis that children's attributes "interact" with relational supports or stressors to determine adjustment—that is, rather than combining in an additive way, the impact of child characteristics or relational ties on adjustment may be conditional. For example, certain child characteristics may make children especially receptive or immune to the effects of interpersonal supports or stressors. Consistent with this proposition, Garmezy et al. (1984) have shown that the achievement of high-ability children suffers more in the context of stressful parent-child relationships than does the achievement of low-ability children. There is also evidence to suggest that the contributions of interpersonal supports or stressors vary as a function of children's gender. Boys appear to be more affected by factors associated with parenting stress than are girls (e.g., divorce and father absence; Hetherington, Cox, & Cox, 1982; Hetherington, 1989) and may, therefore, be more vulnerable to certain types of adjustment problems (e.g., classroom disruption, externalizing disorders; See Felner, Stolberg, & Cowen, 1975). During early school transitions, boys also appear to be at greater risk for classroom peer rejection (Ladd & Price, 1987), which may, over time, increase their risk for various forms of maladjustment (see Parker & Asher, 1987).

The Concept of School Adjustment

Children who are exposed to the challenges of early school transitions must adapt, and it is likely that they will do so with varying degrees of success. However, little agreement exists in the literature as to what constitutes evidence of children's adaptive success following the transition to grade school. One solution to this dilemma is to identify key indicators of children's adaptive success and locate them within a larger system of variables that can be construed as "school adjustment" (see Ladd, 1989; Ladd & Price, 1987). However, previous investigators have tended to use the term *school adjustment* loosely, often to refer to a narrow range of school-oriented or education-oriented variables. Consequently, the concept of school adjustment brings with it some unwanted conceptual baggage.

Until recently, many investigators have equated the concept of school adjustment with measures of children's academic achievement or achievement-related behaviors. Most of what is known about the determinants of early school adjustment has come from research on the socialization of children's cognitive skills, such as studies of the effects of preschool programs and curricula (e.g., Lazar & Darlington, 1982) and the effects of home environments (e.g., Bradley, Caldwell, & Rock, 1988). Few investigators have studied the interpersonal precursors of school adjustment, such as the adaptive significance of children's social competencies and relationships during school transitions.

Another problem is that, conceptually, little effort has been made to link the concept of school adjustment to processes that occur before or during the transition to kindergarten. In part, this problem may be overcome by defining school adjustment in terms of the child's success at coping with specific challenges or demands that occur during school transitions. Moreover, the concept of school adjustment should be expanded to include indices that reflect children's success in dealing with differing types of challenges or task domains, including those that reflect success at interpersonal in addition to academic challenges.

Furthermore, researchers have tended to study potential predictors of school adjustment independently rather than jointly, and in the context of cross-sectional research designs rather than longitudinal ones. The process through which children adapt to school is complex and influenced by many factors; insight into how these factors combine or interact to produce higher or lower levels of school adjustment will not be achieved by studying potential predictors in isolation. Moreover, because the processes through which children adapt to school are undoubtedly not static ones, what researchers can learn from cross-sectional studies is restricted. Rather, it is likely that experiences that prepare children for school and the processes of coping and adaptation are dynamic in nature and can best be explicated within longitudinal investigations.

In view of these limitations, we have proposed that the concept of school adjustment be broadened to encompass not only the degree to which children embrace and succeed in both the interpersonal and academic contexts of the classroom, but also children's perceptions and feelings about the school environment (Ladd & Price, 1987; Ladd, 1990). Specifically, we define school adjustment as the degree to which children become interested, engaged, comfortable, and successful in the school environment. Therefore, as children enter grade school, adjustment is reflected in the degree to which they develop positive versus negative perceptions of school, feel comfortable versus distressed in new classrooms, become involved versus avoid school and school-related activities, and progress versus fall behind at academic tasks (Bogat, Jones, & Jason, 1980; Ladd, 1990; Ladd & Price, 1987). Each of these adjustment dimensions is assumed to be an important precursor of children's subsequent educational progress. For example, children who like school and become involved in classroom activities are more likely to learn and profit from their educational experiences. Conversely, children who develop negative attitudes toward school or an inclination to avoid or withdraw from the school environment are likely to have additional adjustment problems and disrupted progress.

Our efforts to assess school adjustment have been organized around four key concepts, and for each concept, we have attempted to gather information from multiple indicators. Specifically, the measures we have used to tap school adjustment outcomes have been organized into the following categories: (a) children's perceptions of school and various aspects of the school environment, including measures of school liking and attitudes toward classroom activities; (b) classroom affect, including measures of manifest anxiety and loneliness; (c) school involvement, including indicators of school engagement versus avoidance and withdrawal; and (d) school performance, including indices that tap attentional and task-related behaviors and academic "readiness."

Linkages Between Child Characteristics, Relational Supports and Stressors, and Early School Adjustment

The principal aim of our work has been to identify child characteristics and relational supports and stressors within the family, school, and neighborhood that may have an important bearing on children's school adjustment. Although the focus of our empirical work has been concentrated on the transition to grade school, findings we have obtained from studies of earlier ecological transitions (i.e., the transition to preschool; see Ladd, Hart, Wadsworth, & Golter, 1988) are relevant as well and are incorporated into this review.

The Linkage Between Child Attributes and School Adjustment

Children's success in classroom peer relationships depends, in part, on the interaction styles they employ with classmates. Consistent with data gathered with older children (e.g., Younger & Boyko, 1987; Younger & Piccinin, 1989), studies with preschool and kindergarten children show that young children's perceptions of peers' interaction styles, particularly their use of aggressive and prosocial behaviors with peers, are both accurate and stable. These studies also show that young children's behavioral perceptions are related to their liking preferences and friendship choices in the classroom (e.g., see Ladd & Mars, 1986; Masters & Furman, 1981).

Moreover, there is considerable evidence from our work to suggest that the quality of young children's social skills influences the degree to which they succeed at developing supportive peer relationships in the classroom, both before and after the transition to kindergarten. We conducted a short-term longitudinal study of children's entrance into preschool classrooms and examined the relation between children's behavioral styles at the outset of the school year (i.e., prosocial vs. antisocial) and their peer acceptance at the middle and end of the school year (Ladd, Price, & Hart, 1988, 1990). The types of social skills children displayed on the playground among peers during the early weeks of school were predictive of their eventual status among classmates. Whereas children with prosocial styles (e.g., cooperative play) tended to become better liked and less rejected by classmates, those with antisocial styles (e.g., arguing, physical aggression) were more likely to become disliked and rejected. Moreover, children who became rejected by peers had more difficulty finding consistent play companions than did accepted children and were also seen by their teachers as less well adjusted in school. It would seem that in new school environments children's success in establishing supportive peer relationships is partly determined by the types of social skills they display in early social encounters with peers. However, it was unclear from these findings whether children's interaction styles were stable characteristics that they possessed prior to school entry or transient responses to the new school situation.

We gathered further evidence pertaining to this question in a longitudinal study of the transition from preschool to kindergarten (Ladd & Price, 1987). Two aspects of children's behavioral styles were assessed in preschool, including the frequency of their prosocial and antisocial behaviors towards peers and the number of different peers with whom they tended to conduct prosocial versus antisocial interactions. These measures, which reflected children's interactive styles in preschool, were used to predict their emerging peer relations in new schools with unfamiliar kindergarten classmates. Organismic characteristics, such as children's mental age and gender, were also taken into account in analyses designed to evaluate the predictive efficacy of their preexisting social skills.

Results indicated that children's styles of interacting with peers in preschool did, in fact, forecast their peer acceptance and rejection in kindergarten. Children who displayed a broader range of positive peer contacts in preschool—that is, they used prosocial behaviors with many as opposed to only a few peers—achieved more supportive peer relations in kindergarten. Conversely, greater use of antisocial behaviors and a broader range of negative peer contacts in preschool predicted peer rejection in kindergarten. Important sex differences were also found in the relation between children's social skills and their emerging peer relationships. Cooperative play and arguing behaviors in preschool emerged as better predictors of kindergarten peer acceptance and rejection, respectively, for girls than for boys. The stability coefficients obtained for these behavioral measures from preschool to kindergarten were also higher for girls than for boys. In contrast, measures of physical aggression and the range of negative peer contacts observed in preschool were stronger predictors of kindergarten peer rejection for boys than for girls. Moreover, the corresponding stability coefficients were higher for boys than for girls. No relationships were found between children's mental age and their acceptance or rejection in kindergarten.

Another important finding to emerge from the Ladd and Price (1987) study was that children's behavioral styles in preschool also predicted teachers' perceptions of classroom maladjustment in kindergarten. More specifically, children who were aggressive toward peers in preschool tended to be seen by kindergarten teachers as disruptive and hostile in the classroom. The same results were found for boys whose preschool peer interactions had been characterized by a broad range of negative contacts. An additional finding was that boys with more negative contacts in preschool were also seen by kindergarten teachers as hyperactive and distractible.

Taken together, these findings suggest that children's social skills, particularly their styles of relating to peers, are not merely a unique response to a particular setting but rather a social disposition that is maintained across school contexts and predictive of current and later school adjustment. Moreover, there appear to be important gender differences in the types of social skills that place children at risk for adjustment problems in new school environments.

Our data also suggest that organismic variables are associated with academically oriented school adjustment outcomes. In a longitudinal study conducted across the kindergarten school year, Ladd (1990) found that children's mental age was predictive of their early academic performance and progress. As early as the 2nd month of kindergarten, children with higher mental-age scores tended to receive higher ratings from teachers for competence at academic behaviors and scholastic readiness. Mental age also forecasted gains in school performance across the entire kindergarten year. These data are consistent with past findings and suggest that children's mental maturity may underlie both their initial readiness for kindergarten and subsequent progress during the year (see Stevenson, Parker, Wilkinson, Hegion, & Fish, 1976; Worland, Weeks, & Janes, 1984).

The Linkage Between Relational Supports-Stressors and School Adjustment

Consistent with our model, we have also investigated the linkages between several relational supports-stressors and children's school adjustment. Included among these are aspects of children's relationships in family, classroom, and neighborhood environments.

The Family Environment: Socialization Activities That Prepare Children for School

Within the family, the role that parents play in managing children's *informal* peer relations, such as their play contacts in the home and neighborhood prior to school entry, may be an important precursor of school adjustment. We were interested in determining whether parents' management practices, particularly their efforts to initiate children's nonschool peer contacts during preschool, would predict children's school adjustment in kindergarten (Ladd & Golter, 1988). Using a telephone log methodology, we asked parents to report their daily management activities; we derived scores that indexed the frequency of children's neighborhood peer contacts that parents had initiated for the child and had monitored in a direct manner (e.g., watching children closely, guiding their play) versus an indirect manner (e.g., periodically observing children's activities).

Analyses of the initiation data revealed that parents who initiated a larger number of informal peer contacts tended to have children who had a larger range of play partners and a larger number of consistent play companions or friends. In addition, the frequency with which parents tended to arrange play dates was related to children's peer status in kindergarten—but only for boys. Boys whose parents tended to initiate peer contacts during preschool became better liked and less rejected by peers in kindergarten.

In a follow-up study, we (Ladd & Hart, 1992) replicated this finding but also showed that the frequency of parents' initiations was associated with children's classroom behaviors. Specifically, parents who displayed higher levels of initiation tended to have children who were more prosocial and less withdrawn among classmates in school. The Ladd and Hart data also showed that the strategies parents used to initiate play dates were associated with children's efforts to arrange their own peer contacts. The degree to which parents involved children in the process of arranging informal play activities was positively correlated with the frequency with which children initiated their own peer contacts. Children who initiated more of their own play activities, in turn, displayed fewer anxious behaviors in the classroom.

One interpretation of these findings is that parents who sponsor frequent play opportunities at home ensure that their children will have regular contact with certain playmates and develop diverse or extensive peer networks. By participating in these informal relational contexts, children learn many skills that will transfer to classroom settings—for example, the ability to be sociable and prosocial with peers (see Howes, 1983, 1988). Moreover, because extensive social ties appear to be normative among boys (Ladd, 1983; Ladd, Price, & Hart, 1990; Waldrop & Halverson, 1975), boys whose parents foster diverse peer networks may be better able to negotiate multiple peer relationships and group activities in school, and thus, achieve higher levels of peer acceptance in the classroom.

Ladd and Golter (1988) also examined another aspect of parents' management behavior—the extent to which they supervised children's informal peer contacts in a direct versus indirect manner. Parents' styles of monitoring were found to be related to later school maladjustment for both boys and girls. Children whose parents tended to use direct as opposed to indirect forms of monitoring during preschool tended to become less accepted and more rejected by peers in kindergarten and had more classroom behavior problems, such as disruptiveness and aggression.

These findings are consistent with the view that parents' supervisory styles impact children's school adjustment, especially their ability to establish supportive social ties with classmates. For example, it may be the case that direct monitoring represents a type of parental control that prevents children from independently mastering and generalizing peer-related social skills. Another possibility is that children who tend to be directly supervised by parents at home may not be as well prepared for classroom settings that afford less adult guidance and attention and, thus, respond to what is perceived as a lack of structure by becoming more disruptive or unruly.

In addition to managing children's peer relations in the home and neighborhood, parents may help children adjust to school by providing them with opportunities to relate with peers in a variety of community settings such as playground, library, pool, and church school. By exposing children to different settings, peers, and rules for behavior, parents may help children become more autonomous and comfortable in new environments and more skillful at establishing new relationships. To explore this hypothesis, we employed parents' reports of the diversity of community settings in which children had regular peer contact during preschool to forecast children's school adjustment following their entrance into kindergarten (Ladd & Price, 1987). Results showed that children who had participated in multiple peer contexts during early childhood were more comfortable in the new school environment and displayed lower levels of school avoidance. Specifically, the measure of preschool peer contexts predicted lower levels of classroom anxiety and requests to see the school nurse at the beginning of kindergarten and fewer absences from school at both the beginning and the end of kindergarten.

The School Environment: Prior School Experience and Relational Supports and Stressors in the Classroom

We have also investigated several aspects of the *school* environment that are hypothesized to be precursors of children's school adjustment (Ladd & Price, 1987). Measures were obtained of the duration of children's experience in preschool classrooms and the percentage of time that children spent playing with younger, same-age, and older peers in these settings. These measures were deemed to be important antecedents of kindergarten adjustment for the following reasons: First, children with considerable preschool experience may have a head start at mastering important school-related tasks such as separating from parents, meeting new peers, forming relationships with teachers, negotiating the culture of the school, and so on. Children who accumulate this type of experience may face fewer adjustment demands as they enter kindergarten, or they may perceive the demands they do face as less discrepant with their past experience and, therefore, easier to accommodate. Second, because most grade-school classrooms require that children relate with age-mates, children who have demonstrated a preference for younger companions in preschool may be at a disadvantage. Moreover, overinvolvement in this type of relationship may be associated with lower maturity demands and, ultimately, failure to develop age-appropriate social skills and relationships (see Ladd, 1983, 1984).

In fact, we found that both the duration of children's preschool experience and their association with younger companions were associated with their posttransition school adjustment. Children with greater preschool experience displayed fewer anxious behaviors during the early weeks of kindergarten, and those who preferred to relate with younger classmates in preschool developed negative attitudes toward school that endured throughout the school year.

Further efforts to explore these questions revealed that children's preschool experience predicted their academic performance during the early months of kindergarten (Ladd, 1990). After 2 months of kindergarten, children with greater preschool experience tended to receive higher ratings from teachers for academic behaviors and readiness. This study also showed that, although the duration of children's preschool experience was not predictive of their early school perceptions, it did forecast changes in children's perceptions over the course of the school year. Children with more preschool experience tended to develop more favorable views of school and the school environment across the kindergarten year. Perhaps children with greater preschool experience found it easier to adapt to kindergarten routines and, over time, developed more positive views of school.

In addition to these potential antecedents, we hypothesized that interpersonal features of the new school environment, such as the relationships that kindergarten children formed with classmates and teachers, might influence children's school adjustment. Based on past research indicating that friends and familiar peers can be an important source of emotional support in novel situations (e.g., Ispa, 1981; Schwarz, 1972), we anticipated that the proportion of familiar peers in children's kindergarten classrooms would be positively related to their school adjustment. Indeed, children who began kindergarten in classrooms with familiar peers were less anxious at the outset of the school year and made fewer requests to visit the school nurse. These children were also more likely to develop stable, positive attitudes toward the new school environment.

Unfortunately, our familiar peers measure was a global one and did not distinguish among the types of peer relationships children had with their kindergarten classmates. Familiar peers, as they were defined in this study (Ladd & Price, 1987), consisted of all classmates a child had known prior to school entrance. Thus, it was not possible for us to distinguish between the contributions of familiar peers versus friends.

However, in a follow-up study, Ladd (1990) further explored the relation between children's peer relationships in new kindergarten classrooms and their school adjustment. Measures included both the number of acquaintances and the number of "prior" friends, that is, peers who were friends with the child prior to the start of school, who were enrolled in children's kindergarten classrooms at the beginning of the school year. This more differentiated look at the peer composition of children's classrooms revealed that only the classroom friendship measures were associated with early school adjustment. Specifically, the results showed that children with more classroom friends at school entrance developed more favorable perceptions of school by the second month, and children who maintained these relationships tended to like school better as the year progressed. Children who made more new friends in the classroom increased in school readiness over the school year.

The *quality* of the friendships that children form with classmates may also have an important bearing on their adjustment to school. Specifically, the relational or dynamic features of classroom friendships (e.g., degree of validation, aid, conflict) may provide various psychological benefits and costs for children that, in turn, impact their adjustment in this context. Such social "provisions," as Weiss (1974) has termed them, may be present to varying degrees in children's friendships, depending on the nature of the relationship and the characteristics of the partners. Our efforts to probe this aspect of friendship (Ladd, Kochenderfer, & Coleman, in press) reveal that kindergarten children who saw their friends as sources of validation and aid were more likely to develop positive perceptions of their classmates and favorable attitudes toward school. Further, among boys, classroom friendships that were characterized by high levels of conflict were associated with multiple forms of school maladjustment, including higher levels of school loneliness and avoidance, and lower levels of school liking and engagement.

In addition to friendships, Ladd (1990) also explored linkages between children's classroom peer acceptance and their adjustment to kindergarten over the school year. These findings were even stronger than those obtained for friendship and indicated that rejection by one's classmates early in the school year forecasted less favorable school perceptions, higher levels of school avoidance, and lower levels of scholastic readiness by the end of the school year. Supplementary analyses designed to determine whether early differences in school adjustment forecasted changes in children's peer acceptance failed to produce significant findings.

Children may also experience rejecting or abusive relationships with classmates when they become participants in bully-victim interactions or become the targets of classmates' aggressive behaviors. Data we have gathered with kindergarten samples (Kochenderfer & Ladd, in press) suggest that victimization is encountered by a substantial proportion of kindergarten children (i.e., on average, 22% of the children in our samples report moderate to severe levels of victimization) and that this form of abuse is associated with higher levels of loneliness and school avoidance.

The results of these studies suggest that prior friendships may provide an important familiarization function as children enter new classrooms. The presence of prior friends may make the new school environment seem less "strange" and more accommodating to a young child. Moreover, if high-quality friendships are formed and these relationships are maintained, they may provide emotional support that children need as they cope with ever-increasing school demands. In contrast, rejection and victimization by classmates early in the year appear to function as a stressor in the new school context and may impair many aspects of children's school adjustment (Kochenderfer & Ladd, in press; Ladd, 1990).

Classroom peers, however, are not the only figures with whom children can form relationships and seek support on a daily basis in school. Classroom teachers may serve this function as well. In fact, our data suggest that three features of the teacher-child relationship—dependency, conflict, and closeness—may have an important bearing on kindergarten children's school adjustment (see Birch & Ladd, in press). Specifically, Birch and Ladd found that dependency in the teacher-child relationship was associated with children's adjustment difficulties, including poorer academic performance, negative school attitudes, and scholastic disengagement. Teacher-child relationships that were conflictual in nature were also linked to child adjustment difficulties; children who formed relationships of this type tended to like school less, were more school avoidant, and were less engaged in classroom activities. In contrast, teacher-child closeness was positively associated with children's academic performance and teachers' perceptions of children's scholastic engagement. These findings are consistent with the view that multiple forms of relationships impact children's success during early school transitions and that the effect of these relationships on early school adjustment varies depending on the "provisions" (e.g., supports, stressors) they afford young children.

The Neighborhood Environment:
Relational Supports in the Informal Peer Network

As hypothesized in the proposed model of school adjustment, children's peer relations in nonschool settings like the neighborhood may also have an important bearing on their school adjustment. Investigations by Ladd (1983, 1988) and Ladd, Hart, Wadsworth, and Golter (1988) were among the first to describe the features of children's nonschool peer relations during the preschool and early elementary years. These studies reveal that children as young as 3 years old tend to have frequent play companions in the neighborhood and that the number of neighborhood companions increases steadily for boys and girls throughout both preschool and grade school.

In a study of the transition from home to preschool, Ladd et al. (1988) found that children who play primarily among age-mates in the neighborhood, as opposed to those who played among younger or older peers, received higher school adjustment ratings from teachers following their entrance into preschool. Conversely, in our study of the transition from preschool to kindergarten (Ladd & Price, 1987), we found that preschoolers who tended to associate with younger peers in the neighborhood were more likely to develop negative attitudes toward kindergarten.

Besides the form of companionship children pursue, the stability of their peer relationships in nonschool settings may facilitate adjustment to new school environments. We found that children who retained a larger proportion of their nonschool peer relationships, as they moved preschool to kindergarten, tended to develop more favorable attitudes toward the new school environment (Ladd & Price, 1987).

The Transition to Grade School: Emergent Themes and Future Directions

Overall, our findings are consistent with the premise that early school adjustment is a function not only of children's attributes but also of the types of relationships they posses during major shifts in school environments. Attributes that children "bring" to school, such as their peer interaction patterns, appear to be important precursors of school adaptation. Our findings suggest that children who interact cooperatively with a majority of their classmates tend to become better accepted by their classmates. These children are also more successful at finding and maintaining specific play partners, such as consistent companions or "friends," and tend to be seen as well adjusted by their teachers. In contrast, children who behave aggressively toward many of their classmates tend to become disliked by peers early in the school year and are viewed as poorly adjusted by their teachers. It also appears that it is often difficult for children to escape negative peer reputations once they have been formed. Once children become disliked, their reputations tend to persist over time and limit their choice of play partners and activities.

The types of behavioral styles that young children bring to school appear to differ by gender and, especially for boys, may be relatively stable across school contexts. In our studies, aggressive, antisocial styles that were found to forecast school maladjustment were more common and stable among boys than among girls. Thus, it would appear that aggressive boys are at greater risk for early school adjustment problems. Also, the stability of this behavioral style across school settings suggests that, for males in particular, the tendency to engage in antisocial interactions with many peers may be the result of child disposition rather than an idiosyncratic response to a particular setting. Although these findings give us some insight into the precursors of early school adjustment in boys, they do little to illuminate the behavioral antecedents of school adjustment in girls. Clearly, the relation between girls' interpersonal behaviors and their school adjustment needs further attention.

In addition to the child characteristics studied here, our findings are consistent with the view that features of children's interpersonal relationships may have an important impact on their school adjustment. Thus far, our data suggest that supports and stressors occurring in a number of relational contexts, including the family, neighborhood, and school, are linked to early school adjustment. Moreover, it appears that both the relational supports that children possess as they enter school and those that exist prior to school entrance are important.

Before children enter kindergarten, parents' socialization activities may play an important role in preparing children for school. There is evidence to suggest that parents' management of children's informal peer relations at home and in the neighborhood are associated with children's later school adjustment. Our findings reveal that children whose parents tended to foster contact with peers at home and in the community during preschool tended to have higher levels of social adjustment when they entered new kindergarten classrooms. Moreover, higher levels of adjustment were found for children whose parents supervised their peer contacts in indirect, noninterfering ways.

Our efforts to investigate supports and stressors within the school context point to the importance of both prior experience in this setting and the quality of children's relationships with teachers and classmates. Experiential antecedents, such as children's school and peer experiences during the preschool years, may enhance or inhibit their adaptation to new grade-school classrooms. We found that children who associated primarily with younger companions during preschool tended to develop less favorable school attitudes and displayed higher levels of school avoidance once they entered grade school. It appears that, although companionship with younger children may be common and appropriate during preschool when classrooms are often mixed-age, overinvolvement in this type of relationship may not prepare children for the social demands of age-segregated grade-school classrooms.

Greater school experience, as reflected in the duration of children's preschool attendance, also emerged as a significant predictor of early grade-school adjustment. In particular, children who spent more time in preschool classrooms exhibited lower levels of anxiety during the early weeks of kindergarten. This finding is consistent with the hypothesis that prior school experience prepares children for such tasks as separating from parents, spending time away from home, and becoming comfortable with new peers and teachers.

Once children enter grade school, features of the existing classroom environment may also influence school adjustment. Our data suggest that early school adjustment, following the transition from preschool to kindergarten, is enhanced when children begin school in classrooms that offer immediate and lasting relational supports with peers and teachers. In particular, the extensivity and form of children's friendship ties in the classroom, including the number of prior friends enrolled in the same classroom, the extent to which these relationships were maintained, and the degree to which children formed new friendships, were found to forecast higher levels of school adjustment. In addition, rejection or victimization by one's classmates early in the school year was associated with changes in several important school adjustment indices, including perceptions (e.g., increased disliking of school), involvement (e.g., increased avoidance of school), and performance (i.e., decreased achievement in school). Beyond the quality of children's ties with peers, supportive relationships with teachers appear to facilitate adjustment and success in the school setting. Further, conflictual or stressful teacher-child relationships seem to interfere with successful adoption in school contexts.

The peer relationships that children form in their neighborhoods may also serve as relational supports during the transition to grade school. During the transition to kindergarten, the stability of children's ties with neighborhood friends was associated with school adjustment following children's entrance into grade school. The continuity of these relationships may have provided children with an enduring source of support and a greater sense of predictability in an otherwise changing social environment.

Intervention Opportunities

Potentially useful strategies for researchers and educators interested in preventing children's school adjustment problems follow from the research reviewed in the previous sections. In particular, our research on early environmental shifts has led us to think that preventive programming could be most effective if it was designed to assist children both before and during key school transitions. Because much of our past work has been focused on the transition from preschool to kindergarten, we use this period as the basis for examples and illustrations.

Prior to kindergarten entrance, it may be useful to identify children who are prone to exhibit maladaptive behavioral dispositions and involve them in interventions designed to promote prosocial, adaptive behaviors. For example, during preschool, it may be beneficial to help children learn how to inhibit aggressive acts and pursue more extensive positive contacts with peers. Gains in these skills may better enable children to make new friends and achieve higher levels of peer acceptance when they enter grade-school classrooms. Preventive interventions might also be designed to help families provide children with important "formative" experiences in both family and school settings. Parents might, for example, arrange for children to attend preschool and develop neighborhood friendships with age-mates prior to the time they enter grade school. Experiences that help children meet new peers and negotiate new social settings, such as developing ties with peers in a variety of community settings, may also be helpful.

Parents may help children cope with major environmental transitions by fostering as much continuity as possible in children's friendships in nonschool settings, such as the neighborhood. Enduring friendships in the neighborhood may offer children a "secure base" as they cope with radically changing contextual and interpersonal demands in settings such as school. In addition, parents could capitalize on existing interpersonal supports by creating "buddy systems" in which children are paired with friends or familiar peers as they enter school.

These findings may also have important implications for educators and may be especially relevant to policies concerning the composition of kindergarten classrooms in new school buildings and the facilitation of children's ties with classmates during the early weeks of school. In planning the peer composition of new classrooms, school administrators may wish to consider grouping children so as to maximize contact with prior friends. Teachers should consider experimenting with techniques designed to help children maintain existing friendships and form new ones and to prevent early peer rejection and victimization in the classroom (see Ladd, 1981; Mize & Ladd, 1990; Oden & Asher, 1977). Teachers should also recognize that supportive teacher-child relationships may play an important role in children's early school adjustment. In sum, it is important for educators to consider ways to design the school environment so that children receive the resources they need to cope with changing demands and challenges.

To conclude, the research we have reviewed here suggests that early school adjustment is related to children's characteristics and their interpersonal supports within the family, school, and neighborhood. Further studies are needed to explore the unique and combined effects of various child characteristics and relational supports on specific adjustment outcomes. At present, our work suggests that supportive features of new school environments partially compensate for the risks posed by maladaptive child characteristics. However, many other combinations of child characteristics and environmental supports-stressors may operate to influence early school adjustment, and these linkages should be systematically examined in future empirical studies.

Acknowledgments

I wish to thank Sondra Birch and Eric Buhs for their comments on this chapter.

References

Birch, S. H., & Ladd, G. W. (in press). The teacher-child relationship and children's early school adjustment. *Journal of School Psychology.*

Block, J. (1983). Differential premises arising from differential socialization of the sexes. *Child Development, 54,* 1335–1354.

Blyth, D. A., & Traeger, C. (1988). Adolescent self-esteem and perceived relationships with parents and peers. In J. Antrobus, M. Hammer, & S. Salzinger (Eds.), *Social networks of children, adolescents, and college students* (pp. 171–194). New York: Erlbaum.

Bogat, G. A., Jones, J. W., & Jason, L. A. (1980). School transitions: Preventive intervention following an elementary school closing. *Journal of Community Psychology, 8,* 343–352.

Bradley, R. H., Caldwell, B. M., & Rock, S. L. (1988). Home environment and school performance: A ten-year follow-up and examination of three models of environmental action. *Child Development, 59,* 852–867.

Bronfenbrenner, U. (1979). *The ecology of human development.* Cambridge, MA: Harvard University Press.

Bukowski, W., & Hoza, B. (1989). Popularity and friendship: Issues in theory, measurement, and outcome. In T. J. Berndt & G. W. Ladd (Eds.), *Peer relationships in child development* (pp. 15–45). New York: Wiley.

Coie, J. D., & Krehbiel, G. (1984). Effects of academic tutoring on the social status of low-achieving, socially rejected children. *Child Development, 55,* 1465–1478.

Compas, B. E., Malcarne, V. L., & Fondacaro, K. M. (1988). Coping with stressful events in older children and adolescents. *Journal of Consulting and Clinical Psychology, 56,* 405–411.

Connell, J. P., & Ilardi, B. C. (1987). Self-system concomitants of discrepancies between children's and teachers' evaluations of academic competence. *Child Development, 58,* 1297–1307.

Cowen, E. L., Lotyczewski, B. S., & Weissberg, R. P. (1984). Risk and resource indicators and their relationship to young children's school adjustment. *American Journal of Community Psychology, 12,* 353–367.

Dweck, C. S. (1986). Motivational processes affecting learning. *American Psychologist, 41,* 1040–1048.

Dweck, C. S., & Elliott, E. S. (1983). Achievement motivation. In E. M. Hetherington (Ed.), *Handbook of child psychology* (Vol. 4, pp. 643–691). New York: Wiley.

Felner, R. D., Stolberg, A., & Cowen, E. L. (1975). Crisis events and school mental health referral patterns of young children. *Journal of Consulting and Clinical Psychology, 43,* 305–310.

Garmezy, N., Masten, A., & Tellegen, A. (1984). The study of stress and competence in children: A building block for developmental psychopathology. *Child Development, 55,* 97–111.

Heller, K., & Swindle, R. W. (1983). Social networks, perceived social support, and coping with stress. In R. D. Felner, L. A. Jason, J. N. Moritsugu, & S. S. Farber (Eds.), *Preventive psychology: Theory, research, and practice* (pp. 87–103). New York: Pergamon Press.

Hetherington, E. M. (1989). Coping with family transitions: Winner, losers, and survivors. *Child Development, 60,* 1–14.

Hetherington, E. M., Cox, M., & Cox, R. (1982). Effects of divorce on parents and children. In M. Lamb (Ed.), *Nontraditional families* (pp. 233–238). Hillsdale, NJ: Erlbaum.

Howes, C. (1983). Patterns of friendship. *Child Development, 54,* 1041–1053.

Howes, C. (1988). Peer interaction of young children. *Monographs of the Society for Research in Child Development, 53* (1, Serial No. 217).

Howes, C. (1991, April). *Relations between attachment to caregivers and competent play with peers.* Paper presented at the biennial meeting of the Society for Research in Child Development, Seattle, WA.

Ispa, J. (1981). Peer support among Soviet daycare toddlers. *International Journal of Behavioral Development, 4,* 255–269.

Kochenderfer, N., & Ladd, G. W. (in press). Peer victimization: Cause or consequence of school maladjustment? *Child Development.*

Krappman, L. (1985). The structure of peer relationships and possible effects on school achievement. In R. A. Hinde, A. N. Perret-Clermont, & J. Stevenson-Hinde (Eds.), *Social relationships and cognitive development* (pp. 149–166). Oxford, England: Clarendon Press.

Kupersmidt, J. B. (1983, April). *Predicting delinquency and academic problems from childhood peer status.* Paper presented at the biennial meeting of the Society for Research in Child Development, Detroit, MI.

Ladd, G. W. (1981). Effectiveness of a social learning method for enhancing children's social interaction and peer acceptance. *Child Development, 52,* 171–178.

Ladd, G. W. (1983). Social networks of popular, average, and rejected children in school settings. *Merrill-Palmer, Quarterly, 29,* 283–307.

Ladd, G. W. (1984). Expanding our view of the social world: New territories, new maps, same directions? *Merrill-Palmer Quarterly, 30,* 317–320.

Ladd, G. W. (1988). Friendship patterns and peer status during early and middle childhood. *Journal of Developmental and Behavioral Pediatrics, 9,* 229–238.

Ladd, G. W. (1989). Children's social competence and social supports: Precursors of early school adjustment? In B. Scheider, G. Attili, J. Nadel, & R. Weissberg (Eds.), *Social competence in developmental perspective* (pp. 277–291). Amsterdam: Kluwer Academic Publishers.

Ladd, G. W. (1990). Having friends, keeping friends, making friends, and being liked by peers in the classroom: Predictors of children's early school adjustment? *Child Development, 61,* 1081–1100.

Ladd, G. W., & Golter, B. S. (1988). Parents' initiation and monitoring of children's peer contacts: Predictive of children's peer relations in nonschool and school settings? *Developmental Psychology, 24,* 109–117.

Ladd, G. W., & Hart, C. H. (1992). Creating informal play opportunities: Are parents and preschooler's initiations related to children's competence with peers? *Developmental Psychology, 28,* 1179–1187.

Ladd, G. W., Hart, C. H., Wadsworth, E. M., & Golter, B. (1988). Preschooler's peer networks in nonschool settings: Relationships to family characteristics and school adjustment. In J. Antrobus, M. Hammer, & S. Salzinger (Eds.), *Social networks of children, adolescents, and college students* (pp. 61–92). New York: Erlbaum.

Ladd, G. W., Kochenderfer, B., & Coleman, C. (in press). Friendship quality as a predictor of young children's early school adjustment. *Child Development, 67.*

Ladd, G. W., & Mars, K. T. (1986). Reliability and validity of preschoolers' perceptions of peer behavior. *Journal of Clinical Child Psychology, 15,* 16–25.

Ladd, G. W., & Price, J. M. (1986). Promoting children's cognitive and social competence: The relation between parents' perceptions of task difficulty and children's perceived and actual competence. *Child Development, 57,* 446–460.

Ladd, G. W., & Price, J. M. (1987). Predicting children's social and school adjustment following the transition from preschool to kindergarten. *Child Development, 58,* 1168–1189.

Ladd, G. W., Price, J. M., & Hart, C. H. (1988). Predicting preschoolers' peer status from their playground behaviors. *Child Development, 59,* 986–992.

Ladd, G. W., Price, J. M., & Hart, C. H. (1990). Preschoolers' behavioral orientations and patterns of peer contact: Predictive of peer status? In S. R. Asher & J. D. Coie (Eds.), *Peer rejection in childhood.* New York: Cambridge University Press.

Lazar, I., & Darlington, R. (1982). Lasting effects of early education: A report from the Consortium for Longitudinal Studies. *Monographs of the Society for Research in Child Development, 47* (2–3, Serial No. 195).

Lazarus, R. S., Cohen, J. B., Folkman, S., Kanner, A., & Schaefer, C. (1980). Psychological stress and adaptation: Some unresolved issues. In H. Selye (Ed.), *Guide to stress research.* New York: Van Nostrand Reinhold.

Masters, J. C., & Furman, W. (1981). Popularity, individual friendship selection, and specific peer interaction among children. *Developmental Psychology, 17,* 344–350.

Mize, J., & Ladd, G. W. (1990). A cognitive-social learning approach to social skill training with low status preschool children. *Developmental Psychology, 26,* 388–397.

Oden, S., & Asher, S. R. (1977). Coaching children in social skills for friendship making. *Child Development, 48,* 495–506.

Parker, J. G., & Asher, S. R. (1987). Peer acceptance and later interpersonal adjustment: Are low-accepted children at risk? *Psychological Bulletin, 102,* 357–389.

Rutter, M. (1983). Stress, coping, and development: Some issues and some questions. In N. Garmezy & M. Rutter, (Eds.), *Stress, coping, and development in children.* New York: McGraw-Hill.

Sandler, I. N., & Ramsay, T. B. (1980). Dimensional analysis of children's stressful life events. *American Journal of Community Psychology, 8,* 285–302.

Schwarz, J. C. (1972). Effects of peer familiarity on the behavior of preschoolers in a novel situation. *Journal of Personality and Social Psychology, 24,* 276–284.

Stevenson, H. W., Parker, T., Wilkinson, A., Hegion, A., & Fish, E. (1976). Longitudinal study of individual differences in cognitive development and scholastic development. *Journal of Educational Psychology, 68,* 377–400.

Tero, P., & Connell, J. P. (1984, April). *Children's academic coping inventory: A new self-report measure.* Paper presented at the annual meeting of the American Educational Research Association, Montreal, Canada.

Waldrop, M. F., & Halverson, C. (1975). Intensive and extensive peer behavior: Longitudinal and cross-sectional analyses. *Child Development, 46,* 27–38.

Weiss, R. (1974). The provisions of social relationships. In Z. Rubin (Ed.), *Doing unto others* (pp. 17–26). Englewood Cliffs, NJ: Prentice-Hall.

Worland, J., Weeks, D. G., & Janes, C. L. (1984). Intelligence, classroom behavior, and academic achievement in children of high and low risk for psychopathology: A structural equation analysis. *Journal of Abnormal Child Psychology, 12,* 437–454.

Younger, A. J., & Boyko, K. A. (1987). Aggression and withdrawal as social schemas underlying children's peer perceptions. *Child Development, 58,* 1094–1100.

Younger, A. J., & Piccinin, A. M. (1989). Children's recall of aggressive and withdrawn behaviors: Recognition memory and likeability judgments. *Child Development, 60,* 580–590.

CHAPTER SEVENTEEN

Combining Endogenous and Exogenous Factors in the Shift Years: The Transition to School

SHARON L. KAGAN AND PETER R. NEVILLE

Long examined in research, children's development throughout both their earliest years and the shift years here under consideration is marked. Simultaneous and dramatic changes across many domains—physical, cognitive, social, emotional, neurological, cultural, and language—make these years an intense period of biopsychosocial transition. But beyond well-known shifts in endogenous factors, children also experience critical shifts in exogenous factors that, combined with endogenous variables, alter their developmental trajectory. The purpose of this chapter is to focus on the interaction of endogenous and exogenous variables as children approach the shift years by examining the critical period around their transition to formal schooling.

Years ago, one could write about the transition to formal schooling as the movement directly from home to school, pinpointing the "event" as taking place somewhere between late in the 4th and early in the 5th year of life. Today, such precision is difficult. More and more children are entering kindergarten having had some out-of-home preschool experience (U.S. Department of Education, 1993). As a result, the period of transition from home to a more formal out-of-home setting takes place at different times for different children throughout the early years. Even for those few who experience no formal out-of-home care prior to kindergarten, the time of their induction to school also fluctuates owing to school policies and parental decisions. The proliferation of "developmental" or "transition" classes for youngsters deemed "unready" for kindergarten, coupled with a movement for parents to keep their children out of school to give them an additional year to mature, considerably alters the consistency of the chronological age at which children enter kindergarten. Indeed, it is quite common for kindergarten teachers to have children in their classes whose ages span a full 2 years, as well as children who have been "in transition" for perhaps as many as 4 years.

Consequently, today "transition to school" takes on new meaning. It no longer suggests a specified chronological moment in time when all young children enter the portals of the neighborhood school. Nor does it refer to a magic moment when children are deemed (often by a standardized test) "developmentally ready" for school. Instead, rather than a discrete event, transition today connotes an extended process that occurs at different times, over different durations, for different children.

Such differences make *transition to school* difficult to define. For some, transition to school "refers to those activities initiated by schools or preschools to bridge the gap between the preschool and the kindergarten experiences" (Love, Logue, Trudeau, & Thayer, 1992, p. 6). Love et al. (1992) identified three ingredients of the transition process: preschool programs that have the potential for producing benefits worth retaining; an effective elementary school program; and an effective transfer process between preschool and elementary school designed to overcome discontinuities that may disrupt children's continuous learning and development. For others, the transition to school refers to a "process that occurs over several years, and for many children involves the adaptation to a new part of the community culture—namely that culture of the school" (Ramey & Ramey, 1992, p. 1).

Building upon these definitions, we suggest that the transition to school refers to a process, but one that includes not only children adapting to the culture of school but also schools and families adapting to the unique developmental needs and learning stages of young and shift-age children. Indeed, this chapter suggests that for too long transition to school has been too narrowly conceptualized, first as a primarily cognitive transition; second, as an isolated, activity-based, temporal period; and third, as a nonreciprocal adaptation that demands conformity by young and shift-age children to classroom procedures and school policies that have historically been created for older and less culturally diverse populations. We suggest that in order for the transition to be successful it must be understood as an ongoing process of mutual adaptation: that of children adapting to the culture of schools *and* schools and other institutions adapting to the needs of young and shift-age children. The transition to school, therefore, is the joint and durable responsibility of schools, families, and preschools. (In this chapter, we use the generic term *preschool* to include any early care and education setting serving children prior to formal school entry, including child care, Head Start, and for-profit and nonprofit community-based programs.) We come to this conclusion and the recommendations that follow after an analysis of the multiple, historic, and sadly unsuccessful attempts to render the transition to school effective.

The Importance of the Early Years

Well researched, but perhaps less well understood in the practitioner and policy communities, profound changes in endogenous variables characterize young and shift-age children. From other chapters in this volume we know, for example, that during this time period children begin to focus on more than one dimension of a given situation (see Siegler, this volume, chap. 4) and to execute simultaneously certain behaviors and thought processes that had previously been performed sequentially (see Mounoud, this volume, chap. 5). Research indicates that children's memory processes are profoundly affected by increased ability with and use of language, to the degree that only those memories developed during and following the ages of 4 to 7 are retained later in life (see Nelson, this volume, chap. 7). Further, children's perceptions of themselves undergo extensive development during this time, leading to increased abilities to assess their own skills and performance as well as the establishment of a sense of self-worth (see Harter, this volume, chap. 10).

Beyond their importance during this age span, capacities developed during the early and shift years bear critical significance for children's success in school and in later life. Pellegrini and Dresden (1991) noted that developments in problem-solving abilities and in levels of attention and motivation have particular relevance to abilities called for in the school setting. Development of visual-motor integration during this time also bears implications for children's school success in subsequent years (Fowler & Cross, 1986). Capacities for social comparison and self-assessment enable children to incorporate feedback from others and make improvements in performance. In addition, Ladd (see Ladd, this volume, chap. 16; Ladd & Price, 1987) noted that in these years children face such challenges as social acceptance by new peer groups, completion of academic tasks, and demanding performance expectations; Ladd suggested that children's success in meeting these challenges and adjusting to this new setting may have long-term developmental consequences. Moreover, Love et al. (1992) reminded us that beyond inherent developmental advancements, the achievement of abilities in cognitive, social, physical, and other domains during these years is critical for future school success.

Much attention accorded the shift years has focused on endogenous factors (e.g., biological and genetic variables and intrapsychic processes); nevertheless, as ecological and contextual orientations have ascended in popularity (Bronfenbrenner, 1979; Caldwell, 1991), attention has refocused to include the influence of exogenous factors and the interaction of endogenous and exogenous variables. Zigler and Kagan (1982) affirmed the importance of linking endogenous and exogenous variables when they discussed the benefits children derive as they experience a sense of continuity between both the internal time periods of their lives and the external spheres of their lives. Reflecting the urgent need to consider endogenous and exogenous variables together, Bredekamp (1987) noted that environmental change is particularly stressful for those with "limited experience and few well-developed coping strategies" (p. 60). Incorporating a systemic perspective and making the connection between endogenous and exogenous variables even more explicit, Zimiles (1991) reminded us that the early developmental years overlap with a time of similarly significant upheaval in the environment of the child: the movement from the familiarity and intimacy of the home to the more formal and foreign context of preschool and school.

Transitions and Continuity in the Early Years: Important but Absent

Transitions and continuity in the early years must be addressed from a perspective that does not segregate endogenous and exogenous variables. Theoretically, such a perspective begins with the premise that continuity for young children embraces both, thus demanding the nesting of developmental variables within the context of environmental factors. Practically, it demands that we consider what constitutes ideal contextual conditions for children as they pass through the early and shift-age years. What precisely is the significance of the preschool-school transition for the developmental advances being made during this period? What is the nature of the environmental transition children are forced to navigate? How critical is it that the preschool-school transition be characterized by continuity, rather than fragmentation, of experience? How much attention is being paid to the confluence of endogenous and exogenous variables during the transition years?

If one reflects on the current sociopolitical context, it is apparent that such issues have ascended in importance. The need for women to be employed outside the home has given rise to unprecedented numbers of young children being cared for in nonmaternal settings. Although not dispensing with their responsibility for continuity in their children's lives, parents are increasingly aware of the challenges that personal and institutional continuity demand; they want continuity between themselves and the institutions that serve their children as well as continuity among these institutions.

Such sentiments are accelerated by a growing national focus on young children and their transition to school. Given impetus by the National Education Goals Panel's focus on readiness, public discourse has increased regarding what constitutes readiness, where it begins and ends, and who should be responsible for "readying" America's children for school. State governors have established readiness actions teams that are examining the continuity of services for young children and families. The business community has become interested in "learning before school" (Committee for Economic Development, 1993). And new definitions of early development and learning (National Education Goals Panel, 1993) are being debated in the scholarly community.

Not unrelated to these practical efforts, the need for continuity has resurfaced in theoretical circles as scholars try to understand the persistent fade-out of the impact of early intervention efforts. While many studies show short-term gains of high-quality early intervention, particularly for low-income children (McKey et al., 1985) and equally impressive gains of reasonably durable effects

(Berrueta-Clement, Schweinhart, Barnett, Epstein, & Weikart, 1984; Lazar & Darlington, 1982), there appears to be a fade-out of cognitive effects around age 8 or 9 (Caldwell, 1987; Lally, Mangione, & Honig, 1988). Some have suggested that such fade-out may be an artifact of inappropriate testing measures. Others have suggested that because such testing increasingly excludes children in special education classes and those who have been retained in grade, testing has become increasingly selective; it often includes children who are most similar and who show little difference in achievement scores. As a result, children who have had early interventions look quite similar to those who have not, fortifying the appearance of the fade-out of effects of early intervention programs (Barnett, 1993).

Beyond methodological rationales for fade-out, there is growing concern that fade-out is attributable to the discontinuation of enriched services offered in many preschools, including health services, social services, and supports for families. Indeed, this rationale has been so strong that an initial goal of the National Head Start/Public School Transition Demonstration Project, as stated in the Human Services Reauthorization Act of 1990 (Pub. L. No. 101–501), was to make available for low-income elementary students in grades kindergarten through grade 3 and their families "supportive services that build on the strengths of families, including health, immunization, mental health, nutrition, parenting education, literacy and social services" (Fed. Reg., 1991, p. 31818). Others have suggested that fade-out may be attributable to pedagogical discontinuities between preschools and schools (Bredekamp & Shepard, 1988).

That such discontinuities exist has been verified by experience and by a large and recent national study (Love et al., 1992). Culling data from a stratified random sample of 1,003 public school districts and then followed up by visits to a small number of sites, the study combines qualitative and quantitative data to reflect a dismal picture. It concludes that "after assessing the extent of a variety of transition activities, we must conclude that transitions activities are not common place in our nation's schools. . . . Transition activities have achieved the status of formal policy in only 13% of the schools" (p. 119). Moreover, it is clear that schools do not typically provide the kinds of comprehensive services associated with high-quality early care and education programs to their own preschool programs (Marx & Seligson, 1988), much less to kindergarten children.

Different Approaches to Fostering Continuity

Perhaps even more telling than the contradiction between the theoretical and political importance accorded continuity and its absence from practice at present is the degree to which efforts to bridge the preschool-to-school chasm have been part of our history. Indeed, a quick review reveals the tenacity and the polemics associated with such efforts.

Efforts to link preschools and schools, and thereby to ensure greater continuity for shift-age children, can be classified into three broad groups:

1. Those efforts that have taken root as a result of federal initiatives and have been launched largely, though not exclusively, via Head Start or its related services.

2. Those funded efforts that have been launched at the state or local level that have had transition not as a primary goal but as a secondary or tertiary goal.

3. Those policies and procedures that have emerged at the local or district level that have focused on young children and, as a result, have altered the nature of entry or transition to school.

Reflecting these differences in origin, the types differ greatly in their conceptions of continuity and in their approaches to transition.

From the Federal Perspective

Early federal government attempts to create continuity between preschools and schools were stimulated by a desire to disprove the concern that early intervention did not work. Disconcerted by the findings that the positive effects of Head Start disappeared as children moved into elementary school (Holmes & Holmes, 1966), President Lyndon Johnson launched the Follow Through program in 1967 with the goal of providing continuing support to Head Start children as they made the transition to regular school (Rivlin & Timpane, 1975). Originally designed to be a comprehensive national program like Head Start, Follow Through was thwarted by limited funding, so that in reality it became a planned variation experiment to examine whether different curriculum models had different effects on children. Enmeshed with Follow Through, a second continuity effort, the Head Start Planned Variation (HSPV) Program, was launched in 1969. Designed to improve the educational achievement of disadvantaged children, it focused primarily on curricular strategies and included a limited number of Follow Through communities, ostensibly making it feasible to follow children involved in the same curriculum from preschool through the early grades.

Evaluation results from both projects were not particularly informative or encouraging in large part because of implementation and evaluation complexities. The shifts from a comprehensive to a curricular program and from a service to a demonstration program, coupled with methodological problems— incomparable treatment and control groups, tests not equally reflecting the goals of all the models, transient children and teachers, and insufficient sites— rendered the Follow Through evaluation problematic. Moreover, preoccupied with these issues, researchers gave little attention in the Follow Through evaluation reports to the issue of transition (Stebbins, St. Pierre, Proper, Anderson, & Cerva, 1977, cited in Love, 1988). Moreover, HSPV research findings concluded that although children in the planned variations showed substantially greater test gains than did children not enrolled in any preschool, they did not do significantly better than did comparison children in regular Head Start, nor did particular HSPV models emerge as significantly better than others (Rivlin & Timpane, 1975).

Despite the fact that (and in part because) data regarding the benefits of transition were not sufficiently convincing, the Office of Child Development (OCD) tried again in 1974 with Project Developmental Continuity (PDC). This program was a national demonstration with the explicit goals of ensuring continuity of experience for shift-age children from preschool through the early primary years and of developing models for developmental continuity that could be implemented on a wide scale in Head Start and other child development programs and school systems (Love, Granville, & Smith, 1978). Conceptually significant, PDC addressed the comprehensive domains in which transitions needed attention: administrative coordination, curriculum, pre- and in-service training, developmental support services, parent involvement, and services for handicapped and bilingual, culturally diverse children. Although different from its predecessors in vision and breadth, PDC research results were again inconclusive, this time because it was difficult to retain pure "no-treatment" conditions. The evaluation found no significant differences favoring PDC children, although in some sites PDC children showed more positive learning attitudes or styles during the elementary years (Bond, 1982).

Still concerned about the transition issue, the next major initiative launched by the Administration for Children, Youth and Families (ACYF), OCD's successor, was the Head Start Transition Project in 1986. In 1986, all Head Start programs were encouraged to initiate transition activities, with 15 programs receiving special grants to do so. Results obtained from a random sample of Head Start grantees indicated that transition grantees were more likely than regular nontransition grantees to provide more transition activities and that, when such activities were provided, children showed greater resilience through the first months of school, when self-confidence levels typically fall off (Hubbell, Plantz, Condelli, & Barrett, 1987). In addition to yielding information regarding the impact of transition activities on children, the study also identified strategies that worked successfully and specific barriers to establishing continuity.

In an effort to capitalize on this knowledge and to address the current desire to facilitate more linkages among families, preschool programs, and schools, ACYF launched another effort, the National Head Start/Public School Early Childhood Transition Demonstration Project in 1991. Reflecting current political interest in the early years, this congressionally mandated program is designed to "enhance the transition to school experience for children and families affected by economic poverty, especially those served by Head Start" (Ramey & Ramey, 1992, p. 1). The appropriation contained funds to establish 32 demonstration sites and to conduct a comprehensive evaluation of the implementation and outcomes of their work. Because the evaluation is still in process, results from this effort are not yet available.

Two trends emerge from this litany of federal initiatives: First, there seems to be a tenacious commitment to understanding and minimizing the preschool-to-school chasm. In other domains, one or two federal initiatives that had not been particularly productive would have precluded further federal expenditures on similar efforts. Not so with the transition strategies launched from the federal level. They seemed to be incarnated and reincarnated as though they could render some mystical answer to society's yearning for a response to the fade-out effect.

Second, each of these well-intentioned initiatives, while focusing on a series of comparatively minimalist activities, actually tried to serve as a de facto catalyst for the reform of primary education, be it from a curricular or a comprehensive perspective. Yet each was launched from a perch outside the educational hierarchy, with insufficient funding or legitimacy to accomplish the task, leading researchers and policymakers to seriously question the potency of outside change agents armed with only modest artillery.

From the State and Local Perspective

Paralleling efforts at the federal level, there have been a limited number of state and local efforts that have shed considerable light on the transition issue. Unlike those federal efforts discussed in the previous section, these initiatives were not designed solely or even primarily to ameliorate the preschool-to-school chasm; like the federal efforts, however, they typically demanded special funding and were seen as demonstration programs or special efforts.

Notable among the local efforts was the Brookline Early Intervention Project, which offered fairly durable support to families with young children. Children who participated in the program had significantly fewer behavior problems and less difficulty in reading (Pierson, Walker, & Timan, 1984). Caldwells' Kramer School in Little Rock, Arkansas, was a comprehensive effort to improve the quality of experience for young children and their families. As a part of this commitment, Caldwell developed the construct of "educare" and began providing child care and education within the context of the public school. Continuity was improved as children and families had fewer settings to navigate.

At the state or city-state level, several projects warrant note. Consistent effort in New Jersey, embodied by their recent Urban Prekindergarten Pilot Program and the current GoodStarts Program have had components that attempt to link children and families across settings. The New York City Giant Step Program mandated continuity of programming through kindergarten and required teachers to develop continuity plans for children. Today, with help from the regional education laboratories, states are developing continuity plans to span the transition from early care and education settings to schools (Regional Education Laboratories Early Childhood Collaboration Network, 1993). States are launching efforts through funds from the Child Care and Development Block Grant, as well (Blank, 1993). Hawaii has developed a comprehensive state plan linking child care and the schools; Vermont and New York have established similar efforts.

Analysis of such transition efforts provides us with two important lessons: First, though not targeted at the preschool-school chasm directly, efforts to build collaboration in the entire early care and education system can have an impact on the preschool-to-school transition that transcends the conventional categorical emphasis associated with those federal initiatives that have emerged from and are typically directed to Head Start and Head Start–related programs. Second, these initiatives, while emerging from different auspices, demanded additional dollars. Such efforts, whether or not they have targeted transition continuity as a direct goal, do not seem able to sustain themselves without special fiscal supports and programmatic attention.

From the Local Policies and Procedures Perspective

Transition activities that have emanated from local district policies and procedures have embraced a philosophically different, and more narrow, approach to transition. First, school transition efforts seem to have concentrated on a more delimited conception of continuity, stressing cognitive skills rather than the broader range of developmental domains and services considered by preschools. Second, schools have viewed continuity as an issue for only a limited group of children—those deemed unready for school, typically assessed by their scores on standardized readiness tests. Within this context, the need for continuity is conceptualized as a targeted strategy for a subset of children: those with a "readiness" deficit.

Such an orientation is manifest programmatically in schools' attempts to prepare "unready" children for regular school services. Extra-year programs such as readiness classes, transition classes, or 2-year kindergartens are provided for those deemed unready. Alternatively, some districts may raise the school entry age to give younger children additional time to develop. Such transition efforts are generally viewed as positive and beneficial interventions.

Research suggests the opposite, however. The classification of children as unready by schools or their referral to transition classes has had questionable effects and may well hinder rather than help children's development. Shepard and Smith (1987) pointed out that held-out children perform no better than children who enter school with their normal age cohort. Indeed, some data indicate that held-back and retained children fare less well socially and emotionally (Bredekamp & Shepard, 1988). Moreover, such redshirting has hidden effects that transcend the individual—that is, it promotes inequity by further disadvantaging the most economically disadvantaged. When kept out of school, the disadvantaged have few options, and many do not attend alternate placements, thus placing them in double jeopardy. Not only are they out of school, but their more fortunate peers who are in school are advancing even more rapidly. Both groups enter a kindergarten curriculum that has now been retailored to the needs of the more able children (Elkind, 1987; Katz, 1988; Sigel, 1987), making it all the more challenging for the disadvantaged children. In effect, by focusing on children's readiness in addressing the preschool-school transition, schools may have actually widened the chasm to be traversed and created additional barriers to successful development in the shift years.

The Roots of Failure

The various approaches discussed in the previous sections indicate a widespread acknowledgment of continuity as an important issue but also reveal that, with the exception of a few isolated efforts, people have yet to devise a sufficient method for bridging the preschool-to-school gap. In part, the reasons for limited knowledge and programmatic success have already been described: flaws in implementation and research design in the federally initiated efforts, overexpectation of results from too modest an intervention, and questionable effects on children and on the nature of the kindergarten curriculum caused by schools' readiness focus.

However, these explanations belie the influence of much deeper issues, issues that have prohibited sufficient attention to the critical exogenous conditions that shape children's development during the shift years. The first is a naive understanding of the pervasiveness and embeddedness of the systemic roots of discontinuity between preschools and schools, and the second is a misperception of the depths of discontinuity in practice.

Understanding the Systemic Roots of Discontinuity

The roots of discontinuity are not found simply in the failure to create strong bridges to span the chasm between preschools and schools, but in the failure to address the question of why such a chasm exists in the first place. Indeed, examination of the social role of preschools and schools reveals differences in societal commitments to and expectations from them that profoundly differentiate the way they function.

SOCIETAL LEGITIMACY

Schools and preschools differ in the legitimacy they are accorded by society. Enjoying both a clear and agreed-upon mission and a long tradition of legitimacy and support, elementary and secondary education are viewed by society as a rightful and just entitlement granted to all children. Indeed, attendance by children is compulsory, as is the provision of educational services. Contrarily, preschool has never been fully legitimated or regarded as an entitlement by society. Persistent beliefs in the hegemony of the home and the primacy of maternal care have consistently undermined the rationale for providing out-of-home services to children (Cahan, 1989; Kagan, 1991a). Consequently, public endorsement of support for preschool education have been based not on preschool's intrinsic value for families and children but on its value as the handmaiden to greater social causes, such as those that arose during the Great Depression, World War I and II, and the War on Poverty—the times when national commitment to young children was manifest. Indeed, in contrast to education, preschool has suffered a history of legislative capriciousness and sporadic, half-hearted support.

Though federal commitment to preschool and child care has increased recently, preschools still enjoy none of the universal and firmly established support of schools. Rather, public support has been targeted primarily to disadvantaged children (e.g., Head Start; Social Security Act [SSA] Titles IV-A [Aid to Families with Dependent Children], IV-B [Child Welfare Services], and IV-C [Work Incentive Program]; Chapter 1), supporting a system characterized by economic segregation rather than universal entitlement, and with minimal coordination among the multiple involved agencies and funding sources (Kagan, 1991a).

MISSION

Although regular debate ensues regarding the mission of public education in this country, several principles are firmly established. The education system is designed to prepare future citizens for life in a democratic nation. As such, students are encouraged to be learners, competent citizens, wage earners, and contributors to society. Though broadly construed, the mission of public education is clear. For preschool education, the mission is less clear. Some preschools have been established to provide minimal care to children while parents work; essentially, these institutions have the provision of service to parents as their core mission. Alternatively, many preschools see service to children as their primary mission, with a focus either on creating environments that provide cognitive stimulation to prepare for school or on providing havens for socialization where social-emotional development is stressed. Furthermore, a third mission of preschool is to support the development of the child in the context of the family. Often dubbed two-generation programs, these efforts strive to balance services to children and to families. Lacking the clarity of mission that surrounds education, preschools vary in their fundamental orientation, their raison d'être, and as a result, in how they conceptualize their roles.

SUPPORT AND STATUS

These differences in the public recognition, legitimacy, and mission of preschools versus schools have led to commensurate differences in the specific funding structures and public financial supports received by each. Established by constitutional prescription, formal systems for the financial support of schools via taxation exist, allowing for the provision of services free of charge to all within the public sector. The preschool system, on the other hand, is supported by a loose and fragmented patchwork of funding sources—subsidized primarily by parents—and includes a substantial percentage of for-profit providers. Indeed, preschool services are caught in the vortex between being a public good and a market commodity. Such ambivalence has precluded durable public funding.

The Practical Depths of Discontinuity

As might be expected, institutions that vary so in their legitimacy, missions, and level of support vary in the way they conceptualize and carry out their tasks. Preschools and schools vary in their approaches to pedagogy, to parents and families, and in their sense of professionalism.

PEDAGOGICAL APPROACHES

Although it is an overstatement to generalize that all preschools maintain a comprehensive developmental orientation and that all schools focus exclusively on the cognitive domain, it is the overwhelming reality that the content of preschool curricula tend to be more multifaceted, embracing broader domains of development, than those of schools. Recognizing the existence of this pedagogical chasm, Weber (1971) noted what is still largely true today:

> Child development thinking . . . remained isolated from application in the major mass institutions. While it influenced nursery schools, university demonstration schools, experimental private schools, and parent education, developmental thinking within state education—in kindergartens or in the few Dewey schools—suffered from restriction, narrowness of application and lack of influence. (pp. 236–237)

More than just an ideological difference, differences in pedagogy are manifest in instructional strategies, so that, for example, preschools tend to be more learner-focused, more multifaceted, and more integrated than most schools where children are taught subjects (art, science, math, reading) as discrete entities, often in desks in rows, with teachers didactically leading the discourse.

APPROACHES TO PARENTS AND FAMILIES

The distinction regarding breadth of pedagogical orientation between preschools and schools is echoed in their respective approaches to educating and involving parents in their children's learning process. From the parent cooperative movement to the parent empowerment of Head Start (Holloway & Fuller, 1992; Zigler & Valentine, 1979), preschools have put a premium on involving the parents and families of children (Becher, 1986). Recognizing parents as their children's first teachers, preschool has a tradition of both educating parents in child development and encouraging their involvement in substantive program and policy decisions. Further, recognizing the importance of families, most preschools have consciously attempted to respect and reflect their cultural values and beliefs; it is therefore not surprising that many prominent multicultural efforts have their roots in early childhood education (Derman-Sparks, 1989).

In contrast, schools have operated on the premise of serving *in loco parentis,* or "in the place of a parent." Suggesting a more limited conceptualization of parent involvement, this term has in practice come to imply the devolution of parent authority to a school board almost to the exclusion of general parent input or influence (Davies, 1978; Lightfoot, 1978). The ethos of schools, including an emphasis on teacher professionalization and an unwieldy bureaucratic structure, fortifies their lack of receptivity to parents (Grubb & Lazerson, 1977).

It should be noted that schools have attempted to engage parents via parent-teacher associations and via legislative mandates through the Elementary and Secondary Education Act and the Education for All Handicapped Children Act (Pub. L. No. 94–142). Despite these efforts, some of which have had a degree of impact, schools have generally not engendered substantial parent involvement. Indeed, the dichotomy between parents' experience of schools versus parents' experience of preschools is well documented (Grubb & Lazerson, 1977; Kagan, 1991b; Powell, 1989; Schultz, 1993).

PROFESSIONALISM

Given the recognized status of schools as a universal entitlement and the concomitant resources allocated to them, schoolteachers have been able to develop a certain degree of professionalism (Spodek, 1991), including codification of minimum training levels and content at the state level, established pathways for career advancement, and salary levels generally commensurate with the services that they provide to society. As a result, staff turnover is low, there is a certain assurance of minimal levels of service quality, and teachers are able to protect their interests through established collective bargaining units.

Unable to stake such a claim to "professionalism," preschool teachers work under conditions dictated by the limited recognition accorded by society. Training requirements for employment vary greatly, given the multitude of auspices, and state licensing regulations often require little more than a high-school diploma and a criminal record check as a prerequisite for employment. Such minimal entry requirements combine with drastically lower salary levels—several years ago the average child-care teacher forewent $99 to $433 monthly by working in the field (Culkin, Morris, & Helburn, 1991)—to produce an annual staff turnover rate of 42% (Phillips, Howes, & Whitebook, 1991). The fragmented systems of training and employment in preschool have prevented the establishment of clear career ladders, though it should be noted that advancements are being made by numerous organizations such as the Center for Career Development, the Child Care Employee Project, and the National Association for the Education of Young Children (Kagan, et al., 1992). However, the reality remains that preschool is still a fledgling profession and that although those children served by preschool and school teachers may differ only slightly in their ages, variations in the support of these fields contribute to a dramatic difference in the conditions under which preschool and primary teachers operate.

This analysis of the roots of failure to achieve notable advancement in continuity between schools and preschools suggests that it is not simply that their respective roles in society, missions, or strategies are different. Indeed, some differences are to be expected across the age groups. Rather, the point is that the missions and functions are often not complementary and that it is this conflict of ideology that prevents the establishment of real continuity. Although past transition efforts have been tacitly based on assumptions of systemic complementarity, there is a need to envision continuity far more broadly and boldly, based on a deeper understanding of the polemics that segregate the systems.

Rethinking Continuity

A revised approach to transitions cannot be achieved simply through a programmatic strategy or array of discrete transition activities. Instead, future efforts to improve transitions between preschools and schools must be guided both by the demands of the local context and, importantly, by new approaches to continuity that are systemic, attitudinal, and supported.

Systemic Approaches

The observed differences between preschool and school practices are, in fact, deeply rooted in systemic characteristics of the fields. By implication, this suggests that meaningful transition efforts must address both practices and systems. To date, most efforts have addressed practices—that is, providers have concentrated on the more limited, though not unimportant, components of transition (e.g., transfer of records, joint teacher training). Often these activities do produce solid advances, but just as often their effects are mitigated when the special grant ends.

To augment the "practices" or "Band-Aid" approach to continuity, a systems approach needs to be instituted. Such an approach needs to recognize the roots of discontinuity and to establish mechanisms for addressing root causes. Because of the depth of the issues, individual programs typically cannot do this alone. Our embryonic experiences with the newly formed state collaborations and those incepted through the Head Start collaboration grants offer good models. They engage in meaningful, durable collaborations that establish common planning, data collection, and accountability capacities. Supporters of such programs suggest that transitions cannot be conceptualized as the dyadic interaction between two institutions for a specific subgroup of children—but rather that for continuity of transitions to take root, it must be regarded as something needed by all families and children and provided by all institutions and programs. Indeed, the coming-to-school experience, given the inconsistencies in our system, represents an exogenous hurdle that all children need to surmount.

Attitudinal Approaches

More than a question of what people do, discontinuity between preschools and schools extends to what people think, welling up as biases, suspicion, and feelings of superiority between the two domains, conditions both contributing to and reinforced by a lack of communication between school and preschool practitioners. In order to effect transitions that make a difference for children and families, schools and preschools need to acknowledge the depth and pervasiveness of attitudinal differences. Moreover, they need to construct opportunities for open dialogue across systems to surface and address such differences.

Supported Approaches

As noted earlier in this chapter, past transition efforts have failed to conceptualize their mission broadly and to incorporate all relevant parties, including schools, preschools, families, and other institutions and services in the community. In part, such narrowness of vision and strategy has emanated from too weak an understanding of the incongruity of the systems. But in part, such narrowness has also been the result of inconsistent funding commitments and episodic attention to the issue of continuity. Rather than launching national or state demonstrations that are underfunded and too short in duration, new efforts need financial and temporal support—that is, we should recognize firmly that without resources and time the entrenched polarities characterizing the systems will not be overcome.

Moreover, without sustained and systemic attention to fostering continuity for children and their families as they make the transition to formal schooling, children in the United States will suffer. Data clearly support the need for continuity in pedagogy, attitudes, and structures when children are young and are already facing the difficult developmental challenges of the shift years. Experience points out the consequences to children when such supports are missing. Americans need to apply this knowledge to practice, however, institutionalizing the understanding that when children have difficulties in the transition to school, the problem is not in the nature of the child, but in the nature of the child's experiences that have been constructed by adults and sanctioned by society.

References

Barnett, S. (1993, May 19). Does Head Start fade out? [Commentary]. *Education Week, 12* (34), 40.

Becher, R. (1986). Parent involvement: A review of research and principles of successful practice. In L. Katz (Ed.), *Current topics in early childhood education* (Vol. 6, pp. 85–122). Norwood, NJ: Ablex.

Berrueta-Clement, L. R., Schweinhart, L. J., Barnett, W. S., Epstein, A. S., & Weikart, D. P. (1984). *Changed lives: The effects of the Perry Preschool Program on youths through age 19.* Ypsilanti, MI: High/Scope Press.

Blank, H. (1993). *Investing in our children's care: An analysis and review of state initiatives to strengthen the quality and build the supply of child care funded through the Child Care and Development Block Grant.* Washington, DC: Children's Defense Fund.

Bond, J. T. (1982). *Project Developmental Continuity evaluation. Final report:* Vol. 1. *Outcomes of the PDC intervention.* Ypsilanti, MI: High/Scope Educational Research Foundation.

Bredekamp, S. (Ed.). (1987). *Developmentally appropriate practice in early childhood programs serving children from birth through age 8.* Washington, DC: National Association for the Education of Young Children.

Bredekamp, S., & Shepard, L. A. (1988). How best to protect children from inappropriate school expectations, practices, and policies. *Young Children, 44,* 14–24.

Bronfenbrenner, U. (1979). *The ecology of human development: Experiments by nature and design.* Cambridge, MA: Harvard University Press.

Cahan, E. (1989). *Past caring.* New York: National Center for Children in Poverty, School of Public Health, Columbia University.

Caldwell, B. (1987). Staying ahead: The challenge of the third grade slump. *Principal, 66* (5), 10–14.

Caldwell, B. (1991). Continuity in the early years: Transitions between grades and systems. In S. L. Kagan (Ed.), *The care and education of America's young children: Obstacles and opportunities* (pp. 69–90). Chicago: National Society for the Study of Education.

Committee for Economic Development. (1993). *Why child care matters: Preparing young children for a more productive America.* New York: Author.

Culkin, M., Morris, J. R., & Helburn, S. W. (1991). Quality and the true cost of child care. *Journal of Social Issues, 47* (2), 71–86.

Davies, D. (1978). *An overview of the status of citizen participation in educational decision making.* Washington, DC: Institute for Responsive Education and the Education and Human Resources Development Division of Optimum Computer System.

Derman-Sparks, L. (1989). *Anti-bias curriculum: Tools for empowering young children.* Washington, DC: National Association for the Education of Young Children.

Elkind, D. (1987). *Preschoolers at risk.* New York: Knopf.

Federal Register. (1991, July 11). *Department of Health and Human Services, Program Announcement No. ACYF-HS-93600.91-3.* Washington, DC: U.S. Government Printing Office.

Fowler, M. G., & Cross, A. W. (1986). Preschool risk factors as predictors of early school performance. *Journal of Developmental and Behavioral Pediatrics, 7* (4), 237–241.

Grubb, N. W., & Lazerson, M. (1977, November). Child care, government financing, and the public schools: Lessons from the California Children's Centers. *School Review, 86,* 5–37.

Harter, S. (1996). Developmental changes in self-understanding across the 5 to 7 shift. In A. J. Sameroff & M. M. Haith (Eds.), *The five to seven year shift: The age of reason and responsibility* (chap. 10, this vol.). Chicago: University of Chicago Press.

Holloway, S. D., & Fuller, B. (1992, October). The great child-care experiment: What are the lessons for school improvement? *Educational Researcher, 21,* 12–19.

Holmes, D., & Holmes, M. B. (1966). *Evaluation of two associated YM-YWCA Head Start programs of New York City: Final report.* New York: Associated YM-YWCAs of New York City.

Hubbell, R., Plantz, M., Condelli, L., & Barrett, B. (1987). *The transition of Head Start children into public school: Final report* (Vol. *1*). Alexandria, VA: CSR.

Kagan, S. L. (1991a). *United we stand: Collaboration for child care and early education services.* New York: Teachers College Press.

Kagan, S. L. (1991b). Moving from here to there: Rethinking continuity and transitions in early care and education. In B. Spodek & O. Saracho (Eds.), *Yearbook in early childhood education* (Vol. *2,* pp. 132–151). New York: Teachers College Press.

Kagan, S. L., Costley, J., Landesman, L., Marx, F., Neville, P., Parker, S., & Rustici, J. (1992). *Family education and training: Obstacles, opportunities, and outcomes for low-income mothers* (Center Report No. 4). Baltimore, MD: Center on Families, Communities, Schools & Children's Learning, Johns Hopkins University.

Katz, L. G. (1988, Summer). What should young children be doing? *American Educator, 12* (2), 28–33, 44–45.

Ladd, G. W. (1996). Shift ecologies during the 5 to 7 year period: Predicting children's adjustment during the transition to grade school. In A. J. Sameroff & M. M. Haith (Eds.), *The five to seven year shift: The age of reason and responsibility* (chap. 16, this vol.). Chicago: University of Chicago Press.

Ladd, G. W., & Price, J. M. (1987). Predicting children's social and school adjustment following the transition from preschool to kindergarten. *Child Development, 58,* 1168–1189.

Lally, J. R., Mangione, P. L., & Honig, A. S. (1988). The Syracuse University family development research programs: Long-range impact on an early intervention with low-income children and their families. In D. R. Powell (Ed.), *Parent education as early childhood intervention: Emerging directions in theory research, and practice:* Vol. *3. Advances in applied developmental psychology* (pp. 79–104). Norwood, NJ: Ablex.

Lazar, I., & Darlington, R. (1982). Lasting effects of early education: A report from the Consortium for Longitudinal Studies. *Monographs of the Society for Research in Child Development, 47* (2–3, Serial No. 195).

Lightfoot, S. L. (1978). *Worlds apart: Relationships between families and schools.* New York: Basic Books.

Love, J. M. (1988). *Study of public school programs designed to ease the transition of children from preschool to kindergarten: Study overview and conceptual framework.* Hampton, NH: RMC Research Corporation.

Love, J. M., Granville, A. C., & Smith, A. B. (1978). *A process evaluation of Project Developmental Continuity: Final report of the PDC feasibility study, 1974–1977.* Ypsilanti, MI: High/Scope Educational Research Foundation.

Love, J. M., Logue, M. E., Trudeau, J. V., & Thayer, K. (1992). *Transitions to kindergarten in American schools.* Washington, DC: U.S. Department of Education.

Marx, F., & Seligson, M. (1988). *The public school early childhood study.* New York: Bank Street College of Education.

McKey, R. H., Condelli, L., Ganson, H., Barrett, B. J., McConkey, C., & Plantz, M. C. (1985). *Executive summary: The impact of Head Start on children, families and communities.* Washington, DC: CSR.

Mounoud, P. (1996). A recursive transformation of central cognitive mechanisms: The shift from partial to whole representations. In A. J. Sameroff & M. M. Haith (Eds.), *The five to seven year shift: The age of reason and responsibility* (chap. 5, this vol.). Chicago: University of Chicago Press.

National Education Goals Panel. (1993). *Reconsidering early development and learning: Toward shared beliefs and vocabulary.* Washington, DC: Author.

Nelson, K. (1996). Memory development from 4 to 7 years. In A. J. Sameroff & M. M. Haith (Eds.), *The five to seven year shift: The age of reason and responsibility* (chap. 7, this vol.). Chicago: University of Chicago Press.

Pellegrini, A. D., & Dresden, J. (1991). The concept of development in the early childhood curriculum. In B. Spodek & O. Saracho (Eds.), *Yearbook in early childhood education* (Vol. 2, pp. 21–45). New York: Teachers College Press.

Phillips, D., Howes, C., & Whitebook, M. (1991). Child care as an adult work environment. *Journal of Social Issues, 47* (2), 49–70.

Pierson, D. E., Walker, D. K., & Timan, T. (1984). A school-based program from infancy to kindergarten for children and their parents. *Personnel and Guidance Journal, 62* (8), 448–455.

Powell, D. R. (1989). *Families and early childhood programs.* Washington, DC: National Association for the Education of Young Children.

Ramey, C., & Ramey, S. (1992). *The National Head Start/Public School Early Childhood Transition Study.* Washington, DC: Office of Management and Budget.

Regional Educational Laboratories Early Childhood Collaboration Network. (1993).

Elements and indicators of home, school, and community linkages. Publication place not given: Author.

Rivlin, A. M., & Timpane, P. M. (1975). Planned variation in education: An assessment. In A. Rivlin & P. M. Timpane (Eds.), *Planned variation in education: Should we give up or try harder?* (pp. 1–21). Washington, DC: Brookings Institution.

Schultz, T. (1993). *Head Start and public schools: Looking back, looking around, looking ahead.* Alexandria, VA: National Association of State Boards of Education.

Shepard, L. A., & Smith, M. L. (1987). Effects of kindergarten retention at the end of first grade. *Psychology in the Schools, 89,* 135–145.

Siegler, R. S. (1996). Unidimensional thinking, multidimensional thinking, and characteristic tendencies of thought. In A. J. Sameroff & M. M. Haith (Eds.), *The five to seven year shift: The age of reason and responsibility* (chap. 4, this vol.). Chicago: University of Chicago Press.

Sigel, I. (1987). Early childhood education: Developmental enhancement or developmental acceleration? In S. L. Kagan & E. F. Zigler (Eds.), *Early schooling: The national debate.* New Haven, CT: Yale University Press.

Spodek, B. (1991). Early childhood teacher training: Linking theory and practice. In S. L. Kagan (Ed.), *The care and education of America's young children: Obstacles and opportunities: Ninetieth yearbook of the National Society for the Study of Education* (pp. 110–130). Chicago: National Society for the Study of Education.

Stebbins, L. B., St. Pierre, R. G., Proper, E. C., Anderson, R. B., & Cerva, T. R. (1977). *Education as experimentation: A planned variation model: Vol. IV-A. An evaluation of Follow Through.* Cambridge, MA: Abt Associates.

U.S. Department of Education. (1993). *Prospects: The congressionally mandated study of educational growth and opportunity: The interim report.* Washington, DC: Author.

Weber, L. (1971). *The English infant school and informal education.* Englewood Cliffs, NJ: Prentice-Hall.

Zigler, E., & Kagan, S. L. (1982). Child development knowledge and educational practice: Using what we know. In A. Lieberman & M. McLaughlin (Eds.), *Policy making in education: Eighty-first yearbook of the National Society for the Study of Education.* Chicago: University of Chicago Press.

Zigler, E., & Valentine, J. (1979). *Project Head Start: A legacy of the War on Poverty.* New York: Free Press.

Zimiles, H. (1991). Diversity and change in young children: Some educational implications. In B. Spodek & O. Saracho (Eds.), *Yearbook in early childhood education* (Vol. 2, pp. 21–45). New York: Teachers College Press.

CHAPTER EIGHTEEN

Performance in Context: Assessing Children's Achievement at the Outset of School

SAMUEL J. MEISELS

Assessments of children's achievements at the beginning of formal schooling reveal a great deal about theories of development implicit in these assessments. Some assessments appear to imply a social learning perspective, in which children acquire socially appropriate behaviors through exposure to adult role models and to other children who have mastered the complexities of participating in a world where specific behaviors are considered acceptable.

Other assessments suggest that development is primarily maturational—certain expectations are warranted for children at certain ages but are unexpected for children who have not yet reached that point chronologically or developmentally. Still other assessments are consistent with other more varied and heterogeneous views of how children grow and change over time. Apparently, under the mat of assessment technique lies a theory of the developing child.

In this chapter I analyze several widely used readiness and early school achievement tests in order to explore their theoretical assumptions more fully. My contention is that conventional, group-administered assessments that are in widespread use in schools today belie a narrow perspective about child development, a perspective that teaches us very little about what children actually know and can do. I will also describe an alternative approach to assessment of school achievement known as performance assessment. This approach is structured around the concept of developmental continuity and is based on a set of principles that are different from those used by conventional assessments.

Defining Readiness and Early School Achievement

The practice of assessing the social, emotional, cognitive, and motoric achievement of children at the outset of formal schooling is generally described as readiness testing. Unfortunately, *readiness* is a term that is nearly as widely misunderstood as it is frequently used. For example, children are often described as "ready" or "not ready," as if readiness were a within-the-child phenomenon. Yet, readiness is not a biological entity or an ability. Although it undoubtedly reflects higher-order cortical activity, readiness is not a gene, a chromosome, or any other biological "thing."

The term *readiness* is also appended to programs, classes, tests, and curricula. This seems to indicate that readiness is something "out there," that is, something outside the child. Some commentators suggest that readiness refers to how well prepared children are for formal education (see Boyer, 1991). This is a useful component of a readiness definition, but it begs the question of how to define the formal education for which children are to be ready. A similar problem can be seen in national policy debates concerned with school readiness. The first National Educational Goal states, "By the year 2000, all children will start school ready to learn" (National Education Goals Panel, 1991, p. 2). However, this statement was not intended to suggest that all children should start school in readiness classes, tested by readiness tests, and taught using readiness curricula materials. It simply says that all children should be ready to learn when they come to school.

Kagan (1990) offered a helpful distinction by contrasting *readiness for learning* with *readiness for school*. The former, readiness for learning, refers generally to a child's status prior to encountering new information or more advanced skills. From this perspective, children are considered ready to learn something when they have already acquired the simpler skills that enable them to reach higher or more complex skills, as Bruner (1966) once suggested in his definition of readiness. This view conceives of development as the process of advancing toward more sophisticated or complex levels of functioning. However, this view does not strictly imply a within-the-child approach to readiness, because it is consistent with interactional theories that suggest that children's skills, abilities, and knowledge are dependent not only on what the child brings to the situation but also on external experience, stimulation, and the characteristics of the environment in which the child is reared and nurtured (DeVries & Kohlberg, 1987; Sameroff & Fiese, 1990). Thus, thinking about readiness as readiness for learning may bridge the gap between a conception of readiness as an indwelling phenomenon and the perspective that learning is a complex, multidimensional phenomenon that can only be fully understood in context.

Readiness for school is another matter. This view emphasizes specific skills or experiences that the dominant culture values as the precursors to successful school experience. Such precursors include being able to sit still, recognize primary colors, count to 10, distinguish different two-dimensional shapes, and know one's address, among other indicators. Children generally do not acquire these bits of information or skills without external guidance or teaching. Yet, the readiness-for-school perspective suggests that some children have an almost innate ability to acquire these facts and skills. Those who are not successful are not ready for school or need special assistance or enrollment in such extra-year programs as "Developmental Kindergarten" or "Young 5s" programs (see Ilg & Ames, 1972). Those who have these skills are deemed "ready," as if readiness were an absolute state of affairs. This view suggests that our attention should be devoted to whether or not children have mastered these skills and acquired this information, rather than emphasizing the conditions under which children can acquire them (see Meisels, 1992).

This chapter embraces the views inherent in the readiness-to-learn position. My perspective is that readiness and early school achievement are a bidirectional concept that focuses both on children's current skills, knowledge, and abilities and on the conditions of the environment in which children are reared and taught. Because different children are prepared for different experiences, and different children respond differentially to apparently similar environmental inputs, *readiness* is a relative term. Although it can be applied to individual children, it is not something in the child, and it is not something in the curriculum. It is a product of the interaction between children's prior experiences, their genetic endowment, their maturational status, and the whole range of environmental and cultural experiences that they encounter.

This interactional perspective has important implications for how we view assessment at the outset of formal schooling—in the years between 5 and 7. Clearly, if the way that children function at age 5 is related to their prior experiences and to what they are undergoing at that time, as well as to their genetic potential and other factors, and if their achievement potential describes a dynamic rather than static status, then assessment during this period cannot be content to record static "snapshots" of children's responses to highly circumscribed test situations.

Conventional, group-administered assessments of children during the age 5 to 7 year period are highly decontextualized and generally treat the children they are assessing as passive respondents. The dimensions of development that the assessments tap are very limited, as is the behavior that is sampled. Five-year-olds are considered "pre-readers," 6-year-olds are treated as "early readers," and 7-year-olds are expected to be "intermediate readers." In other words, although these tests assume that some children are more advanced than others, qualitative distinctions are in short supply. As I discuss in this chapter, this view of assessment is so narrow that it obscures the phenomena it seeks to elucidate. The next section examines these tests and their fit with the interactionist definition of readiness given earlier in greater detail.

Measuring Readiness and Early School Achievement

School readiness and children's early school achievements are usually measured by norm-referenced, group-administered, objectively scored, paper-and-pencil tests. In this section, I briefly describe readiness tests—those used with 5-year-olds—and characterize their uses and usefulness. Then, in the next section, five early school achievement tests are discussed and critiqued, followed by a presentation of a very different approach to assessment.

Readiness Tests

Readiness tests are designed to assess a child's relative preparedness for a particular school or preschool program. Accordingly, they represent tests of readiness for school, as described earlier.

Analysis of the content of typical readiness tests is illuminating. One such test, the Developmental Tasks for Kindergarten Readiness (Lesiak, 1978), begins with an assessment of social interaction. Table 18.1 presents several of the items from the "Social Interaction" subscale of this instrument. All of the items are objectively scored.

Such items as these are found on many school readiness tests, although the most typical subtests focus on visual discrimination, color naming, counting, alphabet knowledge, and identification of body parts. Table 18.1 displays something else that is worthy of careful consideration. Implicit in many school readiness tests, as well as assessments used with older children, is a cultural and class bias. Nearly all items on these tests are dependent on dominant cultural conventions and on the particular kind of informal, verbally mediated learning that takes place in middle-class homes but may not be part of a particular child's experience.

Empirical research substantiates this claim. One study of six tests of academic readiness that were administered to more than 400 children reported

Table 18.1
Social Interaction Items Selected From the *Developmental Tasks for Kindergarten Readiness*

1. "Hello, my name is (   ). What is your name?" [Child receives credit if first name is given spontaneously.]
2. "Won't you have a seat?" [Credit if child sits down without further urging.]
3. "How are you?" [Credit for a response that is verbal and appropriate.]
4. "How old are you?" [Credit for correct years of age.]
5. "Where do you live?" [Correct number or name of street accepted.]
6. "Would you mind moving your chair closer? I have something I want to show you." [Credit if the child moves closer to the examiner or looks at the test booklet.]
7. "How did you like doing some of the things we did today?" [Credit for appropriate verbal response.]
8. "Thanks for working with me today. I hope to see you again in school." [Credit if child rises from the chair spontaneously.]

Note. Adapted from W. J. Lesiak, *Developmental Tasks for Kindergarten Readiness—III* (Brandon, VT: Clinical Psychology Press, 1994). Used with permission.

significant and substantial racial, ethnic, and class differences (Oakland, 1978). White, Mexican American, and African American children showed differential success on these tests. Moreover, the tests themselves were differentially accurate. Their weakest validity, as demonstrated by correlations with later measures of achievement and intelligence, was demonstrated for African American students. Moreover, within each racial-ethnic group, the tests were more highly valid for middle-class than for lower-socioeconomic (SES) children.

These issues are critical to the meaning of readiness test results, because readiness tests are used to determine a child's potential success in school. If these tests treat children from different ethnic groups and classes differently, their overall meaning and usefulness is severely compromised. The question of the accuracy of the inferences or predictions that can be drawn from a test and its results is precisely the question that validity studies are intended to answer. Every readiness test administration thus contains an implicit prediction. The prediction is that children who pass this test will perform successfully in school; those who fail the test will not be "ready" for formal schooling.

However, Table 18.1 shows how risky predictions can be when made from tests of this type. "Appropriate" behavior in one context, with one specific teacher, and by one particular child may not be appropriate in another situation with another set of conditions. Yet the results of tests that rely on these and other similar items are accorded normative meaning—despite their inherent relativity. This means that a child who is considered "ready" in one school situation might not be "ready" in another—simply because the setting and its attendant expectations differ. Yet the results of the test are interpreted as an indication of the child's lack of readiness, not the school's lack of fit with the child.

All tests that contain implicit or explicit predictive properties must demonstrate the accuracy of their predictions. However, the evidence that is available regarding the psychometric properties of readiness tests is highly questionable. The Metropolitan Readiness Test (MRT) serves as an almost paradigmatic illustration (Nurss & McGauvran, 1986). The MRT is a group-administered test that is designed to assess children's development of prereading skills. Its subtests cover auditory memory, beginning consonants, letter recognition, visual matching, beginning consonants, letter recognition, visual matching, language and listening, and quantitative language. These areas are tested by means of items that are read to children and to which children respond by filling in an oval, bubble, or circle. No context for these items is given. No problems are available for solution. No manipulative materials are used. Only auditory reception and visual discrimination of relatively isolated shapes, sounds, pictures, or numbers is called upon. This methodology is common to nearly all group-administered readiness and achievement tests.

What do the results from the MRT tell us? Technical information reported by the publisher shows strong internal reliability, with Kuder-Richardson formula 20 coefficients ranging from .73 to .88 (Nurss & McGauvran, 1986). However, the MRT's validity data are quite limited. The test manual reports only two small-scale studies. The first, with 183 subjects, provides correlations between the MRT and the Metropolitan Achievement Test (MAT) 7 to 9 months later. Correlations between the MRT prereading composite score and the subtests of the MAT range from .54 to .69. The second study correlated MRT findings with scores from the Stanford Achievement Test ($N = 286$). These correlations were higher, ranging from .68 to .83.

Other validity data concerning the MRT are available from independent sources. A longitudinal study that correlated MRT results with scores from the Comprehensive Test of Basic Skills (CTBS) administered to more than 40 students reported stable correlations through grade 10 (Weller, Schnittjer, & Tuten, 1992). Similar findings are reported for 1-year intervals by other researchers (Nagle, 1979; Rubim 1974). Nevertheless, as is explained in this chapter, these findings are inconclusive.

Two common features of these studies, as well as the validity studies of the achievement tests reviewed in the next section, are important to note. First, the studies are self-referential—that is, the tests under investigation are compared with other forms of the same or very similar tests, rather than with explicitly independent criteria. For example, the MRT is validated in terms of its prediction of the MAT and CTBS scores. The MAT is validated by its comparison with the Stanford Achievement Test (Fortune & Cromack, 1985). The CTBS, in turn, is validated by its correlation with its own "benchmark" form (CTB Macmillan/McGraw-Hill, 1991). The practice of "validating" a test against other forms of the same test is also used by the California Achievement Test (CAT) (Bunch, 1985). The technical circularity of these procedures is highly suspect, given that the validity of the "outcome" may be no better established than that of the predictor. This self-referential practice also calls into question the meaning of these results, since the criterion—other forms of the same or similar tests—does not inform us about what children actually know or can do, which is what we are using the tests to draw inferences about.

A second similarity among these tests concerns their method of reporting validity data. Primarily, they report correlations. But correlations only describe the degree of overlap between two or more domains or measures. They cannot fit individuals into such binary classifications as "ready" or "not ready." For example, a correlation cannot tell us whether a specific child who was low on the MRT (the predictor) was also low on the MAT or the Stanford (the criterion, or outcome). The child who scored low on the MRT may have scored high on one of the outcomes, and another child may have reversed this situation by scoring high on the predictor and low on the outcome. If one wishes to decide whether a test is a good predictor for a binary classification, one needs to examine frequencies of correct and incorrect classifications and their inter-relationships in addition to rank-order correlations. But such data are missing from technical reports about the MRT and from all the other readiness and early school achievement tests that are available for review. Although, as pointed out earlier, most readiness tests intend to describe a child's current level of skill achievement or preacademic preparedness, the tests nevertheless are used to predict who will be successful or ready for school. Hence, they must be evaluated on the quality of their predictive validity, and this information is invariably incomplete. In short, generations of educators and policy makers have been making decisions about children's futures with tests that leave important questions about validity unanswered and significant information about children's success in school unavailable.

The best—and simplest—quantitative means for evaluating a test's ability to make accurate individual predictions are computations of sensitivity and specificity. *Sensitivity* refers to the proportion of children who are correctly identified as having a particular condition or set of characteristics by some test or other indicator in relation to all of the children who actually have that condition. *Specificity* is the converse: It refers to the proportion of those children who are correctly classified as free of the condition being investigated in relation to all children without that specified condition. In other words, if the "condition" we are investigating is readiness, a test with high sensitivity would identify a high proportion of those children who are correctly selected by independent means as "not ready." A test with high specificity would be successful in eliminating these "unready" children from its classification of "ready" children. This classification analysis provides a breakdown of true and false positives, information that is completely unavailable from correlational data but that is essential for selecting between competing predictors (see Sackett, Haynes, & Tugwell, 1985, for further discussion of sensitivity and specificity).

In summary, school readiness and achievement tests do not report sensitivity and specificity, nor do they provide the data necessary to compute these ratios. In this respect and others school readiness tests are of limited value. Their content is generally abstract, verbally mediated, and potentially biased against children unfamiliar or uncomfortable with middle-class manners and mores. Their psychometric data are generally unconvincing, primarily because of their self-referential basis and their incompleteness. Given that most readiness tests appear to test readiness for school, and to imply an absolute concept of readiness, their limitations substantially outstrip their potential positive contributions.

Early School Achievement Tests

Meaningful distinctions between readiness tests and the achievement tests that are used early in children's school careers are difficult to make. Readiness tests are intended to be used at children's entry to school; achievement tests are supposed to reflect a child's accumulation of knowledge and skills. Nevertheless, all of the achievement tests that are in widespread use nationally are also recommended for use at the outset of kindergarten.

With the exception of the MRT, which is nationally normed, perhaps the major distinction between readiness tests and achievement tests is that achievement tests purportedly are applicable to all children and all classrooms, whereas readiness tests generally report a child's preparation for a specific classroom program. For example, the Comprehensive Test of Basic Skills states that its purpose is "to measure students' understanding of the broad concepts developed by all curricula" (CTB Macmillan/McGraw-Hill, 1991, p. 9). The Stanford Early School Achievement Test (SESAT) is intended to "reflect what is being taught in schools throughout the country" (Psychological Corporation, 1990, p. 11). The California Achievement Test is "designed to measure achievement in the basic skills taught in schools throughout the nation" (CTB Macmillan/McGraw-Hill, 1992, p. 1). Similar statements of purpose can be listed for other tests, for example, the Iowa Tests of Basic Skills (ITBS) (Hieronymus, Lindquist, & Hoover, 1982) and the Metropolitan Achievement Test (Prescott, Balow, Hogan, & Farr, 1988). Another difference between readiness and achievement tests is that achievement tests are the first in a series of tests that usually extend through a child's entire school career. Beyond this, readiness tests and achievement tests are nearly indistinguishable in content, purpose, administration, and meaning.

Systematic data are unavailable concerning the actual frequency of use of specific achievement tests or the amount of money spent on them. Bunch (1985) estimated that 11 to 12 million administrations of all levels of the CAT (K–12) take place per year. Several years ago a news article claimed that 10 million students take the CTBS or the ITBS in grades K–12 (Kelly, 1992, p. 8A). Regardless of the actual numbers of administrations, it is clear that large numbers of children take these tests each year, and substantial sums are spent on them. (The National Commission on Testing and Public Policy, 1990, reported that more than 20 million school days are given over simply to taking standardized tests in the United States, with more than $100 million in 1988 dollars spent on direct sales of tests and test services—a threefold increase over the previous 3 decades.)

The most commonly used school achievement tests in early elementary classrooms are those already mentioned: the CAT, CTBS, ITBS, MAT, and SESAT. All of these tests are used with children within the 1st month or 2 of their entry into kindergarten. All five are standardized, norm-referenced, group-administered, multiple-choice, machine-scorable, achievement tests. Each requires many hours to complete. They are usually administered in

Table 18.2
Subtests of Kindergarten Achievement Tests

ITBS[a]	CTBS[b]	CAT[c]	MAT[d]	SESAT[e]
Word analysis	Sound recog.	Word analysis	Reading	Sound recog.
Vocabulary	Vocabulary	Vocabulary	Language	Words
Language	Comprehension	Comprehension	Science	Reading
Listening	Visual recog.	Lang. express.	Social studies	Letters
Math	Math	Math	Math	Math
				Environment
				Listening

[a]Iowa Tests of Basic Skills.
[b]Comprehensive Tests of Basic Skills.
[c]California Achievement Test.
[d]Metropolitan Achievement Test.
[e]Stanford Early School Achievement Test.

small, but timed doses over a period of 1 to 2 weeks and require no educational skill, knowledge, or experience from the person who gives or proctors them.

Table 18.2 lists the subtests for all five tests. It is clear that the major content areas covered by the tests are very similar. The tests were originally formulated to give information about children's reading readiness, and the emphasis on literacy and prereading skills is evident in the table. Also evident from an analysis of the content of the tests is their focus on isolated skills. Each of the subtests listed in the table is tested separately, and little or no effort is made to integrate them. In this respect alone, these tests fail to achieve one of their basic goals: to reflect commonly taught grade-level skills of most state and district curricula. Each skill is tested separately from the context of the subject area in which it is taught. Therefore, anyone who expects these tests to reflect a specific curriculum is likely to be disappointed. Because these skills may be taught in the classroom very differently from how they are presented on the test, students may not do as well on the tests as they do in their classrooms where skills are not taught in a manner that is separate from context.

The CAT and ITBS are particular exemplars of this approach to testing skills in isolation and out of context. At the kindergarten and first-grade level they focus on individual skills and do not evaluate the student's ability to integrate, synthesize, or analyze skills. This problem becomes even greater as the student advances in grade and is asked to do more synthesis and analysis of information in class but continues to be tested on discrete skills on the ITBS, CAT, MAT, and SESAT. The CTBS claims to use a more holistic approach. For example, the reading items for the older levels are stories and questions about

Figure 18.1 Sample items from Level 5, Iowa Tests of Basic Skills, Form J. Copyright © 1990 by the University of Iowa. All rights reserved. Reproduced with the permission of the publisher, the Riverside Publishing Company.

meaning, rather than questions about isolated words and skills. However, at the kindergarten level, the CTBS is generally indistinguishable from all of the other tests under review.

Another characteristic common to these readiness and achievement tests is their appearance to children—that is, the task demands of the testing situation. Figure 18.1 contains two practice items from the ITBS. The manner in which the items are presented and the familiarity of children with this kind of material are likely to affect their success. In other words, the ability to follow the particular directions and task requirements of such tests plays a major role in children's test performance. For some children, the tasks may simply be too novel or abstract for them to demonstrate their actual abilities.

The items depicted in Figure 18.1 are typical of those on all of the tests being reviewed. They seem to show that the real "action" is in following the directions, not in producing the correct response. Here is what you would have to do to complete the ITBS's practice Item 1 shown in Figure 18.1 if you were a typical 5-year-old:

1. Open your booklet to the second page.

2. Find the ducks at the top of the page.

3. Put your marker under the first row on the page.

4. Find the circles under the pictures.

5. Listen to a "story" about the pictures. (The story is "Which animal is best at climbing trees?").

6. Mark the circle under the "picture that best tells about the story."
(Riverside Publishing Company, 1990, p. 14)

If you have learned the difference between a story and a question, this item can be quite confusing because the child is asked to respond to a story but is only asked a question. In any event, it takes six steps to arrive at this ill-defined task. The test manual suggests that this item measures vocabulary skills, but the tasks are so visually cluttered and composed of so many subparts that failure on this item could have many differing etiologies and different meanings.

In an extremely insightful and comprehensive analysis of formal measures of early literacy, Stallman and Pearson (1990) raised still another important point: They argued convincingly that these kinds of reading-readiness achievement tests do not reflect current thinking in the field of early literacy. They noted that children taking these tests are assessed on isolated skills in settings that are devoid of context, rather than being evaluated on "situated" tasks in natural setting in which they are asked to use what they know and have had experience with previously. The entire test-taking experience is dominated by "filling in bubbles, moving the marker, making sure that everyone is in the right place. These activities may be related to test taking, but they have nothing to do with reading" or the skills that are supposedly being tested (Stallman & Pearson, 1990, p. 38).

In short, such tests are unrealistic because they call upon skills that most children have used only in context but here are asked to use in a decontextualized, unintegrated manner. The tests reflect theories of learning that are generally considered to be without scientific merit, for example, children are tested on isolated skills in abstract settings rather than on reading tasks in concrete situations in which they are asked to behave like readers. Moreover, recognition, not production or even identification, is the dominant mode of cognitive processing, although for many years research has supported a theory of reading as one of constructing meaning rather than learning small, component elements that are somehow mysteriously integrated later on (Stallman & Pearson, 1990; Sulzby, 1985).

"Decomposition, decontextualization, and objectivity" are the three constructs that Stallman and Pearson concluded undergird these tests (1990, p. 41). The approach to skills assessment used by all these tests is one in which a complex task, such as reading, is decomposed into its constituent parts. The apparent belief is that in testing these parts, mastery of the whole can be inferred. However, simply by using a task-analysis procedure, the skills are ipso facto taken out of context. They are decontextualized and isolated. Often, they are rendered meaningless and foreign to the child.

Reading, mathematics, and language are not learned well in a decontextualized fashion. They are mastered in context. Yet, those who construct these tests persist in testing isolated skills out of context in part because of the belief that such tests are more "objective" than assessments that are situated in the lives of children's daily activities. How "objective" these tests are is highly questionable (see, e.g., Wodtke, Harper, Schommer, & Brunelli, 1989). Moreover, they reflect very little qualitative shift longitudinally in terms of what children can or should be able to do intellectually. This seems to imply that 7-year-olds are more advanced than 5- or 6-year-olds because they can do more difficult tasks—not because they have qualitatively different abilities.

If one wishes to draw valid conclusions about a student's profile of strengths and difficulties from these types of assessments, one would have difficulty using the data from these tests. They may inform us that a child does not have strong letter knowledge, but they cannot tell us which specific letter the child knows or does not know. They may tell us about a child's overall ability to recognize letters, objects, or sound-symbol combinations, but they will not be able to tell us how children combine these elements into the intellectually more demanding tasks of reading. And, as noted earlier, none of them provides classificational data regarding sensitivity and specificity. No information is available concerning their predictive validity for individuals, and other data (reviewed in a later section of this chapter) suggest that they may actually have negative effects on children's learning. They provide very little documentation of children's patterns of reasoning or conceptualization, and thus their contribution to our knowledge about how children between ages 5 and 7 develop is very limited.

Assessing Young Children's School Achievement With a Performance Assessment System

What is the alternative to these decontextualized, objectified tests that are based on a reductionistic theory of knowledge? One alternative is performance assessment.

Defining Performance Assessment

Performance assessment represents a significant departure from group-administered, objectively scored, skills-focused, product-oriented assessments of achievement. Performance assessments focus on students' actual work and accomplishments, rather than on their responses to formalized, decontextualized test items. Performance assessments consist of actual examples of classroom-based activities, rather than highly inferential estimates of learning. They are "real instances of extended criterion performances, rather than proxies or estimators of actual learning goals" (Shepard, 1991, p. 21). Moreover, they represent an ongoing assessment, rather than a general snapshot taken of narrow academic skills at a single time point. Insofar as they reflect students' capabilities, rather than their programmed responses, they have the potential for demonstrating qualitative and quantitative changes in children's development.

Calfee (1992) has suggested several criteria that performance assessments should meet. First, such assessments should be integrative. Rather than the decomposition of skills that marks conventional assessment paradigms, performance assessments bring together various skills into visible displays and demonstrations of skillful behavior. Hence, in this paradigm we expect to see children construct models, solve problems, and prepare reports that call upon a range of skills, experiences, and knowledge. Second, they should emphasize top-level competence. This means that children are asked to show what they can do in performance assessments, not what they cannot do. It means, as well, that teachers work with their students to help them achieve their best possible products, rather than focusing almost entirely on having students respond to a series of items that may not reflect their special talents or interests.

Third, performance assessments encourage metacognition and the capacity to articulate performance. Students are engaged in the assessment process. They evaluate their own work and select items to be included in the assessment, items that reflect their own sense of progress. Finally, performance assessments are guided by developmental standards. These standards reflect the longitudinal character of children's work that is captured by the continuous progress format of most performance assessments. They also refer to the continuity of development between children at different ages, grades, and levels of functioning. Now, instead of seeing children as members of skills classes that are relatively sealed off from one another except in terms of level of difficulty (i.e., "prereaders," "early readers," "intermediate readers"), people can view them as functioning on a continuum of skill achievement, in which both qualitative and quantitative differences are displayed.

The Work Sampling System

What does performance assessment look like in the years between 5 and 7? In the following pages, I describe the Work Sampling System (Meisels, Jablon, Marsden, Dichtelmiller, & Dorfman, 1994). Work Sampling is a performance assessment system that offers an alternate to product-oriented, group-administered achievement tests in preschool through grade 5. It reflects a very different view of readiness and of how children learn in school. The purpose of Work Sampling is to assess and document children's skills, knowledge, behavior, and accomplishments as displayed across a wide variety of classroom domains on multiple occasions. Work Sampling systematizes teacher observations by guiding those observations with specific criteria and well-defined procedures. It consists of three complementary elements: (a) Developmental Guidelines and Checklists, (b) Portfolios of children's work, and (c) Summary Reports. These elements are all classroom-focused and instructionally relevant. They involve the child, the child's family, the teacher, and the school administration in the process of assessment. Each of the Work Sampling elements is described in turn.

Developmental Guidelines and Checklists

The Checklists are designed to assist teachers in observing and documenting individual children's growth and progress. Each of the eight Checklists, from age 3 to grade 5, covers seven domains:

- Personal and Social Development
- Language and Literacy
- Mathematical Thinking
- Scientific Thinking
- Social Studies
- The Arts
- Physical Development

Each domain (e.g., Language and Literacy) is composed of several functional components (for kindergarten: Listening, Speaking, Literature and Reading, Writing), and each component is defined by a number of performance indicators that refer to children's specific behaviors, skills, or accomplishments. Figures 18.2 and 18.3 present examples of Checklist components and indicators drawn from the Language and Literacy domain; Figure 18.2 provides an illustration of the kindergarten level, and Figure 18.3 shows the analogue for first grade.

These figures show the relationship among the items in the Language and Literature domain of the Checklists. Most indicators can be tracked back and forth chronologically, although some tasks do not appear in all of the Checklists. For example, kindergarten-age children are not expected to demonstrate competence in spelling, as are first graders. Other differences among the Checklist items are incorporated in the Guidelines, which is also described in this section.

Domain	**Functional Component**	**Performance Indicator**

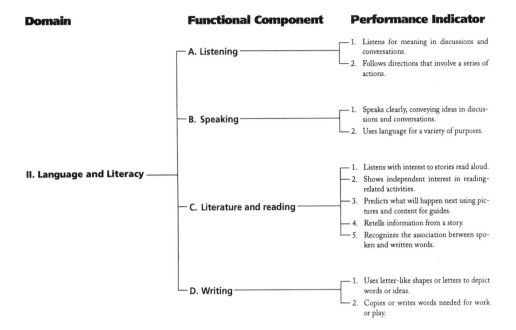

Kindergarten

Figure 18.2 Language and literacy components and performance indicators for the Work Sampling System—kindergarten. Copyright © 1994 by Rebus Planning Associates. Reproduced with the permission of the publisher.

To use the Checklist, the teacher first selects a domain and associated functional component. Then, after observing the student repeatedly, and working with him or her in the classroom, as well as considering other sources of information (e.g., portfolios, notes, parental comments), the teacher indicates how well the student fulfills each of the performance indicators by using a 3-point rating scale (*Not yet, In process, Proficient*). The rating categories reflect a modified mastery-achievement continuum and show the degree to which children have acquired the skills, knowledge, and behavior, or have demonstrated the accomplishments required by each of the performance indicators listed in the Checklist and described in the Guidelines.

As noted, each Checklist is accompanied by a set of Guidelines. The Guidelines are critical for understanding and using the Checklists. The Guidelines clarify the Checklist items by providing a rationale and examples for each performance indicator. They enable teachers to apply the Checklist consistently to a whole class of children and to interpret the Checklist reliably, so that different classrooms will be assessed by different teachers in similar ways. The

Checklists incorporate information from a wide range of resources including local, state, and national standards for curriculum development. Figure 18.4 presents comparative entries from the kindergarten, first-, and second-grade Guidelines.

These Guidelines show clearly how a specific area is assessed differentially across time. The expectations for 7-year-olds are clearly different from those for 5-year-olds, yet overall they form a continuum within the area of language and literacy. Clearly, the view implicit in this approach is that 7-year-olds differ from 5-year-olds in a number of dimensions both qualitatively and quantitatively, yet there is substantial continuity across this period. (It should be noted that although the domain of Language and Literacy was used throughout this section, this continuous structure is reflected in the other domains as well.)

The Checklist is designed to be completed on each child three times during the course of the year. The performance indicators that constitute the Checklists are intended to reflect common activities and expectations in classrooms that are structured around developmentally appropriate activities (see Bredekamp, 1987), but they are not intended to be used to compare the progress of one

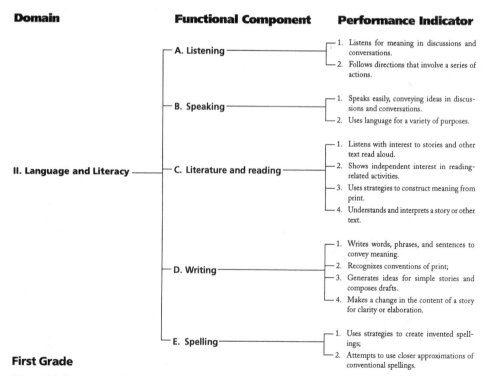

Domain   **Functional Component**   **Performance Indicator**

II. Language and Literacy

A. Listening
1. Listens for meaning in discussions and conversations.
2. Follows directions that involve a series of actions.

B. Speaking
1. Speaks easily, conveying ideas in discussions and conversations.
2. Uses language for a variety of purposes.

C. Literature and reading
1. Listens with interest to stories and other text read aloud.
2. Shows independent interest in reading-related activities.
3. Uses strategies to construct meaning from print.
4. Understands and interprets a story or other text.

D. Writing
1. Writes words, phrases, and sentences to convey meaning.
2. Recognizes conventions of print;
3. Generates ideas for simple stories and composes drafts.
4. Makes a change in the content of a story for clarity or elaboration.

E. Spelling
1. Uses strategies to create invented spellings;
2. Attempts to use closer approximations of conventional spellings.

First Grade

Figure 18.3 Language and literacy components and performance indicators for the Work Sampling System— first grade. Copyright © 1994 by Rebus Planning Associates. Reproduced with the permission of the publisher.

The Work Sampling System

■ Language and Literacy

D Writing continued

Kindergarten	First Grade	Second Grade
2 Copies or writes words needed for work or play.	1 Writes words, phrases, and sentences to convey meaning.	1 Uses writing to convey meaning for a variety of purposes.
Children begin to understand the power of written words when they see that messages, such as "Please Leave Standing" on a sign in front of a block structure, have an impact. Children show that they understand the power of written words by:	For many six year olds, the process of writing is an act of the moment; there is very little sense of writing for a specific audience. The pleasure in the process is usually connected to something else, such as producing a drawing, making a sign, or creating a list. Examples of how six year olds write for a variety of purposes include:	Second grade children can begin to understand that writing is a way to communicate ideas and organize information. Examples of how second graders write for a variety of purposes include:
• copying words to convey messages (for example, "Stop" or "Go");	• telling or writing about a picture, drawing, or painting;	• writing poetry, how-to books, or plays;
• recognizing that putting their names on a product signifies that it was done by them;	• making lists and signs for projects and activities throughout the classroom;	• writing a story about a personal experience;
• realizing that a caption created for a picture or painting can tell a story about the drawing;	• writing a caption to accompany a science observation of the monarch butterfly;	• writing down information collected during a survey;
• copying a note to take home;	• writing a note to the teacher or a friend.	• writing about a math problem in a math journal;
• making a sign, such as "Hospital" or "Shoe Store," for the dramatic play area;		• writing captions or descriptive sentences to accompany a science observation.
• copying labels from around the room;		
• using the keyboard to write their name or a personal message.		

Figure 18.4 Guidelines for the Work Sampling System: Writing Performance Indicator—kindergarten through second grade. Copyright © 1994 by Rebus Planning Associates. Reproduced with the permission of the publisher.

child with that of another. There is no expectation that every child will be in the "Proficient" category in every item by the end of the year. Rather, the Checklists are to be used as part of the complete Work Sampling System to document a profile of children's individualized progress in developing skills, acquiring knowledge, and mastering important behaviors. Variability in development across groups of children—and even across different domains within individuals—is normal and has a place in this approach.

Portfolios

The second major element of the Work Sampling System consists of portfolios of children's work. Portfolios are a purposeful collection of students' work that illustrates their efforts, progress, and achievements and potentially provides a rich documentation of each child's experience throughout the year (cf. Paulson,

Paulson, & Meyer, 1991). Portfolios make possible the active involvement of children in the process of selecting and judging the quality of their own work.

Work Sampling advocates a relatively structured approach to portfolio collection that relies on the identification and collection of two types of work: Core items and Individualized items. Core items serve as work samples representing five domains that are common to all children and also as repeated illustrations of areas of learning engaged in by the same child throughout the year. In addition to the Core items, Individualized items are selected on three occasions throughout the year. These items can be planned in advance, or they can be quite spontaneous. They need not be identical for all children, they can vary across time, and they can be collected at intervals different from those of the Core items. These items will enable the portfolio to be more responsive and individualized and they reflect specific goals and unique interests and abilities of individual children.

Portfolios can only inform and extend the teacher's purposes when they become an integrated part of the teaching-learning process. Portfolio collection in the Work Sampling System is an activity that involves both the student and the teacher. It is an activity in which teachers and students make instructional decisions as they compile the Portfolio and discuss its contents. Portfolio content is intended to parallel classroom activities and is expected to lead to the development of new activities based on joint teacher-student assessment of the child's progress and interests. Indeed, this is one of the distinguishing features of Portfolio collection: It offers an opportunity to preserve an actual moment of the classroom experience. It carries with it a sense of the classroom context that enables both students and teachers to interpret the Portfolio items in terms of a connected and related framework.

The Portfolio is a tool for documenting, analyzing, and summarizing the child's growth and development across the entire school year. As such, the Portfolio affords an opportunity for analysis of intra-individual change in children, as Core items that are collected on multiple occasions are reviewed and analyzed. Assessment of the Portfolio is based on the child's continuous development toward a standard of performance that is consistent with the teacher's curriculum and with appropriate developmental expectations. Critical to this process is the teacher's specification of his or her standards of achievement— standards that the child can show progress in meeting through the longitudinal character of portfolio construction.

Summary Reports

The final element of the Work Sampling System is the Summary Report, completed on each child three times per year. This Report consists of a brief summary of each child's classroom performance. It is based on teacher observations and on records that are kept as part of the Work Sampling System. The

Report contains specific criteria for evaluating children's performance in each of the domains of learning and behavior that are emphasized in the classroom. The Report is intended to accomplish three goals:

1. It helps teachers summarize information from the Checklists and Portfolios regarding the development of individual children.

2. It provides an easily understood accounting to parents about their child's growth and development.

3. It provides general information about individual children's progress that can be used by school administrators and others concerned with children's educational accomplishments.

By summarizing performance and linking it to the evidence accumulated on the Checklist and Portfolio, the Report provides an authentic way of communicating what children accomplished, where their strengths and difficulties lie, and how much progress they made during the year.

Evidence of the Effectiveness of Work Sampling

Relatively little evidence is available to demonstrate the effectiveness of performance assessment (see Shavelson, Baxter, & Pine, 1992), and no studies concerning comprehensive performance assessment with young children have been reported. However, it is unreasonable to expect that major changes in assessment and instructional policy can be undertaken without an empirical foundation for guiding those changes. This section describes a preliminary study of the reliability and validity of the Work Sampling System. The complete report is available in a separate publication (Meisels, Liaw, Dorfman, & Nelson, 1995).

Subjects

A total of 100 children from 10 different classrooms in three school districts were selected for this study. They ranged in age from 4 years 11 months to 6 years 6 months in the fall (mean age = 5 years 7 months). None had been retained or previously enrolled in kindergarten. The three school districts that were represented included one that was primarily middle class and white (40 students), one that was split between working-class and middle-class white (30 students), and one that was urban, poor, and primarily African American (30 students).

Procedures

In the fall and spring two individually administered norm-referenced assessments were given to the children; in the spring, the teacher also completed a child behavior questionnaire about each of the children participating in the study. Throughout the year, the teachers implemented the Work Sampling System. Information from the Checklists, Portfolios, and Summary Reports was used in this study in addition to the standardized data.

The individual assessments were drawn from two comprehensive batteries. One assessment was derived from the Kindergarten Achievement Battery of the Woodcock-Johnson Psychoeducational Battery–Revised (WJ-R) (Woodcock & Johnson, 1989). The following subtests were administered: "Letter Word Identification," "Applied Problems," "Dictation," "Science," "Social Studies," and "Humanities." The second assessment consisted of the Motor Scale of the McCarthy Scales of Children's Abilities (MSCA) (McCarthy, 1972). These assessments were administered by five trained examiners who were blind to the study's purposes. Fall and spring assessments were counterbalanced to avoid bias. In the spring, the teachers also completed a 45-item Child Behavior Rating Scale (Bronson & Love, 1987).

Reliability of the Checklist

Internal reliability data (or, Cronbach's index of internal consistency) demonstrate that the Checklist has extremely high reliability, with α ranging from .84 to .95. The fall Checklist showed the highest internal consistency, with α between .90 and .94.

Validity of the Checklist

The validity of the Checklist was tested by means of correlations, regressions, and computation of sensitivity and specificity. High correlations were obtained between the Checklist and the other assessments given in the fall and spring. The correlations between the total scores of the fall Checklist and the fall Woodcock Johnson–Revised (WJ-R) total by grade are .73 in the fall and .74 in the spring; between the winter Checklist and the spring WJ-R, they are .73; and between the spring Checklist and the spring WJ-R, they are .63. These correlations contrast with those obtained between the Checklist and the motor scale of the MSCA, which range from .43 in the fall to .28 in the spring. It is clear that the Checklist and WJ-R share a great deal of variance in common. The correlations between the spring Checklist and the concurrent Child Behavior Rating Scale were also very high (.79).

Multiple regressions that compared the spring performance on the WJ-R (by grade), the MSCA, and the Child Behavior Rating Scale with the child's gender, age, initial ability, and Checklist scores were also conducted. The results indicate significant associations between the winter Checklist and all but one outcome (i.e., the MSCA Motor) even when the potential effects of gender, maturation (age), and initial ability (i.e., fall test scores) were controlled. The data demonstrate clearly that the Checklist, especially in the winter, makes a significant contribution to predictions of children's performance in the spring.

Sensitivity and specificity analyses of the Checklist and the WJ-R were conducted to indicate the extent to which children's developmental status may have changed or remained constant. The data show that the Checklist has high sensitivity and specificity in predicting the WJ-R. In fact, the prediction of the fall and winter Checklist to the spring WJ-R is substantially more accurate than the prediction of the fall WJ-R to itself in the spring. The Checklist is a poor predictor of only the MSCA from fall to spring.

Reliability and Validity of the Summary Report

The interscorer reliability of the Summary Report consisted of two raters each coding 75 of the Summary Reports. The data show extremely high interrater Pearson product correlations between raters 1 and 2 ($r = .89$ for total score). However, the correlations between each of the raters and the teachers were somewhat lower. The mean correlations for rater 1 and the teachers was .70; for rater 2 and the teachers it was .62. Further data show that the raters' findings uniformly correlate more highly with the outcomes than do the teachers'. This suggests that the raters' findings were more accurate than those of the teachers, probably owing to their greater familiarity with how the two sources of information (Checklists and Portfolios) should be integrated for the Summary Report.

Discussion

These data provide very strong empirical support for the reliability and validity of the Work Sampling System as a measure of children's overall school achievement in kindergarten. Although the sample was relatively small and an earlier version of the Work Sampling materials was used for this study, these findings provide a justification for the continued use of the Work Sampling System and a basis for designing more extensive studies.

Since the study was completed, refinements have taken place in all aspects and all components of the Work Sampling System. The Checklists have been rewritten to enhance their clarity, increase the number of domains, change their scaling, and present a unified perspective from age 3 through age 11. The Guidelines have similarly been rewritten to reflect the changes in the Checklists and to specify more clearly what teachers should be evaluating. The Portfolio materials have also been revised, particularly to clarify the selection of Core items. Finally, the Summary Report has undergone major changes. In conjunction with the ongoing development of training methods and materials, these changes should result in the Work Sampling System's becoming an extremely useful performance assessment for preschool and the elementary grades.

Conclusion

All three of the Work Sampling System elements—Checklists, Portfolios, and Summary Reports—are essential to this assessment approach. Without the Checklists, teachers cannot keep track of children's progress toward widely accepted curriculum goals. Without Portfolios, qualitative differences between children's work are obscured, children's ability to take an active role in evaluating their own work is impaired, and parents are not included in the process of assessment. Without Summary Reports, easily summarizable data for parents, teachers, and school administrators are unavailable. Together, these components constitute a dynamic, authentic performance system in which each element informs every other component and in which each participant is able to obtain useful and easily interpretable data so that instruction can be improved and learning enhanced.

The opportunity to learn more about children's readiness and their development through use of the Work Sampling System should be underscored. The essential character of the readiness definition propounded at the outset of this chapter is that readiness and early school achievement are, at heart, interactional. This definition casts a dual focus on the child's status and on the characteristics of the child's educational setting. These two foci are incorporated into the three elements of the Work Sampling System. The Checklists indicate the child's skills, knowledge, behavior, and accomplishments in relation to a criterion-referenced framework of state and national curriculum standards. The Portfolio displays the child's accomplishments in comparison to classroom expectations. The Summary Reports combine the information from the Checklists and Portfolios, and indicators of the student's progress, into an easily understood and reported summary of the student's performance. The three times per year format of Work Sampling enables teachers to chart over time children's progress—their emergent readiness and evolving mastery—and to use this information to modify their approach to teaching and to individualize their curriculum objectives.

The general method of performance assessment that is represented by Work Sampling is extremely well suited for focusing on the interactive nature of development. It is based on using teachers' perceptions of their students in actual classroom situations while simultaneously informing, expanding, and structuring those perceptions; it involves students and parents in the learning and assessment process, instead of relying on measures that are external to the classroom and family context; and it provides for genuine accountability that systematically documents what children are learning and how teachers are teaching. Moreover, it reflects a view of development that is continuous and that suggests that the transitions at the outset of schooling are regular but occur on multiple qualitative and quantitative levels over time.

Central to all of these elements is the emphasis on recording children's classroom performance, documenting teachers' activities, and understanding and interpreting children's work in context. No other approach to measuring readiness and early school achievement can focus so clearly on what the child brings to the learning situation and what the learning brings to the child. Where these two are joined, children's development can be studied, assessed, and nurtured.

Acknowledgments

This chapter is based on a paper that was commissioned by the National Center for Education Statistics, Office of Educational Research and Improvement, U.S. Department of Education, and on research that was supported in part by the John D. and Catherine T. MacArthur Foundation. Only the author is responsible for the opinions expressed. The Work Sampling System™ reflects the collaborative efforts of Samuel J. Meisels, Judy R. Jablon, Dorothea B. Marsden, Margo L. Dichtelmiller, and Aviva Dorfman. I wish to thank Regena Fails and Dorothy M. Steele for their contributions as well.

References

Boyer, E. L. (1991). *Ready to learn: A mandate for the nation.* Princeton, NJ: Carnegie Foundation for the Advancement of Teaching.

Bredekamp, S. (Ed.). (1987). *Developmentally appropriate practice in early childhood programs serving children from birth through age 8.* Washington, DC: National Association for the Education of Young Children.

Bronson, M. B., & Love, J. (1987). *Child Behavior Rating Scale.* Boston: Abt Associates.

Bruner, J. S. (1966). *Towards a theory of instruction.* Cambridge, MA: Harvard University Press.

Bunch, M. B. (1985). California Achievement Tests, forms C & D. In D. J. Keyser & R. C. Sweetland (Eds.), *Test critiques* (Vol. 22, pp. 111–124). Kansas City, MO: Westport Publishers.

Calfee, R. (1992). Authentic assessment of reading and writing in the elementary classroom. In M. J. Dreher & W. H. Slater (Eds.), *Elementary school literacy: Critical issues* (pp. 211–226). Norwood, MA: Christopher-Gordon.

CTB Macmillan/McGraw-Hill. (1991). *Comprehensive Tests of Basic Skills* (4th ed.). Monterey, CA: Author.

CTB Macmillan/McGraw-Hill. (1992). *California Achievement Test* (5th ed.). Monterey, CA: Author.

De Vries, R., & Kohlberg, L. (1987). *Constructivist early education: Overview and comparison with other programs.* Washington, DC: National Association for the Education of Young Children.

Fortune, J. C., & Cromack, T. R. (1985). Metropolitan Achievement Test (5th ed.). In D. J. Keyser & R. C. Sweetland (Eds.), *Test critiques* (Vol. 3, pp. 427–433). Kansas City, MO: Westport Publishers.

Hieronymus, A. N., Lindquist, E. F., & Hoover, H. D. (1982). *Iowa Test of Basic Skills.* Chicago: Riverside Publishing Company.

Ilg, F. L., & Ames, L. B. (1972). *School readiness.* New York: Harper & Row.

Kagan, S. L. (1990). Readiness 2000: Rethinking rhetoric and responsibility. *Phi Delta Kappan, 72,* 272–279.

Kelly, D. (1992, September 16). Understanding standardized exams. *USA Today,* p. 8A.

Lesiak, W. J. (1978). *Developmental tasks for kindergarten readiness* (Archives of Behavioral Science Monograph, No. 52). Brandon, VT: Clinical Psychology Publishing.

McCarthy, D. (1972). *McCarthy Scales of Children's Abilities.* New York: Psychological Corporation.

Meisels, S. J. (1992). Doing harm by doing good: Iatrogenic effects of early childhood enrollment and promotion practices. *Early Childhood Research Quarterly, 7,* 155–174.

Meisels, S. J., Jablon, J. R., Marsden, D. B., Dichtelmiller, M. L., & Dorfman, A. (1994). *The Work Sampling System: An overview.* Ann Arbor, MI: Rebus Planning Associates.

Meisels, S. J., Liaw, F., Dorfman, A., & Nelson, R. (1995). The Work Sampling System: Reliability and validity of a performance assessment for young children. *Early Childhood Research Quarterly, 10,* 277–296.

Nagle, R. J. (1979). The predictive validity of the Metropolitan Readiness Tests, 1976 edition. *Educational and Psychological Measurement, 39,* 1043–1045.

National Commission on Testing and Public Policy. (1990). *From gatekeeper to gateway: Transforming testing in America.* Chestnut Hill, MA: Boston College.

National Education Goals Panel (1991). *Measuring progress toward the national education goals.* Washington, DC: Author.

Nurss, J. R., & McGauvran, M. E. (1986). *Metropolitan Readiness Tests* (5th ed.). Cleveland, OH: Psychological Corporation.

Oakland, T. (1978). Predictive validity of readiness tests for middle and lower socioeconomic status Anglo, Black, and Mexican American children. *Journal of Educational Psychology, 70,* 574–582.

Paulson, F. L., Paulson, P. R., & Meyer, C. A. (1991). What makes a portfolio a portfolio? *Educational Leadership, 48,* 60–63.

Prescott, G. A., Balow, I. H., Hogan, T. P., & Farr, B. C. (1988). *Metropolitan Achievement Test* (6th ed.). Cleveland, OH: Psychological Corporation.

Psychological Corporation (1990). *Stanford Early School Achievement Test* (3rd ed.). Cleveland, OH: Author.

Riverside Publishing Company (1990). *Iowa Tests of Basic Skills—Administrator's manual.* Chicago: Author.

Rubin, R. A. (1974). Preschool application of the Metropolitan Readiness Tests: Validity, reliability, and preschool norms. *Educational and Psychological Measurement, 34,* 417–422.

Sackett, D. L., Haynes, R. B., & Tugwell, P. (1985). *Clinical epidemiology: A basic science for clinical medicine.* Boston: Little, Brown.

Sameroff, A. J., & Fiese, B. H. (1990). Transactional regulation and early intervention.

In S. J. Meisels & J. P. Shonkoff (Eds.), *Handbook of early childhood intervention* (pp. 119–149). New York: Cambridge University Press.

Shavelson, R. J., Baxter, G. P., & Pine, J. (1992). Performance assessments: Political rhetoric and measurement reality. *Educational Researcher, 21*, 22–27.

Shepard, L. A. (1991). Interview on assessment issues. *Educational Researcher, 20*, 21–23, 27.

Stallman, A. C., & Pearson, P. D. (1990). Formal measures of early literacy. In L. M. Morrow & J. K. Smith (Eds.), *Assessment for instruction in early literacy* (pp. 7–44). Englewood Cliffs, NJ: Prentice-Hall.

Sulzby, E. (1985). Kindergartners as writers and readers. In M. Farr (Ed.), *Advances in writing research: Children's early writing development* (Vol. *1*, pp. 127–199). Norwood, NJ: Ablex.

Weller, L. D., Schnittjer, C. J., & Tuten, B. A. (1992). Predicting achievement in grades three through ten using the Metropolitan Readiness Test. *Journal of Research in Childhood Education, 6*, 121–130.

Wodtke, K. H., Harper, F., Schommer, M., & Brunelli, P. (1989). How standardized is school testing? An exploratory observational study of standardized group testing in kindergarten. *Educational Evaluation and Policy Analysis, 11*, 223–235.

Woodcock, R. W., & Johnson, M. B. (1989). Woodcock-Johnson Psychoeducational Battery–Revised. Allen, TX: DLM Teaching Resources.

Conclusion and Summary

CHAPTER NINETEEN

The 5 to 7 Year Shift: Retrospect and Prospect

MARSHALL M. HAITH AND ARNOLD J. SAMEROFF

What We Have Learned

We came to this exploration of 5- and 7-year-olds with several questions. Compared with 25 years ago, what has changed in our thinking about age differences and the sources of these changes? Do we still see this period of transition as unique or, at least, highly important? How can we best characterize the processes of change in terms of such descriptors as continuous-discontinuous, qualitative-quantitative, reorganizational-emergent? Let's take on these issues and some others that have emerged from this venture.

Changes in Our Thinking Over the Past 30 Years

Shep White's chapter 2 of this volume nicely set the stage for our exploration by laying out the state of affairs 30 years ago when his earlier and well-known chapter was published (White, 1965). His glance through history provided a background of consistency in religious, legal, and cultural views of the 7-year-old as newly coming upon rationality and responsibility. In retrospect, White summarized these views at the time he wrote his earlier chapter: "Children know right from wrong, are first capable of guilt, have minds, reason and are reasonable at age seven" (White, 1965, chap. 2). Although there was occasional interest by researchers at that time in personality and social transitions, for example, in dependency (Sears, Maccoby, & Levin, 1957), by far the largest focus was on the child's cognitive competence. Research was supporting the idea that children thought differently at age 7 than at age 5, having shifted from a stimulus-response associative mentality to one that permitted mediation and the use of concepts and relations. White summarized the transition as "a cognitive shift involving the inhibition of a more juvenile level of thought and the emergence of a more mature form of thought." As several authors in this volume have noted, the picture was of a 5-year-old and a 7-year-old, standing side-by-side, living in an identical world, the only difference being that the 7-year-old had acquired a bigger brain by virtue of her or his 2-year head start, which enabled the child to think more complexly about the physical world. The older child's perspective was enriched by newly acquired tools of "reasoning, symbolic thought, abstract thought, planning, inference, [and] complex conceptualization" (White, this volume, chap. 2).

Scholars, at least in the field of developmental psychology, have undergone a striking, we dare say qualitative, transition in how they think about what is going on in this period. Not only has the study of cognition changed dramatically, but advances have occurred in research and knowledge about underlying biological processes as well as overarching social constraints.

Consider what is new in the domain of cognition. Memory research, not even mentioned in White's 1965 chapter, has exploded over the past 3 decades; we now know that there are remarkable changes in memory style and strategy during early development. Nelson, in chapter 7, reviewed these new findings and alerted us to the acquisition of episodic memory and its significant role in social participation. Also in the cognitive domain, the research on theory of mind has virtually no predecessor in the research arena of the middle 1960s. Chandler and Lalonde articulated this concept for us in chapter 6 by distinguishing an understanding of false beliefs from a truly representational theory of mind; apparently there are layers to the notion, and the deeper levels are comprehended only by the older child.

Research on social and emotional developmental shifts was not well represented in the context of White's pioneering chapter. The work in this area has gone from ground zero to an admirable level of sophistication, as portrayed by Harter in chapter 10, where several dimensions of the development of the self-concept have been uncovered and an orderly theory of development can be tested. Changes in this area have permitted a wide range of exploration, as illustrated, for example, in Dunn's studies of how peer relations affect a child's self-concept (this volume, chap. 12) and Stevenson-Hinde and Shouldice's work on the development of fearfulness (this volume, chap. 11).

Consider the new methods that have been brought to the table. Janowsky and Carper in chapter 3 presented readers with a highly accessible overview of what is known about anatomical, neural, and neuropsychological changes through the years of interest. Several worthwhile hypotheses are now available for testing. One conclusion from chapter 3 is that fairly little is known precisely about changes during this age period, but the technology is virtually there, and we can expect major advances soon. The elegant use of information-processing strategies was almost unknown in the middle 1960s. Siegler (this volume, chap. 4), Morrison, Griffith, and Frazier (this volume, chap. 8), and Olson, Wise, and Forsberg (this volume, chap. 9) demonstrated the power and precision of this approach, and it seems that researchers are finally getting down to some specifiable and understandable processes that might be involved in the change between 5 and 7 years. Behavior genetics research was almost unheard of when the 5 to 7 shift was introduced, and during its explosive growth, this field has taken a developmental turn. Previous linear models of hereditary determinants of behavior are giving way to epigenetic models in which different complexes of genes underlie behavior at different stages of growth; there is an increasing focus on the processes by which biological activity interacts with psychological functioning. Olson et al. demonstrated the exciting use of current strategies in this field, using dyslexia as an example of phenotype that emerges during our period of interest.

As striking as the uncovering of new processes and new methods in cognitive and social development has been over the past 30 years, perhaps the most startling development has been an appreciation that the contextual-life changes that the child experiences between 5 and 7 play a large role in the shift that occurs. Think about our two children, 5 and 7, standing side-by-side in their identical world. What researchers have noticed in the past 3 decades is that their worlds are not identical at all. Probably this development seems so striking because it is so obvious—after the fact.

Life context for a child during these years of concern consists, in large part, of school and family. Ladd (this volume, chap. 16), Meisels (this volume, chap. 18), and Kagan and Neville (this volume, chap. 17) have all discussed the monumental changes that occur in a child's life when school becomes a part of that life. Almost everything changes—the authority figures, the number and kind of social agents and friends, the activities, and the rules. How could investigators have missed the role that such an enormous change plays in a child's life? Perhaps people missed it because they saw school as a result of the endogenous changes that had occurred in the child rather than as an important agent of that change.

There has been very little attention given to the role of the family in the 5 to 7 shift, even now. Weisner (this volume, chap. 14) developed an intriguing evolutionary and transactional story about the changes in the family that occur as the child matures; the family changes in response to the child's changes and, in turn, effects additional changes as the child's role in the family alters, a story that is nicely embellished with cross-cultural evidence. Schooling is seen as a cultural co-opting of this transition, which has evolved and naturally occurs in the relation between child and family. Barth and Parke (this volume, chap. 15) elaborated this picture by reminding us that there is no one "family." Family dynamics are shaped by individual personalities and cultural stresses and support. Marital quality and family economic well-being affect the child's role in the family and parent-child relations.

This volume's authors have not let researchers off so easily as to only admit their blind side and mention school and the family. The authors have increased the conceptual load by introducing systems and their interrelation into investigators' conceptual life. Can anyone remember discussions about systems 30 years ago? Here Stevenson-Hinde and Shouldice emphasized a behavior systems approach in which individual development must be interpreted in a framework that includes the causation, evolution, and function of interactive, self-organizing systems. Not only must researchers acknowledge family and school as systems now, they have to consider how these systems affect one another and, of course, researchers' target of concern, the child. Wrap into this formula the personality of the child, and one has a pretty complex assortment to deal with. Barth and Parke (chap. 15) and Ladd (chap. 16) are the major chefs of this complex brew, but who can deny what they have said? Children come to school as a product of their biology and their experiences; we must all acknowledge that these influences will produce variation in both behavior and developmental transitions in cognitive and social spheres. The relational supports the family can provide, the parental interaction style with the child, and the parental involvement with the school, all of which are moderated by marital quality and family stress, must play a role in the child's adaptation to school. Then there is the school itself, how well it tolerates variation in the child, how it interfaces with the family, and how the family and school affect one another. It all seemed so much simpler when people read White's 1965 chapter.

Furthermore, researchers need to acknowledge a somewhat different perspective on all of this. To this point, the child, family, and school have been treated as separate entities, interacting surely, and even transacting, but still separate. Rogoff offered a contrasting perspective (this volume, chap. 13). Researchers can focus in and out if they like, for purposes of discussion, but actually, the child, family, and school are not separate entities. The unit of analysis is the child's activity in a world context, not abstract mental concepts, whether they be of cognitive or social personality flavor. Behavior and thought are not separable from the context and activity in which they occur.

Has anything changed in the last 30 years in how researchers think about and study the 5 to 7 year age period? Definitely! Researchers have new concepts, new fields of study, new methods, and a new level of theorizing they need to accommodate. We move on now to ask how the field has changed our view of behavioral differences between 5- and 7-year-olds.

Are 7-Year-Olds Different Behaviorally from 5-Year-Olds?

The simple answer is yes. But how? Janowsky suggested that a reorganization of the frontal lobes around this period gives rise to emerging skills in memory and executive functioning, pointing to evidence provided by Nelson concerning changes in memory skills. Nelson, in turn, made the argument that language increasingly becomes a tool for narrative expression that provides a platform for the development of episodic memory. The ability to frame experience as episodic is an interesting correlate of other changes that occur. Once a child appreciates the "me" in his or her experiences, there is a basis for self-reflection on those experiences. Such self-reflection seems key to the metacognitive and executive processes that emerge around the 5 to 7 age period and to some of the behavioral changes that our authors discussed. Recall Chandler and Lalonde's argument that, during this period, a "true" representational theory of mind emerges; we suspect that such an accomplishment might await the child's discovery of his own mind through reflection on his own experiences.

Siegler, Mounoud (this volume, chap. 5), and Harter have all emphasized a transition during this period toward more multidimensional and integrative thinking, an accomplishment that they believe reflects regulation of earlier modes of thought. Whenever one calls up the concept of regulation that includes the possibility of suppression or inhibition, we are inclined to think about executive functions. Certainly, there is plenty of evidence that executive functions improve around this age. These functions are enhanced by the kind of self-critiquing that is only possible through reflection on one's own thoughts. The ability to say to oneself "Is this correct? Should I consider alternatives that might make more sense?" opens up the potential for indefinitely more adaptive behavior in situations than simply making the prepotent response. It seems reasonable to suppose that episodic memory, constituting a personalized knowledge base, would be important for supporting increasingly flexible and reflective thinking.

Not all of the changes we discovered in this book fit readily under the executive functioning umbrella. Morrison et al. documented a host of cognitive improvements during this interval that are not readily accommodated by a single core concept—memory performance and strategies, phonemic segmentation, syllabic segmentation, quantitative skills, letter naming, reading, vocabulary, and general knowledge. However, on the social plane, Harter's notion of the "I" self emerging during this period, taking the "me" self as the object of evaluation and criticism places heavy weight on the child's skills of self-reflection.

It is important to note that not all things change during this age period. Dunn, using dips in age-to-age correlations to examine changes in self-concept and sibling relations, found a change during the 5 to 7 year age period for self-concept but not for sibling relations. Whether one agrees that this methodology addresses the central question we pose here or not, the point is that there are probably many variables that do not change during this age period. Researchers hear less about them, because they are less likely to attract the interests of developmentalists.

We conclude that, on the behavioral level, there is no question but what the 7-year-old behaves differently from the 5-year-old. This conclusion is compatible with the long religious and cultural traditions in thinking about children at these ages that White reviewed, as well as the modern scientific view. Why these changes occur is more open to question. We argue that the ability to reflect on one's thoughts and experiences plays an important role and that such reflectivity itself depends heavily on the ability to have a personalized knowledge base (episodic memory) for evaluation.

How Do We Characterize the Difference Between 5-Year-Olds and 7-Year-Olds?

Is the difference in behavior quantitative or qualitative? Is the transition continuous or stepwise? Is the change restricted to prior capacities, or does it reflect the emergence of new abilities?

The answer to each question is, It depends. Mounoud took the strong position that major transitions are qualitative and emergent, followed by quantitative change. Janowsky made the important point that qualitative and emergent behavioral changes can reflect continuous processes that suddenly exceed threshold; no discrete shifts in brain function have been observed during this period, although continuous changes in myelination and synaptic shaping do occur. Still, a critical threshold or composite critical value might be reached that could trigger significant behavioral alterations.

For the most part, the chapter authors of this volume converge on the reasonable conclusion that whether one sees sudden, discontinuous shifts or more gradual, continuous transitions depends on the grain of analysis and the question one asks.

White argued that past notions are too absolutist. Although he placed a heavy burden on the role of reasoning ability in accounting for the "5 to 7 shift," he did not argue that an absolutely new ability to reason occurs during this period. Rather, "it is an ability to reason with others and to look reasonable in the context of society's demands" (White, this volume, chap. 2).

Siegler's suggestion seems like a happy compromise for many of the findings that our authors presented. One can see qualitative differences between 5- and 7-year-olds in many contexts. On the other hand, scores of experiments have shown that, in some form, one can elicit from a 5-year-old pieces of what appear to be unique 7-year-old accomplishments if one just twiddles enough with the experimental conditions, the form of the questions, and the criteria for qualifying behavior. Siegler offered the possibility that although 5-year-olds can do many of the things that 7-year-olds can do, they just don't—typically. Rather, they have characteristic modes of thought that are more direct, conditioned by their lesser processing capacity, theoretical beliefs, and encoding ability. And, we add, by their nascent skills of reflection. The notion of "characteristic modes of thought" can accommodate a wide variety of findings and data.

To this point, we have focused on the cognitive and social changes that occur in the child. But a central message of this volume is that the child cannot be viewed in a vacuum. What is going on in the child's cultural and social world must be acknowledged.

Are the Environments of 7-Year-Olds Different from Those of 5-Year-Olds?

For the industrialized world, the answer again is obviously affirmative. Key components of the child's changing world during this period are the family and school. The school transition is the easiest to see. Ladd (this volume, chap. 16) and Kagan and Neville (this volume, chap. 17) nicely documented the changes, and one gets the impression that, second to birth and death, this may be one of the most striking transitions that a person experiences during his or her lifetime. New rules, unfamiliar constraints, a radically different physical environment, changes in social density and composition, alterations in activity pacing, and separation from the family are among the transformations that accompany a child's shift from the familiar home life to the unfamiliar school environment. The authors have made a convincing case that to the degree a child negotiates this transition comfortably or uncomfortably, the child's modes of thought about both academic and personal-social matters will be affected. The analysis becomes messier when one has to consider how these new factors play out in transaction with the characteristics of the child and the home. The social skills that the child brings in the form of prosocial and friend-making talents or aggressive and antisocial behavior play a major role in facilitating or impeding the entry into school. The family exerts its influence directly through involvement or lack of involvement with the school and indirectly through support in the home.

Likewise, the family scene shifts, parallel to the transition of the child into school. Weisner pointed to changes in the family system attendant to the emerging competencies of the child, such as reasoning and decision making, social skills, and self-understanding. The daily routine of the family accommodates to these changes through adjusted expectations and increased responsibilities in such matters as caretaking, social support, and domestic tasks. Industrial cultures have complicated this picture by co-opting this period of increasing competency for the purpose of schooling, thus reducing the child's role in family maintenance. Still, the child's changing status impacts the family structure and plays back to affect the child's adjustment in a changing world.

Aside from the important role that the family structure plays in preparing the child for this transition, through the shaping and utilization of social skills, the family's involvement with the school is an important variable in the child's adaptation, especially the child's social adjustment. Barth and Parke reminded readers, however, that there is no prototypical family. Families vary in the stress they experience, the resources they command, the marital quality they maintain, and the relationships that exist between parent and child. All of these factors affect the ease with which this age transition is negotiated.

As stated earlier, one of the key messages of this book is that changes in the child's social ecology during the 5 to 7 year age transition are dramatic and play a critical role in differences in behavior at the beginning and end of this period.

How Do We Characterize the Difference in the Environments of 5- and 7-Year-Olds?

We can ask the same questions about the transitions in environments between 5 and 7 years of age as we did about the child. That is, are the changes qualitative or quantitative, continuous or discontinuous? Curiously, the answers come somewhat easier than do the answers to those questions about the child.

School definitely constitutes a qualitative and discontinuous change for the child. Kagan and Neville reminded us that even for the child who has preschool, theoretically a transition experience, virtually everything about that child's life changes when moving from the primarily family context to the elementary school environment. For example, the degree to which involvement of the family is emphasized, the extent to which the teacher's approach to the child is integrated as opposed to focused on cognitive achievement, and even the relative number of adults that are available to meet the child's needs shift abruptly and dramatically between preschool and elementary school.

Rogoff viewed these ecological shifts from another perspective. The child's role changes in sociocultural activities, but whether this is a qualitative or quantitative shift depends on how the culture is organized and how activities are structured. Thus, shifts in activities might be qualitative and discontinuous in one culture and quantitative and continuous in another. The important thing for Rogoff is not how the environment changes for the child but, rather, how the child's role changes in activities in which he or she engages. This is an interesting take on the interrelation between child and society, and we are curious about how it will affect research and conception in the field.

Morrison, Griffith, and Frazier forced us to acknowledge that we need to exercise caution in striving to formulate valid generalizations about the effects of school on behavior versus other events that occur as a child grows older. Their new methodology, which examines similar-age children just beyond and just before the age criterion for school entry, yielded surprising findings. The effect of schooling on cognition is highly specific, affecting, for example, memory performance but not narrative skills, and syllabic segmentation but not subsyllabic segmentation. The investigator who strives for generalization in this field had better possess a strong degree of frustration tolerance.

Some Qualifications

The authors raised several issues about the validity of characterizing the 5 to 7 year shift as unique and about the use of such terms as *adjustment, readiness,* and *transition.*

Is the 5 to 7 Shift Unique or Is It Special?

The 5 to 7 shift is not unique. Development occurs across the life span, and one could select almost any two age periods and find differences in the child's and even the adult's behavior between them. As Janowsky and Carper reported, central nervous structures are in transition throughout the prenatal period and continue to change noticeably into adolescence. Dunn cited evidence for substantial changes in self-concept during the 5 to 7 year interval but not in sibling relations; however, although finding no evidence for changes in sibling relations during this period, she did find evidence for changes between 3 to 5 and 7 to 9 years of age. Both White and Rogoff pointed to changes that occur during other age brackets, and Rogoff nicely documented some changes that we assume are inherent to the 5 to 7 year shift that occur in other cultures during different age transitions.

The 5 to 7 shift is special. Although acknowledging that other shifts do occur at other ages, we find impressive the extensive, if not uniform, changes in the ways that cultures treat children at these two ages and have treated children throughout history. Sure, pieces of behavior that we might naively have claimed at one time as the exclusive province of the 7-year-old may even be demonstrable in infants. For example, White pointed out that several studies suggest that infants are capable of reasoning, and there are scores of studies that, with special jiggering of the experimental conditions, show components of conservation ability in children before the 5 to 7 transition. But we believe that there is a different quality to the performance of the 7-year-old, both in the level and in the integration of skills that children do not possess before the transition. Critics can pick at the pieces, but the whole picture yields a pretty compelling story. Still, we agree that we must talk about both the child and the culture in painting this picture.

How Good Are Our Concepts?

Meisels, Ladd, and Kagan and Neville all alluded to difficulty in addressing the key questions we posed because of the fuzziness of such concepts as *readiness,*

adjustment, and *transitions.* All this volume's authors encouraged a more interactive view of these concepts rather than assuming that all of the action resides
in the child. *Readiness,* for example, has traditionally been viewed in terms of
the child's maturational status. However, as Meisels suggested, when we ask
about readiness, we have to ask, "Readiness for what?" And, "In what context?" A child's school readiness depends both on the demands of the school
and on how well the school is equipped to adapt to the individual child's needs.
Meisels adopted a sensible definition of *readiness,* that is, readiness to learn in
an interactive and reciprocal context.

The authors' use of the term *school adjustment* has also led to problems.
Ladd offered a useful alternative: "the degree to which children become interested, engaged, comfortable, and successful in the school environment" (this
volume, chap. 16). This interpretation encompasses social-emotional factors as
well as cognitive ones, and it provides a role for the school's adjustment to the
child as well as vice versa.

Furthermore, Kagan reminded us that the transition to school carries many
meanings. Again, the transition does not occur only in the child, nor does it
occur for all children at the same particular age. The fact that some children
experience preschool and others do not makes for considerable age variance in
the transition process. Moreover, the adaptation is not just cognitive, and it is
reciprocal.

Concept definition often seems like a nuisance barrier in attempts to address
more pressing issues. However, without agreement on such terms, confusion
results, and people talk past one another. Especially the admonitions to include
characteristics of the school environment as central to the concepts of readiness, adaptation, and transition to school are important and should condition a
general shift in perspective that incorporates school structure as central to our
characterization of the 5 to 7 year shift.

Individual and Gender Differences

An important new development in approaching the 5 to 7 year shift is the consideration of individual differences. For the most part, investigators have traditionally treated the shift as a universal and uniform event across all children.
But examination of individual differences suggests that such differences do
exist, and this appreciation has implications for intervention for children who
have difficulties during the transition.

Individual Differences in Transition

Children do not march through the 5 to 7 year shift in lockstep fashion. Individual differences exist in the transition in the social, as well as cognitive, domains. Readers were introduced to two additional approaches in Dunn's (this

volume, chap. 12) demonstration that the age-to-age correlation of judged self-concept dips during this period, reflecting rank-order changes, and Olson, Wise, and Forsberg's (this volume, chap. 9) report of analyses of genetic contributions that seem important in the acquisition of reading skills.

A repeated message from our authors is that a recognition of individual differences in age transitions is only a first step. The next step is to analyze the processes that are responsible for individual differences. Olson et al.'s penetrating analysis of reading deficits, which yielded phoneme awareness as the culprit, is a case in point. Meisels (this volume, chap. 18) argued for a dynamic, ongoing assessment in context rather than standard testing procedures, which are decontextualized. Among other advantages, the ongoing assessment approach yields much more specific information about why a child is delayed or exceptional, not just that they are. In the social sphere, Ladd reported evidence that variations in school adjustment reflect earlier dispositions to aggressive, antisocial behavior as well as the ease of making new friends. In turn, some of these dispositions appear to be related to characteristics of the parents and the child-parent interaction, factors emphasized by both Ladd, and Barth and Parke.

Gender Differences

Although the developmental literature is filled with studies of gender differences, there has been little that explicitly examines the interaction between gender and transitions. This lack is evident in this volume. Ladd pointed to gender differences in the way sociable or aggressive children negotiate the transition to school, and Stevenson-Hinde and Shouldice pointed to gender differences in the fears of young children. These few examples underscore the failure of the field to take a clear biopsychosocial approach in attempts to integrate researchers' understanding of the 5 to 7 year transition. The evidence for differences in the socialization of boys and girls has become almost as compelling as the evidence for biological differences between boys and girls. How these differences affect differences in cognitive and emotional and social functioning and their transition across age is a story that now only exists in outline.

Intervention

An understanding of the processes that are responsible for individual gender and group differences in the transition is important for developing interventions. Olson et al., for example, presented encouraging findings with dyslexic children, showing that an intervention program that targeted phoneme awareness training produced a resulting increment in reading skill. There are two important secondary messages to take from this work. One is that the treatment for a deficit need not address the original "cause." Olson et al. presented compelling evidence that a genetic component plays a role in phoneme awareness deficits. Yet, an effective intervention was behavioral, not genetic, in character. Second, environmental interventions can affect processes that are responsible for individual differences. Schooling is the dominant cognitive intervention in our society. In this light, Morrison et al.'s findings are supportive; school was seen to be influential for memory performance, phonemic segmentation, quantitative skills, letter naming, and reading. Meisel's Work Sampling System adopts a similar precept. Continuous monitoring of children's performance provide opportunities for graded and sensitive intervention.

There is a smaller but increasing focus on social and emotional behavior. Ladd noted that, once in school, a child's reputation tends to stick. Thus, he proposed that interventions occur prior to school. The gap in our knowledge and the need for further research to move beyond insightful speculation are obvious. This lack is not restricted to research on the 5 to 7 year transition but is characteristic of psychology as a whole. New preventive-intervention initiatives are in the offing, stimulated by changes in our national research agenda (Mrazek and Haggerty, 1994) and the emergence of the new discipline of intervention science (Coie et al., 1993).

Where Do We Go from Here?

This volume's authors have noted many of the impressive advances in concepts, methods, and findings concerning what changes take place between 5 and 7 years of age, both in children's behavior and in their supporting environment. What will another volume on this topic contain—preserving the current temporal pattern, say 30 years from today?

To start, we see tremendous potential and need for better information about changes in brain function during the 5 to 7 shift, including anatomical, neurophysiological, and biochemical factors. This is not a call for reductionism; rather, the child is a whole functioning system, and the more we know about that system, the better. Ethical and moral considerations will dictate and constrain our methodologies, but the advances in imaging techniques are likely to yield all sorts of valuable information that will enrich our findings and provide guidance for behavioral research and theory, and vice versa.

We also see a need for better articulation of how social and cultural changes specifically affect children's behavior between 5 and 7. There is no doubt but what investigators have come a long way in acknowledging the fact that the child's world changes materially during this time. However, in many cases, we are not much further than simply listing the changes that occur. Even when we can find correlative changes between the environment and the child, we lack specificity of how environmental and child variables operate. Basically, we need a process analysis of environmental effects. This analysis will have to go still further; we need a much better understanding of how the child's characteristics interact or transact with these environmental factors. But it is clear to us that the process analysis we call for will be required before we can make much progress on a comprehensive model of environment-child interaction.

We have a strong expectation that the next volume will be much richer in its portrayal of the social and affective changes that occur during this transition. Although chapters that deal with these domains in this volume are ground-breaking, it still seems obvious that there is an imbalance in what we know about cognitive and social-emotional phenomena. Because methodologies in the social and emotional areas are improving, it is a sure bet that a future analysis will redress at least some of this imbalance.

History should have taught us that the human desire for simplicity is not typically realized in conceptual analyses of human behavior. Rogoff proposed that what we see in the child is only a reflection of what goes on in the culture. Yet Morrison, Griffith, and Frazier provided a clear warning that cultural factors affect some behavioral domains more than others. We suspect that the next volume will report additional evidence for the effects of culture described by Rogoff and the kind of domain specificity that Morrison et al. uncovered. Additionally, we expect reports that document variable domain sensitivity to influences of the family and that demonstrate that some factors but not others are amenable to intervention. And, horror of horrors, we fully expect that each of these considerations differs for different children. The next book may be a long one.

Finally, picking up on this last theme, we see the need for much more attention to individual differences. Although several authors presented chapters mentioning individual differences in the 5 to 7 age transition, there is so much more to do. In fact, there are very few longitudinal studies that bridge the 5 to 7 period. An important question is the extent to which the amount of change or pace of change is predictive of later development and what factors affect amount and pacing. Individual differences will pose a special challenge to perspectives that put a great weight on cultural factors, although ultimately they will stimulate a more complete model for understanding the child in context. We look forward to seeing how this tradition will develop; to our knowledge, the issue of individual differences has not been confronted directly by sociocultural analyses.

There is an old adage that people often cite in business negotiations: "Leave something for the next guy." This volume documents great progress over the previous 30 years. At the same time, there is plenty left for those who follow.

Our Summation

The Piagetian literature fostered a deficit model in which differences between 5- and 7-year-olds were framed in terms of capacities the younger preoperational child did not have. This perspective provided a marvelous stimulus for a new generation of investigators to counterargue that, indeed, children younger than 5 not only had many unrecognized capacities but also that these capacities included those previously granted only to children over 7. What has emerged in the contents of this book is what we hope is a balanced view in which there is room not only for interpretation of both 5- and 7-year-olds as competent children when judged in their own terms, but also for the recognition that development does occur between these two ages. Moreover, rather than a restricted view of cognition as the keystone of this change, biological and social factors make their contributions to this growth.

We were tempted to say biology and society make independent contributions, but part of our new understanding is rooted in the transactional quality of development in which there is no true independence of these factors. Depending on the point of entry into the process, cognitive, biological, or social factors would seem to be at the leading edge. Biological transitions might enhance memory functions, but memory functions might anticipate the biological shifts. Cognitive advances might facilitate the child's understanding of social behavior, but social organization might stimulate and shape cognitive advances. And even if not clearly evident in current studies of 5- to 7-year-olds, evolution offers a comprehensive distal model for how social factors shape biological change through selection pressures. More proximally, comparative studies have demonstrated a multitude of biological changes in other species that result from changes in social interaction.

Is there a 5 to 7 year shift? One answer is that if by 5 you mean 3 and if by 7 you mean 10, there is definitely a 5 to 7 year shift. This answer reflects the study of what might be called *partial accomplishments* (Haith, 1990, 1993). If one asks whether 5-year-olds can attend, remember, have emotions, engage in social interactions, and even take charge of social interactions, the answer is yes. If one asks whether 5-year-olds can fully integrate their physical, cognitive, emotional, and social worlds, the answer is no. But neither can 7-year-olds. In fact, as adults some of us may still be grappling with this task while the rest have given up. Indeed, this may be the exciting message that emerges from the work presented in this volume. What may seem as a final answer, for example, a theory like Piaget's, which explains all of development, may instead be a stimulus for the next breakthrough in our increasing awareness of the determinants and organization of development. The dialectical underpinning of both the development of the child and our attempts to understand these changes offers an exciting prospect for what the future will reveal.

References

Coie, J. D., Watt, N. F., West, S. G., Hawkins, J. D., Asarnow, J. R., Markman, H. J., Ramey, S. L., Shure, M. B., & Long, B. (1993). The science of prevention: A conceptual framework and some directions for a national research program. *American Psychologist, 48,* 1013–1022.

Haith, M. M. (1990). Perceptual and sensory processes in early infancy. *Merrill-Palmer Quarterly, 36,* 1–26.

Haith, M. M. (1993). Preparing for the 21st century: Some goals and challenges for studies of infant sensory and perceptual development. *Developmental Review, 13,* 354–371.

Mrazek, P. J., & Haggerty, R. J. (Eds.). (1994). *Reducing risks for mental disorders: Frontiers for preventive intervention research.* Washington, DC: National Academy Press.

Sears, R. R., Maccoby, E. E., & Levin, H. (1957) *Patterns of child rearing.* Evanston, IL: Row, Peterson.

White, S. H. (1965). Evidence for a hierarchical arrangement of learning processes. In L. P. Lipsitt & C. C. Spiker (Eds.), *Advances in child development and behavior,* (Vol. 2, pp. 187–220). New York: Academic Press.

CONTRIBUTORS

Joan M. Barth
Psychology Department
Skidmore College
Saratoga Springs, New York 12866

Ruth Carper
Department of Neurology
Oregon Health Sciences University
Portland, Oregon 97201

Michael Chandler
Department of Psychology
University of British Columbia
Vancouver, British Columbia
   V6T 1Y7 Canada

Judy Dunn
Institute of Psychiatry
London SE5 8AF
England

Helen Forsberg
Department of Psychology
University of Colorado
Boulder, Colorado 80309

Julie A. Frazier
Department of Psychology
Loyola University of Chicago
Chicago, Illinois 60626

Elizabeth McMahon Griffith
Department of Psychology
University of Denver
Denver, Colorado 80208

Marshall M. Haith
Department of Psychology
University of Denver
Denver, Colorado 80208

Susan Harter
Department of Psychology
University of Denver
Denver, Colorado 80208

Jeri S. Janowsky
Department of Neurology
Oregon Health Sciences University
Portland, Oregon 97201

Sharon L. Kagan
Bush Center in Child Development
  and Social Policy
Yale University
New Haven, Connecticut 06511

Gary W. Ladd
Children's Research Center
University of Illinois
Champaign, Illinois 61820

Chris Lalonde
Department of Psychology
University of British Columbia
Vancouver, British Columbia
  V6T 1Y7 Canada

Samuel J. Meisels
School of Education
University of Michigan
Ann Arbor, Michigan 49109

Frederick J. Morrison
Department of Psychology
Loyola University of Chicago
Chicago, Illinois 60626

Pierre Mounoud
Faculty of Psychology
University of Geneva
Geneva
Switzerland

Katherine Nelson
Department of Developmental
  Psychology
City University of New York
New York, New York 10036

Peter R. Neville
Bush Center in Child Development
  and Social Policy
Yale University
New Haven, Connecticut 06511

Richard Olson
Department of Psychology
University of Colorado
Boulder, Colorado 80309

Ross D. Parke
Department of Psychology
University of California at Riverside
Riverside, California 92521

Barbara Rogoff
Psychology Board
University of California at Santa Cruz
Santa Cruz, California 95064

Arnold J. Sameroff
Center for Human Growth and
  Development
University of Michigan
Ann Arbor, Michigan 48109

Anne Shouldice
Sub-Department of Animal Behavior
Cambridge University
Madingly, Cambridge CB3 8AA
England

Robert S. Siegler
Department of Psychology
Carnegie-Mellon University
Pittsburgh, Pennsylvania 15213

Joan Stevenson-Hinde
Sub-Department of Animal Behavior
Cambridge University
Madingly, Cambridge CB3 8AA
England

Thomas S. Weisner
Departments of Psychiatry and
  Anthropology
University of California at Los Angeles
Los Angeles, California 90095

Sheldon H. White
Department of Psychology
Harvard University
Cambridge, Massachusetts 02138

Barbara Wise
Department of Psychology
University of Colorado
Boulder, Colorado 80309

INDEX OF NAMES

INDEX OF SUBJECTS